TARBELL'S
TEACHER'S GUIDE

TO THE INTERNATIONAL BIBLE LESSONS
FOR CHRISTIAN TEACHING OF THE
UNIFORM COURSE
FOR SEPTEMBER 1971–AUGUST 1972

EDITED BY

FRANK S. MEAD, LITT. D.

SIXTY-SEVENTH
ANNUAL VOLUME

**FLEMING H. REVELL COMPANY
OLD TAPPAN, NEW JERSEY**

Printed in the United States of America

SBN 8007-0450-9

LIBRARY OF CONGRESS CATALOG CARD NUMBER: 5-40811

Old Tappan, New Jersey

CONTENTS

LIST OF LESSONS
SEPTEMBER–NOVEMBER 1971: **The Doctrine of God**

DECEMBER 1971–FEBRUARY 1972: **The Gospel of Luke**

4   CONTENTS

A WORD TO THE TEACHER

LIL' ABNER, in the famous comic strip, had a way of saying, in certain puzzling situations, "It's all amusin' and confusin'." Just in case some of our readers may be still a bit confused, if not amused, at the rather radical change in the arrangement of the lessons in TARBELL'S, it may be helpful to explain once more why and how this change has come about.

It is all based on the stubborn fact that the church school year, in most Sunday schools, begins in September and not, as with the *calendar* year, in January. The Division of Christian Education of the National Council of the Churches of Christ in the U.S.A., which publishes these annual outlines for the International Sunday School Lessons, believed that the lessons should run as the church year runs—beginning with September and continuing through the following August, and they have asked all publishers of lesson guides, such as TARBELL'S to cooperate in making such a change. So—we are making this the 1971–1972 edition of TARBELL'S. The book will be available early in May, this year and in succeeding years.

As in previous years, the lessons cover a wide spectrum of religious interest and subjects, and deal with what our professional educators call "basics." The basics for this year cover The Doctrine of God, The Gospel According to Luke, The Nature and Mission of the Church, and The Bible and Devotional Life. At first glance this seems to cover more territory than any teacher can get over in one year—and it is! You cannot possibly teach your class everything about God in thirteen lessons, so don't try. Nor can very many of the details of church history be considered in the third quarter, nor all about the Bible in the fourth quarter. What we have here is an *introduction* to all this. Don't bite off more than you can chew. Rather, open the door to research and further study on the part of the pupil.

One of the finest teachers this editor ever had was a professor in theological school who came into class one morning and said, with a perfectly straight face, "Gentlemen, I have come to the conclusion that the finest form of government in the world is the Communist form." Now, he didn't believe that, for one moment; he had come to no such conclusion. All he was doing was opening a door. It *flew* open! His statement was so startling that we talked about it and argued about it for weeks, and we came up with the conclusion that it was the very worst form of government—with which conclusion he agreed! He was a wise teacher. He didn't try to indoctrinate or brainwash us, but he did make us *think*, which was exactly what he wanted. That was his basic motive, and it should be the basic motive in all education. Education is not the memorizing or recital of facts and figures, be they living or be they dead; it is a process of growing through thinking.

6

So, with these topics for the coming year, throw open a few doors. That doesn't mean that you are to be as negative as the professor was about it; it doesn't mean that you are to suggest that God is dead, but it might be good for you to find out just how much your students know about a *living* God, and to help fill in a few of the gaps in their thinking. You will not have accomplished much if, at the end of the year, you have taught them only to recite the precepts of some ancient or medieval scholars, but if you have led them through the mystic door to the awareness of a living, relevant God, in faith and reverence and commitment, you will have accomplished much.

Don't depend on this book *exclusively;* your church and public libraries are filled with other equally helpful books. Use them. TARBELL'S isn't a crutch; it doesn't try to explain everything in ten easy lessons. It is a GUIDE calculated to help you glean from the great Scripture-house that strength and Spirit which will give you access to the singing lives enjoyed by the first-century Christians.

It can be done. It is being done by countless teachers everywhere. May it happen to you and through you this year!

Yours for Christ,
Frank S. Mead.

AUDIO-VISUAL MATERIAL RECOMMENDED
FOR THIS YEAR'S STUDY

Symbols: C with R, color filmstrip with record; FS, filmstrip; MP, motion picture; B & W, black and white; C, color; Min., minutes.

SEPTEMBER–NOVEMBER 1971: The Doctrine of God

September 5—Thinking About God
  God of Creation, MP, Moody films, 30 Min., C. Seeing God in the beauty of His Creation.
  Prior Claim, Moody films, 30 Min., C. God is first in all things.
  Each With His Own Brush, FS, Friendship Press: the artists of the world show us the Christ of His own land. C with devotional script.

September 12—God Transcends Our Understanding
  Dust or Destiny, MP, Moody films, 28 Min., C.
  Time and Eternity, Moody Films, 28 Min., C. Two beautiful films depicting the wonders of God.
  By Faith We Understand, FS, United Church Press, C with R. Understanding God a little better through study of the Bible.

September 19—God Reveals Himself
  Signposts Aloft, MP, Moody Films, 28 Min., C. The wonders of God are everywhere.
  The Glory of the Lord, FS, Concordia Filmstrips, C with R. Excellent material for worship or study with this lesson.
  Growth of Our Idea of God, United Church Press, C. The development of man's thoughts of God.

September 26—God Gives Meaning to Life
  Parable, Protestant Council of Churches, MP, 22 Min., C. A thought provoking film for today.
  A New Thing, Burt Martin Associates, 34 Min., C. An open and frank expression of what their faith in Christ has done to change their lives.
  This Sustaining Bread, FS, Friendship Press, C with R. A worship service.

October 3—God Calls Men
  Moses Called by God, MP, Concordia Films, 17 Min., C or B & W. The story of Moses' call.
  Called to Serve, Family Films, 30 Min., B & W. What is meant by the phrase, "called to serve"?
  You Have Been Called, FS, Concordia Filmstrips, C with R. We are reminded that God calls each of us.

October 10—God Creates a Community
  What Is the Church? MP, Family Films, 30 Min., B & W. Can the church prove it is a community under God?
  Workers Together With God, Family Films, 33 Min., B & W. An inspiring film for active church members.
  From the Upper Room to the Crowded Streets, FS, Friendship Press, C with R. A thought provoking discussion springboard.

October 17—God Responds to Prayer
There Was a Widow, MP, Family Films, 30 Min., B & W. An excellent
modern interpretation of the parable Jesus told.
Under His Wing, Concordia Films, 30 Min., B & W. The faith of a child
can embarrass an adult.
Commitment, Prayer and Faith, FS, Family Filmstrips, C with R. A discussion filmstrip that should help make this lesson meaningful.

October 24—God Heals Broken Humanity
Is There a Man in the House? MP, Family Films, 30 Min., C. God assures us
it is never the end of the line.
A World on Fire, Cathedral Films, 30 Min., C or B & W. A Christian has
some responsibility in helping to heal a broken humanity.
The Vision of Isaiah, FS, Cathedral Filmstrips, C with R. A worship service.

October 31—God Judges the World
Faith in Revolution, MP, Broadcasting & Films Commission, 28 Min., C. An
informative film of turbulent Southeast Asia. The present in the light of
the past.
The Great Revolution, Concordia Films, 30 Min., C. Disillusioned by the
Communist creed, José asks, "Do people need something to hate?" Do
they?
The Church Alive in Japan, FS, Friendship Press, C with R. From the
ashes of the past comes something new and vital, relevant to the needs of
her poeple today.

November 7—God Sustains His Creation
Dust or Destiny, MP, Moody Films, 28 Min., C. A wonderful film to use
with this lesson.
God's Wonderful World, FS, United Church Press, C. A worship service.

November 14—God Establishes Moral Order
To Forgive a Thief, MP, Cathedral Flms, 30 Min., B & W. A discussion for
this lesson.
Don't Blame Me, Cathedral Films, 30 Min., C. The sins of omission.
One World, FS, United Church Press, B & W. A fine discussion springboard.

November 21—God Conquers Evil
Mr. Big, MP, Family Films, 30 Min., B & W. A thought provoking film that
should lend a great deal to the lesson.
Painful Confession, Concordia Films, 30 Min., C. The importance of knowing that God does forgive.
Do You Not Care if We Perish? FS, Family Filmstrip, C with R. A discussion filmstrip.

November 28—God Brings the World to Fulfillment
Man on a Skateboard, MP, Family Films, 20 Min., C. What is personal fulfillment?
Freedom Under God, FS, United Church Press, C. The meaning of freedom
today.

DECEMBER 1971–FEBRUARY 1972: The Gospel of Luke

December 5—Luke Tells the Good News
The Second Missionary Journey, MP, Cathedral Films, 30 Min., B & W. Here
we meet Luke as he begins his service to Christ in caring for Paul.
The Many Faces of Mexico, Cathedral Films, 30 Min., C. Today man still
answers the call.
New Day in Nepal, FS, Friendship Press Filmstrip, C. A unique missionary
enterprise.

December 12—God Fulfills His Promises
Birth of John the Baptist, MP, Family Films, 20 Min., C or B & W. A film
for the study of worship.
Holy Night, Cathedral Films, 30 Min., C or B & W. From the prophecies of
Isaiah through the birth of Christ.
The Annunciation, FS, Cathedral Filmstrips, C with R. A worship service.

December 19—Good News of Great Joy

The Other Wise Man, MP, Family Films, 30 Min., C. A beloved Christmas classic beautifully filmed.

Glory in the Highest, Concordia Films, 30 Min., C or B & W. A lovely Christmas film.

Love at Christmas, FS, Cathedral Filmstrip. A meaningful worship service.

December 26—Jesus Overcomes Temptation

Men of the Wilderness, MP, Cathedral Films, 30 Min., C or B & W. The story of the temptations of Jesus and the death of John the Baptist.

Baptism and Temptation, FS, Cathedral Filmstrips, C or B & W. A study guide.

January 2—Jesus Teaches the Way of Love

A Heart of Gold, MP, Concordia Films, 30 Min., B & W. Excellent for to-day's lesson.

I Don't Want to Get Involved, Family Films, 30 Min., C. The overwhelming need for love in this day and age.

How Do You Love Your Neighbor, FS, United Church Press, C. A discussion guide.

Two Great Commandments, Family Filmstrips, C with R. The relevance of Jesus' teaching in today's world.

January 9—Our Compassionate Christ

The Youth Drug Scene, MP, Family Films, 30 Min., C. A true story of the results of the compassion of a few serving Christ.

To Forgive a Thief, Cathedral Films, 30 Min., C. An excellent film to lead a discussion.

The Pressures of Popularity, FS, Family Filmstrips, C with R. A discussion filmstrip.

January 16—The Healing Christ

Jesus Heals the Man Born Blind, MP, Family Films, 20 Min., C or B & W. The Bible story.

More Than Conquerors, Concordia Films, 30 Min. B & W. A discussion film.

The Drama of Redemption, FS, Cathedral Filmstrips, C with R. A discussion starter.

January 23—What Price Discipleship

Discipleship, MP, Cathedral Films, 30 Min., C or B & W. A most beautiful film.

Seven Days a Week, Family Films, 30 Min., B & W. What is it costing you?

Jesus and His Disciples, FS, United Church Press. A teaching strip.

January 30—Faithful With Possessions

Talents, MP, Family Films, 37 Min., B & W. An inspiring film on the use of our possessions.

The Rich Fool, Family Films, 30 Min., B & W. A modern version of the parable.

Stewardship for Adults, FS, Family Filmstrips, C with R. The link between faith and practice.

February 6—Christ's Concern for the City

The City: Where the Action Is, MP, Family Films, 30 Min., C. What are you doing? What is your church doing?

Where the People Are, Broadcasting and Films Commission, 35 Min., B & W. This film will surely stimulate discussion.

The Church Ministers to a New Generation, FS, Family Filmstrips, C with R. Are Christians learning to listen?

February 13—Endurance and Christian Hope

The Captive, MP, Broadcasting and Films Commission, 30 Min., B & W. It is evident that we must endure and lend a hand with the hope.

Syzygy, Broadcasting and Films Commission, 27 Min., C. Where is the hope for today's world? A discussion film.

Living and Working Under Pressure, FS, Family Filmstrips, C with R. A discussion springboard.

February 20—The Death That Changes Lives
The Crucifixion, MP, Family Films, 20 Min., C or B & W. For worship or
study.
Miracle of Love, Family Films, 45 Min., B & W. An inspiring story of the
impact today of Jesus' death.
The Redeemed, Concordia Filmstrip, C with R. The believer and the non-
believer stand at the foot of the cross.

February 27—Walking with the Living Christ
The Lord's Ascension, MP, Family Films, 15 Min., B & W. For study or for
a worship service.
He Lives, Concordia Films, 30 Min., C or B & W. Finding and holding the
promise of Easter morning.
The Upper Room, FS, Cathedral Filmstrips, C with R. A worship service.

MARCH–MAY 1972: The Church: Its Nature and Mission

March 5—The Foundation of the Church
The Second Missionary Journey, MP, Cathedral Films, 30 Min., B & W. The
struggles of the early church.
What Is the Church? Family Films, 30 Min., B & W. Time now to take stock.
The Church in New Testament Times, FS, United Church Press, C. An in-
formative strip.

March 12—The Spirit Empowers the Church
Endued with Power, MP, Family Films, 20 Min., C or B & W. The story of
Pentecost.
A Light That Shines in the Darkness, Cathedral Films, 22 Min., C. The
story of Pentecost filmed with the fluid camera technique.
You Shall Receive Power, FS, Family Filmstrips, C with R. A worship service.

March 19—The Fellowship of the Redeemed
A Faithful Witness, MP, Family Films, 20 Min., C or B & W. The organization of the early Church.
Stephen, First Christian Martyr, Cathedral Films, B & W. The story from
the Bible.
The Church Is Born, FS, Cathedral Filmstrip, C with R. The story of the
early church.

March 26—One Body in Christ
Salvation and Christian Fellowship, MP, Family Films, 20 Min., C or B & W.
Human weakness cropped up early in the new church.
Workers Together With God, Family Films, 30 Min., B & W. Where each
bears his share of the load in Christian fellowship.
The Two Faces of Faith, FS, Friendship Press, C. How Christians express
their faith.

April 2—The Church of the Risen Lord
Dawn of Victory, MP, Concordia Films, 30 Min., C or B & W. The Easter
story closing with Christ's command to carry the gospel into all the world.
The Power of the Resurrection, Family Films, 60 Min., C or B & W. The
Bible story as told by Peter. An inspirational film.
The Resurrection, FS, Cathedral Filmstrips, C with R. A worship service.

April 9—The Church a Worshiping Community
The Other Six Days, MP, Family Films, 30 Min., B & W. The trials of a
seven-day-week Christian.
This Way to Heaven, Concordia Films, 30 Min., B & W. Our answer to a
child's question.
Christian Worship, FS, United Church Press, C. A filmstrip study of the
Protestant worship service.

April 16—The Church Organized for Missions
  Children of the World, MP, Cathedral Films, 30 Min., C. A call to serve in
  a time of need.
  The Faith of Yuan Tai, Concordia Films, 30 Min., B & W. What will you
  do with all the Yuan Tais?
  Point of Contact, FS, Cathedral Filmstrips, C with R. Something to stimulate a discussion.

April 23—The Church a Witnessing Community
  A New Thing, MP, Burt Martin Associates, 34 Min., C. Individual witnessing in today's world. Excellent material for this lesson.
  The Healing Witness, Family Films, 30 Min., B & W. Witnessing in the
  simple things in life.
  The "I and Thou" of It, FS, Cathedral Filmstrips, C with R. Excellent discussion material.

May 7—The Church Responds to Human Need
  The Captive, MP, Broadcasting and Films Commission, 34 Min., B & W.
  The concern of today's church.
  Decision at Delmo, Cathedral Films, 26 Min., B & W. Where should the
  church stand in the social world? A fine discussion film.
  The Church Ministers to the New Generation, FS, Family Filmstrips. A dis-
  cussion FS.

May 11—The Church Proclaims the Gospel
  Is This for Me? MP, Cathedral Films, 45 Min., B & W. Take time today to
  look at the ministry and the minister.
  Called to Serve, Family Films, 30 Min., B & W. Here we witness a young
  man faced with a call, and his response as he looks carefully at what the
  requirements really are.
  An Overview, FS, Cathedral Films, C with R. A review of today's church
  for discussion.

May 21—The Church's Teaching Ministry
  Crossing Point, MP, Family Films, 30 Min., C with R. A most unusual film
  and a must for today.
  The Great Challenge, Cathedral Films, 28 in., C. A challenge for every
  churchman.
  The Importance of Family Teaching, FS, C with R. We must not discon-
  tinue a teaching program that this hour demands.

May 28—The Church's Need for Renewal
  A World on Fire, MP, Cathedral Films, 30 Min., C or B & W. This will help
  stimulate a lively discussion on today's topic.
  Christian Faith in a Confused World, Family Films, 30 Min., B & W. The
  church must answer the call today.
  The Priesthood of All Believers, FS, Family FS, C with R. Today's new
  challenge.

JUNE–AUGUST 1972: The Bible and Devotional Life

June 4—What Is the Devotional Life?
  Faith of Our Families, MP, Concordia Films, 40 Min., B & W. An interesting
  study on methods of personal devotion.
  Does Christ Live in Your Home? Family Films, 30 Min., B & W. This film
  is interesting and thought provoking, and answers many questions on
  family devotions.

June 11—Meeting God Through the Scriptures
  Front Page Bible, MP, Family Films, 30 Min., B & W. An interesting use
  of the Bible; good for discussion.
  A Boy and His Bible, Family Films, 30 Min., B & W. A boy's Bible inspires
  his editor.
  Each With His Own Brush, FS, Friendship Press, C with R. An inspiring
  worship service for today.

June 18—Meeting God Through Prayer
   The Family Altar, MP, Concordia Films, 30 Min., B & W. Leading others
     to Christ through our own close walk with Him.
   Bible on the Table, Family Films, 30 Min., B & W. An experience in faith.
   Family Worship, FS, Family Films, C with R. A helpful approach to the
     problem of developing worship practice at home.

June 25—Hunger for Security
   The Great Revolution, MP, Concordia Films, 30 Min., C. The story of one
     man's search.
   Money for the Master, Concordia Films, 30 Min., B & W. What is the
     security we seek?
   Stewardship for Adults, Family Films, C with R. Presenting man's need for
     God and his need to share.

July 2—Discovering a Meaningful Faith
   Titan 5, MP, Concordia Films, 30 Min., C. Ask the question: where is God
     today?
   Message From Space, Family Films, 30 Min., B & W. New questions enter
     our quest for the answer.
   Freedom Under God, FS, United Church Press, C. A filmstrip study reflect-
     ing the value of freedom and security.

July 9—Finding God's Guidance
   Signposts Aloft, MP, Moody Films, 28 Min., C. The awareness of God's
     guidance in a space age.
   To Walk in Faith, Concordia Films, 30 Min., C. When tragedy enters, Christ
     is always there.
   How God Speaks to Us Today, FS, Family Filmstrips, C with R. God con-
     tinues to seek us, so we need only to turn to Him.

July 16—Praising the Lord
   God of Creation, MP, Moody Films, 28 Min., C. A film of great beauty.
   Hidden Treasures, Moody Films, 28 Min., C. The beauty in the smallest
     things fills our hearts with joy and praise.
   Hymn Stories, FS, Family FS, C with R. The story of four hymns of praise.

July 23—Confession and Forgiveness
   Painful Confession, MP, Concordia Films, 30 Min., C. A timely film, perfect
     for today's study.
   Alibi, Concordia Films, 30 Min., C. A film for discussion: What about a
     sin we know Christ has forgiven?
   A Man Can Change, FS, United Church Press, C. Discussion material.

July 30—Deepening Our Relationship With God
   The Big Account, MP, Concordia Films, C, B & W. A person faces the loss
     of job and social position. What is his reaction?
   Search for Truth, Cathedral Films, 30 Min., C. From the world of science:
     a search for a closer walk with God.
   This Sustaining Bread, FS, Friendship Press, C with R. A devotional film-
     strip for today.

August 6—Worshiping in the Congregation
   Wake Up, Charlie Churchman, MP, Family Films, 20 Min., B & W. A dis-
     cussion film with a new approach.
   Forward With Christ, Family Films, 30 Min., B & W. Congregations must
     search also for new meaning in work and worship.
   Finding Your Place in the Church, FS, Family Filmstrips, C with R. Excel-
     lent for today's discussion.

August 13—Worshiping in the Family
   Does Christ Live in Your Home? MP, Family Films, 30 Min., B & W. Good
     discussion material.
   Who Set Your Standards? Family Films, 30 Min., C or B & W. Finding the
     need for a family to worship together.
   Family Worship, FS, Family Films, C with R. Its importance in our life today.

August 20—Sharing in Christ's Work
The Captive, MP, Broadcasting and Films Commission, 28 Min., B & W.
Working in the mission field.
The Gift, Broadcasting and Films Commission, 23 Min., C. A unique film
on Christian stewardship. It is introduced through a resumé of the life
of Christ.
How Things Hide People and Liberate the Captives, FS, Friendship Films,
C with R. Both excellent discussion strips for today.

August 27—Sharing Through Witness
The Healing Witness, MP, Family Filmstrips, 30 Min., C or B & W. The
most effective way to live and serve.
Winsome Witness, Concordia Films, 30 Min., B & W. Youth carries a responsibility in the work of witnessing.
Digging Deep, FS, Friendship Filmstrips, C with R. A good discussion for
this lesson.

ADDRESSES OF PRODUCERS OF RECOMMENDED MATERIAL

Broadcasting and Films Commission
475 Riverside Drive
New York, N.Y. 10027

Cathedral Films and Filmstrips
2921 W. Alameda Ave.
Burbank, California 91505

Concordia Films and Filmstrips
3558 S. Jefferson St.
St. Louis, Mo. 63118

Family Films and Filmstrips
5823 Santa Monica Blvd.
Hollywood, California 90038

Burt Martin Associates
279 Fifth Ave.
New York, N.Y. 10016

Moody Institute of Science
12000 Washington Blvd.
Whittier, California 90606

United Church Press
Philadelphia, Penna. 19103

Protestant Council of New York City
475 Riverside Drive
New York, N.Y. 10027

Friendship Press
475 Riverside Drive
New York, N.Y. 10027

SEPTEMBER, OCTOBER, NOVEMBER 1971

THE DOCTRINE OF GOD

LESSON I—SEPTEMBER 5

THINKING ABOUT GOD

Background Scripture: Psalms 42, 53; 139; Acts 14:15-17; 17:22-31
Devotional Reading: Psalm 111

KING JAMES VERSION

PSALM 42 As the hart panteth after the water brooks, so panteth my soul after thee, O God.

2 My soul thirsteth for God, for the living God: when shall I come and appear before God?

3 My tears have been my meat day and night, while they continually say unto me, Where is thy God?

PSALM 53 The fool hath said in his heart, There is no God. Corrupt are they, and have done abominable iniquity: there is none that doeth good.

2 God looked down from heaven upon the children of men, to see if there were any that did understand, that did seek God.
PSALM 139 Whither shall I go from thy Spirit? or whither shall I flee from thy presence?

ACTS 17 22 Then Paul stood in the midst of Mars' hill, and said, Ye men of Athens, I perceive that in all things ye are too superstitious.
23 For as I passed by, and beheld your devotions, I found an altar with

REVISED STANDARD VERSION

PSALM 42 As a hart longs
for flowing streams,
so longs my soul
for thee, O God.

2 My soul thirsts for God,
for the living God.
When shall I come and behold
the face of God?

3 My tears have been my food
day and night,
while men say to me continually,
"Where is your God?"
PSALM 53 The fool says in his
heart,
"There is no God."
They are corrupt, doing abominable iniquity;
there is none that does good.

2 God looks down from heaven
upon the sons of men
to see if there are any that are wise,
that seek after God.
PSALM 139 7 Whither shall I go
from thy Spirit?
Or whither shall I flee from thy
presence?
ACTS 17 22 So Paul, standing in
the middle of the Aeropagus, said:
"Men of Athens, I perceive that in
every way you are very religious. 23
For as I passed along, and observed
the objects of your worship, I found

15

this inscription, To the Unknown God. Whom therefore ye ignorantly worship, him declare I unto you.

also an altar with this inscription, 'To an unknown god.' What therefore you worship as unknown, this I proclaim to you."

MEMORY SELECTION: God looks down from heaven upon the sons of men to see if there are any that are wise, that seek after God. Psalm 53:2 (RSV).

HOME DAILY BIBLE READINGS

Aug. 30. M. *The Desire for God's Presence,* Psalm 42:1-5.
Aug. 31. T. *The Need to Seek God,* Psalm 53.
Sept. 1. W. *God's Infinite Knowledge and Power,* Psalm 139:1-10.
Sept. 2. T. *"Wonderful Are Thy Works!"* Psalm 139:14-24.
Sept. 3. F. *Not Without Witness,* Acts 14:8-17.
Sept. 4. S. *All Men Are God's Children,* Acts 17:22-31.
Sept. 5. S. *God Dwells With Man,* Revelation 21:1-6.

BACKGROUND

For the next thirteen Sundays we shall be studying *the Biblical teaching about God,* not in terms of what *we* think about Him, but about what the Bible tells us of His character and His work, His revelation of Himself, the ways in which He speaks and acts as we seek Him in human need. We shall be "searching the Scriptures" all the way from the Psalms through Revelation.

In today's lesson, we start with the Psalms—with what the ancient Hebrews thought and said about God. And that is the place from which to start, for "they show us the human heart laid before God in all its moods and emotions . . ." (Dummelow's *One Volume Commentary*). Nowhere in the Bible do we find such an inspiring and uplifting picture of God, of His perfection, love, power, faithfulness, righteousness—and eternal, unfathomable *mystery*.

In the very beginning, man thought of God, and started wondering what He was like.

NOTES ON THE PRINTED TEXT

I. As the hart panteth after the water brooks, so panteth my soul after thee, O God, Psalm 42:1. The hart was a stag, a male deer (a female deer was a "hind"). Here, the Psalmist pictures a stag dying of thirst in a desert, "panting" for the sight of a water hole and finding every water hole dried up. He is surrounded by enemies—human and animal, waiting to kill and devour him.

Many a man lives like this! Many are lonely, fearful, thirsty, hungry —for *what?* Many find themselves surrounded by enemies who would be glad to kill them, if they could; in that agony of mind they look for help and security to the only source of help left to them—God, "panting for (beseeching) His aid.

Certainly the Psalmist had such a man in mind when he wrote the 42nd Psalm. He may even have been thinking of himself as such a man. In verse 3 he says that tears have been his daily food—that every day of his life he was conscious of the enemies who surrounded him, taunting him with the question, "Where is thy God? If this God of yours is so almighty, why doesn't He help you now?" The Psalmist longs for a sight of the face of The God in whom he believes: verse 2 suggests that he is in the Temple, praying, because he believes that God is to be found there.

Man has a built-in thirst (longing) for God. And whatever he says about it, he is driven to search for his maker until his quest succeeds and he has the security that nothing human can give.

II. The fool hath said in his heart, there is no God, Psalm 53:1. Psalm 53 has been called "the second edition of Psalm 14." Read both Psalms to see how close they are! Perhaps they came from two independent Psalm collections.

Both Psalms are a lament; they are discourses on the folly and wickedness of mankind. If Psalm 14 is the "first edition" we can understand why it is a lament, for this Psalm was written during the Persian period of Israel's history, which was a time for lament. God seemed to have deserted His people; many of them asked, "Where *is* He?" Others said, "We have been wrong; there isn't any God." The priests were almost as bad as the people; they had become materialistic and, in many instances, actually taught what we might call a "practical atheism."

The people were like the priests, or worse; many of them had become irreligious, agnostic, atheisic. Don't condemn them too quickly for that; in our own time, theologians have been telling us that "God is dead!" In our time many are turning from the church, leaving the ministry, ignoring God as though He were not there at all! It is a corruption, an abomination, an iniquity—and a *foolishness.* (Now the *idea* that God is dead seems to be dying among us; it had a *very* short life.)

God looked down from heaven, says verse 2, to see if there were any wise (faithful) men left. He found some, and He still finds them. In or out of the church, the overwhelming majority of people in our world are not fools; God finds enough who do understand, and who still seek Him. He was patient with us when we went through many such eras before; He has always waited with confidence—and He asks confidence of us now.

III. Whither shall I go from thy Spirit? or whither shall I flee from thy presence? Psalm 139:7. What a Psalm is the 139th! It tells us of the omniscience (the infinite knowledge) of God, of His omnipresence (His presence everywhere at once), of His providence for human life, of His hatred of sin. Read the *whole* Psalm to get it all.

Whither shall we go to get away from God? Can we hide from Him in a cave on Everest, or in a submarine in the depths of the sea? Could Jonah escape Him in the belly of a great fish? Could Judas Iscariot escape Him in his hell of remorse? The ultimate folly is to think that we can find a place where God is not. He created us. He knows us—every inch, every thought of us, every movement, every hope and every faith. Ikhnaton, the god of Egypt, was powerful by day, but he was powerless during the night! To the God of the Hebrew, God was with man day *and* night.

IV. Whom therefore ye ignorantly worship, him I declare unto you, Acts 17:23. Paul speaks these words to the Athenians who, with the Hebrews, had long been thinking and debating about the nature of God. But there was a great difference between the thinking of the two peoples. The Greeks had many gods—a whole "pantheon" of deities. There were so many of them that the Greek worshiper seeking the help of one or another of his gods didn't even know which one he should worship! He prayed in ignorance, unable to identify the right god for his special purpose. Hence, the inscription that Paul saw on an altar in Greece—"To the god whose name is not known!" It was ignorant—and superstitious worship.

Paul said to them, "There is no doubt in my mind of who and what God is. There is but one God, not many; He created the world, and every one in it. He has made us all of one blood. All of us are His creation, and we should worship Him together. "Whom therefore ye ignorantly worship, him I declare unto you."

This was a high milestone in the march of man. This is the concept of the one God of all men (verse 28).

SUGGESTIONS TO TEACHERS

Dr. J. Wallace Hamilton has written: "Here is the man who wrote the 42nd Psalm. We don't know who he was, which doesn't matter at all. He is every man, some time, when life gets snarled up and God gets far away. Around him are his pagan enemies, gleefully enjoying his predicament, taunting him day after day, needling him with the question: Where is thy God? All right. Where is He?"

It will take a lot of space and time to answer that question, but during the next three months we will try as we study the question of the existence of God. We start today with four statements about God:

1. There is a universal, undying thirst for God.
2. Some fools say there is no God.
3. We cannot escape the presence of God.
4. There is both mystery and certainty about God.

Memorize these four statements before you begin to teach.

TOPIC FOR ADULTS
THINKING ABOUT GOD

The Sea. "All of us are up against it when we try to comprehend God, because we can't jump outside our own experience. Can we say anything that is adequate to describe God? Of course not! We can no more delineate God than we can pour the ocean into a pint cup. Nevertheless, even a cupful of the ocean reveals its quality. So we go on trying to express what we think is true about God's quality in symbols drawn from our own life.

"Each time I visit my island off the coast of Maine, I fall in love with the sea again. Now I don't know all of the sea—wide areas of it will always be unknown to me—but I know the sea. It has a near range. It washes my island. I can sit beside it and bathe in it and sail over it, and be sung to sleep by the music of it. God is like that. He is so great in His vastness that we can think of Him only in symbolic terms, but He has a near range.

"The nub of the whole question about the nature of God lies in the answer to the question: where do we think in our own lives we touch the near range of God? I believe we come close to God wherever there is beauty, love, integrity, truth. So often, if you ask people where God is, their thoughts go shooting off among the stars; but it is deep down within human life that we find God. *God is love and he who abides in love abides in God, and God abides in Him.*" The simple truth is that we discover the Divine wherever love illumines life." Dr. Harry E. Fosdick, in an interview with Nardi Reeder Campion, *Reader's Digest,* October, 1966. Quoted by permission of *Reader's Digest.*

Small. "Often our God is too small, limited to certain programs, a certain church, a particular denomination. The story is told of a Japanese Christian in this counry who had just heard a sermon by a famous preacher. Asked what he thought of the sermon, he replied, 'From listening to him you get the idea that God is a white man, an American, and a Baptist. But everyone knows that God is a yellow man, a Japanese, and a Methodist' "—David Paul Byram, "Pastor-a-Go-Go," *Christianity Today.*

Well—what do *you* say He is?

The Heavens. "In a little church in the far south of Ireland, every window but one is of painted glass. Through that single exception may be seen a breath-taking view: a lake of deepest blue, studded with green islets and backed by range after range of purple hills. Under the window is the inscripion: 'The heavens declare the glory of God, and the firmament showeth his handiwork.' "—Robert Gibbings.

Looking. "I am reminded of a story about Vallentin: 'The late Munich comedian, Karl Vallentin . . . once enacted the following scene: the curtain goes up and reveals darkness; and in this darkness is a solitary circle of light thrown by a street lamp. Vallentin, with his long-drawn and deeply worried face, walks around this circle of light, desperately looking for something. "What have you lost?" asks a policeman who has entered the scene. "The key to my house." Upon which the policeman joins him in his search; they find nothing and after a while the policeman asks, "Are you sure you lost it here?" "No," says Vallentin, and pointing to a dark corner of the stage he says, "Over there." "Then why on earth are you looking for it here?" "There is no light over there," says Vallentin.' " (Eric Heller, in *The Disinherited Mind.*)

"God is not dead. We have just been looking for Him in the wrong places. He has arisen and gone before us."—Thomas A. Fry, Jr., in *Change, Chaos and Christianity* (Revell).

Questions for Pupils on the Next Lesson: 1. Can any man find and understand God simply by thinking about Him? 2. What is meant by the words in Exodus 33:20: ". . . you cannot see my face; for man shall not see me and live (RSV)?" 3. How do you know there is a God? 4. What do we mean when we speak of "the *glory* of God?" 5. Just how are God's ways not *our* ways? 6. If you had to explain what God is to a heathen who had never heard of Him, how would you do it? 7. Explain, "God is both transcendant and immanent."

TOPIC FOR YOUTH
THINKING ABOUT GOD

There He Goes! During the first World War, two soldiers sat in a wet, muddy trench, looking out across "No Man's Land," that fearful stretch between their trenches and the enemy's. The younger of the two looked bitterly at the dead bodies lying out there and cursed the evil and the madness that had turned men into beasts lusting for the lives of other men. He turned to his commanding officer and asked, "Captain, where is God?" If there was a God, he reasoned, why all this madness?

The captain pointed to two stretcher-bearers climbing up over the top of the trench to pick up a wounded man screaming with pain. The captain said, "Look, son. There He goes, out there."

Mrs. Booth. William Booth is commonly said to be the founder of the Salvation Army. In a way, it was not so much William as his wife Katherine who gave the impetus and the drive to that amazing army. It is told of Katherine Booth that one day, when she was a little girl, she went out to roll her hoop down the main street of her town, and ran into a policeman dragging a helpless drunk to the town jail. On the curb stood a mob more disgusting than the drunk; they hooted at the "culprit" and threw mud at him. Little Katherine watched the scene for a moment, then dropped her hoop and ran out to march down the street with him. She wanted everybody to know that there was one person in the town who cared what was happening to a human being in need. . . .

Perhaps it would sound strange, but may we say that God came down from heaven in the person of Jesus Christ to meet and conquer the pain and degradation of the human race.

God and the Lions. A famous British preacher, Charles H. Hulbert, had a great sermon on "God and Lions."

"It was based on the question put by King Darius to Daniel after his night in the lions' den. . . . 'O Daniel,' he asked, 'is thy God, whom thou servest continually, able to deliver thee from the lions?' In the sermon, Hulbert would line up the gods man worships—pleasure, power, fame, wealth . . . , and measure them against the lions that seek his soul to devour it—greed, lust and power and pride and every form of subtle sin. With piercing logic, he would show that the false gods in which man places his trust are insufficient to deliver him from the lions which lie in wait at every turn. The only God who is worth serving, he would conclude, is one who is bigger than the lions . . . .

"We live in an age which tends to devalue God. What may be regarded as reduced views of His nature and capacities are much in vogue. But we must remember that if they are to be really honest with God, we must be honest with His Word, and take our conception of Him from what is revealed there. What kind of a God are you envisaging and serving today? Is He the God of the speculative theologians, or the God of the Bible? Is He the God who cannot or the God who can? Is He able to deliver you from the lions which beset you? Is He only a god of the hills who leaves you in the lurch down in the valley where you need Him most? Or is your trust in the living and true God, the God who is able to deliver you from the power of the lions, the God and Father of our Lord and Saviour Jesus Christ, the God who gave His Son to die on the cross so that those who look to Him for salvation might have life forevermore? When Christ is ours, this God is ours. There is no other way, for it is our Lord Himself who solemnly assured us that no man can come to the Father but by Him."—*More Sermons I Should Like to Have Preached,* by A. Skevington Wood (Revell).

There Is! Helen Miller Lehman, in a little poem entitled, "Evidence," tells us where God is:

> The fool has said in his heart,
> "There is no God."
> But the fool has not the mind to know.
> Cycles of coppery suns and silvered moons
> Declare the wonderment of God,
> And all the things of earth
> Silently proclaim His handiwork.
> He spoke, and there was light;
> He breathed, and man became a living soul.
> Aeons of time declare the everlastingness of Him.
> The fragrance of a flower,
> And the mystery of a throbbing heart
> Witness to His creative power.
> The wise have not the minds to understand,
> Yet they must say in all humility,
> "There is a God!"

> From *Sourcebook for Speakers,* p. 177;
> quoted by permission of Zondervan
> Publishing House, publishers.

Finding Him. "We may . . . catch a glimpse of God in the experiences of everyday life. To those who have eyes to see, God is in every vista. To those who are tuned to hear, His still small voice whispers in every sound. God is found not only in church or at the Communion table or at some 'holy place.' In Bible times men and women were constantly finding Him in diverse and unexpected places. The Wise Men found Him in a stable. Simeon found Him in the Temple; the thief found Him on a cross. His contemporaries never knew for sure just where they would come upon Him. It is so today. God knocks at the door of our lives in a thousand ways and never twice the same."—Charles B. Templeton, in *Project No. 1.*

Sentence Sermon to Remember: They say God's dead; they say He's black; they say He's white. I say He's everything. He's love.—Pearl Bailey.

Questions for Pupils on the Next Lesson: 1. Why does God remain hidden, and a mystery? 2. Did Moses see God? 3. What powers does God have that are found in no one else? 4. Does anyone but God know the mind of God? 5. What do we mean by "The sovereignty of God?" 6. To whom or what can we compare God? 7. What do we mean when we say that God has "revealed" Himself?

LESSON II—SEPTEMBER 12

GOD TRANSCENDS OUR UNDERSTANDING

Background Scripture: Exodus 33:12-23; Job 11:7-9; 37:23-24;
Isaiah 40:18-26; Romans 11:33-36
Devotional Reading: Psalm 86:8-13

KING JAMES VERSION

EXODUS 33 19 And he said, I will make all my goodness pass before thee, and I will proclaim the name of the Lord before thee; and will be gracious to whom I will be gracious, and will show mercy on whom I will show mercy.

20 And he said, Thou canst not see my face: for there shall no man see me, and live.

ISAIAH 40 18 To whom then will ye liken God? or what likeness will ye compare unto him?

19 The workman melteth a graven image, and the goldsmith spreadeth it over with gold, and casteth silver chains.

20 He that is so impoverished that he hath no oblation chooseth a tree that will not rot; he seeketh unto him a cunning workman to prepare a graven image, that shall not be moved.

21 Have ye not known? have ye not heard? hath it not been told you from the beginning? have ye not understood from the foundations of the earth?

22 It is he that sitteth upon the circle of the earth, and the inhabitants thereof are as grasshoppers; that stretcheth out the heavens as a curtain, and spreadeth them out as a tent to dwell in:

23 That bringeth the princes to nothing; he maketh the judges of the earth as vanity.

24 Yea, they shall not be planted; yea, they shall not be sown; yea, their stock shall not take root in the earth: and he shall also blow upon them, and they shall wither, and the whirlwind shall take them away as stubble.

REVISED STANDARD VERSION

EXODUS 33 19 And he said, "I will make all my goodness pass before you, and will proclaim before you my name 'The Lord'; and I will be gracious to whom I will be gracious, and will show mercy on whom I will show mercy. 20 But," he said, "you cannot see my face; for man shall not see me and live."

ISAIAH 40 18 To whom then will you liken God,
　or what likeness compare with him?
19 The idol! a workman casts it,
　and a goldsmith overlays it with gold,
　and casts for it silver chains.
20 He who is impoverished chooses for an offering
　wood that will not rot;
he seeks out a skilful craftsman
　to set up an image that will not move.
21 Have you not known? Have you not heard?
　Has it not been told you from the beginning?
　Have you not understood from the foundations of the earth?
22 It is he who sits above the circle of the earth,
　and its inhabitants are like grasshoppers;
who stretches out the heavens like a curtain,
　and spreads them like a tent to dwell in;
23 who brings princes to nought,
　and makes the rulers of the earth as nothing.
24 Scarcely are they planted, scarcely sown,
　scarcely has their stem taken root in the earth,
when he blows upon them, and they wither,
　and the tempest carries them off like stubble.

25 To whom then will ye liken me, or shall I be equal? saith the Holy One.

26 Lift up your eyes on high, and behold who hath created these things, that bringeth out their host by number: he calleth them all by names by the greatness of his might, for that he is strong in power; not one faileth.

ROMANS 11 33 O the depth of the riches both of the wisdom and knowledge of God! how unsearchable are his judgments, and his ways past finding out!

34 For who hath known the mind of the Lord? or who hath been his counselor?

35 Or who hath first given to him, and it shall be recompensed unto him again?

36 For of him, and through him, and to him, are all things: to whom be glory for ever. Amen.

25 To whom then will you compare me, that I should be like him? says the Holy One.

26 Lift up your eyes on high and see: who created these? He who brings out their host by number, calling them all by name; by the greatness of his might, and because he is strong in power not one is missing.

ROMANS 11 33 O the depth of the riches and wisdom and knowledge of God! How unsearchable are his judgments and how inscrutable his ways!

34 "For who has known the mind of the Lord. or who has been his counselor?"

35 "Or who has given a gift to him that he might be repaid?"

36 For from him and through him and to him are all things. To him be glory forever. Amen.

MEMORY SELECTION: O the depth of the riches both of the wisdom and knowledge of God! how unsearchable are his judgments, and his ways past finding out! Romans 11:33.

HOME DAILY BIBLE READINGS

Sept.   6. M. *God Can Guide*, Exodus 33:12-23.
Sept.   7. T. *The Deep Things of God*, Job 11:7-9, 13-15.
Sept.   8. W. *God's Wondrous Work in Nature*, Job 37:5-11, 23-24.
Sept.   9. T. *Man's Limited Knowledge*, Job 38:12-21.
Sept. 10. F. *God's Sovereignty*, Isaiah 40:18-26.
Sept. 11. S. *God's Transcendent Knowledge*, Romans 11:33-36; 12:1-20.
Sept. 12. S. *God's Glory and Man's Honor*, Psalm 8.

BACKGROUND

Men have wondered from time immemorial what God is like—what He *looks* like!—and have wished that they might actually *see* Him as a *presence* in their midst. At times, they have even longed to touch Him (see Job 37:23). And no man has ever seen Him.

This is the mystery of God; someone has called it, "The Hiddenness of God." How, then, can we know that there *is* a God? "No man hath seen God at any time" (I John 4:12). That seems to deny man his greatest, fondest wish, doesn't it?

But God and the Scriptures give us one great promise that takes away the sting of disappointment, and explains *why* we cannot see God clearly, completely, with our own *human* eyes. . . .

NOTES ON THE PRINTED TEXT

I. I will make all my goodness pass before thee . . . Exodus 33:19. Moses, leading his people through the wilderness, had just seen those people bow down to a golden calf; he was furious at the sight of the calf, furious at the thought of his people committing the greatest of all sins—the sin of turning their backs on God. He turns to God almost in desperation, only to learn that God is about to refuse to go any farther with His stubborn, fickle people. As Moses pleads, God relents and promises to go on with them, to take them on toward the Promised Land. Thus God speaks to Moses; but even yet Moses does not see the face of God.

So he makes one more request of God—that he might see the "glory" of the Almighty. The word "glory" might be translated "full majesty." He wants a full, convincing, vision of God. If only he could have that, he and his people would be convinced beyond all doubt that God was with them.

No, replied God, that cannot be, *because the full glory of the face of God is beyond the reach of human understanding*, beyond the reach of the human *mind*. No man can ever see God perfectly, completely. (See Job 11:7-9). Not Moses, not even the angels, may see God's face.

But men may and will see the goodness, the grace and the mercy of God at work in the world. There would come the time when they would see such glory in the person of Jesus Christ. The divine *face* is never to be revealed, but there is to be a revelation of His person, will and power among men. There is a limit to the capacity of man to understand the full glory of God; there is no limit to God's capacity to reveal His purpose and power among men.

Should we not be satisfied with that? *Are we?*

II. To whom then will ye liken God? or what likeness will ye compare unto him? Isaiah 40:18. The people of Israel are captives in Babylonia; they are surrounded by the images and idols of a heathen people representing *their* gods—Marduk, Nabu, Shamash. They are a lonely, despairing people wondering whether God has at last deserted them, whether they should bow down to the Babylonian idols; after all, the Babylonians *had* conquered the "children of God," hadn't they? Perhaps there *was* a power in those idols; perhaps they, the Hebrews, should have some such image of *their* God, to worship and to help them conquer, or, at least to escape from, Babylon!

Isaiah the prophet scolds them and scoffs at the idols. Are not the idols and images something made by the hands of men? Are they not made of perishable wood, gold, silver? Do they not fall, and break, and rot, and disappear? How can they compare such perishable images with the God of Israel?

Look at your God, Israel! Is He not manifest in His work as Creator, as guide of the fortunes of men? He laid the foundations of the earth and put men on the earth; He has made kings and kingdoms and prospered or destroyed them; He has made the judges of the earth look like fools. Do you really think you can compare the idols and images of Babylon, the gods of the heathen, with *Him?* Lift up your eyes and see: *who created all this?* Lift up your eyes to the stars of heaven; they are like a great army, like a host of living, intelligent beings led and guided every night across the skies by their Creator, God. He calls them forth in his name. . . .

To whom or what can we compare such a God? He has no equal or equals. He is mighty beyond our understanding. None of us can paint or carve a likeness of Him! Many artists have tried that; their images are vague, unconvincing.

III. How unsearchable are his judgments, and his ways past finding out! Romans 11:33. Paul was a scholar, not often given to ecstacy. But here in Romans 11 he *sings!* He is almost overcome as he contemplates the glorious mystery of God. The very thought of God's ways and power are "past finding out." His wisdom, His knowledge, His judgments are beyond our finite powers to understand. Who has *ever* understood the infinity of His mind?

Who, Paul asks, could give Him advice? (See Isaiah 40:13.) How can any of us ever recompense (repay) Him? (See Job 41:11.) "From him and through him and to him are *all* things." To such a God as this "be glory for ever" (verse 36)!

God remains a mystery too great for us. If He were not that, He would not be God at all.

SUGGESTIONS TO TEACHERS

The subject of this lesson "God Transcends Our Understanding," is confusing. When we say He is transcendent, we mean that He is beyond the world, and if He is beyond the world—how can we be expected to *understand* Him? It reminds us of a professor of philosophy who said to a freshman class, "You are about to undertake a study of the unknown and the unknowable." But as the class progressed it became evident that there was a lot they could learn about life that, before they had met the professor, they never thought they could learn.

And we say, "God is also 'immanent.' " That is, He is *in* the world, as well as beyond or above it. It takes some thinking, but it can be done: we can understand that while God remains hidden from human view, He is everywhere and in everything around us. What we can gain today may not be a full understanding of God, but it can be the beginning of a knowledge of Him on which we can start to build. . . .

TOPIC FOR ADULTS
GOD TRANSCENDS OUR UNDERSTANDING

God in a Box. The late J. Wallace Hamilton spoke eloquently of the majesty and mystery of God. Preaching on our Scripture lesson (Exodus 33:20), and of the denial to Moses of the privilege of seeing the face and form of God, he said:

"What sort of God would He be that you and I could get our minds around or hold inside our little box of brains? The angels must smile often at the glibness of little men who seem to think the human mind is ultimate, that the limit of its reach is the limit of the real. As the little man said as he stood with a curved glass in his hand, 'I have swept the heavens with my telescope and I find no God there.' A God who could be found with a piece of glass could not be God. A God who could be defined in the words of a creed could not be God. And if we could get our minds clear around Him, we would have to begin immediately to doubt Him—for the God who can create galaxies of galaxies, yet whose Spirit pervades all living things, is hardly the sort of God we can 'read like a book' or encompass in our little box of brains. Why bother with a God who is no bigger than our grasp?"

This is the transcendence—no, the incomprehensibility—of God. He is too big for our understanding.

The Image. "What," asks some unknown author, "is your image of God? Is He a long, dull, oblong blur? A celestial Santa Claus?" Or "the Great Disposer of Events," as Lincoln conceived Him? A Father image not needed now that "man has come of age?" "The ground of being?"

"Theodore P. Ferris hopes 'your image of God is of a living Presence . . . a love that sustains you.' You find it in the Bible, if you look in the right places—Psalm 139, Isaiah 40. . . . Begin with Jesus, with the way He lived . . . loved . . . lost His life . . . lives now."—Author unknown.

That is *not* incomprehensible!

Abstractions, Religion. " 'Son,' said the chaplain to the troubled doubter, 'if you believe in good, then you really believe in God. In more than twenty-three languages and dialects, good is a synonym for God. What you really mean when you say you don't believe in God is that you don't believe in the existence of an elderly gentleman with a white beard, seated on a golden throne somewhere in the sky. Well, I don't either. But if you believe in acting according to your best understanding of all that is good, then you believe in God.'

" 'But those things—aren't they just abstractions?' asked the boy.

" 'Not when translated into action. In action, abstractions come to life. That's what we call religion.' "—From *Advance*.

Symbols. "In the Metropolitan Museum of Art in New York there is a fine collection of scarabs, charms which the ancients wore. A beautiful one of dark blue has carved upon it a mystic figure, and under the symbol are these words: 'Fear not, Upwawel is beside thee.' And who is Upwawel? The Jackal God. And in simple faith, twenty centuries ago, the Egyptian carved that symbol. What foolishness! you say. There's no reality to a Jackal God; there is no God like that to protect man. No, and yet this man of the far past was not wholly wrong. He was right in thinking that there was an unseen power on whom he could depend; wrong when he thought that he [the 'unseen power'] lived in the form of a jackal. He was right in thinking that there was a friendly someone; wrong in the symbol which he gave to the one in whom he trusted.

"So through the ages the symbols of God have changed, but the truth which the symbols try to say have become more and more clear. And perhaps the symbol of God as Father is not the final picture which the world will have of Him."—Harry W. Kimball.

Do you agree with that last line? If not, what symbol would you suggest?

Wonders. Every religion ever conceived in the mind of man has found the evidences of God overwhelming. The Psalms are full of that astonishing wonder about God, and the Koran of Islam says, "If all the trees on

earth were pens and if there were seven oceans full of ink, they could
not suffice to describe the wonders of the Almighty."

God's face may be "transcendant"; His works are immanent.

Questions for Pupils on the Next Lesson: 1. What was the "Word"
mentioned in John 1:1? 2. Describe the "light [that] shines in the darkness" (John 1:5). 3. How and when was the Word made flesh, and *why?*
4. Where do *you* look to see God revealed? 5. *Why* do we believe that
there is a creative mind behind the universe? 6. Name three ways in which
the Old Testament prophets gave us a revelation of God. 7. What is the
most perfect revelaton of God the world has ever seen?

TOPIC FOR YOUTH
GOD TRANSCENDS OUR UNDERSTANDING

Candle, Sun, God. In Nevada, the scientists exploded a man-made
candle known as the atomic bomb. The scientists crouched in trenches
miles away from the point of explosion, and held darkened glasses before
their eyes, lest they be blinded by the blazing light; one scientist called
it "a light that concentrated within itself the intensity of a hundred suns."

That was a hundred suns. Now try an experiment. Go out of doors and
try looking at just the *one* sun in the heavens. Don't look very long. It
can *blind* you! You know that sun is there; you can feel it if you cannot
look at it, but you know it is there, and that your very life depends on
the light it spreads over our earth.

If you cannot look at the light of an atomic bomb explosion, or even
at the sun in the sky above you, what makes you think that you can
bear the full light of God? As one minister has asked, "If you cannot face
the candle, how can you look at the sun?" Or at God. . . ?

Seeing. "A boy was taken by his father on a camping trip in the Adi-
rondacks. They hired a guide, left the beaten trails, and spent a week in
the heart of the woods. The boy was greatly impressed by the ability of
the guide to see all sorts of things, invisible to the ordinary eye. One day,
after the guide had been pointing out some of the hidden secrets of nature, the lad asked with an awed voice, 'Mister, can you see God?'

"The old man replied, 'My boy, it's getting so I can hardly see anything
else when I'm out in the woods.' "—Walter D. Cavert.

God is present in His world—for those who have eyes to see. . . .

Searching for God. Leo Tolstoy searched for God a long, long time before he found Him. And then he found God in a most unexpected place:

"I began to draw near to the believers among the poor, the simple and
ignorant, the pilgrims, monks and peasants. The more I contemplated the
lives of these simple folk, the more deeply was I convinced of the reality
of their faith, which I perceived to be a necessity for them, for it alone
gave life a meaning and made it worth living. The more I learned of
these men of faith, the more I liked them and the easier I felt it so to
live. . . . Still I did not find Him whom I sought. Again I was left in
despair.

"Thus did moods of joy and despair come and go until one day in the
early spring, seeking after God in my thoughts, a flash of joy illumined

my soul. I realized that the *conception* of God was not God Himself. I felt that I had truly lived only when I believed in God. Live to seek God, and life will not be without Him. The light that shone then never left me. The simple men around me, the working classes, were the real Russian people. They made the meaning of life clear. I came to know that God is all we need."

A poet whose name is unknown says:

> I sought my soul,
>   But my soul I could not see.
> I sought my God,
>   But my God eluded me.
> I sought my brother,
>   And I found all three.

How long since you saw God in your brother?

God in Space. "I did not see God looking into my space cabin window as I did not see God looking into my car's windshield on earth. But I could recognize His work in the stars as well as when walking among flowers in a garden. If you can be with God on earth you can be with God in space as well."—James V. McDivitt, American astronaut.

Darkness, Light. We pity those people who have lost God somewhere in the darkness of doubt and uncertainty, who try to live as though He were too far away to be of much use to us on earth.

"Helen Keller, beleaguered within the citadel of sense, lets the world in through the postern gates of touch and smell. In *The Story of My Life* she writes: 'Sometimes I go rowing without the rudder. It is fun to try to steer by the scent of the water grasses and lillies, and of bushes that grow on the shore.' She touches the lips of a friend and holds conversation across incredible abysses of silence. She puts her marvelously sensitive fingers under the belly of a violin and thrills in ecstacy over *The Hymn to the Sun.* Helen Keller has found God in the darkness though others have missed Him in the light."—R. H. Miller.

Sentence Sermon to Remember: We are like photographic negatives: the full personality, the image of God, is latent and will not be developed until it is exposed to love.—George Sweazey.

Questions for Pupils on the Next Lesson: 1. What is "grace?" 2. Where should we look to see revelations of God? 3. Did God make the universe in a week or in millions of years? 4. Which of the prophets do you like best, and why? 5. *How* was God revealed in Jesus Christ? 6. Do you think God reveals Himself in nature? Explain. 7. What does the book of Revelation reveal?

LESSON III—SEPTEMBER 19

GOD REVEALS HIMSELF

Background Scripture: John 1:1-18
Devotional Reading: Isaiah 40:21-31

JOHN 1 In the beginning was the Word, and the Word was with God, and The Word was God.

2 The same was in the beginning with God.

3 All things were made by him; and without him was not any thing made that was made.

4 In him was life; and the life was the light of men.

5 And the light shineth in darkness; and the darkness comprehended it not.

9 That was the true Light, which lighteth every man that cometh into the world.

10 He was in the world, and the world was made by him, and the world knew him not.

11 He came unto his own, and his own received him not.

12 But as many as received him, to them gave he power to become the sons of God, even to them that believe on his name:

13 Which were born, not of blood, nor of the will of the flesh, nor of the will of man, but of God.

14 And the Word was made flesh, and dwelt among us, (and we beheld his glory, the glory as of the only begotten of the Father,) full of grace and truth.

15 John bare witness of him, and cried, saying, This was he of whom I spake, He that cometh after me is preferred before me; for he was before me.

16 And of his fulness have all we received, and grace for grace.

17 For the law was given by Moses, but grace and truth came by Jesus Christ.

18 No man hath seen God at any time; the only begotten Son, which is in the bosom of the Father, he hath declared him.

JOHN 1 In the beginnig was the Word, and the Word was with God, and the Word was God. 2 He was in the beginning with God; 3 all things were made through him, and without him was not anything made that was made. 4 In him was life, and the life was the light of men. 5 The light shines in the darkness, and the darkness has not overcome it.

9 The true light that enlightens every man was coming into the world. 10 He was in the world, and the world was made through him, yet the world knew him not. 11 He came to his own home, and his own people received him not. 12 But to all who received him, who believed in his name, he gave power to become children of God; 13 who were born, not of blood nor of the will of the flesh nor of the will of man, but of God.

14 And the Word became flesh and dwelt among us, full of grace and truth; we have beheld his glory, glory as of the only Son from the Father. (15 John bore witness to him, and cried, "This was he of whom I said, 'He who comes after me ranks before me, for he was before me.'") 16 And from his fullness have we all received, grace upon grace. 17 For the law was given through Moses; grace and truth came through Jesus Christ. 18 No one has ever seen God; the only Son, who is in the bosom of the Father, he has made him known.

MEMORY SELECTION: In many and various ways God spoke of old to our fathers by the prophets; but in these last days he has spoken to us by a Son, whom he appointed the heir of all things, through whom also he created the world. Hebrews 1:1-2 (RSV).

HOME DAILY BIBLE READINGS

Sept. 13. M. *God in His Creation,* Psalm 19:1-6.
Sept. 14. T. *Word of Life and Light,* John 1:1-8.
Sept. 15. W. *"The Word Became Flesh,"* John 1:9-18.
Sept. 16. T. *Seen Through Jesus Christ,* John 14:5-11.
Sept. 17. F. *All of God's Fullness,* Colossians 1:15-30.
Sept. 18. S. *"God Spoke . . . by a Son,"* Hebrews 1:1-8.
Sept. 19. S. *The Incomparable Sovereign,* Isaiah 40:21-31.

BACKGROUND

Last week we said that "no man hath seen God at any time." In the New Testament that statement is made twice—in I John 4:12, and in the Gospel of John (1:18). No man has seen God "face to face." But, from time to time, there have been some very definite revelations, or revealings, of God, and it is with these revealings that we are concerned today.

Where do we look for these revelations? Where and when did God reveal to men His character and His purpose with them? John says there are three places to which we can look. . . .

NOTES ON THE PRINTED TEXT

I. In the beginning was the Word, and the Word was with God, and the Word was God, John 1:1. The first place to look for a revelation of God, says John, is in the very beginning of time. "In the beginning," says the very first verse of the Bible, "God created the heaven and the earth." Away back there! Even before the heaven and the earth were formed, God was there; He first *revealed* Himself in His work of creation.

John speaks of "the Word." What was the Word? This is the English translation of a Greek word, "Logos." One of our dictionaries says, "The Word is . . . a form of divine revelation, a means used by God to communicate with men the truth of Himself or the knowledge of His will." Dr. Floyd V. Filson describes the Word as "the active divine agent of God" which entered history the moment history began. We could say that the agent was "one in nature with God," just as Jesus Christ and the Holy Spirit (also God's agent!) are one with Him.

In the beginning—God! If you want to see what God is, and how He works, and what He has done on our earth and for mankind, look at the creation. Many men of many faiths and nationalities have tried to explain the creation of matter, earth and man, and most of them have failed; but the Hebrew did well when he put God at the very foundation of all life. It was revealed to him that the universe and everything and everyone in it *must* have been created by an all-wise, all-powerful mind which they called God, and that it cannot be understood as anything but part of a divine *plan.*

Can we disagree with that? Can we possibly believe that the universe just *happened* to get together? That it was all *accidental?* Can we who wear Swiss watches on our wrists and marvel at their perfection look at sun, stars, moons and planets moving in such perfect order and *not* believe that a Mind (God) made them and guides them? When a cynic said that those who believed in a God-created universe were "credulous," a Christian scholar replied that it took more credulity *not* to believe in it! The universe without the molding hand of God is incredible.

All things were made by Him; He even gave life, the most precious gift of all, and He gave light to illumine life and to make it "livable." His light "shines in the darkness, and the darkness has not overcome it" (verse 5, RSV). That is, the darkness of man's doubt has not yet put out the light that came to earth as it was created—and no better explanation of how the earth and all on it were formed and developed has yet been offered.

II. That was the true Light, which lighteth every man that cometh into the world, John 1:9. Verses 9-13 carry on, or develop, the thought expressed in verses 4-5—that the Word or the Light revealed God and enlightened certain men (prophets) during the Old Testament period. The Word was working then, the Light was here then, but few saw it. It came to "his own"—to Israel, His particularly "chosen" people—but they "received him not." Those who did see it and understand and accept it received His power and became the sons of God (verse 12).

So this is the second place in which God revealed Himself: in the prophets. We must read and study the Old Testament prophets if we want a revelation for ourselves; the prophets were men "tuned in" to God, men who listened for His voice, men who echoed His voice. They were the forerunners of Jesus; many, many times Jesus admitted His debt to them, and He quoted them freely and often. They had visions of God, and visions, while not perfect in revelation or to understanding, are, nevertheless, an important stage in the development of our conception of God. Read Isaiah!

Be sure you understand *this:* this sonship with God came, not by physical creation, by any *human* birthright or tradition, not by physical descent (blood) or physical love (the flesh, or the will of fleshy man) but spiritually, through the action of a redeeming and saving God, through the Word, the Light.

Good as it was, it was incomplete in the Old Testament and all through Old Testament times. Now, John takes a giant step forward as he describes how the *perfect* revelation came.

III. And the Word was made flesh, and dwelt among us, John 1:14. One night, says Dr. Paul Scherer, "God came down the ladder of heaven with a baby in His arms!" Beautiful! This was Christmas; this was the incarnation. This was God in the flesh of man, God in Christ.

Up to this moment, the eye of man had never seen God; now men saw Him incarnate in His Son, saw His grace and truth at work, *saw what God was like.* The prophets had predicted Him; John the Baptist had witnessed to His coming, and now the long-predicted coming was accomplished. Never before, never since, have we so clearly seen the nature of God as we see it in Christ. "For all previous revelations of God suffered from necessary imperfection; only through the Son in intimate relation to the Father could the Fatherhood be fully revealed"—Alfred E. Garvie, in *The Abingdon Bible Commentary,* p. 1067. Quoted by permission of Abingdon Press, publishers.

SUGGESTIONS TO TEACHERS

Over and over again, we hear it said that "the primary need of the world and of mankind is an awareness of God and obedience to Him." Like many another religious maxim, this is "easier said than done." Some seek Him in a definition; we can no more find God in a definition than we can trap a tempest in a paper bag! (A tempest so trapped, if it could be trapped, would be nothing more than a bagful of stale air; definitions have a way of becoming stale, too!) Neither can we trap God in a strictly scientific explanation, for science changes its concepts and findings from day to day and year to year.

Where, then, and how do we find God? We find Him when, first, we understand that *God reveals Himself*, and that He does not depend on man's efforts. He reveals Himself in nature (creation), in the Biblical prophets, above all in Christ Jesus.

And, second, He demands of man only that man open his heart and receive Him, wherever and however He chooses to reveal Himself.

Start with those two propositions. Then find out how and in what God has revealed Himself to men *historically*. . . .

TOPIC FOR ADULTS
GOD REVEALS HIMSELF

Reality. "Studdert-Kennedy, that great English preacher who died a few years ago, has left us a beautiful paragraph in which he describes his experience of finding God. Here is the setting:

" 'I was alone at night on a moor by the sea. Above me was a dark velvet dome and a million stars. Beneath me, moving slowly in a heavy swell, the sea. No sound but the rustling of a breeze through the heather and the boom of waves against the cliff. I was alone, and yet at the same time acutely concious of that vast, shadowy, mysterious other-than-myself looming up out of the darkness over against me—the universe and the world, and all those other worlds that shone like points of light above me.'

"His feelings at that moment he compared to those of another time when he lay alone in No Man's Land, with his heart in his mouth, watching a dark moving object drawing closer to him. Suppose he had whispered to that object, 'Who goes there?' Would the answer be a bullet, a friendly word, or mere silence? Suppose he had whispered to that mysterious object called the universe. Would the answer be a friend, a foe, or just an indifferent mass without either love or hatred at its heart? Then he tells us that he made the cry to the universe and that only one word came back out of the stillness of the night—'God!' At that moment religion was born in his heart. He stood in the presence of a God who had revealed Himself. And it is only in some such moments of solitude that God will become real to you and to me."—Arthur J. Pfohl.

Dawn. "Steadily the wondrous transfiguration went on. Hands of angels hidden from mortal eyes shifted the scenery of the heavens; the glories of night dissolved into the glories of the dawn. Faint streaks of purple soon blushed across the sky, the whole celestial conclave was filled with the inflowing tide of the morning light which came down from above in one grand ocean of radiance; till at length a flash of purple blazed out from above the horizon, and turned the dewey teardrops of flower and leaf into rubies and diamonds. In a few seconds the everlasting gates of the morning were thrown open, and the lord of the day, arrayed in glories too severe for the gaze of man, began his course. I am filled with amazement when I am told that in this enlightened age there are persons who can witness this daily manifestation of the power and wisdom of the Creator and yet say in their hearts, 'There is no God.' "—Edward Everett.

He who fails to see God revealing Himself every morning in the dawn must be blinder than blind.

God Revealed in Christ. "I once attended a reception at which the well-known teacher Dr. William Lyon Phelps was the guest of honor; and, speaking to a small group of us during the course of the evening, he suddenly said, 'You know, I am a unitarian.' All of us were completely surprised, because we knew that he was not only a member of the Calvary Baptist Church in New Haven, but its honorary pastor, having been ordained to the ministry late in life. Then, after Dr. Phelps discerned that we were sufficiently shocked, he added, 'I mean by that, that Jesus is the only God I know.' This, of course, is not at all the position of the Unitarians, but it illustrated how some Christians become so absorbed in the person of Christ that they overlook the fact that He came into the world for the purpose of leading men to God the Father, from whom how many, like the prodigal son, have gone astray. Yet we have much sympathy with Dr. Phelps' statement, for when we have found Christ we feel that we are at the end of our quest. 'He that hath seen me,' said Jesus, 'hath seen the Father.' "—From a sermon by Edward Hughes Pruden.

(Notice that Dr. Phelps used a small "u" in "unitarian" in his statement. Do you see *why?*)

Question for Pupils on the Next Lesson: 1. Why does God allow the wicked to prosper? 2. Describe the mind and mood of the man who wrote Psalm 73. 3. Does crime pay—ever? 4. What kind of prosperity or success does God want us to have? 5. What meaning has God given to *your* life? Explain in detail. 6. Has God been sufficient for all your needs? 7. Do you think God has a life plan for every man in the world?

TOPIC FOR YOUTH
YOU CAN KNOW GOD

God and Man. "Man can meet God in everyday experiences. Jesus was certain of this. When He told about the Kingdom of God, He used as illustration the common, ordinary events of human life: a housewife doing her spring cleaning; a farmer at his regular planting; a merchant conducting his usual business. It is in the day-to-day routine of life that God breaks through with His sovereign claims."—*The Crusader.*

Not Enough. Certainly God reveals Himself in nature. He speaks in the resurrection of every spring; His face is in the flower, His power in the sea breaking over the rocks, in the beauty of trees afire with His coloring in autumn. Some poet has written:

As near as green grass to a hill,
  As petals of gold to a daffodil,
As near as the sunlight is to the sod,
  So near to the human heart is God.

And another:

In the rustling grass
I hear Him pass.

Yes! no matter which way we turn in nature, we hear her whisper of the creator.

But—is this enough? This is evidence of His power as creator, but does not mankind need something more? And does not mankind find cruelty behind the beauties of nature? Do we not find her "red in tooth and claw?" Do we not see poisonous snakes, man-eating beasts, insects feeding on each other in a deadly battle for survival? It would seem, when we look at nature closely, that the God we see here is impersonal and indifferent. . . .

We do not find the *love* of God in nature. We do find that love in the Son of God on His cross. . . . God is more, much, much more personal *there!*

Finding, Losing. "Some years ago a busy layman wistfully told a friend who was a minister that he would like to find God and follow Christ. Then he added, 'How should I go about it?' The minister replied, 'I would start by worshiping God in church and by studying the Gospels.' To this the layman replied, 'Well, I'm sorry, but I haven't time for that.'

"I have never forgotten my friend's reply: 'You cannot find God in your spare moments.'"—*Christ Speaks from the Cross,* by Gardiner M. Day (Seabury Press).

How God Looks. "J. B. Martin in his early years of writing found it necessary to be gone from home for long periods of time, doing research for his articles. When his children were small, they memorized his face from a picture so they would recognize him when he came home. Is that a parable for how it is between us and God? Only we do the traveling here, into many far countries of desire and idolatry, forgetting 'how God looks.' But in Jesus Christ we have a picture to memorize."—*Christian Herald.*

A famous Methodist bishop once wrote a book entitled "The Christlike God." It was a good title, and a good idea. Think about it!

Not . . . But. Dr. Robert H. Hamill has said that "God is not as likely to be found in a burning bush as in a burning issue. Not in water turned to wine but in boredom turned to joy. Not in the life brought from Lazarus' tomb but in life brought from despair. . . ."

He was not denying that Moses heard the voice in the burning bush, or that water was turned into wine at Cana—but only that God has many ways of revealing Himself, and that unless we are aware of this we can miss Him completely. . . .

When He Comes. We do not know who wrote this short verse; we can only wish we had:

Thou shalt know Him when He comes,
Not by any din of drums,

Not by vantage of His airs,
Nor by anything He wears;
Neither by His crown,
Nor His gown,
But His presence known shall be
By the holy harmony
Which His coming makes in thee.

Revealing. The Mosque of Santa Sophia in Istanbul was not always a mosque; it was built by Constantine, and for long years it was a Christian church—the Christian Church of the Divine Wisdom. When the Turks conquered the city in 1453 it became the mosque of Aya Sofia, and the conquerors did their best to destroy all marks and signs that had once marked it as a place of Christian worship.

Just a few years ago we stood under the marvelous dome of the mosque, watching some men high above upon scaffolds, washing the walls and scraping away ancient plaster. They were a team of archeologists from the University of Pennsylvania. As they worked, we saw a revelation: under the old plaster, smeared on centuries ago by the Moslem Turks, there was a beautiful circle of Christian symbols running all around the dome!

God often reveals Himself when men care enough to wash off the accumulated grime of sin, to remove the "plaster" of hatred and intolerance and religious conflict smeared over His name and spirit by the hands of men.

He expects us to do just that; His revelation awaits it!

Sentence Sermon to Remember: To find God in humanity's need is not the only way to find Him, but if one does not find Him there, he is not apt to find Him anywhere else.—Georgia Harkness.

Questions for Pupils on the Next Lesson: 1. Just how is God "good to the upright" (Psalm 73:1)? 2. Why should you be envious of rich wicked men? 3. What did Jesus have to say about the wicked prospering? 4. Does God love the wicked? 5. True or false: "The income tax has made us a nation of cheats"? 6. Where did the Psalmist go to find the answer to his questions? 7. Exactly *what* is meaningful in your life?

LESSON IV—SEPTEMBER 26

GOD GIVES MEANING TO LIFE

Background Scripture: Psalm 73; Ephesians 1
Devotional Reading: Philippians 3:4-16

KING JAMES VERSION

PSALM 73 Truly God is good to Israel, even to such as are of a clean heart.

2 But as for me, my feet were almost gone; my steps had well-nigh slipped.

3 For I was envious at the foolish, when I saw the prosperity of the wicked.

16 When I thought to know this, it was too painful for me;

17 Until I went into the sanctuary of God; then understood I their end.

21 Thus my heart was grieved, and I was pricked in my reins.

22 So foolish was I, and ignorant: I was as a beast before thee.

23 Nevertheless I am continually with thee: thou hast holden me by my right hand.

24 Thou shalt guide me with thy counsel, and afterward receive me to glory.

25 Whom have I in heaven but thee? and there is none upon earth that I desire besides thee.

26 My flesh and my heart faileth: but God is the strength of my heart, and my portion for ever.

EPHESIANS 1 9 Having made known unto us the mystery of his will, according to his good pleasure which he hath purposed in himself:

10 That in the dispensation of the fulness of times he might gather together in one all things in Christ, both which are in heaven, and which are on earth; even in him:

REVISED STANDARD VERSION

PSALM 73 Truly God is good to the upright,
to those who are pure in heart.

2 But as for me, my feet had almost stumbled,
my steps had well nigh slipped.

3 For I was envious of the arrogant,
when I saw the prosperity of the wicked.

16 But when I thought how to understand this,
it seemed to me a wearisome task,

17 until I went into the sanctuary of God;
then I perceived their end.

21 When my soul was embittered,
when I was pricked in heart,

22 I was stupid and ignorant,
I was like a beast toward thee.

23 Nevertheless I am continually with thee;
thou dost hold my right hand.

24 Thou dost guide me with thy counsel,
and afterward thou wilt receive me to glory.

25 Whom have I in heaven but thee?
And there is nothing upon earth that I desire besides thee.

26 My flesh and my heart may fail,
but God is the strength of my heart and my portion for ever.

EPHESIANS 1 9 For he has made known to us in all wisdom and insight the mystery of his will, according to his purpose which he set forth in Christ 10 as a plan for the fullness of time, to unite all things in him, things in heaven and things on earth.

MEMORY SELECTION: He destined us in love to be his sons through Jesus Christ, according to the purpose of his will. Ephesians 1:5 (RSV).

HOME DAILY BIBLE READINGS

Sept. 20. M. *When the Wicked Prosper,* Psalm 73:1-9.
Sept. 21. T. *God Gives Understanding,* Psalm 73:10-20.
Sept. 22. W. *Our Strength and Portion,* Psalm 73:21-28.

Sept. 23. T. *God's Purpose and Plan,* Ephesians 1:1-8.
Sept. 24. F. *"For the Praise of His Glory,"* Ephesians 1:9-14.
Sept. 25. S. *Hope, Inheritance and Power,* Ephesians 1:15-23.
Sept. 26. S. *Christ Is the Answer,* Philippians 3:4-16.

BACKGROUND

The Book of Job and the Book of Psalms may be the oldest books in the Bible, both in point of the times at which they were written and the social and religious backgrounds against which they were written. And as we read it, Psalm 73 seems almost to have been written by Job! Indeed, the gaunt old man who suffered so much for no apparent reason could very easily have written it, for it asks the same questions that *he* asked: Why do the righteous suffer? Why do the wicked prosper? And why does God permit all this?

The Psalm is divided into two parts; in verses 1-14, the Psalmist is a wailing pessimist telling of how he was tempted to desert God and how he nearly lost his faith; in verses 15-28, he is a singing optimist, telling us how he came back to faith and how he found meaning in life.

This is Old Testament material. For the Christian, there are two verses in Ephesians which bring the whole thing sharply up to date. . . .

NOTES ON THE PRINTED TEXT

I. . . . as for me, my feet had almost stumbled, Psalm 73:2 (RSV). The man who wrote this had been a sufferer much like Job. He had not suffered so much physically as Job had, but mentally and spiritually he had been having a hard time of it. He knew in his heart that God had been good to Israel, and good, too, to "such as are of a clean heart," but *his* heart was far from clean, and his mind was twisted with doubt. He was like so many of us today! A bishop said recently that sometimes it seems to him that more are leaving the modern church than are joining it! The devils of doubt are as active now as they were when Psalm 73 was written.

What was it that led this Psalmist into the depths of doubt? What was it that "shook him up"—shook his faith? It was simply that when he looked around at his neighbors, he saw that the wicked ones seemed to be prosperous and happy, while the righteous were poor and often unhappy! He had been taught that it was the other way around: That the righteous prospered, and the wicked were punished. It seemed not to be working out that way where *he* lived! He was "envious" of the arrogant (wicked) as they prospered.

We should know what he means, when he says this. We hear it said that crime doesn't pay—and then we read in the newspapers that a labor leader lives like a king and refuses to explain "where he got it," that in a suburb of Chicago a lot of retired racketeers live in palaces, that a group of Army profiteers stole three hundred thousand dollars a year for who knows how many years . . . and we wonder just as the Psalmist wondered.

Why do the wicked prosper? It's still a bitter question. . . .

II. But when I thought how to understand this, it seemed to me a wearisome task . . . , Psalm 73:16 (RSV). Or he might have said, "It's

all too much for me to understand; I am tired of trying; I give up. . . ."
Many of us do that; we stop trying to figure it out, to think it through;
we just "sweep it under the rug"—turn away from it, begin to tolerate
evil—and then even to respect and practice it!

Our Psalmist couldn't do that; as the King James translation puts it,
he says that the hunt was more "painful" than wearisome. He was a
deeply troubled man—especially troubled when he realized that if he
spoke his thoughts out loud (his thoughts of the apparent failure of God
really to punish the wicked) he might disturb the faith of those who
still believed in God, and upset them, which he did not want to do. He
was a good man, this Psalmist—a compassionate, wistful man who just
couldn't turn a cold shoulder to God, even though he could not understand. . . .

Now he did two things that excite our admiration. First, he grappled
with the problems; he fought off his doubts. He fought them off and
conquered them with this: "I went into the sanctuary of God; then I
understood . . ." (verse 17). He went to *church!* He fell on his knees
before the altar, before God, and there he got things straight. There in
the quietness he saw clearly: "prosperity is but for a day and chastened
character stands out brilliantly against the darkening skies of a day of
reckoning. 'Success,' says Victor Hugo, 'is a very hideous thing, and its
resemblance to merit deceives men.'" (W. A. Shelton.)

He knew then that there would always be evil, *and that there would
always be God.* He put himself on God's side, that he might profit
spiritually.

III. *My heart and my flesh may fail, but God is the strength of my
heart and my portion forever,* Psalm 73:26 (RSV). This is the crux of
the matter, and this is the conclusion to which the troubled Psalmist
came in the quiet of the sanctuary. At times, heart and flesh might fail
him, *but God was sufficient for all his needs.* He wanted to live like a
man of God, not like a beast (verse 22). Thereafter, he would let God,
not lust or greed or money-mad ambition guide him. He would take the
glory of heaven (heaven on earth in righteous living and heaven beyond
the earth) rather than ill-gotten money and success. You can't take it
with you! His doubts died. God gave him the answers he was looking
for. He saw now that the prosperity of the wicked was really *degradation,* and he had felt degraded and filthy and unclean when he entered
the sanctuary to talk it over with God. When he left he was a new
man. . . .

IV. . . . *according to his purpose which he set forth in Christ as a
plan for the fullness of time,* Ephesians 1:9, 10 (RSV). What had happened to the Psalmist kneeling in the Temple, was that he had gained
a new insight into the will of God. The will and the *purpose.* God has
a plan for man in the world, and in the fullness of the times (in God's
own good time) He will work it out. Good and evil are in God's world,
yes; there are conflicting elements in the world and in the universe—
but these are part of the plan. According to Paul in Ephesians, God
planned to reconcile these differences and to bring in Christ a new unity
to man. All the powers in the universe, good and bad, are subject to

God in Christ, who reconciles all the warring powers of the world, both among themselves and to God.

Paul speaks of the "mystery" of God's will for men (verse 9). And in verse 10: he tells how the mystery is explained: "It was God's purpose that all the many strands, all the loose ends of things, all the warring, competing, hating elements of His world should be gathered into one unity and union in Jesus Christ. Jesus came to make this world into one world in Himself" (Dr. William Barclay).

SUGGESTIONS TO TEACHERS

Life can and often does become the horror described by Macbeth in Shakespeare:

> Tomorrow, and tomorrow, and tomorrow,
> Creeps in this petty pace from day to day,
> To the last syllable of recorded time,
> And all our yesterdays have lighted fools
> The way to dusty death. Out, out, brief candle!

Life is a brief candle, but it need not be lived at a petty pace—*provided* we are sensible enough to let God give it meaning and purpose.

The question for *us* is, "What must *we* do to get God's meaning into our lives?" The purpose of this lesson is to suggest a few ways in which this can be done. . . .

TOPIC FOR ADULTS
GOD GIVES MEANING TO LIFE

Faith and God. "Life can do strange things to educated people who try to live by intellect alone, who go their own perverse ways, dashing their heads against the stone wall of God's law in a moral universe. Reason alone is not sufficient to orient a person in this mysterious universe. For a balanced concept of the meaning of existence there must also be faith in a God who cares."—James W. Kennedy.

You want to live "meaningfully?" Then first get yourself a faith in a God who means something!

Objective. That great Quaker Christian, Rufus Jones, once said that "our greatest objective in life is to find the rest of ourselves." To which another adds this:

"The rest of himself, which many a man never comes to know, is that part of self *which he finds only in God.* Tolstoy defines God as 'He with whom we cannot live.'

"We could make an experiment. We could plant some flower seeds in the ground out under the bright sunshine, and some more seeds in a pot of earth kept in a dark room. And yet such an experiment is not necessary. We know what would happen. In my back yard are two hibiscus bushes. One is in the open sunshine; the other is hidden from the sun half a day by a garage. There is a startling difference. The bush which gets the sun reaches out with long healthy branches; its flowers grow full and lovely. The bush which does not get sufficient sun is dwarfed and scrawny, its blossoms only half mature. You see, the *rest* of that bush is in the power of the sun, and it will never be the bush it was meant to be until that extra energy is added to it. Augustine once expressed it: 'The true end of a thing is the highest it can become.'

"Millions of people are existing like that stunted hibiscus bush. The *rest of them* is in God. They will never be all they were meant to be unless they find that larger self in God. They are living as if the three dimensions, length, breadth and thickness, were all, as if the fourth dimension, the spiritual, were not a real and necessary dimension of true life. 'Man shall not live by bread alone,' said our Lord; but some people seem quite sure that they *can* live by bread alone if they try hard enough —and they certainly can if a little cake is added!"—From a sermon by Frank B. Fagerburg.

Any cake in your life? *Analyze it!*

Coming Through. At a moment in World War II, when it looked as though the Germans might win, Winston Churchill went on the air with words that gave a new courage to the whole free world:

"When I look back on the perils which have already been overcome, upon the great mountain waves through which the ship has driven, when I remember all that has gone right, I am encouraged to feel that we need not be afraid that the tempest will overcome. Let it roar, let it rage, we shall come through."

What gives meaning to life? Courage, and faith to stand in the storm, knowing that with God we shall come through *anything!*

Daily Living. "I have found that there is a happy balance which we must have in our twenty-four-hour day, and that is this: part of the day belongs to your God, part to your family, and part to your job; if we can pray as if everything depends on God, and work as if everything depended on work, we cannot help but succeed."—Frank H. Zureick, in *Insurance Salesman.*

. . . and that wouldn't be success as the world thinks of it, either . . . !

Frenzy, Faith. "In a kind of frenzy too many of us rush through our days, not living life but consuming it. Our nervous excesses are responsible for more unhappiness than any other one cause. The haste of modern living is waste in the truest, deepest sense. We are so busy reaching for things beyond us that we miss eternal values which are near at hand. . . . A healthy mind must be housed in an unhurried body. . . . Happy is the man who has learned how to substitute faith for frenzy and rest for rush."—Alfred A. Montapert, in *Grit,* June 8, 1969.

Questions for Pupils on the Next Lesson: 1. How does God call men? 2. How do you interpret the story of the burning bush? 3. To *what* was Moses called? 4. Are business men and lawyers called of God, as well as ministers? Explain. 5. What is meant by the words, "I AM THAT I AM" (Exodus 3:14)? 6. By what names is God known in the Old Testament? 7. How can you be *sure* that God calls you?

TOPIC FOR YOUTH
GOD GIVES MEANING TO LIFE

Cause Above Conflict. "During the late war one of our boys from Orange, New Jersey, became a lieutenant in the Air Force at the age of twenty-six, and also won the Congressional Medal of Honor. When Jay came back, various dignitaries in our state planned a dinner and asked me as his pastor to bring him. I shall never forget how after the talk on his behalf he was asked to say a few words. He rose, visibly unnerved, holding the table for support, a man some six feet in height and prematurely gray, and stuttered out a 'Thank you,' and sat down.

"Afterward, on the way home, I asked him how he became a hero. He said simply that he did not know. One day he had been asked to take some pictures at Bougainville and he had taken them with the help of his men. That was all.

"Of course, having read the magazines and the newspapers, I knew that it was somewhat more complicated than that. He had flown his fortress without guns and filled with cameras some five hundred miles to Bougainville, had been met by some twenty fighter planes of the enemy, plowed right through them, took pictures and came back. Twenty fresh fighters followed him back for some distance.

"He said nothing of the man in the co-pilot's chair who was dead, nor of the men behind him badly wounded. And he said nothing of the fifty pieces of metal which had entered his thigh and were still there, causing a limp in his walk. He did not describe how he had blacked out when they landed and had been unconscious for days. That was all forgotten. They were merely details. He had gone to Bougainville to take pictures.

"In some way, we all have our pictures to take. We have our causes to get absorbed in. They pull our minds from self. They create the courage to seek steadfastly the will of God. Put your cause above the conflict."—From a sermon by Dr. Raymond I. Lindquist, in *The Upper Room Pulpit*, March, 1951.

Beyond and above every conflict in our lives is God—and He can lift us beyond and above if we want it that way. . . .

Seven Things. Mr. John H. Case is head of Berg Electronics. He has the most unusual business card in the business world. On the back of it he lists seven things he has tried in his effort to find meaning and purpose in life, and he tells what happened when he tried them:

1. Laughing at difficulties—and found them disappearing.
2. Attempting heavy responsibilities—and found them growing lighter.
3. Facing a bad situation—and found it clearing up.
4. Telling the truth—and found it the easiest way out.
5. Doing an honest day's work—and found it the most rewarding.
6. Believing men honest—and found them living up to expectation.
7. Trusting God every day—and found Him surprising me with His goodness.

There is real meaning in that!

Sunrises, Cyclones. "It seems to be a general belief that the will of God is to make things distasteful for us, like taking bad-tasting medicine when we are sick, or going to the dentist. Somebody needs to tell us that sunrise is also God's will. There is the time of harvest, the harvest which will provide food and clothes for us, without which life could not be sustained on earth. God ordered the seasons; they are His will. In fact, the good things in life far outweigh the bad. *There are more sunrises than cyclones.*"—Charles L. Allen.

Meaning comes into life when we see God in *every* sunrise.

Square. "Sometimes they hint at it, and sometimes they come right out and say it, 'Dick Van Dyke is a square.' They explain this state of affairs by pointing out that I'm married to my first wife after 16 years, have four chlidren, go to church regularly and spend my spare time with the family. And you know what? I admit it—and I don't mind. 'Square' has a nicer meaning than it used to have. . . . Today it means a person who lives by the rules."—Dick Van Dyke, in *Tarrytown Tidings*, Tarrytown, New York.

Overcoming. "A number of us were talking to a young Chinese Christian who was on his way back to China after World War I. We asked 'Do you think the Christian faith can ever actually influence China?' He answered, 'I do not know about that. But I do know I shall try to make it so.'

"Without that faith we can do nothing; with it there is nothing we dare not try to do. It is the faith that overcomes the world."—*Sermons on the Psalms*, p. 107, by Harold A. Bosley. Quoted by permission of Harper and Row, publishers.

Sentence Sermon to Remember: There is a major theme in every man's life; everything you do in your life is a variation on it.—Preston Bradley.

Questions for Pupils on the Next Lesson: 1. Describe a "call" from God. 2. Are all calls from God alike, or do they come in different ways and words? 3. To what service does God call the Christian *layman?* 4. Is God involved in our human lives? Give evidence. 5. How can you serve God in the church without being a minister? 6. Why are some men reluctant to respond when God calls? 7. What talent or talents have you that God could use?

LESSON V—OCTOBER 3

GOD CALLS MEN

Background Scripture: Exodus 3:1-20; II Timothy 1:8,9
Devotional Reading: Mark 2:13-17

KING JAMES VERSION	REVISED STANDARD VERSION

EXODUS 3 Now Moses kept the flock of Jethro his father-in-law, the priest of Midian: and he led the flock to the back side of the desert, and came to the mountain of God, even to Horeb.

2 And the Angel of the Lord appeared unto him in a flame of fire out of the midst of a bush: and he looked, and, behold, the bush burned with fire, and the bush was not consumed.

3 And Moses said, I will now turn aside, and see this great sight, why the bush is not burnt.

4 And when the Lord saw that he turned aside to see, God called unto him out of the midst of the bush, and said, Moses, Moses. And he said, Here am I.

5 And he said, Draw not nigh hither: put off thy shoes from off thy feet; for the place whereon thou standest is holy ground.

6 Moreover he said, I am the God of thy father, the God of Abraham, the God of Isaac, and the God of Jacob. And Moses hid his face; for he was afraid to look upon God.

7 And the Lord said, I have surely seen the affliction of my people which are in Egypt, and have heard their cry by reason of their taskmasters; for I know their sorrows;

8 And I am come down to deliver them out of the hand of the Egyptians, and to bring them up out of that land unto a good land and a large, unto a land flowing with milk and honey; unto the place of the Canaanites, and the Hittites, and the Amorites, and the Perizzites, and the Hivites, and the Jebusites.

9 Now therefore, behold, the cry of the children of Israel is come unto me: and I have also seen the oppression wherewith the Egyptians oppress them.

10 Come now therefore, and I will send thee unto Pharaoh, that thou

EXODUS 3 Now Moses was keeping the flock of his father-in-law, Jethro, the priest of Midian; and he led his flock to the west side of the wilderness, and came to Horeb, the mountain of God. 2 And the angel of the Lord appeared to him in a flame of fire out of the midst of a bush; and he looked, and lo, the bush was burning, yet it was not consumed. 3 And Moses said, "I will turn aside and see this great sight, why the bush is not burnt." 4 When the Lord saw that he turned aside to see, God called to him out of the bush, "Moses, Moses!" And he said, "Here am I." 5 Then he said, "Do not come near; put off your shoes from your feet, for the place on which you are standing is holy ground." 6 And he said, "I am the God of your father, the God of Abraham, the God of Isaac, and the God of Jacob." And Moses hid his face, for he was afraid to look at God.

7 Then the Lord said, "I have seen the affliction of my people who are in Egypt, and have heard their cry because of their taskmasters; I know their sufferings, 8 and I have come down to deliver them out of the hand of the Egyptians, and to bring them up out of that land to a good and broad land, a land flowing with milk and honey, to the place of the Canaanites, the Hittites, the Amorites, the Perizzites, the Hivites, and the Jebusites. 9 And now, behold, the cry of the people of Israel has come to me, and I have seen the oppression with which the Egyptians oppress them. 10 Come, I will send you to Pharaoh that you may bring forth my people, the sons of Israel, out of Egypt." 11 But Moses said to God, "Who am I that I should go to Pharaoh, and bring the sons of

mayest bring forth my people the children of Israel out of Egypt.

11 And Moses said unto God, Who am I, that I should go unto Pharaoh, and that I should bring forth the children of Israel out of Egypt?

12 And he said, Certainly I will be with thee; and this shall be a token unto thee, that I have sent thee: When thou hast brought forth the people out of Egypt, ye shall serve God upon this mountain.

13 And Moses said unto God, Behold, when I come unto the children of Israel, and shall say unto them, The God of your fathers hath sent me unto you; and they shall say to me, What is his name? what shall I say unto them?

14 And God said unto Moses, I Am That I Am: and he said, Thus shalt thou say unto the children of Israel, I am hath sent me unto you.

Israel out of Egypt?" 12 He said, "But I will be with you; and this shall be the sign for you, that I have sent you: when you have brought forth the people out of Egypt, you shall serve God upon this mountain."

13 Then Moses said to God, "If I come to the people of Israel and say to them, 'The God of your fathers has sent me to you,' and they ask me, 'What is his name?' what shall I say to them?" 14 God said to Moses, "I am who I am." And he said, "Say this to the people of Israel, 'I am has sent me to you.'"

MEMORY SELECTION: *Take your share of suffering for the gospel in the power of God, who saved us and called us with a holy calling, not in virtue of our works but in virtue of his own purpose and the grace which he gave us in Christ Jesus ages ago.* II Timothy 1:8-9.

HOME DAILY BIBLE READINGS

Sept. 27. M. *A Call for a Deliverer,* Exodus 3:1-10.
Sept. 28. T. *A Promise of Deliverance,* Exodus 3:11-20.
Sept. 29. W. *Called to Save His People,* Judges 6:7-14.
Sept. 30. T. *"Be Not Afraid,"* Ezekiel 1:28-2:10.
Oct.   1. F. *From Darkness to Light,* Acts 26:12-18.
Oct.   2. S. *Called to Godly Living,* II Peter 1:3-11.
Oct.   3. S. *Called to Serve,* II Timothy 1:6-12.

BACKGROUND

During the days of Moses, man took a giant step forward in his thinking about God, and that portion of mankind known as Israel gives us much to think about in its account of the religious experience of the great leader. The birth and adoption of Moses by Pharaoh's daughter are described in Exodus 2:1-10; his killing of the Egyptian foreman, his flight to Midian and his marriage to the daughter of a priest of Midian are recorded in Exodus 2:11-22. His time in Midian is spent in brooding, brooding over the fate of his people, over his own place in their history, and, most of all, over his relationship with God.

Out of the brooding came a new name for God, and a new concept of Him. . . .

NOTES ON THE PRINTED TEXT

I. And the angel of the Lord appeared unto him in a flame of fire out of the midst of a bush, Exodus 3:2. Exodus 2:24 says that the children of Israel were "groaning" in slavery in Egypt. Groaning, perhaps, in weariness and fear. Their leader Moses was groaning, too: not so much in fear as in uncertainty. For what purpose had he been brought to Midian? What was he to do here and beyond this hiding place in the mountains? And God, the God who had led him there—was God still with him, was God still guiding him, and to *what?*

In one of the most dramatic moments of the Bible, God explains to the wondering Moses what it is all about, and what he is to do. God appears in a burning bush; (the "angel" in verse 2 was actually the Lord; angels at this period were not personal beings but people or things that temporarily embodied God. See Genesis 21:15-19; Deuteronomy 33:16; Judges 6:11,14; Psalm 104:4). "The word LORD stands for YHWH, probably Yahweh, which in Hebrew is read as 'Adonai,' meaning Lord" (The Interpreter's Bible).

Out of the bush came a *flame* (see Exodus 19:18, Ezekiel 1:27; I Timothy 6:16), which was a *manifestation* of God. The figure of the bush has its root in pagan animism. These *physical* roots and backgrounds are easily explained, but there is something in the spectacle of the burning bush that is not so easily explained. Some scholars have spoken of inflammable gases that arise from certain desert plants and foliage, and others have written of inflammable naptha deposits, but it isn't very convincing. The point of the story is that in this mystical, spiritual experience, Moses clearly heard a call from God to go back into Egypt and lead his people from that land to freedom in a land of their own—to "the place of the Canaanites" (verse 8). Said Professor W. Robertson Smith, "God or His angel (the words are interchangeable) was there, as He is behind all the wonders of this wonderful universe. Through all these things, if we have but the open ear, God is calling *us* by name, as from the bush He called 'Moses, Moses.'"

Moses hesitates. The immensity of the task overwhelms him, and he cries, "Who am I, that I should go . . . ?" This is the humility of greatness; there is no greatness without it. The most courageous leaders of human history have invariably thought themselves too little for great tasks; they have been afraid. The difference between them and lesser men is that with God's help they conquered their fears.

Moses' fear left him when God said to him, "But *I* will be with you . . . !" Moses had no answer for that one—and no further objection. If God be for us, who can be against us?

II. . . . and [when] they ask me, What is his name? what shall I say to them (RSV)? Exodus 3:13. Moses had no fear now about what he has to do—but he had just one more question, and it was a good one. If he were to tell his people that God had commissioned him to lead this great deliverance from Egypt, they would surely ask him, "God? Which god? *What is his name?*"

These were the days of the worship of many gods; there were thousands of gods—all foreign, heathen, pagan, not at all like the "God of their fathers," about whom the Hebrews had been taught from infancy. *How could they know that this God who had talked with Moses was the God of their fathers—the one, true God?*

God answers Moses: "I AM WHO I AM. . . . Say this to the people of Israel, "I AM has sent me to you." *The Abingdon Bible Commentary* explains:

"The answer to Moses' question . . . contains either a new name or a new interpretation of an old name of God already known to Moses. The words, *I am that I am* [KING JAMES VERSION] are evidently intended as an interpretation of the name 'Jehovah,' which was pronounced in Hebrew *Yahweh*. . . . There is no doubt that the name, whatever its original meaning and use may have been, came to designate for Moses and for Israel the living, self-existent God, the One who is and will be, and who has within Himself the exhaustless resources of being. He is not defined by any one event, or by one circumstance, or by the experience of one age or nation, but is ceaselessly renewing the revelation of Himself in the world of nature and in human history. His being is expressed in action. He will be for His people guide, counselor, warrior, lawgiver, and mighty deliverer."—Professor J. F. McLaughlin, in *The Abingdon Bible Commentary*, p. 256. Quoted by permission of Abingdon Press, publishers.

The last two sentences of the above quotation should answer a lot of our questions about our *Christian* God!

SUGGESTIONS TO TEACHERS

We think too much of "the call of God" as being something mysterious, almost incomprehensible, something that comes only to men of unusual spiritual awareness. We tend to think of it as something resembling a sudden, Damascus-road conviction. And often it is just that. But not always is it so dramatic or so sudden.

Someone has said that a "call" is an awareness of humanity's need, and a resolution to do something about it. But it is also an awareness of God's love and concern for humanity—and of His need of *our* help in serving and "saving" humanity. Such an awareness and resolution can come very, very slowly; it comes sometimes early in life, sometimes after long, long thinking and meditation and weighing of values in the adult years. It comes to men in various ways.

But however it comes, it always has this common element: *it is a summons from God to do something.* When He calls us He does not say, "Come aside from the world and rest." He says "Go!"

TOPIC FOR ADULTS
GOD CALLS MEN

The Voice of God. "The first question that has puzzled many (about me) concerns the voice of God. What was it? What did I hear? Did I see any person? If not, how was the voice of God conveyed to me? These are pertinent questions.

"For me, the voice of God, of conscience, of truth, the inner voice or 'the still small voice,' mean one and the same thing. I saw no form; I have never tried, for I have always believed God to be without form. But what I did hear was like a voice from afar and yet quite near. It was as unmistakable as some human voice definitely speaking to me, and irresistible. I was not dreaming at the time I heard the voice. The hearing of the voice was preceded by a terrific struggle within me. Suddenly the voice came upon me. I listened, made certain it was the voice, and the struggle ceased. I was calm. The determination was made accordingly, the date and the hour of the fast fixed. Joy came over me. This was between eleven and twelve midnight. I felt refreshed. . . .

"Could I give any further evidence that it was truly the voice that I heard and that it was not an echo of my own heated imagination? I have no further evidence to convince the skeptic. He is free to say that it was all self-delusion or hallucination. It may well have been so. I can offer no proof to the contrary. But I can say this—that not the unanimous verdict of the whole world against me could shake me from the belief that what I heard was the true voice of God."—Mahatma Gandhi.

Gandhi has been called "The greatest Christian of our age" by a famous American missionary. Was he? And does God speak to men of other faiths than Christianity?

No Refusal. None of us needs to be told who Florence Nightingale was; she was and is still one of the most beloved heroines of all time. Near the end of her life, old and worn out by her sacrificial service to men wounded in war, she said this:

"If I could tell you all, you would see how God has done it all, and I nothing. I have worked hard, very hard, that is all; *and I have never refused God anything.*"

That was a call—and an answer!

The Pull. A minister from Scotland walked through the Cave of the Winds at Niagara Falls. He wrote this about it:

"It is like living amidst the break-up of an old universe or the creation of a new. You are shut off from the whole world of nature and humanity for the time, enwrapt in this wild smother of thunder and foam. Your only link with the entire world of humanity is the presence of the hand of your guide. You cannot see him, you cannot hear him; all that you are conscious of is a hand with a pull in it."

Whoever and whatever we are, we are all conscious, at one time or another, of the "pull" of the hand of God. The hand is always there, calling upon us to take it, but we have a tendency to stuff our ears against the voice and to withold *our* hands. . . .

Calls. Jesus called Peter and Andrew from a fishing boat. He called Matthew from a disgusting, degrading job at a tax collector's table. He called a rich young man who turned away from Him. He called the famous Methodist preacher, Peter Cartwright, in a barn lot at dawn, when he was on his way home from an all-night dance. He stopped Billy Sunday on the street and made him listen to a Salvation Army band. Harry Emerson Fosdick was sitting in church when his call came. He called Bishop Arthur Moore thus: "Christ came into a dirty, smoky railroad caboose and lifted my life out of it. Not only did He forgive my sins, but He completely remade my whole life. There was spiritual transformation, there was also an intellectual awakening." He calls men from the gutter, from worship in cathedrals, from prisons, from college, from palaces and mud huts. . . . He calls all who have open ears and receptive hearts. . . .

Questions for Pupils on the Next Lesson: 1. Describe the call of Moses at Sinai. 2. What did God call on the people of Israel to *do?* 3. What *kind* of community did God ask Moses and his people to organize? 4. What was the difference between the Israelite community and the Christian community? 5. For what purpose was the Christian community formed? 6. What do the Christians do in your community? 7. Can God do His work on earth without the help of a community?

TOPIC FOR YOUTH
GOD CALLS YOU

Generals, Privates. When General Lee invaded Pennsylvania in June of 1863, a man living near Gettysburg sent a telegram to General Halleck, in Washington, offering his services "as a superior officer." He was sure that he could do great things for the Union in a post of high command. He said he knew how to stop Lee.

General Halleck wired back: "We have five times as many generals as we know what to do with, but we are greatly in need of privates. Wire me if interested."

God calls *you*, even to do the humble work of a "private" in His army. It is the men in the ranks who really do the job. . . .

Living for What? "Several years ago a very close friend of mine got off the beam in his thinking. He became very selfish. He magnified some of his problems, which were not unlike the kind that others about him were having. He had missed life. The world was against him. He thought about himself day and night. He quit his job and coddled himself. His physician could find little wrong with him except a deep emotional disturbance. He talked of suicide to his parents and friends, until they were worried sick over him. Then one day he came to spend a few hours with me. After my wife had fed us we drifted across the street to my study at the church and he started to complain.

" 'I'm sick of it all,' he said. 'Life is not worth living. Nobody cares for me. I've come over here today to let you in on a secret. I'm going to kill myself. What do you think of that?'

"I answered, 'Why not?' He turned toward me, his eyes searching my face for some evidence of humor. 'What do you mean?' he shouted. 'I mean that it seems the only thing you can do. Why go on living? You have based your life on selfishness. You have forgotten your family, your job, your responsibilities and your God. *What are you living for?*'

"When I said that he was so angry he could have struck me. He got up and left my study. It distressed me to have to hurt him, but it was necessary. His boasting to so many people that he was planning to kill himself was a certain sign that he didn't intend to. My reaction had shocked him. My question, 'What are you living for?' haunted him. In a few days he was back at work, back with his friends, back in his church and back in the normal path of activities."—*Faith for These Troubled Times*, by D. N. Franklin (Revell).

That is God's way of calling *you;* He is always asking, "What are *you* living *for?*"

Call and Answer. A Sunday-school teacher too modest to sign her name has written this poetic account of what God called her to do, and how she did it:

One day I prayed that God would lay a soul upon my heart;
And in my prayer I promised Him that I would do my part.
I'd call on strangers, write some cards, and use the telephone;
Then trust Him—in His wisdom—to lead me to that one.

Just then my doorbell rang so hard it shook me from my prayer.
Before me stood a ten-year old; his head and feet were bare.
His small, dark face was far from clean, his speech was cold and rough.
His brother said, "He's awful mean"; his manner said, "I'm tough."

But as I stood there at the door, the Saviour whispered low,
"Here is that soul I charge to you. Oh, do not let him go!"
That's why I baked these cookies; I've put them out to cool
For my small friend—no longer tough—he's in our Sunday school.

And *that* is being called of God. . . .

Cowards. General Philip Sheridan was one of the great cavalry leaders in American military history. One of his finest victories came at the Battle of Five Forks. Just before that battle began, Sheridan got to worrying about his men, who were battle-weary and tired of fighting. Tired men, and timid men, never win battles!

So he issued an order before going into action. It was a short one, only five words long: "Cowards to the rear! Forward!" They won. . . .

God never calls a coward; He can use only heroes . . . only men willing to die for their cause, for His cause. . . .

Rent. The purpose of a call is service; it is also proof of the reality of the call. Service! We like the sentiment in the words of an anonymous author: "Service is the rent I pay for the space I fill."

Sentence Sermon to Remember: There is such a thing as a call to the Christian ministry. It comes from the world—a world committing suicide.—Paul Scherer.

Questions for Pupils on the Next Lesson: 1. Define the word "community" and apply it to Christianity. 2. What does the word "chosen" mean in "the chosen people?" 3. How was Israel a "royal priesthood?" 4. Is the social community of our time personal or impersonal? 5. How should Christians "leaven the community?" 6. Is the American nation really "Christian?" 7. Which covenant is mentioned in Exodus 19:5?

LESSON VI—OCTOBER 10

GOD CREATES A COMMUNITY

Background Scripture: Exodus 19; I Peter 2:1-10
Devotional Reading: Matthew 18:10-20

KING JAMES VERSION

EXODUS 19 In the third month, when the children of Israel were gone forth out of the land of Egypt, the same day came they into the wilderness of Sinai.

2 For they were departed from Rephidim, and were come to the desert of Sinai, and had pitched in the wilderness; and there Israel camped before the mount.

3 And Moses went up unto God, and the Lord called unto him out of the mountain, saying, Thus shalt thou say to the house of Jacob, and tell the children of Israel;

4 Ye have seen what I did unto the Egyptians, and how I bare you on eagles' wings, and brought you unto myself.

5 Now therefore, if ye will obey my voice indeed, and keep my covenant, then ye shall be a peculiar treasure unto me above all people: for all the earth is mine:

6 And ye shall be unto me a kingdom of priests, and a holy nation. These are the words which thou shalt speak unto the children of Israel.

7 And Moses came and called for the elders of the people, and laid before their faces all these words which the Lord commanded him.

8 And all the people answered together, and said, All that the Lord hath spoken we will do. And Moses returned the words of the people unto the Lord.

I PETER 2 9 But ye are a chosen generation, a royal priesthood, a holy nation, a peculiar people; that ye should show forth the praises of him who hath called you out of darkness into his marvelous light:

10 Which in time past were not a people, but are now the people of God: which had not obtained mercy, but now have obtained mercy.

REVISED STANDARD VERSION

EXODUS 19 On the third new moon after the people of Israel had gone forth out of the land of Egypt, on that day they came into the wilderness of Sinai. 2 And when they set out from Rephidim and came into the wilderness of Sinai, they encamped in the wilderness; and there Israel encamped before the mountain. 3 And Moses went up to God, and the Lord called him out of the mountain, saying, "Thus you shall say to the house of Jacob, and tell the people of Israel: 4 You have seen what I did to the Egyptians, and how I bore you on eagles' wings and brought you to myself. 5 Now therefore, if you will obey my voice and keep my covenant, you shall be my own possession among all peoples; for all the earth is mine, 6 and you shall be to me a kingdom of priests and a holy nation. These are the words which you shall speak to the children of Israel."

7 So Moses came and called the elders of the people, and set before them all these words which the Lord had commanded him. 8 And all the people answered together and said, "All that the Lord has spoken we will do." And Moses reported the words of the people to the Lord.

I PETER 2 9 But you are a chosen race, a royal priesthood, a holy nation, God's own people, that you may declare the wonderful deeds of him who called you out of darkness into his marvelous light. 10 Once you were no people but now you are God's people; once you had not received mercy but now you have received mercy.

50

MEMORY SELECTION: You are a chosen race, a royal priesthood, a holy nation, God's own people, that you may declare the wonderful deeds of him who called you out of darkness into his marvelous light. I Peter 2:9-10 (RSV).

HOME DAILY BIBLE READINGS

Oct. 4. M. *Keep My Covenant,* Exodus 19:1-9.
Oct. 5. T. *Prepared to Receive God's Law,* Exodus 19:16-25.
Oct. 6. W. *God Keeps His Promise,* Joshua 23:1-8, 14-16.
Oct. 7. T. *Promise of a New Covenant,* Jeremiah 31:27-34.
Oct. 8. F. *Members of One Body,* I Corinthians 12:12-21.
Oct. 9. S. *God's Own People,* I Peter 2:1-10.
Oct. 10. S. *Agreement in Community,* Matthew 18:10-20.

BACKGROUND

The Israelites have come 150 miles from Egypt to Sinai; at Sinai, they remain eleven months, during which a great event, important historically, is recorded. They came to Sinai a poorly organized crowd; they left it a deathless community created at the hand of and through the grace of God—a religious and moral community with a special purpose in the world.

God cannot do His work on this earth without consecrated communities based on covenants between Himself and the people He chooses for the communities. Many have *thought* they were chosen for such a community and purpose, but they were *not.* The Israelites almost lost their standing as such a community because they misunderstood the terms God laid down for them. . . .

We are to study those terms today. . . .

NOTES ON THE PRINTED TEXT

I. You have seen what I did to the Egyptians, and how I bore you on eagles' wings and brought you to myself, Exodus 19:4. God didn't discover the children of Israel at Sinai; He had arranged their destiny and He had been with them in a past they had almost forgotten. He had watched over them and He had led them out of their greatest troubles (in Egypt) toward the mountain near which they were now encamped. He had "purchased" them for a great work. (See Exodus 15:16ff.) And when they fled from Egypt, like so many young eagles making their first attempt to fly, He had hovered over and around them, lifting them up when they were in danger of falling, supporting them when they were exhausted, feeding them when they were hungry (Deuteronomy 32:11).

All this God had done for them; they must have known that, but there were times when they seemed a bit ungrateful for it all.

II. Now therefore, if ye will obey my voice indeed, and keep my covenant, then ye shall be a peculiar treasure unto me . . . , Exodus 19:5. According to a tradition already old in the wilderness, God had made a promise to the people of Israel (see Deuteronomy 7:6; 14:2 and 26:18) that he would choose them out of all the peoples of the earth for a special service. That service was for them to be "a light to [all] the nations . . ." (Isaiah 49:6). *The people were to serve Him!*

To be chosen as a community of God means to be chosen to *serve* God—to *do* something for Him. It does not give the "chosen" the privilege of sitting down and boasting of their peculiar relationship to God —as though they were "God's pets!" They are not to boast in pride, but to *obey in humility.* They had no "corner" or monopoly on God's favor, no security in His promise to make them a peculiar treasure *unless they obeyed Him.*

Yes, the Jews were to be "a kingdom of priests and a holy nation" (verse 7)—but that meant only that every member of the nation was consecrated to the service of God. The designation expressed the high calling of Israel; it also called for a high standard of morals and faith in the lives of every individual in Israel. This was to be the covenant: God on His part would make them a great people bearing His lamp across the world; on their part, they would obey Him implicitly, faithfully and forever.

Moses brought them all together and explained everything to them as he had received it from God in the clouds of Sinai, the God who had brought the people to Himself at that mountain in order to have them agree on the covenant. And the people answered and said, "All that the Lord hath spoken, we will do."

It was a promise easy to make, difficult to keep. . . .

III. *Which in time past were not a people, but are now the people of God,* I Peter 2:10. On the whole, Israel did well in fulfilling the duty of communicating the knowledge of God and His will to the world. In spite of all their stumblings, in spite of the dark periods in their history when the Israelites' great prophets felt compelled to condemn the apostasy and unfaithfulness of the people to the God of the covenant, they did spread abroad the knowledge of the one universal God. In their dispersion over the earth, they spread a faith over the earth—a new faith and a new concept of God. And they gave Jesus Christ to the world. "The people of God," it might be said, fulfilled their destiny and kept the covenant.

But now something happened. In Christian teaching, it is believed that when Israel rejected the Messiah, its sacred function and mission passed to the Christian church. (See Revelation 1:6.) The Christians now became an "elect" race, with a new covenant to replace the old (Old Testament) covenant and receive the mantle of the "chosen" in the same sense as the Israelites had previously been chosen, that is, to spread the light of God *in Christ* throughout the world. They were chosen, not to enjoy any special, exalted privileges, but to "tell out the excellences" of God to others.

Verse 10 relies on Hosea 1 and 2; it refers to a *united* community which, as Gentiles, the Christians never had previous to the work of Christ, and a unity the Jews lacked (or lost) in their rejection of Christ.

So, in order to build His kingdom, God created two communities and instituted two covenants. He needs that community to work out His will; man needs God's community, particularly *now*, when the sacredness of the individual is being lost or destroyed in collective disinterest and spiritual apathy.

SUGGESTIONS TO TEACHERS

The "community" created by God in the Old Testament was Israel—the whole nation, the whole people. The community created in the New Testament was a little body of Christians working like leaven in the "lump" of Jewish, Roman, and Greek society. The "community" for us today is the Christian church, working in our nation and our world to produce a better nation and a better world.

God has plans for this modern community of ours, just as He had plans in His previous Biblical communities. Mankind needs to know those plans; mankind also needs to understand that if we are to survive this "church community" must work once more in an impersonal and often cruel society to "accentuate the *personal*" as Jesus did.

God has created a new community in the church; in it He has given us new joys and new responsibilities. Now let us look sharply at the responsibilities to see whether we are meeting them as God wants us to meet them. . . .

TOPIC FOR ADULTS
GOD CREATES A COMMUNITY

Club or Community? Malcom Boyd is the controversial author-priest who wrote a best-selling book of prayers entitled, "Are you Running With Me, Jesus?" It is a startling book, as, are his words elsewhere about the church community:

"The church is a corporate community relating to Jesus; it is a group of persons with a commitment to follow Jesus. What this means to me is that Jesus represents the fact that God isn't in a cloud over Las Vegas or somewhere else. He's here, radically here, involved in the sweet commitment of life's deepest realities and revolutions. That's why there is meaning and purpose in life. The community that shares this life and hope together is a community of faith in terms of the biblical witness. It is no longer a private club. Rather, it's a community which has a style of life that demands involvement in God's healing activity in the world."

Well—how would you describe the style of life of *your* church? Is it a community or a club?

In Diptipur. Anyone who has traveled in India has been startled by the presence of a small Christian community in the midst of more than 500,000,000 Hindus, Moslems, Buddhists and other non-Christians. It is so overwhelming that many ask what this little Christian community can possibly accomplish. It has accomplished miracles.

Mrs. Joseph M. Smith wrote an article entitled "Water, More Precious Than Gold," in which she described one effort to help this minority community:

"In Diptipur, Orissa, India, we watched Bob Larson supervise the digging of a reservior which we were told would change thousands of Indian lives. We had earlier attended a baptismal service in a village not far from Diptipur where the only available water is the algae-covered pond. . . . Water, literally, is the life-giving element in India. Some villagers walk a quarter of a mile for water. The reservoir in Diptipur would not only provide water for household needs and for irrigation; Mr. Larson is also hopeful of beginning a fish culture if the monsoons bring enough rain to fill the 'dig.' All of this would mean a steadily improved diet and strength for frail bodies as the result of the church in action. I let myself dream of what a well for every village in India could do. . . ."

We read also of two American Protestant doctors who went into the Congo to open a hospital that would serve 100,000 people. With them went a group of nurses in a Roman Catholic order!

That is "community."

Involvement. The racial problem and the civil rights struggle in our own country has been and still is a desperate problem and struggle; it has divided the church, even set brother against brother, and the end is not yet. One Christian writer, however, sees an unfolding brother-hood and sense of community developing in it all. Dr. Earnest A. Smith writes in *Concern*:

"The involvement of the church in the civil rights struggle of 1963-65 will go down in history as the one great time when all churches, all religionists, joined together in a cause they believed to belong to their aspirations for the Kingdom of God. There has never been a more thrill-ing sight than the robed ministers walking with bearded students and the severe nuns in step with modern coeds. For once in this life, men were caught up in a common human involvement in which many tradi-tional customs were forgotten. Communion was for all faiths at the crude table in a Selma church—and all faiths took the common cup before they made their overt witness to their living faith. Some clergy-men paid the supreme sacrifice in this effort. They were set upon, bat-tered, bruised and killed. They are the martyrs who are indeed the ever-sprouting seeds of the church. For once the church reached its supreme height—witnessing, servicing, worshiping, healing."

Any comments on this as a community?

Church. Howard E. Butt is a leading Christian layman with clear eyes and a good witness. Recently he said something that should be copied and put up on every church bulletin board in the country: "The church was intended to be a vibrant, redeeming community of compassion, mission, service, witness, love and worship—not a fra-ternity of the fans of the faith."

Amen!

Competitors, Commission. Many modern Christians seem afraid of the host of competitors who seem to be taking over many of the functions of the church. They shed tears over the competition of TV, Sunday sporting events, the automobile which takes whole families away from church, etc., etc.

Says W. T. Purkiser in *Herald of Holiness* (September 3, 1969): "The church, it is true, has many critics in these days. But it has no competi-tors. No other institution—whether government, school, service club or civic association—attempts to or can do what the church is commis-sioned to do."

Name a few of those commissions.

Questions for Pupils on the Next Lesson: 1. Can you be a Christian without belief in answered prayer? 2. Define the word "prayer." 3. Describe your attitude in prayer. 4. Can a prayer be *wordless*? Explain. 5. Why is Hebrews 11 called "the Westminster Abbey of the Bible?" 6. Why was Abel's offering better than Cain's? 7. What should we believe about God before we address Him in prayer?

TOPIC FOR YOUTH
GOD CREATES A NEW PEOPLE

Property. "Undaunted by opposition to earlier suggestions that parish property be turned over to the Federal government for use by the poor, Roman Catholic Bishop Fulton J. Sheen [has] suggested that under-utilized Catholic churches become dispensaries, cinemas and depots for food and clothing. . . . Bishop Sheen asked the church to 'dispossess herself of some of her real property by giving it to the poor for housing.' . . . Bishop Sheen's remarks . . . were followed the next day by the issuance of a new set of guidelines to govern erection of parish structures in the Rochester (N.Y.) diocese. Among the guidelines:

1. The cost of a rectory must not exceed that of an average house in the parish.
2. The type of church building to be erected must never depend on the ability of a parish to pay for it.
3. The right of the poor to have a decent home enjoys priority over the church's right to erect tax-exempt structures that exceed the bare minimum of cost."

Condensed from an item in
Presbyterian Life, August 15, 1968.

Tax exempt church property! That is under serious criticism today. The churches of the United States own land and buildings worth at least eighty *billion* dollars—all tax exempt! That is almost double the combined assets of the nation's five largest industrial corporations. In Dallas a Baptist church's property includes a 7-story parking and recreation building with a skating rink, a gym and 4 bowling lanes. A church near Willis, California, operates a $500,000 motel and other enterprises. Other churches in the country own newspapers, radio and TV stations, department stores, restaurants, shopping centers and hotels, and the Cathedral of Tomorrow owns an electronics firm, a wire and plastics company and (!) the Real Form Girdle Company!

Question: Can the church community really witness to the gospel of the Penniless Prince of Peace against such a background?

St. Francis of Assisi was perhaps the most influential saint we have ever known; his first rule for his order was, "No property!" Let's think it over.

Proud of Her Town. "I'm proud of my town of North Platte, Nebraska, because of the help and hope which it has given to a transient family in need. A family of nine was living in an automobile near the railroad tracks. They stopped in our town because they could not find work in California and did not have enough money to take them back to Iowa, where they came from. A railroad man saw their predicament and gave the SOS.

"A house was located for them, and new paint was applied by volunteers in the community. Mowers came in to cut the weeds. Two trucks brought in groceries, bedding, furniture, clothing, toys, an electric washer and dryers and other gifts. 'Everything is beautiful,' the children shouted, but the parents just choked up.

"You probably have guessed the ending. They want to live permanently in our town. The head of the household now has work, but he is still befuddled because he cannot yet understand the love and compassion which a town extended to him—a stranger."—Mrs. Russell Grandey, in *Grit*, November 23, 1969. Quoted by permission of *Grit*.

We'd call that a good community. "I was a stranger, and ye took me in!"

Caring. "Really to belong to the church is to care about what God cares about, to fall in love with His Kingdom. We must be ready to risk our hearts for its sake. And that is never easy or cheap. It means, for example, that if we become aware of some evil force in the community seeking to trap persons and take away their manhood or their womanhood and to destroy their dignity, we will not simply wring our hands and shed a tear and say, 'That's too bad!' Because we care as God cares, we will say, 'That's too bad, so let's do something about it. Let's hit that thing and hit it hard!' It is risky business to speak up in some communities today. But it is the cost of caring."—*Reach for the Sky*, by Robert E. Goodrich (Revell).

The Cat. Bishop Kennedy tells a good little story about a mother who heard the family cat yowl in pain. She knew where to look: she looked for her son Tommy, and said, "Tommy, stop pulling his tail." Replied Tommy, "I'm not pulling his tail. I'm just standing on it. He's doing the pulling."

Comments the bishop: "So we put the blame on the cat, or on the poor, or on the White House, or on the union. This is the age of the alibi. Where does one find an honest facing of facts and a true picture of the situation? Only in the church."

Is this true in your town and your church?

Sentence Sermon to Remember: The church is not to be a settlement but a pilgrimage, not an estate but an embassy, not a mansion but a mission.—Paul S. Rees.

Questions for Pupils on the Next Lesson: 1. Why do you pray? 2. What proportion of your prayers is answered? 3. How many of your prayers are for yourself? 4. Distinguish between prayers of intercession and prayers of petition. 5. Are Matthew 7:8 literally true? Give evidence. 6. What was Paul's thorn in the flesh? 7. Should we boast of our weaknesses (II Corinthians 12:9)?

LESSON VII—OCTOBER 17

GOD RESPONDS TO PRAYER

Background Scripture: Matthew 7:7-12; Romans 8:26-27;
II Corinthians 12:1-10; Hebrews 11:6
Devotional Reading: Psalm 42

KING JAMES VERSION

HEBREWS 11 6 But without faith it is impossible to please him: for he that cometh to God must believe that he is, and that he is a rewarder of them that diligently seek him.

MATTHEW 7 7 Ask, and it shall be given you; seek, and ye shall find; knock, and it shall be opened unto you:

8 For every one that asketh receiveth; and he that seeketh findeth; and to him that knocketh it shall be opened.

9 Or what man is there of you, whom if his son ask bread, will he give him a stone?

10 Or if he ask a fish, will he give him a serpent?

11 If ye then, being evil, know how to give good gifts unto your children, how much more shall your Father which is in heaven give good things to them that ask him?

12 Therefore all things whatsoever ye would that men should do to you, do ye even so to them: for this is the law and the prophets.

II CORINTHIANS 12 7 And lest I should be exalted above measure through the abundance of the revelations, there was given to me a thorn in the flesh, the messenger of Satan to buffet me, lest I should be exalted above measure.

8 For this thing I besought the Lord thrice, that it might depart from me.

9 And he said unto me, My grace is sufficient for thee: for my strength is made perfect in weakness. Most gladly therefore will I rather glory in my infirmities, that the power of Christ may rest upon me.

ROMANS 8 26 Likewise the Spirit also helpeth our infirmities: for we know not what we should pray for as we ought: but the Spirit itself maketh intercession for us with groanings which cannot be uttered.

REVISED STANDARD VERSION

HEBREWS 11 6 And without faith it is impossible to please him. For whoever would draw near to God must believe that he exists and that he rewards those who seek him.

MATTHEW 7 7 "Ask, and it will be given you; seek and you will find; knock, and it will be opened to you. 8 For every one who asks receives, and he who seeks finds, and to him who knocks it will be opened. 9 Or what man of you, if his son asks him for a loaf, will give him a stone? 10 Or if he asks for a fish, will give him a serpent? 11 If you then, who are evil, know how to give good gifts to your children, how much more will your Father who is in heaven give good things to those who ask him? 12 So whatever you wish that men would do to you, do so to them; for this is the law and the prophets."

II CORINTHIANS 12 7 And to keep me from being too elated by the abundance of revelations, a thorn was given me in the flesh, a messenger of Satan, to harass me, to keep me from being too elated. 8 Three times I besought the Lord about this, that it should leave me; 9 but he said to me, "My grace is sufficient for you, for my power is made perfect in weakness." I will all the more gladly boast of my weaknesses, that the power of Christ may rest upon me.

ROMANS 8 26 Likewise the Spirit helps us in our weakness; for we do not know how to pray as we ought, but the Spirit himself intercedes for us with sighs too deep for words. 27 And he who searches the

27 And he that searcheth the hearts knoweth what is the mind of the Spirit, because he maketh intercession for the saints according to the will of God.

hearts of men knows what is the mind of the Spirit, because the Spirit intercedes for the saints according to the will of God.

MEMORY SELECTION: This is the confidence that we have in him, that, if we ask any thing according to his will, he heareth us. I John 5:14.

HOME DAILY BIBLE READINGS

Oct. 11. M. God Answers Prayer, Psalm 34:1-10.
Oct. 12. T. God Hears His People, Psalm 102:1-4, 12-22.
Oct. 13. W. How to Pray, Matthew 6:5-15.
Oct. 14. T. Ask, Seek, Knock, Matthew 7:7-12.
Oct. 15. F. The Spirit Intercedes, John 16:7-14; Romans 8:26-27.
Oct. 16. S. When Weakness Is Strength, II Corinthians 12:1-10.
Oct. 17. S. Thirst for the Living God, Psalm 42.

BACKGROUND

Those who believe in God believe in prayer; they *must,* for prayer is communion or talking with God. The last verse of Psalm 42 explains *why* we pray—in spite of all that happens to us that seems unjust, in spite of our occasional wondering whether God is there or not—we *pray.* ". . . I shall *yet* praise him!" We pray because praying is our contact with God, and in our hearts we know that we need God!

But there are certain attitudes we must have as we approach God in prayer. Prayer is a two-way street: God *listens,* and the petitioner *speaks.* The selections in our lesson for today describe the conditions under which God will listen to our prayers, or not listen; they also tell us how to speak to Him, and what to ask Him, and what we may expect Him to answer. . . .

NOTES ON THE PRINTED TEXT

I. But without faith it is impossible to please him, Hebrews 11:6. Hebrews 11 lists four notable Bible characters who approached God in prayer away back in the "days of the beginnings": Abel, Enoch, Noah and Abraham. We can't go back much further that *that!* And all four of these great men of God approached Him with one great characteristic in common: "By *faith,*" Abel, Enoch, Noah and Abraham went to God in prayer. They had faith that they were speaking to a God who was real, not to a God who was a creation of the human mind, not a figment of the imagination, not a "ghostly spirit up there somewhere." They spoke in the conviction that God was *living,* that He heard what they said in their prayers, and that He would answer them.

Abel brought an offering to his God, certain that God would see and approve and accept that offering. He wasn't making his offering to the *idea* of God but to God's reality in his life. Enoch was so sure of God that he *walked* with Him! (See Genesis 5:22.) Noah *talked* with God, and did what God told him to do (Genesis 6:13-22). Abraham left the security of his home in Ur and set out across desert and wilderness to a new land promised him by God; when God called him to do that, he asked no questions, and *went.* God must have been *very* real for Abraham to do a thing like that. Abraham went *in faith.* . . .

It is necessary that we believe in God before we pray to Him; it is even more necessary for us to believe that He is a God who *cares*, who is involved in our human lives, and that He came to our world to demonstrate His care and love for us in one named Jesus Christ. We must *believe* this *before* we pray.

II. *Ask, and it shall be given you,* Matthew 7:7. This idea of prayer is too often misunderstood. It does *not* mean that anyone (Christian or non-Christian) can ask God for *anything* and get it. One commentator says of the passage: "We are not told that no matter what petitions men offer, they will be granted. Matthew's entire discourse applies only to the children of the Kingdom, to those who hunger and thirst after righteousness and the mercy of God, to those whose whole hope is in Him. *They* may with assurance ask their Father who is in heaven for every need of their lives. If they seek Him, they will find Him. If they knock on His door, He will respond. This presumes on the part of those who ask, seek, and knock, *an intensity and a seriousness of desire.* (See Luke 11:5-8.)"—Suzanne de Dietrich, in *The Layman's Bible Commentary,* Vol. 16, p. 47. Quoted by permission of John Knox Press, publishers.

In verses 9-11, Matthew compares the love of men to the love of God—which is immeasurably greater. This little parable deals with both His love and with our praying, with our asking Him for help in our human needs. Matthew is stressing the necessity of *asking*—but he makes it clear that we must not always expect to get what we ask for! God knows what is good for us; He will give us that. He also knows what is bad for us; He will *not* give us that. Either way, He always responds, always answers prayer.

Verse 12—the "Golden Rule"—seems out of place in the context, but actually it isn't. It deals with the question of *neighborly* love, and love is the theme of this whole section on prayer. Jesus uses it to demonstrate how limited our love can be without this neighborly spirit and impulse; to Him, it summed up "the law and the prophets" and re-emphasized the ancient principle laid down in Leviticus 19:17-18.

Pray *in love!*

III. *And lest I should be exalted above measure through the abundance of the revelations . . . ,* II Corinthians 12:7. Paul had several great mystical experiences, or revelations, and while that was good, it held a great danger—namely, that he might become boastful, or conceited, or overly pious, about it. To keep him from falling into that trap, Paul says, God sent him "a thorn in the flesh." Just what that thorn was we do not know. It could have been his physical ugliness; he had epilepsy, and tradition says that he had bad eyes. Or it may have been mental—doubt, or temptation, or temper. Some believe it was a temptation to impurity; by the Protestant it is thought to have been some physical defect or painful affliction. Paul called it "the messenger of Satan to buffet me." Poor Paul was certainly buffeted, in more ways than one!

But the affliction—or the "messenger"—also brought a message that must have come from God: "My grace is sufficient for you, for my power is made perfect in weakness" (RSV). Paul probably resented this affliction, whatever it was; he probably prayed that it be taken from him. But he is telling us in these words in Corinthians that God sometimes says, "No," to such a prayer, that he may "refuse to give us what we want in order to give us what we need" (Kenneth J. Foreman). God may withhold some gifts for our own good. He may "afflict" us with other more undesirable gifts to make us struggle toward perfection. If Paul had been physically perfect he just might have been boastful, proud and conceited, and that would have destroyed him!

In prayer, we need to understand that the gift of God's grace is sufficient to overcome any handicap, to make any prayer worthy and effective. Prayer should be humble, contrite, modest and meek. God's grace is sufficient to overcome physical pain, the opposition of the enemies of God, the cruel treatment and persecution of man by his foes. It was sufficient to make Paul disregard what men thought of him and did to him. His extremity was God's opportunity.

IV. . . . for we know not what we should pray for as we ought . . . , Romans 8:26. These two verses from Romans 8 may be the most important statement on prayer in the New Testament. It states two propositions. (1) We cannot pray as we should because we cannot see the future. We may pray for things that will not be good for us tomorrow; we cannot know what may happen tomorrow. But God knows, and acts according to His knowledge. (2) We cannot know, either, what is best for us. Once, Socrates said that we should pray simply for "good things, and not attempt to specify them, but to leave it to God to decide just what the good things are." We cannot always know our *real* need; we cannot always understand God's purpose with us. We should leave it to the Spirit to intercede with God for us.

"As Paul saw it, prayer, like everything else, is of God. He knew that by no possible human effort can a man justify himself; and he also knew that by no possible effort of the human intelligence can a man know for what to pray. In the last analysis the perfect prayer is simply, 'Father, into thy hands I commend my spirit. Not my will, but thine be done'" (William Barclay).

SUGGESTIONS TO TEACHERS

When we talk of prayer, there are endless possibilities for discussion; prayer has many faces, all of them good! For the purposes of this lesson, the following emphases are suggested:

1. God's fatherly concern.
2. Why men pray.
3. How God answers the needs of men who pray.
4. The place of petition in prayer.
5. The Spirit's intercession for us.

Generally, today, we shall emphasize points 2 and 3.

TOPIC FOR ADULTS
GOD RESPONDS TO PRAYER

Heartbreak, Heart's-ease. "I base my whole life on prayer. A hundred times a day my thoughts go to the one human life that so supremely influenced the world and I renew my faith in my relationship with the

Saviour of mankind. I have silently prayed during great battles, during crises in the nursery, at glittering dinner tables and as a speaker on flag-draped platforms.

"Gradually, the miracle has been forced on me that no prayer goes unanswered. It may be answered by seeming disappointment, even humiliation. It is often answered in a totally unexpected way, or when it has been forgotten even by the suppliant. The insufferable has disappeared, the unbearable has become precious and right, the heartbreak has become hearts' ease."—Kathleen Norris, novelist.

She has found the true, constant answer to prayer—and it is a completely unselfish answer. . . .

Rules. There should be great freedom in prayer—but there *are* certain rules for prayer that seem good to follow. For instance:

1. Begin with God. If you can learn to forget self and saturate your mind with thoughts about God, prayer will be more meaningful.

2. Thank God for His blessings. This helps to develop a grateful heart.

3. Prayer that God will forgive our sins. Ask Him to forgive *specific* sins.

4. God's rules for prayer are the same for all. No person has any specific privileges in prayer.

5. God wants His children to have the best.

6. The door to the Father's house is always ajar. You may go in and out of your Father's house through prayer at any hour of the day or night.

7. God answers all our prayers in one of three ways: (a) More often than we deserve, God says yes to our prayers. (b) God answers some prayers in this fashion: "I cannot say either yes or no. I will do my part and if you do yours the prayer will be answered in the affirmative. However, if you fail to do your part, the answer will be in the negative." (c) God says no distinctly to many of our prayers.—*But God Can*, by R. V. Ozment (Revell).

Two Virtues. "There are two main pitfalls on the road to mastery of the art of prayer. If a person gets what he asks for his humility is in danger. If he fails to get what he asks for he is apt to lose confidence. Indeed, no matter whether prayer seems to be succeeding or failing, humility and confidence are two virtues which are absolutely essential."— A Trappist monk.

How humble are you, and how confident that God hears and will answer when you pray?

Why? Why do we pray? This may not be a complete listing of the reasons, but think about them, anyway:

1. Many of us pray because we are afraid. God is a lawyer to us, to be consulted only in time of trouble.
2. We pray because we are weak and want to be strong. Maybe we can lose that inferiority complex in prayer.
3. We pray because we know God is there, and we'd like His companionship.
4. We pray because it's the thing to do; everybody else does it, so why not we, too?
5. We pray because we know that human hands can let us down, and that God's hand never does.

6. We pray because inherently we want to be good, and we know that
only God is really good.

Right or wrong?

Questions for Pupils on the Next Lesson: 1. What did God ask Isaiah
to do for his fellow man? 2. What disturbed Jesus most about people?
(See Matthew 9:36.) 3. How far does God go in His compassion for
humanity? 4. Is there much compassion left in our world? Be specific. 5.
What does the church do for suffering people? 6. How does God go
about healing a broken heart? 7. Is your church interested in the underprivileged in your community? Give instances.

TOPIC FOR YOUTH
GOD ALWAYS ANSWERS

Color Scheme. "The story is told that an elderly lady, visiting New
York went to pay her respects to the United Nations. She asked that
the UN flag be shown to her, and she remarked, 'The United Nations is
such a wonderful organization that I should like to display its flag in my
living room.' When she saw the flag, however, she exclaimed, 'Oh, this *is*
a beautiful flag, but it would clash with the color scheme in my living
room; can I get it in another color?' The clerk explained that this was
impossible, and very politely suggested, 'Perhaps it would be easier to
change the color scheme in your living room.' "—Julius Kerman, in *The
Treasury of Inspirational Anecdotes, Quotations and Illustrations.* (Revell).

The moral of the story is this: in prayer, adjust your life to the colors
in which God has painted you. If any change is necessary, let Him tell
you how to make it.

Harmony With God. ". . . of course, you will not think of prayer as
just a means of getting something you want. Prayer is the means by
which we get what God wants us to have. What we want for ourselves
may be wrong; what God wants for us is right. So, in prayer, it is always
well to ask ourselves, 'What is it that God wants for me?'

"I remember talking once with a very rich man who was having
trouble sleeping. 'I believe if I can just get near to God everything will
be all right,' he said. 'But I have been trying to find Him and I can't.
Do you think I might, if I gave a lot of money to the church?'

" 'How much are you willing to give?' I asked.

" 'I would give $100,000 if you can suggest how I can find God.'

" 'You will have to give a good deal more than that,' I replied. 'You
must give Him your whole self, your entire life. Your idea seems to be
that all you need to do is to press a button and God will appear, like
a glorified bellboy. There is only one way you can find God, and that is
to confess your sins, tell the Lord that you are not asking Him to come
to you, but that you are giving yourself to Him. One hundred thousand
dollars won't buy Him, but if you give yourself to Him, He will give
Himself to you!'

"He said, 'Lord, I do not want to dictate to you. All I want is to have
you and to serve you.'

"That is the way to get the power of God in our lives. We can tell

Him what we want; that is perfectly proper. But we must always add, 'If this isn't what you want for me, then I want only what you want to give me.' When you achieve that kind of harmony with God, then things will really begin to move in your life."—Dr. Norman Vincent Peale, in *Pulpit Preaching*, July, 1967.

Long ago, George Macdonald wrote, " 'O God!' I cried, and that was all. But what are the prayers of all the universe more than expansions of that one cry? It is not what God can give us, but God that we want."

No Help. "The story is told of the famed Professor Eliot of Harvard. The students in his class were asked to sign a statement when they took their examination that they had received no help in answering the questions.

"One of the bright lads approached the professor's desk and said with a straight face, 'I can't sign that statement, sir. While I was working on the exam I frequently asked God for help.'

"Dr. Eliot let his glance run over the boy's examination paper. Then, also with a straight face, he said, 'Go ahead and sign it, son. You didn't receive any help.' "—*Liguorian*.

In case you missed it, the point of the story is that in prayer we should never ask God to do something for us that we can and should do for ourselves.

Running Scared. While they were plowing their garden, a farmer and his son were caught in a thunderstorm; the lightning struck a tree near the garden, and the father turned and ran for the barn. He looked back and saw his son standing still, looking up into the sky.

"What are you doing?" he shouted.

"I'm prayin'."

"Prayin'! A scared prayer ain't worth nothin', son. *Run!*"

Isn't it? Shouldn't we pray when fear overtakes us? Is it better to run scared . . . ?

Sentence Sermon to Remember: Nothing is so beautiful as a child going to sleep while he is saying his prayers.—Charles Peguy.

Questions for Pupils on the Next Lesson: 1. What is the greatest pain or suffering in the world? 2. How much time or money did you give last year to helping those in need? 3. Is Isaiah describing Jesus in chapter 61? 4. Explain what Paul meant by ". . . continue in the faith . . ." (Colossians 1:23)? 5. Is our government all wrong in its program of foreign relief? 6. Should we show compassion to the Communists? 7. Name one Good Samaritan in your town.

LESSON VIII—OCTOBER 24

GOD HEALS BROKEN HUMANITY

Background Scripture: Isaiah 61; Ephesians 2:11-19;
Colossians 1:21-23
Devotional Reading: Isaiah 42:1-9

KING JAMES VERSION

ISAIAH 61 The Spirit of the Lord God is upon me; because the Lord hath anointed me to preach good tidings unto the meek; he hath sent me to bind up the broken-hearted, to proclaim liberty to the captives, and the opening of the prison to them that are bound;

2 To proclaim the acceptable year of the Lord, and the day of vengeance of our God; to comfort all that mourn;

3 To appoint unto them that mourn in Zion, to give unto them beauty for ashes, the oil of joy for mourning, the garment of praise for the spirit of heaviness; that they might be called Trees of righteousness, The planting of the Lord, that he might be glorified.

4 And they shall build the old wastes, they shall raise up the former desolations, and they shall repair the waste cities, the desolations of many generations.

COLOSSIANS 1 21 And you, that were sometime alienated and enemies in your mind by wicked works, yet now hath he reconciled 22 In the body of his flesh through death, to present you holy and unblamable and unreprovable in his sight:
23 If ye continue in the faith grounded and settled, and be not moved away from the hope of the gospel, which ye have heard, and which was preached to every creature which is under heaven; whereof I Paul am made a minister; . . .

REVISED STANDARD VERSION

ISAIAH 61 The Spirit of the Lord God is upon me,
because the Lord has anointed me
to bring good tidings to the afflicted;
he has sent me to bind up the brokenhearted,
to proclaim liberty to the captives,
and the opening of the prison
to those who are bound;
2 to proclaim the year of the Lord's favor,
and the day of vengeance of our God;
to comfort all who mourn;
3 to grant to those who mourn in Zion—
to give them a garland instead of ashes,
the oil of gladness instead of mourning,
the mantle of praise instead of a faint spirit;
that they may be called oaks of righteousness,
the planting of the Lord, that he may be glorified.
4 They shall build up the ancient ruins,
they shall raise up the former devastations;
they shall repair the ruined cities,
the devastations of many generations.
COLOSSIANS 1 21 And you, who once were estranged and hostile in mind, doing evil deeds, 22 he has now reconciled in his body of flesh by his death, in order to present you holy and blameless and irreproachable before him, 23 provided that you continue in the faith, stable and steadfast, not shifting from the hope of the gospel which you heard, which has been preached to every creature under heaven, and of which I, Paul, became a minister.

MEMORY SELECTION: But when he saw the multitudes, he was moved with compassion on them, because they fainted, and were scattered abroad, as sheep having no shepherd. Matthew 9:36.

HOME DAILY BIBLE READINGS

Oct. 18. M. *The Healer From God,* Isaiah 61:1-9.
Oct. 19. T. *Rejoicing in God's Care,* Isaiah 61:10-62:5.
Oct. 20. W. *Supported and Protected,* Isaiah 62:6-12.
Oct. 21. T. *God's Compassionate Steadfast Love,* Isaiah 63:7-14.
Oct. 22. F. *God's Restoring Love,* Zephaniah 3:14-20.
Oct. 23. S. *Peace From God,* Isaiah 60:17-22; Colossians 1:21-23.
Oct. 24. S. *Assurance in God's Promise,* Isaiah 42:1-9.

BACKGROUND

To many people of the Old Testament, as with many people of today, God meant many things. To some He was the object of admiration and worshiped as the Creator of all men and all things; to others He was a more personal and loving guide; some thought of Him as a God of battle, others said He was a God of peace; to some He was a stern, avenging judge, dispensing justice; but to others His mercy was more important than His justice.

It is with this last idea that we deal in this lesson: God is a God of compassion, engaged in healing a broken and suffering humanity. As far back as the days of the Psalmists men were aware of His compassion: "O give thanks unto the Lord, for he is good: for his mercy endureth for ever. . . . For he satisfieth the longing soul, and filleth the hungry soul with goodness" (Psalm 107:1,9).

The prophets spoke often of God's righteousness and judgment, of His impatience with His fickle, wandering people, but God seemed nearer when they spoke of His mercy, forgiveness and compassion, as Isaiah spoke when he talked about a "suffering servant.". . .

NOTES ON THE PRINTED TEXT

I. He hath sent me to bind up the broken-hearted . . . , Isaiah 61:1. Isaiah stood as a prophet in the desperate days after the Babylonian exile, just before or during Nehemiah's return to Jerusalem. Earlier (in chapters 41, 42, 49, 50, 52 and 53) we hear the prophet talk about Israel as "the suffering servant" of God; here, in chapter 61, the prophet reminds his suffering people of their historic mission as the servant, and while he does not call himself *the* servant, he represents himself as one sent to the downhearted and discouraged people of God, to remind them of the *everlasting, divine compassion.*

The people of Israel had been afflicted during the Exile; they had become what we would call "underprivileged." They are broken-hearted. They had been in prison either in Babylon or in their ruined Jerusalem. They had struggled in poverty and under misgovernment; they had suffered moral and spiritual loss, and even physical degeneration. And Isaiah the prophet gets up and says to them, "It is to the poorest and most afflicted and most disheartened and underprivileged that I come in the name of God to bring you good tidings from Him; I come in His name to preach liberty to you, to announce that He will punish your afflicters and comfort all you who mourn." After all their years of suffering, he said, there would be "the acceptable year of the Lord," or, as the REVISED STANDARD VERSION translates, a "year of the Lord's favor," in which they would wear garlands instead of ashes (symbols of triumph instead of symbols of despair). They would be strong once more (strong as "oaks of righteousness" (verse 3, RSV), and they would glorify once more the God they thought had deserted them. They would rebuild their ruined cities, and restore the glory of Israel.

It is an important statement, this declaration of the compassion of God—so important that Jesus repeated it almost word for word in His famous sermon at Nazareth (Luke 4:18-19). Both Isaiah and Jesus stood out clear and sharp as men divinely commissioned to heal and restore and set free *the poor and the disheartened.* They did not come to preach to the privileged but to those who mourned—to the captives, the lonely, the oppressed, the meek and the broken-hearted.

In an old English church there is cut into the wall the figure of a hand reaching up in supplication; above the pleading hand is the word "God," on one side of which are the words, "I can," and on the other side the words, "I will." That's it! That is what Isaiah is saying: that God reaches down to heal and help through the hands of the prophet and the concerned lover of God and man. Both individuals and the church are divinely commissioned to "Go and do likewise"—go and comfort and heal and help and lift and love.

One of the most brilliant young men we know has just graduated with honors from the University of Chicago; a dozen well-paid jobs in industry—in highly technical and scientific work—were offered to him; but he turned them all down to accept a job teaching young high-school "dropouts" in a school maintained by seven Christian churches in the city.

That's it! In the name of a compassionate God, *we* must be compassionate—or stop calling ourselves Christians.

II. *And you, that were sometime alienated and enemies in your mind by wicked works, yet now hath he reconciled,* Colossians 1:21. This is to say that "God acts supremely through the life and death of Christ to heal humanity's hurt." In the new American Bible translation of the New Testament (*"Good News for Modern Man"*), this passage reads: "At one time you were far away from God and made yourselves his enemies by the evil things you did and thought. But now, by means of the physical death of his Son, God has made you his friends, in order to bring you, holy and pure and innocent, into his presence. You must, of course, continue faithful on a firm and sure foundation, and not allow yourselves to be shaken from the hope you gained when you heard the gospel. It is of this gospel that I, Paul, became a servant—this gospel which has been preached to everybody in the world," page 450. Quoted by permission of the American Bible Society.

In other words, it is good to be saved, but being saved (or "reconciled" with God) must be followed by being active in the work of compassion dramatized by Christ dying on His cross for all men. "Reconciliation," says Dr. Barclay, "demands loyalty; and reconciliation demands that through sunshine and shadow we never lose confidence in the love of

God. Out of the wonder of reconciliation are born the strength of unshakeable loyalty and the radiance of unconquerable hope."

Maybe that is what is the matter with us in our present world chaos: maybe we have lost our faith in the love and compassion of God. . . .

SUGGESTIONS TO TEACHERS

We might well look in today's lesson for answers to the following questions:

1. Is there really a "broken" humanity inhabiting our world? *How* is it broken? *Who* suffers, and why?
2. How can God do *anything* about broken humanity until we put on the bandages with our own human hands?
3. What did Jesus do, or tell us to do, about people who suffer? Give chapter and verse.

Why should the church worry about broken people?

TOPIC FOR ADULTS
GOD HEALS BROKEN HUMANITY

Hunger. A bitter critic said the other day that the most pressing need in our world was not more churches to worship in but more food for the hungry. Before we get angry at that, we might look at certain facts about the hunger that has given us a broken and bitter humanity.

"Arnold Toynbee may have missed the mark when he guessed that our age would go down in history as the first in which it became thinkable that the whole human race could make use of the benefits of civilization. Instead, unless we do something about the people who don't get enough to eat, our period may be remembered as the Age of Hunger, which seems wildly paradoxical when you consider our technological advances. Here we are all set to fly to the moon, here we are with marvelous machines doing most of our work and apparently a good bit of our thinking for us, here we are with nothing to do over the week ends but have fun and watch ball games—while half the people on earth suffer from hunger and malnutrition."—Bowman Doss, in *Minutes* (Nationwide Insurance).

Check it. Half of our world *is* hungry. We have made it to the moon, since the above was written, but we have not yet had compassion enough to go all-out in feeding the hungry. Jesus told us to feed them, but they'll just have to wait—perhaps until we get to Mars. And then—what?

What God Does. In the days just before World War II began, a worn-out minister went down to Florida to "get away from it all." He was tired, physically and mentally, if not spiritually, so tired that he was on the edge of a nervous breakdown. So he took his wife and drove down to a Florida beach. The first night of his "vacation" he fell off to sleep thanking God that he was away from all the furore about possible war, away from the voices that disturbed him at home, "away from it *all*." But in the middle of the night he was awakened by a voice which said, "Europe shall be bathed in blood. Her beaches shall be piled high with the carnage of war and human wreckage. Millions will be homeless and hundreds of thousands will die." He discovered that it was the voice of a woman holding a spiritualist seance in an adjoining room.

But—was it just her voice? Could it have been God speaking through her to a tired minister? Why do God and troubled conscience keep us awake? Why can't we sleep and forget the broken ones in our world? Why doesn't Jesus let us alone, let us just enjoy ourselves? Why can't we get Him out of our minds?

This is how God alerts us to the needs of broken humanity. . . .

Welfare. A few years back, a disturbed Christian looked at our welfare program in the United States and found it wanting. Starting with the Bible text, "Depart from me . . . into the eternal fire . . . for I was hungry and you gave me no food . . . naked and you did not clothe me . . . ," he made this reply on behalf of a Christian who thought he was helping the poor with welfare:

"But, Lord, what kind of talk is this? We didn't really let you go hungry. We gave you $23 a month for food, plus $5 a month for clothing, to say nothing of $9 for personal incidentals and $3 for laundry! We admit you couldn't live every well on it, but we didn't let you starve! We even paid your doctor bills. We kept you alive. What kind of ingrate are you? After all, if you wanted more, you should have gone to work and earned it!"

He concludes with this: ". . . it seems to me imperative that the churches should begin to hear and respond to the voice of the Lord saying, 'I was hungry, thirsty, naked and sick, and your small welfare checks kept me that way. I was a stranger and you preferred that I remain one. I was in "prison," and you decided to keep me there. How long will you treat me so?' "—(Adapted from *Christian Century*, February 24, 1965. Quoted by permission.)

Is it worse now than it was in 1965? What should we be doing in Christ's name to change it?

Questions for Pupils on the Next Lesson: 1. Was Habakkuk a negative thinker? 2. Against what did Habakkuk protest? 3. Who was king when Habakkuk prophesied, and what kind of king was he? 4. Why did God let the Chaldeans run wild over smaller nations? 5. Would you let Habakkuk preach in your church? If not, why not? 6. How do you think God will judge the United States? 7. Do you think God determines the destiny of nations? Give illustrations.

TOPIC FOR YOUTH
GOD HEALS MAN'S DEEPEST HURTS

Healing the Hurts. Sergeant Richard Kirkland isn't very well known as a great war hero. Not one in a million of us know anything about him, and that's too bad, for he was a soldier appointed by God to heal the hurts of man.

The sergeant fought on the Confederate side in the batle of Fredericksburg in the Civil War, December, 1862. His unit defended a stone wall against which the Union soldiers came in waves and died in waves; the ground in front of the wall on both sides was covered with the bodies of the dead and the wounded. The sergeant fought well—and he went to his commanding officer and asked that he be allowed to go out at night with water for "those poor people out there." The reluctant officer gave his permission; all night long, Dick Kirkland moved around in the dark with his canteens of water, offering them to both friend and enemy. A strange thing happened: both sides stopped firing while he was out there, and resumed firing when he came back behind the wall.

They promoted the sergeant to lieutenant; he was killed later at Chickamauga. A slab marks his grave in Camden, South Carolina, and there is a plaque bearing his name in the Prince of Peace Episcopal Church at Gettysburg. That's all.

How does God heal man's deepest hurts? As Lieutenant Kirkland did . . . ! And with men like him. . . .

Humanity. "One day Abraham Lincoln stopped to confer with a group of physicians in an army hospital. The president listened to one of these men indicating the difficulty of the operation which had been performed. It was one which had required the amputation of a soldier's arm at the shoulder joint. As this surgeon went into much detail, his fellow physicians gave him strict attention. It was obviously a difficult operation. When the doctor had finished his description, the other physicians began asking questions relative to techniques and methods. Lincoln, unable to restrain himself, burst out with one question, the one which at the moment no doctor had thought to ask: 'But what about the *soldier?*'

"In the midst of wholesale killing and suffering, in the midst of difficult operations, this man, Abraham Lincoln, was more concerned with humane problems than with any which were related to techniques and methods.

"If Christianity means anything at all, the inescapable interrogation is always: 'What happens to people?' An Old Testament writer etched it unforgettably on the lips of a father: 'How is the young man?' [See II Samuel 18:32—Ed.] Because people count more than things, the real issue today is not a scientific one which has to do with machines or atoms or hydrogen bombs; it is one which has to do with the welfare of people. There is never any progress until the humane problem is met and the welfare of humanity is not merely faced, but adequately handled."— G. Ray Jordan.

Jesus would agree. To Him, man was the beginning and the end of it all.

Reparations. In recent years we have been witnessing a strange and disturbing thing. We have heard James Forman, chairman of the United Black Appeal of the National Black Economic Conference, demand "reparations" of $500 *million* from the churches of the United States as token of the "repentance of the churches" for their neglect of the Negro in this country and for the suffering of the ancestors of the modern Negroes in slavery. And an American Indian demanded payment of $150 million by the National Council of Churches, as "reparations" for Indian suffering.

Certainly both Negroes and Indians have suffered—but is this the way to "atone" for their suffering? Or is it blackmail? Are the great-great-great-grandchildren to pay cash for the mistakes of their great-great-great-grandfathers? Or is there a better way? Perhaps we should move up from the abuses of years ago to a *voluntary* and *concerted* Christian effort—in which Negroes could join hands—to make life better for the descendants of the slaves.

How would you reply and react to the demands of Mr. Forman and the Indian?

The Vote. "The assistant superintendent (of a school) broke his leg and was hospitalized. Most of his get-well messages he tossed away after reading: But one he kept. It was a telegram which read: 'The executive board of the County Education Association has instructed me to send you its wishes for a speedy recovery, by a vote of 7 to 5.' "—*Mississippi Educational Advance.*

That's good for a laugh, yes; it could also be a painful reminder that while most of us vote for sympathy for the sick and broken and oppressed, we do not even send a card. . . !

Healing. Marta Korwin-Rhodes, a concert pianist, worked in a wartime hospital. She writes: "Late one night, going through the wards, I noticed a soldier whose face was buried in his pillow. In his agony, he was sobbing and moaning in the pillow so he would disturb no one. How could I help him? I looked at my hands. If I could transmit vibrations in harmony through the piano, why could I not transmit harmony directly, without an instrument? When I took the boy's head in my hands, he grabbed them with such force I thought his nails would be imbedded in my flesh. I prayed that the harmony of the world would come to alleviate his pain. His sobs quieted. Then his hands released their grip, and he was asleep."

Sentence Sermon to Remember: Charity is a virtue of the heart, not of the hands.—Joseph Addison.

Questions for Pupils on the Next Lesson: 1. Is God as concerned for the life of a nation as He is for the life of an individual? 2. What would God condemn in our morality? 3. For what purpose is God using the United States? 4. For what purpose is God using Russia and North Korea? 5. Has God helped us to win our wars? Explain how. 6. Describe what you think is an ideal Christian nation. 7. How do we know that God directs the rise and fall of nations?

LESSON IX—OCTOBER 31

GOD JUDGES NATIONS

Background Scripture: Habakkuk 1-2; Acts 17:22-31
Devotional Reading: Isaiah 40:12-17

HABAKKUK 1 5 Behold ye among the heathen, and regard, and wonder marvelously: for I will work a work in your days, which ye will not believe, though it be told you.

6 For, lo, I raise up the Chaldeans, that bitter and hasty nation, which shall march through the breadth of the land, to possess the dwelling places that are not theirs.

7 They are terrible and dreadful: their judgment and their dignity shall proceed of themselves.

8 Their horses also are swifter than the leopards, and are more fierce than the evening wolves: and their horsemen shall spread themselves, and their horsemen shall come from far; they shall fly as the eagle that hasteth to eat.

9 They shall come all for violence: their faces shall sup up as the east wind, and they shall gather the captivity as the sand.

10 And they shall scoff at the kings, and the princes shall be a scorn unto them: they shall deride every stronghold; for they shall heap dust, and take it.

11 Then shall his mind change, and he shall pass over, and offend, imputing this his power unto his god.

12 Art thou not from everlasting, O Lord my God, mine Holy One? We shall not die. O Lord, thou hast ordained them for judgment; and, O mighty God, thou hast established them for correction.

13 Thou art of purer eyes than to behold evil, and canst not look on iniquity: wherefore lookest thou upon

HABAKKUK 1 5 Look among the nations, and see;
wonder and be astounded.
For I am doing a work in your days
that you would not believe if told.

6 For lo, I am rousing the Chaldeans,
that bitter and hasty nation,
who march through the breadth of the earth,
to seize habitations not their own.

7 Dread and terrible are they;
their justice and dignity proceed from themselves.

8 Their horses are swifter than leopards,
more fierce than the evening wolves;
their horsemen press proudly on.
Yea, their horsemen come from afar;
they fly like an eagle swift to devour.

9 They all come for violence;
terror of them goes before them.
They gather captives like sand.

10 At kings they scoff,
and of rulers they make sport.
They laugh at every fortress,
for they heap up earth and take it.

11 Then they sweep by like the wind and go on,
guilty men, whose own might is their god!

12 Art thou not from everlasting,
O Lord my God, my Holy One?
We shall not die.
O Lord, thou hast ordained them as a judgment;
and thou, O Rock, hast established them for chastisement.

13 Thou who art of purer eyes than to behold evil
and canst not look on wrong,

them that deal treacherously, and holdest thy tongue when the wicked devoureth the man that is more righteous than he?

HABAKKUK 2 6 Shall not all these take up a parable against him, and a taunting proverb against him, and say, Woe to him that increaseth that which is not his! how long? and to him that ladeth himself with thick clay!

7 Shall they not rise up suddenly that shall bite thee, and awake that shall vex thee, and thou shalt be for booties unto them?

8 Because thou hast spoiled many nations, all the remnant of the people shall spoil thee; because of men's blood, and for the violence of the land, of the city, and of all that dwell therein.

why dost thou look on faithless men,
and art silent when the wicked swallows up
the man more righteous than he?
HABAKKUK 2 6 Shall not all these take up their taunt against him, in scoffing derision of him, and say, "Woe to him who heaps up what is not his own—
for how long?—
and loads himself with pledges!"
7 Will not your debtors suddenly arise,
and those awake who will make you tremble?
Then you will be booty for them.
8 Because you have plundered many nations
all the remnant of the peoples shall plunder you,
for the blood of men and violence to the earth,
to cities and all who dwell therein.

MEMORY SELECTION: He made from one every nation of men to live on all the face of the earth, having determined allotted periods and the boundaries of their habitation, that they should seek God in the hope that they might feel after him and find him. Acts 17:26-27 (RSV).

HOME DAILY BIBLE READINGS

Oct. 25. M. God's Punishment Through Other Nations, Habakkuk 1:1-11.
Oct. 26. T. God's Sure Judgment, Habakkuk 1:12-13; 2:1-5.
Oct. 27. W. The Covetous and Grasping, Habakkuk 2:6-14.
Oct. 28. T. Dishonoring Neighbors and Worshiping Idols, Habakkuk 2:15-20.
Oct. 29. F. Awe Before the Lord, Habakkuk 3:1-9.
Oct. 30. S. God Rules the Nations, Acts 17:22-31.
Oct. 31. S. The Nations, a Drop From a Bucket, Isaiah 40: 12-17.

BACKGROUND

About Habakkuk we know almost nothing except that he was a great prophet with great words to speak at the moment when the heathen Babylonians were conquering the world and destroying all that was good in Judah and Israel. He asks some questions for which we still have no really satisfactory answers; he also provides one of the greatest thoughts in religion (Habakkuk 2:4). *That thought sparked the Reformation!*

This questioning of Habakkuk is loaded with spiritual as well as political dynamite. Handle it with care!

NOTES ON THE PRINTED TEXT

1. Look among the nations, and see. . . . For lo, I am rousing the Chaldeans . . . Habakkuk 1:5,6 (RSV). Habakkuk prophesied, approximately, about the year 600 B. C. And this is what he saw in those days: he saw Babylon becoming a conquering world power such as had never been seen before. Babylon—or "the Chaldeans"—had conquered mighty Assyria, and at the battle of Carchemish Babylon had defeated and almost destroyed Egypt. Naturally, little Judah had no chance against such military might; she became a vassal of Babylon. A contemptible puppet, a "king" named Jehoiakim, "ruled" Judah under the fists of the Babylonian conquerors. He was corrupt, apostate and oppressive. But he was only one of the oppressors at work in helpless Judah. Other native sons of Judah moved like vultures among the people, waxing fat as the nation suffered. And from without were the Chaldeans, so terrible that they defy description even by the prophet; a bitter and hasty nation (hasty in that the Chaldean Empire was built so quickly), the Chaldeans were vicious, cruel plunderers who respected no law and had no pity. They were irresistible in their evil; their horses were as swift as leopards; the destroyers leveled castles and hovels and stole everything in sight; they enslaved the people or killed them; they moved as swiftly as an evil wind as they trampled down one nation after another, "gathering their captives as the sand." Among the nations of the world, Babylon was an evil beast running wild and out of control. Wrong was on the throne, there was no law or justice, the wicked ruled and the righteous suffered.

Habakkuk asks of God one question: *"Why?"* Why had God permitted this? Why did He allow the Chaldeans—who had made a God of might *their* might—to do this to other nations, particularly to Judah? God seemed to be looking on in silence, doing nothing. *Why?* "Art thou not from everlasting?" (See verse 12.) Are you not God—the God of Judah?

Why? Why do evil nations go on tearing the world apart? Why Caesar, Alexander, Hitler, Stalin? Why Buchenwald and Dachau? Why this rape of nations?

II. O Lord, thou hast ordained them as a judgment, Habakkuk 1:12 (rsv). This is the answer to Habakkuk's question and complaint. God has ordained (destined) such nations as Chaldea to be a chastisement for other nations—other nations in peril of going wrong. Assyria was created by God as "the scourge of Israel." Chaldea was the scourge of Judah—the chastising, correcting whip of the Lord against the oppressors *both within and without.*

With Chaldea, as His instrument, God is punishing the oppressors who were Judeans! The ruling classes of Judea are as much "out of line" as were the pagan Babylonians. This is Habakkuk's arresting idea—and one that takes hard thinking to understand and accept. One phase of it bothers us: if Chaldea is the chosen weapon in God's divine purpose, why should Chaldea be punished? Why was Nebuchadnezzar's army wiped out if it was God's instrument?

What answers have you for *that* question?

III. Woe to him who heaps up what is not his own—for how long? Habakkuk 2:6 (rsv). Now, Habakkuk has a flash of inner light and illumination. From some *spiritual* watchtower (2:1) his questioning gives way to faith—to a triumphant faith in a God who is not watching the debacle in silence and doing nothing about it, but a God who, in His own time, will see truth restored to the throne and righteousness replacing the wickedness of Babylon. "Though it tarry, *wait* for it" (verse 3). God has it all firmly in control, though even as good a man as Habakkuk cannot see it. The purpose will be worked out. When the kingdom will come is not clear to man, but come it will, at the hands of God. "For the earth shall be filled with the knowledge of the glory of the Lord, as the waters cover the sea" (verse 14).

This section of Habakkuk is a series of "woes"—woes sung to the oppressors, to any nation with a lust for conquest, to any plundering people. The Chaldeans will be punished—but the punishment should be left to God.

The central teaching here is that God guides *all* history and the destiny of man. Man himself cannot do that; he has no knowledge of the future. God knows the past, the present *and* all that is to come, and those with faith in God will leave all in His hands.

It was certainly valid teaching for the people of Israel; how valid is it in *our* minds?

SUGGESTIONS TO TEACHERS

Shakespeare says in *Hamlet*, "There's a divinity that shapes our ends, rough-hew them how we will." For whom or what did he mean that—for individuals, or for nations, or for both? Does God guide the nation as He guides private life? Will He destroy Russia and bless the free nations of the world?

It is a question as old as the oldest nation, and important to the youngest. Wrapped up in these questions are the mystery of God's use of evil forces in certain nations for His own purpose, the dynamic and dramatic nature of God's judgment on *all* nations, the need for trusting in God when He seems absent or slow to act. Think on these things.

Think, too, of the godless evil of Communism in our time; under it nearly half of our world is wearing chains inflicted by Marx and Lenin. Which will win? For more than forty years, the Communists have won; how will it be tomorrow, next year?

What purpose, if any, does God have in Russia? And is His hand in history as it unfolds *today?*

TOPIC FOR ADULTS
GOD JUDGES NATIONS

The Bee. Dr. Charles A. Beard, dean of American historians, has said that in our study of history we must remember that "The bee always fertilizes the flower it robs." To put it in other words, that is, the conviction that even the evil wrought by nations which seem completely bad has been and can be used of God for a good purpose.

"Out of evil," writes Dr. John A. Redhead, Jr., "good emerges; and that, because in history there is a God who makes even the wrath of men praise Him. It is a matter of history that in 1866 Prussia took away a part of the territory of Denmark. What happened? The Danes determined they would make up in quality what they lacked in quantity. It actually turned out that they produced more on the remaining acres than they had on the larger territory, and the great progress of modern Denmark is said to have begun from that national wrong. The bee fertilized the flower which it robbed.

"So often has that experience occurred that students of history are able to set it down as a principle of life. For example, I found it recently written down in this abstract form:

'The invading culture (in a war) is not always the invading culture. Military victors are sometimes civilized and practically absorbed by the subject people whom they have enslaved; and in the process of conquering its conquerors, a civilization which has become effete and sophisticated is infused with new life.'

"I found it also in the concrete in a form which can be easily appreciated in the South. 'We enslaved the Negro and succeeded only in starting him on the road to an astonishing progress.' You have only to compare that great man George Washington Carver with the savages in central Africa today to see how well the bee fertilized that flower which it robbed."

Danger! "The gap between the rich countries and the poor countries grows at a frightening rate and there are as yet no persuasive signs on the horizon to suggest that the growth of this spread is being slowed down, let alone reversed. It seems increasingly apparent that unless something is done about this situation, and done soon, there will be a series of explosions among the deprived peoples of the world which could in the end wreck civilization as we know it."—John F. Melby, in *Rotarian*, June, 1969.

Is God's hand in prosperity for one nation and starvation for the other—or has man alone done this? Has the "series of explosions" already begun? Is God tired of our civilization? Does He have another, better one in mind? Is there divine purpose in all this, or only human greed and error?

Alternatives. "The only way in which some nations will be saved from Communism is for them to develop alternatives to it. Failure of comfortable nations to realize the depth of the neglected social problems of half the world is the chief ally of Communism and unless this is understood, our military power and alliances will be of little avail. . . .

"The very atheism of Communism is a judgment on the churches which for so long were unconcerned about the victims of the industrial revolution and early capitalism and which have usually been the ornaments of *the status quo*, no matter how unjust it has been."—President John C. Bennett, Union Theological Seminary.

What was the condition of the Russian church when Communism overthrew it? Did that church deserve to survive? Did it serve people and Christ, or only a corrupt government and itself?

Read up on this before you render judgment! Perhaps God had a great purpose, in letting that church fall.

Questions for Pupils on the Next Lesson: 1. Describe the honor and majesty of God (Psalm 104:1). 2. List five ways in which you see God sustaining the universe. 3. How was Psalm 104 used by the ancient Hebrews? 4. Name two common elements found in the creation stories of the Hebrews and the Babylonians. 5. Is Psalm 104 science or poetry? 6. Describe the relevance of faith in God in the light of nuclear threat and space exploration. 7. Why do you think God created the sun and the moon?

TOPIC FOR YOUTH
GOD WORKS THROUGH NATIONS

Aliens. We are suspicious of "alien" nations today, but. . . .

"It was a Jew who brought the Gospel to Rome, a Roman who took it to France, a Frenchman who took it to Scandinavia, a Scandinavian who took it to Scotland, a Scotsman who evangelized Ireland, and an Irishman who, in turn, made the missionary conquest of Scotland.

"No country ever originally received the Gospel except at the hands of an alien."—*Survey Bulletin.*

To put it otherwise, God has used every nation and nationality in the world to spread His word!

The Cross in History. "One of the illustrious paintings of the world is Fra Angelico's *Crucifixion.* It was hung in the monastery of St. Marco in Florence. Like all the pictures of this artist, it is a painting of great charm and simple devotion. All the distracting elements of the original scene at Calvary have been omitted. The rude soldiers, the noisy rabble, the malefactors—these have no part in the scene. Instead, around the cross, grouped in attitudes of silent meditation and devotion, are figures of the great saints of the church: John the Baptist, Mark, Ambrose, Jerome, Augustine, Bernard, Francis of Assisi. Indeed, all who in the painter's day were considered the great and glorious luminaries of the church are included in the painting. In this painting, however, the usual elevation of the cross causes it so to dominate these great figures of history that they all seem dwarfed and inconspicuous. It is as if the artist were calling on all beholders to see these great and revered personalities—all of whom had served the church and many of whom made Florence famous in the church's story—in correct proportion, since all of them were but humble devotees of the cross."—Ernest Wall, p. 251, *The Minister's Manual,* edited by Charles L. Wallis. Quoted by permission of Harper and Row, publishers.

The cross and the man upon it are still the hub of history.

Governor, President. Robert G. Ingersoll, a famous American agnostic, isn't very well known to our younger generation, but their fathers knew him as one of the most colorful agnostics in American history. He was a brilliant man, with a rich and brilliant vocabulary and a great gift of oratory. But he left a rather negative mark on the history of his time. Once, he ran for governor of Illinois—and lost. Soon after that election, a group of men were arguing about the values of Christianity. One of them said, "Just show me one good thing that Christianity has accomplished."

Another man replied, "It kept Ingersoll from becoming governor of Illinois."

Ingersoll himself not only bewailed his loss of the governorship; he said in later life that his beliefs—or nonbeliefs—had kept him from running for president of the United States. While it is dangerous to say that God brings about the election or defeat of any candidate at the polls, it is certainly true that no agnostic has ever been seriously considered for the highest office in the gift of the American people. Why?

Confrontation. Once Dr. Fosdick said in a magazine article that Communism might teach us great lessons in forcing us to defend our religious faith. He wrote:

"Jesus said that when you have enemies that 'hate you . . . and reproach you and cast out your name as evil' you are to 'rejoice in that day and leap for joy.' That is asking a good deal! I have not yet been able to 'leap for joy' because of the Communists, but this much seems clear: if we should rise to the occasion, it might turn out that one of the best things that ever happened to American democracy was the confrontation of Communism, with its blazing faith, its pitiless attacks on our failures, to endeavor by personal conversion to win the world. We are up against that confrontation. Can we, like Wordsworth's *Happy Warrior,* 'turn our necessity to glorious gain'?" Quoted from "What Communism Is Doing for Me," in *Together,* November, 1956. Quoted by permission of *Together* magazine.

Idols. One of the great dangers in nationalism is that we become nation-worshipers instead of God-worshipers, that we come to put our faith in "chariots," or in military power, rather than in God. Nations which have done that in the past, have all crumbled into dust. You know their names. . . .

We in America have the most formidable armaments ever known to any nation in history. Yet—military airplanes are often obsolete six weeks after they take to the air! We develop bigger and better intercontinental missiles—and before we can use them other nations have anti-intercontinental missile defenses worked out, so then we develop an anti-anti-missile . . . and inflict taxes on the tax-paying public that are staggering. There is even talk of a rebellion against rising taxes. . . .

Can we win by this method? Has any nation ever won by using it? What does history tell us about *that?* . . . And what must God think of it?

Sentence Sermon to Remember: God governs in the affairs of men; and if a sparow cannot fall to the ground without His notice, neither can a nation rise without His aid.—Benjamin Franklin.

Questions for Pupils on the Next Lesson: 1. For what purpose was Psalm 104 written? 2. Do you take Psalm 104:3 literally. If not, how do you interpret it? 3. What is the "bound which they should not pass" (verse 9)? 4. How many planets did God create? How many stars? 5. Does true science deny true religion? Explain. 6. Did our landing on the moon strengthen your faith in God? 7. Is the universe stable and fixed, or does it grow?

LESSON X—NOVEMBER 7

GOD SUSTAINS HIS CREATION

Background Scripture: Psalm 104; Acts 14:15-17; Colossians 1:15-17
Devotional Reading: Job 38:1-11

KING JAMES VERSION

PSALM 104 Bless the Lord, O my soul. O Lord my God, thou art very great; thou art clothed with honor and majesty:

2 Who coverest thyself with light as with a garment: who stretchest out the heavens like a curtain:

3 Who layeth the beams of his chambers in the waters: who maketh the clouds his chariot: who walketh upon the wings of the wind:

4 Who maketh his angels spirits; his ministers a flaming fire:

5 Who laid the foundations of the earth, that it should not be removed for ever.

6 Thou coveredst it with the deep as with a garment: the waters stood above the mountains.

7 At thy rebuke they fled; at the voice of thy thunder they hasted away.
8 They go up by the mountains; they go down by the valleys unto the place which thou hast founded for them.
9 Thou hast set a bound that they may not pass over; that they turn not again to cover the earth.

27 These wait all upon thee; that thou mayest give them their meat in due season.
28 That thou givest them they gather: thou openest thine hand, they are filled with good.

29 Thou hidest thy face, they are troubled: thou takest away their breath, they die, and return to their dust.

REVISED STANDARD VERSION

PSALM 104 Bless the Lord, O my soul!
O Lord my God, thou art very great!
Thou art clothed with honor and majesty,
2 who coverest thyself with light as with a garment,
who hast stretched out the heavens like a tent,
3 who hast laid the beams of thy chambers on the waters,
who makest the clouds thy chariot,
who ridest on the wings of the wind,
4 who makest the winds thy messengers,
fire and flame thy ministers.
5 Thou didst set the earth on its foundations,
so that it should never be shaken.
6 Thou didst cover it with the deep as with a garment;
the waters stood above the mountains.
7 At thy rebuke they fled;
at the sound of thy thunder they took to flight.
8 The mountains rose, the valleys sank down
to the place which thou didst point for them.
9 Thou didst set a bound which they should not pass,
so that they might not again cover the earth.

27 These all look to thee,
to give them their food in due season.
28 When thou givest to them, they gather it up;
when thou openest thy hand, they are filled with good things.
29 When thou hidest thy face, they are dismayed;
when thou takest away their breath, they die
and return to their dust.

| 30 Thou sendest forth thy spirit, they are created: and thou renewest the face of the earth. | 30 When thou sendest forth thy Spirit, they are created; and thou renewest the face of the ground. |

MEMORY SELECTION: Nevertheless he left not himself without witness, in that he did good, and gave us rain from heaven, and fruitful seasons, filling our hearts with food and gladness. Acts 14:17.

HOME DAILY BIBLE READINGS

Nov. 1. M. God's Majesty, Psalm 104:1-9.
Nov. 2. T. God's Providential Care, Psalm 104:10-23.
Nov. 3. W. Sustainer of the Universe, Psalm 104:24-30.
Nov. 4. T. Shepherd of His Sheep, Psalm 95:1-7.
Nov. 5. F. Lord of the Universe, Psalm 74:12-17.
Nov. 6. S. Thanksgiving for God's Bounty, Psalm 65.
Nov. 7. S. God, the Creator, Job 38:1-11.

BACKGROUND

The Psalmists were singers; a Psalm is a sacred song or hymn (there are 150 of them in what we call the Book of Psalms) sung either by an individual in private devotions or by a group of worshipers. They are poetry, not history or science.

Psalm 104 is one of four hymns which center on the praise of God *as Creator of heaven and earth.* (The hymns are found in Psalms 8; 19:1-6; 29 and 104.) Some scholars say that Psalm 104 was a hymn sung in celebration of the annual New Year Festival, as it may have been. But some others like to think of it as a music which burst out of the heart of one singer, one poet who could go out at night and look at the star-studded sky and sing, "When I consider thy heavens, the work of thy fingers, the moon and the stars, which thou hast ordained —what is man, that thou art mindful of him?" (Psalm 8:3,4.)

He is singing both of God and *to* God. . . .

NOTES ON THE PRINTED TEXT

I. . . . thou art clothed with honor and majesty, Psalm 104:1. The author of this Psalm (it may have been David, but we are not told who he is) knew well the ideas and the myths about creation that were current in his day. There were many versions, written by Babylonians, Egyptians, Persians, Canaanites—and by the Hebrews in Genesis 1. There are common elements in all of them, for, in their own words and against their own cultural and religious backgrounds, the peoples were all trying to give special accent to the honor and glory of the creator. The Egyptians, for instance, sang a hymn to the sun composed by the Egyptian Pharaoh Amenhotep IV (Ikhnaton), which made the *sun* the creator. They had a "sun god." The Babylonians sang of how Marduk, the god of Babylon, destroyed his enemy Tiamat, who was a dragon (devil) causing confusion in the world. But the (Hebrew) author of Psalm 104 made one great, supreme God *creator of the sun,* and a God so almighty that, at that time, He had no Tiamat to oppose His creation.

Notice how this author describes the creation of the heavens (verses 1-4). First of all, he says that God has covered Himself with light, "as a garment." According to Genesis 1:3, light was created *first;* it was the basic element (who can think of life without *light*?); God *was* light, and it gleamed from Him like a radiant "garment." He made and stretched out the heavens as a man would make and stretch out a curtain or a tent. He laid deep in the waters below the beams which supported the heavens; these are the waters *above* the firmament, which are the source of rain (see Genesis 1:7 and Psalm 148:4, also Psalm 104:13). He created chariots of the clouds; they are driven on the wings of the wind. He made the winds His messengers, He made flame and fire His ministers (see the Revised Standard Version here). These elemental forces of nature were in His hands, to be used as He pleased.

No—it is not a *scientific* explanation; the Psalmist wasn't writing a textbook on science. He was singing in ecstatic praise. He was simply putting all creation in the hands of one God. (If we cannot put it there —where *shall* we put it, with all our science?)

II. Thou didst set the earth on its foundatons . . . , Psalm 104:5 (rsv). All ancient peoples (Babylonians, Canaanites and Hebrews alike) believed that there was a time when there was nothing but chaos. We have already mentioned the chaos which, in the Babylonian account of creation, ruled the unfolding universe when the great god Marduk created heaven and earth out of the carcass (!) of his enemy Tiamat, the goddess of confusion. The Canaanites believed that their god, Baal, crushed the sea dragon Yam, or Tannin, and Lotan (Leviathan), and "Shalyat of the seven heads." The Babylonians and the Canaanites believed these myths; the Hebrew Psalmist did not.

He did believe that the waters once covered the earth. (It could be; we have picked up perfectly round stones in Leadville, Colorado, 10,200 feet above sea level, which some scientists say was once under water!) But the Psalmist says that God simply separated the waters from the earth—"And God called the dry land Earth; and the gathering together of the waters he called Seas" (Genesis 1:10, rsv). There was no great battle between gods in this version, no long struggle. The Psalmist discards the Babylonian and Cananitish myths; he has a God who simply spoke, and the waters separated from the earth. It is language close to that used in the story of the flood in Genesis 7 and 9.

Geologists and other scientists in our day may have other theories, but that makes little difference. The point is that there came a time when, in the wisdom of the creator of both, earth and the seas *were* divided.

III. These all look to thee, to give them their food in due season, Psalm 104:27 (rsv). "These all" are the ones described in Psalm 103, including animals and men. God created every one of them—and He did *not* create them and set them down in the world, and then *leave* them. That would be like an engineer opening the throttle of his engine and then jumping out of the cab. God made them and He knew when He made them that they were utterly and completely dependent on Him—and He sustained them. He sustained them with the fruit of the tree and the water in the spring. He sent His rain on just and unjust alike; He made His sun to shine that food could grow. He gave us all we need.

Now, if God were to "hide his face" from us—if He were to withdraw all contact with us, including His sun and rain and rich soil and food—what then? Then, said the Psalmist, we would all die. (See Job 34:14,15.) Without the breath of life He gave us and without His sustenance, we would die. Fortunately for us, He does not do that; instead, He sends His creative Spirit to renew our faith—*and* our lives.

So says the Psalmist. Has it ever been said better?

SUGGESTIONS TO TEACHERS

Creation, we say, is evidence of the existence of God. True. We could also say, as this lesson teaches, that God's care of His children *after* creation is further and perhaps greater proof of His existence and His love. That is the first teaching of this lesson!

Second: we live in an age of nuclear threat and space exploration. How do we find God in such an age? What has the atom bomb and the conquest of space done to our faith in God—if anything?

These are things to think about. . . .

TOPIC FOR ADULTS
GOD SUSTAINS HIS CREATION

Prop. "When Martin Luther's friends wrote despairingly of the negotiations at the Diet of Worms, Luther replied from Coburg that he had been looking up at the night sky, spangled and studded with stars, and had found no pillars to hold them up. And yet they did not fall. God needs no props for his stars and planets. He hangs them on nothing.

"So, in the working of God's providence, the unseen prop is enough for the seen."—Augustus Hopkins Strong.

If God created the stars and keeps them in their courses, how much more has He done for His crowning creation—man!

Change, Stability. There has probably never been an age in the history of man when so much has changed so fast. *Everything* is changing; we need not specify, but only observe, the truth of that. Speaking of the place of God in such a time, a New York minister says:

"As we travel with Him along the way there are no permanent rest stations, no secure havens, no hiding places from which, after a time, He will not beckon us to follow Him, to serve with Him, to tackle with Him the loneliness and hurt, the estrangement among men. For . . . as He has done for ages, so will He smash our idols now. He has told us that He is a jealous God, that security and hope are to be in no one and no thing but Him. In Christ He has shattered our grip on the past and present and has released us to live for the future. In Him we are enabled to expect and to manage the unexpected. Our hope and our security rest in His promise to be present among us as we struggle through change and face uncertain futures. As Dr. King said, 'We know not what the future holds, but we know who holds the future.'

"We have learned . . . that great American folk hymn, 'We Shall Overcome.' It is perhaps only half right. For the message of the New Testament is that God *has* overcome, and that in our behalf He will continue to overcome. In that hope and confidence we are released and invited to a life of freedom, of challenge, of creativity."—James W. Crawford, in *Pulpit Digest,* October, 1968.

Adaptation, God. The woodcock is an odd bird. It eats earth worms.

It has a three-inch-long beak with a hinge in the middle, so that the bird can spring his beak open *underground*.

Brown snakes have a natural camouflage which makes them practically invisible as they move about on brown rocks or on brown desert soil. Green snakes are green because they run in green places—in thick foliage, or deep grass. Polar bears have long, heavy hair to protect them against the cold; lions have short hair because they live in warm climates. Eagles have great wing spreads because they must fly high over mountains; sparrows have tiny wings because they feed mostly on the ground. Monkeys have tremendously agile hands and feet, for they live in trees; fish have fins and scales because they live in water.

Some call it "the adaptation of nature." Others call it God's providence. What do you call it?

Laurence Sterne said that "God tempers the wind to the shorn lamb." What did he mean by that?

The Spinal Cord. "Dr. Joseph P. Evans, Director of the Division of Neurological Surgery at the University of Chicago, finds his faith confirmed by a study of the spinal cord. He says:

"I have had recurrent occasions to expose at operation the upper cervical spinal cord. After removing the bony protective layer, the tough membrane which encompasses the cord is brought into view. When this is opened a truly impressive sight is revealed. The surgeon sees, through a transparent jacket, a clear fluid bathing the cord from which arise the nerve roots that carry impulses in and out of the cord. There is also a fine tracery of blood vessels that is beautiful to behold. But overshadowing everything is the great order apparent in this.

"If one reflects how orderly this is, and how much more elaborate is the brain, whose secrets are even more deeply hidden than those of the spinal cord, the reality of great order is almost overwhelming. . . . From the objective evidence of order in the cord one is led, in my opinion, directly to a consideration of the old argument concerning a First Cause. It is this line of thinking that gives me a deep belief in a Creator. . . . And so I believe that just as the maker of a chair has a purpose in mind, so, too, the Maker of man has an end in mind for man himself. This, in turn, leads me to think of the Creator as a Personal God, one who is interested in individuals as such, and from this, of course, follows my belief in the dignity of man."—*Illustrate!* by J. C. Hefley. Quoted by permission of Zondervan Publishing House, publishers.

The purpose goes on working after the man is born: this we call *providence!*

Questions for Pupils on the Next Lesson: 1. Under what moral system did the ancient Hebrews live? 2. Do all moral systems come from God? 3. Are the teachings of the Sermon on the Mount ethical or spiritual? 4. How do you tell the law of God from the law of man? 5. Explain how you practice the morality of Romans 12:14. 6. Does the moral precept of Galatians 6:7 always work out in every man's life? 7. Why is Judaism sometimes called "an ethical monotheism"?

TOPIC FOR YOUTH
GOD IS IN CONTROL

The White Temple. "A Denver reporter and photographer discovered the secret hide-out of a religious group known as the Brotherhood of the White Temple, in the foothills of the Rockies. It is reported that several hundred members of the cult have retired there to await 'Armageddon.' The leader and founder of the group expects a Russian atomic attack on the United States this year; he bases his prediction largely on his study of the prophecies of Nostradamus, a 16th century astrologer, and on the measurements of the Great Pyramids.

"The retreat consists of about 100 new homes, a glistening white two-story temple building and two structures that had a barracks-like appearance. . . . The temple interior was illuminated with an eerie blue light; 200 overstuffed chairs faced a great dais topped by a throne, on which was a headdress of gold cloth. Three gongs stood on a pedestal beside the throne and an incense burner stood before it. There were indications that great supplies of food were stored in a near-by cave.

"Outside the leader's house was a gleaming yellow . . . Buick. And atop a 50-foot tower is a television aerial, presumably to enable him to watch Armageddon being fought.

"The great need today is not for a mountain hide-out, but a strong faith in the Lord and His Word, which cannot be destroyed by atomic bombs. The Psalmist had such a faith. He said, 'God is our refuge and strength, a very present help in time of trouble. Therefore will not we fear though the earth be removed and the mountains be carried into the midst of the sea; though the waters thereof roar and be troubled, though the mountains shake with the swelling thereof.' "—From *Now*, Le Tourneau Tech publication.

You want security in the atom age? Where do you expect to find it but in the God who controls . . . ?

Providential Care. Man needed food, so God gave him soil in which to raise food.

The soil needed encouragement, so God provided sun and rain.
The soil needed protection from wind and erosion; God provided grass.
Man needed heat for his comfort, and fuel for his fire; God gave him coal, buried deep in the earth.
Man needed a shelter over his head; God gave him wood and stone.
Man needed clothing; God gave him the hides of animals.
Man needed beauty; God gave him the orchid and the rose.
Man needed hope and faith; God gave him Jesus Christ.
Man needs nothing that God does not supply.

God Up There. Testifying before the Senate Committee on Aeronautical and Space Sciences, Colonel John Glenn had this exchange with Senator Wiley (we quote from the official transcript):

"Senator Wiley. 'From what you have said on other occasions, I was wondering whether you felt that God was up there as well as down here, and that in Him you lived and moved and had your being?'

"Colonel Glenn: 'Absolutely; I think that to try to limit God to one particular section of space . . . is a very foolish thing to do. I don't know the nature of God any more than anyone else, nor would I claim to because I happened to have made a space ride that got us a little above the atmosphere. God is certainly bigger than that, and I think He will be wherever we go.' "

Space? Why worry about it? God is up there as well as down here, if we have eyes and ears. . . .

At Work. Many of us, shocked and disturbed at the explosions of our atomic and nuclear bombs, have been saying that "we have stolen the secret of God hidden in the atom, and that it will destroy us." Maybe. Whether or not we destroy ourselves depends, not on the discovery of nuclear power, but on man's use of it. And God may have other secrets in atomic activity that we haven't discovered yet!

"The atom is already at work in everyday peacetime uses. More than 1000 industrial firms now employ the atom in factory operations, while in hospitals and clinics, atomic medicines are being administered on a growing scale. It is estimated that more lives have already been saved by the atom than were wiped out in the Hiroshima and Nagasaki A-bomb blasts."—*The Survey Bulletin.*

Man proposes, God disposes. His hand is still on the throttle!

Sentence Sermon to Remember: Behind the dim unknown, Standeth God within the shadow, Keeping watch above His own.—James Russell Lowell.

Questions for Pupils on the Next Lesson: 1. Do our moral laws depend on our environment? 2. What is meant by "God is not mocked?" 3. Is God's moral law unchanging, the same forever and everywhere? 4. What four moral precepts are laid down in Romans 12:12-16? 5. Why can't we live morally as we please? 6. What does Paul mean by "Rejoice with them that do rejoice, and weep with them that weep?" 7. Is the Golden Rule "all we need in religion," as some people think?

LESSON XI—NOVEMBER 14

GOD ESTABLISHES MORAL ORDER

Background Scripture: Exodus 20:1-20; Romans 2:12-16; 3:21-26;
Galatians 6:7-10
Devotional Reading: Psalm 75

KING JAMES VERSION

ROMANS 12 12 Rejoicing in hope; patient in tribulation; continuing instant in prayer;

13 Distributing to the necessity of saints; given to hospitality.

14 Bless them which persecute you: bless, and curse not.

15 Rejoice with them that do rejoice, and weep with them that weep.

16 Be of the same mind one toward another. Mind not high things, but condescend to men of low estate. Be not wise in your own conceits.

GALATIANS 6 7 Be not deceived; God is not mocked: for whatsoever a man soweth, that shall he also reap.

8 For he that soweth to his flesh shall of the flesh reap corruption; but he that soweth to the Spirit shall of the Spirit reap life everlasting.

9 And let us not be weary in well doing: for in due season we shall reap, if we faint not.

REVISED STANDARD VERSION

ROMANS 12 12 Rejoice in your hope, be patient in tribulation, be constant in prayer. 13 Contribute to the needs of the saints, practice hospitality.

14 Bless those who persecute you; bless and do not curse them. 15 Rejoice with those who rejoice, weep with those who weep. 16 Live in harmony with one another; do not be haughty, but associate with the lowly; never be conceited.

GALATIANS 6 7 Do not be deceived; God is not mocked, for whatever a man sows, that he will also reap. 8 For he who sows to his own flesh will from the flesh reap corruption; but he who sows to the Spirit will from the Spirit reap eternal life. 9 And let us not grow weary in well-doing, for in due season we shall reap, if we do not lose heart.

MEMORY SELECTION: Be not deceived; God is not mocked: for whatsoever a man soweth, that shall he also reap.—Galatians 6:7.

HOME DAILY BIBLE READINGS

Nov. 8. M. *Reverence for God,* Exodus 20:1-11.
Nov. 9. T. *Reverence for Persons Under God,* Exodus 20:12-20.
Nov. 10. W. *God Will Judge All Men,* Romans 2:6-16.
Nov. 11. T. *All Men Need Redemption in Christ,* Romans 3:19-26.
Nov. 12. F. *Keeping on Faithfully,* Galatians 6:1-10.
Nov. 13. S. *God Vindicates Righteous Living,* Psalm 62:5-12.
Nov. 14. S. *Exalting the Righteous,* Psalm 75.

BACKGROUND

The early Christians were surrounded by people who were *not* Christians, and before their conversion to Christ *they* were not Christians either. When they accepted Christ, they found themselves with two problems: (1) just what were they to believe in this totally new faith, and (2) what were they to *do* about what they believed and how were they to do it? To understand their problem we might think of ourselves as going to Japan or India to live. How would we conduct ourselves in India and Japan?

Now, Paul, who writes to certain Romans and Galatians about this problem, was a most practical man. Great theologian that he was, he had no use for a theology that did not become translated into *practice*. He thought that there were certain obligations following conversion, that there were certain *ethical* implications to salvation, certain things the saved one must do, a certain way in which he must *live*.

Christians, he said, were not to pattern themselves on (not to *conform* to) the moral or ethical standards of the world, but on the moral and ethical standards of *God*. But . . . just what were those standards? What *were* the moral demands of God . . . ? This is what we are to discover in this lesson.

NOTES ON THE PRINTED TEXT

I. Rejoicing in hope; patient in tribulation; continuing instant in prayer . . . , Romans 12:12. If Paul is hard to understand theologically (and he *is!*) he is easy to understand when he tells us what a Christian is. He is painfully clear in *that* department. The main thrust of his thinking is found in Romans 12:12-16, in which he describes the characteristics of the Christian man.

First, the Christian man is no kill-joy, no melancholy pessimist. He is always *an optimist*. Paul said that to a people writhing under the heel of the Roman conqueror, a people unhappy with much of their traditional precepts in morals and religion. "You have no business sitting around weeping like a lot of children; you should be rejoicing in your hope!" When everything else is gone, many of us find that we have nothing left *but* hope! There are times when we can only pray—provided we still have hope (confidence) in the God to whom we pray. There is no such thing as a hopeless Christian. Said someone, "There are no hopeless situations; there are only men who have grown hopeless about them." It is hope *in action* that has given us a better world to live in than the old Romans and Hebrews had—and that will give us a yet better world tomorrow. Without hope—*nothing*.

The Christian man has a patience with trouble that often makes the world laugh while God approves. The Christian man doesn't complain, "What have I done to deserve this trouble?" He says, as he gets up from the blow, "There must be a lesson in that for me somewhere." When Beethoven was made the victim of complete deafness he said, "I will take life by the throat . . . ," and he did, and he is one of our greatest composers. When the Son of God bled to death on a cross, He said, "Into thy hands. . . ." Patience! It has made many a sufferer a triumphant hero. Impatience has produced more disaster than progress.

The Christian is *constant* in prayer, Romans 12:12 (RSV). He doesn't pray just in church at 11 o'clock on Sunday morning; he prays before sleeping and on greeting the dawn, he prays as he walks to work, rides the bus or sits at his desk. The man who doesn't do that cheats himself of the strength of God. And he adds giving to praying. He doesn't growl that he has no money to give to starving or underprivileged people, near or far, while "there is so much to do right here at home." He sees any man in need as his brother. He doesn't turn his back on a stranger; he takes the stranger in. His home is a harbor, not a hide-out.

He is always hospitable, never hostile; his religion is the religion of the open hand.

Verses 14 and 15 in this chapter go back to the teachings and almost the language of the Sermon on the Mount; they should not need explanation here, but they are good to study and reflect upon in a day when every nation in the world seems driven by hate. We look at pictures of riot and bloodshed every day of our lives right here in Christian America, and if we are Christian we ask ourselves, "Dear God, what has happened to us, anyway? Why are we like this? Why must we curse each other?"

What does Paul mean by, "Rejoice with them that do rejoice, and weep with them that weep?" He means that a Christian cannot possibly be jealous; he will rejoice when good things happen to his friend, as well as when good things happen to himself. He weeps when his friend weeps in sorrow; he takes the pain of others into *his* heart. People who cry together know what true friendship is, what love is. It is in sorrow that we find our best friends.

Lastly, the Christian is no snob. He is a stranger to conceit. He has no (spiritual) superiority complex. He lives as Christ and St. Francis lived —humbly, and *with* the humble. He refuses to hate or to "look down his nose" at any man; he lives in harmony with those around him.

Measured by all this, how would you rate as a Christian?

II. Be not deceived; God is not mocked, Galatians 6:7. Some people —including some Christians—have a queer idea that God is something and somehow like a tolerant old grandfather who will forgive his grandchildren, no matter what they do, no matter what they are. That makes of God something like a soft, sentimental fool. Paul despised the idea of God being like that. He cried out that no man could mock (sneer at) God; no man could burn life's candle in the service of the devil and blow its smoke in the face of God. He said that each of us could live as we choose to live—but we must expect to reap as we sow. We don't sow thistles and reap roses. We don't live in the gutter and walk easily into heaven. If we sow to our own nature (or live by a low moral standard) we will reap a rotten harvest. Sow to the Spirit and we reap everlasting life. We are recompensed, one way or another.

So—"let us not be weary in well-doing" (verse 9). "The sum of the matter is that we are to miss no chance of doing good to all men, remembering especially the 'household of faith' (Galatians 6:10)—that is, the children in God's family, the members of the church. This is the Christian version of the proverb which says that 'charity begins at home'" (Archibald M. Hunter).

SUGGESTIONS TO TEACHERS

The teacher could very well start this lesson with a background discussion on the moral order of God. In terms of human behavior, what does that "order" embrace? What are its fundamentals? (Here, look at the Ten Commandments and the Sermon on the Mount.)

Then—he might stress the basic and *unchanging* nature of God's moral law, and the law of sowing and reaping in moral and immoral living (a *very* important concern!).

Let the latter half of your class discussion revolve around the question, "What is the relation of God's moral order to the problems of our day?" If they have no relation to each other, why talk about it at all?

TOPIC FOR ADULTS
GOD ESTABLISHES MORAL ORDER

Stealing. Stealing, we hold, is immoral as well as illegal; that was laid down in the Ten Commandments. With very few exceptions, that is still universally accepted as a moral principle. It is one of the "planks" of God's moral order.

Late in the year 1885, an organization known as the American Copyright League accepted this as their motto:

> In vain we hold old notions fudge
> And bend our conscience to our dealing.
> The Ten Commandments will not budge
> And stealing will continue stealing.

But, some say, stealing is "relative," and our concepts of it change from country to country, from time to time. "All morality is relative," they say. Is it? What is relative about burglary, murder or a little plain lie? Will God accept "just a little" immorality? What provision did He make for relative sin in the Commandments, or in the Sermon on the Mount?

Purse Snatchers. Our neighbor's wife had her purse snatched yesterday afternoon at 2 o'clock. It happened in broad daylight, on the main street of one of our largest cities. Three teen-age boys (playing hookey from school because this was Friday, when most down-town workers in the city got paid) pushed her into a doorway, and one of them tore her purse out of her hand. In doing that, he broke three fingers, which will remain crooked and crippled until she dies. It happens so often, the police and the courts say, that they just can't keep up with it, or bring all the offenders to justice.

They were teen-agers. They lived in a pig-sty tenement. Two of them did not know who their fathers were. One was a dope addict. One had served time in a reformatory for looting during a riot. One had been fired from seven successive jobs. They were wrong. Criminally wrong. Morally wrong. But . . . was there also immorality and guilt on the part of a community which had done nothing to get them out of those slums and out of a crime-ridden environment, but had depended on policemen's clubs for "law and order?"

Who's immoral here? How many of *God's* laws were broken . . . ?

The Higher Ups. There's more trouble in this city where our friend lost her purse: the Federal government is investigating the mayor and the whole city council, who have been charged with corruption and protection of the Mafia!

"Don Herold once wrote: 'Moralizing and morals are two entirely different things—always found in entirely different people.'

"We are in danger of becoming a nation of moralizers rather than the moral nation we must be if freedom is to live in this world. Perhaps the time has come when something like Jesus' denunciation of the scribes

and Pharisees is needed in our midst. One looks almost in vain, however, for men in public life with sufficient courage to reaffirm the moral
faith of the nation's founders."—Jack Mendelsohn, "Legislating for God,"
in *Progressive*.

How much can you tell about the moral faith of the founders?

Killing. The Ten Commandments made it moral law (revealed by
God) that men should not kill. Jesus went further when He said that
we should not even kill our enemies; we should love them! Both were
developing aspects of the moral law of God.

But—twenty centuries after Jesus—we Americans were shocked and
stunned at the report of a massacre said to have been staged by American soldiers at My Lai in Vietnam. As we write, the story is being in-
vestigated. The investigation may come to nothing or find the report
untrue or grossly exaggerated. But this truth remains: all war is an immoral business, and all those involved in its battles tend to become something less than men and more like animals. Subject any man, anywhere,
to training in the art of killing, and he is bound to become a killer, even
after the war is over!

Jesus was trying to save us from this immorality when He bade us
love our enemies. He was trying to build respect for the law of God.

The Scarlet Letter. Nathaniel Hawthorne wrote a great, poignant story
in *The Scarlet Letter*. His heroine was Hester Prynne, an adulteress; as
punishment, she was condemned to wear an embroidered "A" on her
dress, so that the community could never forget or forgive her sin. The
women of the community thought that wasn't enough; they demanded
that she be branded with the letter on her forehead. She might have
been branded, except for the interference of one woman with a Christian heart, who said, "Let her cover the mark as she will. The pangs of
it will always be in her heart."

Paul said that "whatsoever a man soweth, that shall he also reap."
The harvest of immorality, the penalty of breaking God's moral law, is
horrible, suffered mainly in the deep recesses of the heart. . . .

Questions for Pupils on the Next Lesson: 1. Just how does God conquer evil? 2. What does it mean to be "justified by faith?" 3. What is
grace, and how does it help us face temptation? 4. What "strength"
(Romans 5:6) does the crucifixion of Christ give us? 5. Does your religion help you to rise above circumstance? How? 6. What is accomplished in the life of a man who lets God take over his life? 7. Did Jesus
die for the godly or the ungodly? Why?

TOPIC FOR YOUTH
GOD'S MORAL ORDER

Breaking. "It is not unusual to hear someone refer to the breaking of
one or more of the commandments. E. Stanley Jones points out that it
is impossible to break any of the commandments. They are unbreakable.

"What really happens is that the commandments break *us* when we
violate them. It is against natural law for a man to butt his head against
a stone wall. In the act, the man does not break the law or the wall; he
breaks his head. Sin has a boomerang action; it comes back on the
sinner."—C. H. Spurgeon.

Narrow-Minded. We talk a great deal, these days, about "the new morality," and those who champion it too often condemn those who see nothing "new" in it as being squares, reactionaries, Victorians, or just plain narrow-minded. But . . .

"The preacher is sometimes accused of being narrow-minded because he insists on the Christian's forsaking all to follow Christ. But all of life is narrow, and success is to be found only by passing through the narrow gate and down the straight way.

"There is no room for broad-mindedness in the chemical laboratory. Water is composed of two parts hydrogen and one part oxygen. The slightest deviation from that formula is forbidden.

"There is no room for broad-mindedness in the mathematics classroom. Neither geometry, calculus nor trigonometry allows any variation from exact accuracy, even for old times' sake. The solution of the problem is either right or it is wrong—no tolerance there.

"There is no room for broad-mindedness in the garage. The mechanic there says that the piston rings must fit the cylinder walls within one-thousandth part of an inch. Even between friends there cannot be any variation if the motor is to run smoothly.

"How, then, shall we expect that broad-mindedness shall rule in the realm of religion and morals?"—From *The Log of the Good Ship Grace.*

The question is important. Should every generation be bound by the morals of the preceding generation? Should twentieth century morality be the same as fourth century morality? Or should morality change and grow—from an immovable base of truth and proven principles laid down by experience and faith in God? Beware of snap judgments!

Retribution. In the Spanish-American War, a great naval victory was won by Admiral Schley, who all but put the Spanish Navy out of action at the battle of Santiago. Someone asked the admiral what he was thinking about during that battle (aside, we presume, from thinking about sinking the Spanish ships!). He replied:

"As we brought destruction to Cervera's fleet, my mind went back three hundred years to the time when the Spaniards drove my ancestors out of Spain. I thought how strange that years later I would be the one to help pay that debt to a wicked nation for such a humiliating action."

While it may be a bit dangerous to figure out exactly how, when, where and by whom retribution comes, the fact is that it *comes.* It is God's law that it shall come, that He shall not be mocked, and that the sins we commit two by two we shall pay for one by one.

Conduct. "Fundamentally, the force that rules the world is conduct, whether it be moral or immoral. If it is moral, there may be hope for the world. If immoral, there is not only no more hope, but no prospect of anything but destruction of all that has been accomplished during the last 5,000 years."—Nicholas Murray Butler.

Diamonds. We read in the paper just the other day that a Hollywood star received as a Christmas gift a set of diamond-studded golf clubs. We play golf, too, but we can't imagine looking down at a diamond in the head of our driver just as we are about to hit the ball!

But that's beside the point. The point is illustrated in another item in the same paper, which reported that babies and children were starving to death by the hundreds in a war-torn country.

"For I was an hungered, and ye gave me no meat . . ." (Matthew 25:42).

And *that* is breaking God's moral law.

Sentence Sermon to Remember: The first article of my creed is that I am a moral personality under orders.—William L. Sullivan.

Questions for Pupils on the Next Lesson: 1. Have you any interest in justification? 2. Did Jesus Christ ever stop you from doing anything wrong? 3. What should suffering produce in our lives? 4. Are any of us worthy of the sacrifice of Christ on the cross? 5. Do you know of anyone who does not struggle against evil? 6. How have you found peace in an evil world? 7. Tell in fifty words what Christ means to you.

LESSON XII—NOVEMBER 21

GOD CONQUERS EVIL

Background Scripture: Romans 5; 8:28-39; II Corinthians 4:7-18
Devotional Reading: Psalm 85

KING JAMES VERSION

ROMANS 5 Therefore being justified by faith, we have peace with God through our Lord Jesus Christ:

2 By whom also we have access by faith into this grace wherein we stand, and rejoice in hope of the glory of God.

3 And not only so, but we glory in tribulations also; knowing that tribulation worketh patience;

4 And patience, experience; and experience, hope:

5 And hope maketh not ashamed; because the love of God is shed abroad in our hearts by the Holy Ghost which is given unto us.

6 For when we were yet without strength, in due time Christ died for the ungodly.

7 For scarcely for a righteous man will one die: yet peradventure for a good man some would even dare to die.

8 But God commendeth his love toward us, in that, while we were yet sinners, Christ died for us.

9 Much more then, being now justified by his blood, we shall be saved from wrath through him.

10 For if, when we were enemies, we were reconciled to God by the death of his Son; much more, being reconciled, we shall be saved by his life.

11 And not only so, but we also joy in God through our Lord Jesus Christ, by whom we have now received the atonement.

REVISED STANDARD VERSION

ROMANS 5 Therefore, since we are justified by faith, we have peace with God through our Lord Jesus Christ. 2 Through him we have obtained access to this grace in which we stand, and we rejoice in our hope of sharing the glory of God. 3 More than that, we rejoice in our sufferings, knowing that suffering produces endurance, 4 and endurance produces character, and character produces hope, 5 and hope does not disappoint us, because God's love has been poured into our hearts through the Holy Spirit which has been given to us.

6 While we were yet helpless, at the right time Christ died for the ungodly. 7 Why, one will hardly die for a righteous man—though perhaps for a good man one will dare even to die. 8 But God shows his love for us in that while we were yet sinners Christ died for us. 9 Since, therefore, we are now justified by his blood, much more shall we be saved by him from the wrath of God. 10 For if while we were enemies we were reconciled to God by the death of his Son, much more, now that we are reconciled, shall we be saved by his life. 11 Not only so, but we also rejoice in God through our Lord Jesus Christ, through whom we have now received our reconciliation.

MEMORY SELECTION: *In all these things we are more than conquerors through him that loved us.* Romans 8:37.

HOME DAILY BIBLE READINGS

Nov. 20. S. Hope Beyond This Life, II Corinthians 5:1-9.
Nov. 21. S. The Final Victory, Revelation 7:9-17.

BACKGROUND

There are great words all through the first four chapters of Romans: sin, faith and justification, for instance. On these themes great sermons have been preached, great books written. Just one phrase, "The just shall live by faith," has fascinated Christians and Christianity for nearly two thousand years.

Paul is fascinated by it, too, but even more is he concerned with what happens in the life of the Christian *after* the act of justification by, or through, faith. What happens *then?* Kenneth J. Foreman has put it beautifully when he says, "Indeed, it would be better to say that faith simply opens the door to God, *letting God take over.*"

All right—what is *accomplished* in the life of the man who lets God take over his life? There are certain definite results, summed up in four words which we will think about in this lesson: peace, joy, reconciliation, love.

Perhaps we could sum it up, generally, by saying that *God conquers evil in us when we give Him a free hand in our lives.*

NOTES ON THE PRINTED TEXT

I. Therefore, since we are justified by faith, we have peace with God through our Lord Jesus Christ, Romans 5:1 (RSV). Peace? It is the great hunger of mankind. Many of us, struggling against evil—against the temptation to live easily instead of nobly—would give *anything* for it. Even good Christians fight a lifelong battle to gain "the peace that passes all understanding."

In a way, they do not need to battle at all. As Christians, they *have* peace, even when they do not know it. You may remember from your study of American history, that General Andrew Jackson fought and won the battle of New Orleans, in the War of 1812, *after* the war was over, after peace had been declared. It was a totally useless battle. Just so, it is useless, or unnecessary, for the Christian to go on fighting for peace once he realizes that through the redeeming sacrifice of Christ he *has* peace already planted in his soul. Once he really understands that he has been reconciled (brought back) to God through Christ, he should *know* that he is at peace with man and God. In the person of Jesus Christ, God has come all the way to him. God is at peace with us; we should understand that therefore we are at peace with Him, and His peace should bring us into a wider peace with men. We sing, "I *know* that my Redeemer liveth." If only we would stop fighting and listen, we would know that His peace *is* in our hearts; but we can't listen while we are fighting!

We don't deserve it; it is the free gift of a God who loves us even when we are at our worst.

II. We rejoice in our hope . . . in our sufferings, Romans 5:2,3 (RSV). The Christian life is a life of joy—of *rejoicing.* We should be so happy that we could sing from the housetops about it all. We should be happy that we have tribulations to help us—yes, help us! Tribulation is the fire that burns out the dross from the metal of life, that *purifies* it, that, through testing, makes us strong and patient. We should rejoice, too, that after the tribulation, after the suffering and the struggling, we shall have a glory so great that our small minds cannot grasp it. Paul never says much about heaven, but here he says that *in the future—* even after we are gone from this earth—we shall *share the glory of God.* After this life, the glory! We have no reason to be sad about anything in life, even sad about the prospect of death, for God has given us hope, and "hope does not disappoint us" (verse 5).

The most evil thought in life is that death ends everything. Jesus Christ conquered that evil for us on the first Easter morning. . . . Let there be joy over death, not despair!

III. While we were yet helpless, at the right time Christ died for the ungodly, Romans 5:6 (RSV). Jesus Christ didn't die to help the righteous; He died for men who were *ungodly*—for men who made no claim whatever of righteousness, for sinners who never even knew Him! For the ungodly and the unlovable. He loved the unlovable; He made us see that they were the object of Calvary, the object of the love of a holy God.

It is never easy to die, even for one's friends. "Greater love hath no man," said Jesus about the man who died for His friends. But He also said, "Love your enemies . . ." and *He died* for His enemies! There never can be a greater love than that.

"While we were yet sinners, Christ died for us." Well, we are all sinners, and always have been. We are still sinners in the sense that we still fall far short of the glory of God. We still struggle against sin, against the evil that surrounds us. Some win the struggle when the peace and love of God gets into their hearts; some lose when that peace and love is locked out of their hearts. But when the man plagued by evil lets God in, then the *desire* to be evil, to do the ugly or dishonest or mean thing, is gone out of him. The converted drunkard drinks no more; the thief steals no more, the liar tells the truth, the bigot hates no more— all because Christ has saved them from even the desire to drink and steal and lie and hate. This is salvation while yet we live—while we are still sinners. Salvation being saved from *doing* what is sinful—does not wait on death; it comes not only after death, but often as we *live.*

God loved us enough to send His Son to save us from all this. His Son, said someone, did not come to change God's attitude toward us, but to prove that His attitude toward us was one of love—even in moments when we are at our lowest and worst.

It is incredible, but it is true. "God so loves us that . . ." He opens the gates of heaven and rids us of the evil in our hearts while we walk the earth *before* death . . .

SUGGESTIONS TO TEACHERS

Ambition is "a thing strongly desired or sought after," and usually we identify it with money or material success. But there is another ambition that fascinates and drives men all through their lives: this is a *spiritual* ambition, and it could be summed up in the words, "I am never good enough!" However we fail or succeed, there is always the gnawing longing or aspiration or ambition to be better than we are—*if only we knew how!*

This lesson is a "how" lesson. It tells us how and where to get the help we need to be better than we are; it tells us that with God—often *only* with God—can we conquer the bad or unworthy in us, and be lifted up into a more abundant life. God conquers evil. Think of it under these suggested lesson emphases:

1. The power of God's love over evil.
2. Christ's victory on the cross empowers the Christian to win victory over evil.
3. The redeemed person can rise above *any* adverse circumstance.
4. We are saved, not by any law, but by simple faith.

TOPIC FOR ADULTS
GOD CONQUERS EVIL

Salvation. "Salvation" is an abused and often misused term, in a selfish sense. For those who haven't quite thought it through, it means simply believing a certain creed or teaching about God and Christ, and thereby gaining admission to heaven after death. To others, it means being saved from something *now*. Dr. H. F. Rall puts it in these words:

"'Salvation' is one of religion's great words. It is well to see what is its true and full meaning. To some it means a drunkard saved from the ditch, to others escape from hell or reaching heaven. . . . This is true, but not enough. Salvation means three things:

1. Deliverance from evil of every kind, within and without, now and to come.
2. The gaining of good, good of every kind but especially the highest good, the life with God and all that this brings.
3. The help of God.

"In a word, salvation is deliverance and life by the help of God. . . . 'You did he make alive,' Paul writes. That is salvation—being alive to God and to every good which God's world can bring us." Quoted by E. Paul Hovey in *Treasury of Inspirational Anecdotes, Quotations and Illustrations* (Revell).

Transformation. Albert W. Palmer has described the power of God over the evil in our lives in two short, beautiful sentences: "Salvation is not something that is done for you but something that happens within you. It is not the clearing of a court record but the transformation of a life attitude."

One attitude says, "Sure, I do evil things occasionally. I'm only human, you know, and I can't help it. . . ."

The higher attitude says. "I am human, too, but I have God to help me, and to keep me from trying to excuse the evil in my heart. . . ."

Image. We have always wondered about those little statuettes of Christ which we see on the dashboards of automobiles driven by our Roman Catholic friends. For a time, we were suspicious of their value; we saw too many cars wrecked in collisions along the road to take them seriously! But one day a Catholic friend explained to us that this image of Christ in the car was not supposed or expected to save any man from collisions caused by his own or some other's carelessness. He put it this way:

"I don't expect any miracles of that little statue. I don't believe it will prevent me from being hurt by stopping the laws of motion and propulsion when I set myself on a collision course. But I have found that it *does* prevent something else—another sort of collision. I used to swear like a mule driver; I could outcurse any ten men with the same talent. But, you know, since I put Christ up there on the dashboard, I just couldn't swear or take His name in vain any more. There He was, *looking right at me*—and I just couldn't do it. . . ."

Well, it's worth a lot of Protestant thought . . . !

Sick, Stable. As do so many of us, Dr. Arthur House Stainback likes to fish, but he doesn't like to get seasick when he goes deep-sea fishing. We know what he means! He describes one fishing expedition:

"Some years ago in Miami, I decided to take a day's fishing on a drift boat. The sea was rough, and I became desperately sick. And I do mean desperately! All day the boat rolled and tossed, and the degree of my sickness surpassed human knowledge. Finally, the day ended and we were back on land. Wobbly, and fearful of fainting any minute, I walked down the gangplank. I was amazed at what happened as soon as I stepped on solid ground; my sense of balance returned and at last a stability of stomach. I had been brought ashore.

"When a person accepts Christ the tossing and rolling of the world leading to spiritual sickness suddenly stops, and there is a stable peace in Christ." From *Illustrating the Lesson* (Revell).

Like a Clock. We have always admired, even envied, those people who have mastered the art of keeping a cool and calm mind in the midst of furore and excitement. Christ set an example of the serene mind when men came to arrest him in Gethsemane.

Robert Louis Stevenson was not what we'd call a church-going Christian, but he had a great Christian mind and soul. He said once, "Quiet minds cannot be perplexed or frightened, but go on in fortune or misfortune at their own private pace, like a clock in a thunderstorm."

A clock! Do a little meditating on the clock. . . .

Questions for Pupils on the Next Lesson: 1. We talk a lot about "fulfillment." What do we mean by that? 2. Is there such a thing as perfect fulfillment in life? 3. What was Utopia? 4. Where did Paul say we would all find fulfillment? 5. What kind of fulfillment do you expect to find in heaven? 6. Is Revelation 11:15 a dream or a reality? 7. How does the whole creation groan in travail (Romans 8:22)?

TOPIC FOR YOUTH
GOD CONQUERS EVIL

The Power of God. Donald Lester has said that "we are saved by someone doing for us what we cannot do for ourselves." That someone is God.

We thought of this when we talked with an old friend who had been a hopeless drunk and gambler in his younger days. Then he would boast that he could "drink any man under the table." In his later days he didn't boast about anything; he became the superintendent of a rescue mission on the Bowery.

We asked him once how many drunks he knew who had been able to conquer the evil of drunkenness without the help of religious faith. His answer was short: "I never knew any man to conquer it without faith."

He mentioned the two requirements for membership in Alcoholics Anonymous: first, the alcoholic must admit that the problem has whipped him; second, he must admit that of himself he can do nothing, but with the help of God he can get up and stand tall again. . . .

God conquers evil when we can't!

Cleaning. An unnamed poet gives us this:

> We cleaned our little church today—
> Wiped all the dust and dirt away.
> We straightened papers, washed the floors;
> Wiped off the lamp and painted doors.
> We brushed the dirt stains from the books
> And whisked the cobwebs from the nooks.
> We polished windows so we'd see
> The newly greening shrub and tree.
> The menfolks, too, raked up the yard—
> They laughed and said it wasn't hard,
> And, oh, it felt so very good
> To have the place look as it should.
> We said, "How wonderful 'twould be
> If we cleaned out what we can't see—
> Such things as grudges, hates and lies,
> And musty thoughts much worse than flies."
> Selected from *Christian Witness.*

Men's hearts are swept clean when they meet Christ. It would be good for men to let Him sweep us clean, not just once, but every day. . . .

Skid Row. Few of us go to live on Skid Row. But often, though we do not realize it, descend to the gutters of Skid Row in thought, if not in deed.

Dr. J. Vernon McGee has the truth when he writes: "When we say, 'Something should be done about Skid Row,' God is saying the same thing about us. That is why He sent His Son to help us."

Peace. God conquers the conflicts born of evil in our minds. He expells the conflict, the turbulence of evil, and in its place puts—peace, the most precious possession of human life.

"Augustine, seeking peace, plunged into the wilderness expecting to find in it solitude and quiet. In the desert he found calm, tranquillity, everywhere but in his heart; when peace finally found him he was back in the strenuous life of old Milan. Wesley had this peace though he traveled more than five thousand miles a year on horseback and preached half a dozen times a day. Fitzgerald, the translator of the *Rubaiyat* of Omar Khayyam, seems to have missed it, though he lived the life of a recluse and kept doves. It is not dependent on circumstances. We have seen it in the face of the old-age pensioner and missed it in the gaze of the rich. We have marked its presence in people standing beside the open grave of their dead, and missed it in others who had no obvious care in the world. It is not to your circumstances but to your hearts that the apostle prays the peace of God may gain admission.

"Have you ever met a soul in whom the peace of God fully dwells? You have not forgotten the meeting. Life has few things to show more beautiful than this. They are poised: it is not in the power of circumstances to force them from their balance. . . . They display that 'toil unsevered from tranquillity' that Matthew Arnold praised; a hundred duties claim their notice but are powerless to dislodge that central calm: the surface waters swirl and foam, but the hidden depths are still and tranquil. They are not irritable or impatient; they neither boast of themselves nor complain about life . . . and if you ask their secret they smile and say, 'He keeps them in perfect peace whose mind is stayed on Him.'"—From *Daily Readings of W. E. Sangster* (Revell).

The Idols. We love the story of the old Chinese lady who was converted; the conversion was genuine enough, she told the missionary, but what bothered her was, "How does Christ *work*?" He tried to explain, but she wasn't quite sure about it. . . .

Then she had a dream, in which she saw Jesus standing in the doorway of her bedroom. She saw Him clearly, she said—and she also saw all the old idols on her shelf climb down and run out of the room. Then she understood: "When Jesus comes, the idols go."

What halfgods, or petty gods or just plain idols has Christ driven out of your life? What little evils fled for their lives? It *should* happen. . . .

Sentence Sermon to Remember: Every evil comes to us on wings and goes away limping.—French proverb.

Questions for Pupils on the Next Lesson: 1. In how many worlds do you live? 2. Describe what "the age to come" is in Jewish thinking. 3. Will this world ever be perfect? 4. Do you think of the next world as a continuation of this world? Explain. 5. Explain the doctrine of adoption. 6. Has Christianity made our world a better one? Give details. 7. When do you think that "Christ's glorious reign" will begin?

LESSON XIII—NOVEMBER 28

GOD BRINGS THE WORLD TO FULFILLMENT

Background Scripture: Micah 4:1-7; Romans 8:18-25;
I Thessalonians 5:1-11; Revelation 11:15
Devotional Reading: Micah 4:1-5

KING JAMES VERSION

ROMANS 8　18 For I reckon that the sufferings of this present time are not worthy to be compared with the glory which shall be revealed in us.

19 For the earnest expectation of the creature waiteth for the manifestation of the sons of God.

20 For the creature was made subject to vanity, not willingly, but by reason of him who hath subjected the same in hope;

21 Because the creature itself also shall be delivered from the bondage of corruption into the glorious liberty of the children of God.

22 For we know that the whole creation groaneth and travaileth in pain together until now.

23 And not only they, but ourselves also, which have the firstfruits of the Spirit, even we ourselves groan within ourselves, waiting for the adoption, to wit, the redemption of our body.

24 For we are saved by hope: but hope that is seen is not hope: for what a man seeth, why doth he yet hope for?

REVELATION 11　15 And the seventh angel sounded; and there were great voices in heaven, saying, The kingdoms of this world are become the kingdoms of our Lord, and of his Christ; and he shall reign for ever and ever.

REVISED STANDARD VERSION

ROMANS 8　18 I consider that the sufferings of this present time are not worth comparing with the glory that is to be revealed to us. 19 For the creation waits with eager longing for the revealing of the sons of God; 20 for the creation was subjected to futility, not of its own will but by the will of him who subjected it in hope; 21 because the creation itself will be set free from its bondage to decay and obtain the glorious liberty of the children of God. 22 We know that the whole creation has been groaning in travail together until now; 23 and not only the creation, but we ourselves, who have the first fruits of the Spirit, groan inwardly as we wait for adoption as sons, the redemption of our bodies. 24 For in this hope we were saved. Now hope that is seen is not hope. For who hopes for what he sees?

REVELATION 11　15 Then the seventh angel blew his trumpet, and there were loud voices in heaven, saying, "The kingdom of the world has become the kingdom of our Lord and of his Christ, and he shall reign for ever and ever."

MEMORY SELECTION: *The kingdom of the world has become the kingdom of our Lord and of his Christ, and he shall reign for ever and ever.* Revelation 11:15 (RSV).

HOME DAILY BIBLE READINGS

Nov. 22. M. A Prospect of Peace, Micah 4:1-7.
Nov. 23. T. The Fulfillment of the Law, Romans 8:1-10.
Nov. 24. W. The Hope of Coming Glory, Romans 8:11-17.
Nov. 25. T. A Promise for All Creation, Romans 8:18-25.
Nov. 26. F. Assurance in Christ, Romans 8:28-39.

Nov. 27. S. *A Time of Glad Reunion,* I Thessalonians 4:13-18.
Nov. 28. S. *The Day of the Lord,* I Thessalonians 5:1-11.

BACKGROUND

In the eighth chapter of Romans, Paul says more about the Spirit than he says in all the rest of his writings put together, and it is therefore one of the most important chapters in the whole Bible. As we read it we notice that Paul does not explain to us *who* the Spirit is; perhaps he thought that wasn't necessary. Neither does he tell us *why* the Spirit is necessary, or why He is at work in the world. It would help all of us to take the several ideas of the Spirit in this chapter and put them together, and thus draw up or outline a *personal* conception of the Holy Spirit. . . .

There are two points in the background of Paul's thinking which we must keep clearly in mind in this lesson. One is that He believed that the Spirit was at work as a visible, present Power. The other is that the Spirit was at work, in not just one world, but in *two* worlds. There was to him a vast difference between these two worlds, as we shall see. . . .

NOTES ON THE PRINTED TEXT

I. I consider that the sufferings of this present time are not worth comparing with the glory that is to be revealed to us, Romans 8:18 (RSV). The Jew divided time into two ages and two worlds. There was to him the present age, the age in which he lived; then there was an age to come, a future age in which men and things would be changed and different *and better.* Let us look first at what he thought of the present (his) age.

It was completely *bad.* It was a troubled, insecure, unlovely, corrupt and sinful age. This Jew could have sung with the Christian, "Change and decay in all around I see." The old standards and traditions were in decay—rotting. Men were anything but godly; they were a miserable lot who lied and stole and practiced all manner of deceit and went to war and killed each other. Religion was a thin veneer covering the old animal instincts. This was their age; this was their world. And the more we think of it, this is *our* world and age, too, isn't it? Every day, almost every hour, some fine old tradition or ideal or principle comes crashing down.

Then there was that other age and world—the new one. There would come, said the Jews, a "Day of the Lord," a day of judgment in which the old world would be shattered, changed and rebuilt. Isaiah cried that God would "create new heavens and a new earth" (Isaiah 65:17). All through the days between the Old and the New Testaments the Jews dreamed of this glorious new age to come.

The text speaks of the "eager longing" (or, better, eager "expectation") in which "creation" awaits the coming of the new day and age. By "creation" is meant "nature." Nature was as bad as, even worse than, men. Man sinned, and nature was affected by that sin. "Cursed be the ground for thy sake," said God to Adam after Adam's sin (Genesis 3:17). So all nature also waited for the great change when it would be free from the decay to which man's sin had brought it.

II. . . . and not only the creation, but we ourselves, . . . groan inwardly as we wait for adoption as sons . . . , Romans 8:23 (RSV). Paul turned here from nature to man, and to man's adoption into the family of God. This "doctrine of adoption" is a complicated, and important one to Paul and the Christian. Legally, adoption is the procedure by which an adult person assumes to a child the relationship of a parent. To Paul, in a Christian sense, it is the act by which God receives the believer into the relationship of a child, His child. And Paul says that the final phase of this adoption comes in the redemption of the *body* of man. In the world to come, in the world of glory, the total man—body and spirit—will be saved, redeemed, changed, made more glorious than he ever was physically. The body will be changed and "fashioned like unto his glorious body . . ." (Philippians 3:21). "It is sown a natural body; it is raised a spiritual body" (I Corinthians 15:44).

The only hope for man in this sort of a world was that such a change would be worked in him—that, in the wisdom of God, this spiritual change would completely renovate him. Hope! Aren't we all still hoping for this? Don't we all want a re-creation at the hands of God? Of course we do. Paul says that we are *saved* by this hope (verse 24). We hope not to go on as we are, not to go on as hopeless puppets in a dying world, but as something better in a better world. We do not look at the present world as the best of all possible worlds; we look beyond the world to God, who through us can build a better world in a better age.

H. G. Wells said once that mankind began in a cave and would end in "the diseased-soaked ruins of a slum." No man who believes in God believes anything like that; intelligent men believe in the redeeming power of God, and they dare to go on living in hope of it, no matter how bad things are.

We are the adopted children of a God who cares, who has made life in His world a thrilling, throbbing experience. *We* should make of life a thrilling, throbbing *hope*. We may have been born into a world in which *men* (not God) have created conditions of decay, but we need not approve of the decay; *we can stop it*. We go to grammar school and graduate from grammar school; we do not *stay* in grammar school. We go to high school but we do not *stay* there. We go to college, and we graduate to something beyond college. We are born prone to sin, but we need not live forever in sin; we can move up to something better. We may have a rotten world on our hands, but we need not contribute to its rottenness. With God's help, we can burn out the rottenness with the help of His flaming Holy Spirit. And we all live in the divine hope that we shall do just that—with the help of God.

III. The kingdom of the world has become the kingdom of our Lord and of his Christ, Revelation 11:15 (RSV). This passage is difficult of interpretation, since it seems to describe something that has not yet happened. It says that a great victory has been accomplished, when as a matter of fact it hasn't; the kingdom of this world has not yet become the kingdom of God in Christ. It is really a way of saying that the Messianic reign has begun; it Looks ahead to the time when God will actually become the supreme ruler of the world, in fact as well as in prophecy.

Dr. Lynn Harold Hough says: "From the time of the Greeks there have been many books telling the tale of an ideal state made real in human life. The Book of Revelation reminds us that such hopes can become real only as part of the kingdom of God. All utopias lack the last quality unless they express the will of Christ. But the man of Patmos reminds us that in spite of all the evil there is something in history which leads forward to Christ's glorious reign. There is a good in the kingdom of this world which can find its fulfillment only in the kingdom of God."—From *The Interpreter's Bible*, p. 450, Vol. 12. Quoted by permission of Abingdon Press, publishers.

SUGGESTIONS TO TEACHERS

To "fulfill" means to finish or to complete a task or a life mission. For most of us that seems impossible; our cemeteries are filled with men who, though they worked hard all their lives, did *not* complete their work, and we could carve on their tombstones the words, "They still had work to do." We live only once, the cynics say; we never get a second chance.

But the Christian believes that we *do* get that second chance, and maybe a third or fourth or fifth chance; to him, there is a "going on" after we leave this earth; there will be things happening in another, better world. It will be Christ's world, and He will rule it "for ever and ever." All the hopes within us that have been frustrated will be realized there. This is Bible teaching.

So we live, not in just one world, but in two: the present world and the one to come. Some call it heaven and earth, and hold them to be vastly different. But perhaps God made one the training ground for the other. At any rate, there is another, future, better world waiting. . . . God promises it.

TOPIC FOR ADULTS
GOD BRINGS THE WORLD TO FULFILLMENT

Not Good Enough. Mankind has made great progress on his earth; it has been a long, long road from the cave man to now, and it is a road of accomplishment. Along this road we find the glory that was Greece, where the human mind reached heights never known before Greece came into being. And there is Rome, which brought peace to a world based on firm law and order; and the Middle Ages, the ages of great cathedrals and scholars, the age when the Christian fully realized that, after all, there was one world made up of many peoples who were all working out the purpose of their creator. There is the Reformation, when mankind rose in splendid spiritual dignity to cast off the shackles which must always go before any real freedom can come; there is the Renaissance when man's soul soared in a new burst of creativeness and beauty. Mankind might have stopped at the end of any one of these ages and said, "We have come far enough. This is the perfect, the golden age." But mankind has never done that; instead, he has always said, "*It is good, but not good enough.*" He has longed, struggled toward a still better world. He has never been satisfied. His heart yearned for something finer, nobler. . . .

Jesus called it the Kingdom of God, and He promised that if man kept on trying, *he would reach it.*

Our earth is a halfway house; the mansions of God are hidden in the mists of the future. God dares us to enter the mists and find these mansions and live in them.

The Mind Beyond. Iona Henry McLaughlin has a little book called *Triumph Over Tragedy,* in which she describes the tragic deaths of her husband and two children; it seemed like the end of the world to her. But she made it through the shadows to a new, confident faith. She says:

"Only faith in a caring, loving, impartial God makes sense. It is not reasonable for me to think that God gives life and light to creative human minds—to a Raphael, a Brahms, a Newton—only to drop them in a grave at the end of threescore years, more or less, with a 'That's all. This is the end.' Why should He bother to create us at all if *that* is the end? A creative energy which could be that wasteful is not much of a force to worship or be guided by, or even to love. Will I shock you when I say that I—or you—could have devised a better system than that, and organized a more competent use of human material?

"But the solid fact is that I could not have devised man and the universe as they are, nor could you.

"A mind beyond, greater than anything we tiny Lilliputians could conceive of, brought all that into being, in a most orderly way. It is for us to fit into the order, not for the order to fit *us.*"

There just *must* be another world, a going-on of life . . . !

Wilderness. Says someone, "The trouble with most people these days is that they want to reach the Promised Land without going through the wilderness." Correct! *This* world *is* a wilderness, so dark and bleak and frightening that we all wonder sometimes if we'll get through it at all. But God promised that we would, just as the old Israelites got through it, and that we would find a Promised Land awaiting us beyond the wilderness. When we understand and accept that, we find fulfillment and purpose; but if we have eyes only for *this* world, we spend our lives in shallows and in miseries.

Questions for Pupils on the Next Lesson: 1. What *was* the Good News? 2. Who was Theophilus? 3. What did Luke want to tell us about Jesus? 4. What was Luke's occupation? 5. What were the "infallible proofs" mentioned in Luke 1:3? 6. Did Luke write any Scripture other than his Gospel? 7. Explain the words, ". . . after he had given commandment through the Holy Spirit" (Luke 1:2).

TOPIC FOR YOUTH
WHAT'S THE WORLD COMING TO?

The Hill. At times, it does seem that the world and we who live in it are coming to nothing good. Every morning's newspaper reminds us that we are in anything but good condition, and that if we go on the way we are going now there can be nothing but disaster. That's what the pessimists say, and some of them are very, very intelligent men. . . .

But some other very intelligent men are optimists about it. They say something like this:

". . . There often occur what appear to be rude interruptions, sense-less losses, tragic endings. When something like this happens—the death of a loved one, a personal disaster, or anything of the sort—it is as though we were in a valley. All of life now seems to lie under the darkened lea of the enveloping hills. But when one once ascends the hill he sees that the valley is but incidental in the totallity of the landscape. What had seemed major and decisive is now seen in true perspective as something minor and incidental. *When the perfect comes, the imperfect will pass away*.

"Does this mean that a soul in heaven has seen everything, thought everything, done everything? That there is nothing more to look forward to? By no means. If a composer attains a perfect mastery of technique, harmony and rhythm, does that mean he is washed up and can compose no more? Of course not. It means that he is now equipped to do signifi-cant work. And the writer who has developed an exquisite style—does that mean the end of his creative work? No; it means the beginning of it, for now he is qualified to do it."—C. Stanley Lowell, in *The Pastor*.

This world is only the beginning; we consummate and fulfill in a world beyond. . . . So says God.

New Life. Man's need to be vitally related to someone or something of eternal significance is answered in Christ's triumph over sin and death. In His death on the cross we were made *alive;* there is no miracle to com-pare with that!

A century ago, a British archeologist picked up a vase lying at the side of a mummy in an Egyptian tomb. He brought it to the British Museum, where it was on exhibition for several years—until the awful day when a museum worker dropped it on the floor and broke it into a hundred pieces.

That was irreparable loss—but in the dust on the floor, the worker picked up a few dried peas, as hard as rock, which had been entombed with the vase and the mummy. He took the peas out of doors and planted them in the ground. They had been in that tomb for more than 3,000 years—but within a month after their new planting, they sprouted into new life! And the new peas were good to eat.

If God could do this with a few peas, what must He plan to do with a whole world? It is all a part of the mysterious wisdom of God. Worlds, like seeds, or peas, have a *future*.

Present, Future. "A converted Japanese artist said to a missionary, 'I suppose the reason English artists put so much perspective into their drawings is that Christianity has given them a future; and the reason Oriental artists fail to do so is that Buddha and Confucius do not raise their eyes above the present."—A. J. Manning.

Dr. George W. Truett once said, "I do not know what the future holds, but I do know who holds the future." There wouldn't be much sense in living if there were no future.

The Stars. We look up at the stars, and think of eternity; they must have been there forever! An anonymous poet thinks they may *not* be eternal, but. . . .

> The stars shine over the earth,
>   The stars shine over the sea;
> The stars look up to the mighty God,
>   The stars look down on me.
> The stars have lived for a million years
>   A million years and a day,
> But God and I shall love and live
>   When the stars have passed away.

Question: If our world should disappear some day, would there be another world . . . ?

Never Finished. "Whenever I think of the future, I think of Mr. R. E. Olds, who made the Oldsmobile and the Reo cars. About 1902 he announced a new model which he called his Farewell Car. He implied that this automobile was the ultimate, that after it, nobody could ever bring improvement to the motorcar. How wrong he was! There's always more to be done. You can never catch up. You can never finish."—Karl L. Prentiss.

That is really comforting. There is nothing more desolate than the artist who believes that he painted his masterpiece while he was still young! We are dead only when the masterpiece is behind us. God promises work on yet another masterpiece tomorrow. . . .

Sentence Sermon to Remember: The world has forgotten, in its concern with Left and Right, that there is an Above and Below.—Glen Drake.

Questions for Pupils on the Next Lesson: 1. Did Luke write his Gospel for Jews or Gentiles? 2. Describe Luke's background. 3. Luke has been called the finest Gospel writer. Explain that. 4. True or false: Mark tells us what Jesus did; Luke tells us what He said. 5. According to Acts 1, what was Luke's purpose in writing his Gospel and portions of Acts? 6. Was Luke an eyewitness of the work of Jesus? 7. About when did he write his Gospel?

DECEMBER, 1971, JANUARY, FEBRUARY, 1972

THE GOSPEL OF LUKE

LESSON I—DECEMBER 5

LUKE TELLS THE GOOD NEWS

Background Scripture: Luke 1:1-4; Acts 1:1-5
Devotional Reading: II Timothy 1:8-14

KING JAMES VERSION

LUKE 1 Forasmuch as many have taken in hand to set forth in order a declaration of those things which are most surely believed among us,

2 Even as they delivered them unto us, which from the beginning were eyewitnesses, and ministers of the word;

3 It seemed good to me also, having had perfect understanding of all things from the very first, to write unto thee in order, most excellent Theophilus,

4 That thou mightest know the certainty of those things, wherein thou hast been instructed.

ACTS 1 The former treatise have I made, O Theophilus, of all that Jesus began both to do and teach,

2 Until the day in which he was taken up, after that he through the Holy Ghost had given commandments unto the apostles whom he had chosen:

3 To whom also he showed himself alive after his passion by many infallible proofs, being seen of them forty days, and speaking of the things pertaining to the kingdom of God:

4 And, being assembled together with *them,* commanded them that they should not depart from Jerusalem, but

REVISED STANDARD VERSION

LUKE 1 Inasmuch as many have undertaken to compile a narrative of the things which have been accomplished among us, 2 just as they were delivered to us by those who from the beginning were eyewitnesses and ministers of the word, 3 it seemed good to me also, having followed all things closely for some time past, to write an orderly account for you, most excellent Theophilus, 4 that you may know the truth concerning the things of which you have been informed.

ACTS 1 In the first book, O Theophilus, I have dealt with all that Jesus began to do and teach, 2 until the day when he was taken up, after he had given commandment through the Holy Spirit to the apostles whom he had chosen. 3 To them he presented himself alive after his passion by many proofs, appearing to them during forty days, and speaking of the kingdom of God. 4 And while staying with them he charged them not to depart from Jerusalem, but to wait for the promise of the Father, which, he said, "you heard from me, 5 for John baptized with water, but before many days you wait for the promise of the Father, which, *saith he*, ye have heard of me.

5 For John truly baptized with water; but ye shall be baptized with the Holy Ghost not many days hence.

shall be baptized with the Holy Spirit."

MEMORY SELECTION: . . . *it seemed good to me* . . . *to write an orderly account* . . . *that you may know the truth concerning the things of which you have been informed.* Luke 1:3-4 (rsv).

HOME DAILY BIBLE READINGS

Nov. 29. M. A Witness to the World, Isaiah 43:8-13.
Nov. 30. T. The Lord's Messenger, Malachi 3:1-12.
Dec. 1. W. The Good News, Luke 4:16-21.
Dec. 2. T. "You Shall Be . . . Witnesses," Acts 1:6-11.
Dec. 3. F. Salvation for All Men, Romans 1:8-16.
Dec. 4. S. Let the Redeemed Speak, Psalm 107:1-9.
Dec. 5. S. Not Ashamed, II Timothy 1:8-14.

BACKGROUND

We begin today a three-months' study of the Gospel According to Luke. It is a Gospel or book written by a man who was a physician before he became a Christian—a well-educated man! He wrote, not one book but two—the Gospel of Luke, and the book called The Acts of the Apostles; these two books originally formed a two-volume work on the origin of Christianity and the spread of the Christian church.

Luke was not an eyewitness to the ministry of Jesus; he wrote this Gospel about A.D. 80, long after Jesus was gone. He wrote beautifully; here is the best Greek in the New Testament, the most readable and enchanting of all four Gospels, and in some ways the most inspired. He dedicated his books to a man named Theophilus, about whom we know very little indeed; most likely he was an intelligent, searching Gentile who wanted to know the truth about Jesus Christ. Luke wrote for the Gentiles, that they might know the truth. And he put the manna down where they could get it—within reach of the common man as well as within reach of the scholar.

It is an epic of beauty—*and research.*

NOTES ON THE PRINTED TEXT

I. Forasmuch as many have taken in hand to set forth in order a declaration of those things which are most surely believed among us . . . , Luke 1:1. There was at first nothing more than an oral tradition describing the work of Jesus; like all oral tradition, it was enlarged upon, and contained much legend and fancy as well as much fact. Then came men who saw the necessity of getting it all down in writing; there were many such "scribes" before Luke wrote *his* story. The eyewitnesses died off slowly; the apostles were martyred; it became important that some accurate written record be made of the ministry of Jesus, since, in the main, those made previous to Luke, were fragmentary and *not* accurate. Some few were: Luke used both Mark and Matthew in writing his account, together with a source known only as "Q," material which both Luke and Matthew used. ("Q" is the first letter of the German word for "source.") But Luke wasn't satisfied with what had been written; he was anxious to separate fact from fancy, to write a more accurate account of "all that Jesus began both to do and to teach." So he sat down to write.

He wrote as *a historian.* He wrote carefully, *after long research.* He consulted every reliable source he could find—the few remaining eye-witnesses of Jesus' ministry, the books or parchments available; he was a literary detective, searching out the "facts of the case." Diligently, he separated fact from oral tradition. He traced everything from its beginning; he aimed at accuracy above all. This is not "a flash in the pan" sort of book, written to make money! It is a carefully planned and executed book. Luke demanded proof for every line he wrote. (See Luke 1:3.)

Luke had probably read the Roman and Greek histories written by Dionysius of Halicarnassus (7 B.C.?), who was a model of excellence. Dionysius said, "Before beginning to write I gathered information, partly from the lips of the most learned men with whom I came in contact, and partly from histories written by Romans of whom they spoke with praise." Luke followed the formula of Dionysius. He wrote the best story of Jesus because he was never satisfied with any but the most reliable sources.

This is not to say that Mark and Matthew were *inaccurate.* The three men wrote the same thing *for different audiences.* Matthew was a Jew who wrote primarily for Jews to convince them of the messianic nature of Jesus. Mark wrote down what Peter told him about Jesus, and he wrote to convince other non-Jewish readers of the power of a Christ who was quite human and still the only begotten Son of God. Luke wrote as a companion of the great Paul, who moved out into the hostile Gentile world to convince the Gentiles—*and* posterity—"of the authenticity and trustworthiness of the Christian faith for concerned, seeking Gentiles" (Donald G. Miller).

While others wrote historical treatises or theology, the little Gentile doctor wrote an inspiring story based on the infinite love of God for the common people of a sick and brutal world. If ever we doubted the idea of "the inspiration of the Scriptures" we cannot doubt it here, or doubt that "the beloved physician" was inspired when he wrote what has become the most inspiring account of the life and work of Jesus yet written. But let us not forget this, too: it is inspiration based on painstaking historical research. It is proof positive that an adequate and intelligent appreciation of Jesus does not come to or from a lazy mind; it comes to the mind that seeks and sweats and toils and weighs and analyzes, that is never satisfied with a half-truth. "Seek, and ye shall find."

We do not know when or where or how Luke came under the influence of Jesus, but we do know that the Christ he found is the most beautiful and reasonable Christ pictured in all Scripture.

II. In the first book, O Theophilus, I have dealt with all that Jesus began to do and teach . . . Acts 1:1 (RSV). We have already said that Luke and Acts, which Luke also wrote, together form a two-volume work on the ministry of Jesus and the rise of the church. Here we have the introduction to the second volume. It is quite similar to the introduction we have already studied in Luke 1. Theophilus—"the most *excellent* Theophilus"—is mentioned again, and the wording of both paragraphs is quite similar. Luke opens his second volume (Acts) with mention of his first volume (the Gospel), so that the reader will know he is reading the second chapter of a "continued" story that has not yet been finished. He sums up the teachings of his first book in a beautiful condensation, reminding us that up to this point he had covered the life of Jesus to the hour of His ascension; *now* he will tell us how the life of Jesus goes on *in His church.*

Verse 3 is the key verse to the passage: ". . . you shall be baptized with the Holy Spirit." Luke was telling the apostles to wait on the coming of the Spirit, for, as old Isaiah had said long before, "They that wait upon the Lord shall renew their strength" (Isaiah 40:31). Wait. Don't be in a hurry. Make haste slowly when you study Christ and His church, lest in your haste to get all the truth you miss most of it! No sensible man gobbles down a steak dinner in the shortest possible time; he eats a bit at a time, enjoying every morsel of it. Study your Bible in the same way: give its truth time to be digested; get the most out of every "morsel."

In that way you build a *firm* foundation.

SUGGESTIONS TO TEACHERS

This is introductory material on Luke and his Gospel; it is *background* for what is to follow in later lessons. It is a picture of Jesus painted in words for Gentiles who were so despised by the Jews and so loved by Jesus. It is good news for both Jew *and* Gentile—such news as they had never heard before.

The Jesus of Luke is the divine Saviour of *all the world and all men.* It is for Jews, Samaritans, cynical Greeks, brutal Romans; for the poor rather than for the rich, for women and children, saints and sinners, for the finest of minds, and, above that, for the common man who needed it most.

The following lesson emphases are suggested:

1. Why the Gospel of Luke was written.
2. The universality of the Gospel message—not for a privileged race, class, sex or age.
3. The Gospel speaks to the complex problems of modern man.
4. How shall we share the good news with others, *now?*

TOPIC FOR ADULTS
LUKE TELLS THE GOOD NEWS

Luke. "He may once have been a slave; slaves were often physicians. He came from Antioch. He met Paul at Troas and became his personal physician and missionary companion. A scientist and a theologian, globe-trotting for God! Science and religion joining hands, casting their nets to snare men for Christ. Two kindred, cultured, brilliant minds with but a single thought—to save a sick world in the name of the great physician. They followed the long trail together, came down to the end of the road where Paul cried out, 'Only Luke is with me!'

"He gave us the third Gospel and parts of Acts. He gave Paul admiration and affection, professional care and personal faithfulness. He misses seeing Jesus; he came too late to travel with the band. But when he slipped across death's gulf to be with Paul again, he surely heard the Master say, 'Well done . . . inasmuch as ye have done it unto the least of these . . . ye have done it unto me.'

"A good doctor, Luke. He faced storm, heat, cold, peril, death itself to tend the sick. The first medical missionary!"—*Who's Who in the Bible,* by Frank S. Mead, Harper & Row, publishers.

Unique. What does Luke give us in his Gospel that the other Gospel writers do not? He gives us a great deal! He gives us five great hymns of the church: the *Ave Maria,* the *Magnificat,* the *Gloria in Excelsis,* the *Nunc Dimittis,* the *Benedictus.* Only in Luke do we find accounts of the birth of the Baptist, the presentation of Jesus in the Temple, the adoration of the shepherds, the visit of the 12-year-old Jesus to the Temple.

Luke is the only evangelist who records all seven of the great events of Jesus' life: His birth, baptism, temptation, transfiguration, death, resurrection and ascension. To Luke we are indebted for the parables of the two debtors, the Good Samaritan, the friend at midnight, the rich fool, the barren fig tree, the builder of the tower, the king going to war, the lost coin, the prodigal son, the unjust steward, the rich man and Lazarus, the unprofitable servant, the importunate widow, the Pharisee and the publican, the pounds; and for the miracles of the draught of fishes, the raising of the widow of Nain's son, the cure of the woman with a spirit of infirmity, the cure of the man with the dropsy, the healing of the ten lepers, the restoration of Malchus' ear; and events such as the visit to the house of Mary and Martha, the sending out of the seventy disciples, the sojourn at the house of Zacchaeus, etc.; and also for the records of our Lord's prayers at His baptism, after the cleansing of the leper, before the call of the twelve disciples; at the transfiguration, and Jesus' death on the cross of His enemies.

This is very, very careful writing! *Can you think of anything important about Jesus that Luke left out?*

Versions. Luke gave us one version of the life and ministry of Jesus, and there have been many "new" versions of Luke's account since he died. Look back now and see how many versions of the Bible we have had. All of them were written to correct inaccuracies, to make the meanings clear and clearer, to put the gospel in language we can all understand. Our Revised Standard Version of the Bible is the work of thirty-two scholars who worked for fourteen years on this one version!

It has all been in the interest of *accuracy,* legibility, relevance and understanding. May we ask a question? Have these new versions improved upon Luke's account?

Questions for Pupils on the Next Lesson: 1. Who sang the hymn in Luke 1:68-79? 2. Why is this section of Luke called "The Benedictus?" 3. Why do you suppose God chose Zacharias and Elisabeth as the mother of John the Baptist? 4. What do we know of the lineage or genealogy of Zacharias and Elisabeth? 5. What was the "horn of salvation" in Luke 1:69? 6. For what purpose was Zacharias' son born?

7. Who spoke the words in Luke 2:29-32? What do the words, *Nunc Dimittis* mean?

TOPIC FOR YOUTH
THAT YOU MAY KNOW

Doctor, Christian. "Yesterday I heard John Golden, playwright, actor and producer, tell a New York audience that there are 6,000 actors in our country of whom only 1,000 are earning a living. So he advised young people not to go into acting, because they would likely starve to death. But, said he, the stage will always need plays, so you write plays. This is one field in writing—television and radio plays, short stories and novels, research articles and books, etc. For the Christian with a flare for writing there is also work to be done. Many Christian people may not be able to earn their living that way, but they can make real contributions to their own church publications, or for secular magazines, giving them material that is 'different.' A good deal of evangelism is done by means of the printed page; much of the material is good, but a lot of it is poorly done, and there is room for something better.

"Dr. Luke was a Christian. There are still a few benighted souls who believe that a medical doctor cannot be a Christian. That is nonsense, of course, and the trend among medical students is away from the materialism of a generation or two ago toward a much more reverent view of life and man and the ministry of medicine. Christian doctors have a high duty to make their witness clear wherever they minister, and our young people who plan to go into medicine as a profession ought to make up their minds *now* that they are really going to be *Christian* doctors, just like Luke."—Winfield Burggraff, in *Earnest Worker*.

Has any man in our generation made a finer contribution to Christianity than Dr. Schweitzer?

Writers. Come to think of it—we probably would never have had our Bible if it hadn't been for good editors and good writers! We would never have had *any* book without them. And what a contribution Christian writers have made ever since Luke sat down to write about Jesus Christ.

Those who wrote the Bible produced a book that has been a best-seller for *centuries*. No other book can make that claim.

We think of Dr. Lloyd Douglas, author of *The Robe* and of seven other best-sellers, all dealing with religious faith. And of Dr. Charles M. Sheldon, who wrote *In His Steps*, and saw it translated into 23 languages and sell in the millions. And of the lovable, Jewish Sholem Asch, who wrote and reached millions of readers with his *Nazarene, The Big Fisherman*, and *Mary*.

Or think, too, of the numberless writers for TV and radio who in writing Christian scripts have reached more people on one broadcast than heard Jesus and Paul put together in their lifetimes! Only yesterday we watched, with our minister, a TV broadcast starring Peter Ustinov and a black youngster, dealing with race prejudice. We both shed a tear or two, and at the end of it the pastor remarked, "That was worth a thousand sermons."

There is a great work waiting to be done by Christian writers!

Wrestling With Words. One of the finest preachers of our time—and one of the finest Christian writers, too—was the late Dr. J. Wallace Hamilton of St. Petersburg, Florida. In an appreciation of his brilliant preaching and writing, used as preface to his latest book, *The Trumpet Still Sounds,* we read these words about him:

"He had a deep, compelling conviction that the preacher was obligated not only to tell the Good News but to tell it well, clearly and vitally. He said that a sermon should *sing.* 'If in any part of a sermon you have a word that doesn't sing, then find one that does. . . . It is a frightening thing to see how dull and tame we have made the words of Christ. . . . We must make [them] *live.* No word has meaning until it comes alive, and every effort you make to find the right word to say the right thing brings you head-on into the divine imperative which is the incarnation—the Word made flesh. This is the pain of preaching. . . . None of us has the words yet to convey the Word adequately. . . . We must find the word for it, we must wrestle with the words, must sit with our heads in our hands. . . .'

"He was not just a born preacher. . . . Preaching was anything but easy to him; it was an agony before it was an ecstasy. His startling language was born in sweat and struggle, and he always thought there was a better word beyond the one he used. Once he said to his editor, 'You know, I should rewrite *Ride the Wild Horses* (his first book); I think I could do a lot better with it now. . . .' By this time, that book had been selling all across the country for 16 years. On the same book his editor had sat with him for thirty-five minutes trying to find exactly the right words for just one page of the manuscript."

It sounds like Luke struggling for perfection.

Sentence Sermon to Remember: Of all priesthoods, aristocracies, governing classes at present extant in the world, there is no class comparable for importance to the priesthood of the writers of books.—Carlyle.

Questions for Pupils on the Next Lesson: 1. Was the birth of John the Baptist a fulfillment of Old Testament prophecy? Explain. 2. Explain the meaning of Luke 2:30. 3. What is the *Magnificat?* 4. Was John the Baptist personally related to Jesus? 5. Who was "sitting in darkness" (Luke 1:79)? 6. What does the experience of Zacharias and Simeon tell us about in revealing God's will to men? 7. Why was it necessary for John the Baptist to "announce" the coming of Christ? 8. Did Christ fulfill the Old Testament promises mentioned in Luke 1?

LESSON II—DECEMBER 12

GOD FULFILLS HIS PROMISE

Background Scripture: Luke 1:5-80
Devotional Reading: Isaiah 9:2-7

KING JAMES VERSION

REVISED STANDARD VERSION

LUKE 1 68 Blessed be the Lord God of Israel; for he hath visited and redeemed his people,

69 And hath raised up a horn of salvation for us in the house of his servant David;

70 As he spake by the mouth of his holy prophets, which have been since the world began:

71 That we should be saved from our enemies, and from the hand of all that hate us;

72 To perform the mercy promised to our fathers, and to remember his holy covenant;

73 The oath which he sware to our father Abraham,

74 That he would grant unto us, that we, being delivered out of the hand of our enemies, might serve him without fear,

75 In holiness and righteousness before him, all the days of our life.

76 And thou, child, shalt be called the prophet of the Highest: for thou shalt go before the face of the Lord to prepare his ways;

77 To give knowledge of salvation unto his people by the remission of their sins,

78 Through the tender mercy of our God; whereby the dayspring from on high hath visited us,

79 To give light to them that sit in darkness and in the shadow of death, to guide our feet into the way of peace.

LUKE 2 29 Lord, now lettest thou thy servant depart in peace, according to thy word:

30 For mine eyes have seen thy salvation,

31 Which thou hast prepared before the face of all people;

LUKE 1 68 "Blessed be the Lord God of Israel,
for he has visited and redeemed his people,

69 and has raised up a horn of salvation for us
in the house of his servant David,

70 as he spoke by the mouth of his holy prophets from of old,

71 that we should be saved from our enemies,
and from the hand of all who hate us;

72 to perform the mercy promised to our fathers,
and to remember his holy covenant,

73 the oath which he swore to our father Abraham, 74 to grant us
that we, being delivered from the hand of our enemies,
might serve him without fear,

75 in holiness and righteousness before him all the days of our life.

76 And you, child, will be called the prophet of the Most High;
for you will go before the Lord to prepare his ways,

77 to give knowledge of salvation to his people
in the forgiveness of their sins,

78 through the tender mercy of our God,
when the day shall dawn upon us from on high

79 to give light to those who sit in darkness and in the shadow of death,
to guide our feet into the way of peace."

LUKE 2 29 "Lord, now lettest thou thy servant depart in peace, according to thy word;

30 for mine eyes have seen thy salvation

31 which thou hast prepared in the presence of all peoples,

| 32 A light to lighten the Gentiles, and the glory of thy people Israel. | 32 a light for revelation to the Gentiles, and for glory to thy people Israel." |

MEMORY SELECTION: Mine eyes have seen thy salvation, which thou hast prepared in the presence of all peoples, a light for revelation to the Gentiles, and for glory to thy people Israel. Luke 2:30–32 (RSV).

HOME DAILY BIBLE READINGS

Dec. 6. M. The Messiah Foretold, Isaiah 9:2-7.
Dec. 7. T. The Birth of John Promised, Luke 1:5-17.
Dec. 8. W. The Annunciation, Luke 1:26-38.
Dec. 9. T. Mary Visits Elisabeth, Luke 1:39-45.
Dec. 10. F. The Magnificat, Luke 1:46-55.
Dec. 11. S. John the Baptist Born, Luke 1:57-66.
Dec. 12. S. My Song of Confidence, Psalm 27:1-6.

BACKGROUND

For the background of this lesson read the first chapter of Luke all the way through. It contains the story of Zacharias (or Zecharias), a member af a great priestly line, and of Elisabeth his wife, a daughter of the Aaronic line and a cousin of Mary the mother of Jesus. They were old when they appear in Luke's story—old and childless, and despairing of ever having a longed-for child. But one day an angel spoke to aged Zacharias in a vision, telling him that "Elisabeth shall bear thee a son, and thou shalt call his name John."

John the Baptist! The name meant "Jehovah's gift," or "God is gracious." Gracious indeed was God to give them such a son as this in their old age. The neighbors, marveling at the birth of this John, at the vision of Zacharias and the other things that happened to him, wondered, "What manner of child shall this be?" *They* didn't know, but Zacharias did, thanks to the angel (Gabriel). To tell the curious neighbors and the whole world who this son was, the old priest burst into a song of praise and thanksgiving in which he made it clear that this his child was to be the forerunner of Jesus the Christ, the fulfillment of Israel's messianic hope. We call it the *Benedictus,"* and it is still sung in many of our churches. . . .

NOTES ON THE PRINTED TEXT

I. Blessed be the Lord God of Israel; for he hath visited and redeemed his people, Luke 1:68. The birth of John was a great event and a great moment in the life of Zacharias and Elisabeth, in the life of the nation Israel and in the life of future mankind. It was great for the parents of the baby because, as John's name implied, God had been "gracious" to them in giving them this child; it was great for Israel because it was the beginning of the fulfillment of the promise of God that He would save (protect, guide, lead) Israel out of her troubles to a new day of triumph; it was great for all history in that it gave mankind a Saviour who would save erring men, regardless of race, color or condition. Blessed be God!

Zacharias sang that with all his heart. His *Benedictus* (this word is the first word in the Latin Bible) had two great emphases, or themes.

One was that salvation would arrive in the person of a babe soon to be born in Bethlehem (Luke 1:36 seems to indicate that John was born about six months before Jesus was born). How long Israel had waited for this! How long ago it was that the holy prophets had predicted this moment! How long ago it was that Isaiah had promised the light of a Saviour to a people who walked in darkness, but he never quite gave up hope! How many weary years had passed since he had said, "For unto us a child is born . . . and his name shall be called Wonderful, Counsellor. . . . !" How long they had waited for this son of the house of David! Even before the prophets they were waiting: ever since the covenant of Abraham!

Now the fulfillment of that covenant, of those promises of God, was to be announced by Zacharias' child. After what had seemed a long period in which God was "inactive," He was about to redeem His people and save them from their enemies. (Was Zacharias thinking of the most recent enemy—Rome?)

The redemption, Zacharias says, was a "visit." God was "visiting" men, coming down to live with them in the flesh of Jesus Christ. God, says Luke, had "raised up a horn of salvation . . . in the house of his servant David" (verse 69, RSV). Many of the ancient kings wore the horns of the bull or the rhinoceros as a symbol of great strength and prosperity. Michelangelo put such a horn on the head of Moses, in one of the great statues of all time. (Read Psalms 18:2-3; 132:17, and Ezekiel 29:21.) It was a mightly salvation, so strong as to be over-whelming, as strong as the Almighty Himself! Just as the Almighty had been strong enough to overwhelm the Egyptians and bring Israel out of slavery and through the wilderness, so now ,in the Redeemer about to be born, the same God would give them a new exodus from Roman might and power and make them free to serve Him without fear in holiness and righteousness. There is no mention of vengeance on their enemies here, no mention of a Christ who would crush the foes of Israel with force of arms. No violence! The Christ came swordless; against Him Rome eventually fell.

II. *And thou, child, shalt be called the prophet of the Highest: for thou shalt go before the face of the Lord to prepare his ways,* Luke 1:76. This is the second emphasis of the *Benedictus,* and it is an emphasis on John and his mission. John had been sent to prepare the way for Christ in the hearts of men, to remind the people of their sins and to announce God's forgiveness for their sins—a God of mercy who was something new in a nation which had so long thought of Him as stern judge, a punisher rather than a forgiver. John would call his people to repentance. (He did just that, in words of fire that seared their souls!) Note here that Luke says nothing of John's work as a baptizer, nothing of his violent death at the hands of his enemies, nothing even of the sufferings of the Redeemer. Luke concentrates on the *announcer.*

Luke was a quiet, sensitive man; through his words we sense a loathing of all violence, a mistrust of human force and brutality. Maybe this is why he says nothing about a John who came out of the desert breathing fire. Maybe this is why he ends his passage here with quiet words about mercy and the rising of the sun for the people "that sit in darkness." He does not stress the dark bitterness of the long night, but the happy bursting of the dawn which gives light for the escape of the people out of the shadows and into the peace of God.

Jesus is the sun, appearing in splendor. Said the prophet Malachi, looking forward to this moment: "But unto you that fear my name shall the Sun of righteousness arise with healing in his wings . . . (Malachi 4:2). The sun, the Son, had risen!

How many of them of that day understood the meaning of these words? How many understand them *now?*

Lord, now lettest thou thy servant depart in peace . . . , Luke 2:29. Enter Simeon, the good, devout and godly man (a rabbi?) who all his life had waited in faith for the coming of "the consolation of Israel"— for the coming of the Messiah. When Mary and Joseph brought their baby into the Temple to present Him to the Lord, there was Simeon, who had been promised by God and the Spirit that he would not die until he had seen the Messiah, the Lord Christ. And Simeon took the Lord Christ in his arms and turned to the altar to give Him unto God, and held Him there, and sang, "Lord, now lettest thou thy servant depart in peace." He could die now. He had seen the Lord.

For centuries, the *"Nunc Dimittis"* (these words about departing) has been the great, tender, moving evensong of the church. And ever since then Christ's ministers have offered babyhood at the altars. . . .

Luke dipped his pen in love, joy, mercy, tenderness and beauty, all of which are as lovely for us today as they were then. . . .

SUGGESTIONS TO TEACHERS

One salient fact stands out about both Zacharias and Simeon: they were old men who had trusted God to send His Redeemer to save Israel, trusted Him long after their contemporaries had lost hope, and God rewarded them; their hopes were realized when Jesus Christ was born. Trust in God! Whom else *can* we trust?

There is also this truth in their stories: *God uses people to reveal Himself and His will to men.* We see God most clearly revealed in the unconquerable faith and love of men who not only know Him but actively do His will. "God has no hands but our hands." God solves the problems and the ills of human existence with the help of men who love and trust Him.

We might sum it up thus: Historically and personally, God keeps His promises.

TOPIC FOR ADULTS
GOD KEEPS HIS PROMISE

Long-Term Faith. Undoubtedly, people laughed at Simeon and Zacharias—a pair of doddering old men with an impossible dream! But in the end . . . !

" 'Bishop,' said Thomas Carlyle to his friend Bishop Wilberforce on an occasion when they were talking about death—'Bishop, have you a creed?'

" 'Yes,' replied the bishop, 'I have a creed, and the older I grow the firmer it becomes; there is only one thing that staggers me.'

" 'What is that?' asked Carlyle.

" 'It is the slow progress,' said the bishop, 'that that creed seems to make in the world.'

"Carlyle remained silent for a moment, and then said slowly and seriously, 'Ah, but if you have a creed you can afford to wait.'

"Yes, if we have a faith or a creed, we can afford to wait. Remember that the great scientist Kepler was prepared to wait for his recognition. Said he, 'I may well wait a hundred years for a reader, since God has waited six thousand years for a discoverer.' "—*A Treasury of the Christian Faith,* p. 276; by Harry Taylor.

Children of Hope. All over our world, millions of children are starving—and hoping against hope that help will come.

"Bob Pierce watched the ragged war orphans digging through army garbage in Korea. His missionary companion moaned, "There are so many of them. What can we do?'

"Softened to tears, Pierce suddenly pulled out his wallet and handed over his last five dollars. 'It isn't much,' he said, 'but it's all I have.' He came home to start World Vision, which began caring for orphans through a unique sponsorship program. . . .

Everet Swanson saw the same tragedy while visiting missionaries after the Korean War. . . . Arriving home, he was met by a pastor who offered him $50 and said, 'Use it for the orphans.' Swanson started Compassion, which follows the same system of sponsorship as World Vision. The two organizations together now care for over forty thousand children who might otherwise be starving or dead. . . ."—*Thinkables,* by James C. Hefley (Revell).

So forty thousand children who were prisoners of hope for so long got a glimpse of the saving love of God in two men sent by Him. . . . God does use people!

Believing. "P. T. Barnum was not only a great showman, but also something of a homely philosopher. He once observed that more people were humbugged into believing too little than were humbugged into believing too much. The danger today is that people should be humbugged into believing nothing."—Clarence E. Macartney.

Zacharias and Simeon *believed* in the promise of God. Their trust in God didn't "die on the vine." Has yours?

Questions for Pupils on the Next Lesson: 1. Describe the Good News in twenty words or less. 2. Why was Jesus born in Bethlehem? 3. What is uniquely beautiful about Luke's story of the birth of Jesus? 4. How was Jesus' birth a declaration of war against Caesar? 5. How far was Bethlehem from Nazareth? 6. Just when did you clear out the "inn of your heart" and let Jesus be born there? 7. Will your celebration of Christmas this year be worthy of Christ?

TOPIC FOR YOUTH
GOD KEEPS HIS PROMISE

Forty Years. "My father, when in Litchfield (Mass.), lived on a salary of eight hundred dollars a year, with a family of eleven growing children. How ministers lived at that time I cannot conceive. I remember his saying once at the table . . . something that made a deep impression on my mind. Having poured his tea into a saucer to cool, he was resting his two elbows on the table. Mother sat opposite to him, murmuring, in her sweet, refined, gentle, sad way that the bills were due; that she had no money; that, indeed, she did not see how they could get along; that for her part she expected to die in the poorhouse. At that father dropped his hands to the table, and his eyes sparkled, and he said, 'My dear, I have trusted God for forty years, and He has never forsaken me; I am not going to distrust Him now.' That waked me up; it sank into me, and during my earlier life I went through perils of sickness and poverty and all forms of limitation and trouble, but I never lost sight of that scene and that sentence."—Phillips Brooks.

Check back now. When did God ever break a promise to *you?*

Like a Clock. "In one of his poems, Peguy makes God say, 'I don't like the man who can't sleep. He doesn't trust me.' It is a striking way of saying what Jesus said: 'Why are ye fearful, O ye of little faith?' The simple truth is that fear is the opposite of faith. Either we live fearfully or we live trustfully, one way or the other. If we live fearfully, our anxieties come in bunches. We have more worries than a cat has lives. On the other hand, as Robert Louis Stevenson wrote, 'Trustful, quiet minds cannot be perplexed or frightened, but go on in fortune or misfortune at their own private pace, like a clock during a thunderstorm.'"—Harold Blake Walker, *Praying Hands,* July-August, 1968.

Believers in God live like that. . . .

Hope. There must have been many times when Zacharias and Simeon "had their doubts" about the promises God had made to them and to Israel. But there is no record that they ever gave up in doubt or despair. . . .

"Robert Louis Stevenson, making a list of his sufferings and sadness and sorrow, said: 'I still hope; I still believe; I still see the good in the inch and cling to it.' Having experienced one inch of goodness, he is compelled to believe in its intrinsic worth for all men. On another occasion he wrote:

To go on forever and fail and go on again,
And be mauled to the earth, and arise,
And content for the shade of a word, and a thing not seen with the eyes,
With the half of a broken hope for a pillow at night,
That somehow the right is the right,
And the smooth will blossom from the rough. . . .

There it is again: half of a broken hope for a pillow at night: broken—only half of it left—but it is the pillow on which he rests his weary faith—his faith that things must come out right. Ah! We have felt the worth of our Christian ideals all too seldom, all too fitfully. But at Christmas time it sweeps over our souls with a compulsion that cannot be denied. And we dare not give it up. It is our way out and up. It is the hope of redemption for this disillusioned and weary old world.

This Christian hope is not a passive thing. It is active. We hope and then we go to work to make the hope a reality. We hope

Till hope creates
From it own wreck the thing it contemplates.
—Ilion T. Jones.

Great Enough. "How . . . can you actually start trusting God? How . . . can you 'put your hand in the hand of God?' Tonight, when the long day has finally ended, go to your room and lock the door. Then stand beside the window, and in the darkness watch the moon and the stars. Then deliberately yield yourself—with all your needs, problems, secret anxieties—to the God who is holding this vast universe together. If He is great enough to do that, He is great enough to care for you."—James Gordon Gilkey.

The High Wires. "When I was eight I went to the circus in Boston and marveled at the trapeze artists, soaring impossibly through space, always catching the flying swing from each other. 'Aren't they scared?' I whispered to my mother.

"A man in the row ahead turned to answer: "They aren't scared, honey,' he said gently. 'They trust each other.'

" 'He used to be on the high wires himself,' someone whispered."—Ardis Whitman, in *Christian Herald,* December, 1968.

If you really want to know how trust in God gives a man a security that no other man can give him, talk with that man who has dared to trust God in the hard experiences of his life—and has found in God just such a security . . . !

Sentence Sermon to Remember: Henry Kaiser called the number one rule for getting along harmoniously with other people: simply recognizing that every single person you meet is a child of God, and that makes him important.—Les Giblin.

Questions for Pupils on the Next Lesson: 1. When was Caesar Augustus emperor in Rome? 2. Describe the general world condition when Jesus was born. 3. For what purpose did Joseph and Mary travel to Bethlehem? 4. What did the word "Saviour" mean to the Romans? 5. Are we certain that Jesus was born December 25? 6. Who were the first visitors at the manger? 7. Did Jesus bring peace to the world?

LESSON III—DECEMBER 19

GOOD NEWS OF GREAT JOY

Background Scripture: Luke 1:26-38; 2:1-20
Devotional Reading: Philippians 2:5-13

KING JAMES VERSION

LUKE 2 And it came to pass in those days, that there went out a decree from Caesar Augustus, that all the world should be taxed.

2 (And this taxing was first made when Cyrenius was governor of Syria.)

3 And all went to be taxed, every one into his own city.

4 And Joseph also went up from Galilee, out of the city of Nazareth, into Judea, unto the city of David, which is called Bethlehem, (because he was of the house and lineage of David,)

5 To be taxed with Mary his espoused wife, being great with child.

6 And so it was, that, while they were there, the days were accomplished that she should be delivered.

7 And she brought forth her firstborn son, and wrapped him in swaddling clothes, and laid him in a manger; because there was no room for them in the inn.

8 And there were in the same country shepherds abiding in the field, keeping watch over their flock by night.

9 And, lo, the angel of the Lord came upon them, and the glory of the Lord shone round about them; and they were sore afraid.

10 And the angel said unto them, Fear not: for, behold, I bring you good tidings of great joy, which shall be to all people.

11 For unto you is born this day in the city of David a Saviour, which is Christ the Lord.

12 And this shall be a sign unto you; Ye shall find the babe wrapped in swaddling clothes, lying in a manger.

13 And suddenly there was with the angel a multitude of the heavenly host praising God, and saying,

14 Glory to God in the highest, and on earth peace, good will toward men.

REVISED STANDARD VERSION

LUKE 2 In those days a decree went out from Caesar Augustus that all the world should be enrolled. 2 This was the first enrollment, when Quirinius was governor of Syria. 3 And all went to be enrolled, each to his own city. 4 And Joseph also went up from Galilee, from the city of Nazareth, to Judea, to the city of David, which is called Bethlehem, because he was of the house and lineage of David, 5 to be enrolled with Mary, his betrothed, who was with child. 6 And while they were there, the time came for her to be delivered. 7 And she gave birth to her first-born son and wrapped him in swaddling cloths, and laid him in a manger, because there was no place for them in the inn.

8 And in that region there were shepherds out in the field, keeping watch over their flock by night. 9 And an angel of the Lord appeared to them, and the glory of the Lord shone around them, and they were filled with fear. 10 And the angel said to them, "Be not afraid; for behold, I bring you good news of a great joy which will come to all the people; 11 for to you is born this day in the city of David a Savior, who is Christ the Lord. 12 And this will be a sign for you: you will find a babe wrapped in swaddling cloths and lying in a manger." 13 And suddenly there was with the angel a multitude of the heavenly host praising God and saying,

14 "Glory to God in the highest,
    and on earth peace among men
        with whom he is pleased!"

MEMORY SELECTION: And the angel said unto them, Fear not: for, behold, I bring you good tidings of great joy, which shall be to all people. For unto you is born this day in the city of David a Saviour, which is Christ the Lord. Luke 2:10-11.

HOME DAILY BIBLE READINGS

Dec. 13. M. The Birth of Jesus, Matthew 1:18-25.
Dec. 14. T. The Presentation, Luke 2:22-32.
Dec. 15. W. The Redeemer Has Come, Luke 2:33-40.
Dec. 16. T. Visit of the Wise Men, Matthew 2:1-12.
Dec. 17. F. Jesus in the Temple, Luke 2:41-52.
Dec. 18. S. Invitation to All, Isaiah 55:1-7.
Dec. 19. S. The Example of Christ, Philippians 2:5-13.

BACKGROUND

The parents of Jesus lived in Nazareth, but Jesus was not born there. Why? Why in *Bethlehem?* Some Bible scholars say, "Because it was prophesied that He be born there"—prophesied in Micah (5:2). Some others say that it was due to the accident of the Roman census, which required Joseph and Mary to be in Bethlehem—David's town, a "headquarters town" of the census. Others say that Matthew and Luke *contrived* to have Him born here in order to fulfill the old prophecy.

Luke does not mention the prophecy of Micah. He simply states the fact that Jesus was born in Bethlehem. Neither does Luke set the date on which He was born. He had in mind something far more important than a mere date. *He was getting God into human history.* Some good preacher has said, "The history of mankind was split in two on the roof beam of a Bethlehem stable."

NOTES ON THE PRINTED TEXT

1. And it came to pass in those days that there went out a decree from Caesar Augustus, that all the world should be taxed, Luke 2:1. Think of it: the redeeming, liberating Son of God entered the world at the moment when a Caesar was levying a tax on his (captive) subjects! Christ against Caesar: it was a declaration of war in that stable.

This enrolling for tax purposes was an old Roman custom, carried out all across the Roman world. The census of the "payers" was taken every fourteen years; this census in Palestine came in 8 B.C. and the year in which the Saviour was born. To comply with the command of Caesar Augustus, Joseph and Mary traveled the 80 miles from Nazareth to Bethlehem, which, we might say, was "the chief city of their tribe"— the tribe in which David was the greatest of them all. In this, Luke was being meticulously and historically correct.

Luke calls Jesus "Saviour" (verse 11). Augustus, too, had been called Saviour, in arrogance and pride; but what a fall that arrogance and pride were to suffer later on! The kingdom of Augustus crumbled and rotted away; few traces of it are left. Of the kingdom of the babe in the manger there is no end.

With Mary about to give birth to her child, the anxious father could find no room in the inn. It was His first rejection! No room inside *any* inn—so Jesus was born in a stable behind an inn. The Eastern "khan" was a series of open-air courtyards, with stalls and stables for the animals of the travelers. In one of these stables Mary, unattended, brought her child.

The good news of His birth came first to a group of the most despised people in the land—shepherds, who were "watching their flocks by night." Nobody loved a shepherd; shepherds were unclean, literally unwashed, and therefore unable to keep the precious ceremonial law. The orthodox looked down on them as we would look down on a dirty Bowery tramp. The richest treasure of heaven was announced first, not to Caesar Augustus, not to the priests of the Temple, nor to the "respectable" leaders of the people, but to the shepherds. They were of low degree who heard the words, "to *you* is born . . . a Saviour." They were rather special shepherds, yes; they were shepherds who provided the lambs for Temple sacrifices—but they were still *shepherds*, lowly, rejected, second-class citizens. What a touch that was! The sacrificial Lamb of God was announced first to those who took care of the sacrificial lambs of the Temple.

Now in Judea, when a child was born, it was the custom to celebrate the event with music—unless the family was too poor to arrange for it. Usually a group of local musicians gathered at the home to play and sing their very simple folk tunes by way of welcome to the new arrival. And if the musicians were at all typical of most such local singers and players one can imagine what some of the music must have been like. . . . But Jesus was born, not in the house of his parents, back in Nazareth, but in a common *stable* 80 miles away from home, where no musicians were available in the middle of the night! So, for the lack of an earthly "choir," God substituted a heavenly choir. "And suddenly there was . . . a multitude of the heavenly host praising God and saying . . ." (verse 13). They sang a song that the local singers could not possibly have sung, for the local ones did not know what was happening that night. The heavenly choir sang, "Glory to God in the highest, and on earth, peace, good will toward men" (verse 14). It had pleased God to send His Son into the world to make a prospect of peace available (and how that world wanted peace!)—but with one condition: the *Revised Standard Version* translates this verse, . . . "and on earth peace among men *with whom he is pleased*." It was no offer of peace to men who loved conflict, who hated, who did not *want* peace! Even God cannot give peace to a man who deliberately rejects it.

Peace? We read later in the life of Jesus that He came, not to bring peace but a sword—a sword that would divide families, and set brother against brother *over the question of loyalty to Him*, whether they would accept or reject his offer of peace. It was not a political peace, much as Israel wanted that, and much as the people had dreamed that the Messiah would bring them political peace. It was not the peace of a mawkish, sentimental "good will" which prays humbly for peace, begs God in church for it, and then does nothing to bring it about. God is hardly pleased with men who make no effort to do that. He *is* pleased with men who understand that peace is a "right relation to

God, through the forgiveness of sin." May peace begin with *our* forgiveness!

So God sent Mary's baby as the harbinger, the Prince of peace, but made it painfully plain that peace is possible only among men of good will. How good is your good will? How good is your devotion to the inspiring teachings of Jesus Christ? If God were to ask you, "What have you done for peace through Christ?" what would you answer?

SUGGESTIONS TO TEACHERS

Christmas! What does it mean? What *should* it mean?

The following emphases are suggested:

1. Contrast the good news of Christmas with the bad news in tomorrow's newspaper.
2. Christmas, as the celebration of the incarnation, should be observed—*how?*
3. The incarnation is tangible evidence of God's compassion and concern for people.
4. As the Prince of peace, Jesus has brought peace to whom, where, when?

TOPIC FOR ADULTS
GOOD NEWS OF GREAT JOY

Peace, Christmas. "On many a popular greeting card is this message: 'Glory to God in the highest, and on earth peace, good will toward men.' Many agree that a more accurate translation is: 'Glory to God in the highest, and on earth peace among men in whom he is well pleased.' Think now—the angels did not *prophesy* peace—they proclaimed it! And this is the difference between heaven and the hell on earth we now see all about us. The 'popular' view that Christianity stands for peace, the brotherhood of men and the prosperity of nations is true in a general sense. But if we look at the picture from the viewpoint of Jesus Christ, that somewhat Pollyanna view falls apart at the seams! And the critic of Christianity understandably demands, 'What does all this talk about peace on earth really amount to? Where is the peace?'"

"From the human viewpoint this criticism is stingingly just. But—God became a baby so that we might be brought into the viewpoint of Christ. 'And they shall call his name Emmanuel, which being interpreted is, God with us.' Jesus Christ is the God-man, by Him any man can be transformed into a son of God. This fact is at the heart of the Christian revelation. And the cross of Christ is in the heart of God. By faith in the Christ we are literally born from above and brought—not by intellectual comprehension but by direct action of the Holy Spirit—into the viewpoint of the One who calls us to press on beyond a mere commemoration of His earthly birth. Jesus of Nazareth was not *becoming* God; He *was* God incarnate . . . Emmanuel . . . God with us in human flesh. Jesus Christ is not 'the best human being!' . . . His life is God's life, which stooped that night nearly two thousand years ago to enter by a humble gate into our suffering, sin-shocked world.

"But mere acceptance of it will not bend our stiff necks or break our stubborn religiosity until Jesus Christ has actually been born again in us. He must come into us from outside us. 'If any man will . . . open the door, I will come in.'

"Christmas is for *our* sake? Yes. And may we join hearts and minds at this time, remembering His historical birth, and yield ourselves so completely to God that our lives become new birthplaces for Christ! This Christmas and forever, we have no choice but to remember, if we are facing reality, that the deepest meaning of the redemption of Jesus Christ is that in us He can again walk this needy old earth, with healing in His hands and peace for all men who follow Him . . . because those are the men in whom God is well pleased. Christmas is for our sake! 'Unto *us* a child. . . .'" *The Burden Is Light,* by Eugenia Price (Fleming H. Revell Company).

> The Carpenter of Galilee
> Comes down the street again,
> In every land, in every age,
> He still is building men.
> On Christmas Eve we hear Him knock;
> He goes from door to door:
> Are any workmen out of work?
> The Carpenter needs more.
> —Hilda W. Smith.

God Made Known. "Historians tell us that Horace Mann was the first president of Antioch College in Ohio. To read the record, you would wonder that the school lasted beyond thirty days. Of the first one hundred and fifty applicants, only eight passed the entrance examinations. The school's buildings had no doors, running water or heat. Animals wandered into the lecture halls and livestock roamed the fenceless campus. In spite of this bleak beginning, it became a pioneer in coeducation and in welcoming young people of every race.

"Consider the grubby beginnings of the first Christmas: the bare stable, the harsh winter, the flight to Egypt. God calls us to consider His ways, for He is indeed made known in weakness."—Harry Atkinson, in *Christian Herald.*

No Room in the Inn. "Millions of us today say that we are too busy to give much time to religion; there are so many demands on our time, so many other things to do, such pressure. . . . What we are really saying is that we haven't saved any room for Christ in our lives and in our living. . . .

"'No room, no room.' The Mad Hatter shrieked this at Alice in the celebrated wonderland tea party, even though room abounded. No room in many of our neighborhoods for those of a minority race. No room in our agricultural economy for just wages and good conditions for the migrant worker. No room in our bomb shelters. No room for talk about peace, despite the appeal of the angels from the midnight sky, because this is a day (so many tell us) when only tough talk and suspicion of neighbor will do. No room, or at least not sufficient priority, in many a Christian church for the spirit of unity to which He calls His church." —John H. Burt, in *Pulpit Preaching.*

Questions for Pupils on the Next Lesson: 1. What did God have in mind when He allowed Jesus to be tempted? 2. Did Jesus conquer temptation once and for all in the wilderness? 3. Did Jesus know what was to happen to Him at His baptism? 4. Where was the wilderness?

5. Do you have wilderness areas in your life in which you are tempted? Describe them. 6. What would have been wrong if Jesus had turned stones into bread? 7. Are you ashamed of being tempted—and was Jesus ashamed?

TOPIC FOR YOUTH
GOOD NEWS OF GREAT JOY

Good News. "Once upon a time, a certain man armed with a gun, a strong pocket knife and the permission of a cottager at the foot of a mountain went up through the snow after . . . meat and a free Christmas tree. . . . He laid his gun down, took his knife and stopped to cut down a tiny but sturdy tree. To the hunter's dismay, a cottontail scampered from under the tree.

"Nearby . . . the man found the green bones of a doe gnawed clean. Out there, nature was 'red in tooth and claw.' Even the tree was lopsided from struggling against the rocky mountain. Everything seemed to be having a hard time on that cold mountain, yet right there, *right then,* the man began to catch the Christmas spirit!

"To you accustomed to a crackling fireplace, expectant stockings, wide-eyed children, the laughter of those you love, and carols in the church back home, Christmas away from home may not have the feel of the real thing. The dismal dormitory, or the barren barracks, and the longing for loved ones and for home, and the wild fury of the war still raging chill your spirit. Yet the true Christmas spirit thrives under difficulties, for it is the Christ spirit: the forgetting of self in doing something difficult for others.

"Long ago the first Christmas spirit was caught by folks who also were having a hard time—a peasant woman bearing a beautiful burden and finding no place in the inn to lay Him down; wise men who had spent all they had while searching for Him; ragged shepherds shivering on the plains . . . and war-weary humble peoples across the centuries yearning for 'peace on earth, good will among men.' "—*Something for Everybody,* by Paul Hortin. Quoted by permission of Droke House.

The good news came first to people in stables, to shepherds. . . .

Keeping Christmas. "There is a better thing than the observance of Christmas Day and that is keeping Christmas.

"Are you willing

to forget what you have done for other people, and to remember what other people have done for you;
to ignore what the world owes you and to think what you owe the world;
to put your rights in the background, and your duties in the middle distance, and your chances to do a little more than your duty in the foreground;
to see that your fellowmen are just as real as you are, and try to look behind their faces to their hearts, hungry for joy;
to own that probably the only good reason for your existence is not what you are going to get out of life, but what you are going to give;
to close your book of complaints against the management of the universe, and look around you for where you can sow a few seeds of happiness—
"are you willing to do these things even for a day?

"Then you can keep Christmas.

"Are you willing to stoop down and consider the needs and the desires of little children

>   to remember the weakness and loneliness of people who are growing old;
>   to stop asking how much your friends love you, and ask yourself whether you love them enough;
>   to bear in mind the things that other people have to bear;
>   to try to understand what those who live in the same home with you really want, without waiting for them to tell you;
>   to trim your lamp so that it will give more light and less smoke, and to carry it in front so that your shadow will fall behind you;
>   to make a grave for your ugly thoughts and a garden for your good thoughts, with the gate open—
>   are you willing to do these things even for a day?

"Then you can keep Christmas.

"Are you willing to believe that love is the strongest thing in the world —stronger than hate, stronger than evil, stronger than death—and that the blessed life which began in Bethlehem nineteen hundred years ago is the image and brightness of the eternal love?

"Then you can keep Christmas. And if you keep it for a day, why not always? But you can never keep it alone."—Henry Van Dyke.

While Shepherds Watched. Does anyone recall offhand who was poet laureate and historiographer to Queen Anne at the turn of the eighteenth century? No?

His name was Tate and he died in a debtor's prison. But never mind. He has his immortality among us when we sing one of the simplest, most direct and moving of the nativity hymns:

>   While shepherds watched their flocks by night,
>   All seated on the ground,
>   The angel of the Lord came down,
>   And glory shone around.

Sentence Sermon to Remember: When the light of faith gives the dark of any night a sparkle—it's Christmas.—William B. Taylor.

Questions for Pupils on the Next Lesson: 1. Why did Jesus go into the wilderness to be tempted? 2. Did Jesus believe in a personal devil? 3. How many temptations were there? 4. Why can't man live by bread alone? 5. Is it *always* wrong to compromise? 6. How much sensationalism is there in your church? 7. Do all great leaders of men face the three temptations of Jesus?

LESSON IV—DECEMBER 26

JESUS OVERCOMES TEMPTATION

Background Scripture: Luke 3:15-22; 4:1-15
Devotional Reading: Psalm 91

KING JAMES VERSION

LUKE 3 21 Now when all the people were baptized, it came to pass, that Jesus also being baptized, and praying, the heaven was opened.

22 And the Holy Ghost descended in a bodily shape like a dove upon him, and a voice came from heaven, which said, Thou art my beloved Son; in thee I am well pleased.

LUKE 4 And Jesus being full of the Holy Ghost returned from Jordan, and was led by the Spirit into the wilderness,

2 Being forty days tempted of the devil. And in those days he did eat nothing: and when they were ended, he afterward hungered.

3 And the devil said unto him, If thou be the Son of God, command this stone that it be made bread.

4 And Jesus answered him, saying, It is written, That man shall not live by bread alone, but by every word of God.

5 And the devil, taking him up into a high mountain, showed unto him all the kingdoms of the world in a moment of time.

6 And the devil said unto him, All this power will I give thee, and the glory of them: for that is delivered unto me; and to whomsoever I will, I give it.

7 If thou therefore wilt worship me, all shall be thine.

8 And Jesus answered and said unto him, Get thee behind me, Satan: for it is written, Thou shalt worship the Lord thy God, and him only shalt thou serve.

9 And he brought him to Jerusalem, and set him on a pinnacle of the temple, and said unto him, If thou be the Son of God, cast thyself down from hence:

10 For it is written, He shall give his angels charge over thee, to keep thee:

REVISED STANDARD VERSION

LUKE 3 21 Now when all the people were baptized, and when Jesus also had been baptized and was praying, the heaven was opened, 22 and the Holy Spirit descended upon him in bodily form, as a dove, and a voice came from heaven, "Thou art my beloved Son; with thee I am well pleased."

LUKE 4 And Jesus, full of the Holy Spirit, returned from the Jordan, and was led by the Spirit 2 for forty days in the wilderness, tempted by the devil. And he ate nothing in those days; and when they were ended, he was hungry. 3 The devil said to him, "If you are the Son of God, command this stone to become bread." 4 And Jesus answered him, "It is written, 'Man shall not live by bread alone.'" 5 And the devil took him up, and showed him all the kingdoms of the world in a moment of time, 6 and said to him, "To you I will give all this authority and their glory; for it has been delivered to me, and I give it to whom I will. 7 If you, then, will worship me, it shall all be yours." 8 And Jesus answered him, "It is written,

'You shall worship the Lord your God,
and him only shall you serve.'"

9 And he took him to Jerusalem, and set him on the pinnacle of the temple, and said to him, "If you are the Son of God, throw yourself down from here; 10 for it is written,

'He will give his angels charge of you, to guard you,'

11 and

'On their hands they will bear you up,
lest you strike your foot against a stone.'"

12 And Jesus answered him, "It is said, 'You shall not tempt the Lord your God.'"

11 And in their hands they shall bear thee up, lest at any time thou dash thy foot against a stone.

12 And Jesus answering said unto him, It is said, Thou shalt not tempt the Lord thy God.

MEMORY SELECTION: It is written, Thou shalt worship the Lord thy God, and him only shalt thou serve. Luke: 4:8.

HOME DAILY BIBLE READINGS

Dec. 20. M. The Messenger to Come, Isaiah 40:1-5.
Dec. 21. T. Preparing the Way, Luke 3:1-6.
Dec. 22. W. The Preaching of John, Luke 3:7-14.
Dec. 23. T. The Wilderness Temptation, Matthew 4:1-11.
Dec. 24. F. God Is Faithful, I Corinthians 10:1-13.
Dec. 25. S. The Secret Place, Psalm 91:1-8.
Dec. 26. S. Honored of God, Psalm 91:9-16.

BACKGROUND

Jesus was twelve years old when He first became aware of His unique relationship to God. Then *for eighteen years,* we hear nothing about Him; these are "the hidden years" of His life, during which He worked and thought and dreamed at Nazareth. Not until He was thirty do we have another recorded event in His life; at thirty He came to John to be baptized, and it was immediately after the baptism that He was tempted.

Up to that moment, He had never preached a sermon, worked a miracle, or made a public announcement about Himself or His work. He was not yet ready to do that. But when He came out of the waters of Jordan and out of the wilderness of temptation, He *was* ready. Today we are to find out what it was in those two experiences that *made* Him ready.

NOTES ON THE PRINTED TEXT

1. Thou art my beloved Son; in thee I am well pleased, Luke 3:22. Before Jesus left Nazareth, a wave of religious revival had started under the preaching of John. John was winning converts, making men aware of their sins and their need of repentance, and crowds flocked to hear him and to fall under his spell. Jesus heard this good news in the carpenter shop at Nazareth, and, hearing it, He knew that He had to become a part of this movement toward righteousness and God. In John's voice He heard God's call to action—and He accepted the call, and went to John to be baptized as a public announcement of His acceptance and of His identification with the people and their cause. The divine Jesus was answering the call and will of the Father; the human Jesus was answering the call of the people.

But the baptism turned out to be something greater than perhaps even Jesus expected. *God spoke directly to Him as He stood in Jordan.* God said to Him, "Thou art my beloved Son; in whom I am well pleased." You have done the right thing, made the right decision. "Thou art my beloved Son" was an echo of Psalm 2:7—long accepted as a description of the Messiah! "In whom I am well pleased" is derived from Isaiah 42:21, and is a description of the suffering servant of the Lord!

When Jesus heard these words of God, He *knew* He was the Messiah; He also knew that He would suffer terribly. He saw the cross and He accepted it. And He knew that He would need great strength and courage along the road that was to lead to the crucifixion.

He knew that there would be enemies along that road, waiting to destroy Him. He knew that the voices of doubt and temptation would threaten Him. So from Jordan He went directly into the wilderness to listen to these voices, and to prepare Himself to fight them and conquer them.

II. And Jesus . . . was led by the Spirit into the wilderness, being forty days tempted of the devil, Luke 4:1,2. According to tradition, the "wilderness" was a barren, rocky mountain some eight miles west of Jericho; it was called "Quarantania," which meant "a place of forty days." To this lonesome, almost fearsome spot went Jesus, in an effort to "think things through," to face up to the power of the enemies who awaited Him, *and to decide on the methods He would use in His ministry.* (We get our word "quarantine" from the name of this mountain; think about that!)

Here He meets the devil, face to face. Jesus believed in the devil with all His heart; there is no doubt about that. He had read in His people's Scriptures of the presence, power and work of "Diablos," or Satan; the word "Satan" meant "adversary, opposer"; the word "Diablos," strictly, meant "false accuser." And the purpose of this devil was to obstruct or destroy the work of God, to prevent God from saving men, and thus make it impossible for Him to establish His kingdom. The devil "goes to work" on Jesus; he tries to corrupt and weaken Jesus at the start. He tries three times, in three ways, with three arguments.

First, He said, "If you are the Son of God command this stone that it be made bread" (verse 3). Be a bread king! Give the people that for which they long most: food, bread, things. The people will love a leader who *feeds* them; turn one of these stones on your mountain (stones shaped like loaves of bread) *into* bread, and they'll clamor to follow you. Supply their human needs, and they'll love you. Be a social worker! Give them food and pay their rent, and you will win. Jesus had the perfect answer for that one: He quoted Deuteronomy 8:3: "Man shall not live by bread alone, but by every word of God" (verse 4). Man needs bread, yes; but he needs more *fellowship with God.* With the help of God he can be a *new man*—and who does not long for *that?* It is more important to feed the heart and soul of a man than it is to feed his body. None of us would be satisfied with the meeting of just our physical needs; that would produce boredom. But give a man spiritual bread, and his whole life sings.

The devil tried again. He tempted Jesus to *compromise,* to become a merely political Messiah. The devil pointed to the land of Israel which lay at the foot of their mountain, and promised to give Jesus *that* if Jesus would "worship" him—use *his* methods, do things *his* way. Your people long for freedom from Rome: give them freedom, and I will give you not only Israel but all the kingdoms of this world! Don't be an idealist, a dreamer. Be a good politician, statesman, military leader. That's what the people want—a good strong man who will give them "welfare!" Don't be stiff-necked; give a little here and there, compromise a little. . . .

Don't fight the devil; compromise with him! The devil said the world was his to give—that he was "overlord" of it all. (He does seem to control a great deal of it!)

Jesus wasn't impressed with the offer. He denied the devil's claim of ownership of the nations of the world; they were not his, but God's. And God is right, and you the devil are wrong, and "right is right and wrong is wrong," and I will not do that which is wrong, however well it "pays off." "Thou shalt worship the Lord thy God, and him only shalt thou serve." That included worship by the devil as well as by man. That includes all of us who must decide whether to serve the devil for temporary gain or serve God for eternal gain. Jesus rejected the devil's offer of "power and glory" and chose the way of the cross, which, in the end, will give us all greater glory and power.

Once more the devil tried his wiles. He brought Jesus to the Temple at Jerusalem and told Him to jump from its highest pinnacle. If He were truly the Son of God, God and His angels would save Him! What a sensation that would be. How the people would cheer! The people love sensations, and tricks. Give them what they want. Be spectacular. Be a nine-days' wonder. That will get them.

It might have gotten them, but Jesus was not interested in getting them that way. He knew that sensationalism was a fraud, a mockery of God, and He remembered "Ye shall not tempt the Lord thy God." (See Deuteronomy 6:16.) The protecting care of God comes to a man not at his request when he is doing foolish things; it comes when he is doing sensible, righteous things with the help of God. Don't tempt your God with tricks! It is not sensationalism that saves a man; it is service and suffering and faith above suffering—as we saw it on the cross.

So Jesus put aside the temptations to win a cheap, transient, worthless victory in using the cheap tricks of the compromiser, the scheming politician, the sensationalist. He had a better, if harder, way. He had come, not to amuse men, or meet their physical needs; He had come to save them with His blood, and save them He did.

SUGGESTIONS TO TEACHERS

Eric Hoffer has said, "Man staggers through life yapped at by his reason, pulled and shoved by his appetites, whispered to by fears, beckoned by hopes." That isn't a very optimistic picture of the state of man— but it just happens to be true. Man is tempted every day of his life, perhaps every hour, to be something less than he should be. His problem is to steer his reason constructively, to control his appetites so that they do not turn him into a selfish pig, to make his fears work for him instead of against him, and to hope for the highest and not the lowest.

Jesus in the wilderness was plagued by all the negative values that Hoffer mentions—with a difference. *He had a power within Himself that helped Him conquer them.* List his three temptations: to turn stones into bread, to leap from the Temple pinnacle, to gain all the kingdoms of the earth. List them on your blackboard—and ask your class what they mean *in terms of their own lives.* There was a definite purpose in Jesus' temptations. They had a definite relation to His mission on earth. Outline that mission carefully; then ask about the mission of every student in your class.

How do their temptations fulfill or destroy that mission?

TOPIC FOR ADULTS
VICTORY OVER TEMPTATION

Stones Into Bread. Jesus' first temptation was to turn stones into bread. In effect, the devil was really saying to him, "The animal needs come first in most peoples lives; help them satisfy those needs, and you can dominate them." The animal needs do come first, all too often.

In Miami there is a monstrosity called Biscaya; it is a house that cost millions, a Caesar's palace filled with "treasure" brought from the ends of the earth. Artistically, it is a nightmare; Chinese rugs and vases are found in the same room with French tapestry and Roman furniture. Middle East mosaic floors are covered with Western gadgets. There are gardens all around the place, packed with ancient statues from Rome and Greece. There is a dock at the water's edge modeled after the dock to which some dead Caesar brought his slave-driven galleys.

We went through it not long ago; we talked with one of the attendants who explained things to the tourists. He said to us, "You know, to me, this is the most vulgar exhibition of useless wealth in the civilized world."

The owner of it all was unmarried. He spent only a few weeks every year in the place. He piled it all up, and then he died, and now Miami doesn't know what to do with it.

The animal needs come first? Jesus turned His back on them!

Gun Worship. The devil offered Jesus a compromise: if He would just bow down to Satan, just compromise a little on His allegiance to God, then Jesus could have "all the kingdoms of the world." That sounded like a good bargain—but it wasn't. Jesus didn't want all the kingdoms of this world at such a fantastic and repulsive price.

Actually, this was an appeal to Jesus to capitalize on the patriotic fervor of His people, and to use His power as a military leader. Adolf Hitler made such a compromise with the devil—and got, not kingdoms but a coward's death. Soviet Russia today controls nearly half the world —and in that half Russia faces almost constant rebellion and disorder, and her whole "empire" shows signs of coming apart at the seams.

Perhaps, late as it is, the church has caught up with Jesus in His opposition to military power and misdirected patriotism! As never before, the church is fighting war and military establishments.

Jesus couldn't be a nationalistic patriot; He sought the allegiance of men of every nationality on earth. What a contrast there is between Hitler and Jesus: the one has had his ashes scattered to the winds, the other still rules from His cross!

Compromises. Speaking of compromise: ". . . on account of its compromises Christianity is bankrupt. I have written, and I believe firmly, that if Christianity had really prevailed and if it had really fulfilled the teaching of Christ, there would be no question of communism—there would indeed be no social problem at all.—André Gide.

Can it possibly be true? Think carefully on this thing!

Questions for Pupils on the Next Lesson: 1. Define the word "love." 2. Who are the real enemies of Christ? 3. Was the Golden Rule original with Jesus? 4. Can we live with other people without judging them? 5. Have you ever literally practiced the teaching in Luke 6:29? 6. Who has a right to take vengeance, according to Jesus? 7. How has the United States practiced forgiveness of its enemies?

TOPIC FOR YOUTH
JESUS ALSO WAS TEMPTED

Jump! The last and supreme temptation of Jesus was to bend God's love and power to His own ends. The devil said, "Jump!" Jump from the highest Temple pinnacle. God in His love will save you from all harm. Besides, the people will just love a sensational trick like that!

It was—and is—blasphemy. Asking God to do you a great favor, to perform a great miracle in order to make you a "great" leader, is the worst sin you can commit against God.

Recently we have read three books, all written by rich men who wrote those books to prove that they made fortunes in business by following the principles laid down in the Bible! Was *that* what the Bible was written for—to make men rich? They seem not to understand that God makes men rich in other, *spiritual* ways, and that all through the Bible men rich in gold seemed to have a hard time of it getting into the kingdom! They seem also to have missed the story of the man with bigger and bigger barns, and the rich young ruler, and so many others who tried to use God's power for their own profit.

God rushes to the aid only of those who *sacrifice* for Him. His help is not to be bought at any price.

Possessions and Power. Ensworth Reisner writes of the temptations of possessions and power: "We don't think of prosperity as being particularly deadly, but it can be. It took a radio and television personality to bring it home to me. I heard Dave Garroway quoting some government figures showing that the prosperous Americans spent twenty times as much for luxury items as they spent for education; two and a half times as much on liquor as on health, welfare and religion put together. These simple effects of prosperity can be more . . . dangerous to America than can communism or Russia. Yet are there many of us who would not enjoy being tempted by prosperity? Lord, help us not to be led into temptation!"

Mothballs. "In *Reader's Digest* several years ago there was an article on our rusty and leaky Merchant Marine fleet. It stated that after World War II 5,500 American flagships were swathed in cocoons of grease and mothballed in shipping boneyards. By September of 1966, 135 had been resurrected for sailing to Vietnam. Their repairs cost one billion two hundred thirty thousand dollars. A Bethlehem Steel Corporation shipbuilding executive described their condition: 'The preservative grease on the hull and superstructure had usually hardened and could be removed only by sandblasting or with chemicals.' It is a tragic and sickening picture of our once-proud maritime condition.

"I could not, however, help thinking that this is what happens to a man when he denies his destiny and mothballs his purpose. Man was made for climbing, for doing, for viewing life from the top. *When he becomes content with compromise,* then he loses the desire to do his best, even if no one is looking. When he hears no distant drummer because he has stopped up his ears with mediocrity, he becomes a leaky pipeline to God until one day he is no pipeline at all, and by the time that has happened he probably has forgotten how to call the plumber."—Neil Wyrick, Jr., in *The Presbyterian Outlook,* February 26, 1968.

Perspective. "Anyone who has struggled with temptation knows how easy it is to rationalize. 'Everybody is doing it today," you tell yourself. To put your temptation in proper perspective, ask yourself these questions:

1. If I engage in this activity, will it degrade my own or someone else's personality?
2. Once begun, where will this activity lead me?
3. Could my engaging in this activity cause someone else to stumble?
4. Would I be willing to permit those I love to engage in this activity?
5. If I yield to this temptation, will it meet the standards of God's will for my life?"—*But God Can,* by Robert V. Ozment (Fleming H. Revell Company).

Parable. "I read the other day about some safe-crackers in a little town in Canada who broke into a business office and used so much dynamite to blow the safe that it destroyed the thirty-six dollars in bills they might have had, caused two thousand dollars' worth of damage to the office—and they found five cents!"—Source unknown.

If Jesus had fallen for the devil's temptations, He would have blown His kingdom to bits before He started—and gotten something hardly worth a nickel in return. That's the way temptation works!

Sentence Sermon to Remember: Temptations are like tramps; treat them kindly and they return, bringing others with them.—*The Link.*

Questions for Pupils on the Next Lesson: 1. Is it possible for us to love those with whom our country is at war? 2. What did Jesus mean by, "Judge not . . . ?" 3. Is Jesus' principle of love *too* revolutionary? 4. Are there any limitations to a Christian's charity? 5. How did Jesus' idea of righteousness differ from that of His Jewish contemporaries? 6. For what reason should we be merciful, according to Jesus? 7. Is the Golden Rule religious or ethical teaching?

LESSON V—JANUARY 2

JESUS TEACHES THE WAY OF LOVE

Background Scripture: Luke 6
Devotional Reading: I Corinthians 13

KING JAMES VERSION

LUKE 6 27 But I say unto you which hear, Love your enemies, do good to them which hate you,

28 Bless them that curse you, and pray for them which despitefully use you.

29 And unto him that smiteth thee on the one cheek offer also the other; and him that taketh away thy cloak forbid not to take thy coat also.

30 Give to every man that asketh of thee; and of him that taketh away thy goods ask them not again.

31 And as ye would that men should do to you, do ye also to them likewise.

32 For if ye love them which love you, what thank have ye? for sinners also love those that love them.

33 And if ye do good to them which do good to you, what thank have ye? for sinners also do even the same.

34 And if ye lend to them of whom ye hope to receive, what thank have ye? for sinners also lend to sinners, to receive as much again.

35 But love ye your enemies, and do good, and lend, hoping for nothing again; and your reward shall be great, and ye shall be the children of the Highest: for he is kind unto the unthankful and to the evil.

36 Be ye therefore merciful, as your Father also is merciful.

37 Judge not, and ye shall not be judged: condemn not, and ye shall not be condemned: forgive, and ye shall be forgiven:

38 Give, and it shall be given unto you; good measure, pressed down, and shaken together, and running over, shall men give into your bosom. For with the same measure that ye mete withal it shall be measured to you again.

REVISED STANDARD VERSION

LUKE 6 27 "But I say to you that hear, Love your enemies, do good to those who hate you, 28 bless those who curse you, pray for those who abuse you. 29 To him who strikes you on the cheek, offer the other also; and from him who takes away your cloak do not withhold your coat as well. 30 Give to every one who begs from you; and of him who takes away your goods, do not ask them again. 31 And as you wish that men would do to you, do so to them.

32 "If you love those who love you, what credit is that to you? For even sinners love those who love them. 33 And if you do good to those who do good to you, what credit is that to you? For even sinners do the same. 34 And if you lend to those from whom you hope to receive, what credit is that to you? Even sinners lend to sinners, to receive as much again. 35 But love your enemies, and do good, and lend, expecting nothing in return; and your reward will be great, and you will be sons of the Most High; for he is kind to the ungrateful and the selfish. 36 Be merciful, even as your Father is merciful.

37 "Judge not, and you will not be judged; condemn not, and you will not be condemned; forgive, and you will be forgiven; 38 give, and it will be given to you; good measure, pressed down, shaken together, running over, will be put into your lap. For the measure you give will be the measure you get back."

MEMORY SELECTION: As ye would that men should do to you, do ye also to them likewise. Luke 6:31.

BACKGROUND

Luke leads us quickly, almost too quickly, into the preaching of Jesus. As Luke tells the story, Jesus went into a mountain place to pray alone; this was the moment when His ministry began, and He approached it by way of communion with the Father. In the morning, He chose twelve disciples, "whom also he named apostles" (6:13). Then "he came down with them, and stood in the plain . . ." (6:17). The "plain" could have been a level spot between two peaks or hills; here He preached to them, and to "a great multitude of people . . . which came to hear him, and to be healed of their diseases." He preached to them what has been called the Sermon on the Plain.

Was this Luke's abbreviated account of the Sermon on the Mount? It would seem so. The setting is the same—a place called the Horns of Hattin, a level place between two hills at the foot of a mountain. Luke does not give us as much of the sermon as Matthew gives; it is a partial collection of the same materials in Matthew's version, and Luke scatters other parts of Matthew's version through his Gospel.

Whether the two sermons are different sermons, or two versions of the same sermon, it began and ended with a word that has become the password of the Christian faith: *love.*

NOTES ON THE PRINTED TEXT

I. But I say unto you which hear, Love your enemies, do good to them which hate you, Luke 6:27. This word "love" is often a word of derision for the enemies of Christianity, and, truth be told, the friends of Christianity have often made it quite the same thing! It has gained a sentimental, Pollyanna-ish, soft, mawkish tone. It has become almost an effeminate word. But for Jesus it was anything but that. When He said, "Love your enemies," He made of love a most heroic, courageous, masculine, challenging word. Just try loving your enemies if you think it is easy! It isn't enough, He said, to love your friends; the Christian must love his enemies. Love is not a weak sentiment; it is "good will in action for the good of others." Love is something you *do,* not something you *profess.* It is not passive; it is strong, aggressive action in a desire to redeem those who offend or insult us.

Love our enemies? We've tried hating our enemies, and it has left us in a horrible, global mess. Maybe, just maybe, we should have the courage to try Jesus' idea of so loving the enemy that he becomes our friend. It *has* been done; nations we once hated we now love! It has happened to individuals; atheists have gone to the cross and become believers!

In verses 20-30, Jesus gives four concrete illustrations of what He means by love in action. If a man strikes you, don't descend to his level by striking back. It takes far more courage *not* to retaliate, but if you can do it, you prove that you are the better man. If a man steals your cloak, give him your coat also; he needs clothes more desperately than *you* do. A clerk in a department store said to us of shoplifters, "We often see them steal, but we don't arrest; the thief must need what he steals more than we do!" Do you "buy that?" Jesus did!

Give to the beggar; he may be a fraud, a profiteer capitalizing on human sympathy—but he *may* be one who will be hungry if you do not help him. You never know! What you give is a pittance, anyway; you will never miss it. "And when a man has taken what belongs to you, don't demand it back" (Phillips' translation). We know a superintendent of a rescue mission who became that because a rich man refused to prosecute him for stealing the rich man's silver and financed his education instead! It does work, but few there be who dare try it. . . .

Jesus sums it all up in verse 31: the Golden Rule. That rule wasn't original with Him; Hillel the great Jewish teacher, Philo of Alexandria, the Stoics and Confucius, all stated the same rule but *negatively:* "do *not* do unto others. . . ." Jesus made it positive; He suggested that good Christian conduct does not consist in not doing evil but in actively doing *good.* Millions say they believe it; few actually care to live by the rule.

II. For if you love those who love you, what credit is that to you? Luke 6:32. In verses 32-36, Jesus tells why He believed in this sort of love-in-action. *He believed in it because it is a principle rooted in God.* God loves like this; therefore men should love like this, therefore men *should imitate God.* This is love at its highest—at its divine best. It is also perfectly *unselfish* love. It asks nothing in return. It denies all selfishness. It isn't love expended in order to get love or anything else in return. Love or righteous living extended for the sake of getting some sort of reward is not love at all; it is just another form of selfishness. *Love others because God loves you.* Be merciful to others because God has been merciful to you; refuse mercy to others, and you are a greater atheist than the man who doesn't even believe in the existence of God! Don't "give out" in order to *get* something; any sinner can do that. Love your enemies because God loves them; He is as kind and merciful to the wicked as He is to you.

III. Judge not, and ye shall not be judged, Luke 6:37. Why shouldn't men judge? Because God and God alone is the final judge of all men and all behavior. *He* forgives, or levies justice; it is His prerogative, not ours. What makes us think that we have any right to steal that divine prerogative? Who or what gives us the authority to condemn or avenge? "Vengeance is mine, saith *the Lord.*" God alone knows the heart of man, the good and evil circumstances that fill that heart and direct that behavior; He alone is able to judge, approve or condemn.

What Jesus is saying is that the secret of Christian living is to forgive freely and to give freely, not in order to get forgiveness or to gain the whole world, but because God has forgiven us and given us treasure beyond counting. When we do that, the reward will be unbelievable, even though we have never thought of any reward. Dr. Barclay says: "Verse 38 has the strange phrase, 'People will give into your bosom' (*English*

Revised Version). The Jew wore a long loose robe down to the feet, and round the waist was a girdle. The robe could be pulled up so that the bosom of the robe above the girdle formed a kind of outsize pocket in which things could be carried. So the modern equivalent of the phrase would be, 'People will fill your pocket.'" *The Gospel of Luke,* Daily Bible Study Series, by William Barclay. Quoted by permission of John Knox Press, publishers.

That says it well!

SUGGESTIONS TO TEACHERS

A friend recently said to us, "This Sermon on the Mount stuff is certainly beautiful, but in our kind of world it's just impossible to practice." *Is it?* Is it really impossible to turn the other cheek, to love a man who has been your enemy? I asked myself this about my friend: "Had he ever really *tried* to put the principles of the Sermon on the Mount to work— or was he just too lazy and selfish even to try?"

Was Jesus just daydreaming when He preached this sermon? Is it too much to expect of humanity? Is it more blessed to hate than to love? Is forgiveness even of one's enemies a sign of weakness or a sign of *maturity?*

There is more revolutionary dynamite in the Sermon on the Mount than there is in communism. If we sincerely put these principles of Jesus to work—would we have had communism at all?

Where are we putting these principles to work today?

TOPIC FOR ADULTS
LOVE IS . . .

The Other Cheek. Before Martin Luther King was murdered an Australian observer wrote this about him:

"The son of a minister and descendant of slaves, Martin Luther King has never lifted a hand against white people, although he has been knifed and beaten and his home has been bombed. He has insisted on turning the other cheek, whatever they did. When the "Freedom Riders" arrived in Montgomery and were mercilessly beaten by white hoodlums, the 50,000 Negroes in the city, heeding the advice of the young preacher, clenched their fists and stoically refused to join battle. So they are winning the admiration and sympathy of the vast majority of white Americans. Their battle is being won, not by violence, but by turning the other cheek to the many insults which whites see fit to mete out."—*Difficult Sayings of Jesus,* by Gordon Powell (Fleming H. Revell Company).

True—but what happened after Dr. King was shot? The black extremists took over; they turned to violence, riots, arson, threats of armed guerrilla warfare. And when they did that, they set their cause back a hundred years. They lost both the respect and the co-operation of white people who had suffered much to help them, but now hesitated to help at all.

While the blacks were turning the other cheek, they gained more freedom than they had known for over a century. But now . . . ?

Judging. " 'Judge not.' But the manager of a baseball team must judge, for example, when to send in a new pitcher; the voters must judge between candidates and platforms; and a judge on the bench must judge as to the innocence or guilt of an accused man. Can we help judging? No.

"But our English word, 'judge,' is like the Greek word in this instance: it has many meanings. The context . . . leaves little doubt as to Christ's meaning: 'Do not judge censoriously.' Yesterday I heard a mother say to her teen-age daughter, 'Don't go picking people apart.' That is the meaning. 'Picking people apart seems to us not a very serious sin, or we would not spend so much time in carping gossip. But Jesus wanted us to understand that it carries the issues of life and death.'"

"Picking people apart itself makes our sin as big as a log for . . . we thus deeply wound people: 'Give a dog a bad name, and you hang him.' The folk in a French village, so the story goes, condemned one neighbor as a miser, only to find on his death that the money he had (stingily?) saved he had willed to the village to build an acqueduct from a mountain lake so that the village might always have a supply of pure water. Carping criticism increases our sin until it is like the main beam of a house." —From a sermon by Dr. George A. Buttrick.

And *what* a house!

Love or Go Mad. "England was my last stop before going home. The hotel was next to a bombed-out crater where, perhaps, a beautiful building had once stood. I stared out of the window, and wondered how it must have been back there in 1944 to have no place of safety as Hitler's bombs fell. . . . The English hostess of the hotel had joined me as I stood gazing at the empty crater. 'Don't you find yourself still hating those who did this to your country?' I asked.

"She looked at me for a moment and replied, 'No, not now. At first I did. But spending night after night in bomb shelters, I discovered that one had to acquire a faith in a power greater than himself or go berserk. I learned to pray, as many did, and God became real to me. I found that hatred had to go if I was to have peace.' Amazing!"—Author unknown.

Love or go mad! So much of our world seems to have gone mad today —and we wonder why!

Lord, Catch Me! Believe it or not, a 12-year-old girl named Teresa Turner, in Torrance, California, wrote this about love:

"Love is an emotion a friend has for a friend, a brother has for a brother, a mother has for a child. It is an emotion God has for each of us. Love is a warm, wonderful glow. It is a power that sweeps the world, catching men in its glory. Oh, Lord, catch me!"

Can you beat it?

Questions for Pupils on the Next Lesson: 1. Who was the Levi of Luke 5:29? 2. Why was Jesus criticized for eating in Levi's house? 3. How did Jesus answer the criticism? 4. How many publicans attend your church? 5. Is Christian compassion a passive characteristic, or an aggressive one? 6. What sympathy did Jesus offer the widow of Nain at her son's funeral? 7. What compassion have you offered to someone else in the last month?

TOPIC FOR YOUTH
LOVE IS . . .

The First Stone. ". . . we want . . . people to overlook our faults and forgive us for our failures. If we do that for others, they will do it for us. The Golden Rule will surely work.

"Have you ever visited Lincoln's tomb at Springfield? There have been many wonderful things said about Lincoln but the appraisal of Lincoln selected to be carved on his tomb is this: 'Now he belongs to the ages.' Do you recall who said that about Lincoln? It was Stanton, the same Stanton who once referred to Lincoln as 'this great ignoramus from Illinois, a baboon who doesn't have brains enough to be President.'

"But Lincoln kept Stanton in office because, he said, 'He is the greatest Secretary of War we ever had.' Lincoln looked beyond Stanton's faults and saw his real abilities. Eventually Stanton did the same for Lincoln.

"I know a man who keeps on his desk an ordinary rock. He is very careful to keep it in plain view and within easy reach. He doesn't keep it there for the purpose of hitting someone with it. On the contrary, it is there to stop him when he is tempted to hit someone—to hurl a criticism, to judge too quickly, to return evil for evil. This man was deeply moved by the story of that one who had done wrong and a crowd which would have stoned her to death. He keeps the stone on his desk so that when he is tempted to stone another, it is his reminder of Jesus' words, 'He that is without sin among you, let him first cast a stone at her.' "—C. L. Allen.

Sound (?) Advice. "An itinerant preacher one night read a passage to a small group of listeners wherein they are admonished to turn the other cheek. Then, closing the Bible, he began his interpretation.

" 'Now, brethren and sisters, the Good Book tells us that if an enemy smacks you on one cheek, you turn the other cheek and let him smack you on that. But, brethren and sisters, the third lick, *the third lick,* I say, *belongs to you.*' "—*Coronet,* April, 1958.

Funny? Not so funny. This is the preacher's idea, not Jesus' idea. Jesus didn't even strike back after being smitten on both cheeks.

But it is an idea widely accepted among some folks. Do you accept it?

Pompidou. Not so long ago, President Pompidou of France came to the United States for discussions with our President. His mission turned out to be almost a disaster; he was picketed, shouted at, jostled by Jewish crowds in our streets because France had recently sold war planes to Israel's enemies, the Arabs. It was perhaps the most discourteous reception ever afforded a foreign dignitary in our country.

Selling arms to any country is bad business—but, in all truth, we in the United States should think twice before condemning any foreign country for doing exactly what *we* have been doing for some time. It is the bitter truth that the United States sold arms to both Arabs and Israeli. The biggest and most prosperous "merchant of death" among nations selling arms to other nations is not France; two, the Soviet Union *and* the United States surpass all the others!

Judge not, that ye be not judged. Look in the mirror before you throw any stones.

Love. "I have an old-fashioned formula: it sounds corny, but I think we have to have more love in the world. By 'love' I mean the kind of affection that endears us to our brothers, of whatever color they are and whatever language they speak. We have to recognize them as human beings. We have to have compassion. We have to put ourselves in their place. I shorten all that down to love. It certainly isn't love in the sense that a man and a woman love, although that's part of it. It's love for the whole being and the whole scope of life, the whole respect for the inner man, for his spirit. Until we have that love, until it supplants greed and grasping and combativeness and abrasiveness, we're going to have trouble everywhere."—Roy Wilkins, in an interview in *Urban Review,* June, 1969.

Love Them. Once we asked our good friend Fulton Oursler, a great author and a good Roman Catholic, "Why does the Catholic church keep the institution of the confessional alive? A Catholic can commit all the sins in the catalogue, go to confession on Saturday and be forgiven of them all and the church knows that he is going out the next week and commit the same sins all over again."

"Ah," he said, "that is because the church is a mother to us. A mother knows, when she punishes her child for some misbehavior, that he will probably do it again. But she forgives him, and goes on trying. . . ."

That is good. Forgiveness, as Jesus saw it, is *divine.* God forgives us all —knowing well that we will stumble and fall again, but . . . He loves us. He hates the sin, but loves the sinner.

That is better than judging and condemning. . . .

Sentence Sermon to Remember: Live every day as if it were your last; do every job as if you were the boss; drive as if all vehicles were police cars; treat everyone else as if he were you.—*R & R Magazine.*

Questions for Pupils on the Next Lesson: 1. Was Jesus interested in any particular class of people more than in others? 2. What was the occupation of Levi? 3. Jesus talked often about taxes: why? 4. Why did Jesus defy convention and prejudice in order to eat in Levi's house? 5. True or false: "The widow's son was in a cataleptic trance"? 6. Why did Jesus perform the miracle at Nain? 7. Does He perform such miracles today?

LESSON VI—JANUARY 9

OUR COMPASSIONATE CHRIST
TEMPERANCE

Background Scripture: Luke 5:27-32; 7:11-23, 36-50; 10:25-37
Devotional Reading: Luke 10:25-37

KING JAMES VERSION

LUKE 5   29 And Levi made him a great feast in his own house: and there was a great company of publicans and of others that sat down with them.

30 But their scribes and Pharisees murmured against his disciples, saying, Why do ye eat and drink with publicans and sinners?

31 And Jesus answering said unto them, They that are whole need not a physician; but they that are sick.

32 I came not to call the righteous, but sinners to repentance.

LUKE 11   And it came to pass the day after, that he went into a city called Nain; and many of his disciples went with him, and much people.

12 Now when he came nigh to the gate of the city, behold, there was a dead man carried out, the only son of his mother, and she was a widow: and much people of the city was with her.

13 And when the Lord saw her, he had compassion on her, and said unto her, Weep not.

14 And he came and touched the bier: and they that bare him stood still. And he said, Young man, I say unto thee, Arise.

15 And he that was dead sat up, and began to speak. And he delivered him to his mother.

16 And there came a fear on all: and they glorified God, saying, That a great prophet is risen up among us; and, That God hath visited his people.

17 And this rumor of him went forth throughout all Judea, and throughout all the region round about.

REVISED STANDARD VERSION

LUKE 5   29 And Levi made him a great feast in his house; and there was a large company of tax collectors and others sitting at table with them. 30 And the Pharisees and their scribes murmured against his disciples, saying, "Why do you eat and drink with tax collectors and sinners?" 31 And Jesus answered them, "Those who are well have no need of a physician, but those who are sick; 32 I have not come to call the righteous, but sinners to repentance."

LUKE 7   11 Soon afterward he went to a city called Nain, and his disciples and a great crowd went with him. 12 As he drew near to the gate of the city, behold, a man who had died was being carried out, the only son of his mother, and she was a widow; and a large crowd from the city was with her. 13 And when the Lord saw her, he had compassion on her and said to her, "Do not weep." 14 And he came and touched the bier, and the bearers stood still. And he said, "Young man, I say to you, arise." 15 And the dead man sat up, and began to speak. And he gave him to his mother. 16 Fear seized them all; and they glorified God, saying, "A great prophet has arisen among us!" and "God has visited his people!" 17 And this report concerning him spread through the whole of Judea and all the surrounding country.

MEMORY SELECTION: *Those who are well have no need of a physician, but those who are sick; I have not come to call the righteous, but sinners to repentance.* Luke 5:31-32 (RSV).

HOME DAILY BIBLE READINGS

Jan. 3. M. *The Call of Matthew,* Matthew 9:9-13.
Jan. 4. T. *The Example of Christ,* Romans 15:1-6.
Jan. 5. W. *The Law of Love,* James 2:8-13.
Jan. 6. T. *Concern for Others,* Galatians 6:1-6.
Jan. 7. F. *The Mercies of God,* Psalm 103:6-13.
Jan. 8. S. *The Sinful Woman Forgiven,* Luke 7:36-50.
Jan. 9. S. *The Good Samaritan,* Luke 10:25-37.

BACKGROUND

It *must* have been a physician who wrote Luke 5 and Luke 7; these are chapters about healings, showing careful organization of a working staff interested in good health and the art of healing. Read Luke 5:1-26 for this background. Take especial care to see *who* were healed, and *why.*

Here we have a picture of the compassion of Jesus—a compassion that still walks the corridors of the modern hospital in His name and in His spirit. He *came* to heal, to comfort, to lift up and inspire. It was a compassion as wide and deep as the sea—limitless.

Jesus could get angry; usually, He was angry with the self-righteous. But He hadn't come to minister to the self-righteous, to the religiously proud and conceited. He came to be a great physician to those who were *sick.* And He asked no questions about creed or condition when He paused to heal. . . .

NOTES ON THE PRINTED TEXT

I. And Levi made him a great feast in his own house, Luke 5:20. Levi was Matthew; dual names are frequent in the New Testament. Matthew had been a tax collector before he accepted Christ. A tax collector! That made him the most unpopular man in town. *Any* tax collector was a parasite, a pariah, a leech, a traitor, a thief, in the eyes of the Jews. They were men of Jewish birth appointed (for a price), by the Romans to collect taxes for the empire. The highest bidder got the job—and proceeded to make himself a fortune at the expense of the people. The taxes they levied were unbelievable. There was a poll tax on both men and women, who paid just because they were alive. There were taxes on the ground they lived on, on the grain and fruit they raised, taxes for the use of the roads and highways, a tax of one per cent on every income. There were taxes on markets, on horses and carts, and beyond that there was extortion and graft. The people hated the tax collectors and the Pharisees despised them. They were excluded from the synagogue. They were about as popular as a Nazi in modern Jerusalem would be.

Matthew the collector—now Matthew the Christian—invited Jesus to a banquet in his house. At the banquet was "a great company of publicans"—Matthew's tax collecting pals. And Jesus *went,* and sat down with them to eat. In the East, to eat with a man was to accept him in fellowship, and here was Jesus accepting the tax collectors, eating with "evil" men.

The community was stunned; the Pharisees and the scribes were furious. This was *most* unorthodox. It was something good Jews *never* did. They demanded that Jesus tell them why He stopped to eat, to fellowship, with such unworthy and unclean rascals. And Jesus told them: "I came not to call the righteous, but sinners to repentance." Sinners! These were the people—the sick people—who needed Him most. The Pharisees thought they had no need of Jesus; they saw no need for Him, and so He could do little or nothing for them. But He could do a lot for men who *knew* they were sinners and needed help. Help He gave them, while the "respectable" people howled.

This was compassion—fighting, fearless compassion. Jesus loved the little men, the weak, burdened, sinning, sick men. He lived for them, even died for them. He was living evidence of God's compassion for men.

II. Now . . . there was a dead man carried out, the only son of his mother, and she was a widow, Luke 7:12. Is there anything worse than that? The only son of a widow—dead! No sorrow in the world is equal to this.

It happened at Nain—a day's journey from Capernaum. It was a funeral procession, heart-rending with its wailing by professional mourners, the melancholy music of flutes and clashing cymbals, and the neighbors doing their sorrowful best to hold up and comfort a widowed mother now left alone and desperate in a bitterly cold world. What can be said to a woman like this? What can be done for such sorrow?

Most of us try to *say* something that we hope will "comfort." Jesus said almost nothing: only two words, "Weep not." That was all. But no—not quite all; if it had been all, the incident would never have been reported in Luke's Gospel. Jesus did more. *In compassion for the widow,* He turned to the bier on which the young man lay, and said *to the young man,* "I say unto thee, arise!" And he that was dead "sat up, and began to speak."

Some "explainers" of the incident would tell us that the young man was in a "cataleptic trance," and that Jesus, with his deeply perceptive and penetrating eyes, saw this. But Luke doesn't say that. Luke says the man was *dead.* Take it or leave it, that is what the record says, and that is what the early church believed. To the first Christians it was a historic event. And it was an event that brought many of them to confess Jesus as the Messiah. If it had been only a man brought out of a trance, we would think that Jesus would have said something about premature burial. He didn't.

"And he delivered him to his mother" (verse 15). Get things in order here. First, there was the bitter *human* agony and pathos of the mourners —especially of the mother. It was to *her* more than to the dead son that Jesus extended His compassion. To His compassion He added His power over death. "Explain" it as you wish, the stubborn fact remains that Jesus gave life to one marked for death.

Even the people were impressed with that power, with that act of Messiahship. They were first gripped by fear; then they cried, ". . . a great prophet is risen up among us; and . . . God hath visited his people" (verse 16). Phillips translates this, ". . . and God has turned his face toward his people." That was all that was really important— God in Jesus Christ turning His compassionate face toward a people living in the darkness of death and sorrow.

Do we, with all our scientific knowledge, with all our professional medical and surgical ability to prolong life—do we understand Jesus as well as they understood Him that day?

SUGGESTIONS TO TEACHERS

Years ago we had a great friend in a good doctor; in those years we had little money—and the doctor refused to let us pay him for his services until we had the money to pay! He gave a dollar a day out of every five to a charity clinic to heal people who *never* paid him. He said, "This is why I became a doctor."

Jesus was just such a physician. He played no favorites; He was more interested in the poor and in the outcasts of society than in those who were "well off." He gave help without discrimination; He never knew a color line.

As Christians, He asks that we do that, too. He demands not subscription to belief in a creed, but *compassion for others.* Self-centered Christians get in His way. Those who are compassionate in their personal, family, church and community relations are *His* chosen people.

He doesn't ask which church we belong to; He asks, "What are you doing for me in love and compassion—and for your fellow man?" It is the first rule of the Christian life, it is the key to the kingdom. . . .

TOPIC FOR ADULTS
OUR COMPASSIONATE CHRIST

Matthew. Matthew was a man despised and rejected. Nobody had any compassion for him—except one man from Galilee. Dorothy Sayres tells of Christ's compassion for Matthew, and of what it did for him:

" 'I shan't forget my first sight of him neither' [says Matthew]. 'Well, I'll tell you, I was a tax-gatherer . . . one of the dirty dogs that works for the government and makes his profit out of selling his countrymen. . . . When he came down our street the other day, I don't mind telling you I'd had a pretty good morning. . . . And I looked up—and there he was. "Hullo," I thought, "here's the Prophet. I suppose he'll start calling me names like the rest of 'em. Let him. Hard words break no bones." So I stared at him, and he stared at me—seemed as though his eyes were going straight through me and through my ledgers, and reading all the bits that weren't for publication. And somehow or other he made me feel dirty. That's all. Just plain dirty. I started shuffling my feet. And he smiled—you know, the way he smiles sometimes all of a sudden—and he says, "Follow me." I couldn't believe my ears. I tumbled out of my desk, and away he went up the street, and I went after him. I could hear people laughing—and somebody spat at me— but I didn't seem to care. . . .

" 'I said to him, "Master, I'm coming with you." And he said, "Come along" ' "—*The Man Born to be King*, by Dorothy Sayres, pp. 109-10. Quoted by permission of Harper and Row, publishers.

He came to do just that for Matthew—and all others despised and rejected. He had a *redemptive* interest in them. . . .

Our Drunks. How do we treat our drunks—our alcoholics? Generally, we avoid them, stay out of their way, laugh at their pitiful antics, tell ourselves that it's a man's own business; if he wants to get drunk, not ours. If he's as weak as that, well. . . .

Earl (Red) Cook was a gambler in Phenix City, Alabama, in the early 1950's. He went to prison on a murder charge, sentenced to ten years as a confirmed alcoholic. It looked like the end of the road—but an itinerant preacher got into his cell, prayed with him, led him in compassion to the compassionate Christ—and Earl "bought" it. For the next nine years he was the prison chaplain's assistant, organizing prayer and Bible study groups behind the bars. Released, he became a counselor with Alabama's Division of Alcoholism. . . .

Compassion did it. An unhonored and unsung and unknown preacher proved that Christ cared about Earl Cook, and. . . .

Not many drunks are so fortunate—and not many Christians are like that preacher. . . .

Prejudice. Jesus faced bitter prejudice in the scribes and Pharisees; it was both religious and racial prejudice. It did much toward nailing Him to the cross.

Sam Levenson says of prejudice today: "Of all the obstacles to a human being's growth to full stature prejudice is the worst. It destroys more individuals than war. It is hereditary, not in the blood stream, but in the stream of conversation within the home. Out of the mouths of babes come adult slanders, repeated word for word."

Prejudice isn't born in a new-born baby; it is *taught*. Bigotry is the product of bad education. People who hate other people are taught to hate them.

How go the conversations in your home?

Caring. In our time, something has happened to the teaching of compassion. We say we love the compassionate Jesus, but we read only the other day that while a U.S. Senator from Mississippi collects $13,000 *a month* for not raising cotton a kid from that same state gets $8.50 *a month* welfare.

Why?

Condolence, Compassion. When a daughter of Senator Percy of Illinois was cruelly murdered the whole country was shocked, and hundreds of thousands wrote the Senator in condolence. Mr. Percy told James M. Minifie, the political analyst, during Percy's campaign for election to the Senate, that of all the thousands of letters he received, the most comforting one came from Robert Kennedy. When Minifie told Mr. Kennedy about that, Kennedy replied, "We've had more experience."

Someone asked Senator Kennedy's widow after *his* murder whether she hated his killer. She replied, "No, I pity him."

The word for it is (Christian) compassion. Judge not . . . !

Questions for Pupils on the Next Lesson: 1. Did those healed by Jesus always have faith in Him? 2. How do you explain the act of the woman touching Jesus' robe? 3. What qualifications do you look for in a "divine" healer today? 4. Would Christ's failure to heal you destroy your faith in Him? 5. What is your reaction to the reports of the healings at

Lourdes? 6. Is the modern surgeon a worker of miracles? 7. Was the child of Jairus dead or only in a trance?

TOPIC FOR YOUTH
JESUS' CONCERN FOR EVERYONE

Shoes. "Jo-Jo was pointed out to me as the president of the Coney Island Dragons, one of the largest gangs in the city. The boy who pointed him out wouldn't introduce us. 'Little Jo-Jo might not like it, Dave.' So I walked up to this boy alone and stuck out my hand.

"Jo-Jo's first act was to slap me across the palm. Then he leaned over and spit on my shoes. In the gangs this is the highest sign of contempt. He walked away and sat down on a bench with his back to me.

"I walked over and sat beside him. I said, 'Jo-Jo, where do you live?'

" 'Preacher, I don't want to talk to you. I don't want to have anything to do with you.'

" 'But I want to have something to do with you,' I said. 'I'm going to stay here until I find out where you live.'

" 'Preacher,' said Jo-Jo, 'you're sitting in my parlor.'

" 'Well, where do you go when it rains?'

"He said, 'I move down to my suite in the subway.'

"Jo-Jo had on a pair of old canvas shoes. His toe was sticking out on the right foot and he had a dirty black shirt on and a too-big pair of khaki trousers. He looked down at my shoes. They were brand new. . . .

"Jo-Jo said, 'Look, rich man, it's all right for you to come here to New York and talk big about God changing lives. You've got new shoes and you've got a suit of clothes that match. Look at me! I'm a bum. There are ten kids in my family. We're on relief. They kicked me out—there wasn't enough food to go around.'

"Jo-Jo was right. Then and there, on the public park bench, I took off my shoes and asked him to try them on.

" 'What's the gimmick? What are you trying to prove? That you got a heart, or something? I'm not going to put your stinking shoes on.'

" 'You've been griping about shoes. Put them on.'

"Jo-Jo said, 'I ain't never had new shoes.'

" 'Put them on.'

"So, sullenly, Jo-Jo put on the shoes.

"Then I got up and walked away. I walked down the block in my stocking feet, about two blocks, to the car. It was quite a circus, people laughing and joking, and as I got to the car, Little Jo-Jo came up behind me and said, 'You forgot your shoes.'

" 'They're your shoes.' I got into the car.

" 'Preacher,' Jo-Jo said, reaching inside the open window, 'I forgot to shake your hand.'

"So we shook. Then I said, 'Look, you don't have any place to live. I'm bumming a bed myself right now. But there's a couch out in the living room. Maybe the folks who took me in will take you in too. Let's go ask them.'

" 'O.K.,' said Jo-Jo, just like that."—David Wilkerson, in *The Cross and the Switchblade* (Fleming H. Revell Company).

Helps. Dr. Harrison Ray Anderson offers "a handful of helps" for anyone trying to help an alcoholic:

1. Bring yourself up to date with the new facts about alcoholism.
2. Encourage a meeting at which a trained person can speak and answer questions.
3. Find the persons around you who can help and use them in a threefold approach to a threefold problem—physical, social, moral.
4. Know the active groups at work in this field—Alcoholics Anonymous —Alateen—Alanon, and others. Use them.
5. Ask yourself what position you, a Christian (not the other man) should take—heavy drinker, social drinker, abstainer?—*Presbyterian Outlook,* December 22, 1969.

Fools. Many of us stay away from funerals—even from "paying our respects" to the sorrowing *before* the funeral—we feel so helpless in trying to help! Others rush in and say the wrong thing! What is right for us to do?

"Stephen Paget, referring to Pope's familiar lines, 'Fools rush in where angels fear to tread,' makes this turn of thought: 'I am sure that angels rush in where fools fear to tread. There are many fools who are afraid of treading anywhere. . . . For instance, when the people next door lost their only child, there was a fool who left his card because he was afraid to go in: but there was an angel who rushed in and broke down and cried, so that the other two found their tears; it was time they did, or one of them would have gone out of her mind.' "—Robert Luccock, in *Christian Herald,* May, 1969.

Notice how Jesus approached it: He did not rush in, but neither did He hesitate to go; and when He went, He was all compassion, not for the dead son, but for the living mother. We don't have to "be sure of saying the right thing" when death comes to our friends; just the fact that we *go,* even though we can say nothing, shows the compassion the sorrowing ones need!

Sentence Sermon to Remember: Next to love, sympathy is the divinest passion of the human heart.—Edmund Burke.

Questions for Pupils on the Next Lesson: 1. Were Christ's healings mostly *mental* or *physical* healings? 2. Can anyone with a good Christian faith heal the sick? 3. Did Jesus heal people only because they were sick, or for some other purpose? 4. Who was Jairus? 5. What do you think was the matter with the daughter of Jairus? 6. What would a modern doctor call "an issue of blood" (Luke 8:43)? 7. Tell the story of Aimée Semple McPherson; was she a sincere healer?

LESSON VII—JANUARY 16

THE HEALING CHRIST

Background Scripture: Luke 4:31-40; 5:12-26; 8:1-3, 26-56
Devotional Reading: Isaiah 61:1-7

KING JAMES VERSION

LUKE 8 40 And it came to pass, that, when Jesus was returned, the people gladly received him: for they were all waiting for him.

41 And, behold, there came a man named Jairus, and he was a ruler of the synagogue; and he fell down at Jesus' feet, and besought him that he would come into his house:

42 For he had one only daughter, about twelve years of age, and she lay a dying. But as he went the people thronged him.

43 And a woman having an issue of blood twelve years, which had spent all her living upon physicians, neither could be healed of any,

44 Came behind him, and touched the border of his garment: and immediately her issue of blood stanched.

45 And Jesus said, Who touched me? When all denied, Peter and they that were with him said, Master, the multitude throng thee and press thee, and sayest thou, Who touched me?

46 And Jesus said, Somebody hath touched me: for I perceive that virtue is gone out of me.

47 And when the woman saw that she was not hid, she came trembling, and falling down before him, she declared unto him before all the people for what cause she had touched him, and how she was healed immediately.

48 And he said unto her, Daughter, be of good comfort: thy faith hath made thee whole; go in peace.

49 While he yet spake, there cometh one from the ruler of the synagogue's house, saying to him, Thy daughter is dead; trouble not the Master.

50 But when Jesus heard it, he answered him, saying, Fear not: believe only, and she shall be made whole.

51 And when he came into the house, he suffered no man to go in, save Peter, and James, and John, and the father and the mother of the maiden.

REVISED STANDARD VERSION

LUKE 8 40 Now when Jesus returned, the crowd welcomed him, for they were all waiting for him. 41 And there came a man named Jairus, who was a ruler of the synagogue; and falling at Jesus' feet he besought him to come to his house, 42 for he had an only daughter, about twelve years of age, and she was dying.

As he went, the people pressed round him. 43 And a woman who had had a flow of blood for twelve years and could not be healed by any one, 44 came up behind him, and touched the fringe of his garment; and immediately her flow of blood ceased. 45 And Jesus said, "Who was it that touched me?" When all denied it, Peter said, "Master, the multitudes surround you and press upon you!" 46 But Jesus said, "Some one touched me; for I perceive that power has gone forth from me." 47 And when the woman saw that she was not hidden, she came trembling, and falling down before him declared in the presence of all the people why she had touched him, and how she had been immediately healed. 48 And he said to her, "Daughter, your faith has made you well; go in peace."

49 While he was still speaking, a man from the ruler's house came and said, "Your daughter is dead; do not trouble the Teacher any more." 50 But Jesus on hearing this answered him, "Do not fear; only believe, and she shall be well." 51 And when he came to the house, he permitted no one to enter with him, except Peter and John and James, and the father and mother of the child. 52 And all were weeping and bewailing her; but he said, "Do not weep; for she is not

52 And all wept, and bewailed her: but he said, Weep not; she is not dead, but sleepeth.

53 And they laughed him to scorn, knowing that she was dead.

54 And he put them all out, and took her by the hand, and called, saying, Maid, arise.

55 And her spirit came again, and she arose straightway: and he commanded to give her meat.

56 And her parents were astonished: but he charged them that they should tell no man what was done.

dead but sleeping." 53 And they laughed at him, knowing that she was dead. 54 But taking her by the hand he called, saying, "Child, arise." 55 And her spirit returned, and she got up at once; and he directed that something should be given her to eat. 56 And her parents were amazed; but he charged them to tell no one what had happened.

MEMORY SELECTION: *Thy faith hath made thee whole; go in peace.* Luke 8:48.

HOME DAILY BIBLE READINGS

Jan. 10. M. Miracles at Capernaum, Luke 4:31-40.
Jan. 11. T. The Leper Cleansed, Luke 5:12-16.
Jan. 12. W. A Paralytic Healed, Luke 5:17-26.
Jan. 13. T. A Mind Restored, Luke 8:26-39.
Jan. 14. F. On the Sabbath, Luke 13:10-17.
Jan. 15. S. The Ten Lepers, Luke 17:11-19.
Jan. 16. S. Good News for Needy Men, Isaiah 61:1-7.

BACKGROUND

This is one lesson for which the teacher *must* read the Home Daily Bible Readings. All the Readings except the concluding one from Isaiah are in Luke, and all deal with the work of the healing Christ. Again, it took a sensitive physician, aware of the pain and suffering of his people, to write these stories of Christ the Healer. Ask yourself this—and ask your students to read the Daily Readings in *class* and then ask themselves the same question: *how many of those healed were believers in Christ*—believers *before* they were healed?

In this period of Jewish history and society physicians were a luxury few could afford. Most people were poor; many were outcasts, and few, if any, cared whether they lived or died! Medicine as we know it was unknown then. Many healers were charlatans. And many died who should have recovered. In those days life was grim. But, with the coming of Jesus, *sorrow and suffering and even death were far less grim.*

NOTES ON THE PRINTED TEXT

I. . . . the people gladly received him: for they were all waiting for him, Luke 8:40. Jesus and His disciples had been in "the country of the Gadarenes." Look at your map. Find the city, or town of Gergesa. It was from Gergesa, in the land of the Gadaranes, or Gerasenes, that Jesus set sail for home—probably for Capernaum, at the upper end of the Lake of Galilee, where the people were "waiting for him." They waited in almost painful expectancy; they had heard of His healings in towns and cities around the lake. The waiting people remind us of the crowds that today await miracles of healing at Lourdes. Among them were people with all manner of diseases, and some healthy ones who were merely curious, and some who were hostile. Among those who were sick and in need of healing there was budding faith and a last hope of being made whole again by this healing miracle-worker from Nazareth.

Two of them were used by Luke to illustrate the method and mind of Jesus the Healer. One was an obscure, unnamed woman with a "flow of blood" which, over twelve long years, no physician had been able to heal. The other was a well-placed, successful and highly respected man named Jairus, who held the honored post of "ruler of the synagogue." They were alike in some ways and different in others. Let us look at the woman first.

With the shadow of doom and death in her eyes, she came up behind Jesus and touched the fringe of His garment. What a gesture that was! Without saying a word, she reached out of her prison house of pain and despair and wordlessly, tearfully, hopefully, just touched the hem of His gown. Was it desperation or faith? Probably it was both. . . .

Jesus did not see her; she came up behind Him. But, with His divine intuition, He knew somehow that someone had touched Him. He asks, wistfully, "Who touched me?" Those packed in around Him denied that *they* had done it; the woman hid her face and at the moment said nothing. Peter was there, and Peter was angry. (Naturally!) Angry and a little incredulous. He resented the pressure of the crowd; why didn't they leave Jesus alone? Hands off, people!

But Jesus' heart had been touched as well as His clothing. His *heart* knew, and His heart responded to the touch, no matter whether it was from faith or despair. "I perceive that power has gone forth from me," He said. Power to heal, even though He could not see the pain-filled face. Perhaps the woman was thinking of some magic in the gown or in the Christ; but Jesus wasn't bothered even by that. The fact that she had touched Him was enough. It was faith, however blind, however inspired. "And immediately her flow of blood ceased" (RSV).

Think of this: to Jesus, the act of healing a physical disorder was *not as important as the woman's relationship to Him!* He took that little ounce of faith and built on it; He wanted to lead her into full confession and fellowship with Him as Messiah. Once she had that, she would be restored spiritually as well as physically. She was restored both ways: ". . . thy faith hath made thee whole; go in peace." Peace for the first time in twelve years!

II. *And Jairus . . . fell down at Jesus' feet, and besought him that he would come into his house,* Luke 8:41. The healing of the woman took place while Jesus was on His way to the home of Jairus, whose daughter was dying. At least, everyone thought she was dying; some said she was already dead (verse 49). Like the woman with the issue of blood, Jairus reached out for Jesus as a last resort. Up to the moment, as ruler of a synagogue, it is not very likely that he had much use for the rebel prophet and healer from Nazareth. But now death had struck in his own house, at his own twelve-year-old daughter. Come to my house, Jesus Christ! In just such a moment, millions since have asked Him in prayer to come to their house.

Jesus looked at the man and said, "Fear not: believe only, and she

shall be made whole." He went home with Jairus the Jew; He looked
at the child and said, "Weep not; she is not dead, but sleepeth." Dead?
The wailers had already arrived; in Palestine burial had to come within
hours after death, and many, the scholars say, were buried before they
were actually dead. But Jesus did not accept the fact of death—here
or at any other time. He touched the girl's hand, "and she arose straightway." He ordered that she be *fed!*

Some say, "The girl was not dead at all; she was only in a trance,
and about to be buried alive, and Jesus knew it. . . ." Maybe so; Luke
doesn't say so. To him, it was no "miracle of diagnosis." Luke accepted
it as a demonstration of the power of Jesus over the last enemy, death.

There is another important angle in this story. It is the angle of Jairus.
Here was a man born a Jew, raised in the old Jewish faith, a "one hundred percenter," in the best sense. "In his hour of need," says Campbell
Morgan, "he pocketed his pride and asked for help." In spite of the
funeral arrangements already being made, he hoped against hope, and
he centered that hope on Jesus. Jesus did what He did in that house
for a double purpose: to restore life to the child and to build the faith
of Jairus into complete and lasting devotion.

When some of us were young, we used to sing a hymn, "You never
know what Jesus can do." We don't sing it much any more—and some
of us wonder why. You never know—until you reach out in what young,
trembling, uncertain faith you have, and just *touch* Him. . . .

SUGGESTIONS TO TEACHERS

We need a new approach to the healings of Jesus. If we tell the stories
of His healing miracles, and stop there, we are not helping our students
very much—but when we get them to thinking of how Christ heals
today we are "reaching them where they live." That should be the main
concern of the lesson.

Does Christ heal people today? How? *Through whom?*

How should we in the church seek His help, in sickness or in death?
Should we always ask for a miracle? What if He does *not* heal us? Is our
faith lost then?

What evidences of His healing do you see in modern individuals and
society?

And what can we do to *help* Him heal?

TOPICS FOR ADULTS
LOVE AND MAN'S BROKENNESS

Love and Healing. "Physical healing by direct spiritual power lies in
a realm which is beyond our full knowledge. To this particular sufferer,
Jesus said, 'Daughter, your faith has made you well.' In a number of
Christian churches there are special services to which men and woman
come to pray that the living Christ will do for them what Jesus did for
the sick and sad in Galilee. We dare not say to any one of them, 'If you
believe it positively enough, then your bodily infirmity will be healed.'
It may be that the greater purpose which the love of God holds for some
human life is to enable it to become radiant through accepted suffering.
But this is certain: there is a grace for body and soul which will be

found by those—and by those only—who reach out for it with the most intense desire. In this scene from Luke the crowd whose interest in Jesus was no more than curious and casual never made contact with His reality. But the woman did, because her soul was hungry for what only God could give; and that sort of hunger the divine compassion will recognize and answer as Jesus responded to the woman's touch with His outgoing power and bade her, 'Go in peace.' "—*The Compassionate Christ,* by Walter Russell Bowie, p. 128. Quoted by permission of Abingdon Press, publishers.

Abiding Faith. Dr. Robert C. Peale, who is a surgeon and physician, says this:

"Because of the abiding faith and trust the injured or sick person has in Almighty God, as a surgeon I constantly see recoveries that were thought impossible. I also see poor results because of an attempted cure by religion or science alone. I am therefore convinced that there is a definite and fixed relation between science and religion, and that God has given us both as weapons against disease and unhappiness, but, administered together for the benefit of mankind, their possibilities are unlimited."

The Greater Physician. "Over four centuries ago, Dr. Ambrose Pare said, 'I dressed the wound, but God healed it.' Surgical progress has outmoded almost all of his other pronouncements, but that statement remains with no need of change.

"People look to us doctors as sources of healing, but we have no such power of ourselves. The simple truth is that the best of us are only trying, in a very crude and humble way, to do something practical to assist the Greater Physician. Take, as an example, the healing of the skin after an operation. We use sutures or . . . ordinary thread to bring the severed edges closer to each other, but there isn't a living thing we can do to make the skin heal. Homeostasis takes care of that, and I want to underline the inescapable conclusion that homeostasis is the work of the wisdom of God in our bodies. The right materials are brought to the spot, the right things are done with them, and the newly manufactured scar tissue grows in the right directions. Why? The God we surgeons assist is at work."—Dr. Frederick Lee Liebolt.

Such miracles of healing happen in our hospitals every day. Ask any surgeon!

God's Area. Some years ago we heard a woman tell a fantastic story about being cured of curvature of the spine. Frankly, we didn't quite believe it—until she showed us two X-ray pictures of her spine. The first—taken before she went to a faith-healing service in Pittsburgh— showed her spine definitely crooked. The second, taken after her faith healing, was as straight as any normal, healthy spine.

We asked a doctor for his reaction. He said, "Don't ask me; ask God. There are some areas in healing which are beyond our powers of understanding. These are God's areas. Ask Him, not me!"

The woman's faith had made her whole; that was the *only* explanation.

Questions for Pupils on the Next Lesson: 1. Name the twelve disciples without looking at your Bible. 2. What two tasks did Jesus assign to each of the twelve? 3. Could a modern disciple of Jesus obey, literally, the command in Luke 9:3? 4. How does a disciple save his life by losing it? 5. What excuse do you give for not following Jesus Christ? 6. Is Christ more important to you than your family? 7. Is Luke 9:58 still true? Explain.

TOPIC FOR YOUTH
CHRIST'S LOVE AND YOUTH'S BROKENNESS

Love. Modern youth is in rebellion against what they call a sick world. Surely, it *is* sick; we agree! But when those extremists among the youthful rebels try to cure the sickness by setting college buildings on fire, or exploding bombs in public buildings, or forcibly taking over a local church, or in interrupting church services to shout their resentments, we think they are doing their cause more harm than good. Many of them cry, "Make love, not war." But what kind of love are they talking about? That word *love* is important.

"The way to find love is not by waiting until you find something very lovable. You find love by loving according to your present opportunities. John Haynes Holmes tells of an Italian fruit vendor. He had made his little pushcart a dream of beauty, with the fruits and candies arranged just right. Attractive as it was, the peddler seemed not to be satisfied. He was bending over his wares, giving a little extra polish to an apple here, making a little different arrangement there. Dr. Holmes wondered if he was not losing customers by being so absorbed in his little cart. 'But,' concluded Dr. Holmes, 'there was a light of sheer joy on his face which perhaps was better than any sale.'

"Love has the power to transform and remake life. To the weak it gives strength. *To the sick it gives health.*"—C. L. Allen, in *Pulpit Preaching*.

The Cold. "I remember landing in France with a group of people and being ridiculously held up at customs because I had an ancient typewriter with me. It seemed to dislocate the equilibrium of the French inspector that an alien should cross the country to Switzerland with a typewriter in his possession, and to me this was so delaying and absurd that it upset me, too.

"Arriving in Paris, we had a few hours to spare and decided to drive to Chartres for a visit. By the time we arrived, I had a terrible cold. I admitted that the irritation in Cherbourg caused it. But I handed it over to God, and by the time we returned to Paris the cold was gone.

"That seemed to me a Christian way to handle a minor sickness. It had nothing in it of punishment. I broke a law of God and suffered the consequences for what I had done."—Samuel M. Shoemaker, "How to Be Sick in a Christian Way," *The New Christian Advocate,* December, 1958.

Doesn't most sickness come when we disobey the laws of God? And who can heal it better than God?

Three Courses. The son of Sir Harry Lauder was killed in World War I. When he was informed of the death, Sir Harry said:

"In a time like this there are three courses open to a man. He may give way to despair, sour on the world, and become a grouch. He may endeavor to drown his sorrow in drink or by a life of waywardness and wickedness. Or he may turn to God."

Jairus and the widow turned to God—and found healing.

Society, Jesus. "About 20,000 people from New York City are sent to state mental hospitals every year, and most of them are processed through Bellevue or Bellevue's counterpart in Brooklyn, King's County Hospital. Obviously, a patient's first contact with a mental hospital may determine the speed of his recovery. Yet, judging from my experience at Bellevue, which spans, in all, ten years, I would say that conditions there convey one basic message to the incoming patient: Society does not care a damn about you or your illness."—Frank Leonard, "An Attendant's View," *Fact.*

Rough language, isn't it? Never having been a patient in either hospital, we wouldn't know whether this is "fact" or not—but we do know that society as such seems to care very little about a lot of the problems that plague the individual. Contrast this attitude with that expressed in the following words by Dr. Charles E. Jefferson:

"Nowhere does Jesus' brotherliness come out more clearly than in His treatment of the sick. He could not pass a sick man without His soul going out to him. Pain in its every form appealed to Him, misery drew virtue from His heart. A large proportion of all the recorded miracles are miracles of healing. He could not look on the deaf and dumb, the palsied, the blind, without putting forth His power to help them. . . . Travelers through the Orient tell us that we people of the West have no conception of the indifference of the Oriental heart to human woes and miseries. Jesus, by being brotherly, has set an example after which the life of the world is slowly being patterned."

The pattern hasn't been worked out completely yet, even in the hospitals—but we should never overlook the fact that more people are being healed every day and restored to health, both in the hospitals and by the followers of Jesus in the sickrooms of the world, than Jesus ever healed—just as He promised when He said that His disciples would do greater things than He had done!

The Healing Journey. Dr. Paul Rees calls the life of the Christian a "healing journey," made according to ability and not according to expediency. He explains:

> Expediency says: "I must look after my own safety."
> Ability says: "At all costs, I must rescue this drowning man."
> Expediency asks: "How little can I get by with?"
> Ability asks: "How much can I do?"
> Expediency mumbles: "I must save up for a rainy day."
> Ability cries: "I must give now, for this may be my last day."

"For the Good Samaritan life was a healing journey. He took the wounded of the way and made them whole.

"The Great Physician is looking for more 'Samaritans' who will walk the way of the wounded with Him."—Paul R. Rees, in *World Vision Magazine.*

Sentence Sermon to Remember: But unto you that fear my name shall the Sun of righteousness arise with healing in his wings.—Malachi 4:2.

Questions for Pupils on the Next Lesson: 1. What is the difference between a disciple and an apostle? Define both. 2. Name three essentials of good discipleship. 3. Could you leave a fatally sick father to become a missionary? 4. What are the risks of Christian discipleship for our generation? 5. Name five living men you think Jesus would pick as disciples. 6. Explain the psychology of Luke 9:62. 7. Is Jesus being bitter or sarcastic in Luke 9:5?

LESSON VIII—JANUARY 23

WHAT PRICE DISCIPLESHIP?

Background Scripture: Luke 9:1-6, 23-25, 57-62; 10:1-12
Devotional Reading: Matthew 19:16-22

KING JAMES VERSION

LUKE 9 Then he called his twelve disciples together, and gave them power and authority over all devils, and to cure diseases.

2 And he sent them to preach the kingdom of God, and to heal the sick.

3 And he said unto them, Take nothing for your journey, neither staves, nor scrip, neither bread, neither money; neither have two coats apiece.

4 And whatsoever house ye enter into, there abide, and thence depart.

5 And whosoever will not receive you, when ye go out of that city, shake off the very dust from your feet for a testimony against them.

6 And they departed, and went through the towns, preaching the gospel, and healing every where.

23 And he said to them all, If any man will come after me, let him deny himself, and take up his cross daily, and follow me.

24 For whosoever will save his life shall lose it: but whosoever will lose his life for my sake, the same shall save it.

25 For what is a man advantaged, if he gain the whole world, and lose himself, or be cast away?

57 And it came to pass, that, as they went in the way, a certain man said unto him, Lord, I will follow thee whithersoever thou goest.

58 And Jesus said unto him, Foxes have holes, and birds of the air have nests; but the Son of man hath not where to lay his head.

59 And he said unto another, Follow me. But he said, Lord, suffer me first to go and bury my father.

60 Jesus said unto him, Let the dead bury their dead: but go thou and preach the kingdom of God.

61 And another also said, Lord, I will follow thee; but let me first go bid them farewell, which are at home at my house.

REVISED STANDARD VERSION

LUKE 9 And he called the twelve together and gave them power and authority over all demons and to cure diseases, 2 and he sent them out to preach the kingdom of God and to heal. 3 And he said to them, "Take nothing for your journey, no staff, nor bag, nor bread, nor money; and do not have two tunics. 4 And whatever house you enter, stay there, and from there depart. 5 And wherever they do not receive you, when you leave that town shake off the dust from your feet as a testimony against them." 6 And they departed and went through the villages, preaching the gospel and healing everywhere.

23 And he said to all, "If any man would come after me, let him deny himself and take up his cross daily and follow me. 24 For whoever would save his life will lose it; and whoever loses his life for my sake, he will save it. 25 For what does it profit a man if he gains the whole world and loses or forfeits himself?"

57 As they were going along the road, a man said to him, "I will follow you wherever you go." 58 And Jesus said to him, "Foxes have holes, and birds of the air have nests; but the Son of man has nowhere to lay his head." 59 To another he said, "Follow me." But he said, "Lord, let me first go and bury my father." 60 But he said to him, "Leave the dead to bury their own dead; but as for you, go and proclaim the kingdom of God." 61 Another said, "I will follow you, Lord; but let me first say farewell to those at my home." 62 Jesus said to him, "No one who puts his hand to the plow and looks back is fit for the kingdom of God."

62 And Jesus said unto him, No
man, having put his hand to the plow,
and looking back, is fit for the kingdom of God.

*MEMORY SELECTION: If any man will come after me, let him deny
himself, and take up his cross daily, and follow me. Luke 9:23.*

HOME DAILY BIBLE READINGS

Jan. 17. M. Confessing Christ, Luke 9:18-22.
Jan. 18. T. The Transfiguration, Luke 9:28-36.
Jan. 19. W. Powerless Disciples, Luke 9:37-42.
Jan. 20. T. Commissioned Disciples, Luke 10:1-12.
Jan. 21. F. Lesson on Humility, Luke 9:46-56.
Jan. 22. S. Costly Discipleship, Mark 10:35-45.
Jan. 23. S. The Great Refusal, Matthew 19:16-22.

BACKGROUND

From the start of His ministry, Jesus knew that He was working
against time and the hatred of His enemies; anyone who talked as He
did, who defied both civil and religious authorities, was bound to run
into trouble. He had to look forward to the time when His personal
work on this earth would be ended, and someone else would have to
"take over." There were no newspapers; books, as a medium of communication, were too expensive for the ordinary man. There was no
radio, no T.V.! His message had to be carried from man to man by word
of mouth, orally.

So He picked twelve disciples or apostles to carry on after He was
gone. He picked them fairly early in His ministry, so that they would
have the benefit of personal contact with Him, and He have time to
train them and get them ready. He laid down certain rules of conduct
for them, certain methods they were to employ in spreading His Good
News. . . .

NOTES ON THE PRINTED TEXT

*I. And he sent them to preach the kingdom of God, and to heal the
sick, Luke 9:2.* Before a man starts work with any firm or any cause,
he should know just what he is expected to *do,* just what the cause stands
for. A poet has no business taking employment with a firm specializing
in industrial engineering, nor should an engineer try to write poetry
for a living! The disciples were called to a specific, specialized work.
What was it?

Jesus gave them "power and authority over all demons and to cure
diseases" (verse 1, RSV). This is Dr. Luke speaking! First, they were to
heal, because sickness was the great curse of the land. Second, they
were to preach the kingdom; the kingdom had been the hope of the
sick for generations. Preach and heal! Be concerned with the health of
both the bodies and the souls of men. Protest against anything and
anyone who threatens any man's health. Change men, change things,
change environments, customs, ideas *here on earth.* You are not here
to preach pie-in-the-sky, but salvation *now!* Do that which will help
save men—feed them, clothe them, visit them in prison, take in the
stranger, go to them when they are sick. . . . Preach, but don't stop

there; add *deeds* to your preaching! Mahatma Gandhi said once that he believed in Christian conversion when it was genuine: "If a man has really found God through discovering Jesus Christ, then he must be baptized and show the world that he is a follower of Jesus, or else he will be a living lie." Show the world, disciples!

II. *Take nothing for your journey, no staff, nor bag, nor bread, nor money; and do not have two tunics,* Luke 9:3 (rsv). In other words *travel light.* Have you ever noticed an experienced world traveler? He carries so little luggage that the inexperienced often laugh at him. But he knows what he is doing. He does not overburden himself with a lot of excess baggage he will never need. This command of Jesus sounds a little ridiculous under modern conditions of life; no church leader ever goes out with no money or without a change of clothing! But these disciples were not living under modern conditions; this age was almost primitive. And they were going out on only one short trip, not on a long one. They were to depend on the generosity of those to whom they were sent. They were not to be richly gowned preachers traveling in Cadillacs; that would never find much sympathy among the poor.

Travel light. Accept hospitality; if hospitality is not extended, leave that place and move on. If there is no chance to witness to your Christ in one home, go to another. Don't *press!* You are an announcer of Christ's presence; announce it. If those to whom you make the announcement reject it, shake off the dust of the inhospitable city and go elsewhere.

This was not an encouragement to "quit quickly," or to cowardice. It was just common sense. . . .

III. *If any man will come after me, let him deny himself, and take up his cross daily, and follow me,* Luke 9:23. Jesus was to suffer on the cross. He knew it, even now. He denied Himself the possibility of escaping the cross and accepted it. And here He warns His followers that they, too, will suffer as they preach and heal. People will misunderstand and the authorities will scourge and crucify. So be it! Let the disciple be warned: he, too, will be scourged and crucified. It happened. Few if any of the disciples escaped violent death. Few, if any, refused to deny Christ; instead, they denied their own human, selfish desires and rejected the possibility of gaining a world, lest the world crush them and destroy their mission. They all lost their lives in His service— but how we honor and love them today! They shared His humility and His cross—*daily.* Can we do less?

IV. . . . *a certain man said unto him, Lord, I will follow thee whithersoever thou goest,* Luke 9:57. Here we have three would-be followers of Christ, three candidates for discipleship. The first one made a wild, unconsidered promise in a moment of emotional enthusiasm: "I will follow thee whithersoever thou goest!" Peter did that. A lot of us do that, in such moments of conviction and conversion, but when the emotion wears off and the going gets rough, we tend to fall out of His ranks in a hurry. Jesus said to this first man, "Be careful. Count the cost of what you are saying! Don't make promises you cannot keep. What you are promising may mean the sacrifice of all that you hold dear. Be sure you *want* to sacrifice it!"

The second candidate was willing to follow Him, but before the man began following there were some things he had to take care of. He had to give his dead father a funeral. I'll follow you, Lord—but not just *yet!* Let me make a little money first. The great moment with you can wait awhile; I'll come along later. The trouble is that people who say this seldom come along at all. They put it off until.tomorrow— and tomorrow never comes, and they *never* follow Him. Jesus wasn't telling the man that he should not take care of his father's funeral; He was telling the man that there is a crucial moment in everything—and that if one does not do what he must do *in that moment,* he will probably never do it at all. Preaching eternal life is far more important than burying a body!

The third candidate had a somewhat similar statement to make: he, too, would like to be a disciple, but "let me first say farewell to those at my home" (verse 61, rsv). Jesus seemed harsh with this man when He told the man to look ahead and not back—like a plowman plowing a furrow. But perhaps He looked deep into the man's heart and saw there a resolution that was too weak for the rigors of discipleship. This could have been only a desire to postpone his loyalty. Our first loyalty should be to Christ; our second, to our families. Our first duty is to plow a straight, clean-cut furrow for Him; our second, to plow it *now.*

If you saw a man drowning in deep waters, you would not run home to say to your family, "I may drown if I try to save him, so I have come to say good-by to you." No—you jump in and swim, and save the drowning one. He would die if he waited for you to run home and back!

Men, said Jesus, souls are dying; save them before it is too late!

SUGGESTIONS TO TEACHERS

Jesus chose only twelve men to be His close, intimate disciples; that was high honor. Then He gave them unusual powers and authority "over all demons and to cure diseases"—which was a still greater honor. Finally, He told them what they must be and do as disciples; He laid down rules for their discipleship which demanded more of them than had ever been demanded before. *The demands apply to us too,* if we plan to be His disciples.

Consider those demands one at a time—and find out how many of your pupils are ready to meet them. Start with these:

1. There can be no discipleship without *complete* self-denial.
2. Discipleship permits no wavering or turning back.
3. Christ's claims take priority over family and social obligations.
4. No excuses are recognized by Christ when He calls.
5. There are risks involved in serving Christ which should be faced *before* we promise to follow Him.

Step up, volunteers!

TOPIC FOR ADULTS
WHAT PRICE DISCIPLESHIP?

The Rev. John Jones. "The other day in Emporia (Kansas), the longest funeral procession that has formed here in ten years followed the Rev. John Jones three long miles in the hot July sun out to Dry

Creek Cemetery. Now, a funeral procession may mean little or much. When a rich and powerful man dies, the people play politics and attend his funeral for various reasons. But here was the body of a meek, gentle little old man—a man 'without purse or script.' It won't take twenty minutes to settle his estate in probate court. He was a preacher of the gospel—but preachers have been buried before this in Emporia without much show of sorrow.

"The reason so many people lined up behind the hearse that held the kind old man's mortality was simple: they loved him. He devoted his life to helping people. In a very simple way, without money or worldly power, he gave of the gentleness of his heart to all around him. We are apt to say that money talks, but it speaks a broken, poverty-stricken language. Hearts talk better, clearer, and with a wider intelligence. This old man with the soft voice and the kindly manners knew the language of the heart and he spoke it where it would give zest to joy. He worked manfully and with a will in his section of the vineyard, and against odds and discouragements he won time and again. He was infinitely patient and brave. He held a simple, old-fashioned faith in God and His loving-kindness.

"When others gave money—which was of their store—he gave prayers and hard work and an inspiring courage. He helped. In his sphere he was a power. And so when he lay down to sleep hundreds of friends trudged out to bid him good-by with moist eyes and with cramped throats to wish him sweet slumber.

"And then they turned back to the world to make money—to make money—what a hollow, impotent thing! What is a man profited if he gain the whole world and lose his own soul?"—An editorial by William Allen White in the *Emporia Gazette*.

Such a discipleship is open to *all* of us!

Giving Up. Sometimes, we are puzzled when Lent rolls around on the calendar and we hear good folks in the church talk about "giving up something for Lent." They give up smoking; they give up eating candy, going to the theater, throwing parties in their rumpus rooms, playing bridge or golf, etc., etc. It sounds quite "sacrificial," but it isn't. Jesus would never have settled for any such sacrifice among His followers.

All He asks us to give up—every day in the year, not only at Lent—is our selfishness, greed, laziness, lust for money, unconcern for others, pride, fear, doubt, lying, insincerity, skepticism, etc., etc!

He would like to see us give up all that 364 days a year, and perhaps reverse it and have one day (in Lent) when we give up nothing!

Sacrifice. "The salt loses its own identity in order to preserve; the oil is entirely consumed to give the light; the yeast is completely lost in the dough it transforms. Each sacrifices itself so that its function may be fulfilled."—*A Faith to Live By*, by Stuart Leroy Anderson.

Questions for Pupils on the Next Lesson: 1. What possessions do you cherish that you do not really need? 2. Is it impossible to serve God and worship money at the same time? 3. What was "the greater condemnation" to Jesus? 4. Do you share Jesus' idea in Luke 21:3? 5. Is our use of money a reflection of our faith and religion? 6. Is it wrong to be rich and right to be poor? Explain your answer. 7. What will happen to your money when you die?

TOPIC FOR YOUTH
WHAT PRICE DISCIPLESHIP?

No Bread, No Money. A strange thing has just happened in the home of one of our friends. There is a boy in that family who has a fine mother and father; his parents sacrificed much to put him through school, to provide the money for his college education; they gave him a love that knew no limit. But he has just quit college in the middle of his freshman year! He has just written his parents that he was "fed up" with college, that he intended to buy a cheap car and just "hit the road," and traveling across the country as a penniless tramp. He said, "I want to know what poverty is, what it means to be poor and insecure. I want to know what it means to have nothing. Just send me some money to buy the car—and I'm off."

At first, we were outraged; this was ingratitude, cruel, stupid, selfish. How could a boy treat his parents like *this*? What that kid needed was a good spanking . . . !

But then we got to thinking: the disciples of Jesus did exactly the same thing! They left their families, their friends; they left jobs that provided security for themselves and their wives and children. They became deliberately poor, insecure, wanderers on the face of the earth. Our favorite saint—Francis of Assisi—did the same thing. . . . Now we're wondering about this boy. . . .

Was he a fool? Did he have to do *this* to find out what it meant to be poor? Could he have contributed more to conquering poverty if he had trained himself in college for a life of service? How would you rate him—as a fool or a Christian?

We are not telling you what we think; we are asking you what *you* think about him. Should we *all* do this?

Conversion. The twelve were converted (won to Christ) before they became disciples. A group of ministers once asked Mahatma Gandhi about conversion, and he replied:

"I believe in Christian conversion if it is genuine. On the other hand, there is nothing worse than being something on the outside that you are not on the inside. If a man has really found God through discovering Jesus Christ, then he must be baptized and show the world that he is a follower of Jesus, or else he will be a living lie."

Gandhi had been a successful lawyer in his early days. But when he said this he drank a breakfast of goat's milk, wore a cheap loin cloth and carried a dollar watch. No script!

Consecration runs hand in hand with conversion—consecration to *others*.

Crosses. " 'Dear Abby,' begins a letter that appeared recently in our newspaper, 'I have been going steady for six months and my boy friend's religion doesn't permit him to go to movies or dances. There is nothing much for us to do except to sit out in a car and court. I like him a lot, but this is getting dangerous. What should I do?'

"The reply by the columnist was a good one: it suggested scrabble, picnics and activities with other couples. Yet I could not help wondering about that fine fellow. I wondered if he thought that giving up movies and dancing was some kind of cross-bearing!

"We find it so convenient to use phrases about the cross, but when people start talking about their own self-denial we begin to flinch. We don't like it. . . . *Jesus Christ offers us a cross to carry.* King David says to Araunah the Jebusite, in II Samuel 24:24: 'Neither will I offer . . . unto the Lord that which dost cost me nothing.' This 'giving up' business can become quite tricky; it can be quite subtle; it can actually lead to self-righteousness. But taking up the cross does not mean simply giving up this or that; it is not just a moral rearrangement of our lives; it means absolute identification with Jesus Christ in His death and resurrection. And a lot of times we *will* give up things, and they *will* be costly. They will not be insignificant.

"This point has been a hard one for me to get, I must confess: that we are saved only by receiving the life of our Lord and letting him live through us,"—From "The ABC of Discipleship," by Howard E. Butt, in *Decision,* September, 1962.

Excuses. Most of our excuses for not following Christ are lame, silly excuses. For instance, ponder this from *Today:*

"Church Member X: 'We really shouldn't be out here fishing on prayer-meeting night.'

"Church Member Z: 'Oh, well, I couldn't be at church tonight, anyway. I've got a sick child at home!' "

Silly? Yes. But typical!

On the other hand: "Let us never forget that most of the great accomplishments in the history of the race, most of the important contributions made to Christ's cause have been made by men and women who had excuses if they had wished to use them."—Rev. John A. Maclean.

Sentence Sermon to Remember: I beseech you, be ye followers of me.—I Corinthians 4:16.

Questions for Pupils on the Next Lesson: 1. Explain the meaning of Luke 16:10. 2. Who or what was mammon? 3. How can we be "faithful" to something unrighteous (Luke 16:11)? 4. Why did the Pharisees scoff at Jesus? 5. What made Jesus suspicious of the scribes? 6. Does Jesus say we should have no possessions at all? 7. If you were a millionaire how would you use your money to gain happiness? 8. How much was two mites?

LESSON IX—JANUARY 30

FAITHFUL WITH POSSESSIONS

Background Scripture: Luke 16:1-15, 19-31; 20:45-21:4
Devotional Reading: II Corinthians 8:1-9

KING JAMES VERSION

LUKE 16 10 He that is faithful in that which is least is faithful also in much: and he that is unjust in the least is unjust also in much.

11 If therefore ye have not been faithful in the unrighteous mammon, who will commit to your trust the true riches?

12 And if ye have not been faithful in that which is another man's, who shall give you that which is your own?

13 No servant can serve two masters: for either he will hate the one, and love the other; or else he will hold to the one, and despise the other. Ye cannot serve God and mammon.

14 And the Pharisees also, who were covetous, heard all these things: and they derided him.

15 And he said unto them, Ye are they which justify yourselves before men; but God knoweth your hearts: for that which is highly esteemed among men is abomination in the sight of God.

LUKE 20 45 Then in the audience of all the people he said unto his disciples,

46 Beware of the scribes, which desire to walk in long robes, and love greetings in the markets, and the highest seats in the synagogues, and the chief rooms at feasts;

47 Which devour widows' houses, and for a show make long prayers: the same shall receive greater damnation.

LUKE 21 And he looked up, and saw the rich men casting their gifts into the treasury.

2 And he saw also a certain poor widow casting in thither two mites.

3 And he said, Of a truth I say unto you, that this poor widow hath cast in more than they all:

4 For all these have of their abundance cast in unto the offerings of God: but she of her penury hath cast in all the living that she had.

REVISED STANDARD VERSION

LUKE 16 10 "He who is faithful in a very little is faithful also in much; and he who is dishonest in a very little is dishonest also in much. 11 If then you have not been faithful in the unrighteous mammon, who will entrust to you the true riches? 12 And if you have not been faithful in that which is another's, who will give you that which is your own? 13 No servant can serve two masters; for either he will hate the one and love the other, or he will be devoted to the one and despise the other. You cannot serve God and mammon."

14 The Pharisees, who were lovers of money, heard all this, and they scoffed at him. 15 But he said to them, "You are those who justify yourselves before men, but God knows your hearts; for what is exalted among men is an abomination in the sight of God."

LUKE 20 45 And in the hearing of all the people he said to his disciples, 46 "Beware of the scribes, who like to go about in long robes, and love salutations in the market places and the best seats in the synagogues and the places of honor at feasts, 47 who devour widows' houses and for a pretense make long prayers. They will receive the greater condemnation."

LUKE 21 He looked up and saw the rich putting their gifts into the treasury; 2 and he saw a poor widow put in two copper coins. 3 And he said, "Truly I tell you, this poor widow has put in more than all of them; 4 for they all contributed out of their abundance, but she out of her poverty put in all the living that she had."

MEMORY SELECTION: No servant can serve two masters: for either he will hate the one, and love the other; or else he will hold to the one and despise the other. Ye cannot serve God and mammon. Luke 16:13.

HOME DAILY BIBLE READINGS

Jan. 24. M. The Peril of Wealth, Luke 18:18-27.
Jan. 25. T. The Parable of the Pounds, Luke 19:11-26.
Jan. 26. W. The Rich Fool, Luke 12:13-21.
Jan. 27. T. The Folly of Anxious Care, Luke 12:22-34.
Jan. 28. F. The Rich Man and Lazarus, Luke 16:19-31.
Jan. 29. S. Faithfulness in Stewardship, I Corinthians 4:1-7.
Jan. 30. S. Liberal Christians, II Corinthians 8:1-9.

BACKGROUND

Luke 15, 16 and 17 give us a glimpse of the teaching Jesus. Sometimes He taught in parables—in little illustrative stories about very common little things and people which His listeners could understand—about sheep and a boy who got lost, a woman who lost a coin and a steward who made the best of a bad situation when his master fired him. These were everyday illustrations out of everyday life.

Notice that the parables we have mentioned were all about either money or possessions; In His teaching, Jesus talked more about these two things than about anything else. (That statement is no exaggeration; check it with the text.) Money and possessions! How do we *use* money and possessions? Is it wrong to *have* money and possessions? Should all Christians be penniless, iterant saints? Is it wrong to be well off? Is all money "dirty?"

The prodigal son made a selfish (wrong) use of his father's money; he is a good illustration of how *not* to use money. The unjust steward (Luke 16:1-9) made a slightly better use of it. In our use of it we could improve on both of them if we could keep in mind the teaching of Jesus. . . .

NOTES ON THE PRINTED TEXT

I. He who is faithful in a very little is faithful also in much, Luke 16:10 (RSV). Read now the story of the steward in Luke 16:1-9. This story is the background for this verse. A clever steward "pulled a clever trick" when his master fired him for poor use of the master's money; the shrewd steward falsified his books, made friends for himself of his former debtors, and secured his own financial future. It was so clever that even the master who had fired him now praised him! In this story neither steward nor master is a very admirable character, but Jesus told it, not to praise them or approve of what they did *but to illustrate a principle.* He disapproved of the faithlessness of the steward (see verse 10), using him only to make clear the principle that *the proper use of money and material possessions is to use them for the welfare of others.* The steward helped the men who were in debt to him and to his master; consciously or unconsciously, he made good use of the money involved.

Here, Jesus is saying, "If you do well with the small, common tasks of life you are fit to be trusted with a larger task and responsibility.

Prove yourself honest and intelligent in the little thing, and you are ready to handle the greater thing. If you can be trusted with a little money, you can be trusted with a fortune. You (we, all of us) are *only stewards* of our money. Learn to use it well—unselfishly, for good and not evil purposes."

Jesus speaks (verse 11) of "unrighteous mammon [money]." This does not mean *stolen* money; it means unrighteous *use* of money. The world puts great value on money and things; it is so anxious to get fortunes that it sacrifices everything else in life. God despises that. Money is "filthy lucre" only insofar as we get and spend it selfishly or unwisely. It has no value to God; He isn't interested in rich or poor, but only in *men.*

It isn't wrong to make money; it is wrong only to *lust* for it at the expense of everything else. It is wrong only to think more of wealth and possessions than we think of God. You cannot serve both God and money; it is one or the other. Earn it—then use it to make friends for yourself in a Christian way.

The Pharisees, "who were covetous," disagreed with Jesus on this. He silenced them quickly, saying, "God knows your hearts!" They valued wealth; it was to them a sign that the man who possessed it "had done well." That isn't necessarily true. They identified riches and prosperity with goodness; the rich man had the approval of God! This is nonsense. He and his riches, ill-gotten and ill-used, can be an abomination to God. It was exactly that to Jesus! To be rich isn't to be righteous. But we *can* be both.

II. Beware of the scribes . . . which devour widows' houses, and for a show make long prayers, Luke 20:46, 47. The scribes were proud, pious, haughty men. They were most ambitious men, wearing expensive clothes, coveting the highest seats in the synagogue, demanding preference and bows in the street and pay for services they should have rendered for nothing. They were greedy, making profit out of holy office. The very law in which they piously instructed the people made special provision for the widows and the fatherless (see Exodus 22:22-24), and here these so-called "religious" men were exploiting for gain those they were supposed to protect! Jesus loathed their greed and ambition and profiteering; *of all men, they knew how wrong they were.* The man who uses his power and position to enrich himself for his own comfort is as evil as the snake in the Garden! It is especially repulsive when it is done behind a mask of false piety.

Sometimes, we wonder what Jesus would have to say to those modern businessmen who tell the world so proudly, "I followed the teachings of the Bible and made a lot of money!" *What* teachings?

III. . . . Of a truth I say unto you, that this poor widow hath cast in more than they all, Luke 21:3. Jesus sat one day outside the Temple, near the collection boxes into which men and women cast their offerings for the Temple and the Lord. Some wealthy men came by and dropped in a contribution—money that was a pittance to them. And a widow came by and cast in two "mites"—or two *lepta.* A *lepta* was worth one-sixteenth of a penny. Not much, was it? *But it was more than the poor widow could afford to give,* and when Jesus saw the money He praised the widow as much as (in the preceding verses) He had condemned the selfishness of the scribes.

The two stories belong together; they contrast hypocritical piety with giving in the love of God. It is never the size of a contribution or a gift to God that makes it good; it is the spirit in which it is given, and the sacrifice involved for the giver. A millionaire who gives a church a million dollars out of his fifty million to build a church is entitled to no more credit than the poor man who gives a dollar to help buy robes for the choir! In fact, he is entitled to less.

It isn't what you *give* but what you have *left*, that God notices. The widow probably had very little left after giving those two mites. The haughty scribe who gave a hundred times as much probably went home to a good dinner in a fine house. . . .

SUGGESTIONS TO TEACHERS

Think on these things:

1. If God gives man the ability to make money, what's wrong with making all we can?
2. "Every great American fortune is rooted in piracy." True or false? Name some widow's houses that are being devoured *now* in man's lust for wealth.
3. Some people give too much when they give ten per cent; others do not give enough when they give fifty per cent.
4. Our use of money tells more about our characters than our religious professions.
5. Christ said more about money and possessions than He said about anything else. Check your New Testament.
6. None of us owns anything; we are only stewards holding something God has put in our hands for a purpose.

TOPIC FOR ADULTS
FACING FINANCIAL RESPONSIBILITIES

Money Isn't Everything. "Bruce Barton wrote many years ago something that expresses a great truth: 'As one grows older in fishing, even as one grows older in living, there comes the same consoling truth: that one need not catch big fish in order to be happy, that the spirit of the fishing is more important than the catch, that he who fishes well must fish with a calm and tranquil soul, drawing his reward from the joy of his fishing rather than from the weight of his fish.'

"In fishing for dollars, the same philosophy applies. Happiness comes, not from the number of dollars we 'catch' but from the fun we have as we go along. . . .

"As for being 'as rich as a king,' modern man is more than a king. A chariot pulled by the finest horses isn't in the running with one of today's automobiles. Old-time kings would have looked on men flying through the air as gods, yet it is commonplace for us. Candles threw a faint light compared with the brilliance of the electric light we enjoy today. Kings had gold but little else. The miracles worked with money are what count!

"The most valuable riches of all cannot be measured by any material standard. The world's greatest thinkers are at our command to pour out the treasures of their wisdom into our minds. One way to live many lives during one lifetime is to read biographies and autobiographies. To see the beauties of nature we need but to open our eyes. To hear the greatest symphonies we need but to flip a dial and listen. We are surrounded by riches that are ours for the taking.

" 'The man who never entertains poor thoughts is a rich man,' writes Theodore Dreiser. And it was Emerson who said, 'Without a rich heart, wealth is an ugly beggar.' To a great extent, true wealth consists of having rich thoughts and rich emotions. Our richest experiences often come not from getting but from giving."—National Research Bureau.

Two Hands. "God has given us two hands—one to receive with and the other to give with. We are not cisterns made for hoarding; we are channels made for sharing. If we fail to fulfill this divine duty we have missed the meaning of Christianity."—Billy Graham.

Widows' Houses. Jesus condemned those who "devoured widows' houses" in order to gain wealth and possessions for themselves. It is a complaint as old as mankind, and it still goes on. For instance:

There are many wealthy men who pay little if any income taxes; they hire good lawyers to help them evade that expense. But *someone* has to pay taxes to finance the government, and while those able to pay do not pay, the poor and the middle-class (widows, for instance) pay more than they are able to pay!

Great industrial establishments pour poisonous waste and chemicals into the rivers of our land, robbing all of us of natural resources which are supposed to be "public property." The poor in tenements die from breathing foul air poisoned by the smoke from factory chimneys. The smoke, however, is very profitable to some others!

Arms manufacturers in our country make huge fortunes selling their arms abroad; occasionally, our sons are expected to die in wars abroad to protect American "investments." Their widows get very small pensions.

Oh, My Aching Money! "More wiseacres have got off more quips about money than any other subject.

"Aristoxenus, a wise man of the eighth century, said: 'Money makes the man.'

"Now a Boston physician, Dr. William Kaufman, amends this; he says that money makes the man sick.

"Money sickness, he claims, 'is the most common psychosomatic illness of our times, but is rarely recognized by medical diagnosticians.'

"Dr. Kaufman, feeling our purse, says this money sickness makes no distinction among victims. 'Them as has can get it as well as them that hasn't.'

"Symptoms: Headache, stomach ache, muscle ache, joint ache or emotional disturbances."—*New York World Telegram and Sun.*

Apportioning. "Most people apportion their giving according to their earnings. If the process were reversed and the Giver of all were to apportion our earnings according to our giving, some of us would be very poor indeed."—*The Christian.*

Questions for Pupils on the Next Lesson: 1. For what *purpose* did Jesus ride into Jerusalem? 2. What "power groups" opposed Jesus in Jerusalem? 3. What power groups oppose Him in the United States today? 4. Why did Jesus weep over Jerusalem? 5. Why are so many Christian churches dying in our cities? 6. Was Jesus mixing religion and business in Luke 19:45? 7. Where is Protestantism stronger: in our cities or in our suburban areas? Why?

TOPIC FOR YOUTH
FAITHFUL WITH POSSESSIONS

Character. "A person's attitude toward money tells much about the person himself. How a person gets his money indicates his character. If he steals to 'get rich quick' we call him a thief, dishonest, untrustworthy. If he 'works hard to make a living' we call him industrious and ambitious. If he 'figures the angles' we call him shrewd. If he tries to make all the overtime he can we call him 'hungry.' If he makes a lot of money we call him successful, regardless of how he earned it. *How a person spends his money indicates his values.*"—Wayne Saffen, "Money and Your Life," *This Day*, June, 1960.

Time. Some folks talk of stewardship as though it had to do only with money. They are wrong.

"A former city employe mailed Frank J. O'Brien, city treasurer of Albany, New York, a $100 bill marked 'money for stolen time.'

"We are stewards of our time as much as we are stewards of our money. We are going to give an account of our moments as well as of our words. One of the most terrible thoughts ever devised by man is that which is inherent in the common phrase that this or that occupation is engaged in as a 'pastime.' Usage may well have dropped the second 's' from the spelling, but the idea is that we must find something to pass the time away. May God help us to change our thinking that the idea of 'pass time' is to 'steal time.' In stealing it, we rob both ourselves and God."—Donald Grey Barnhouse.

Rule of Living. "Over the entrance to an old cathedral in France these words stand out clearly: 'He who bringeth no gift to the altar, beareth no blessing away.' It is a rule for the worshiper; it is a rule for all of life.

"When we go into the classroom, we must take the gift of attention, the discipline of duty, the joy of work well done, [and] the enthusiasm of an earnest searcher if we would bear the blessings of an education away with us.

"When we go to a concert, we must take the gift of appreciation, understanding, deep feeling, and a desire for the best if we would carry the blessing of real art away with us.

"When we go into a friendship, we must take the art of understanding, the joy of making another happy, the skill of objectivity, [and] the power of versatility if we would carry the blessing of a growing friendship away with us.

"In other words, *we can receive only by giving*. It is one of the great rules of living."—*The Broadcaster*.

Youth and Money. "The young today, on the whole, despise business for the same reason that the young of my own day despised it: that it *seems* to be concerned only with making money by processes which *seem* to be intellectually and emotionally unsatisfying. If the young do not despise the making of money at an age when they have no responsibilities . . . then God . . . have mercy on us."—Henry Fairlie, "How Is Youth to Be Served?", *The New Republic.*

Study this paragraph carefully. Does modern youth despise business? Should they despise it? If so, why? What careers do they seem to prefer to that of businessmen?

Designs With Money. "A pile of pennies had been given to a four-year-old girl. . . . She was quiet for several minutes and then she called to her father in the next room, 'Daddy, come and see. I'm making designs with my money.' The father, although he had always had a multitude of designs *on* money, had never heard of making designs *with* money. He went to see what the child had done. Unknowingly, she had made a design with her pennies across the top of a table in the form of a large cross!

"One need hardly say more than that. That child's manipulation of a few pennies had spelled out in unforgettable language what every person can do with all his money, and all his possessions. We can use our money to make Christian designs in the life of the world. In fact, it was for that purpose that wealth and possessions were given us. For the wise ones of the earth have always known that a man never 'owns' his wealth or his possessions entirely for his own use. They have been loaned to him by the Creator of all wealth to be used in the service of humanity and of God."—Robert E. Luccock, in *Sunday Digest.*

Pennies and the cross! It is an intriguing picture. And it poses a problem: *how can we use our pennies* (*100 to a dollar!*) *to do the work of the cross?*

Sentence Sermon to Remember: Money is not required to buy one necessity of the soul.—Henry David Thoreau.

Questions for Pupils on the Next Lesson: 1. What did the people of Jerusalem mean when they called Christ a king? 2. Why is the Christian church having such a hard time in the modern city? 3. Would Jesus have been crucified if He had *not* ridden into Jerusalem? 4. Would you call the triumphal entry a protest march? 5. Memorize Luke 13:34. 6. Should the whole church program in the modern city be changed? How? 7. Why do so few young ministers want to serve churches in our cities?

LESSON X—FEBRUARY 6

CHRIST'S CONCERN FOR THE CITY

Background Scripture: Luke 13:31-35; 19:28-48
Devotional Reading: Psalm 122

KING JAMES VERSION

LUKE 19 37 And when he was come nigh, even now at the descent of the mount of Olives, the whole multitude of the disciples began to rejoice and praise God with a loud voice for all the mighty works that they had seen;

38 Saying, Blessed be the King that cometh in the name of the Lord: peace in heaven, and glory in the highest.

39 And some of the Pharisees from among the multitude said unto him, Master, rebuke thy disciples.

40 And he answered and said unto them, I tell you that, if these should hold their peace, the stones would immediately cry out.

41 And when he was come near, he beheld the city, and wept over it,

42 Saying, If thou hadst known, even thou, at least in this thy day, the things which belong unto thy peace! but now they are hid from thine eyes.

43 For the days shall come upon thee, that thine enemies shall cast a trench about thee, and compass thee round, and keep thee in on every side,

44 And shall lay thee even with the ground, and thy children within thee; and they shall not leave in thee one stone upon another; because thou knewest not the time of thy visitation.

45 And he went into the temple, and began to cast out them that sold therein, and them that bought;

46 Saying unto them, It is written, My house is the house of prayer; but ye have made it a den of thieves.

47 And he taught daily in the temple. But the chief priests and the scribes and the chief of the people sought to destroy him,

48 And could not find what they might do: for all the people were very attentive to hear him.

REVISED STANDARD VERSION

LUKE 19 37 As he was now drawing near, at the descent of the Mount of Olives, the whole multitude of the disciples began to rejoice and praise God with a loud voice for all the mighty works that they had seen, 38 saying, "Blessed be the King who comes in the name of the Lord! Peace in heaven and glory in the highest!" 39 And some of the Pharisees in the multitude said to him, "Teacher, rebuke your disciples." 40 He answered, "I tell you, if these were silent, the very stones would cry out."

41 And when he drew near and saw the city he wept over it, 42 saying, "Would that even today you knew the things that make for peace! But now they are hid from your eyes. 43 For the days shall come upon you, when your enemies will cast up a bank about you and surround you, and hem you in on every side, 44 and dash you to the ground, you and your children within you, and they will not leave one stone upon another in you; because you did not know the time of your visitation."

45 And he entered the temple and began to drive out those who sold, 46 saying to them, "It is written, 'My house shall be a house of prayer'; but you have made it a den of robbers."

47 And he was teaching daily in the temple. The chief priests and the scribes and the principal men of the people sought to destroy him; 48 but they did not find anything they could do, for all the people hung upon his words.

MEMORY SELECTION: *O Jerusalem, Jerusalem, which killest the prophets, and stonest them that are sent unto thee; how often would*

I have gathered thy children together, as a hen doth gather her brood under her wings, and ye would not! Luke 13:34.

HOME DAILY BIBLE READINGS

Jan. 31. M. *Christ's Lament for the City,* Luke 13:31-35.
Feb. 1. T. *A City Man Finds Salvation,* Luke 19:1-10.
Feb. 2. W. *Preparing to Enter the City,* Luke 19:28-36.
Feb. 3. T. *Unrepentant Cities,* Matthew 11:20-24.
Feb. 4. F. *Wickedness in the City,* Psalm 55:4-11.
Feb. 6. S. *A Prayer for the City,* Psalm 122.

BACKGROUND

For months, there had been a growing hostility to Jesus on the part of the priests, the scribes, and the leaders of the religious life of the people. Short of Jesus suddenly ceasing His preaching or running off into hiding, there was no stopping this hostility. He could do neither; as the opposition increased, so did his determination to face it squarely and publicly increase. Jesus was a man of courage; He never ran from trouble. So we are told that months before Palm Sunday, ". . . when the time was come that he should be received up [taken back into heaven], he steadfastly set his face to go to Jerusalem" (Luke 9:51).

But—*why Jerusalem?* He surely knew that death awaited Him there; this was the citadel, the headquarters, of His bitterest enemies. He knew that a trap had been set for Him there which, if He were caught in it, would take Him to His death. Why walk into the trap?

NOTES ON THE PRINTED TEXT

I. And when he was come nigh, even now at the descent of the mount of Olives, the whole multitude of the disciples began to rejoice . . . , Luke 19:37. This triumphal entry into Jerusalem had been carefully planned; it was no spontaneous, emotional demonstration. Jesus planned the *time:* Passover, when the city would be filled with thousands of pilgrims. He chose the *place:* He would stand on the mount of Olives because to stand there was to fulfill the words of Zechariah the prophet: "And his feet [the feet of the Messiah] shall stand in that day upon the mount of Olives. . . . And the Lord shall be king over all the earth" (Zechariah 14:4, 9). This was "that day," and Jesus was determined that everyone should know it. Jerusalem, with its Passover crowds and its position as the central city of His people, politically and spiritually, was the perfect stage on which to play out the last act of the divine drama.

The triumphal entry was a messianic act. For days past bands of pilgrims had marched into the city singing the ancient Psalms of Israel, singing their hopes of a great national deliverance. This was the moment of Messiah's coming!

Jesus believed that. So did the people, who with the disciples threw their garments under the feet of His colt—an act performed only for royalty. They sang, "Blessed be the *King* who comes in the name of the Lord (Luke 19:38)!" They had sung the same words (see Psalm 118:26) for generations as they went up to the Jerusalem feasts. They had sung it in hope; now they sang it in ecstatic fulfillment. The King had come.

The Pharisees objected (verses 39-40). They thought it might stir up a riot, and bring Roman vengeance down on their heads. Jesus ignored them and their fears: if the people did not cry out on this day, He said, the very stones of the streets would cry out! The blood on the stones of this already bloody, long-suffering city would burst into cheers! The voice of Messiah would be heard, no matter who tried to oppose it.

II. *And when he was come near, he beheld the city, and wept over it* . . . , Luke 19:41. We have two occasions in the Gospels, when Jesus is said to have broken into tears. One is in John 11:35 (the shortest verse in the Bible), on the occasion of the death of Lazarus; the other is here in Luke 19, just before Jesus entered Jerusalem. Where the road from Bethany bends around the southern shoulder of the Mount of Olives, the traveler can look down and see the whole dramatic panorama of Jerusalem, its walls and towers and its Temple area. The heart of Jesus broke, as He looked down on it that day. Here was the city of all cities chosen of God to reveal His presence among men; here was the heart of the Jewish faith—the Temple, the law, His people. It was a city of great hope among men—and it was a city gone blind to God, rebelling against Him, a city that might have inspired God's peace but did not, the city in which the people had cried, "Lift up your heads, O ye gates, and be ye lifted up, ye everlasting doors, and the King of Glory shall come in," was now ready to scream, "Crucify him!" Jesus saw that clearly—and He wept. Wept, not for the suffering He was about to undergo in the Holy City, wept, not for Himself but for the people He had come to save, who were now refusing to be saved. He knew what would happen to this precious city if the political maneuver and intrigue and open immorality and wickedness went on; He knew it would be destroyed and that it would lie "even with the ground" (verse 44)—with them and their children under it. It was leveled with the ground by the Romans in A.D. 70; it was so devastated that a plow was drawn through the middle of it. "The tears of Jesus are the tears of God when He sees the needless suffering in which men involve themselves through their foolish rebellion against His will" (Dr. Barclay).

Oh, Jerusalem! Oh, London, New York, Cairo, Peking! . . . Jesus looks at them, and *weeps* . . . ! Weeps as He wept for Mary and Martha . . . in complete heart-rending compassion. . . . Why do so few of us see His tears, hear His weeping?

III. *And he went into the temple, and began to cast out them that sold therein, and them that bought,* Luke 19:45. At Passover time, the pilgrims flocked into Jerusalem—and paid their taxes. The taxes were outrageous. From these people—mostly poor—exorbitant levies were demanded, outrageous prices were charged for every service. They came with different currencies in their pockets; according to where the people lived, the currency could be Greek, Roman, Syrian, Egyptian which must be changed into Jewish money. Hence, the money-changers—a gang of human vultures who changed the coins, and charged fees for the changing that made their "take" anywhere from twenty to forty thousand dollars a year in *our* coinage. They also sold sacrificial animals; a pair of doves cost fifteen times as much in the Temple area as they cost outside the city walls. Lambs had to be without spot or blemish; the animal merchants charged impossibly high prices for them. All this went on in the Court of the Gentiles, where the chief priests presided and enjoyed a complete thieving monopoly. One of the chief priests, the real head of the business, was a man named Annas!

Jesus was infuriated over the spectacle of His Father's house being turned into headquarters for an economic racket—which is what it was. He thought of the prophetic words of the prophet Malachi: "And he shall sit as a refiner and purifier of silver: and he shall purify the sons of Levi, and purge them . . ." (3:3). After careful deliberation (this was not an act of spontaneous anger) He went into the Temple court with a whip of cords and drove out the thieves, accusing them, as Isaiah had accused them long before, of turning what God meant to be a house of prayer into a den of thieves. (See also Jeremiah 7:11.)

This was an act born after careful deliberation. This is one of the things we love about Jesus: He became furiously angry at an injustice, and He did use a whip, but there He stopped, there He gained control again over His temper and His anger. When He drove the thieves out of "the booths of Annas," as they were called, He was striking out in righteous indignation; He was also fulfilling Scripture and prophecy. He went just so far and no further.

Annas and the high priests howled in indignation, and began laying their plans to destroy Him (verse 47). The refining fire had burned them, and they turned like wolves on Him who had defied them and struck them down while all Jerusalem watched. In the meetings of the Sanhedrin they planned His arrest and death. Kill Him!

But Jesus went calmly on, teaching daily in the Temple; and the people "were very attentive to hear him." He knew what was about to happen to Him. It meant nothing. He held His peace, went on calmly, waiting. . . .

SUGGESTIONS TO TEACHERS

Two truths stand out in this lesson like two long thorns standing out from the stem of a rosebud: *Jesus rode*, and *He rode into a city*. Take them in that order: Palm Sunday and the city.

Ask first why Jesus rode into Jerusalem; why, when He must have known that He was riding to His death? Was He mad? And the city— how did it welcome Him? Pick out personalities standing on the curb, watching Him go by—and tell how they felt about Him.

Then have Him ride down Main Street in any modern city in the world. Would the reception be the same? How would the city welcome Him?

He rode, and into a city. What would He find if he did it *now*? What is "the problem of the cities" for Jesus Christ?

TOPIC FOR ADULTS
CHRIST IN THE CITY

Cities. "The city is no longer the preferred residence of the polite, the civilized, and the urbane. . . . They have fled to the illusion of the suburbs, escaping neon vulgarity, usurious landlords, crime, violence, and corruption. Thus the city is the home of the poor, who are chained to it and to the repository of dirty industry and the commuter's automobile. Give us your poor and oppressed and we will give them Harlem and the lower East Side."—Ian L. McHare.

This editor happens to live near Newark, New Jersey—which has all the appearance of a dying city. Thousands of middle-class wage earners and businessmen have moved out—deserted it, left it to the poor. There are scores of "fine old churches" deserted, too—either torn down, or remodeled into business establishments, or just standing there with the doors locked, rotting away.

Why? Why have so many of our city churches come to this? And *what do you suggest that we do about it—if anything?* Is it hopeless?

Locked Doors. When a minister suggested that it might be a good thing if Jesus could come back and ride down Wall Street on another Palm Sunday, a Wall Street broker replied, with a surprised look on his face, "It would be a lonely ride. Every door on Wall Street is locked tight on Sunday!"

Only on Sunday? Someone has said that what made Jesus weep over Jerusalem was the fact that as He was riding along on Palm Sunday people did not kneel to surrender their hearts to Him in repentance and in faith; that was the tragedy of Palm Sunday.

Is the modern city more unfriendly to Him than Jerusalem was?

Mobilization. In the report of a recent meeting of prominent American churchmen studying the problem of the cities, we read that ". . . they called for church mobilization to reshape city life . . . [pointed to] the need to face up to the crises in the ghettos . . . [said that] we must either produce jobs for the city unemployed, or we are in for trouble . . . [that] we are rapidly approaching the brink of armed conflict in our cities . . . [and] must somehow prevent that conflict and the escalation of conflict . . . [that] we need a crash program."

Well—how do the churches go about all *this?* How do they organize for that mobilization? *Should* they mobilize? And exactly what, in the name of Christ, should they do?

The Ghetto. Long ago we memorized a little verse, the author of which we do not know. It read;

> He walked
> The sandy shore
> Of Galilee until
> The ghetto of Jerusalem
> Called Him.

Question: What did Jesus do for the ghetto?

Questions for Pupils on the Next Lesson: 1. How would you describe "the Christian hope?" 2. *When* were all the horrible things mentioned in Luke 21:11-12 to happen? 3. Did they happen, as Christ predicted? 4. Are you patient or impatient in your religious faith—and activity? 5. Does persecution help or hinder the work of the church? 6. Right or wrong: "The blood of the martyrs is the seed of the church"? How? 7. Have you *ever* suffered for your faith? Give place, date, particulars!

TOPIC FOR YOUTH
CHRIST IN THE CITY

People. Jesus was always aware of people as *individuals:* it was to help the individuals in the sick city of Jerusalem that He went to them on Palm Sunday. Perhaps He was aware that in Jerusalem there were the kind of people Willa Cather describes in her book, *O Pioneers!*

"Freedom often means that one isn't needed anywhere. Here [in the country] you are an individual, you have a background of your own. . . . But off there in the cities there are thousands of rolling stones like me. We are all alike; we have no ties, we know nobody, we own nothing. When one of us dies, they scarcely know where to bury him. Our landlady and the delicatessen man are our mourners, and we leave nothing behind us but a frock coat and a fiddle, or an easel, or a typewriter, or whatever tool we get our living by. . . . We have no house, no place, no people of our own. We live in the streets, in the parks, in the theaters. We sit in restaurants and concert halls and look about at the hundreds of our own kind and shudder."

There *are* people like that in our cities—millions of them! It was for such that Jesus wept, as well as for the wickedness of the city.

Not long ago, a militant organization of young Puerto Ricans in New York City took over a church by force; they literally broke into the place and "took over." Their reason for doing that was that this church, they said, had never even tried to help the suffering people who lived all around it. Of course, they were wrong in what they did: none of us has any right to take the law into his own hands, or to violate the property rights of others. We do not know that they were right when they said this church had done nothing . . . but we do know of *other* churches that have been guilty of that sin.

If you were a young preacher called to a church in the city that did nothing but keep itself alive,—what sort of program would you put on?

Christ's church, like its founder, is (or should be) primarily interested in people—especially Willa Cather's kind of people. . . .

Betrayal. John Oxenham has a stirring poem which he titled "He-They-We."

They hailed Him King as He passed by,
They strewed their garments in the road,
But they were set on earthly things,
And He on God.

They sang His praise for what He did,
But gave His message little thought;
They could not see that their soul's good
Was all He sought.

They could not understand why He,
With powers so vast at His command,
Should hesitate to claim their rights
And free the land.

Their own concerns and this world's hopes
Shut out the wonder of His news;
And we, with larger knowledge, still
His way refuse.

He walks among us still, unseen,
And still points out the only way,
But we still follow other gods
And Him betray.

JOHN OXENHAM

Getting Our Arms Around. "Ross Greek, who spends most of his time working as a youth minister on Los Angeles' Sunset Strip, spoke of a gathering of church women on a Thursday morning. He said that part of the answer to trouble there lay in having the parents take greater responsibility and in knowing where their children were during the late hours. Following his talk a woman came up to him . . . and remarked, 'This is not our problem. Our young people . . . know how to entertain themselves without going to the Strip.' Sunday at 2 A.M. Ross's telephone rang. It was the same woman's voice on the other end. Through tears she stammered out a request: 'My daughter was one of several teen-agers arrested last night in a riot on the Strip. Will you meet us at the jail, and see what you can do to help?'

"The health of all America's cities . . . depends on the willingness of people to accept the city's total life as part of their responsibility and to become involved with it. The suffering of one is the peril of all. That is the lesson many communities have learned since the angry, smoky summer of 1965.

"When people we care about are knocked down by adversity, we go where they are. We put our arms around their shoulders to transfuse hope. We look into their faces and remind them of our confidence in them. Today our cities need this kind of embrace. To become serious about loving people, even by the millions, is to help snatch them from the fire. In the process, something dramatic and good may happen to the way we feel about ourselves."—*Put Your Arms Around the City,* by James W. Angell (Fleming H. Revell Company).

That doesn't apply *just* to the city, either!

Sentence Sermon to Remember: The people are the city.—Shakespeare.

Questions for Pupils on the Next Lesson: 1. In what way are Christ's words eternal? 2. What does Luke 21 tell us about Christ's second coming? 3. What are we to do before He comes again? 4. Can we predict the course of our future history? 5. Is patience always a virtue, or is it sometimes a sign of weakness? 6. Do you have complete confidence that Christianity will win the whole world? 7. Explain the meaning of this: "In your patience possess ye your souls" (Luke 21:19).

LESSON XI—FEBRUARY 13

ENDURANCE AND THE CHRISTIAN HOPE

Background Scripture: Luke 17:20-37; 21:5-38
Devotional Reading: II Timothy 4:1-8

KING JAMES VERSION

LUKE 21 10 Then said he unto them, Nation shall rise against nation, and kingdom against kingdom:

11 And great earthquakes shall be in divers places, and famines, and pestilences; and fearful sights and great signs shall there be from heaven.

12 But before all these, they shall lay their hands on you, and persecute you, delivering you up to the synagogues, and into prisons, being brought before kings and rulers for my name's sake.

13 And it shall turn to you for a testimony.

14 Settle it therefore in your hearts, not to meditate before what ye shall answer:

15 For I will give you a mouth and wisdom, which all your adversaries shall not be able to gainsay nor resist.

16 And ye shall be betrayed both by parents, and brethren, and kinsfolk, and friends; and some of you shall they cause to be put to death.

17 And ye shall be hated of all men for my name's sake.

18 But there shall not a hair of your head perish.

19 In your patience possess ye your souls.

33 Heaven and earth shall pass away; but my words shall not pass away.

34 And take heed to yourselves, lest at any time your hearts be overcharged with surfeiting, and drunkenness, and cares of this life, and so that day come upon you unawares.

35 For as a snare shall it come on all them that dwell on the face of the whole earth.

36 Watch ye therefore, and pray always, that ye may be accounted worthy to escape all these things that shall come to pass, and to stand before the Son of man.

REVISED STANDARD VERSION

LUKE 21 10 Then he said to them, "Nation will rise against nation, and kingdom against kingdom; 11 there will be great earthquakes, and in various places famines and pestilences; and there will be terrors and great signs from heaven. 12 But before all this they will lay their hands on you and persecute you, delivering you up to the synagogues and prisons, and you will be brought before kings and governors for my name's sake. 13 This will be a time for you to bear testimony. 14 Settle it therefore in your minds, not to meditate beforehand how to answer; 15 for I will give you a mouth and wisdom, which none of your adversaries will be able to withstand or contradict. 16 You will be delivered up even by parents and brothers and kinsmen and friends, and some of you they will put to death; 17 you will be hated by all for my name's sake. 18 But not a hair of your head will perish. 19 By your endurance you will gain your lives. 33 "Heaven and earth will pass away, but my words will not pass away."

34 "But take heed to yourselves lest your hearts be weighed down with dissipation and drunkenness and cares of this life, and that day come upon you suddenly like a snare; 35 for it will come upon all who dwell upon the face of the whole earth. 36 But watch at all times, praying that you may have strength to escape all these things that will take place, and to stand before the Son of man."

MEMORY SELECTION: Heaven and earth shall pass away; but my words shall not pass away. Luke 21:33.

HOME DAILY BIBLE READINGS

Feb. 7. M. The Coming Kingdom, Luke 17:22-23.
Feb. 8. T. Hope for Trying Times, Luke 21:7-19.
Feb. 9. W. Living in Readiness, II Peter 3:9-14.
Feb. 10. T. On the Alert, Matthew 24:42-51.
Feb. 11. F. Patient Waiting for Christ, II Thessalonians 3:1-13.
Feb. 12. S. Sharing Our Hope, Titus 2:11-15.
Feb. 13. S. Paul's Charge to Timothy, II Timothy 4:1-8.

BACKGROUND

Luke 19-21 contains the last teachings of Jesus—or, better, the teachings of the last days of His life, when He was moving nearer and nearer to the cross. In these days He talked much of the future, and of what would happen on earth after He was gone from it. The past was the past—dead; let it be dead! There was tomorrow to think about, and the tomorrow He pictured was not exactly pleasant.

One day He predicted that "the days will come, in the which there shall not be left one stone [of the Temple] upon another . . ." (Luke 21:6). That shocked the disciples—and everyone else! In fear and trembling, the disciples asked Him, "*When?*" When was this to happen? And ". . . what sign will there be when these things come to pass?" How will we know it is about to happen?

Like many others, the disciples misunderstood this prediction. Jesus went on to explain it carefully, and to tell them how to behave before the disaster struck.

NOTES ON THE PRINTED TEXT

I. Nation shall rise against nation . . . and great earthquakes . . . and famines, and pestilences; and fearful sights, and great signs shall there be from heaven, Luke 21:10, 11. Think what the destruction of the Temple must have meant to the Jews! Here was one of the most beautiful buildings in the world—a masterpiece of religious architecture, with 40-foot columns cut out of single stones, with gleaming gold-covered dome and walls and inner appointments. It shone like a priceless diamond in the heart of the city; it was the pride and joy of all Jewry, and it was the center of their hopes. And this was to be *destroyed?* When? And, more important, *why?*

In previous lessons, we have mentioned the belief of the Jews in two ages of time: the present age, which was bad, and the age to come, which was to be the goldren age of God and of the dominance of the Jewish people. Now, *in between* these two ages there would be what they called the day of the Lord—and it was a terrible day indeed. It would be a day of judgment, of the destruction of the old and the beginning of the establishment of the better age—the Messianic Age. This is the time when Jerusalem would be destroyed (and destroyed it was), when earthquakes would be a sign of the end of the old order (Vesuvius erupted in A.D. 63, and there were earthquakes in this period in Greece, Asia Minor and Palestine), famine (there was always famine somewhere), pestilences, and "terrors and great signs from heaven" (verses 10-11). In the Bible and in Jewish thought, the idea of "signs" of coming disaster go back to the prophets. (Read Joel 2 and Acts 2:19, 20.) Signs in the heavens were warp and woof of apocalyptic writing—and are not always to be taken literally.

Jesus did not name the day or the hour. Some modern scholars attempt this, but usually their predictions are frustrated, or never quite work out. All Jesus said was that this terror and destruction would come. He was right about that. Josephus the historian says that when Jerusalem was destroyed, 1,100,000 people perished and 97,000 more went into captivity, the Temple was burned and its walls leveled with the ground and the whole city was made a desolation. Jesus and the prophets were right about *that!*

II. But before all these, they shall lay their hands on you, and persecute you . . . , Luke 21:12. Before the fall of Jerusalem, the young church would be called on to suffer, to be tested to prove whether it was worthy of survival. God himself could not protect the people from that! And here is the basic truth of the whole passage: out of this refining fire the people of the new church—of the new age—would rise to bear "testimony" of their faith (verse 13). They would suffer, yes— they would suffer even after this disaster was over, suffer again and again. Jesus promised them no immunity from this trouble and suffering and persecution; He only called on His people to endure it with patience, to refuse to hate and to build a new kingdom based on love. The only help or encouragement He gave them was that *all this was for His sake.* On their loyalty to Him, on their willingness to die for Him, He would build his kingdom. In their sacrificed blood and lives lay the seed of the church for tomorrow, for all ages to come. Suffer as I shall suffer: this is your challenge, and your glory.

When He said, "But there shall not a hair of your head perish" (verse 18), He was not offering them protection from physical harm; He had already told them that in the holocaust some of them would surely die (verse 16). His meaning, rather, must be the same as the meaning of Paul when that apostle said that no "height, nor depth, nor any other creature, shall be able to separate us from the love of God, which is in Christ Jesus our Lord" (Romans 8:39). Dying for Christ, dying for the love of God as we saw it in Christ, is not so much physical death as it is spiritual victory. Is there a better way for a man to die?

So, Christians—be patient. "By your endurance you will gain your lives" (verse 19, RSV). For he who loses his life for Christ's sake shall save his *soul!*

III. Watch ye therefore, and pray always . . . , Luke 21:36. Everything changes, or it dies. Today, our world is changing so fast that many of us are bewildered by it all, wondering "where it will all come out." Jesus had this in mind when He cautioned us that while almost everything on earth would eventually change (or "pass away"), His truth and His words would *never* change. This is the rock to which the Christian clings while the storms of change roar all around him: it is the Rock of Ages. He must cling to faith in Christ and confidence in the ruling hand of God over the storms and over history. Cling, and watch, and pray, in utter confidence. If he doesn't, he isn't in Christ, or of Him.

That the end would come was clear to Jesus; He didn't say when or where or how—so it is futile to keep on asking Him *that*. He said, only, "Have faith, and hope, and watch, and *be prepared for it when it comes.* Don't waste your time in surfeiting and drunkenness"—drunkenness in the lust for material things—and then have the day of the end catch you unprepared, like a rabbit with its foot caught in a snare. Live as though it were to come tomorrow, or even today. Watch (your conduct) and pray, and you will be able to "stand tall" in the presence of the Christ—at the judgment, and *now*.

SUGGESTIONS FOR TEACHERS

There are three possible themes for discussion today:

1. The second coming of Jesus—and the attitude required of His followers as they wait for it.
2. The cardinal Christian virtue of *patience*. This may take some careful explaining, especially to a younger generation that seems to want everything *now!*
3. *Hope*—without which Christianity would have perished in its cradle seems to be lost today in a world that has almost stopped hoping even for peace. . . .

TOPIC FOR ADULTS
ENDURANCE AND THE CHRISTIAN HOPE

Being Involved. "An adequate religious faith does not insure that life will be easier or better for us; it only makes it possible for us to face whatever life may hold. . . . The faith we need is that which comes from being involved in life. Our roots of confidence and hope do not grow deeper from *avoiding* the struggles but from being *involved* in them, particularly when we give our influence and effort on behalf of others. In giving ourselves we discover the meaning of love, and become like a tree planted by rivers of water, whose roots reach the overflowing streams of the divine love."—Rev. R. N. Wells, in *Ohio Grange*, January, 1970.

Like Winston Churchill, Jesus offers His followers only "blood, sweat and tears"—and all He asked of us was the courage to *endure,* and never to lose hope.

Hope of the World. Norman Cousins wrote this about a man we all should know—he was the perfect disciple of our day:

"He never thought much about happiness or unhappiness in terms of his own life. Generally, he thought in terms of what had to be done, and the time required for doing it. Now and then, something would happen that would give him a sense of fulfillment and deep reward. Only a few days earlier . . . he received word from a professorial colleague in France about an examination paper turned in by a nineteen-year-old boy. The question that had been put was: 'How would you define the best hope for the culture of Western Europe?' The answer given by the student was: 'It is not in any part of Europe. It is in a small African village and can be identified with an eighty-two-year-old man.'"

Can you identify the man? He was a missionary, a musician, a philosopher who gave up careers at home in which he would surely have been highly successful to go out to the jungle of Africa and work as a missionary doctor. His own generation called him the greatest man in the world. He worked in Lambarene. . . .

He had a great hope—and what he did about it is the hope of the world. . . .

Stopping God. "Woodrow Wilson, during his last illness, was talking with Ray Stannard Baker. Despite his rebuffs and defeats, Wilson was certain that an international organization like the League of Nations was bound to come. 'Don't worry, Baker,' he said, 'they can't stop God!' Wilson was a Christian, and that is the Christian's confidence."—Raymond E. Balcomb.

The League of Nations *was* organized—and it failed. But then came the United Nations, and it has not failed. Even if it does fail there would come another organization for peace, and another, and another. Some say that the United Nations lacks power in our world because Jesus Christ does not sit at its conference tables. Perhaps He does—perhaps He has come there again—and we just don't recognize Him!

He promised to come, and eventually He will.

Make Haste, O Lord! "In a theater we saw a comedian watering his garden and the plants growing instantly to flower and fruit. The sight was comic because it was absurd. We know that life of that kind is absurd. If this earth is a home where God lives with His children, then a home cannot be hurried. Spring and summer must come and who would wish their swift exit? Fall and winter must come and they also must tarry, if only to show that God can turn these also to His purpose. Children may cry meanwhile, 'Make haste, O Lord.' and perhaps must so cry, being children; but God knows that family love and family life become blasphemy if they are hurried. This truth holds in any worthy realm. Music in a hurry? The inspiration by which it is composed may be swift, but not unless comes the flash of cherished discipline and listening and waiting. A French surgeon used to say to his students in medical school: 'Gentlemen, don't be in a hurry, for there is no time to lose.' A striking phrase! The time we save, even the time we save through time-saving gadgets, may be time lost; for any time is lost that is not savored and that does not carry us toward life's true goal."—From a sermon by George A. Buttrick.

Someone has said that most of the trouble and defeats in our world come because we are in a hurry, and God isn't!

Persecution. "Time and again history reveals how God has made the wrath of men to praise Him. The early Christians had failed to obey the great commission. Had it not been for the persecution that broke out against the church, it might have become a short-lived, narrow sect, and not a universal religion. Persecution kept the church from stagnation. Persecution set many to work who otherwise would have remained comparatively useless, and called forth from them powers and characteristics that before had lain dormant. Persecution scattered the early Christians, but as they went they preached and thus the church was greatly enlarged."—Paul E. Holdcraft, in *Cyclopedia of Bible Illustrations*, p. 227. Quoted by permission of Abingdon Press, publishers.

Questions for Pupils on the Next Lesson: 1. Why was Jesus Christ crucified? 2. What did He accomplish in His death that He could not accomplish some other way? 3. Who was Demas? 4. What happened to Joseph of Arimathea as a result of the crucifixion? 5. Was the centurion converted at the cross? 6. For what crime were two others crucified with Christ? 7. Is it ever too late for a man to repent and be saved?

TOPIC FOR YOUTH
BEING SURE IN CHRIST

Inventor. "Migaly Seidner is an active inventor at the age of 92. His latest invention provides the means to cool turbo-generators. When asked how long it took to develop, he replied, 'I gave 50 years of my life to it. And that's the main lesson of my life. If you start something and believe in it, stick to it to the end.'

"In the Christian experience those who are faithful to the end find God giving life and hope, as He did in the beginning."—Daniel A. Poling.

We might call that being sure in Christ.

Courage, Patience. "A man writing about David Lloyd George, Prime Minister of England . . . records him as saying, 'Courage is the first of political virtues.' Then the man suggested, 'What about patience?' Lloyd George replied, 'Patience is the highest form of courage.'

"Patience is not exciting. But it is a divine quality which counts enormously in any good achievement, in an individual life, or in the larger life of the Kingdom of God on earth. To be patient is to be brave enough to believe; to believe in one's cause and its ultimate victory, and to believe in one's call to serve the cause."—John R. Simmons.

Press On. Calvin Coolidge was nicknamed Silent Cal by newspaper men who had difficulty getting him to talk. He seldom talked unless he had something to say, such as this: "Nothing in the world can take the place of persistence. Talent will not; nothing is more common than successful men with talent. Genius will not; unrewarded genius is almost a proverb. Education will not; the world is full of educated derelicts. Persistence and determination alone are omnipotent. The slogan 'press on' has solved and always will solve the problems of the human race."

Do you suppose he had been reading Philippians 3:14?

Harvest, Hoeing. "This practical supplication hangs on the wall of the vocational agriculture classroom at Gamaliel High School, says Charles Arterburn: 'Pray for a good harvest, but keep hoeing.' "—Joe Creason, in the *Louisville Courier-Journal.*

Seven Years of Hope. "She costs $5,000,000 a year to operate—less than the price of one jet bomber. More than 8,450 major operations have been performed aboard her and some 100,000 persons treated. When she goes to a port she stays in the harbor for ten months, a symbol of America's concern for suffering. She is manned by men in white, not khaki, and perhaps her greatest accomplishment is the training of 3,450 local doctors and nurses in the latest techniques—sometimes fifty years in advance of theirs. Her name is the S.S. *Hope,* and in the seven years she has been at sea she has visited seven nations on three continents and become the most welcome ship in the world.

"In an insane world of idiotic spending for fratricidal wars and 'defense,' the comparatively small expenditures for the S.S. *Hope* have lighted a tiny, inexpensive candle in the darkness. Imagine America's image, to say nothing of the world's health, if a thousand ships of *Hope* moved on the waters of the earth for the alleviation of the ills of mankind. The possibilities for peace in a healthy world stagger the imagination."— From an editorial in the *Saturday Review*, by Richard L. Tobin.

Patience, Persistence. "Let me tell you the story of one of America's most outstanding failures.

"In 1831 he failed in business.

"In 1832 he was defeated for the Legislature.

"In 1833 he again failed in business.

"In 1834 he was elected to the Legislature.

"In 1838 he was defeated for speaker; in 1840 defeated for elector; in 1843 defeated for Congress; in 1846 elected to Congress; in 1855 defeated for the Senate; in 1856 defeated for Vice President; in 1858 defeated again for the Senate; in 1860 he was elected President of the United States.

"His name? Abraham Lincoln."—*How to Make a Habit of Succeeding*, by Mack A. Douglas. Quoted by permission of Zondervan Publishing House, publishers.

Some people still think that Jesus was defeated as He hung on the cross. But . . . !

Not Consumed. "Out of the persecution of the Reformation the old Reformed Church of Europe took as its motto, 'Nevertheless, it was not consumed.' Every chapter of Christian history can conclude with this same statement."—Arthur House Stainback.

Sentence Sermon to Remember: The trouble with people these days is that they want to get to the promised land without going through the wilderness.—Faith Forsyte.

Question for Pupils on the Next Lesson: 1. Was the "good" thief sincere in his request to Jesus, or just afraid? 2. What does the word "paradise" mean? 3. How long did Jesus suffer on the cross? 4. Couldn't Jesus have redeemed us without the cross? Explain why, or why not. 5. Why did the people smite their breasts (Luke 23:48)? 6. Tell what you know about Joseph of Arimathea. 7. Is the cross "the heart of Christianity" now?

LESSON XII—FEBRUARY 20

THE DEATH THAT CHANGES LIVES

Background Scripture: Luke 23
Devotional Reading: Romans 5:1-11

LUKE 23 39 And one of the malefactors which were hanged railed on him, saying, If thou be Christ, save thyself and us.

40 But the other answering rebuked him, saying, Dost not thou fear God, seeing thou art in the same condemnation?

41 And we indeed justly; for we receive the due reward of our deeds: but this man hath done nothing amiss.

42 And he said unto Jesus, Lord, remember me when thou comest into thy kingdom.

43 And Jesus said unto him, Verily I say unto thee, To-day shalt thou be with me in paradise.

44 And it was about the sixth hour, and there was a darkness over all the earth until the ninth hour.

45 And the sun was darkened, and the veil of the temple was rent in the midst.

46 And when Jesus had cried with a loud voice, he said, Father, into thy hands I commend my spirit: and having said thus, he gave up the ghost.

47 Now when the centurion saw what was done, he glorified God, saying, Certainly this was a righteous man.

48 And all the people that came together to that sight, beholding the things which were done, smote their breasts, and returned.

49 And all his acquaintance, and the women that followed him from Galilee, stood afar off, beholding these things.

50 And, behold, there was a man named Joseph, a counselor; and he was a good man, and a just:

51 (The same had not consented to the counsel and deed of them:) he was of Arimathea, a city of the Jews; who also himself waited for the kingdom of God.

52 This man went unto Pilate, and begged the body of Jesus.

LUKE 23 39 One of the criminals who were hanged railed at him, saying, "Are you not the Christ? Save yourself and us!" 40 But the other rebuked him, saying, "Do you not fear God, since you are under the same sentence of condemnation? 41 And we indeed justly; for we are receiving the due reward of our deeds; but this man has done nothing wrong." 42 And he said, "Jesus, remember me when you come in your kingly power." 43 And he said to him, "Truly, I say to you, today you will be with me in Paradise."

44 It was now about the sixth hour, and there was darkness over the whole land until the ninth hour, 45 while the sun's light failed; and the curtain of the temple was torn in two. 46 Then Jesus, crying with a loud voice, said, "Father, into thy hands I commit my spirit!" And having said this he breathed his last. 47 Now when the centurion saw what had taken place, he praised God, and said, "Certainly this man was innocent!" 48 And all the multitudes who assembled to see the sight, when they saw what had taken place, returned home beating their breasts. 49 And all his acquaintances and the women who had followed him from Galilee stood at a distance and saw these things.

50 Now there was a man named Joseph from the Jewish town of Arimathea. He was a member of the council, a good and righteous man, 51 who had not consented to their purpose and deed, and he was looking for the kingdom of God. 52 This man went to Pilate and asked for the body of Jesus. 53 Then he took it down and wrapped it in a linen shroud,

53 And he took it down, and wrapped it in linen, and laid it in a sepulchre that was hewn in stone, wherein never man before was laid.

and laid him in a rock-hewn tomb, where no one had ever yet been laid.

MEMORY SELECTION: By this we know love, that he laid down his life for us; and we ought to lay down our lives for the brethren. I John 3:16 (rsv).

HOME DAILY BIBLE READINGS

BACKGROUND

Jesus is dying on His cross; His work on earth is done, yet now, in death, He is to perform the greatest work of all. It is "The Death That Changes Lives." Millions of men had died before Jesus, and more millions were to die after Him, but never before or after Calvary has any man accomplished so much in his dying!

Luke is not "wordy," and neither is he mystifyingly theological as he tells his version of the story of the death of Jesus. His account does not emphasize the grim, bloody details of the crucifixion; instead he writes in great compassion of the dying of Jesus, the redeemer of human lives and souls. He makes even the malefactors on their crosses attractive; he makes us love the centurion in charge of the execution squad; he makes glorious the figure of Joseph of Arimathea—a likable, gentle man who was redeemed *after* the crucifixion.

Here, Luke the beloved physician is at his best.

NOTES ON THE PRINTED TEXT

I. Jesus, remember me when you come in your kingly power, Luke 23:42 (rsv). Two "malefactors" died that day with Jesus, one on his left and the other on His right. Mark and Matthew call them thieves; they were more likely Zealots, convicted of rebellion against Rome. But they were still criminals, and there was calculated insult in having them die in company with Jesus. This was supposed to humiliate Him further in the eyes of the people. But it did not do that at all. Rather, it gave Jesus the chance to demonstrate, at the very door of death, His power and His compassion in the saving of men. They hoped to make Him look like a common criminal; they made Him the Saviour of mankind instead!

As the agony of the nails increased, one of the criminals cried out in terror, "If you are the Christ, save us!" No penitence here! Only *fear*. He is a man who knows he has done evil but still expects God to save him with a miracle at the moment of death. Jesus makes no reply to him. The other malefactor is different; he admits his guilt; he tells the screaming one quietly that they are getting only what they deserve. And he says as quietly to Jesus, "Remember me. . . ." He sensed something deeper in Jesus than his companion saw; He confessed, repented, asked forgiveness—and *got* it! Jesus welcomed him into "paradise"—the abode of the righteous. Paradise is a Persian word meaning "garden." Persian kings honored men they loved and trusted by inviting them to walk with them in their walled gardens. Jesus was saying, "Come, walk with me in the garden of the King!"

It is never too late to turn to Christ.

It was a dark hour, yes; Luke says that there was a darkness "over all the earth," and that the sun was lost behind the clouds. He also says that "the veil of the temple was rent in the midst" (verse 45). This was the veil that was hung before the Holy of Holies in the Temple; here was the Holy of Holies, the very presence of God, where no man save the High Priest might go, and he only once a year—on the Day of Atonement. God was so hidden from the people! But now, at the moment of the Redeemer's death, the veil was torn away, split down the middle, and the way to God was cleared and made open to all people. Jesus died with His arms stretched wide as if in welcome.

II. Now . . . the centurion . . . glorified God, saying, Certainly this was a righteous man, Luke 23:47. It is the moment of death; Jesus cried, "Father, into thy hands I commend my spirit!" And with that He died. It was a little prayer that he had learned as a child, a prayer said every night by the good Jew; you will find it in Psalm 31:5: "Into thy hands I commit my spirit: thou hast redeemed me, O Lord God of truth." It was the prayer of the trusting child, the "Now I lay me down to sleep" of His people. Only here, He was not lying down to sleep forever in death: He was committing Himself to the Father and to an endless work of redemption over the ages to come. The work of redemption began the moment He "gave up the ghost."

Near the cross stood the Roman centurion who had been in charge of the execution; he was obeying orders as He put Christ to death, but something beyond a military order tore at his heart. The Romans picked unusually capable and talented men for centurions. (Read Luke 7:1-9 for a good description of them.) This one was unusually sensitive to what was happening that day; he looked into the face of Jesus Christ and saw something that his companions missed. "Certainly," he said in the split seconds after Jesus died, "Certainly, this was a righteous man."

No, we cannot say that it was sound conversion to Christ—but it was certainly close to that.

No man is too bad, too "lost," to come to Christ. This centurion was no Jew; he was a despised Gentile, the officer in charge of the murdering of his Lord, and yet. . . .

III. And, behold, there was a man named Joseph . . . , Luke 23:50. A man named Joseph! Joseph of Arimathea—a town now thought to be Ramah, the birthplace of Samuel. He was a counselor—a member of the Sanhedrin that sent Jesus to His death. But Joseph was not there with them the day the vote for death was taken. Perhaps he sensed the innocence of Jesus, and by staying away refused to vote for His execution. He just stayed clear of the whole thing; he didn't want to be involved!

But a man with such a heart and mind *had* to be involved. Call it conscience, call it remorse, call it fear, call it what you wish: even though this Joseph failed to raise his voice in disagreement or protest, he could not stay clear of the grim, evil business. So after the death he went to Pilate (that took rare courage), and asked that the body of Jesus be turned over to him for burial, and gave Jesus his tomb in his own garden.

We are not quite certain where the garden was, and we probably shall never know. But that is unimportant. What is important is that Joseph came, though so late—came with a heart in which Christ was not yet dead. Poor tardy, courageous Joseph! He is like those of us who send flowers to the funeral of a man we might have honored when the man lived! He came; he gave Jesus his tomb.

SUGGESTIONS TO TEACHERS

To start the discussion, ask your class these three questions:

1. What did the cross mean to the Romans and the Jews who put Christ on it? They had put many other men on crosses: was *this* crucifixion something different from all the others?
2. What did the cross mean to Jesus' disciples? Only something horrible that might have been prevented?
3. What did the cross mean to Jesus?
4. And what was the purpose of the cross in the mind of God?

Get this one truth across, *the cross was redemptive: it changed lives.*

TOPIC FOR ADULTS
THE DEATH THAT CHANGES LIVES

The Point. "A master violinist visits a pawnbroker. He has fallen on evil days; his funds are low and he reluctantly finds it necessary to seek a loan.

"With the precious instrument in his hands, he calls at the shop with the three balls over the door. The pawnbroker appraises the violin and the transaction is made. The master violinist leaves with the money he needs, and a pawn ticket . . . as the pawnbroker places the violin on the shelf.

"Two things are true of the violin as long as it remains in the pawnshop. It is in the possession of one who is not its rightful owner—and it is not being used for the purpose for which it was created. It gathers dust on the shelf.

"But better days come when the violinist is able to claim his instrument. He hurries to the pawnshop, presents his ticket and the money to redeem it. In return, his violin is given him, and he rushes home. Breathlessly he enters his studio, opens the violin case, dusts off the valuable instrument, tightens the strings and resins the bow, and begins to play the exquisite music the violin was created to produce.

"Now the violin belongs once more to its rightful owner. Now it is doing that for which it was originally made to do.

"This is redemption! It is the theme of the Bible and it is precisely what Jesus Christ came into the world to do. Redemption is at the heart of Easter, for man was in the possession of one who was not his rightful master—Satan. He was not being used to do that for which he was created—to glorify God. A man who is unredeemed may be ethical, cultured, refined, even religious, but until he surrenders his heart to Christ his life is being used for something less than was intended.

"Don't let yourself miss the point. . . . Jesus Christ came into the world as the 'Lamb of God'—*the* sacrifice for sin. We must accept Him on His terms—not on diluted human terms. All His teaching all His life points to the cross . . . for He was born to die. By virtue of His willing sacrifice, *all men who place their trust in Him will live—forever.* . . . 'I am come that they might have life, and have it more abundantly.' "—Richard C. Halverson, in *The Gold Star Family Album,* edited by Arthur and Nancy De Moss (Fleming H. Revell Company).

Closed Case? "In the movie *The Life of Zola* there is a remarkable scene. Zola was battling to reopen the Dreyfus affair, but his evidence was not admitted and his witnesses were not allowed to testify. Finally, the judge declared that it was a closed case. As they were leaving the courtroom, Zola's lawyer pointed to a mural above the judge's head. It was a painting of the crucifixion. The lawyer said, 'That, too, was once regarded as a closed case.'

"That 'closed case' of nineteen centuries ago was opened by the hand of the Eternal. God manifested His limitless power in the resurrection of His Son, who stepped forth from the shadows of the tomb in the power of an endless life. The disciples became new men. Cowards were changed into heroes; pigmies became giants; broken reeds became pillars of iron."—John Sutherland Bonnell, quoted in *The Freedom to Fail,* by G. Don Gilmore (Revell).

Three Crosses. Amos L. Boren writes in *Highroad* of the three crosses on Calvary:

> I saw three crosses lifted high,
> In silhouette against the sky.
> > And on each cross in bold relief
> > I saw a man in deepest grief;
> > Three types of men in deepest grief.
>
> The right cross bore a man whose mind
> Rejected faith of every kind;
> > He jeered at love, and wailing, cried,
> > "Come, save thyself and us," and died.
> > Cursing God and love, he died.
>
> The cross upon the left-hand bore
> Another thief; but something more,
> > For to the center One, said he,
> > "In Paradise, remember me."
>
> And Christ, in all-redeeming love,
> Cried, "Them forgive! My God, above."
> > The prayer of Him upon the tree
> > Goes still to God for them—and me.
> > Prevails with God for them and me.
> > > > AMOS L. BOREN

Questions for Pupils on the Next Lesson: 1. Where was Emmaus? 2. Explain: "Their eyes were *holden.*" What made them "holden"? 3. What had the prophets spoken (Luke 24:25)? 4. *When* did Christ meet the two on the Emmaus road? 5. How many appearances did Jesus make after His resurrection? 6. Why did Jesus "vanish out of their sight" so quickly?" 7. Is Christ alive in *our* world? Explain.

TOPIC FOR YOUTH

Contact. The Death that Changes Lives. "Hubert Simpson tells of a picture painted for the Royal Corps of Signallers. It shows a signaller unarmed, sent out into no man's land to repair a cable snapped by shell-fire, sent out to restore the broken contact. The picture shows him dead in the fulfillment of his task, but in either hand he holds a fragment of the cable, even in death holding them together, the living current passing *through* his dead frame.

"That is a vivid illustration of what Jesus did for man by His death. Sin had severed the living contact between man and God. The fellowship was broken, the contact interrupted. Alone in no man's land, and with no weapon save His love, Christ brought the two ends together. Beneath the cross one can write the one word 'through' from death to life, through from sin to the possibility of moral victory, through to the very throne of grace, through Jesus Christ our Lord."—Leslie Badham, quoted in *The Minister's Manual,* p. 109, 1969; edited by Charles L. Wallis (Harper and Row).

Pearl Harbor. "Five minutes before eight o'clock on the morning of December 7, 1941, is a time that will live in infamy. At that moment Commander Mitsuo Fuchida led Japanese bombers in a surprise attack on Pearl Harbor. Nineteen naval vessels were sunk or severely damaged, one hundred eighty-eight United States aircraft destroyed, and twenty-two hundred eighty service men killed.

"But the crippling blow did not bring America to its knees. Three and a half years later Fuchida's Empire of the Rising Sun surrendered after atomic bombs were dropped on Hiroshima and Nagasaki.

"By unusual providence, Fuchida was in Hiroshima and left the day before the atomic bomb leveled the city. His escape moved him to ask, 'Why was my life spared?'

"Japan's defeat left millions of Japanese disillusioned who had upheld their emperor as a god. Fuchida was one. And he was bitter against the Americans for dropping the bomb on his country.

"He felt certain that Americans, like the Japanese, had tortured prisoners of war. While searching for evidence, he met a Japanese friend who had been detained in a hospital in Utah, and asked, 'What did they do to you?' The friend surprised him by saying, 'I was not tortured, but treated kindly by a nurse who helped me to regain my health. All the time she knew that her missionary parents had been shot by Japanese soldiers in the Philippines while they knelt in prayer.'

"This shook Fuchida. He wondered if he might have been wrong. He thought that there still might be hope for the world if enough people could be like the forgiving nurse. Back in Tokyo, a missionary handed him a printed tract of testimony. He read about an American bombardier named Jacob DeShazer who had been captured and tortured by the Japanese in a prison camp. After reading the Bible, the American began showing love to his persecutors in every way he could. More than that, after his release and return home, he had come back to Japan as a Christian missionary.

"Fuchida eagerly looked for and found a Japanese Bible. He began reading through the Gospels. 'When I reached Luke 23,' he later testified, 'and read Christ's prayer just before He died on the cross, I learned the meaning of God's love.'

"Transformed into an apostle of love, Fuchida met . . . DeShazer. The two teamed together and spoke to large crowds across Japan about the love of Christ that made them brothers. The man who led the attack on Pearl Harbor subsequently became a minister and declined the highest position in the Japanese Air Force so he could devote full time to Christian service.

"December 7th, then, is a good day on which to remember how God's power changed the man who led the infamous attack into an apostle of love. The new Mitsuo Fuchida's message is, 'On Christ's behalf, we beg you, let God change you from enemies into friends' (Corinthians 5:20)."—*Thinkables,* by James C. Hefley (Fleming H. Revell Company).

Three. "There were three crosses on Calvary, each declaring its own message. The one proclaims the fate of an impenitent world. Refusing to recognize its own guilt and neglecting its day of salvation, the world goes to its doom without a word of comfort from the Saviour of mankind. It dies without hope.

"A second cross demonstrates that 'whosoever believeth in him shall not perish but have everlasting life.' Even the criminal, the person who has lived his life away from God, will find mercy when in penitence he turns to the Saviour who died also for him.

"It is the third cross in which we glory. This supplies the answer to the question, 'What shall I do to be saved?' Through the ages and to all people it declares: 'Believe in the crucified Lord Jesus Christ and you will be saved.' "—E. Paul Hovey.

Sentence Sermon to Remember: The cross is the only ladder high enough to touch Heaven's threshold.—George Dana Boardman.

Questions for Pupils on the Next Lesson: 1. Can you name either of the two who met Jesus near Emmaus? 2. How many people saw the risen Christ? 3. What evidence is there that Jesus is alive *now?* 4. What problems about the resurrection troubled the two men Jesus met? 5. How did He tell them to answer their questions about Him? 6. Would the world have forgotten Jesus if there had been no Easter? 7. How can we bring others into a belief in the risen, living Christ?

LESSON XIII—FEBRUARY 27

WALKING WITH THE LIVING CHRIST

Background Scripture: Luke 24:1-49
Devotional Reading: I John 1-7

KING JAMES VERSION

REVISED STANDARD VERSION

LUKE 24 13 And, behold, two of them went that same day to a village called Emmaus, which was from Jerusalem about threescore furlongs.

14 And they talked together of all these things which had happened.

15 And it came to pass, that, while they communed together and reasoned, Jesus himself drew near, and went with them.

16 But their eyes were holden that they should not know him.

25 Then he said unto them, O fools, and slow of heart to believe all that the prophets have spoken:

26 Ought not Christ to have suffered these things, and to enter into his glory?

27 And beginning at Moses and all the prophets, he expounded unto them in all the Scriptures the things concerning himself.

28 And they drew nigh unto the village, whither they went: and he made as though he would have gone further.

29 But they constrained him, saying, Abide with us; for it is toward evening, and the day is far spent. And he went in to tarry with them.

30 And it came to pass, as he sat at meat with them, he took bread, and blessed it, and brake, and gave to them.

31 And their eyes were opened, and they knew him; and he vanished out of their sight.

32 And they said one to another, Did not our heart burn within us, while he talked with us by the way, and while he opened to us the Scriptures?

33 And they rose up the same hour, and returned to Jerusalem, and found the eleven gathered together, and them that were with them,

34 Saying, The Lord is risen indeed, and hath appeared to Simon.

35 And they told what things were done in the way, and how he was known of them in breaking of bread.

LUKE 24 13 That very day two of them were going to a village named Emmaus, about seven miles from Jerusalem, 14 and talking with each other about all these things that had happened. 15 While they were talking and discussing together, Jesus himself drew near and went with them. 16 But their eyes were kept from recognizing him.

25 And he said to them, "O foolish men, and slow of heart to believe all that the prophets have spoken! 26 Was it not necessary that the Christ should suffer these things and enter into his glory?" 27 And beginning with Moses and all the prophets, he interpreted to them in all the scriptures the things concerning himself.

28 So they drew near to the village to which they were going. He appeared to be going further, 29 but they constrained him, saying, "Stay with us, for it is toward evening and the day is now far spent." So he went in to stay with them. 30 When he was at table with them, he took the bread and blessed, and broke it, and gave it to them. 31 And their eyes were opened and they recognized him; and he vanished out of their sight. 32 They said to each other, "Did not our hearts burn within us while he talked to us on the road, while he opened to us the scriptures?" 33 And they rose that same hour and returned to Jerusalem; and they found the eleven gathered together and those who were with them, 34 who said, "The Lord has risen indeed, and has appeared to Simon!" 35 Then they told what had happened on the road, and how he was known to them in the breaking of the bread.

MEMORY SECTION: But if we walk in the light, as he is in the light, we have fellowship with one another. . . . I John 1:7.

HOME DAILY BIBLE READINGS

Feb. 21. M. The Empty Sepulcher, Luke 24:1-11.
Feb. 22. T. Jesus Appears to the Apostles, Luke 24:36-48.
Feb. 23. W. The Ascension of Jesus, Luke 24:49-53.
Feb. 24. T. The Great Commission, Matthew 28:16-20.
Feb. 25. F. Pressing Toward the Goal, Philippians 3:7-16.
Feb. 26. S. New Life in Christ, Colossians 3:1-11.
Feb. 27. S. Fellowship With the Living Christ, I John 1:1-7.

BACKGROUND

The body of Jesus was placed in Joseph's tomb late on Friday; Luke suggests that only the Roman guards were near the tomb on Saturday, which was the Jewish Sabbath. On Sunday, several women came with aromatic spices which they had prepared—*and they found an empty tomb* (verse 3). They ran back into the city to tell this amazing news "unto the eleven, and to all the rest" (verse 9). They were stunned. Only one of them—the impetuous Peter—got up and ran out to verify their fantastic story; he, too, found the tomb empty, and he "departed, wondering in himself at that which was come to pass" (verse 12).

The empty tomb was overwhelming, but it was not completely convincing evidence of the resurrection; it meant only that Jesus was not *there.* The two men in shining raiment (angels?) at the tomb had tried to tell them that Jesus was risen and had gone into Galilee—but we wonder if, in their almost hysterical condition, the apostles heard the women. In their minds raged the question, "If he is not there, then where *is* he?"

To tell where, Luke (and only Luke, of all the Gospel writers) tells us the story of walking to Emmaus. This is the first post-resurrection appearance of Jesus, the first conclusive evidence that He had risen. It was a *living* Christ who met and walked with two unnamed, bewildered men (some say one was a woman) whose eyes were not yet opened to what had happened. . . .

NOTES ON THE PRINTED TEXT

I. *And it came to pass, that, while they communed together and reasoned, Jesus himself drew near* . . . , Luke 24:15. According to the best authorities, Emmaus lay some seven miles west of Jerusalem. If the two men were walking from Jerusalem *west* to Emmaus, they were walking with the sun in their eyes, and so probably could not see clearly anyone standing between them and the setting sun.

Who were these men? Luke names only one of them: Cleopas, of whom we know nothing. They were sad men, confused men. Their own religious leaders had brought about Jesus' crucifixion. *Why?* They had refused to accept Him as the promised deliverer. *Why?* God had not saved Him from the cross. *Why?* And that empty tomb—what did *that* mean? They argued, wondered, reasoned, trying to get it all straight, and in perspective. They still did not understand. They were still thinking of a national redeemer, and, apparently, Jesus had not convinced them, even after all this, that He was not this (expected) national political deliverer of Israel. Their eyes were "holden" (held back) from the truth of what and who He really was. They were blind, too, against the blinding sun when He suddenly appeared before them on the road. They did not recognize Him at all. He was only a stranger they met on the road. . . .

He is still a stranger to most of us.

II. And beginning with Moses and all the prophets, he interpreted to them in all the scriptures concerning himself, Luke 24:27 (RSV). As they walked with Him along the road, they asked Him questions. Who was this crucified one? Was He or was He not "he which should have redeemed Israel?" (verse 21). This vision of the angels at the empty tomb—what did *that* mean? (That someone might have stolen the body?) Had He been a prophet, or just another rabbi (teacher)? They did not know; they wanted to know. . . .

Gently, Jesus took over the conversation, telling them that they were foolish of mind and sluggish of heart. They had read the Scriptures? Yes, they had. But had they understood what they read there? No, they had not. They believed in the old prophets about the coming of Messiah, yes—but they had not believed *all* the prophets said! Had they forgotten that the prophets had stressed the suffering and the death of the promised one, His persecution, His rejection? It was all there, in the Scriptures: had they missed it? This crucifixion in Jerusalem—did they not see it as the fulfilling of prophecy, as the plan of God. Did they not see that His victory over death in Joseph's garden was a greater victory than any He might have won by force over the Romans? Beginning with Moses in the Scriptures, He interpreted it all, from the foreshadowing in the prophets to the consummation in the garden.

His words enthralled them, but did not yet *convince* them. Different people have different interpretations of Scripture, and this might just be another (stranger's) interpretation. They wanted to talk more, to hear Him more, and so they invited Him into one of their houses, "for it is toward evening . . . And he went in to tarry with them" (verse 29).

It was fortunate for them that He did, for when He sat down to break bread with them "their eyes were opened." Then they knew Him! Perhaps they saw His pierced hands? Perhaps they caught at last the glory of God on His face? Whatever it was—it *convinced* them; the guest at their humble table was He, eating common bread with them in an ordinary place—and their eyes were opened at last to the reality of His presence.

It is a story typical of Luke; it is filled with compassion, patience and humility. Christ's first post-resurrection appearance was to lowly men seeking His truth, and not to scholars, kings or priests! His breaking of bread reminds us of His last supper, with a difference: it took place in a kitchen or a dining-room that was like *our* kitchens and dining-rooms. It was an extraordinary revelation in an ordinary place. We meet Him in the most unexpected places!

As quickly as His true nature was revealed to them He "vanished" from their sight; He was gone from them. . . . Almost, but not quite. A resurrection had taken place *in their hearts*, and they rushed back to Jerusalem to tell the eleven about it, and to tell all others who would listen. They could not keep the good news to themselves; they had to share it.

He who sees Christ clearly and knows Him intimately *must* go to others to tell them. . . . And only He in whose heart Christ is a risen, living presence really knows Christ; only for him is the resurrection *reality*.

SUGGESTIONS TO TEACHERS

In a Sunday-school class we once had a brilliant and beloved teen-ager who was obsessed with the passion to "prove" everything. He would say, "I won't believe anything I can't prove." We were glad that he was in that class: he stirred our minds, and kept us from foolish and unfounded statements. He was always at his best on Easter Sunday; he said to more than one teacher, "But how do you prove that Christ rose from the dead, and lives *now?*"

It was a good question, and it deserves a worthy answer. Try these for answers:

1. The risen Christ appeared *more than once,* according to the Bible.
2. The risen Christ has appeared countless times to men and women whose plans and dreams had collapsed.
3. He has appeared in the lives of men who have given their lives to prove that Christ lived in them as they shared their lives and their faith with others.
4. We see Him today in the eternal resurrection of nature, in every spring after every winter, in the lives of evil men who have been transformed into good men at His touch, in a church that errs often but somehow cannot die. . . .

And where else? Lead your class to discover other evidences of the living Christ—for if He is not alive, he is of little help to anyone. . . .

TOPIC FOR ADULTS
WALKING WITH THE LIVING CHRIST

Transformation. Dr. Paul E. Scherer tells us of the transforming power Jesus Christ had in the lives of His disciples *after* the crucifixion and the resurrection. While He lived, they had many doubts about Him, and asked Him many rather foolish questions; with His death the doubts increased; badly frightened, they huddled in hiding in Jerusalem. But once they *saw* the risen Christ, they no longer doubted.

"So it was with Peter, James and John, Andrew, Philip, Bartholomew, Matthew, and Thomas. They were not as little as they thought—not by a long shot! They saw now what poor fractions of reality they had been crawling into most of the time, hiding there, and trying to pull the whole in behind them. . . . They had lost their faith in the present, locking themselves in a room, like a child shut up indoors on a rainy day, not caring for its toys, pressing its nose against the glass, looking out on a dismal world. They thought it was the end! But it was the beginning! . . .

"Even our own dull spirits should be able to catch the sheen of it. There is One who is far more alive than we are, hoping often against hope to persuade us that life is not ugly and pointless, not even when we can hardly stand it; not silly and brutish and of no account; not filled with bleak and spotty anecdotes. . . ." Paul E. Scherer, in *Missions,* April, 1954.

The risen, living Christ has changed lives just like that in more people than we shall ever be able to count. Who wants more "proof" than that?

The Power. Peter Marshall was one of the outstanding preachers of our generation. He preached this about the living Christ:

"This is the fact that we in the twentieth century cannot ignore. . . . [During] the nineteen centuries before this one there [were] men and women who felt the same power in their lives . . . who had the same peace and inner serenity . . . who had the same joy and radiant victory.

"They were not crackpots, morons or lunatics. Included among them were some of the greatest minds the world has ever known . . . brilliant thinkers, philosophers, scientists, scholars. . . . They were not frustrated personalities who fled the world of reality. . . .

"This is the reality . . . to the man in the street . . . to the government clerk . . . to the anxious mother . . . to the confused schoolboy or schoolgirl. This is the real meaning of Easter. Forget the bunny rabbit and the colored eggs. Forget the symbols of spring that so often confuse and conceal the real meaning of what we celebrate on that day. No tabloid will ever print the startling news that the mummified body of Jesus of Nazareth has been discovered. Bringing the resurrected Christ into our lives, individual and national, is the only hope we have for making a better world. This . . . is the message for Easter."

Peter Marshall was too young to die, but he died well. The day they took him to the hospital—from which he was never to return—he said to his wife, "I'll see you in the morning."

On a Day Like This. There are those among us who believe in the "second coming" of Christ, but believe with equal joy that Christ has never left us! He is here, everywhere, now. Fay Inchfawn, a British poet, puts such a faith in these words:

> Sometimes, when everything goes wrong;
> When days are short and nights are long;
> When washday brings so dull a sky
> That not a single thing will dry.
> And when the kitchen chimney smokes,
> And when there's naught so "queer" as folks!
> When friends deplore my faded youth,
> And when the baby cuts a tooth.
> While John, the baby last but one,
> Clings round my skirts till day is done;
> And fat, good-tempered Jane is glum,
> And the butcher's man forgets to come.
> Sometimes, I say, on days like these,
> I get a sudden gleam of bliss.
> Not on some sunny day of ease,
> He'll come . . . but on a day like this!

Dr. William Barclay says, "The Christian lives forever and everywhere *in a Christ-filled world.*"

Questions for Pupils on the Next Lesson: 1. What or who would you say is the true foundation of the Christian church? 2. Do you agree with the Roman Catholic that the church is founded on Peter? 3. Who were the "strangers and foreigners" in Ephesians 2:19? 4. Of what was Christ "the chief cornerstone?" 5. Who holds the keys of the Kingdom of Heaven? 6. How does the Old Testament differ from the New, in its concept of the church? 7. How does our understanding of our Christian heritage help us to relate to the church's ongoing mission?

TOPIC FOR YOUTH
WALKING WITH CHRIST TODAY

Meeting Christ. "We shall never find Jesus through a factual investigation; we shall not find Jesus even on Easter Sunday in the church, with choirs singing, Scriptures being read, sermons being preached, and prayers being intoned. Jesus is an experience to be lived, and He goes before us. . . . [But] we shall find Him, again and again, if we know how to look for Him.

"Each of us must see and experience the living Christ in his own way in our own day. Even as He appeared at different times, at different places, in different forms, so shall it be for us.

"Mary Magdalene met Him in the garden; the disciples saw Him in an upper room, in the breaking of bread on the Emmaus road, at breakfast by the Galilean shore.

"St. Francis saw Him as a beggar on the road.

"John Wesley met Him at a small gathering in London.

"Luther met Him during a thunderstorm in Germany.

"Handel met Him in his study as he worked days without stopping in composing 'The Messiah.'

"Tom Dooley saw Him in the sick, suffering, weary people of Laos.

"And so it goes that each must meet and experience the living Christ daily as He meets us in life. Indeed, He is not 'way-back-there-when,' not *my* Lord. He goes ahead of us."—Landon K. Owen, Jr., "I Saw the Risen Christ Last Week—And it Wasn't Easter!" *Pulpit Digest,* April, 1968. Quoted by permission.

In the Darkest Hours. "Some of you remember James Gordon Gilkey, a Christian leader in Portland, Oregon. A few years ago he was told by his physician that he had fallen victim to an incurable disease. There was no possible way by which death could be averted or even long delayed. What did he do? Here is his account:

"'I walked out to my home five miles from the center of the city. There I looked at the river and the mountain which I love—and then as the twilight deepened—at the stars glimmering in the sky. Then I said to them, 'I may not see you many times more. But River, I shall be alive when you have ceased running to the sea. Mountain, I shall be alive when you have sunk down into the plain. Stars, I shall be alive when you have fallen in the ultimate disintegration of the universe.' Gilkey knew that one of the shining possibilities of eternal life is that God can be trusted even in our darkest hours.

"Let us hear . . . the conversation between Longinus and Pilate's wife, Procula (in Masefield's play, *The Trial of Jesus*). She asks, 'What do you think the man believed, centurion?' 'He believed that He was God, they say.' 'What do you think of that claim?' 'If a man believes anything up to the point of dying on the cross for it, he will find others to believe it.' 'Do you think He is dead?' 'No, lady, I don't.' 'Then where is He?' 'Let loose in the world, lady, where neither Roman nor Jew can stop His truth.'

"... A whole family of ideas cluster about this central faith (in the resurrection): a universe whose doors are open; a love that does not discard its highest creations; a God who can be trusted at all times—whatever comes. We see them all focused on the central figure of the resurrection. Christ has opened to us the shining possibilities of the life that is eternal. . . . 'He is not dead. He is alive forevermore. He has in His hands the keys of death and hell. Hallelujah! The Lord God Ominipotent reigneth!'"—Robert J. Arnott, in *Pulpit Preaching*, March, 1968.

Inviting. "If we desire to recognize and accept the presence of the Living Christ, we must reach out and grasp for it. We, too, as the men of Emmaus, must invite the Stranger to stay with us. The invitation must turn back the curtain surrounding our lives so that He can come and live in every room in the house. . . . You know what I mean. When guests come, we dust the rug, clean the pictures in the living room, and invite them there only. . . . However, Christ must be more than a house guest. He must settle in our house. He must be a 20-hour-a-day companion. He must be invited to see how we act with our husbands and how we treat our wives or children. Young people, he must be invited on our dates. Men, he must be invited to help transact business. He must be invited to the dinner table as well as to the family altar. That is what it means to invite Christ to stay with you."—Rev. Jimmie L. Gentile.

Sentence Sermon to Remember: I find the name of Jesus Christ written at the top of every page of modern history.—George Bancroft.

Questions for Pupils on the Next Lesson: 1. Where and when is the word "church" first used in the Bible? 2. Some say that Jesus never meant to leave a church: true or false? 3. Describe the organization of the first Christian churches. 4. Is "the church" a building, a people, a mission or a message? 5. How does Paul (in Ephesians 2) describe the foundations of the church? 6. Define the word "church." 7. Is the modern church similar to or quite different from the church of the New Testament?

MARCH, APRIL, MAY, 1972

THE CHURCH: ITS NATURE AND MISSION

LESSON I—MARCH 5

THE FOUNDATION OF THE CHURCH

Background Scripture: Isaiah 28:16; Jeremiah 31:31-34;
Matthew 16:13-20; Ephesians 2:19-22
Devotional Reading: Jeremiah 31:31-34

EPHESIANS 2 19 Now therefore ye are no more strangers and foreigners, but fellow citizens with the saints, and of the household of God;

20 And are built upon the foundation of the apostles and prophets, Jesus Christ himself being the chief corner stone;

21 In whom all the building fitly framed together groweth unto a holy temple in the Lord:

22 In whom ye also are builded together for a habitation of God through the Spirit.

MATTHEW 16 13 When Jesus came into the coasts of Caesarea Philippi, he asked his disciples, saying, Whom do men say that I, the Son of man, am?

14 And they said, Some say that thou art John the Baptist; some, Elias; and others, Jeremias, or one of the prophets.

15 He saith unto them, But whom say ye that I am?

16 And Simon Peter answered and said, Thou art the Christ, the Son of the living God.

17 And Jesus answered and said unto him, Blessed art thou, Simon Barjona: for flesh and blood hath not revealed it unto thee, but my Father which is in heaven.

18 And I say also unto thee, That thou art Peter, and upon this rock I will build my church; and the gates

EPHESIANS 2 19 So then you are no longer strangers and sojourners but you are fellow citizens with the saints and members of the household of God, 20 built upon the foundation of the apostles and prophets, Christ Jesus himself being the chief cornerstone, 21 in whom the whole structure is joined together and grows into a holy temple in the Lord; 22 in whom you also are built into it for a dwelling place of God in the Spirit.

MATTHEW 16 13 Now when Jesus came into the district of Caesarea Philippi, he asked his disciples, "Who do men say that the Son of man is?" 14 And they said, "Some say John the Baptist, others say Elijah, and others Jeremiah or one of the prophets." 15 He said to them, "But who do you say that I am?" 16 Simon Peter replied, "You are the Christ, the Son of the living God." 17 And Jesus answered him, "Blessed are you, Simon Bar-Jona! For flesh and blood has not revealed this to you, but my Father who is in heaven. 18 And I tell you, you are Peter, and on this rock I will build my church, and the powers of death shall not prevail against it. 19 I will give you the keys of the kingdom of heaven, and whatever you bind on earth shall be bound in heaven, and whatever you loose on earth shall be of hell shall not prevail against it.

19 And I will give unto thee the keys of the kingdom of heaven: and whatsoever thou shalt bind on earth shall be bound in heaven; and whatsoever thou shalt loose on earth shall be loosed in heaven.

20 Then charged he his disciples that they should tell no man that he was Jesus the Christ.

loosed in heaven." 20 Then he strictly charged the disciples to tell no one that he was the Christ.

MEMORY SELECTION: I am laying in Zion for a foundation a stone, a tested stone, a precious cornerstone, of a sure foundation. Isaiah 28:16.

HOME DAILY BIBLE READINGS

Feb. 28. M. *Thou Art the Christ,* Matthew 16:13-20.
Feb. 29. T. *The Chief Cornerstone,* Ephesians 2:17-22.
Mar. 1. W. *The Living Stone,* I Peter 2:6-10.
Mar. 2. T. *A Basis for Christian Living,* Matthew 18:15-20.
Mar. 3. F. *The Master Builder,* I Corinthians 3:10-15.
Mar. 4. S. *The Superior Covenant,* Hebrews 8:8-13.
Mar. 5. S. *The New Covenant,* Jeremiah 31:31-34.

BACKGROUND

It is about the year 62—some thirty years after the crucifixion of Jesus. Paul is now the leading apostle of the church, and he has organized churches from Jerusalem to Rome. From his prison in Rome, he writes the letter we call "Ephesians," a letter which was probably circulated through all the churches. It is a letter with one purpose: to establish the centrality of Christ as founder of all the churches that bear His name. The apostle is writing to churches filled, not with ex-Jews, but with Gentiles—a fact that accounts for the peculiar wording of the epistle.

Matthew quotes Jesus in chapter 16:13-20 to lay further emphasis on Christ as the foundation of the Christian church. Notice that he, too, speaks in *Gentile* territory—Caesarea Philippi, a Gentile city north of the Sea of Galilee. This was the seat of the old Roman nature cult of Pan, and before that of the old Canaanitish deities.

So in order that the world outside Jewry might clearly understand, the foundations of the church are explained in both passages in terms the people could not possibly misunderstand. They were a little confused about it then—and some of us still are—but that is the people's fault, not the fault of Jesus or of Paul.

NOTES ON THE PRINTED TEXT

I. *Now therefore ye are no more strangers and foreigners . . . ,* Ephesians 2:19. Gentiles hated Jews, and vice versa, from Moses to Jesus—which was a long time! Living under the Old Testament covenant, the Jews were a most exclusive people. Sure that they were "the chosen people," they built high religious, social and economic fences to keep out anybody (mainly the Gentiles) who might have a disastrous influence on their religion, and those "foreigners" whose blood might bring an evil taint to theirs by way of intermarriage. The Gentiles threw up some fences, too; they were bitter toward the Jews, resenting the "inferior" status the Jews had applied to them. So, separated from the Jews in religious ceremonials and beliefs, mutual animosity and contempt was the order of the day. The Gentiles were "strangers and foreigners"—which made a pretty bad situation and a poor foundation on which to build any unity in religion—or, for that matter in anything else.

But now, through Christ, they had become "fellow citizens with the saints and members of the household of God" (verse 19 RSV). Paul uses the word "saints" to denote Christians in general. In Christ, they were no longer either Jews or Gentiles, no longer separated, no longer different from each other: they were one family in a new faith. They broke bread together; met and sang and prayed together. One faith, one *family*. With such people only Christ could have brought that about.

Paul uses another figure: he says that they are all part of one house, or *building*. They are being built into one great structure upon the foundation of "the apostles and prophets." (Here, the prophets are not those of the Old Testament but the New—all gifted with the Holy Spirit, all inspired teachers of the church.) All kinds of men were in this "structure," bound together in a unity that broke through the old prejudices, hatreds and bitterness. It was one big, growing family, one big growing building.

There was one thing these dwellers in the new house of faith were supposed never to forget unless they wanted the whole structure to collapse: this was that it was Christ Jesus himself, nothing and no one else, who was the cornerstone of the structure. It was this cornerstone that held the whole thing together. Realizing this, the people knew that their house would become something more than a house: "a holy temple" (verse 21). It was a temple built, not on any one man among them, not on any one doctrine or creed, *but only on their unity in Christ. That* is the foundation of the church.

This temple actually was "a house not made with hands, eternal, in the heavens" (II Corinthians 5:1 RSV). ". . . the real temple surpasses any building made by hands. Its massive foundation and glorious walls are composed of living souls. Every believer who is united with Christ has a place in this structure. It thus included men of all races and times. This sanctuary God has made to be His dwelling place. Some day the building will be completed, and will become a source of blessing and rejoicing for the whole world."—Dr. Charles R. Erdman.

II. Thou art the Christ, the Son of the living God, Matthew 16:16. The scene shifts back to Jesus talking with His disciples, asking them who and what they and the people generally think He is. He needed to know what was the general feeling about Him. The disciples replied that some (including Herod, in Matthew 14:2) thought He was John the Baptist raised from the dead. Others thought He was Elijah, returned to earth (as prophesied in Malachi 4:5) to appear as forerunner of the promised Messiah. Or Jeremiah, the great prophet renowned for his sufferings.

Now the Baptist and Elijah and Jeremiah were all good men. Inspired, yes—but still men, flesh and blood, *human*. And that, Jesus wanted His disciples to know, was not enough when they thought of Him. He was human, yes—and a lot more. Peter saw it in a flash, and he burst out with, "Thou are the Christ, the Son of the living God." Perhaps every one of the disciples had hoped that Jesus was the Messiah when they "joined up" with the band, but Peter was the first to shout it to the world. According to Mark, he said simply, "Thou art the Christ." He meant, "Thou art the *Messiah!*"

It was the answer Jesus wanted to hear; He turned to Peter and said, "Simon, son of Jonah, you are favored indeed! You did not learn that from mortal man; it was revealed to you by my heavenly Father" (*New English Bible* translation). Jesus also said something then that has created argument in His church ever since: ". . . you are Peter, and on this rock I will build my church." That verse and saying is found only in Matthew, and scholars wonder if it really was spoken by Jesus. He probably wouldn't have used the word "church," for at that time there was no church as we know it. But many Christians and Christian churches accept and believe it literally—especially the Roman Catholic Church, which teaches that at that moment the church was literally founded on Peter. Others—Protestants for instance—see it as a play on the word "rock" as applied to Peter. These are two views or interpretations, and there are arguments to support both.

But the first church did not recognize Peter *the man* as its highest leader or authority. Paul "opposed [Peter] to his face" (Galatians 2:11). It appears that James was the "top man" in the church and not Peter. All honor to Peter as the first one to cry, "Thou art the Messiah!" All honor to him for his tremendous contribution to the faith! But to most of us, *it was the confession and not the fisherman that was the rock on which the church was founded.*

Peter was a man; Jesus was man *and more.* He was both human and divine, both son of man and Son of God. In the end, it is our faith in Him that matters, not our faith in Peter. In Jesus is the power and the glory of the church; lacking that power, the church would never have survived the centuries of persecution, error and corruption that followed. From His hands we take the keys of the Kingdom. He promised those keys not only to Peter, but to all the disciples (see Matthew 18:18). "To bind or loose, in Jewish usage, meant to declare certain actions either forbidden or permissible" (Rhoda C. Edmeston).

Christ *founds* Christian churches; men merely *organize* them.

SUGGESTIONS TO TEACHERS

Socrates, we are told, was one of history's greatest teachers—and he taught by asking his students questions. Questions and answers: that was the "dialogue." Try it today with this lesson on the founding of the Christian church:

1. How was the Christian church different from its Old Testament antecedents?
2. Why is personal confession of Christ so important to membership in the church?
3. What establishes Christ as "the church's *one* foundation?"
4. Would the ideals of the New Testament church work in our churches today?
5. What, in your opinion, is the *mission* of the church?

Other questions will come from your students: start with these. . . .

TOPIC FOR ADULTS
THE FOUNDATION OF THE CHURCH

The True Church. "The true church is discovered by means of the personality of Christ. One does not enter the true church by joining the Roman Catholic Church or the Methodist Church or by joining any one of the hundreds of churches. Various churches are only varied expressions of the true church. The true church is a reality which cannot be contained within an institutional strait jacket. Jesus possessed no organizational form; He didn't have a Sunday school or a choir or even a Bible as we know it today. He had no creed, no doctrine as outlined by shrewd theologians. Indeed, He said, 'Unless ye become like a little child you cannot enter the true church, the kingdom of heaven.' The little children He spoke of knew only that they liked Him. . . .

"The true church is not something founded by Simon Peter, or Martin Luther or John Wesley or Mary Baker Eddy. The true church is founded by individuals who recognize what Peter and a myriad of saints through history have recognized: 'Thou art the Christ, the Son of the living God.' Wherever you recognize personality as being godly and desire to be as that personality, to be like him, then you are part of the true church and Jesus will say to you just as surely as He said to Peter, 'Thou art the rock, and upon this rock I will build my church.' If you want to find fulfillment of the urge for community you may do it through Christ and only through Christ."—Ensworth Reisner, in a sermon, "The Search for the True Church."

The Original Church. "Dr. A. J. Gordon transformed a cold Boston congregation into a flaming New Testament church. He did not do it by starting a new church down the street, or by excommunicating the unfaithful, but by developing 'a church within the church.' He was a New Testament Christian; he preached New Testament Christianity and he built a New Testament church. Today, we are a long way from the original. 'This' is not 'that!' I have heard of a man who boasted that he possessed an ax that dated back to George Washington's time. 'Of course,' he admitted, 'it has worn out two heads and five handles!' Much of modern Christianity is just about that original."—*Why Not Just Be Christians,* by Vance Havner (Revell).

Well—do we *want* a New Testament church. Would you be happy in it or not? Do you see any tendencies in the modern church to restore its New Testament form and content? What is this thing that today we call "the underground church?" Is that a step back to the New Testament church . . . ?

What Goes On? Here are two very short reports on the modern church:

A prominent Methodist preacher tells of going to an upstate New York conference to give a series of sermons. As he walked up the steps into the church where the conference was meeting, he saw three boys— aged ten or twelve—looking in through an open window. One of them turned to him and said, "What goes on in there, Mister?" What a question!

The minutes of an unnamed church meeting contained the following item: "The Lord's Prayer was read and approved."

Put the two together: is *approving* of an old prayer or of what a blessed Someone said centuries ago all that is going on in your church? Is that *all* the early church did? What did the disciples' church do that we aren't doing?

What goes on in your church that makes it a good church? Let us add one more short report: when a preacher shook hands with a strange man at the door after the service he asked the stranger to "come again," and the stranger replied with one sharp, stinging word: "Why?" Why should anyone come to *your* church?

Questions for Pupils on the Next Lesson: 1. What does the word "Pentecost" mean? 2. What time of the year did the Jews celebrate Pentecost? 3. How did the New Testament Pentecost differ from that of the Old Testament? 4. Has the experience of the church in Acts 2:2-3 ever been repeated? 5. What is meant by "speaking in tongues?" 6. What was "The Day of the Lord?" 7. Name five "Pentecostal" churches or denominations.

TOPIC FOR YOUTH
HOW THE CHURCH BEGAN

How It Began. How did the church begin? There have been thousands of books and magazine articles written on that question, and we could not read them all in a lifetime. But we like the two short little verses written by an unknown poet that ring a bell in our souls when we think of the building of the Christian church and churches:

> God builds no churches! By His plan
> That labor has been left to man;
> No spires miraculously arise,
> No little mission from the skies
> Falls on a bleak and barren place
> To be a source of strength and grace;
> The church demands its price
> In human toil and sacrifice.
>
> The humblest spire in mortal ken
> Where God abides, was built by men;
> And if the church is still to grow,
> Is still the light of hope to throw
> Across the valleys of despair,
> Man still must build God's house of prayer.
> God sends no churches from the skies;
> *Out of our hearts must they arise.*

We like that, not because of its inspiring lines but because of what is between the lines. Men build churches *because they must have them,* because something within them cries out for the message of the church. The church began in this awareness of human need and the need of the human for the divine—and because One came and preached and was crucified in God's effort to meet and conquer the deepest needs of the human heart. The church began with a Christ inspiring men to *build*— and they still build, forever in hope and faith. . . .

Steeples. Have you ever wondered why they put steeples on churches?

"In the historic town of Annapolis Royal, Nova Scotia, there stands a small church edifice with a unique top piece on its spire. It is not a weather vane, or a rooster, or any of the various things found as decorative finish for church spires. Glistening there in the light is the form of a human hand, closed, with the index finger pointing straight up.

"This meaningful symbol is preserved with gold leaf and may be seen in full view at any angle of approach. There it has stood for many decades, giving its silent message to every passer-by."—Frederick P. Freeman.

The church was founded *to make men look up.* . . .

Who Needs It? "A cartoon showed a young lady speaking to a friend on the telephone: 'We're going to have a New Year's party for people who hate New Year's Eve parties.'

"Just so, to some persons, the church is just another thing to do, another organization to join. PTA, League of Women Voters, Little League, Civic Music Association, Community Chest, Red Cross, women's clubs, bridge clubs, reading clubs, political party, business or professional association, United Nations, English Speaking Union—church!

Who needs the church? Those who have a need for it, perhaps, who are not too involved in other good organizations.

"Who needs the church? Every man, every woman, every boy and girl needs the church. Why? Why because the church is the gift of God to His human children. The church is not just another organization of idealistic people, of sincere or insincere 'do-gooders.' It was not created by a group of people who banded together to form it.

"*Through the resurrection of Jesus Christ God created the church.* Therefore, the man and woman outside the Christian fellowship need it in order to have the new life, eternal life, open to all who receive it by their trusting faith."—David A. MacLennan.

I Will Build. "The church's preoccupation must be Christ. Jesus did not say, 'I will build *your* church,' or '*You* will build my church,' He said, '*I* will build my church.'"—Arthur F. Fogartie, in *Presbyterian Journal.*

We sympathize with the minister who asked his people never to say, "*My* church," but always to say, "*Christ's* church," for that is exactly what it is.

The Humble Beginnings. "It began as a small movement among the obscure section of the despised population of a remote province of the Roman Empire. Its leader died the death of a criminal. Its first leaders were hated by their own countrymen. It was limited almost entirely to the slums of the great cities and to the unlearned in the small towns. It quickly drew upon itself ridicule and persecution. It had no rewards or honors to confer. Yet underneath the pomp and power of the Roman Empire the ferment of Christian truth was working, till Rome itself was gone and the leaven of Christ's Kingdom had utterly transformed the world. The stone which the builders rejected has become the head of the corner."—Halford E. Luccock.

Perhaps it was because the builders were so quick to pick up the rejected stone that they found power to do all that . . . !

Sentence Sermon to Remember: A church is God between four walls.
—Victor Hugo.

Questions for Pupils on the Next Lesson: 1. Describe the Holy Spirit.
2. How would you react to Peter's sermon if it were preached in your
church? 3. Why has Chirstian interest in Pentecost declined? 4. Why
do we refer to the Holy Spirit as "He" and not "It?" 5. Under what
conditions may we expect the blessings of the Holy Spirit? 6. Describe
the Jewish Feast of Pentecost. 7. What great lessons do you find in the
Christian Pentecost?

LESSON II—MARCH 12

THE SPIRIT EMPOWERS THE CHURCH

Background Scripture: Acts 1:1-2:42
Devotional Reading: Acts 1:1-8

KING JAMES VERSION

ACTS 2 And when the day of Pentecost was fully come, they were all with one accord in one place.

2 And suddenly there came a sound from heaven as of a rushing mighty wind, and it filled all the house where they were sitting.

3 And there appeared unto them cloven tongues like as of fire, and it sat upon each of them.

4 And they were all filled with the Holy Ghost, and began to speak with other tongues, as the Spirit gave them utterance.

14 But Peter, standing up with the eleven, lifted up his voice, and said unto them, Ye men of Judea, and all ye that dwell at Jerusalem, be this known unto you, and hearken to my words:

15 For these are not drunken, as ye suppose, seeing it is but the third hour of the day.

16 But this is that which was spoken by the prophet Joel;

17 And it shall come to pass in the last days, saith God, I will pour out of my Spirit upon all flesh: and your sons and your daughters shall prophesy, and your young men shall see visions, and your old men shall dream dreams:

18 And on my servants and on my handmaidens I will pour out in those days of my Spirit; and they shall prophesy:

19 And I will show wonders in heaven above, and signs in the earth beneath; blood, and fire, and vapor of smoke:

20 The sun shall be turned into darkness, and the moon into blood, before that great and notable day of the Lord come:

REVISED STANDARD VERSION

ACTS 2 When the day of Pentecost had come, they were all together in one place. 2 And suddenly a sound came from heaven like the rush of a mighty wind, and it filled all the house where they were sitting. 3 And there appeared to them tongues as of fire, distributed and resting on each one of them. 4 And they were all filled with the Holy Spirit and began to speak in other tongues, as the Spirit gave them utterance.

14 But Peter, standing with the eleven, lifted up his voice and addressed them, "Men of Judea and all who dwell in Jerusalem, let this be known to you, and give ear to my words. 15 For these men are not drunk, as you suppose, since it is only the third hour of the day; 16 but this is what was spoken by the prophet Joel:

17 'And in the last days it shall be, God declares,
that I will pour out my Spirit upon all flesh,
and your sons and your daughters shall prophesy,
and your young men shall see visions,
and your old men shall dream dreams;
18 yea, and on my menservants and my maidservants in those days
I will pour out my Spirit; and they shall prophesy.
19 And I will show wonders in the heaven above
and signs on the earth beneath,
blood, and fire, and vapor of smoke;
20 the sun shall be turned into darkness
and the moon into blood,
before the day of the Lord comes,
the great and manifest day.

21 And it shall come to pass, that whosoever shall call on the name of the Lord shall be saved.

21 And it shall be that whoever calls on the name of the Lord shall be saved.' "

MEMORY SELECTION: But ye shall receive power, after that the Holy Ghost is come upon you: and ye shall be witnesses unto me both in Jerusalem, and in all Judea, and in Samaria, and unto the uttermost part of the earth. Acts 1:8.

HOME DAILY BIBLE READINGS

BACKGROUND

The word "Pentecost" means "fiftieth"; in the Jewish calendar of holy days it came 49 days after Passover; in the Christian calendar, fifty days after Easter. It was perhaps the most popular feast of the Jewish year; it came in the early days of June, just at the time when the grain harvest was completed. Some called it "The Feast of Weeks," some others, "The Day of First Fruits." Pilgrims by the thousand flocked into Jerusalem from the country within a fifty-mile radius, cramming the streets and the Temple courts. It was a great, *happy* day.

The disciples of Jesus were in town that day, meeting in an upper room near the Temple. What happened to them on this happy morning changed the whole meaning of Pentecost; it became through them the first birthday of the Christian church.

Some very strange things happened that morning. . . .

NOTES ON THE PRINTED TEXT

I. And suddenly there came a sound from heaven as of a rushing mighty wind . . . and there appeared unto them cloven tongues like as of fire . . . , Acts 2:2, 3. The very air of the room was filled with something tense, electric, exciting. The disciples themselves were filled with excitement, *for they expected something to happen.* They were "all with one accord in one place." Their hearts were fixed on the risen Christ, whom they had just seen ascend into heaven; they wondered, "What now? Is it all over—or have we a great work yet to do?" Their hearts were on fire with hope and expectancy—but they knew that if they were to do the great work of establishing the Kingdom of the Lord, they would need a greater courage and strength than they had ever had before this day. They sat there praying. . . .

And as they sat, there came upon them "a sound from heaven like the rush of a mighty wind." Not wind itself, but the *sound* of a wind. It was the symbol of the Holy Spirit—mighty, mysterious, heavenly, unseen. Many of us have felt it in a precious moment of religious experience and conviction, when our hearts were overwhelmed as this powerful, mysterious Spirit took hold of us and shook us. "And there appeared unto them cloven tongues like as of fire." There was no fire, but upon *each one of them* there was a "luminous tongue, symbolic of the fervent, zealous witness each would be empowered to bear" (C. R. Erdman). John Wesley had had that happen to him: in such a moment he felt "a strange warming of the heart." Isaiah had hot coals put on his tongue and Jeremiah had a fire break out in his heart. Fire and wind were and still are symbols of the presence of the Spirit and of God; they set us ablaze, and they burn with a supernatural power that we can feel but never adequately describe.

Its effect was dramatic and indescribable. They began to "speak in other tongues." Just what this means we are not certain. Luke describes it as a gift of speaking in foreign languages, and many still think of it the same way; the room was filled with men who came from different parts of the country, with different accents and even different languages, and to Luke it was a bedlam of "foreign" languages spoken or shouted by "foreigners." Others believe that it was a case of ecstatic excitement in which the disciples burst into a speech which was "a temporary endowment granted for a special purpose, one of the miraculous gifts which marked the age of the apostles" (Erdman).

In trying to interpret what happened at Pentecost we can take either position. Dr. Erdman's interpretation seems the more logical to most of us, but however we explain this phenomenon (or don't explain it), the thing to remember is that the disciples realized at Pentecost that the Spirit of God had come into their hearts, and that He was to inspire and guide them in doing His work on earth. John Kelman once explained that "the Holy Spirit is just God making man understand Him, God making Himself intelligible to men, God speaking to each man in His own tongue."

And God speaks today in many tongues to many people. . . .

II. *And it shall come to pass in the last days* . . . , Acts 2:17. It remained for Peter to clear the air at Pentecost, to quiet the confusion of the tongues with the preaching of the first recorded Christian sermon. What a sermon it was! First, he blasted the rumor that the Christians speaking in tongues were drunk: this was nine o'clock in the morning, and even an alcoholic would have difficulty getting drink *that* early in the day! They were not drunk; they were only ecstatic, burning with enthusiasm. Peter himself was aflame with zeal and joy, but his head was cool, and his logic was devastating as he began to preach.

He told the gathering first that the miraculous events of the morning were only the fulfillment of the prophecy of Joel (see Joel 2:28-32), in which the old prophet described what was to happen on "the terrible day of the Lord." This day was important in the faith of Israel and later in the faith of the Christians. We have mentioned elsewhere that the Jews divided time into two ages: the disastrous "present age," which was evil and therefore doomed to destruction, and "the age to come," which would be the glorious, triumphant age of God. In between these two ages was to come "the day of the Lord," which would be a *terrible* day. Read Joel to understand its horror; it is condensed in Acts 2:17-21, but the central thought of "the day" is kept clear and sharp in Peter's sermon. The central thought is that the day had arrived on this

Pentecost, in which God had poured out His Spirit not only on a few exceptional people but on all the "chosen" people of Israel. The day was *here;* in Jesus, God had walked personally and purposefully into human history.

The terror prophesied for the day is lost in the promise that "your young men shall see visions, and your old men shall dream dreams" (verse 17). There lay the hope of tomorrow: in the dreams of the old and the vision of the young! Dr. Francis G. Peabody says of this: "How natural it is for some modern man to say, 'But that is what keeps me from the religious life! It is a thing of visions and dreams, and the world I live in is not made of visions but of facts. My God is the God of things as they are.' All this sounds plausible enough, but one of the profoundest facts of experience is this: that one's career is in the main determined not so much by things as they are, but by one's vision of things as they *ought* to be; not by one's possessions, but by one's dreams. 'Man' an English philosopher said, 'is an idea-forming animal.' What distinguishes a man from a brute is precisely this possession of the faculty of vision."

The Spirit of God giving power and vision to the young: *God puts His trust in that!*

SUGGESTIONS TO TEACHERS

We clipped this item from our morning newspaper: "Glasgow, Ky.— Leslie Puckett, after struggling in vain to start his coupé, lifted the hood and discovered that someone had stolen the motor."

Today we are to think about the motor that drives the church. Some folks seem to think that the church needs a new "power," and they talk about "renewal." It isn't that anyone has stolen the motor; we have just let the old one deteriorate. . . .

The original motor was installed at Pentecost; it was a combination of prayer, expectancy and the free gifts of God. Study it, we suggest, under the following themes:

1. The significance of Pentecost.
2. What *is* the Holy Spirit?
3. The need in the church for the Holy Spirit.
4. The Holy Spirit in Peter's sermon.
5. Churches without the Spirit are dying churches.

TOPICS FOR ADULTS
EMPOWERED BY THE SPIRIT

What They Had. "There are millions of Christians in our world population of three billion—a far greater percentage today than the early church had at Pentecost. They had only 120 Christians to go out and win their world. They didn't have automobiles; they didn't have airplanes; they didn't have the printing press; they didn't even have Bibles. They had no churches, no seminaries, no schools. They didn't have even a well-trained clergy. These men had spent just three years with Jesus. Of course, that is plenty, but they did not have university degrees before they went to Jesus' seminary. They were just ordinary businessmen and fishermen and laborers, but they had something we seem to be missing. They had the power of the Holy Spirit. They had disciplined lives. They had commitment and dedication. No wonder they turned their world upside down!"—Billy Graham, in *Sunday School Times*.

How did they turn it upside down?

The Breeze. "On landing in Africa, one of the first lessons we learned was to find out on which side of the house the wind was blowing. Coming out the front door to sit on a porch, we walked first to one end and then to the other. Generally, a breeze would be blowing in one place or the other, and there we placed our chairs. When there was a calm we stifled; when the breeze blew fresh and strong we sighed with joy. The movement of air made life livable.

"Thus we must seek the motions of the Spirit. When we realize that the Holy Spirit moves as He desires, then we know that a revival cannot be pumped up by human effort but must come from God. At times, the wind blows a tempest; at times, there is a gentle breeze; at times, there is a dead calm of the doldrums. At times, He has been pleased to blow us a Luther, a Calvin or a Wesley—great tempests of spiritual movements; at other times, the church has been in a hot, suffocating calm, where the true believers almost gasped for life."—D. G. Barnhouse.

Taking. Explaining the power of his ministry, Dr. F. B. Meyer told of a prayer experience in which he sought the power of the Holy Spirit: "I felt no hand laid upon my head, there was no lambent flame, there was no rushing sound from heaven; but by faith, without emotion, without excitement, I took of that power, and took for the first time, and I have kept on taking ever since."

Dr. Arthur House Stainback comments on this: "The Holy Spirit does not move upon all men in the same way."

Can you describe more than one way in which He comes?

Let Him Work. "Wallace Speers, that unique Christian businessman, tells of a Swedish engineer who had heard for the first time a plea by a Christian leader *that he begin wherever he might be to become a Christian.* The thought haunted this man. His own life was all tangled up. Finally morning came. Each day there was friction with his wife over the radio. She wanted her program; he wanted his. The words of the speaker haunted him: 'Begin where you are, right where you are.' That morning he reached over and snapped on her program. He was starting right where he was.

"Immediately she looked aghast. She felt his brow to discover if he had a fever, but he had none save the fever of a new spirit stirring within him. At the office similar little things began to happen. Soon the headquarters of the concern inquired whether he'd discovered some new gadget by which he boosted production.

"What is the answer? Surely we should know the answer. This old world of ours cries for the transforming power of the Holy Spirit. Let Him work! Give Him a chance; receive the power that we have so often missed and lost—the power of the Holy Spirit, the power to become the sons of God."—From a sermon by Frederick E. Christian.

Pentecost was meant for the individual as well as for the church!

Questions for Pupils on the Next Lesson: 1. Who are "the redeemed?" 2. Does ". . . they had everything in common" (Acts 4:32) mean that there was a touch of communism in the early church? 3. Would you sell your house (see Acts 4:34)? 4. What do you share with people weaker than you are? 5. How would you characterize the faith and work of the early church? 6. Explain the meaning of Romans 15:3. 7. Explain how your church works as a redemptive fellowship.

TOPIC FOR YOUTH
HOW GOD GIVES POWER TO HIS CHURCH

How? J. B. Phillips has a stirring sentence about how the power of God comes to men and churches. He says: "Every time we say, 'I believe in the Holy Spirit' we mean that we believe that there is a living God able and willing to enter human personality and change it." *The power comes out of that faith.*

You don't turn on a dynamo and say. "I hope it works." You turn it on *knowing* that it will work and produce the power you want.

Do we really *believe* in God's power . . . ? Was any church ever built on doubt?

The Fire. "An African travel book tells of something unusual found in the heart of the jungle. In a clearing, to the surprise of Major Lewis Hastings, he came upon sticks carefully piled in the fashion to make a good fire. How did they come to be there, and why were they so well arranged? The explanation was not far to seek. Chimpanzees!

"But why had they not kindled a fire? They had gone as far as they were able. They had watched humans arrange sticks that way. They might squat on their haunches and wait for fire, but their best initiative skills could not produce fire. The miracle of smoke and fire refused to appear. The vital spark was lacking, and without it their patient labors failed. So much they could do, but it was not enough.

"In some ways we humans are like those chimpanzees. Have we not seen a man build a beautiful house, and then fail to touch that house with the fire that makes it into a home? Too often, like the chimpanzees, we make our plans. We build, we wait—but nothing happens.

"We have seen people whose lives are like that. They make fine plans. They follow out the plans. They wait—and nothing happens. They are modern, active, competent, but they lack what is most important. There must be fire, or all endeavor is practically lost.

"A Psalm begins, 'Unless the Lord builds the house, those who build it labor in vain. Unless the Lord watches over the city, the watchman stays awake in vain' (Psalm 127:1-2 RSV). Whether you build a house or establish a city, it is only a pile of sticks unless the Lord is permitted to touch it with spiritual fire. Thus it is with our own lives; we discover that something is lacking unless we let the Spirit of God apply fire to our lives.

"Today is the anniversary of the day of Pentecost, when in Jerusalem the disciples of Jesus experienced spiritual kindling in their lives. After that they were new men and women, quickened by the Spirit, full of light and warmth and energy. They went out and turned the world upside down. We are not chimpanzees; we are God's children, and He will give us fire."—Adapted from Rita F. Snowden, in *The Minister's Manual* for 1969, pp. 2, 5, 6. Edited by Charles L. Wallis. Quoted by permission of Harper & Row, publishers.

Esperanto. "The language of Pentecost is the true *Esperanto,* or universal speech. Everybody understands it. What is it? *It is the language of Christian love.*

"Everybody understands this language. When our soldiers moved into France and the Netherlands, into Italy and Germany, many of them wished to talk to the frightened, needy children they met there. Soon they found the secret. A chocolate bar, a share of their ration or of the food parcel from home, given to a hungry youngster, translated their foreign speech into words the children understood. It is so everywhere.

"Before our Christian doctors, teachers, and evangelists become proficient in the tongue of a new country, their actions, their interest, their friendliness, are understood. They speak the language of the universal Christ, the tongue of the Spirit of God: *love.* Here at home it is the passport, the speech that disarms suspicion or shyness, when we meet folk from backgrounds different from our own. Strangers no longer feel out of place when we try our best to act in a Christian manner."—David A. MacLennan, in *Revell's Minister's Annual,* 1968.

Lighted Up. "I recall a remark made by Sir Walter Scott as he stood before a statue of Robert Burns. He looked at it for a moment and then he said, 'Yes, the luster is there, but it is not lighted up.' It seems to me that what Scott missed in the statue of the poet we miss in our own lives and in the church."—John Bishop.

Sentence Sermon to Remember: To build temples is easier than to be temples of the Holy Spirit.—Anonymous.

Questions for Pupils on the Next Lesson: 1. What was "redemptive" about the New Testament church? 2. Should the modern church "hold all things in common?" 3. Would the early Christians approve of our expensive churches and cathedrals? 4. What is a "likeminded" church (Romans 15:5)? 5. *How* did the apostles give their "testimony" to the resurrection? 6. What does your church *share?* 7. What did the name "Barnabas" mean?

LESSON III—MARCH 19

THE FELLOWSHIP OF THE REDEEMED

Background Scripture: Acts 4:32-37; Romans 15
Devotional Reading: I Peter 1:3-9

KING JAMES VERSION

ACTS 4 32 And the multitude of them that believed were of one heart and of one soul: neither said any of them that aught of the things which he possessed was his own; but they had all things common.

33 And with great power gave the apostles witness of the resurrection of the Lord Jesus: and great grace was upon them all.

34 Neither was there any among them that lacked: for as many as were possessors of lands or houses sold them, and brought the prices of the things that were sold,

35 And laid them down at the apostles' feet: and distribution was made unto every man according as he had need.

36 And Joses, who by the apostles was surnamed Barnabas, (which is, being interpreted, The son of consolation,) a Levite, and of the country of Cyprus,

37 Having land, sold it, and brought the money, and laid it at the apostles' feet.

ROMANS 15 We then that are strong ought to bear the infirmities of the weak, and not to please ourselves.

2 Let every one of us please his neighbour for his good to edification.

3 For even Christ pleased not himself; but, as it is written, The reproaches of them that reproach thee fell on me.

4 For whatsoever things were written aforetime were written for our learning, that we through patience and comfort of the Scriptures might have hope.

5 Now the God of patience and consolation grant you to be likeminded one toward another according to Christ Jesus:

6 That ye may with one mind and one mouth glorify God, even the Father of our Lord Jesus Christ.

7 Wherefore receive ye one another, as Christ also received us, to the glory of God.

REVISED STANDARD VERSION

ACTS 4 32 Now the company of those who believed were of one heart and soul, and no one said that any of the things which he possessed was his own, but they had everything in common. 33 And with great power the apostles gave their testimony to the resurrection of the Lord Jesus, and great grace was upon them all. 34 There was not a needy person among them, for as many as were possessors of lands or houses sold them, and brought the proceeds of what was sold 35 and laid it at the apostles' feet; and distribution was made to each as any had need. 36 Thus Joseph who was surnamed by the apostles Barnabas (which means, Son of encouragement), a Levite, a native of Cyprus, 37 sold a field which belonged to him, and brought the money and laid it at the apostles' feet.

ROMANS 15 We who are strong ought to bear with the failings of the weak, and not to please ourselves; 2 let each of us please his neighbor for his good, to edify him. 3 For Christ did not please himself; but, as it is written, "The reproaches of those who reproached thee fell on me." 4 For whatever was written in former days was written for our instruction, that by steadfastness and by the encouragement of the scriptures we might have hope. 5 May the God of steadfastness and encouragement grant you to live in such harmony with one another, in accord with Christ Jesus, 6 that together you may with one voice glorify the God and Father of our Lord Jesus Christ.

7 Welcome one another, therefore, as Christ has welcomed you, for the glory of God.

214

MEMORY SELECTION: Welcome one another, therefore, as Christ has welcomed you, for the glory of God. Romans 15:7 (RSV).

HOME DAILY BIBLE READINGS

Mar. 13. M. *In Unity of Spirit,* Acts 4:32-37.
Mar. 14. T. *Bear One Another's Burdens,* Galatians 6:1-10.
Mar. 15. W. *All Peoples Are Welcome,* Romans 15:7-13.
Mar. 16. T. *The Gospel for All Nations,* Romans 15:14-21.
Mar. 17. F. *Gentiles Share With Jews,* Romans 15:22-33.
Mar. 18. S. *The Fellowship of Witness,* I Thessalonians 1:2-9.
Mar. 19. S. *A Living Hope,* I Peter 1:3-9.

BACKGROUND

In the Scripture verses immediately preceding those in this lesson (Acts 4:23-31) we find the little Christian community singing and praising God in high hope and exultation. The Spirit was moving in them, shaking them: "the place was shaken where they were assembled together; and they were all filled with the Holy Ghost" (4:31). It was a prayer meeting. . . .

Prayer meetings can send those who become enthusiastic in prayer down different roads and to different emphases and effort. They lead to cloistered activity, which is mainly and often isolated or cut off from any activity in the world—like the prayer or worship of a cloistered nun. Such prayer and worship are never wasted, but, to their credit, the first Christians saw that, in these first dangerous days of the church, it was necessary to add action to praise and prayer. What they did when the meeting was over set a standard for the Christian church, a guideline to true Christian living that, alas, has been ignored too much by the church in Christian history, and is neglected even now. . . .

NOTES ON THE PRINTED TEXT

I. Not a man of them claimed any of his possessions as his own, but everything was held in common . . . , Acts 4:32 (*New English Bible* translation). What we have in Acts 4:32-37 is a description of how the Christians lived in the first New Testament church. (There is a similar description in Acts 2:43-47). Luke says that they held all things (all possessions) "common." That is, *they were a sharing fellowship.* But immediately he adds that they also held in common great *spiritual* gifts, thanks to the resurrection. They were, comparatively, a very small group blessed with gifts from God which they knew they did not deserve; they were so grateful for this that they refused to claim their money or possessions as their own: these they had by the grace and goodness of God. They also felt that no man among them had any right to *hoard* his possessions or his gift of the Spirit. They even sold their houses and their land, and came and laid the profit at the feet of the apostles.

Some call it "communism". It wasn't communism. It was *communal sharing*—something that other groups had practiced before them. For instance, the covenanters in the Dead Sea community did the same thing; it was *required,* demanded there, that every covenanter turn over everything he had to the community.

But the sharing of the property and possessions of the early church was *not* required, not compulsory at all. These Christians gave all they had because they wanted to give all they had; nobody forced them to do it—nobody, that is, but the Holy Spirit. They *wanted* to follow the example of the Christ who called upon the rich young ruler to sell all he had and give it to the poor. They looked around in their community, their Christian fellowship, and they said to themselves, "We see some who are poor. We have no right to keep more than we need, so long as any brother is in want, so we will share it with him."

Private property, however, was not completely abolished. That would have been a mistake—for when you *completely* abolish private property you destroy the possibility of giving anything! It was left to each man to give as he wished, and most gave more than generously.

Of course, it didn't last very long, even among such highly principled men. Some appeared who abused it (one was named Ananias, who stood in sharp contrast to a disciple named Barnabas, who gave his money and his life to Jesus Christ), and the custom seems to have become moderated after the events of Acts 6. That was probably for the best; the little community would not have lasted very long if it had liquidated all its assets! But it had great spiritual values while it lasted; it inspired the spirit of stewardship in the Christian church.

The early church was an unselfish, giving, sharing *fellowship*.

II. We then that are strong ought to bear the infirmities of the weak, and not to please ourselves, Romans 15:1. Here, the driving of the Spirit led the first Christians into another emphasis and effort that had nothing to do with possessions; it had to do with the moral (and spiritual) responsibility of the strong to help the weak in the fellowship. Not only did those who were poor in possessions need help; those weak in faith or conviction or Christian behavior needed help, too. "Each of us," the record reads, "must consider his neighbor and think what is for *his* good and will build up the common life" (Romans 15:2, *New English Bible*). Even as Christ lived not to please himself, so the Christian layman must live. . . .

The church, then as now, includes in its fellowship all kinds of men —some strong, some weak. They are men with varying opinions and ideas, which is good. We can imagine nothing worse than a church in which everybody agrees about everything; such a fellowship would suffer sudden, justifiable death! But all of us in the church, whatever our opinions or ideas, should and *must* live and work together in unity and in spiritual harmony with Christ and "with one another, in accord with Christ Jesus" (Romans 15:2). There is no room, no place, for religious superiority or inferiority in the church. All ground is level at the foot of the cross!

We grow sick at the spectacle of a church fight; how many have been lost to the church forever because others in the church have crucified their Christ in brawls and arguments that would never have come at all if those involved had looked at their problems in the light of Christ's *love!* How little, how foolish, how blasphemous that can be.

First of all, the Christian fellowship should be characterized by a knowledge of the Scriptures, by an understanding of the promises of God to those within the fellowship, by a patience and a tolerance to understand our brother and help him when he is wrong instead of merely condemning him. It should be a collective fellowship with one mind: the mind which was in Christ; "with one mind and one mouth" (verse 6) we should not only glorify God but serve Him.

Read this passage in the *New English Bible*; it is one of the finest translations ever published. And memorize the last verse of our Scripture portion in Romans 15 as a guide to your behavior and spirit in the fellowship of *your* church: "In a word, accept one another as Christ accepted us, to the glory of God."

Beautiful!

SUGGESTIONS TO TEACHERS

One of the meanings of the word "redeem" is *"to reclaim."* When we look closely at the fellowship which was the first church, we find it to be both a fellowship *of* the redeemed and a *redeeming* (reclaiming) fellowship. They were a group of people imbued with the mind of Christ and with His concern for the lost.

They reached out to meet human need; and that need was both sacred and secular. Driven by the Holy Spirit, they worked in both these areas with only two weapons, love and sympathy!

TOPIC FOR ADULTS
THE REDEMPTIVE FELLOWSHIP

The Church Fellowship. On a trip across the country, one of our best friends went four times to one big city church; he wrote his wife: "I did not go back the fifth time; nobody spoke to me the four times I was there, so . . . !" That was a bad church; it was a cold church, a frozen fellowship. . . .

Contrast that church with what E. Stanley Jones said about the church of his youth: "I am quite sure that I would not have survived as a young Christian had I not had the corporate life of the church to hold me up. When I rejoiced, they rejoiced with me. When I was weak they strengthened me, and once when I fell—a rather bad fall—they gathered around me in prayer and love, and without blame or censure they lovingly lifted me back to my feet again." That was a *warm* church, a good church!

Jesus practiced a fine fellowship with those who followed Him; but He talked and worked more among the outcasts—the publicans, the undesirables, the harlots, the hungry who were not being fed by the religious "establishment" of the day.

The fellowship responsibility of the church does not stop at the door of the church: it bursts out into the street. . . .

Necessities. Usually, we speak of "human need" as something identified with poverty. It is more than that.

"If you made a list of the things you believe are vital to you, and then sat and looked at it, I'm sure you would cross off a number of items, leaving only the *necessities.* I've listed these elsewhere as common to us all. I'll do it again: love, worship, work, a roof over our heads and food on our tables."—Faith Baldwin.

Sit down now and *list your most pressing needs*. Are we right in thinking that you would consider the roof and the food as less pressing needs than love and worship?

The church is in the business of meeting all these needs, but, probably, the latter two first. Right, or wrong?

The Weeping Woman. "The church for me is no longer an institution which demands my acceptance of certain abstractions, hallowed by history or decree. . . . The church I know is a small community of human beings who have caught the contagion of Christ's freedom and among whom I can be accepted for myself as I am: all of them ministers who, with their own wounds bound, are free to go out into society, sensitive to the cries of other human beings in their multitudinous needs. I cannot forget that the first person who encountered the risen Jesus was not Peter, the man of action, or John the intellectual, or James the organizer, but a weeping needy woman whose only resource was persistent love."—*The Restless Church*, by Elizabeth Kilbourn (Lippincott).

Who was that weeping woman? Was what she wanted from Christ what we all want? And do we get it in our church fellowships?

The True Church. We hear many Christians who are better denominationalists than they are Christians, saying that theirs is "the one true church." But what *is* a "true" church?

John M. Drescher sees the church in Acts 2:42-47 as a true church, and he describes it in these words:

"It was a *learning* church. They persisted in listening to the apostles as they taught.

"It was a church of *fellowship*. There was a great quality of togetherness—having the same care for one another.

"It was a *praying* church. The members always spoke to God before they spoke to men.

"It was a *reverent* church. . . . The church walking in the fear of the Lord caused a sense of awe in the community.

"The early church was a church where things *happened*. They expected great things from God and attempted great things for God.

"It was a *sharing* church. . . . One Christian could not have too much while another had too little.

"This church was a *worshiping* church. Both in the Temple and from house to house they continued to teach unceasingly and to proclaim the good news of Jesus Christ.

"This church was a *happy* church. Gladness abounded. You cannot overcome a rejoicing church.

"The early church was a *growing* church. It placed little value on any organization not contributing to worship, teaching and alms . . . and the Lord added to the church daily those who were being saved."
—John M. Drescher, in *Gospel Herald*, Mennonite Publication Board, Scottdale, Pa.

Measure your church by these standards; how does it "shape up" as a true church?

Questions for Pupils on the Next Lesson: 1. What was the cause of the quarrel in the Corinthian church? 2. How is the church "the body of Christ?" 3. Why is there so little unity among our modern churches? 4. Was Paul being sarcastic in our Scripture lesson? 5. Is any one member in your church more important than another? 6. Name two of the most common causes of friction in the church. 7. What do we mean by "disparity in unity" in the church?

TOPIC FOR YOUTH
WHAT MAKES CHURCH FELLOWSHIP DIFFERENT?

Different. What makes the fellowship of the church different?

"The church," says H. C. Meserve in the Houston *Times,* "is the main highway of religion. It is not a society of the perfect, but of the admittedly imperfect; a fellowship not of saints, but of people who know they are sinners and wish they were not."

Do you know of any other organization or "fellowship" in your town or city which makes the first requirement for membership the confession that none of us is really good enough to join it? This church fellowship starts with the admission that *all* of us are sinners, but that with the help of the fellowship we do not need *stay* that way. We can be better —with the help of Christ and church.

Burdens. Paul puts upon the strong Christians an obligation to help the weak ones carry their burdens. He claims that the church should be a body of burden-sharing people. . . .

"I shall never forget the first days of Ralston Young's new life; how was he to express this, carrying bags in Grand Central Station? First, he caught the spirit of other men who were seeing in their jobs a spiritual opportunity, not just a spiritual necessity. Then he began thinking of all the people he met day after day; and it came to him that he must 'carry their burdens as well as their bags.' Quietly, and under the Spirit, this began to happen, till he started calling the station his 'cathedral' and chaffing me by saying, 'A lot more people go through my cathedral than go through your church.' And for more than sixteen years his ministry has continued in this emporium of travel. I cannot think of a more difficult field, with people in such a hurry all the time; but that is where his life is set, and that is where he wins people for Christ."—*With the Holy Spirit and With Fire,* by Samuel M. Shoemaker (Harper & Row).

So Ralston Young, a "Redcap" at Grand Central Station, New York, shares the burdens of others. . . .

More, Fewer. We like the short and sharp lines of a little verse written by an unknown poet on "What the Church Needs Is." It reads:

> More *action* and less *faction,*
> More *workers* and fewer *shirkers,*
> More *burden-bearers* and fewer *talebearers,*
> More *backers* and fewer *slackers.*

The Unsatisfied Church. A little boy listened to his Sunday-school teacher tell the story of the lost sheep—the one sheep that was lost while the ninety and nine were safely gathered into the fold; his only comment was, "Teacher, I think a ninety-nine per cent score is a pretty good score in any man's language." It *is* a good score; how many of us fall far short of a mark of ninety-nine in our school exams! But is it good enough when we are dealing with *people?*

"A crowd had gathered at the intersection of two streets. A man and his wife passed. The husband detoured a little to look over the heads of those forming the crowd in an effort to see the center of attraction. In a disgusted manner, he returned to his wife and said, 'It's only a drunk!'

"Only a drunk? . . . He is a child of God. He is a person upon whom God places infinite worth. He is a person who needs to be won to Jesus Christ and His way of life. The church must be dissatisfied until that last and least one has been won."—From a sermon by Harry O. Ritter.

That was the glory of the early church: while it was still hardly more than a small fellowship it set out to find and help those who most needed help. Is that the purpose of the church today? Prove it!

Impressions. "There are, I suppose, almost endless ways in which we make an impression on others. A visitor to the United States from a hungry, impoverished part of the Orient was asked to give his principal impression of this country of the Stars and Stripes. His terse answer: 'The size of your garbage cans!'

"Recently I was conducted through a church building that is nearing completion in a Midwestern state. It will cost a million and a half dollars. Its elaborate dancing studio made more of an impression on me than its worship room—though I refrain from telling you what *kind* of impression it was."—*Christian, Commit Yourself!* by Paul S. Rees (Fleming H. Revell Company).

Can you imagine a New Testament church with a dance studio?

Sentence Sermon to Remember: The church with no great anguish on its heart has no great music on its lips.—Karl Barth.

Questions for Pupils on the Next Lesson: 1. Who is the most important person in your church—and why? 2. How is the Christian church like a human body? 3. What different gifts of God are at work in different people in your church? 4. What should be the main concern of every member of your church? 5. From what discords does your church suffer? 6. Does Paul say in I Corinthians 12 that there should be no difference of opinion and judgment in the church? 7. Without looking it up, give your definition of the mission of the church.

LESSON IV—MARCH 26

ONE BODY IN CHRIST

Background Scripture: Romans 12:1-5; Ephesians 4:4-8; I Corinthians 12
Devotional Reading: Romans 12:3-13

KING JAMES VERSION

I CORINTHIANS 12 12 For as the body is one, and hath many members, and all the members of that one body, being many, are one body: so also is Christ.

13 For by one Spirit are we all baptized into one body, whether we be Jews or Gentiles, whether we be bond or free; and have been all made to drink into one Spirit.

14 For the body is not one member, but many.

15 If the foot shall say, Because I am not the hand, I am not of the body; is it therefore not of the body?

16 And if the ear shall say, Because I am not the eye, I am not of the body; is it therefore not of the body?

17 If the whole body were an eye, where were the hearing? If the whole were hearing, where were the smelling?

18 But now hath God set the members every one of them in the body, as it hath pleased him.

19 And if they were all one member, where were the body?

20 But now are they many members, yet but one body.

21 And the eye cannot say unto the hand, I have no need of thee: nor again the head to the feet, I have no need of you.

22 Nay, much more those members of the body, which seem to be more feeble, are necessary:

23 And those members of the body, which we think to be less honorable, upon these we bestow more abundant honor; and our uncomely parts have more abundant comeliness.

24 For our comely parts have no need: but God hath tempered the body together, having given more abundant honor to that part which lacked:

25 That there should be no schism in the body; but that the members should have the same care one for another.

REVISED STANDARD VERSION

I CORINTHIANS 12 12 For just as the body is one and has many members, and all the members of the body, though many, are one body, so it is with Christ. 13 For by one Spirit we were all baptized into one body —Jews or Greeks, slaves or free—and all were made to drink of one Spirit.

14 For the body does not consist of one member but of many. 15 If the foot should say, "Because I am not a hand, I do not belong to the body," that would not make it any less a part of the body. 16 And if the ear should say, "Because I am not an eye, I do not belong to the body," that would not make it any less a part of the body. 17 If the whole body were an eye, where would be the hearing? If the whole body were an ear, where would be the sense of smell? 18 But as it is, God arranged the organs in the body, each one of them, as he chose. 19 If all were a single organ, where would the body be? 20 As it is, there are many parts, yet one body. 21 The eye cannot say to the hand, "I have no need of you," nor again the head to the feet, "I have no need of you." 22 On the contrary, the parts of the body which seem to be weaker are indispensable, 23 and those parts of the body which we think less honorable we invest with the greatest honor, and our unpresentable parts are treated with greater modesty, 24 which our more presentable parts do not require. But God has so adjusted the body, giving the greater honor to the inferior part, 25 that there may be no discord in the body, but that the members may have the same care for one another. 26 If one member suffers, all suffer together; if one member is honored, all rejoice together.

26 And whether one member suffer, all the members suffer with it; or one member be honored, all the members rejoice with it.

27 Now ye are the body of Christ, and members in particular.

27 Now you are the body of Christ and individually members of it.

MEMORY SELECTION: Now you are the body of Christ and individually members of it. I Corinthians 12:27 (RSV).

HOME DAILY BIBLE READINGS

Mar. 20. M. *Absolute Oneness,* Ephesians 4:1-8.
Mar. 21. T. *Fellow Heirs,* Ephesians 3:1-6.
Mar. 22. W. *The Spirit Unifies,* I Corinthians 12:1-6.
Mar. 23. T. *Unity in Diversity,* I Corinthians 12:7-13.
Mar. 24. F. *All Members of Equal Value,* I Corinthians 12:14-26.
Mar. 25. S. *God Appoints Specialists,* I Corinthians 12:27-31.
Mar. 26. S. *Many Members, One Body,* Romans 12:3-13.

BACKGROUND

The New Testament Church is often held up as the ideal church, and many Christians today feel that "if only we could get a church like *that* . . . *!*" To them it seems perfect! But it wasn't if the church at Corinth is an example. This was one of the churches organized by Paul, and shortly after it began, a church quarrel—or a number of church quarrels—broke out among the "saints" in the congregation which Paul thought serious enough to write two letters to them in order to get things straightened out. We call those letters I and II Corinthians.

In the first letter, written from Ephesus about A.D. 54, the apostle refers to certain rivalries and jealousies that had developed among them; there was an unrestrained individualism and a lack of moral standards that was disgraceful; those who had special gifts such as visions and "speaking in tongues" were envied by those who lacked them. Petty fights over who should be what in the church organization raged like little tempests.

Paul told them that in the church there should be both dependence and interdependence, unity and diversity—and that it was about time they began to settle their petty little arguments in a spirit of *love.* . . .

NOTES ON THE PRINTED TEXT

I. For just as the body is one and has many members, and all the members of the body, though many, are one body, so it is with Christ, I Corinthians 12:12 (RSV). Paul is often hard to understand; he was a theologian, and not many in the church were trained or skilled as theologians. But here there was no misunderstanding his language or his thinking. He put it down where anyone with half a mind could get it.

The church, he says, is a body, an organism; in the church every Christian is a "member"—a unit of one put there to work in unity with all the other members. In Romans 12:5, he had talked about Christians being "one body *in* Christ"; now he talks about them as being the very body *of* Christ. Notice that he says "Christ," not "church." But in his thinking, Christ is the church; it is the body of Christ—a body into which the members had been baptized through the Spirit. Being so baptized, they were united as *Christians;* they were no longer Jews, Greeks, slaves or freemen.

This was a new *unity,* but it did not mean that in this church there should be *uniformity:* there could be and should be individual variety in the collective unity; the individual should still be respected as an individual working together with other members in the church just as the legs of a man work together with his eyes and ears in the human body.

The church was a spiritual workshop in which those who loved Christ worked together to establish His way.

II. If the foot should say, 'Because I am not a hand, I do not belong to the body . . .' I Corinthians 12:15 (RSV). In one of the few instances in which Paul actually poked fun at his brethren in the church he strikes out at them here with an argument that is both funny, absurd—and as sharp as the point of a knife. He goes into a dialogue in which he has the various parts of the human body arguing with each other. The speeches are ridiculous; the Corinthians must have laughed at the arguments between parts of the body when they read them, and laughed at themselves, too! Imagine a foot saying to an ear, "I am more important than *you* are; you couldn't get along without *me!*" (Suppose the feet and the ears were exactly alike: what would the body look like then?) Or suppose the eyes got the idea that they were more important than all the rest of the body, so important that they wouldn't take any advice from the brain or the ears or the legs. Suppose every part of the human body decided to live independently of every other part, what then?

Said Dr. Kenneth J. Foreman: "To sum it up bluntly, it is no more possible for one to be a lone independent *Christian* apart from the church than it is for an ear or an eye to be a lone independent ear or eye, with no body. *An eye in a head is priceless; an eye in a glass jar is a curiosity.*"

We in the church need each other; we need to recognize our interdependence more than our independence. The eye in a man's head cannot say to the feet, "I have no need of you." Neither can any church member say to another, "Who needs *you?*" A church needs *all* its members, for each of them has a contribution to make to the work of the church.

Paul turns the whole thing into a farce. Did the quarreling Corinthians see themselves as clowns in the farce? Do we understand what he means when we either get our own way in the church or pull out and go to some other church—where we repeat the same thing all over again? It is farcical, yes; for the church it is also tragedy.

III. But God has so adjusted the body . . . that there may be no discord in the body . . . , I Corinthians 12:24, 25 (RSV). No discord in the body! The church without discord—without its members engaging in fits of jealousy because one is elected President of the Board and another to a "lesser" office—the church *without that* would be Christ's idea of a church. Both the President of the Board and the little fellow who does a humble, obscure work are part of the body of the church. Actually, they are parts of the body of Christ, some helping Him with their hands, some serving Him with their feet, running His errands, some using a special talent that the others lack. "He has no hands but our hands to do His work today." He can use the skilled surgeon, the nurse—and the lowly church visitor at the hospital. He can use a teacher —and a wide-eyed boy who listens to the teacher.

Many members, one body! We are all part of His body, His church. Let there be no discord in the body, no self-cultivated sickness or envy. Let there be no boasting. When one part of the body is poisoned by a tiny germ the whole body suffers. So keep the *whole* body healthy.

No one member in the church is more important than any other member. No one with great spiritual gifts has any right to boast about his superiority in the church; he has only an obligation to use those gifts for the benefit of all. For "to each is given the manifestation of the Spirit for the common good" (I Corinthians 12:7).

SUGGESTIONS TO TEACHERS

Long ago, Marcus Dodds said of I Corinthians 12: "This epistle is well fitted to disabuse our minds of the idea that the primitive church was in all respects superior to the church of our own day. We turn page after page and find little but contention, jealousies, errors, immorality, fantastic ideas, immodesty, irreverence and profanity." These were practices within the local churches—and some of them were small and petty and quite unbelievable in any Christian! The same is true among us: we split churches over trifles, we impede the work of the church with our childish sins, prejudices and opinions.

There is much of all that among us—so much that it seems a waste of time and space to condemn it further than we have already condemned it. Instead of losing ourselves in the petty quarrels of our local churches, suppose we concentrate on something bigger and more important: suppose we make this lesson one on the larger church unity which Paul advocated—unity *among all denominations*. Ours has been called "The Ecumenical Age." Start the lesson by finding out what "Ecumenical" means; go on to find out why so many of us are *not* ecumenically minded, and why there is so little unity among our various church divisions—why we have dared to divide the body of Christ. . . .

TOPIC FOR ADULTS
ONE BODY IN CHRIST

The Ship. Dr. Ralph W. Sockman says that the only way he can understand this passage in I Corinthians is to think of it in terms of a ship:

"There are parts of a ship which, taken by themselves, would sink. The propeller would sink. The engines would sink. But when the parts of a ship are built together they float. So with the events of my life. Some have been tragic. Some have been happy. But when they are all built together they form a craft that floats . . . and that is going somewhere!"

So with the church. When some little "splinter" group pulls out of a church because it disagrees with the majority in some minor detail, the ship could, and often does, *sink*. It's like the propeller leaving the ship—leaving it helpless, while the propeller sinks of its own weight!

We need to be welded together to make the church ship sail.

Unity. "The question of Christian unity is not a question of the size or number of the churches. It is a question of the quality of our church-manship. It is a question of recovering the true lineaments of a body in which men of every sort and kind are baptized by one Spirit into one fellowship. . . . The quest for Christian unity is the quest for a church whose charity is broad enough to embrace all men. . . . Those beloved ecclesiastical traditions of ours in their separateness hide from men the true lineaments of the family of God. We have no right to barter for any earthly advantage, and if the Lord bids us lay them at His feet in order to give us something greater, we dare not refuse."—From an address by Bishop J. E. Leslie Newbigin.

What "beloved ecclesiastical tradition" would you be willing to give up for the sake of denominational unity? If interchurch unity ever comes, we will all have to give up something in order to get something better. . . . Are we ready to pay that price?

First Steps. Union of all the churches may be a long way off; we still have to decide whether we want it or not, what we are willing to sacrifice for it, and how we are to go about really getting it! We suggest the following preliminary steps:

1. We can recognize other denominations as equal with us in sincerity, intelligence and common purpose.
2. We can at least discuss our differences with each other, and stop gossiping about each other.
3. We can admit that the sacraments of other churches are as valid as ours.
4. We can stop interfering with each other and start co-operating with each other.
5. We have common ground in faith: we should find it and stand on it.

Do this, and church unity will come of its own accord—and faster than we think!

For All Men. "Whose side is Jesus Christ on? Is He on ours? Or theirs? Christ came to this planet to show mankind light, love and the way to peace on earth. He did not see the labels which we attach to certain groups of men: friend, enemy, Oriental, Western, capitalist or communist. *Christ sees only men.* He sees their lives, knows their attitudes, judges their actions—offers mercy, forgiveness and the new life. For all men. Everywhere."—Doug Hostetter, in *Alive,* March 1970.

Could it be that God has no interest whatever in our churches, but is interested only in the people *in* the churches?

Rivals in the Church. "Once older people stop regarding the young as rivals and enemies, they can realize that their task as Christians is complementary to that of the young. Both need each other, and neither could produce a sane or human society alone. It takes humility to realize and manage that, and it's hard—but here again older people *should* be more easily able to face their own limitations, and so make it easier for the young to do the same."—Rosemary Haughton, in *Catholic World* March, 1970.

Recently we have been losing youth from our churches at an alarming rate. Why is that?

Questions for Pupils on the Next Lesson: 1. What did the word "Easter," mean originally, and where did we get it? 2. Why was the resurrection of *first* importance to the early church? 3. What *purpose* did Paul see in the resurrection? 4. Does Paul think it enough for a Christian merely to *hope* for *his* resurrection? 5. Which Scriptures are indicated in I Corinthians 15:4? 6. List the appearances of Jesus after Calvary. 7. Is any preaching effective if it is not based on the resurrection?

TOPIC FOR YOUTH
ONE CHRIST, ONE CHURCH

"All denominations pray to the same God and serve the same Christ. We all read the same Bible and are guided by the same Spirit of truth. We are all trying to reach the same heavenly goal. There will be no denominational barriers in paradise. Since we shall all be one in the church triumphant, we should express our unity more in the church militant.

"The Christian Church (Disciples of Christ) originated as an association for the promotion of Christian unity on the basis of a return to the practices of the New Testament Church. The document which stands at the beginning of this American religious movement was called, 'The Declaration and Address,' by Thomas Campbell. The foremost proposition of that message was, 'The Church of Christ is essentially, intentionally and constitutionally one.' *The church is one.* All who are servants of Christ belong to the one Lord. 'All one body we.'"

What has happened to Campbell's conviction? Is it passé, forgotten, lost? *What do all our denominations, the Disciples included, have in common?*

Co-operation Does It! "This week we heard a student from Southern Rhodesia studying in the United States tell the story of a young man whose village needed meat. He went out hunting and killed an elephant. He tied a rope to the elephant, and, as the custom of his people is, as he pulled, he began to sing, 'My elephant! My elephant! My elephant!' But he couldn't budge the animal. So he went to the village and got all the men and women to bring their ropes to help him. As they pulled, they sang, 'Our elephant! Our elephant! Our elephant!'

"The elephant began to move, until at last they had almost reached the village. Then the young hunter began to think that it was his prowess that had made it possible to bring the elephant home, and so he began to sing again, 'My elephant! My elephant! My elephant!'" The others, hearing him, let him do the pulling alone.

"Progress stopped. Soon the young man saw his mistake, and took up the refrain, 'Our elephant! Our elephant! Our elephant!' At once the others joined him, both in singing and in pulling. So they got their elephant home.

"Applications of this delightful story come readily to mind. . . .

Are you thinking what we're thinking?"—From *The Free Methodist,*
March 3, 1964.

Protestants, Catholics. The modern interest in ecumenism has gone
far in our day; even Roman Catholics and Protestants are talking about
"getting together." That will take time; our generation may never see
these two divisions in Christianity unite under one roof, but. . . .

"Why doesn't everyone take it just a little easier? There are things right
with Catholics, there are things right with Protestants, just as there are
things we both need to do to be better Catholics and better Protestants.
We don't have to fall over each other; Catholics don't have to keep
downgrading themselves and upgrading Protestants and Protestants
don't have to downgrade themselves and upgrade Catholicism.

"We still have theological differences and many of them originated
with Luther. But we don't have to attack Luther.

"We need to talk to each other. . . . We need to face up to our
differences; they exist. But we don't have to club each other."—in
Voices of Our Brethren, by Dale Francis.

Not many years ago the Ku Klux Klan was burning crosses on the
lawns of Roman Catholic churches. Now at Easter, the Roman Catholics
and the Protestants in our town hold a community service in the local
high-school auditorium.

Which method, would you say, is the better method?

Unite or Die. Among his other accomplishments, Benjamin Franklin
was America's first cartoonist. His first cartoon, published in *The Pennsylvania Gazette,* was a picture of a serpent cut into 13 sections, representing the 13 American colonies, every one of which was struggling
for its own autonomy and freedom. Beneath the drawing were the words,
"Unite or die!"

We are told that many churches are giving up today—dying. And that
congregations are falling off badly and budgets being cut drastically.
Would we rather die than unite?

Sentence Sermon to Remember: The real unity of the church must
not be organized, but exercised.—Johannes Lilje.

Questions for Pupils on the Next Lesson: 1. True or false: "The church
stakes its life on the resurrection"? 2. Was Christ's resurrection prophesied in the Old Testament? 3. About how many people saw Jesus after
His resurrection? 4. Are we all promised the same resurrection that
Jesus experienced? 5. Is our personal faith "futile" (I Corinthians 15:17)
without belief in the resurrection? 6. What do you look forward to doing
next Easter? 7. What *sort* of resurrection body do you think you will
have?

LESSON V—APRIL 2

THE CHURCH OF THE RISEN LORD (EASTER)

Background Scripture: I Corinthians 15:3-10
Devotional Readings: I Corinthians 15:51-58

KING JAMES VERSION

I CORINTHIANS 15 3 For I delivered unto you first of all that which I also received, how that Christ died for our sins according to the Scriptures;

4 And that he was buried, and that he rose again the third day according to the Scriptures:

5 And that he was seen of Cephas, then of the twelve:

6 After that, he was seen of above five hundred brethren at once; of whom the greater part remain unto this present, but some are fallen asleep.

7 After that, he was seen of James; then of all the apostles.

8 And last of all he was seen of me also, as of one born of due time.

9 For I am the least of the apostles, that am not meet to be called an apostle, because I persecuted the church of God.

10 But by the grace of God I am what I am: and his grace which was bestowed upon me was not in vain; but I labored more abundantly than they all: yet not I, but the grace of God which was with me.

11 Therefore whether it were I or they, so we preach, and so ye believed.

12 Now if Christ be preached that he rose from the dead, how say some among you that there is no resurrection of the dead?

13 But if there be no resurrection of the dead, then is Christ not risen:

14 And if Christ be not risen, then is our preaching vain, and your faith is also vain.

15 Yea, and we are found false witnesses of God; because we have testified of God that he raised up Christ: whom he raised not up, if so be that the dead rise not.

16 For if the dead rise not, then is not Christ raised:

17 And if Christ be not raised, your faith is vain; ye are yet in your sins.

18 Then they also which are fallen asleep in Christ are perished.

REVISED STANDARD VERSION

I CORINTHIANS 15 3 For I delivered to you as of first importance what I also received, that Christ died for our sins in accordance with the scriptures, 4 that he was buried, that he was raised on the third day in accordance with the scriptures, 5 and that he appeared to Cephas, then to the twelve. 6 Then he appeared to more than five hundred brethren at one time, most of whom are still alive, though some have fallen asleep. 7 Then he appeared to James, then to all the apostles. 8 Last of all, as to one untimely born, he appeared also to me. 9 For I am the least of the apostles, unfit to be called an apostle, because I persecuted the church of God. 10 But by the grace of God I am what I am, and his grace toward me was not in vain. On the contrary, I worked harder than any of them, though it was not I, but the grace of God which is with me. 11 Whether then it was I or they, so we preach and so you believed.

12 Now if Christ is preached as raised from the dead, how can some of you say that there is no resurrection of the dead? 13 But if there is no resurrection of the dead, then Christ has not been raised; 14 if Christ has not been raised, then our preaching is in vain and your faith is in vain.

15 We are even found to be misrepresenting God, because we testified of God that he raised Christ, whom he did not raise if it is true that the dead are not raised. 16 For if the dead are not raised, then Christ has not been raised. 17 If Christ has not been raised, your faith is futile and you are still in your sins. 18 Then those also who have fallen asleep in Christ have perished. 19 If in this life we who

19 If in this life only we have hope in Christ, we are of all men most miserable.

are in Christ have only hope, we are of all men most to be pitied.

MEMORY SELECTION: Thanks be to God, which giveth us the victory through our Lord Jesus Christ. I Corinthians 15:57.

HOME DAILY BIBLE READINGS

Mar. 27. M. Christ "Appeared Also to Me," I Corinthians 15:1-11.
Mar. 28. T. If There Were No Resurrection, I Corinthians 15:12-19.
Mar. 29. W. Christ Triumphant Over Death, I Corinthians 15:20-28.
Mar. 30. T. My Experiences Prove It! I Corinthians 15:29-34.
Mar. 31. F. What Sort of Resurrection Body? I Corinthians 15:35-41.
Apr. 1. S. "Raised a Spiritual Body," I Corinthians 15:42-50.
Apr. 2. S. The Complete Victory, I Corinthians 15:51-58.

BACKGROUND

In our lesson for February 27 we discussed the resurrection story as Luke tells it; now, some twenty years later, we are to discuss it from the viewpoint of Paul. Paul's generation was two decades removed from the exciting days of the resurrection and the Ascension; the Christians of this day heard the stories of those two awesome events, not so often from eyewitnesses as from apostles who took up the gauntlet of the faith from the original disciples and spread it abroad. They spread it to Corinth, which was some 800 miles from Jerusalem.

Now, in Corinth (a Roman city in a Roman province, as deeply influenced by Greek thought as by Roman) lived a cosmopolitan people speaking many languages and interesting themselves in many religions. Their concepts were Greek and Gentile. Their whole thinking and background was vastly different from Christianity, and Paul had a very, very difficult time of it trying to win them to belief in the resurrection and the presence of a risen Christ. He met the same sort of resistance that the modern missionary meets among the modern Moslems. . . .

But he tried. He won many of them. More important, he established the fact that the resurrection was the central, basic truth of Christianity. If there were no resurrection, there could be no Christianity. It is interesting to see how Paul went about among the inhabitants proving the case for a *risen* Lord. . . .

NOTES ON THE PRINTED TEXT

I. For I delivered to you as of first importance what I also received, that Christ died for our sins in accordance with the scriptures . . . , I Corinthians 15:3 (RSV). Writing to the people in the church at Corinth, Paul reminds them that it was he who, for their salvation, had brought the gospel to them. Did they still believe and preach that gospel? If they didn't, their "conversion" was worthless. "First and foremost," Paul says, "I handed on to you the facts that had been imparted to me" (*New English Bible*). What facts?

There were two facts: first, that "Christ had died for our sins in accordance with the Scriptures," and, second, also in accordance with the Scriptures, that Christ had risen on the third day. Period! That was the starting point: the Jewish Scriptures were fulfilled in the resurrection of Jesus Christ. He is, of course, referring to the prophesies of the Old Testament. (See Psalm 22; Isaiah 53; Zechariah 12:10; Hosea 6:2.)

"And he appeared to Cephas. . . ." Cephas! This was Peter, called Cephas (rock or stone) in John 1:42—Peter, whom Paul *knew*, and worked with; Peter, who had *seen* the risen Christ. We might doubt gossip, but it is hard to contradict the statement of an eyewitness!

It is more than interesting that Paul names Peter first as he lists the postresurrection appearances of Jesus. Jesus came to Peter first—to the Peter who had denied Him, not once but thrice, to the Peter who, next to Judas, had probably hurt Jesus more than any other of the twelve. He might have dismissed Peter from the band if He had not been Christ; instead, because He knew what was going on in the broken heart of the big fisherman, He went to Peter to heal the broken heart, to give him a faith and a courage that led him, too, to die on a cross. He went to Peter—and Peter told Paul all about it. . . .

". . . he was seen of James . . ." (verse 7). James was His own brother, one of Jesus' family who once thought Jesus mad! In only one other account—the apocryphal *Gospel According to the Hebrews*, which did not get into the Bible—is this appearance to James mentioned. The resurrection had turned James from disbelief in his own brother to belief and devotion to Him. His brother came back to forgive James. It is an arresting thought that the grace and love of Christ is extended to those who need Him most!

Yes, there were other proofs of His resurrection: The other disciples saw Him (verse 5), and more than five hundred others saw Him (verse 6), and some of them were still alive, and their witness was convincing.

But, important as these eyewitnesses were, they were not important at all compared with one other: Paul says, "Last of all . . . he appeared also to *me*" (verse 8). That was on the Damascus road. He says, "It happened to *me!*" He is speaking now, not of what others had told him, but *out of his own experience.* Once he had persecuted those who followed Christ; because he had done that, he was the most unworthy of all the apostles—and yet Christ had appeared to him personally and asked, "Why persecutest thou me . . . ?" He deserved less at the hands of Jesus than any other living man, yet Jesus had spoken personally to him and personally forgiven him. He was, after the Damascus road experience, the most powerful advocate of Jesus of Nazareth, the greatest of the apostles. "By the grace of God, by the forgiveness of the risen Christ whom I saw with my own eyes "I am what I am. . . ." Saint Paul, in I Corinthians 15:10.

No one could tell *him* that the resurrection was a myth, or an old wives' tale. It was a power in his heart.

II. But if there be no resurrection of the dead, then is Christ not risen, I Corinthians 15:13. That is, "If Christ is not risen in *you,* the resurrection means nothing to you."

But the glory of the resurrection is that *it will happen to you as it happened to Jesus.* It is not a reality merely to Peter and James and the five hundred and the apostles; it can be reality to *you.* If it isn't, then the rest of the teachings of Christianity mean little or nothing. ". . . if Christ was not raised, then our gospel is null and void, and so is your faith. . . . If it is for this life only that Christ has given us hope, we of all men are most to be pitied" (verses 14-19, *New English Bible*).

SUGGESTIONS TO TEACHERS

A very young preacher, just out of seminary, preached an Easter sermon which dealt *only* with what the resurrection of Jesus meant to His disciples in energizing them to spread His gospel. It was, the preacher thought, a good sermon. But a very old man came up to him after the service and said, "Sir, we all know what the resurrection meant to the disciples . . . but what should it mean to us—and to *me?*"

On a previous Sunday (February 27), we discussed the stroll certain disciples took with the risen Christ; today we discuss the possibility of *our* walking with Him! Phillips Brooks put it well when he said that the importance of Easter is not only that it promises life beyond the grave, but that it also empowers us *now* to live by and under the power of faith in His resurrection.

If He is not risen in us with His power of eternal life then, *so far as we are concerned*, His resurrection means nothing!

TOPIC FOR ADULTS
THE CHURCH OF THE RISEN LORD

Mary and We. "This is the miracle of Easter—the miracle of human transformation! Mary Magdalene is the miracle of Easter: she and everyone else like her who has found a transformed life through the resurrected Christ. I know something of what power it takes to transform human life. I have lived long enough and dealt with men and women long enough to know what a grip the habits of the years can get on a person, and how weak mere human resolve is in the face of it. And when I see what Mary Magdalene has become, and remember what she used to be, I stand in husky awe in the presence of God. And what He did for Mary He can do for us. The resurrection happened two thousand years ago—*but has it happened to you?*"—From a sermon by Charles B. Templeton.

The Church. "The people . . . were certain that He became alive again. They saw Him. They talked with Him. Without a single exception, the apostles staked their lives on the fact of Christ's resurrection. When a man as brilliant as Paul, a man as kind and noble as John, a man as sincere and down to earth as Peter, tells me that he saw the risen Christ and speaks of the profound and blessed influence conviction concerning resurrection had on his own life, I'll believe him. I'll believe him long before I'll believe the wisest philosopher who tries to explain life's mysteries without God. When I study the history of the Christian church, beginning with the relatively few men and women who were certain they had a Lord who was alive, who was with them always, and in whom they would live forever; when I observe the growth of the Christian church over the centuries, overcoming all opposition, outliving its enemies, exerting an ennobling influence wherever it has touched human history, I'll confess with unswerving faith, 'Christ is risen,'—period."—Armin C. Oldsen, on The Lutheran Hour.

Fitted for Easter. "In big black type an advertisement of a big department store in an Eastern city has been urging people to 'get fitted for

Easter!' Then the ad goes on to say, 'If you want to look your best on Easter come in and be fitted for a suit or topcoat.'

"Easter is a time for new clothes. But let that plea, 'Get fitted for Easter,' go far deeper than that. We get fitted for Easter in the fullest spiritual sense by realizing anew the greatness of God's love, and the greatness of the gift of eternal life. May those thoughts in our hearts fit us to receive the joy of Easter."—*Christian Herald.*

New Garments. Our preachers sound off loud and clear about the full-dress show that many have made of Easter. But. . . .

"One custom that appears to be universal is the donning of new clothes. The crowds who join in Easter parades are doubtless unaware that they represent a last dim survival of the conferring of white robes upon the newly baptized. In the far-off days this was the general practice, and those already baptized put on new or clean garments at Easter as a reminder of their own baptism."—Victoria A. Banks, in *Church Management.*

At Easter, in the thinking of early church, God gave man new, white, gleaming, spotless clothes for his *soul.* . . .

Open Windows. "John Henry Jowett once called on a cobbler whose home was in a little seaside town in England. The cobbler worked alone in an exceedingly tiny room. Jowett inquired if sometimes he did not feel oppressed by the imprisonment in his little chamber. 'Oh no,' he said, 'if any feeling of that sort begins, I just open this door.' And he opened a door that gave him a glorious view of the sea.

"Easter morning flings life's windows open toward God's omnipotent purpose and power. God confronts man with an open tomb."—Paul L. McKay.

That was the door through which the disciples and the apostles passed from Jerusalem and spread out across the world.

No Doubt. "There may be some dispute between biologists and psychologists as to the precise moment when life begins. But in the mind of the Christian there is no doubt whatever. Life begins at Easter! The solemn declaration, 'He is not here, but is risen,' marked the dividing line between life and death, between hope and hopelessness, in human affairs."—Roy L. Smith.

Questions for Pupils on the Next Lesson: 1. Describe the worship of the church in apostolic days. 2. How many did it take to make a church in those days? 3. How important was prayer in the worship of the early church? 4. What do we mean by worshiping God "in spirit and in truth?" 5. Is worship in your home as effective as worship in your church? 6. What two main features of worship does Luke describe in Acts 2? 7. Do you know of any modern churches in which the people "break bread together?"

TOPIC FOR YOUTH
THE CHURCH LIVES BECAUSE CHRIST LIVES

Difficult to Believe? "We must admit . . . that modern man finds it difficult to believe in the resurrection. It runs counter to all of his every-day assumptions. He is like the sophisticated Athenians who listened respectfully to St. Paul's interpretation of the gospel until he proclaimed the resurrection, when they no longer took him seriously. The minister of today is, therefore, tempted to put no emphasis on the resurrection, and to treat it almost as if it were an optional part of the Christian faith, a sort of addendum which the modern Christian may ignore.

"If we do so, we part company with the central conviction which brought the Christian church into existence. As a distinguished New Testament scholar has said, 'The entire early church moved out from the realization that Jesus Christ had risen. It shaped all its faith, its worship, life and thought in the light of this fact.' The church did not get started because the disciples decided to organize a society to perpetuate the ideals of a lost leader. It sprang into existence, as the *Book of Acts* makes clear, because of an unshakable assurance that they had a living Lord. The early preaching of the Christian message—as the *Book of Acts* also shows beyond question—was so centered in the resurrection that we might say that to proclaim Christ and to proclaim His resurrection were virtually the same thing."—An editorial in *Pulpit Digest* by Samuel M. Cavert.

The Final Part. "In March of 1946 some people in New York City gathered together for an official dinner to pay public tribute to Winston Churchill. Among the guests was a sixteen-year-old boy, Johnny Gunther, in a dinner jacket, sitting between his author-father, John Gunther, and his mother, Frances. A month later, a report from Columbia-Presbyterian Medical Center said: 'Your child has a brain tumor.'

"Sixteen months of heart-rending agony for them, while the boy struggled with death. Somehow, they got through it, though the boy went down before it. When it was all over, Frances wrote in her diary: 'Look death in the face. Death is a part of life, like birth, *but not the final part.*'

"That is the Easter message: death is not the final part. Immortality is the final part. The seal is off the stone definitely and forevermore. Thanks be to God, which giveth us the victory through our Lord Jesus Christ."—From a sermon in *The Pastor* by Harrison Davis.

Hope, Love. We maye have quoted this before, and perhaps we should not have quoted it at all, inasmuch as it came from a man who may have been the greatest American agnostic. But there is Easter in it. Here it is:

"Life is a narrow veil between the cold and barren peaks of two eternities. We strive in vain to look beyond the heights. We cry aloud and the only answer is the echo of our wailing cry. From the voiceless lips of the unreplying dead there comes no word. But in the night of death, Hope sees a star, and listening Love can hear the rustle of a wing."—Robert G. Ingersoll.

The Great Adventure. "Death is a great adventure, but none need go unconvinced that there is an issue in it. The man of faith may face it as Columbus faced his first voyage from the shores of Spain. What lies across the sea he cannot tell; his special expectations all may be mistaken; but his insight into the clear meanings of present facts may persuade him beyond doubt that the sea has another shore. Such confident faith, so founded upon reasonable grounds, shall be turned to sight when, for all the disbelief of the unbelieving, the hope of the seers is rewarded by the vision of a new continent."—Harry Emerson Fosdick.

More. Dr. Rufus Jones, the great Quaker teacher, lost his son at eleven years of age; it was a blow from which he thought, at first, that he would never recover. But later he wrote this:

"When my sorrow was at its most acute stage, I was walking along a city highway. Suddenly I saw a little child come out of a great gate, which swung to and fastened behind her. She wanted to go back into her home behind the gate, but it would not open. She pounded in vain with her little fist. She rattled the gate. She wailed as if her heart would break. The cry brought her mother, who caught the child up in her arms and kissed away the tears. 'Didn't you know I would come? It's all right now.' All of a sudden I saw with my spirit that there was love behind my shut gate. Where there is so much love, there must be more."

The Scripture says, ". . . this mortal *must* put on immortality." It is in the *imperative* mood!

Sentence Sermon to Remember: Easter is God's way of looking at Good Friday.—John M. Krumm.

Questions for Pupils on the Next Lesson: 1. Explain the meaning of Matthew 18:19. Do you accept it literally? 2. Where did the Christians worship before they had churches? 3. Right or wrong: "I can worship God in the forest as well as in a church"? 4. What is the plan of worship in your church services? 5. Is worship a natural instinct, or is it something we must be taught? 6. How have you grown in worship during the last ten years? 7. From what old English word do we get our word, "worship," and what did the English word mean?

LESSON VI—APRIL 9

THE CHURCH: A WORSHIPING COMMUNITY

Background Scripture: Matthew 18:19-20; John 4:19-24;
Acts 2:41-47; Colossians 3:14-17
Devotional Reading: Revelation 19:5-10

KING JAMES VERSION

MATTHEW 18 19 Again I say unto you, That if two of you shall agree on earth as touching any thing that they shall ask, it shall be done for them of my Father which is in heaven.

20 For where two or three are gathered together in my name, there am I in the midst of them.

JOHN 4 24 God is a Spirit: and they that worship him must worship him in spirit and in truth.

ACTS 2 41 Then they that gladly received his word were baptized: and the same day there were added unto them about three thousand souls.

42 And they continued steadfastly in the apostles' doctrine and fellowship, and in breaking of bread, and in prayers.

43 And fear came upon every soul: and many wonders and signs were done by the apostles.

44 And all that believed were together, and had all things common;

45 And sold their possessions and goods, and parted them to all men, as every man had need.

46 And they, continuing daily with one accord in the temple, and breaking bread from house to house, did eat their meat with gladness and singleness of heart,

47 Praising God, and having favor with all the people. And the Lord added to the church daily such as should be saved.

REVISED STANDARD VERSION

MATTHEW 18 19 "Again I say to you, if two of you agree on earth about anything they ask, it will be done for them by my Father in heaven. 20 For where two or three are gathered in my name, there am I in the midst of them."

JOHN 4 24 "God is spirit, and those who worship him must worship in spirit and truth."

ACTS 2 So those who received his word were baptized, and there were added that day about three thousand souls. 42 And they devoted themselves to the apostles' teaching and fellowship, to the breaking of bread and the prayers.

43 And fear came upon every soul; and many wonders and signs were done through the apostles. 44 And all who believed were together and had all things in common; 45 and they sold their possessions and goods and distributed them to all, as any had need. 46 And day by day, attending the temple together and breaking bread in their homes, they partook of food with glad and generous hearts,

47 praising God and having favor with all the people. And the Lord added to their number day by day those who were being saved.

MEMORY SELECTION: God is a Spirit: and they that worship him must worship him in spirit and in truth. John 4:24.

HOME DAILY BIBLE READINGS

Apr. 3. M. The Spirit's Presence, I Corinthians 14:1-5.
Apr. 4. T. The Correct Approach to Worship, John 4:19-24.
Apr. 5. W. Worship for Cleansing and Strength, Hebrews 10:19-25.
Apr. 6. T. Unity and Power Through Worship, Acts 2:41-47.
Apr. 7. F. Fellowship Through Singing, Ephesians 5:15-20.

Apr. 8. S. Praising the Name of Christ, Philippians 2:5-11.
Apr. 9. S. Worship God, Revelation 19:5-10.

BACKGROUND

While Jesus lived, the disciples worshiped with Him wherever He happened to be: on a hillside, on the shores of Galilee, in an upper room in Jerusalem. We are not told *how* they worshiped with Him; there was no one pattern. For some time after His ascension there was confusion and little organization; the disciples were now a loosely organized group of disciples who knew what they must do but were undecided how to do it. Gradually, a unity came, and gradually out of that unity came a "church" or an organization in which the disciples could work to better effect than they could have worked as individual missionaries.

We who are members of that church today can downgrade and criticize "organized religion" if we wish, but, with all its faults, we should be honest enough to admit that if there had been no organized Christianity in the first century there would be no Christianity at all in the twentieth century.

This first church was founded on the firm foundation of *worship.* Today we are to find out just what that worship was like.

NOTES ON THE PRINTED TEXT

I. For where two or three are gathered together in my name, there am I in the midst of them, Matthew 18:20. The Jews had a saying which went, "Where two sit and are occupied with the study of the law, the glory of God is among them." The glory of God, which some of them had seen on the face of Jesus Christ, was in the midst of those who came together to worship Him after Pentecost. He was *there,* in their little prayer groups, in their homes, in their secret meeting places. The consciousness of the presence of Christ was a chain of iron that bound them together in a time of uncertainty and even terror.

Where is the church? It is wherever two or three kneel to pray to or worship Him. It is in a little family circle; it is in the huge mass meeting. The church isn't a building. It is a communing, worshipful spirit.

This, then, is the beginning of the Christian church: little groups of Christians meeting with a risen Christ to *worship.* And that worship was primarily *prayer.*

Now, regarding prayer, the Christians had the word of Jesus Himself that if only two of them agreed together to ask something in prayer, "it [would] be done for them of my Father which is in heaven" (verse 19). In our interpretation, we must be careful of this verse, for if we interpret it literally we are in trouble. Many a time two people have prayed that a friend with cancer might be cured—and the friend died. Or they prayed that a soldier son or friend might come safely through a battle—and he was killed. Farmers have prayed for rain and rain did *not* fall. Prayers in our worship are not always answered as we want them answered, which might even be bad!

Here, Jesus is saying several things about prayer. He is saying that it should always be unselfish, that we should pray as members of a fellowship, and for the good of the fellowship. Prayer shouldn't encourage our selfishness; it should wash it out of our minds and hearts. We should pray, not for *escape* from our problems but for a will and a spirit to *conquer* them. We should pray as Jesus prayed in Gethsemane—pray to be spared pain, suffering and sorrow, "but, *nevertheless*, . . ." If the agony must come, give us the Christian courage to bear it, to conquer it.

In worship, we should never be beggars of God, but. . . !

II. God is a Spirit, and they that worship him must worship him in spirit and in truth, John 4:24. Worship can be—and too often is—as false and "phony" as a counterfeit bill. It can be hypocritical—and too often is. We can praise God beautifully and endlessly in worship, flatter Him to the point where He must resent it—and then go out and live as though He were dead! That is *not* worshiping Him in truth.

In this passage, Jesus was talking with a woman of Samaria about *worship*, and He accused her and the Samaritans of worshiping they did not know what. The Samaritans were guilty of that; they took what they wanted out of the Scriptures and ignored the rest; they were guilty of racial prejudice and bigotry (yes, and at times so were the Jews); they worshiped in superstition—and so do many of *us*. Jesus told the woman that true worship of God should supersede all local rituals, both Samaritan and Jewish; that God was not confined to any one place, to any one temple, and that to insist upon worship of God in *our* church and in *our* ritual and in *our* language is wrong. True and honest and sincere worship is worship in which the spirit (which is immortal in man) meets and communes with an immortal and invisible God who is God of all people, all races, all nations everywhere. It is a moment of honest confrontation of man with God; the liturgy doesn't matter, because man created the liturgy, while God created the heart and the immortal soul as meeting places for man and Himself.

Let worship be true and sincere before it is anything more.

III. And they devoted themselves to the apostles' teaching and fellowship, to the breaking of bread and the prayers, Acts 2:42 (RSV). Here we are in a later period. The young church had really begun to grow! There were at least "about three thousand souls" in the membership, and there were works of healing and casting out of unclean spirits that not only amazed the general population outside the church, but even created respect and fear for what it was doing. "Signs and wonders" awed the people, and for a time at least quieted the opposition.

In verses 44 and 45, Luke describes the community spirit of the growing fellowship, and enlarges on this in Acts 4:32-5:11, which we have already studied.

Luke describes two main features of this worship. The first was the emphasis on prayer; even while the new "Christians" were beginning to meet for prayer and worship in their little groups, they were still attending the regular prayer services in their old Jewish temples. It wasn't easy to stop that; we all change our beliefs before we change our worship habits. They still went to the Temple—in a separate and distinct group.

But they also "broke bread together" in a *new* worship. These were meals of common fellowship in the homes of the Christians; it was a custom connected with the sharing of their possessions. They shared even their food. Perhaps it was done in remembrance of the Christ who once had fed five thousand on a hillside, or perhaps it was a sacramental fellowship with Jesus, who had instituted a "Last Supper." At these fellowship meals (we might call them "sit-ins!"), they sat and ate in expectancy of His return: they prayed, beautifully, "Maranatha: our Lord, come!"

They left some fine guidelines in prayer and worship.

SUGGESTIONS TO TEACHERS

Man's worship began the day the first man on earth looked up and saw the sun, or when he sensed the presence of a tremendous unseen power working in and beyond his visible world. But most men (and women and children!) *still* seem not to know exactly what worship *is*, or what it is supposed to *do*. Start the lesson by asking your class about this.

The word "worship," according to one of our dictionaries, comes from the Old English word "weorthscipe"—*weorth*, meaning *worth*, and *scipe*, meaning *ship*. Worthship! Think about that.

Our worship can be a formality. It can be a habit. It can be an act of desperation performed only when we are in trouble. But if it is worthy worship, it is *a seeking and a finding;* what we find in worship determines what sort of Christians we are, and what sort of *church* we are. . . .

TOPIC FOR ADULTS
THE WORSHIPING COMMUNITY

The Chapel. J. B. Priestly, British novelist and playwright, writes this about worship:

"People like my parents—to use their own matchless phrase—attended places of worship. Now that I see that old phrase with a fresh eye, I also see how astonishing it is. Places of worship. How much we have lost, we of the younger generations, by having no places of worship! Perhaps this new world must remain desolate at heart until it achieves new places of worship. Then the spirit of man will come home again to the universe.

"What is certain is that the absence of church or chapel from these young people's lives has vastly increased their sense of detachment and their feeling of loneliness. When I was a boy, the chapel played a very important part indeed in the communal life. It was the great focal point, the center, the meeting place. Something was always happening there. If the chapel had been taken away, there would have been an enormous gap, and I fancy not all that gap has been filled. It is possible that the moderns living in their laborsaving (apartments) of natty bungalows will not live richly and deeply again, will continue to feel that there is something sterile and faintly desolating in their lives, until some central institution like the old chapel, with the same focusing of interests and the same sense of community, is created once more. And if this new institution can be dedicated to men's profoundest beliefs and emotions, to their conviction that they need not be lost in the universe, then so much the better."—From *Rain on Godshill*.

Someone else has said that if we take away the worship practices of the church all the Rocky Mountains would not fill the gaping hole left in human society. Worship lies at the base of religion—and of almost everything else!

No Funds. "The human mind and the human life are like a checking account. Keep putting enough money in the bank and your checkbook is the most magic book in the world . . . dip your pen in ink, make a few flourishes, and your check becomes the open sesame to your heart's desires. But just stop making ample deposits in your account and the magic evaporates with a curt message from the bank—'No funds!' "— Oliver Wendell Holmes.

You get out of worship what you put in. It takes thought and heart searching to make worship worth while and spiritually profitable; it takes only a little carelessness and squandering of time and thought to go bankrupt.

The Bells. When Albert Schweitzer was a young man he went out with some of his companions on a bird shoot. He had never shot birds before, so he did not know very much about it. But now he learned about it in one blazing second. . . .

He got a flying bird in his sights, and was just about to squeeze the trigger when he heard the bells of a little country church across the meadows, and he could not fire. He threw down the gun and went home; later, he said, "Whenever I have been tempted, since that day, to loosen my convictions about the sacredness of life, I have remembered the call of those church bells across the meadows of Alsace that had kept my soul."

That is worship! That is *worth-ship*—a sense of the worthship of God and of God's creatures. That is communion with God—it is life's most important seeking and finding. . . .

The Window. We have all known moments of worship in unexpected places—in the quietness of a home, or in a moment of inspiration in the schoolroom, or. . . .

"Phillip II of Spain had a window placed in the office where he worked that allowed him to see into his private chapel next door. As he worked at his desk, considering the affairs of State, he would often lift his eyes and see the cross on the altar of the chapel. He worshiped as he worked; he received as he gave; he was strengthened as he served." —Alan Walker.

A few weeks ago, in the National Museum of Art in Washington, we saw for the first time the face of Peter in Rembrandt's "Descent From the Cross." For fifteen minutes, we were held spellbound and motionless by that face. It was a great moment of worship, a great religious experience—in an art gallery!

Questions for Pupils on the Next Lesson: 1. We are emphasizing the words, "The Church as Mission," today; what do we mean? 2. Who were the Hellenists, and what did they do? 3. Was Stephen a minister? 4. What was "the equipment of the saints" (Ephesians 4:11)? 5. What different kind of church leaders does Paul mention? 6. May a layman serve as a minister without being ordained? 7. What gift have you refused to give in the service of the church?

TOPIC FOR YOUTH
WHY WORSHIP TOGETHER?

Three Ships A-Sailing. "Sounds like a Christmas song, doesn't it? But I am thinking of a remark made by a good minister of Christ in Southern California. He was a veteran and speaks out of a long experience. 'Three "ships" carry the freight in a living church,' he observed. 'One is worship, the next is fellowship, and the third is stewardship.' When members worship every week they know more intimately the great God who created and saved and sustains us. They find resources to carry every burden and handle every situation. In fellowship we lose our loneliness and have adventured together in love and friendship. Stewardship makes us responsible Christians, and we know the satisfaction of being working members of the crew of the ship of the Spirit. Welcome aboard!"—Revell's Minister's Annual, 1969.

The Highest Experience. "Three men were discussing the most inspiring worship services they had ever been in.

"One spoke of a revival service in his church with a famous preacher.

"Another remembered a brush-arbor revival meeting from his youth when the people shouted.

"The third said, 'In the highest worship experience of my life I do not remember that there was any weeping or shouting. Understand, I don't particularly object to either; I just don't remember that as a part of the service. In fact, strange as it may seem, I do not even remember the preacher's name. I remember only that there was a message on missions, and when the offering was received it contained a man's gold watch and a woman's diamond ring. That winter mother didn't get the new coat she had been saving for, and we drove the old car for another year."—An editorial in *The Baptist Messenger*, May 29, 1969.

Worship is good only when it goes with you after the service!

Practice. "A distinguished theologian told a gathering of laymen: 'Our assembled, corporate worship is, so to speak, a rehearsal. Here on Sunday at 11 o'clock we worship God in a practice session among ourselves in order that we may more skillfully worship Him the rest of the week dispersed among other people. The rest of the week it is our ministry to adore Him and intercede for the world in the midst of the world."
—Source unknown.

Results. Church worship has "paid off" in great movements and events after the worship was over. For instance:

It was worship that inspired the erection of the world-famous statue known as the Christ of the Andes on the border between Chile and Argentina. Since it was erected, there has never been a war between Chile and Argentina.

On the Sunday after Aaron Burr shot and killed Alexander Hamilton in a duel at Weehauken, New Jersey, a minister in Albany, New York, preached a sermon on the wickedness and folly of duelling; it inspired the first law that put an end to duelling in the United States.

Harriet Beecher Stowe attended a communion service in her church which drove her to write *Uncle Tom's Cabin*—a book which had tremendous influence in the outlawing of slavery. . . .

Visions gained in worship *can* be translated into action. . . .

Seek, Knock. " 'Prayer is not easy and never was,' declared Ardis Whitman. 'The ancient dilemma—man's need to talk to God and his difficulty in doing so—continues. But there is hope in the very gropings of this generation. . . . Contemporary prayer at its best is a thanksgiving for life and love . . . a hallelujah that creation is still going on and we are a part of it.'

"An ancient proverb reminds us that God does not listen to the lazy. "Seekers find; knock, doors open; ask, you receive."—C. Harry Atkinson.

No Urge. Discussing the claim of those who say they can worship God on the beach as well as in the pew, Eleanor Doan says: "When a fellow claims that he can worship as well out in the country, in a mountain resort or at the beach as he can at church, it seems that he probably feels no particular urge to worship at all." Right or wrong?

> A room of quiet, a temple of peace,
> The home of faith where doubtings cease,
> A house of comfort where hope is given,
> A source of strength to make earth heaven,
> A shrine of worship, a place to pray—
> I found all this in my church today.
> —Author unknown.

Sentence Sermon to Remember: This world can be saved from political chaos and collapse by only one thing . . . worship to quicken the conscience by the holiness of God, to feed the mind with the truth of God, to devote the will to the purpose of God.—William Temple.

Questions for Pupils on the Next Lesson: 1. Have your requests in prayer always been answered, as promised in Matthew 18:19? 2. Is God a personality, a spirit or both (John 4:24)? 3. How did the early church organize for *service?* 4. Does your church select leaders to meet specific needs *in your community?* 5. How would you change the organization of your church if you could? 6. What should your church be doing that it isn't doing? 7. Did the New Testament church really have "favor with all the people" (Acts 2:47)?

LESSON VII—APRIL 16

THE CHURCH ORGANIZED FOR MISSION

Background Scripture: Acts 6:1-7; Ephesians 4:11-16; I Timothy 3
Devotional Reading: Luke 10:1-9

KING JAMES VERSION

ACTS 6 And in those days, when the number of the disciples was multiplied, there arose a murmuring of the Grecians against the Hebrews, because their widows were neglected in the daily ministration.

2 Then the twelve called the multitude of the disciples unto them, and said, It is not reason that we should leave the word of God, and serve tables.

3 Wherefore, brethren, look ye out among you seven men of honest report, full of the Holy Ghost and wisdom, whom we may appoint over this business.

4 But we will give ourselves continually to prayer, and to the ministry of the word.

5 And the saying pleased the whole multitude: and they chose Stephen, a man full of faith and of the Holy Ghost, and Philip, and Prochorus, and Nicanor, and Timon, and Parmenas, and Nicolas a proselyte of Antioch:

6 Whom they set before the apostles: and when they had prayed, they laid their hands on them.

7 And the word of God increased; and the number of the disciples multiplied in Jerusalem greatly; and a great company of the priests were obedient to the faith.

EPHESIANS 4 11 And he gave some, apostles; and some, prophets; and some, evangelists; and some, pastors and teachers;

12 For the perfecting of the saints, for the work of the ministry, for the edifying of the body of Christ:

13 Till we all come in the unity of the faith, and of the knowledge of the Son of God, unto a perfect man, unto the measure of the stature of the fulness of Christ: . . .

14 That we henceforth be no more children, tossed to and fro, and carried about with every wind of doctrine, by the sleight of men, and cun-

REVISED STANDARD VERSION

ACTS 6 Now in these days when the disciples were increasing in number, the Hellenists murmured against the Hebrews because their widows were neglected in the daily distribution. 2 And the twelve summoned the body of the disciples and said, "It is not right that we should give up preaching the word of God to serve tables. 3 Therefore, brethren, pick out from among you seven men of good repute, full of the Spirit and of wisdom, whom we may appoint to this duty. 4 But we will devote ourselves to prayer and to the ministry of the word." 5 And what they said pleased the whole multitude, and they chose Stephen, a man full of faith and of the Holy Spirit, and Philip, and Prochorus, and Nicanor, and Timon, and Parmenas, and Nicolaus, a proselyte of Antioch. 6 These they set before the apostles, and they prayed and laid their hands upon them.

7 And the word of God increased; and the number of the disciples multiplied greatly in Jerusalem, and a great many of the priests were obedient to the faith.

EPHESIANS 4 11 And his gifts were that some should be apostles, some prophets, some evangelists, some pastors and teachers, 12 for the equipment of the saints, for the work of ministry, for building up the body of Christ, 13 until we all attain to the unity of the faith and of the knowledge of the Son of God, to mature manhood, to the measure of the stature of the fulness of Christ; . . . 14 so that we may no longer be children, tossed to and fro and carried about with every wind of doctrine, by the cunning of men, by their craftiness in deceitful wiles. 15 Rather, speaking

ning craftiness whereby they lie in wait to deceive;

15 But speaking the truth in love, may grow up into him in all things, which is the head, even Christ:

16 From whom the whole body fitly joined together and compacted by that which every joint supplieth, according to the effectual working in the measure of every part, maketh increase of the body unto the edifying of itself in love.

the truth in love, we are to grow up in every way into him who is the head, into Christ, 16 from whom the whole body, joined and knit together by every joint with which it is supplied, when each part is working properly, makes bodily growth and upbuilds itself in love.

MEMORY SELECTION: . . . . his gifts were that some should be apostles, some prophets, some evangelists, some pastors and teachers, for the equipment of the saints, for the work of ministry, for building up the body of Christ. . . . Ephesians 4:11, 12.

HOME DAILY BIBLE READINGS

Apr. 10. M. Selecting Gentile Leaders, Acts 6:1-7.
Apr. 11. T. The Church in Council, Acts 15:1-6.
Apr. 12. W. Paul's Procedure in Asia, Acts 20:17-24.
Apr. 13. T. Dispersion of Leaders, Titus 1:5-9.
Apr. 14. F. Qualifications of Bishops, I Timothy 3:1-7.
Apr. 15. S. Qualifications of Deacons, I Timothy 3:8-13.
Apr. 16. S. Appointed to Mission, Luke 10:1-9.

BACKGROUND

Someone has said, "The minute you organize an idea, that minute you organize trouble." It might be better to say, "The minute you get an organization, that minute you get *problems*." Every problem is solvable —all have solutions, but, in some situations, it takes patience and good humor to find them.

As it grew larger, a situation arose in the church which threatened its peace. Oddly enough, it arose out of the effort to share the food that was held "in common" and was supposed to be shared without favor or preference. It might have been deliberate or accidental, but whichever it was, it had all "the makings" of a good church quarrel almost before the church was well organized.

A little prejudice may have been involved here, too. . . .

NOTES ON THE PRINTED TEXT

I. . . . there arose a murmuring of the Grecians against the Hebrews . . . , Acts 6:1. The *RSV* text says that "the *Hellenists* murmured against the Hebrews." The word "Hellenist" means "one who lives as a Greek." Or one who may have lived as a 'foreigner" in some Greek territory outside Jerusalem and Palestine. Actually, there were two kinds of Jews—the Greek-influenced foreign Jews living abroad and the strict, orthodox Palestinian Jews. Many of the foreigners even spoke Greek in preference to Hebrew, and little frictions between the two groups were frequent, in both the synagogue and in the church.

The trouble in the church came when the Hellenistic Jews thought there was some discrimination against their widows in the distribution of food. This food distribution was an old Jewish practice; every Friday morning "collectors" appointed by the Jewish congregations made their rounds, collecting money to buy food for the needy, and "receivers of alms" made their rounds in the markets, collecting both money and food. The Christians simply picked up the custom in the church. Perhaps there was a "Hellenistic" collector or two who saw to it that his "Greek" widows were cared for *first*. (Even among us there is some favoritism in our charity!) Or maybe it was the other way round. The church fathers saw the danger in the problem, and moved quickly and intelligently.

They held an election in which seven of their number (seven of "good repute, full of the Spirit and of wisdom") were chosen to see that the food was distributed fairly and regularly. They are sometimes called "deacons," but notice that they are not called that in our Scripture. They were simply seven good men set aside to "serve tables" as helpers or almoners to look after the needy.

This is odd: all seven of them had Greek names! Was there a little "politicking" in their election, or was it a gesture of good will by the orthodox Hebrew churchmen?

This is important: the first concern of the church was to put its faith to work *in practical action*. They appointed officers, not to preach, but to "serve tables"; they may have been remembering the Christ who took a towel at a supper and "served. . . ."

II. *And he gave some, apostles; and some, prophets; and some, evangelists; and some, pastors and teachers*, Ephesians 4:11. This is an important passage; it gives us a clear picture of the organization and administration of the church in the apostolic period. We find in this organization three kinds of officials, or three kinds of *ministries"; one had to do with the *whole* church, another with only the *local* church, and a third with a sort of "free-lance" preaching and teaching through all the churches. Paul says that God gave certain "gifts" to certain men to carry on the work of the church.

To some He gave the gift of *apostleship:* these apostles had authority over all the churches; they were men like Paul, James and Barnabas; they were men of intimate experience with Christ, men who had taken into their lives the power of the *risen* Christ. To some others He gave the gift of prophecy; the *prophets* were free-lance "wanderers" who held no local pastoral post but moved through all the churches, "foretelling" the will and way of God; they had no homes, no families, no salaries; they were both popular and unpopular; they often got into trouble with the civil authorities; they did not last very long as a separate group in the church. Some others were *evangelists*—the first missionaries of the church; few of them are remembered by name; they were the first, anonymous "spreaders of the Word." There were also *pastors* and *teachers*—and, as such, perhaps the most important workers in the whole church; they taught in a day when few could read, when few had books or parchments *to* read; they told the story of Jesus by word of mouth and passed down an oral tradition about Him that was later put in writing; they explained the Scriptures; they were most often *pastors*, or shepherds of the scattered flocks of Christians in the church; they kept the "sheep" from wandering, defended them, educated them, often died for them. Following the example of the chief shepherd, Christ, they immortalized the word "shepherd" and wrote it indelibly into the New Testament record.

It was a good and wise organization—and it had but one purpose: it was all for "the equipment of the saints, for the work of the ministry, for building up the body of Christ" (Ephesians 4:12, rsv). The body of Christ—or the church! And the goal of this upbuilding was "the unity of the faith and of the knowledge of the Son of God" (4:13, rsv). That word "unity" was of paramount importance in the church from the first moment of its existence; it should be of primary importance today—but what has happened to it—the "unity" of the church?

What has happened has been tragic—and largely because so many of us have refused to "grow up"—to live like mature men and women (see verse 13), and not like children "tossed to and fro, and carried about with every wind of doctrine" (verse 14). Living as worthy Christians demands that we live by the truth of Christ, that we have His mind, that we "grow up in every way into him who is the head" (verse 15).

How goes the unity in your church? And how much have you grown lately?

SUGGESTIONS TO TEACHERS

How was the early church *organized?* List the officers—the "official board." What did these officers *do?* The church picked leaders to meet specific needs: what *were* those needs? Were they quite the same as our needs today? If you were in charge of electing the leaders of your church what would you look for in those you selected?

We know a man in a certain church who says he can't be bothered with work on *any* of the boards or commissions of the church. He says, "I have enough troubles already!" He feels that the minister is paid to take care of the religion of the congregation: "let him do it." Can any church succeed in its mission with such men? Point this out, and write it large in the minds of your students: *every Christian is involved in the mission of the church.*

TOPIC FOR ADULTS
ORGANIZED FOR MISSION

Mission. The word "mission" means "sending or being sent on some special work." And it is a word that makes us think of another word—missionary—every time we see it. We are *all* missionaries for something or other.

In China years ago, we visited a little cemetery in which three generations of missionaries were buried. We were impressed with a statement of our guide: "This cemetery is divided into two parts; half of it holds the graves of the first generation, which was strictly evangelical; the other holds the graves of those who built on the work of the early evangelists in other directions. . . ." We thought about that for a long, long time. The missionary is the perfect example of the church changing its methods but not its message to meet new needs as they arise.

The first generation of missionaries, which was just about 100 per cent evangelical, had come to save men in the name of Jesus Christ. But almost in the next generation came men who realized that if the saved were to *stay* saved some other work must be done. There must be schools where the convert could learn to read his Bible; there must be hospitals where the sick could be healed in His name; there must be Christian farmers to provide food for a nation half of which was starving to death! So, when you go abroad now, you find missionaries who are preachers, evangelists, doctors, agricultural experts, nurses, engineers, writers, printers, athletic instructors . . . *anything and everything*.

Ours is a church organized for *mission*. Is there anyone in the church who cannot be a missionary in one category or another?

Institutional. "In recognition of the fact that there are all kinds of churches—effective and ineffective—I want to make clear four of my convictions about the institutional church:

"(1) I believe that the church, as a worshiping, learning, witnessing, serving body of believers, is still a part of God's redemptive plan for God's world.

"(2) I believe that the church needs always to seek and to know and to do God's will contemporaneously, but it need not throw away its entire heritage for that which is momentarily called 'modern' or 'relevant.'

"(3) I believe that the church, to minister adequately—locally and globally—must continue to provide an exceedingly broad approach to the life of its people and to its community.

"(4) I believe that the church must not insist on unrestricted theological systems, work methods, church organizations or church ministries. Rather, the church must constantly relate meaningfully that which is eternal to that which is temporal."—Rev. Dean R. Kirkwood, in *Eternity*, January, 1968.

What does he mean in point 3 by "an exceedingly broad approach?"

Shrouded Up. "An American writer, seeking a quiet and inspiring setting for his work, built a home in the Blue Ridge Mountains of Virginia. Nestled against the mountainside, it overlooked a glorious valley. One day while on a hike the writer met an old woman, a native of the region. With shy courtesy but surprising directness, she asked, their dark valleys, are saying to the church, 'You aren't going to let 'em be shrouded up, are ye? Or be ye?'

"Over the world there are millions of people who, looking across their dark valleys, are saying to the church, 'You aren't going to let your lights be shrouded up, are you?' "—Everett W. Palmer.

Notice that Dr. Palmer says "lights"—plural. What lights have we lighted in the church that we dare not let go out? What was the nature of the lights first set aflame in the early churches? Did they deal only with the darkness of the human soul, or with all the broader physical problems of their society?

And how many people with different talents are required to keep the lights aglow *now*? Can the minister do it all—alone?

Questions for Pupils on the Next Lesson: 1. What are you witnessing *to* in your church? 2. What instructions did the man in Mark 5 get from Jesus about his witnessing? 3. Was Philip a minister or a lay healer? 4. Was Apollos a good witness for Christ or a poor one? 5. What risks are involved in witnessing? 6. True or false: "If religion ends with the individual, it *ends*"? 7. Is witnessing only an oral exercise?

TOPIC FOR YOUTH
ORGANIZED TO SERVE

Pay Up! A youth of 21, Albert Schweitzer heard a voice within his heart say, "You must pay."

He asked, "Pay? Me? How?"

The voice replied: "In service to those who have not known happiness, to those who are starving in body and soul, to those who are writhing in pain. You who are not starving, you who do not know what pain is, you—laden down with blessings—owe a debt."

He asked what kind of service he was supposed to render; the voice told him: "The day-in-and-day-out giving of yourself to people who cannot possibly return what you give."

It is the mission of the church so to serve.

Once we sat in the executive meeting of a large men's Bible class. The treasurer, giving his last report for the year, announced that the class was "in a very comfortable financial position"; it had nearly $400 in the treasury.

A fine old man got up and asked: "What right do we have to hoard $400 in the bank while there are kids in this town so hungry that they go to sleep in school?"

How dare any church be rich?

God's Purpose. You may have some trouble understanding the following, or even accepting it, but think about it:

"Several years ago a Christian youth group in East Berlin gave up their free time to join with a communist youth group in building an orphanage. When the communists asked the Christians why they were helping them, knowing that Christianity and communism were at cross-purposes, the Christians replied, 'You are doing God's work in the world and we want to help you.' The communists were furious! But think of the impact of that witness. The Christians did *not* say that being a communist was God's purpose but that caring for homeless children is always God's purpose in the world."—*Dare To Live Now*, by Bruce Larson.

Dr. Larson also says: "We can co-operate with Him [God] and perhaps interpret what He is doing to fellow workers who may not be Christian." Question: what would happen to the godless communist movement if such a Christian witness came to them from *all* of us?

Growth. We are hearing much today about the decline of religion, and the "death" of Christianity. But the facts tell another story. From the time when "the number of the disciples multiplied in Jerusalem greatly" there has been a steady multiplying greatly far beyond those in Jerusalem, To wit:

At the end of the second century there were
2,000,000 Christians.
At the end of the fourth century there were
10,000,000 Christians.
At the end of the tenth century there were
50,000,000 Christians.
At the end of the fifteenth century there were
100,000,000 Christians.
At the end of the eighteenth century there were
200,000,000 Christians.
At the end of the nineteenth century there were
500,000,000 Christians.
Today it is estimated that there are nearly
one billion Christians.

We can criticize "institutional" or "organized" religion all we wish, but the fact remains that this religion today far outnumbers all others in membership. Such popularity must be deserved!

No, we cannot estimate the value of a faith in numbers alone. All we have to do now is to estimate the value of this faith in its impact on all mankind. That isn't a bad record, either!

Sitters, Doers. Says Dr. Ralph Sockman: "The early church began as a lay movement, each person telling what the Lord had done for him. But now the church program has deteriorated into a kind of propaganda financed by silent spectators. We hire preachers to deliver our sermons and read the Bible for us, we engage professional singers. . . . The laity sits back and pays the bills—and some just sit back."

Decide for yourself: as a layman, are you sitter or doer? There is work for all of us; there is good fighting all along the line. Stand up and be counted!

Sentence Sermon to Remember: The church does not need to change its message—just its method of approach; twentieth-century man will not recognize the truths presented in fourteenth-century garb.—Jack M. Coke.

Questions for Pupils on the Next Lesson: 1. What prompted the commissioning of the man who had been healed (Mark 5)? 2. Specifically, *how* was he to witness for Christ? 3. Why do some Christians *never* witness? 4. Who was the Philip mentioned in Acts 8:5? 5. What was wrong with the early witnessing of Apollos? 6. Is there any kind of witnessing other than oral witnessing? 7. Has the gospel, historically, been passed along more by word of mouth than by writing?

LESSON VIII—APRIL 23

THE CHURCH: A WITNESSING COMMUNITY

Background Scripture: Mark 5:1-20; Acts 8:4-40; 18:24-28
Devotional Reading: Acts 8:26-35

KING JAMES VERSION

MARK 5 18 And when he was come into the ship, he that had been possessed with the devil prayed him that he might be with him.

19 Howbeit Jesus suffered him not, but saith unto him, Go home to thy friends, and tell them how great things the Lord hath done for thee, and hath had compassion on thee.

20 And he departed, and began to publish in Decapolis how great things Jesus had done for him: and all men did marvel.

ACTS 8 4 Therefore they that were scattered abroad went every where preaching the word.

5 Then Philip went down to the city of Samaria, and preached Christ unto them.

6 And the people with one accord gave heed unto those things which Philip spake, hearing and seeing the miracles which he did.

7 For unclean spirits, crying with loud voice, came out of many that were possessed with them: and many taken with palsies, and that were lame, were healed.

8 And there was great joy in that city.

ACTS 18 24 And a certain Jew named Apollos, born at Alexandria, an eloquent man, and mighty in the Scriptures, came to Ephesus.

25 This man was instructed in the way of the Lord; and being fervent in the spirit, he spake and taught diligently the things of the Lord, knowing only the baptism of John.

26 And he began to speak boldly in the synagogue: whom when Aquila and Priscilla had heard, they took him unto them, and expounded unto him the way of God more perfectly.

27 And when he was disposed to pass into Achaia, the brethren wrote, exhorting the disciples to receive him: who, when he was come, helped them

REVISED STANDARD VERSION

MARK 5 18 And as he was getting into the boat, the man who had been possessed with demons begged him that he might be with him. 19 But he refused, and said to him, "Go home to your friends, and tell them how much the Lord has done for you, and how he has had mercy on you."

20 And he went away and began to proclaim in the Decapolis how much Jesus had done for him; and all men marveled.

ACTS 8 4 Now those who were scattered went about preaching the word. 5 Philip went down to a city of Samaria, and proclaimed to them the Christ. 6 And the multitudes with one accord gave heed to what was said by Philip, when they heard him and saw the signs which he did.

7 For unclean spirits came out of many who were possessed, crying with a loud voice; and many who were paralyzed or lame were healed. 8 So there was much joy in that city.

ACTS 18 24 Now a Jew named Apollos, a native of Alexandria, came to Ephesus. He was an eloquent man, well versed in the scriptures. 25 He had been instructed in the way of the Lord; and being fervent in spirit, he spoke and taught accurately the things concerning Jesus, though he knew only the baptism of John. 26 He began to speak boldly in the synagogue; but when Priscilla and Aquila heard him, they took him and expounded to him the way of God more accurately. 27 And when he wished to cross to Achaia, the brethren encouraged him, and wrote to the disciples to receive him. When he arrived, he greatly helped those who through grace had much which had believed through grace:

28 For he mightily convinced the Jews, and that publicly, showing by the Scriptures that Jesus was Christ.

believed, 28 for he powerfully confuted the Jews in public, showing by the scriptures that the Christ was Jesus.

MEMORY SELECTION: Go home to thy friends, and tell them how great things the Lord hath done for thee, and hath had compassion on thee. Mark 5:19.

HOME DAILY BIBLE READINGS

Apr. 17. M. Telling Good News to Friends, Mark 5:15-20.
Apr. 18. T. Philip in Samaria, Acts 8:1-8.
Apr. 19. W. Simon Weaned from Black Magic, Acts 8:9-13.
Apr. 20. T. Simon Converted to Christ, Acts 8:14-25.
Apr. 21. F. Aquila, Priscilla, and Apollos, Acts 18:24-28.
Apr. 22. S. Peter Witnessing to Romans, Acts 10:34-43.
Apr. 23. S. The Ethiopian Eunuch, Acts 8:26-35.

BACKGROUND

A book publisher said recently that books that become best sellers reach that status, not because of highly expensive advertising in newspapers and magazines, but because of "word-of-mouth" repetition—one reader telling another that this is a good book. This is as true in the field of religion as in the field of fiction. The gospel, for instance, was spread across the Middle East and into Europe by word-of-mouth witnessing. There were no newspapers then, no radio or TV. Men and women were told about the gospel and won to it *one by one.* Only a few of the witnesses knew or saw Jesus, but they spread the good news all across their world.

Our lesson describes three such witnesses: a man who had once been possessed of demons and healed by Christ, one of the seven "overseers of the poor" mentioned in our last lesson, and a husband-and-wife team in Ephesus. There were some odd circumstances connected with all three of these witnesses, and all of them played a crucial part in the spread of early Christianity and the building of the early church.

NOTES ON THE PRINTED TEXT

I. Go home to thy friends, and tell them how great things the Lord hath done for thee, Mark 5:19. The story of the healing of the Gadarene demoniac (in Mark 5:1-13) ends, for most of us, with the swine rushing into the sea. Not one in a million of us ever ask, "But what ever happened to the man who was healed, from whom Jesus cast out the devils?" This man deserves something better than that at our hands, for he did something very, very important *after* the healing.

Jesus is talking with him (verse 19). Deeply grateful to Jesus, the man wanted to go with Him in the boat that had brought Jesus to Gadara. It was a natural inclination: he wanted to be with Christ. But Jesus said, "No, go home and tell your friends what has happened to you." Don't just rest or bask in the shadow of Jesus. Go and *witness!* Go and tell others. And he went.

He "went away and began to declaim in the Decapolis" (verse 20).

Decapolis was not just one town or city; "Decapolis" means "ten cities," and ten cities it was (Scythopolis, Pella, Dion, Gerasa, Philadelphia, Gadara, Raphana, Kanatha, Hippos and Damascus). All but one of these cities were in Syria, and, all were essentially Greek cities. They had Greek gods and temples and a Greek way of thinking and living. This was hardly good soil for the seed of the gospel, but Jesus sent the man there, and the latter's departure for Decapolis was a sign that the gospel would never be confined to any narrow geographical area or to any little racial group. It was Christianity bursting through the doorway of the Greek world. It was Christianity's first real contact with Greek civilization.

This one man may have thought that he could never do very much; after all, he was just one man in hostile territory. But, in time, out of his witnessing came a harvest of converts; "all men did marvel" at the witness of the ex-demoniac, and some were convinced.

It is almost awesome to think that such a harvest could be reaped through the witness of a man despised and shunned in a Decapolis which produced Philodemus the great Epicurean philosopher, Meleager the famous epigrammatist, Menippus the satirist, and Theodorus the rhetorician, who was tutor to the emperor Tiberius. (Incidentally, all four of these great ones came from Gadara!). What a witness this man was!

II. *Then Philip went down to the city of Samaria, and preached Christ unto them* . . . , Acts 8:5. This was not Philip the Disciple; it was the Philip of the seven "deacons" whom we met last week. When Stephen, perhaps the most famous of the famous seven, was killed and the persecution spread, the believers "were scattered abroad . . . preaching the word." Philip, the friend of Stephen, went into Samaria. He might have gone in any of a dozen other directions and found a more hospitable reception, but he chose to go into Samaria—and to witness there.

What a place for a converted Jewish Christian to go! There had been years of bitterness between the Samaritans and the Jews; they hated each other in an unbelievable passion. Jesus lost a lot of popular favor when He sat and talked with a Samaritan woman and when He told the parable of a "good" Samaritan. There were no good Samaritans to the Jew, and vice versa. But to Philip—one of the great unhonored and unsung heroes of the church—the Samaritans were a people living in darkness and needing the light of Christ—and to them he went.

In Philip, Christianity took a great leap forward. In the name of Christ he served notice that the whole world was His parish, that all people were candidates for Christ's Kingdom, and that the Christian must go and witness to the whole world. Philip went. That's about all we know about him. It is enough. He preached and healed and conquered unclean spirits, "and there was great joy in that city." He changed the very atmosphere of Samaria from one of poisonous hatred to singing joy.

But, like the healed demoniac, he was just one obscure man, witnessing. . . .

III. And a certain Jew named Apollos, born at Alexandria, an eloquent man, and mighty in the Scriptures, came to Ephesus, Acts 18:24. Apollos was a scholar from a city of scholars—Alexandria. Most of the scholars there held to an allegorical interpretation of the Old Testament, and Apollos, before he met John the Baptist, probably held similar ideas. He was baptized by John into the new faith, and he gained some fame and popularity as a good preacher and as an authority on the Old Testament. But there was something lacking in Apollos and his preaching. He may have sensed it himself, or he may have been unaware of it until he met Aquila and Priscilla in Ephesus. They were two humble witnesses for Christ—weavers of cloth, tentmakers, Christian layman and laywoman who had entertained Paul and employed him in their craft, and traveled with him at least from Corinth to Ephesus. Paul left them in Ephesus, apparently to organize a church. To them, in Ephesus, came Apollos, to preach—and they sensed immediately what was wrong with Apollos and his preaching. He had been baptized of John and that was good—but he had not yet been baptized of the Spirit into a thorough understanding of Jesus as the Messiah. They "expounded unto him the way of God more perfectly," and after that enlightenment he "mightily convinced the Jews . . . showing by the Scriptures that Jesus was Christ" (Acts 18:28).

Think of it! Here were two humble, unprofessional, unordained "commoners" changing the mind of an Alexandrian scholar. That was *really* witnessing. It is not always the learned who open the kingdom door; more often, we think, the lowly have the keys.

The ex-demoniac, Philip, and Aquila and Priscilla: *all humble witnesses in hard places,* just plain men and women, with fires kindled in their hearts, passing on the fire. They say to us, "Witness now, *where you are.* You are not 'only one'; with Jesus Christ, you are a majority of two." On such early witnessing was the church established, and so it must continue.

SUGGESTIONS TO TEACHERS

Some years back a publisher was disappointed in the sales of a little book called *Man Does Not Stand Alone*—a fine little religious book. It was piled up in his basement, and he was about ready to give up on the book when the famous Fulton Oursler ran an excerpt from it in *Reader's Digest*—and the book began to sell faster than it could be printed! Mr. Oursler only "witnessed to the fact" that this was a good book, and so it became a best seller.

Many a good book has been lost and has failed for want of someone to speak up for it; many a Christian has been lost because someone who might have spoken a word for Jesus Christ didn't speak. Witnesses! Christianity was built on them and their work and their graves; they are uncountable, unsung, unhonored—and the real heroes of the Christian crusade. Most of them worked in obscure places, simply saying a word for the Lord. . . .

There is more than one way to witness. The first Christians witnessed as individuals, as a community, orally, and in service to those who needed Christ and didn't even know it. . . .

TOPIC FOR ADULTS
THE WITNESSING FELLOWSHIP

Quartus. At the end of his Epistle to the Romans, Paul speaks of "Quartus, a brother." That's all: just a brother. But Quartus must have meant something to Paul, because Paul used that word "brother" to describe him. A great American preacher, Maltbie Babcock, had a good sermon on Quartus, in which he said:

"Jesus Christ, to whom we owe our lives, sends us out to do His work in the world. We are to be His hands and feet. How is the world going to learn from Christ the good news of forgiveness and hope and power, the comfort of love—how to live the filial and fraternal life? 'Ye are my witnesses,' says the Master. 'Behold, I send you forth.' That is your commission, to represent your Lord.

"Who can go into all our stores, banks, hospitals, schools, colleges, factories, courts? Who can go into all our homes? Who can go into the councils of labor or of capital, among promoters and politicians? Who can attend directors' meetings? Who knows the password? Who has the right of way? Quartus! Quartus the brother can go everywhere.

"He can enter every department of life—legal, commercial, political, educational, social—and take his seat there and say what he thinks and vote as he believes. He can uphold the good and oppose the bad. He can stand, 'a faithful witness.' Stand up, then, as a brother should, and greet the right and grapple with the wrong. When a thing is bad, say it is bad; when you see a good thing, acknowledge it; where business methods are vicious, rebuke them, and either get out yourself or be put out. Be a grain of salt, a ray of light. Encourage the man who is weakening; sympathize with the troubled. Be a brother."

Another sensitive preacher says of this: "This is the church's mission, *through the laymen.*" And this is *witnessing*.

Harder. Soren Kierkegaard, the Danish theologian and philosopher, wrote this about the church as a witnessing fellowship:

"When the Christian witness ceases to astonish the world it will be a sign that the church has lost its mission. The church is not established to make it easier to become a Christian, but harder."

Witnessing may be the hardest thing you have to do in the church—but there is nothing more important for you to do.

Take My Life. Frances R. Havergal was a quite obscure lady; for several years of her life she lived in a small boarding house with ten other people. Some of them were Christians; most of them were not. But they had one thing in common: they were all living depressed lives, thanks to the gloomy atmosphere of the boarding house. Miss Havergal prayed often in her room: "Lord, give me all in this house for thee." One by one, through her witnessing, they all came to new, rich religious experiences, and to acceptance of Christ.

The night she won her last two converts she could not sleep; certain words kept running through her mind, and she could not put them out of her mind. Finally, she got up and wrote them down, polished and improved them until she had them right and clear. It was a hymn; most of us know it well:

> Take my life and let it be
>   Consecrated, Lord, to thee;
> Take my moments and my days;
>   Let them flow in ceaseless praise;
> Take my hands, and let them move
>   At the impulse of thy love;
> Take my feet, and let them be
>   Swift and beautiful for thee.

Questions for Pupils on the Next Lesson: 1. To *what* did Jesus send out His disciples to witness? 2. With whom did the Christian missionary enterprise really begin? 3. Was the church at Antioch a "missionary" church by accident or by design? 4. What did the Holy Spirit mean by ". . . set apart for me Barnabas and Saul?" 5. Are missions as important to us as they were to the early church? 6. What does a good missionary do? 7. What are the main foreign missionary fields of the church today?

TOPIC FOR YOUTH
SHARING THE GOOD NEWS

Plans. Dr. S. D. Gordon imagines the following conversation between Christ and the angel Gabriel:

GABRIEL: Master, you died for the whole world, didn't you?
CHRIST: Yes.
GABRIEL: You must have suffered very much.
CHRIST: Yes, Gabriel. I cannot talk about it, even to you; it goes too deep.
GABRIEL: And do they know about it down there?
CHRIST: Oh, no—just a little handful in Syria know about it thus far.
GABRIEL: Well, Master, what is your plan? What plan have you made to tell the world that you died for them? What arrangements have you made?
CHRIST: Well, I asked Peter and James and John, and some more of them down there, just to make it the business of their lives to tell others; and the others, yet others, and still others, until the last man in the farthest reach has heard the story, and has been caught, thrilled and thralled by the power of it.
GABRIEL: Yes, Master, but suppose that, after a while, Peter forgets. Suppose that John, after a bit, simply doesn't tell the others. Suppose their successors away down there in the twentieth century get so busy about things—some of them good things, church things maybe— suppose they get so busy that they do not tell others—what then?
CHRIST: I haven't made any other plans. I am counting on them."

What was it we said about transmitting the gospel from mouth to mouth, person to person . . . ?

Joey. "Joey was not quite bright. He would never leave the tabernacle at night until he could shake my hand. He would stand right next to me until the last man was gone, in order to say good night. It was embarrassing at times. One evening a man came forward to speak to me. He said, 'I want to thank you for being so kind to Joey. He isn't quite bright, and he has never had anything he enjoyed so much as coming here and singing in the choir. He has worked hard during the day in order to be ready in time to come here at night. He has coaxed us to come, too, and it is through him that my wife and our five children have been led to Christ. His grandfather, seventy-five years old, and an infidel all his life, and his grandmother have come tonight, and now the whole family is converted. Eleanor Doane, in *The New Speaker's Sourcebook*, p. 382. Quoted by courtesy of Zondervan Publishing House, publishers.

The man who told this story was Homer Rodeheaver, who was choir leader for Billy Sunday's campaigns. There were dramatic conversions by the thousand in those campaigns, but there was nothing especially dramatic about Joey or his method. It was just good witnessing. . . . And if Joey could do that, how about the rest of us . . . ?

Protestants. Most Protestants seem to think that the word "Protestant" means to protest against something. It doesn't mean that at all. It might mean "to protest *for* something," but even that is not accurate enough.

In the very early days of the Protestant movement, the word meant "one who bears witness to his faith," or "one who testifies to his inner spiritual experience." If we go back to the original Latin, we find that it comes from two words—"pro" and "testare," which mean "to *testify* for."

The Christian witness is one who stands up in the court of the world and says, "I am here to testify to the truth of the resurrection, to the power of Christ in me, to. . . ." *To what else?*

Acting. Out of the mouths of children often come gems of wisdom and startling questions. One little girl sat in a hotel lobby with her parents, staring across the lobby at a very beautiful lady standing near the clerk's desk. Suddenly she jumped up and walked across to the desk, stood in front of the lady and asked, "Aren't you an actress?"

The woman was startled, but she recovered quickly, and said, "Yes, I am an actress."

There was a moment's silence, and then the child asked, "Well, if you're an actress, why aren't you acting?"

It may have been funny in that lobby, but it isn't funny when someone asks us the same question in other words: "If you are a Christian, why aren't you acting like a Christian?" The purpose of being Christian is not to be a member of a church but to be *actively* witnessing for Christ.

But how many of us honestly do anything like that?

Sentence Sermon to Remember: Do not expect God to use you as a lighthouse somewhere else if He cannot use you as a candle where you are.—*The Survey Bulletin.*

Questions for Pupils on the Next Lesson: 1. What do we mean by "the mandate of missions?" 2. How important is the foreign missionary program to your *local* church? 3. True or false: "There's enough to do right here at home, without sending missionaries abroad"? 4. List five important services rendered by missionaries. 5. Would you call the Peace Corps a missionary project? 6. What contributions did these men make to the missionary cause: Paul, William Carey, Sam Higginbottom, Grenfell, Schweitzer, Laubach, E. Stanley Jones? 7. Why are there fewer missionaries abroad today than there were five years ago?

LESSON IX—APRIL 30

THE CHURCH'S MISSIONARY IMPERATIVE

Background Scripture: Luke 24:45-49; John 17:6-23; Acts 13:1-3
Devotional Reading: John 17:18-26

LUKE 24 45 Then opened he their understanding, that they might understand the Scriptures,

46 And said unto them, Thus it is written, and thus it behooved Christ to suffer, and to rise from the dead the third day:

47 And that repentance and remission of sins should be preached in his name among all nations, beginning at Jerusalem.

48 And ye are witnesses of these things.

49 And, behold, I send the promise of my Father upon you: but tarry ye in the city of Jerusalem, until ye be endued with power from on high.

JOHN 17 18 As thou hast sent me into the world, even so have I also sent them into the world.

19 And for their sakes I sanctify myself, that they also might be sanctified through the truth.

20 Neither pray I for these alone, but for them also which shall believe on me through their word;

21 That they all may be one; as thou, Father, art in me, and I in thee, that they also may be one in us: that the world may believe that thou hast sent me.

ACTS 13 Now there were in the church that was at Antioch certain prophets and teachers; as Barnabas, and Simeon that was called Niger, and Lucius of Cyrene, and Manaen, which had been brought up with Herod the tetrarch, and Saul.

2 As they ministered to the Lord, and fasted, the Holy Ghost said, Separate me Barnabas and Saul for the work whereunto I have called them.

3 And when they had fasted and prayed, and laid their hands on them, they sent them away.

LUKE 24 45 Then he opened their minds to understand the scriptures, 46 and said to them, "Thus it is written, that the Christ should suffer and on the third day rise from the dead, 47 and the repentance and forgiveness of sins should be preached in his name to all nations, beginning from Jerusalem. 48 You are witnesses of these things. 49 And behold, I send the promise of my Father upon you; but stay in the city, until you are clothed with power from on high."

JOHN 17 18 "As thou didst send me into the world, so I have sent them into the world. 19 And for their sake I consecrate myself, that they also may be consecrated in truth.

20 "I do not pray for these only, but also for those who are to believe in me through their word, 21 that they may all be one; even as thou, Father, art in me, and I in thee, that they also may be in us, so that the world may believe that thou hast sent me."

ACTS 13 Now in the church at Antioch there were prophets and teachers, Barnabas, Symeon who was called Niger, Lucius of Cyrene, Manaen a member of the court of Herod the tetrarch, and Saul. 2 While they were worshiping the Lord and fasting, the Holy Spirit said, "Set apart for me Barnabas and Saul for the work to which I have called them." 3 Then after fasting and praying they laid their hands on them and sent them off.

MEMORY SELECTION: As thou hast sent me into the world, even so have I also sent them into the world. John 17:18.

HOME DAILY BIBLE READINGS

Apr. 24. M. The Disciples Have God's Word, John 17:6-14.
Apr. 25. T. Jesus Sends His Disciples Out, John 17:15-19.
Apr. 26. W. Christ's Fulfillment of Scripture, Luke 24:45-49.
Apr. 27. T. The Church Consecrates Persons, Acts 13:1-5.
Apr. 28. F. Invitation From Europe, Acts 16:6-10.
Apr. 29. S. Singing One's Witness, Acts 16:25-34.
Apr. 30. S. Christ's Prayer for Oneness, John 17:20-26.

BACKGROUND

All four of the Gospels agree that Jesus spent His last hours on earth and made His last postresurrection appearance among His disciples. Details differ as they tell the story, but they all agree that the disciples were the last to see Him alive. Jesus had good reason for that; *He had final instructions to leave with them.* He wanted to leave in their minds a knowledge of the cross and an unconquerable faith in His resurrection —and He wanted them to know exactly what they were to do with that knowledge and conviction.

They were to *go and teach all people:* they were to be *missionaries.* In these last appearances He was commissioning them as witnesses to His crucifixion and resurrection. It was the climax of all that He had taught them: His victory over sin and death must be announced to the ends of the earth.

It was His last commission to them, His first to *us.* . . .

NOTES ON THE PRINTED TEXT

I. Then he opened their minds to understand the scriptures, Luke 24:45 (RSV). The Scriptures were the Old Testament Scriptures; up to now, there was not any New Testament. Jesus' resurrection was the fulfillment of Old Testament revelation and prophecy: it was the climactic fulfillment of the law, the prophets, and the writings (Psalms). (See verse 44.) These ancient scriptures said that the Messiah would die and rise again (verse 46), and that "repentance and forgiveness of sins should be preached in his name *to all nations.*" That could not very well be preached without a knowledge of the scriptures.

So the disciples were commissioned as missionaries.

Now, there are three phases or periods involved in this working out of God's purposes in Christ: (1) His purpose as *stated* in the Old Testament, (2) its *fulfillment* in Jesus, and (3) its *proclamation* by the church. It was something like the Trinity: each part depended upon the other two, yet "the three were one." They must understand this and build upon it: it was the basic foundation of the Kingdom and the church.

One thing more was necessary: they needed *power* to make this witness effective. They lacked such power if they were to be no more than weak human beings; such beings are fickle, fearful, often weak, sometimes cowardly. They must have more "power from on high." Such power had been promised them: ". . . ye shall be baptized with the Holy Ghost . . . (Acts 1:5). They were not to rush out preaching until they were certain that they had this gift: "I am sending upon you my

Father's promised gift; so stay here in this city [Jerusalem] until you are armed with the power from above" (verse 49, *New English Bible*).

The Scriptures, the church, the Holy Spirit burning in the church missionary—these were and are God's weapons on earth.

II. As thou hast sent me into the world, even so have I also sent them into the world, John 17:18. These words are spoken by Jesus in His prayer to the Father (John 17) following the farewell discourses (John 13-16). In this prayer (John 17), He prays for Himself (verses 1-5), for His disciples (6-19), and for those who will be led to Him by the witnessing of the disciples (20-26). For the sake of all these, He has died on the cross; He has sanctified (consecrated) Himself in the ultimate sacrifice, that they, too, might be consecrated "through the truth" (verse 19). Let them be one in spirit and in love. Let there also be a unity among those the disciples have led into the church as warm and close as the unity which exists between the Father and the Son. Let them all be *one* in their belief that the Father was in Christ, and that Christ was one with the Father, and that they (the Christians in the church) are one *in* the Father and the Son. Then, and only then, says Dr. Floyd V. Filson, "the world will believe that the Father has sent Jesus and that the gospel is true."

There's that word again: *unity*. Unity, *in depth*, not shallow. This unity is not a sentimental lip service to "the fatherhood of God and the brotherhood of man." It has nothing to do with uniformity in creed, organization or administration. It is a unity born in the heart, in personal relationship with God and our fellow man. It is the unity of *love*, greater than any unity in creed, ritual, form. Said John Wesley, "If your heart is as my heart, give me your hand!" That's it!

We haven't done it yet—we haven't arrived at any such unity in the church, even though these words of Jesus have been on record for nearly two thousand years. That may be because we are not yet willing to pay the price in sacrificial love for each other that Christ paid for us. We have enough truth—common truth mutually held—on which to unite— *if we honestly want to unite on such a basis.*

III. Now in the church at Antioch there were prophets and teachers . . . , Acts 13:1 (RSV). The church at Antioch was a great church, even in its earliest days. It was one of the very first churches to smash the barrier between Jews and Gentiles; it led the way in Christian charity by sending famine relief to "the brethren in Judea." It had from the start the unity prescribed by Jesus Christ—unity in the truth, regardless of color, or race, or "previous condition of servitude." It had a famous group of teachers and prophets. The teachers taught in Antioch; the prophets moved out as missionaries. . . .

Look at this list of notables in the Antioch church: Paul (Saul) and Barnabas were Jews; Simeon (called "the black") may well have been a Negro; Lucius came from North Africa; Manaen had important royal connections with Herod the tetrarch—an aristocrat. If *that* wasn't unity, what is? Men of vastly different cultural, racial and religious backgrounds, they found new unity and purpose in Christ.

Paul and Barnabas we might classify as "prophets"—or men with unusual spiritual gifts. (Today, we might call them "charismatic" leaders.) Together with the others, these two received a revelation of the Spirit as they all prayed together, and they were sent off and away from Antioch as missionaries. They were valuable men in the work of the Antioch church; some might have thought them too valuable to that church to be sent on such dangerous work, but to Paul and Barnabas that thought never occurred. They accepted the laying on of hands from their companions in Antioch, and went off down a road that seemed to have no end—two pioneers in the work of making Christ international, and not tragically Antiochan or even Jewish. . . .

SUGGESTIONS TO TEACHERS

If it were in our midst today, we would call the First Church of Antioch "queer," or something worse. It was a church that undoubtedly needed money and plenty of it to do what had to be done in Antioch— and one of the first things it did was to *organize and finance a foreign missions crusade!* Maybe there was good publicity in the news that they were sending Paul and Barnabas out as missionaries, but in that church they didn't know what "publicity" meant! They sent out two missionaries because they *had* to; they had orders from Jesus Christ.

Start there in discussing today's lesson: start with Christ Himself as a missionary in command of others going into all the world. Analyze the work of the missionaries of the church then and now: What did they do? What *do* they do? *And why?* Study the question of the responsibility of the *modern* church to maintain a missionary program.

And make it clear that the layman who supports the missionary program is as much a missionary as—?

TOPIC FOR ADULTS
THE MISSIONARY IMPERATIVE

The Dry Shell. "The early church was not an institution but rather a mission, a bold and seemingly fantastic mission of a little group of Jews setting out to claim the whole world for their Lord. . . . Whenever it ceased to be a mission and has become content to be merely a religious institution, it has withered and died. But again and again it has happened that out of the dry shell a new missionary impulse has broken forth with important consequences for the world."—James D. Smart.

"Missions" seems to be in something of a dry shell right now, with so many saying that, with all the missionaries out of China and many of them out of India, "the day of missions is over." No missionary says that —and a missionary should know! One phase of missionary work may be over—but God has a habit of cracking the shell and producing *new* plans and methods to renew the church. Missions will not die because of a few faint hearts; the life of the church depends on missions, and God does not want the church to die!

The First Missionary. Do we think that Paul was the first missionary? If we do, we are wrong.

Christ was a home missionary in the house of Lazarus.
He was a city missionary when He taught in Samaria.

He was a Sunday-school missionary when He opened the Scriptures and set men to studying the Word of God.

He was a children's missionary when He took them in His arms and blessed them.

He was a missionary to the poor when He opened the eyes of a blind beggar.

He was a missionary to the rich when He opened the eyes of Zacchaeus.

Even on the cross Christ was a missionary to the robber, and His last commandment was the missionary commitment.—Amos R. Wells.

He was a foreign missionary when the Greeks came to him.

So God started His missionary purpose in the Old Testament, fulfilled it in His Son—and left the rest to us!

Recruits. No army ever succeeded without a constant effort to secure recruits or replacements. No world enterprise ever succeeded with a declining birth rate, or with its defenders dwindling in numbers and enthusiasm. Perhaps Jesus was conscious of this when He told His disciples to go out and get more, and more, and *more* converts to His cause, even after He was gone.

"When Bishop James Thoburn, pioneer missionary, was enroute to India, a businessman aboard the ship said to him one day, 'Thoburn, you've got as much chance saving the heathen as I have taking this teaspoon and using it to empty the Pacific Ocean.'

"The bishop's reply is a classic: 'My job is not so much to *use* a spoon as it is to *make* spoons.' "—*Illustrated Weekly of India,* December 28, 1969.

Judging by what has happened in India in recent years, the bishop was right—and the missionary effort has apparently produced a lot of "spoons." Gandhi has been called "the greatest Christian in the world," and India's dearly purchased independence has a strong Christian complexion!

Support. In any war, there must be ten men working behind the lines to support the man at the front. In the missionary enterprise, the support of the home church, or the lack of it, means death or success to the missionary in the front lines.

Said James Gilmour, missionary to Mongolia: "Unprayed for, I feel like a diver at the bottom of a river with no connecting airline to the surface, or like a fireman wielding an empty hose on a burning building. With prayer, I feel like David facing Goliath."

It takes prayer—the kind of prayer that opens the pocketbook.

Questions for Pupils on the Next Lesson: 1. What is "need" in the Christian sense? 2. Name three specific human needs which your church tries to meet. 3. Explain the teaching of Luke 22:26. 4. What four church efforts are suggested in Hebrews 13:1-3? 5. How would you answer the question of James: "Can his faith save him?" 6. Does the church sin when it stops short of serving *community* needs? 7. Are strangers comfortable or uncomfortable in your church?

TOPIC FOR YOUTH
WHY GO?

Why Go? Why go abroad as a missionary? Well, John R. Mott gave us one good reason why we should go abroad with the gospel of Jesus

Christ. He saw trouble building up in Asia (this was thirty years ago!), and he warned us, "We will either send a few thousand missionaries out there now, or a million bayonets tomorrow." We sent the bayonets—and where are we now? We said, "Why should we worry about China? Let the Chinese settle their own problems; let them stew in their own juice." We did just that, and now the pot is boiling over, and we're getting burned, and we don't like it!

But we are selfish when we send out missionaries just to protect peace for *ourselves;* we should go as missionaries because we want the peace of God to descend on *everybody.*

Is there any other way to get such (world) peace?

A Large Basket. Some critics of missions say, "You have been sending out missionaries for two hundred years—and you haven't really accomplished very much, have you?" Well, we've had soap a lot longer than that, and there are still a lot of dirty faces, but we haven't stopped washing. . . .

"A missionary talking with a native man about the wonderful revivals in Angola during the past months said, 'Eight hundred converted? It doesn't seem possible. If only *all* of them would stand' (stand up and be converted)!

"The native replied, 'Well, it's just like when you go into the garden and dig a big basketful of peanuts. . . . Some fall off before you even get home with the basket. Then you hull them and you lose some more. You put them away and the rats get some, but even with all that, you still have a very large basket of peanuts.' "—*South African Missionary Advocate.*

It is quite a basketful: a total of one billion *living* Christians won to Christ as a result of the outgoing missionary effort of the church isn't a bad record at all! (Yes, every country on earth heard the Word first from some missionary!)

Humility. It takes a lot of humility to go out as a missionary. Most of us are not *that* humble. . . .

"If I gave a large part of my income to the hungry all around me, I'd feel that I was doing my duty. If I imperiled my life to stalk through mosquito-infested jungles to find people who never heard of Christ, I'd feel that it was God's work. If I were separated from my family for a month at a time without my family knowing whether I was dead or alive, I'd feel that my calling was at least partly fulfilled. But if I did all these things . . . well, I'm not courageous enough to do them all. Yet our missionaries are, *and they say almost nothing about it.*"—Charles A. Stuck, in *Arkansas Methodist,* July 4, 1961.

If you haven't that much humility, don't go.

Challenge. Today, youth says it wants to be "challenged." Challenged to be *what,* to *do* what?

"To be a missionary in one of those 'regions beyond' is the greatest privilege and highest honor that God ever confers. Who has not heard of the Northamptonshire cobbler, William Carey, who became the father of our modern era of world missions? William Carey had a brilliant son named Felix, who became British ambassador to India, a position of great importance, responsibility and dignity. Wouldn't any father be proud of such a son? But in a letter to a friend William Carey commented, 'Felix has shriveled into an ambassador.' "—J. Sidlow Baxter.

What did he mean?

No Apologies. You probably never heard of Isaac Owen. Few people ever heard of him, or ever will hear of him. He was an early missionary in California. When he was asked to write a biographical sketch of his life and work, he wrote this:

"Isaac Owen was born in Vermont; raised in Coonrange on White River in the wilderness of Indiana; costumed in buckskin; fed on pounded cake; educated in a log schoolhouse—the principle study in the course was Webster's spelling book; converted to God in the woods; licensed to preach on a log; first circuit embraced a part of five counties. Last heard of, a missionary in California, and, on a review of his life, has no apologies to offer for having been born."

Not bad! Most of us would have a lot more to apologize for when we look back at the record of our lives, and few of us will accomplish as much. . . .

Grape Juice. A young fellow named Welch wanted very much to be a Christian missionary; he tried hard, but, for one reason or another, no missions board would have him. So he did the next best thing: instead of resenting his rejections, he went into the grape juice business with one purpose: to make a lot of money and give it to foreign missions.

He did well in the business; many of us of the older generation can remember the great popularity of Welch's grape juice. It led the field. But thousands of people overseas who never met him and never drank his product would never have heard of Jesus Christ had it not been for him. . . . He still blesses them *in absentia* with abundant life.

Sentence Sermon to Remember: God had only one Son, and He was a missionary.—David Livingstone.

Questions for Pupils on the Next Lesson: 1. What prompted the argument in Luke 22:24? 2. Did Jesus condemn all benefactors? 3. Why is a servant often a "greater" man than his master? 4. What do we mean by "brotherly" love? 5. Name one neighbor you love as much as you love yourself. 6. What is the prison program of your church, and what do you do on that program? 7. How does James describe pure and undefiled religion? 8. Is a man saved by faith alone or by works alone, or by both? Quote Scripture to prove your opinion.

LESSON X—MAY 7

THE CHURCH RESPONDS TO HUMAN NEED

Background Scripture: Matthew 25:31-46; Luke 22:24-27;
Hebrews 13:1-3; James 1:27; 2:14-17
Devotional Reading: Matthew 25:31-40

KING JAMES VERSION

LUKE 22 And there was also a strife among them, which of them should be accounted the greatest.

25 And he said unto them, The kings of the Gentiles exercise lordship over them; and they that exercise authority upon them are called benefactors.

26 But ye shall not be so: but he that is greatest among you, let him be as the younger; and he that is chief, as he that doth serve.

27 For whether is greater, he that sitteth at meat, or he that serveth? is not he that sitteth at meat? but I am among you as he that serveth.

HEBREWS 13 1 Let brotherly love continue.

2 Be not forgetful to entertain strangers: for thereby some have entertained angels unawares.

3 Remember them that are in bonds, as bound with them; and them which suffer adversity, as being yourselves also in the body.

JAMES 1 27 Pure religion and undefiled before God and the Father is this, To visit the fatherless and widows in their affliction, and to keep himself unspotted from the world.

JAMES 2 14 What doth it profit, my brethren, though a man say he hath faith, and have not works? can faith save him?

15 If a brother or sister be naked, and destitute of daily food,

16 And one of you say unto them, Depart in peace, be ye warmed and filled; notwithstanding ye give them not those things which are needful to the body; what doth it profit?

17 Even so faith, if it hath not works, is dead, being alone.

REVISED STANDARD VERSION

LUKE 22 24 A dispute also arose among them, which of them was to be regarded as the greatest. 25 And he said to them, "The kings of the Gentiles exercise lordship over them; and those in authority over them are called benefactors. 26 But not so with you; rather let the greatest among you become as the youngest, and the leader as one who serves. 27 For which is the greater, one who sits at table, or one who serves? Is it not the one who sits at table? But I am among you as one who serves.

HEBREWS 13 1 Let brotherly love continue.

2 Do not neglect to show hospitality to strangers, for thereby some have entertained angels unawares. 3 Remember those who are in prison, as though in prison with them; and those who are ill-treated, since you also are in the body.

JAMES 1 27 Religion that is pure and undefiled before God and the Father is this: to visit orphans and widows in their affliction, and to keep oneself unstained from the world.

JAMES 2 14 What does it profit, my brethren, if a man says he has faith but has not works? Can his faith save him? 15 If a brother or sister is ill-clad and in lack of daily food, 16 and one of you says to them, "Go in peace, be warmed and filled," without giving them the things needed for the body, what does it profit? 17 So faith by itself, if it has no works, is dead.

MEMORY SELECTION: Inasmuch as ye have done it unto one of the last of these my brethren, ye have done it unto me. Matthew 25:40.

HOME DAILY BIBLE READINGS

May 1. M. The Serving Fellowship, Luke 22:24-30.
May 2. T. Food for the Hungry, Acts 11:27-30.
May 3. W. Planning to Meet Human Need, II Corinthians 9:1-6.
May 4. T. Gifts for a Needy Preacher, Philippians 4:14-19.
May 5. F. Service, Not Good Wishes, James 2:14-24.
May 6. S. Hospitality for Strangers, III John 2-8.
May 7. S. Even to the Least, Matthew 25:31-40.

BACKGROUND

If the fellowship of the early church is to be taken as our model for the modern church, we had better understand just how it *was* a fellowship. It was a fellowship based on two convictions: faith in Christ and His demand that we live as servants. That should shake up any Christian who sits in church in company with a (spiritual) superiority complex—as so many of us do! We sit in pride, while hungry people walk past the church without our ever even seeing them.

The first church saw them and went out of its way to help them—first, within the fellowship, and then beyond it. This church was concerned primarily with four things: service, love, faith and works. It was a church created, not to shelter a few saints, but to meet human need *wherever it was to be found.*

NOTES ON THE PRINTED TEXT

I. But I am among you as one who serves, Luke 22:27 (RSV). In the world of the Gentiles which surrounded the New Testament Jew there were countless tyrant kings (the Jews had a king or two like that, too!) who "exercised lordship," the power (authority) of life and death, over their subjects (verse 25). When they dropped a few crumbs to their suffering people they were called "benefactors." (Some of the greatest tyrants in history have given their enslaved subjects such "gifts" as great highways, bridges, resplendent temples and public buildings—all bearing the tyrant's name!)

At public banquets, of course, the king sat at the head of the table, and there was always great attention given to protocol and preference in assigning seats to his favorites; the most favored sat nearest him, on right or left; the least sat down at the end of the table. Everybody wanted to be a king; everybody wanted a seat at the head of the table. It was the way of the world.

The disciples had all this "protocol and preference" nonsense in mind when they quarreled one day over the great (!) question of "which of them should be accounted the greatest." It was sad and disgusting, and Jesus put a quick end to it. He said, in effect, "That may be the way of the world—but it isn't *my* way. There are no kings in the Kingdom of heaven, only God is sovereign; but in earthly kingdoms it is the servant who is important. If you would follow me in my Kingdom you had better forget the world, with all its emphasis on human power. What the world needs is not more kings but more humble *service.* He Himself, He said, had come as a servant.

Some folks in the church feel that they *must* be "leaders" in everything, on every committee, on every board. He who gives "generously" must have the church named for him, or see his name cut in the cornerstone. At church banquets, they *must* sit at the head table! It must break the heart of Christ—the servant.

If we truly love the church, we will use it as His servant's headquarters. It might be a good idea to stop calling them "churches" and call them, as Bruce Barton suggested, "Service Stations." Yes—we all love the church; perhaps we should prove our love by picking up a towel, as He did. . . .

II. Let brotherly love continue, Hebrews 13:1. It was love that held the first Christian fellowship together and determined its character. *Brotherly* love. It was important that these Christians recognized brothers outside the fellowship, as well as within it. The author of Hebrews describes that here when he says that it was the duty of the fellowship (of the churches) to offer hospitality to strangers and to remember those who were in prison. He doesn't say that such love was to be expended only on people in the churches.

First, the strangers. The stranger is the loneliest person in the world—in any world. The wanderer, the man away from home and knowing no one in a city not his own—these should receive Christian hospitality. Every church should be a Church of the Open Door, and every such door should be open around the clock. Find a church maintained only for the pleasure and prayer of an exclusive few, and you have a church ready for burial. That man alone on the street—take him in; you may be helping an angel "unaware!"

The prisoner: do you know of anyone who needs Christ more than he? In Christ's day, they imprisoned men for debt—or because they were poor; they imprisoned men for advocating something other than the "accepted" religion; they imprisoned slaves and courageous men who defied tyrants and corrupt officials. To their credit, the first Christians remembered "those in bonds." They were prison visitors. No state prison is without its chaplain; no man behind bars, guilty or innocent, is without the consolation of the Scriptures and the help of the "brotherly," concerned Christian. Those who are "ill-treated" are remembered, even on their way to the electric chair! It is a Christian obligation—even when no other person or institution in the community sees or accepts such a responsibility. It is Christian service—and Christian love.

III. Pure religion . . . is this, To visit the fatherless and widows in their affliction, and to keep himself unspotted from the world, James 1:27. This is an echo of Psalm 68:5: "A father of the fatherless, and a judge of the widows, is God in his holy habitation." And it echoes, too, Micah's declaration that the Lord *requires* that we do justly and love mercy and walk humbly with Him.

Those of us who think that God requires only church prayers and attendance are wrong; the best prayer you can offer to God, the finest ritual, is in your service to the poor and your personal purity. No ritual or ceremony can take the place of Christian charity. *Nothing can substitute for service and sacrifice.*

James 2:14-17 is in the same vein; it says that words without deeds are an insult to God. It says that faith without works, faith standing in isolation, is a dead faith and quite useless. It says that we are hypocrites when we say to a hungry man, "Go in peace, be warmed and filled," and then neglected to *feed* him.

The little General Epistle of James is hard reading for those who worship God only with their lips; most lip worshipers read this Epistle as little as possible. But those who do read it and understand it have made religion a power for God outside the church as well as within it. If we all listened a little more carefully to James we would have a far better world than we have now.

SUGGESTIONS TO TEACHERS

If you are one who believes that the church has no responsibility in the world beyond believing, praying and worshiping—just skip this lesson. But if you believe that the church is obligated to do all it can to relieve human need, the following ideas might be emphasized:

1. Christ the servant demanded that His church be a servant church, filled with servant Christians.
2. The charity of the church should never be a mechanical reaction, but an impulse born of *love*.
3. Not all of us can preach, but as laymen we can do much more than the preacher in relieving human pain, hunger, frustration and fear.

TOPIC FOR ADULTS
INVOLVED WITH HUMAN NEED

Need. "One fifth of our citizenry live a marginal or submarginal existence—ill-housed, ill-clad, and ill-nourished. The army of the poor today exceeds the number of Americans who have served in all the wars fought by the U.S.—including the Revolution. They number more than twice the combined populations of New York, Chicago, Los Angeles, Philadelphia and Detroit."—Walter S. Valverde, in *Washington World*.

And that includes only the United States! Not a very good record, is it, for a "Christian" nation?

Fish. "Powerful movements, good and bad, are often symbolized by drawings or initials. The mark of Nazism is the swastika, communism is represented by the hammer and sickle. . . . However, the earliest symbol of Christianity was probably a fish instead of a cross. The Greek word, *icthus,* meaning fish, is an ancient acronym for *Jesus Christ, Son of God, Saviour.* . . . The symbol of the fish could be seen throughout the Graeco-Roman World following the crucifixion of Christ.

"Today this ancient symbol has reappeared to identify a loosely organized but far-flung fellowship of Christians from all denominations working under the motto: 'Help Thy Neighbor.' Members of Fish groups give quick spur-of-the-moment emergency aid to those in need.

"For example, Mrs. Brown has just moved to a suburban neighborhood and knows no one well enough to call for emergency baby-sitting at two A.M. She has just learned by long-distance telephone that her widowed mother has had a stroke and is calling for her. The answer girl (when she phones for help) calls the captain of the Fish team (in her church) on duty that day. The team captain calls a Fish housewife who lives near Mrs. Brown. Fifteen minutes later, this Fish woman is at Mrs.

Brown's home writing down instructions for child care. Within the hour, Mrs. Brown is in a taxi on her way to the airport. . . .

"Often Fish simply gives information and direction. Every member has a list of public and private services available in the area. Any emergency job is referred to an existing agency that can handle it.

"Personal Fish service means most often transportation for needy people—to clinics, to alcoholic rehabilitation centers, to food relief agencies, etc. Home care is the next greatest request; for instance, child care when a parent suddenly becomes ill or must respond to an outside emergency need. A less frequent but more dramatic opportunity for service may involve talking an unwed mother out of suicide and finding her a home and a job.

"Naturally, a few people take advantage of the willingness of Fish members to serve. But this doesn't bother them. As one says, 'We'd rather have this happen than to take the chance of failing to help one person in real need.'"—*Thinkables*, by James C. Hefley (Fleming H. Revell Company).

Let brotherly love continue!

Sharing. "An elderly Negro woman was struggling through the crowded railroad station burdened with a heavy suitcase. A gray-haired porter touched his cap and reached for her bag.

"'Thank you for wantin' to help,' she said. 'But I can't pay for your services.'

"'Ma'am,' he said, gently taking her arm, 'I wasn't offerin' my services —I was just wantin' to share your company out to the train.'"—Pete La Roche.

Sharing doesn't always mean sharing food or possessions; more often it means sharing your heart. . . .

Charity. "Charity has become a cliché. But in its simplicity, it still expresses the love and compassion that makes man something apart from other creatures. Be charitable with your time. If someone needs you in a moment of distress, be there. If someone needs to talk over a problem with you, listen. Be charitable with your affections. Let those you love know you love them and that you care about their happiness. Be charitable with your understanding. Don't let disagreements fester into resentment. Don't let anger replace reasonableness. Be charitable with your kindness, courtesy and sense of humor. An act of kindness, a smile, a joke to be shared are often all it takes."—Norman Vincent Peale, in *Salesman's Opportunity*, March 19, 1970.

"Meeting human need" isn't such a complicated thing; it can mean such little things such as going out of your way to shake hands with a stranger visiting your church.

Questions for Pupils on the Next Lesson: 1. Just what is the gospel we are called upon to proclaim? 2. Why did Jesus read from *Isaiah* on that Sabbath in Nazareth? 3. What did Jesus mean by His words in Luke 4:21? 4. Could the gospel be spread without preachers (see Romans 10:14)? 5. Do you completely agree with Romans 10:17? 6. Was Jesus "a regular churchgoer?" Prove it! 7. What was the result of Jesus' words that day in Nazareth?

TOPIC FOR YOUTH
HOW REAL IS YOUR RELIGION

Peace. "When Floyd Patterson was a little boy growing up in Brooklyn, he would hide in a subway station tool room. Reflecting on this childhood escape, he told a newspaper man, 'The total blackness was my hideaway from the bitterness of the world. I'd spread papers on the floor and I'd go to sleep and I'd find peace.'

"May God give us a large vision of the lonely and neglected youth that are found in subway stations, suburban shopping plazas and village gas stations."—David Poling.

Where do the needy in your town hide out? And would *you* find "peace" sleeping in the dark hole called the subway? How and through whom do such people find peace?

The Poor. In a street demonstration march, we saw one poor woman carrying a sign which read, "We Want *Money!*" She and many others in the line of march looked as though they needed money, but—didn't they need something else, something more?

"If you gave a guaranteed income to all marginal families for a full year, almost none would have got out of poverty at the end of the year. They would be poor, not because they lacked money, but because money doesn't buy skills, motivation, or hope."—Dr. Joseph T. English, Assistant Director of the Office of Economic Opportunity for Health Affairs.

True. More than money, the needy of this country need understanding, sympathy, dignity and recognition as human beings, whatever their color or condition.

We heard a fine young Roman Catholic priest say a startling thing when he was asked, "What word, as a priest, would you give us in our present furors of rioting, burning and killing?" He answered, *"Listen to each other!"*

Jesus listened well; He *heard* the pain of man.

The Prisoner. Oscar Wilde was a great writer; he ruined his whole life and career in breaking a British law, and was sent to prison:

"When I was brought down from my prison to the Court of Bank-ruptcy, between two policemen, ——waited in the long dreary corridor that, before the whole crowd, whom an action so sweet and simple hushed into silence, he might gravely raise his hat to me as, handcuffed and with bowed head, I passed him by. Men have gone to heaven for smaller things than that. It was in this spirit, and with this mode of love, that the saints knelt down to wash the feet of the poor, or stooped to kiss the leper on the cheek. I have never said one single word to him about what he did. I do not know to the present moment whether he is aware that I was even conscious of his action. It is not a thing for which one can render formal thanks in formal words. I store it in the treasure house of my heart. I keep it there as a secret debt that I am glad to think I can never possibly repay. . . . When wisdom has been profitless to me, philosophy barren, and the proverbs and phrases of those who have sought to give me consolation as dust and ashes in my mouth, the memory of that little, silent act of love has unsealed for me all the wells of pity . . . and brought me out of the bitterness of lonely exile into harmony with the wounded, broken, and great heart of the world."

Have you ever been in prison—*to help the prisoner?*

Need. Sal Lazzarotti sat in a subway train in New York City and watched an attractive young girl get up from her seat and walk toward the car door. Suddenly he saw her whirl and scream at an 18-year-old boy, "You fresh young punk! Don't look so innocent. I know you touched me!" She struck the boy with both fists, pursued him out on the platform, shrieking, "Police, police!" Sal was certain the boy had *not* touched her; he saw the whole thing.

Lazzarotti left the train and walked to his office. He couldn't get the girl—or the boy—out of his mind. His common sense said, "Don't get involved!" His conscience said, "That boy was innocent." The boy had been arrested; his case came up in court a week later: during that week, Sal Lazzarotti did some research on the boy, and offered to come as a witness when the case was called.

The girl told a wild, completely false story of "what had happened"; Sal shook his head in disbelief. Finally, when the story became more and more unbelievable, the judge said to her, "There is a witness to the incident present, so be sure of what you say!"

That did it. The girl panicked, stumbled and contradicted herself so badly that the case was thrown out of court. She was sent to a psychiatrist!

That is responding to human need. Most of us wouldn't have done it. (No other passenger in the car did it!) But Sal Lazzarotti did; on his way home that night, he said, "Thank you, God, for giving me the courage to act. Help me to be more sensitive to others in need." (Adapted from an article in *Guideposts,* May, 1970.)

Sometimes it seems that a sin worse than lying or stealing or even personal injury is the sin of *indifference;* that sin can kill, too. . . .

Sentence Sermon to Remember: Sympathy is your pain in my heart.— Anonymous.

Questions for Pupils on the Next Lesson: 1. What was unusual about Jesus' sermon at Nazareth? 2. Name the three principal parts of a synagogue service. 3. Who was "Esaias?" 4. What was "the acceptable year of the Lord?" 5. Why did Jesus add words of His own to the reading of Scripture? 6. Some say that preaching is disappearing from the modern church; do you agree? 7. What do you ask for in a sermon?

LESSON XI—MAY 14

THE CHURCH PROCLAIMS THE GOSPEL

Background Scripture: Luke 4:16-21; Romans 10:14-18;
Ephesians 3:7-13
Devotional Reading: Ephesians 3:7-13

KING JAMES VERSION

REVISED STANDARD VERSION

LUKE 4   16 And he came to Nazareth, where he had been brought up: and, as his custom was, he went into the synagogue on the sabbath day, and stood up for to read.

17 And there was delivered unto him the book of the prophet Esaias. And when he had opened the book, he found the place where it was written,

18 The Spirit of the Lord is upon me, because he hath anointed me to preach the gospel to the poor; he hath sent me to heal the broken-hearted, to preach deliverance to the captives, and recovering of sight to the blind, to set at liberty them that are bruised,

19 To preach the acceptable year of the Lord.

20 And he closed the book, and he gave it again to the minister, and sat down. And the eyes of all them that were in the synagogue were fastened on him.

21 And he began to say unto them, This day is this Scripture fulfilled in your ears.

ROMANS 10   14 How then shall they call on him in whom they have not believed? and how shall they believe in him of whom they have not heard? and how shall they hear without a preacher?

15 And how shall they preach, except they be sent? as it is written, How beautiful are the feet of them that preach the gospel of peace, and bring glad tidings of good things!

16 But they have not all obeyed the gospel. For Esaias saith, Lord, who hath believed our report?

17 So then faith cometh by hearing, and hearing by the word of God.

18 But I say, Have they not heard? Yes verily, their sound went into all

LUKE 4   16 And he came to Nazareth, where he had been brought up; and he went to the synagogue, as his custom was, on the sabbath day. And he stood up to read; 17 and there was given to him the book of the prophet Isaiah. He opened the book and found the place where it was written,

18 "The Spirit of the Lord is upon me,
because he has anointed me to preach good news to the poor.
He has sent me to proclaim release to the captives
and recovering of sight to the blind,
to set at liberty those who are oppressed,

19 to proclaim the acceptable year of the Lord."

20 And he closed the book, and gave it back to the attendant, and sat down; and the eyes of all in the synagogue were fixed on him. 21 And he began to say to them, "Today this scripture has been fulfilled in your hearing."

ROMANS 10   14 But how are men to call upon him in whom they have not believed? And how are they to believe in him of whom they have never heard? And how are they to hear without a preacher? 15 And how can men preach unless they are sent? As it is written, "How beautiful are the feet of those who preach good news!" 16 But they have not all heeded the gospel; for Isaiah says, "Lord, who has believed what he has heard from us?" 17 So faith comes from what is heard, and what is heard comes by the preaching of Christ.

18 But I ask, have they not heard? Indeed they have; for

270

the earth, and their words unto the ends of the world.

"There voice has gone out to all the earth,
and their words to the ends of the world."

MEMORY SELECTION: For I am not ashamed of the gospel of Christ; for it is the power of God unto salvation to every one that believeth; to the Jew first, and also to the Greek. Romans 1:16.

HOME DAILY BIBLE READINGS

May 8. M. Preaching to Israel, Matthew 10:5-15.
May 9. T. Christ the Head of the Corner, Acts 4:5-12.
May 10. W. Preaching to Parliament, Acts 5:27-32.
May 11. T. "Receive My Spirit," Acts 7:51-60.
May 12. F. Paul Preaches in Pisidia, Acts 13:26-33.
May 13. S. The Necessity of Preaching, Romans 10:14-18.
May 14. S. Unsearchable Riches, Ephesians 3:7-13.

BACKGROUND

In the Jewish synagogue, the service was divided into three parts. First, there was *prayer,* which was the devotional part; second, there was the *reading of the Scriptures;* this was read from the old Hebrew, then translated into the common tongue (Greek or Aramaic); the law was read and translated one verse at a time, and the prophets three verses at a time. Third, there was the *teaching* part of the service. It was during the third part that Jesus almost disrupted the service one Sabbath day in Nazareth. . . .

NOTES ON THE PRINTED TEXT

I. . . . as his custom was, he went into the synagogue on the sabbath day, and stood up for to read, Luke 4:16. Directly from the scene of His temptations, Jesus went into Galilee and began to teach—and preach —in the synagogues. Naturally, He would go to the synagogue; He had done that since His mother took Him there as a child. It was "his custom." It was the center of the life of His community; every good Jew went to the synagogue. And in these days "there went out a fame of him through all the region round about" (Luke 4:14). What He had to teach and preach roused a sparkling interest in what was usually a stereotyped synagogue performance.

On this Sabbath in Nazareth—His "home town"—He was invited by the president of the congregation to read the Scriptures. This, too, was an established custom; there was no *professional* ministry; any layman could be called up to read the sacred scrolls and to lead the discussion that followed. This day, the brilliant young man from their own town was called. He stood up and read the first two verses of Isaiah 61. Was that "the Scripture reading for the day," or was it a reading selected by Jesus for a particular purpose? Probably, the latter, for when Jesus came to comment on those two verses He exploded a bomb.

In these two verses, the old prophet described the deliverance of the Israelites from their Babylonian captivity in terms of the year of Jubilee —a year in which all debts were canceled, all slaves set free, and in which all property was returned to its original owner. (See Leviticus

25.) Jesus read it accurately; He quoted *Isaiah* as saying, "The Spirit of the Lord is upon *me*, because he hath anointed *me* to preach the gospel to the poor; he hath sent *me* to heal the broken-hearted, to preach deliverance to the captives, and recovering of sight to the blind, to set at liberty them that are bruised, to preach the acceptable year of the Lord" (verses 18-19).

So far, so good. The reading was orthodox enough to suit any Jew. It was all written down in Isaiah, so. . . . But did Jesus put unusual emphasis on that word "*me?*" His listeners must have sensed something like that, for "the eyes of all . . . were fastened on him" as He sat down. And what He said when He sat down (synagogue teachers always sat down to comment and teach) shook them as they hadn't been shaken in years. It was then that He said, "This day is this Scripture fulfilled in your ears" (verse 21).

That was preaching! That was a new kind of preacher giving the gospel (the good news of deliverance) to the people. *Now,* with His coming, captives would be freed from sin, the oppressed lifted up, the sick healed, the (spiritually) blind made to see. This very year in which He spoke was the year of the Lord's favor, the year of grace mentioned in Isaiah 61:2. Isaiah's promise of such release had not come true; the "year" had not come. But now that Christ was here it *had* come. Today this Scripture has been fulfilled. . . ." The preaching of the Christian church was meant to be like that: courageous, lively, *explosive,* in its announcement of the good news. It was never intended to be as uninspiring as a babbling, ritualistic brook run dry through constant reference to the past, but as startling as the sudden blast of a trumpet in a quiet church.

Preaching—such preaching—was important to the early church. It should be as important to us as it was to them—and not something people say should be dropped because of "disinterest in the pew." If the preacher has good news to preach, the pew will come alive.

II. And how are they to hear without a preacher? Romans 10:14 (RSV). The passage, Romans 9 through 11, has the unenviable reputation of being the most difficult to understand and interpret in the whole of the New Testament. It deals with several vexing problems that haunted the mind of Paul: Why had the good news failed to reach and convert the Jews? Had God forsaken them? What was the matter with them that more of them didn't "get it?"

There was nothing the matter with the good news. Perhaps the trouble was twofold: it has never been easy to lift men from selfishness to sacrifice and to a nobler way of life, and perhaps Paul and his preacher missionaries were a bit impatient. Rome wasn't built in a day; the Kingdom of God hasn't arrived *yet* for most of us! But this was and is no excuse for the preacher to stop preaching.

If there were no preachers, Paul says in (the very *clear* passages) in verses 14-18, how then would *anyone* hear the gospel at all? How can it be done unless some are called to preach it and to exemplify it in their living? "How beautiful are the feet of those who preach good news (RSV)!" That is in verse 15; read Isaiah 52:7 to see where he got it. Of course, the people had listened to Isaiah, but poor Isaiah complained, "Lord, who has believed what he has heard from us" (Romans 10:16, RSV)? And people had listened to Christ and to Paul but insofar as changing their lives was concerned they seemed not to have heard or understood a word that had been told them.

True—but suppose all preaching were to stop because some did not listen? Suppose no trained, consecrated preacher were to stand any longer in the pulpit of your church: how would the church attendance record look *then*? The point is that *all* of the Jews had not rejected Him; they simply had not heard Him or of Him from some preacher coming after Him. Pity the preacher, and know his problems before you condemn him; he has always preached against a tide of disinterest, smugness, closed-mindedness and apathy. He has not always preached well or effectively, but he has preached, and he must go on preaching if the Kingdom is *ever* to arrive. The *New English Bible* translates the latter half of verse 17, "We conclude that faith is awakened by the message, and the message that awakens it comes through the word of Christ."

They have preached, and they will—and, Paul says, "Their voice has gone out to all the earth, and their words to the ends of the world" (verse 18, RSV). Preaching *is* important; after all it may just be the most important part of the worship of the church.

SUGGESTIONS TO TEACHERS

Decide for yourself whether you want to invite your minister to sit in on this discussion; it's about *him,* and it might be uncomfortable for him, or it might help him. . . .

What is a preacher for, anyway? What is he supposed to do and be? The congregation has a lot to do with the success or failure of his preaching; how does your congregation receive him?

Study the preaching of Jesus. You will find that it was

1. Disturbing.
2. Often infuriating.
3. In a language everybody could understand.
4. It had one main purpose: *what was that?*

Would you drop the sermon from your worship services? If not, why not?

TOPIC FOR ADULTS
PROCLAIMING THE GOSPEL

Light! In *If Winter Comes,* A. S. Hutchinson has one of his characters say about preaching and preachers:

"I tell you, Hapgood, that plumb down in the crypt and abyss of every man's soul is a hunger, a craving for other food than this earthly stuff. And the churches know it; and instead of reaching down to him what he wants—light, light—instead of that, they invite him to dancing and picture shows, and you're a jolly good fellow and religion's a jolly fine thing and no spoilsport, and all that sort of latter-day tendency. . . . He can get all that outside the churches and get it better. Light! Light! He wants light . . . and the longer it's withheld the lower he'll sink."

The preacher is something like the lady who holds a torch high above New York harbor—Lady Liberty. He holds high a lamp of faith and understanding at the door of the Kingdom of heaven. He is trained to do that, called to do that. But he needs help. He needs a responsive congregation. Does he have it in our church?

Sermons. The editor of a religious magazine received the following letter:

> "Dear Sir: I have been a regular worshiper for over 30 years, and I calculate that I must have heard over 3,000 sermons. I can honestly say that I do not now remember one of them. I wonder if I should have lost much if those sermons had never been preached. I raise the question in no carping or hypocritical spirit. I know how much labor and effort (preachers) spend on the preparation of their sermons. Might not the time so spent be better employed with no real loss to the congregation?"

The editor answered:

> "Dear Sir: I have been married for over 30 years. Every night when I get home my wife has ready for me a nicely prepared meal. Looking back over the years of my married life, I can honestly say that I cannot remember a single one of those meals. But I am quite sure that if I had not had them, I should not be the happy and healthy man I am today."—From *The Anglican Digest,* Summer, 1958.

Well said! A fine preacher said recently that he had been led into the ministry by the worst sermon he ever heard. And Paul asked (Romans 10), "How shall they hear without a preacher?" Think it over!

The Gap. Dr. Clarence Hall, a senior editor of *Reader's Digest,* told 800 North Carolina Baptist preachers that there is no wider gap in Christendom than the ten or fifteen feet between the preacher in the pulpit and the congregation in the pews. He gave three reasons for the gap: growth of clericalism, failure to sell laymen on their responsibilities, and widespread feeling among lay people that they had no real communication with the pastors.

The gap—whose fault is it? The preacher's, or . . . ?

Preachers. "A medical doctor can slice and/or dose his patients and be done with them, except for collecting the bill. A lawyer can draw a will or sue. A teacher can bore his classes three or four hours a day and spend his evenings with a pipe and a detective story. We live in a time of the specialist.

"Not so the preacher. He is supposed to be an orator, administrator, business man, psychologist, school superintendent, scholar, community leader, fund raiser, teacher, after-dinner speaker and master of ceremonies, to name a few of the trades in which he needs some degree of proficiency."—*How to Become a Bishop Without Being Religious,* by Charles Merrill Smith.

So you get a poor sermon once in a while; aren't you surprised that you don't get more?

Questions for Pupils on the Next Lesson: 1. Just what is a church schoolteacher supposed to do? 2. Describe the best teacher you ever had. 3. What "godless and silly myths" are referred to in I Timothy 4:7? 4. Are young teachers the best teachers (I Timothy 4:12)? 5. How important is the teacher's life and living in his teaching? 6. Could the church exist without the church school? 7. Was Jesus more of a teacher than a preacher?

TOPIC FOR YOUTH
LISTENING AND RESPONDING

Listening. "No truly Christian minister preaches *himself.* For Jesus once said, 'He that heareth you, heareth *me.*' Therefore, as you sit in your pew and the minister begins to preach, let the man in the pulpit fade from your view, and hear no one but Jesus only. That is the way to listen to a sermon."—Oswald Riess, in *This Day,* June, 1961.

Billy Bray was a famous British evangelist; when he stood up to preach he would always say to himself, "Back, back, Billy Bray; forward, Jesus Christ!"

Talking Sense. "An English clergyman, after many years devoted to an urban ministry, was called to a rural pastorate. There he set himself to the task of learning the language of his new flock. He jotted down every word he heard the farm folk use. In time, he listed a vocabulary of 300 words. Then, after preparing his weekly sermon, he would translate it into the local dialect.

"Results? Within a few months not merely his church but the church-yard also was filled with people who had come to listen to 'the parson who talked sense.'"—Fred E. Luchs, in *Church Management,* April, 1960.

Jesus preached like that: He talked about fish, yeast, sheep, flowers, lost coins, lost boys, children, wheat and tares, candlesticks, plowing, reaping, sickness. . . .

People respond to sermons like that.

Popular, Unpopular. Crowds came to hear Jesus preach—and what they heard didn't always make them glad they came! His sermons were not calculated to flatter, but to win men to God. Sometimes He had to make them angry. (When John Wesley held his first Methodist conferences in his churches he would always ask about the incumbent minister, "Has he made anyone *angry?*" If he hadn't, Wesley moved him. . . .)

An old lady in the Kentucky mountains seemed to be enjoying her pastor's sermon that Sunday morning. When he talked about bobbed hair and lipstick, when he struck out at "dancin', drinkin' and runnin' around," she shouted, "Amen!" But when he started talking about corn-cob pipes, she leaped to her feet and shouted back at him in a rage. She said, "He has quit preachin'. He has gone to meddlin'."

He had. But Jesus was most effective when He was "meddlin'" about the hypocrisy of the Pharisees, the injustices of the rulers, the bigotry of the religious leaders. If He had never meddled so—would they have crucified Him?

If you're looking for a good preacher, don't look for the *popular* preacher; he may have all the words—and nothing to say.

The Great Ones. Dr. S. Parkes Cadman was probably one of the most widely-heard preachers of his generation. But he too was suspicious of fame and popularity in the pulpit. When a young theological student asked him to name the greatest preachers of his time, he said, "I don't know their names. They are in small churches in obscure parishes all over the world. Some of us are more widely known, and we preach to larger congregations, but these men feed the flock of Christ every week. Their people love them. They are the great preachers in every age."

The Sinner. Daniel Webster was a man of many words—one of American history's most fluent orators. He could speak for hours when he had to. But once he said something really great in the fewest possible words.

"A friend asked him why he generally went to hear a poor country preacher instead of the more brilliant clergymen in Washington.

"'Well, you see,' he replied, 'in Washington they preach to Daniel Webster the renowned individual; but this country preacher preached to Daniel Webster the sinner.'"—Harold Helfer, in *Coronet.*

What do you go to church to hear? Something that leaves you just as you have been for years—or something that makes you "raise your sights?" To be told how nice you are, or . . . ?

Sermons. "It is a fine thing to preach a sermon, but it is a still finer thing to be a sermon. You may remember the incident of Francis of Assissi saying to a young monk, 'Let's go down into this village and preach.'

"They walked through the village and returned to the monastery, and the puzzled young monk asked the old saint, 'Brother Francis, when do we preach?'

"And Francis answered, 'We just did.'"—Arthur Terry, in *Arkansas Methodist.*

That may be what Edgar Guest had in mind when he said that he would rather see a sermon than hear one any time. . . .

Did you think the minister is the only one who preaches? We all preach sermons every day, without saying a word. . . .

Sentence Sermon to Remember: Preaching is truth mediated through personality.—Phillips Brooks.

Questions for Pupils on the Next Lesson: 1. How do we train ourselves in godliness? 2. When should the religious education of a child begin? 3. Why did Paul consider teaching so important to the future of the church? 4. Is Sunday school enough for the religious education of American youth? 5. From whom did you learn most about religion? 6. Shouldn't church schoolteachers be paid? 7. Which means most in the development of a man: spiritual growth or physical growth?

LESSON XII—MAY 21

THE CHURCH'S TEACHING MINISTRY

Background Scripture: Matthew 28:19-20; I Timothy 4:6-16; II Timothy
2:1-2; 3:10-17
Devotional Reading: II Timothy 3:14-4:2

KING JAMES VERSION

I TIMOTHY 4 6 If thou put the brethren in remembrance of these things, thou shalt be a good minister of Jesus Christ, nourished up in the words of faith and of good doctrine, whereunto thou hast attained.

7 But refuse profane and old wives' fables, and exercise thyself rather unto godliness.

8 For bodily exercise profiteth little: but godliness is profitable unto all things, having promise of the life that now is, and of that which is to come.

9 This is a faithful saying, and worthy of all acceptation.

10 For therefore we both labor and suffer reproach, because we trust in the living God, who is the Saviour of all men, specially of those that believe.

11 These things command and teach.

12 Let no man despise thy youth; but be thou an example of the believers, in word, in conversation, in charity, in spirit, in faith, in purity.

II TIMOTHY 2 Thou therefore, my son, be strong in the grace that is in Christ Jesus. 2 And the things that thou hast heard of me among many witnesses, the same commit thou to faithful men, who shall be able to teach others also.

REVISED STANDARD VERSION

I TIMOTHY 4 6 If you put these instructions before the brethren, you will be a good minister of Christ Jesus, nourished on the words of the faith and of the good doctrine which you have followed. 7 Have nothing to do with godless and silly myths. Train yourself in godliness; 8 for while bodily training is of some value, godliness is of value in every way, as it holds promise for the present life and also for the life to come. 9 The saying is sure and worthy of full acceptance.

10 For to this end we toil and strive, because we have our hope set on the living God, who is the Savior of all men, especially of those who believe.

11 Command and teach these things. 12 Let no one despise your youth, but set the believers an example in speech and conduct, in love, in faith, in purity.

II TIMOTHY 2 You then, my son, be strong in the grace that is in Christ Jesus, 2 and what you have heard from me before many witnesses entrust to faithful men who will be able to teach others also.

MEMORY SELECTION: All scripture is given by inspiration of God, and is profitable for doctrine, for reproof, for correction, for instruction in righteousness: that the man of God may be perfect, thoroughly furnished unto all good works. II Timothy 3:16, 17.

HOME DAILY BIBLE READINGS

May 15. M. Home Teaching, II Timothy 1:3-7.
May 16. T. The Pastoral Teaching Ministry, II Timothy 3:10-17.
May 17. W. God Creates Only Good, I Timothy 4:4-10.
May 18. T. God Uses Youth, I Timothy 4:11-16.
May 19. F. Teaching Through Pastoral Correspondence, I Corinthians 4:14-20.
May 20. S. Stressing an Old Commandment, I John 2:1-11.
May 21. S. Profitable for Teaching, II Timothy 3:14-4:2.

BACKGROUND

Paul's two letters to Timothy were, probably, his last letters, written about A.D. 65-67. Paul is an old man now, waiting to die in Rome; in II Timothy 4:6-18 he says farewell to his favorite helper and his spiritual son, Timothy: "I have fought a good fight, I have finished my course, I have kept the faith." It is the courageous shout of a conqueror. That verse also contains the gist of his instructions to the much younger disciple.

In the Scripture portions of our lesson, taken from I and II Timothy, he concentrates on Timothy's duty to *teach* more than to *preach*. He realizes that the spread of the good news depends upon those teachers in the church, both laymen and ordained apostles, who will pass on the torch in an unbroken line from generation to generation. *They are chosen to preserve the truth of God in all its purity.* In order to do this, they must have certain qualifications as teachers and do certain things. . . .

What Paul has to say was of great value to Timothy, and should be of equal value to us, for in one way or another we are *all* teachers in the church. . . .

NOTES ON THE PRINTED TEXT

I. If you put these instructions before the brethren, you will be a good minister of Jesus Christ, I Timothy 4:6 (RSV). "These instructions" refer the reader specifically back to the instructions in 3:14, 15 on the way people should behave themselves in the Christian fellowship. Generally, they are the instructions mentioned in the whole letter, which warn the preachers and the teachers and the people against the sins of heterodoxy (denying the accepted doctrines of the church) and asceticism (abstaining from eating meat, conjugal intercourse, etc.). The good teaching preacher will be firmly founded and loyal to "the words of faith and of good doctrine" which have been handed down to him by *his* Christian teachers.

He will refuse to teach the "profane and old wives' fables," the godless and silly myths of the false teachers (such as, for instance, the foolish and misleading stories that some old women had been teaching the children, or the unbelievable stories in the apocryphal books of the 2nd century which became the mythology of the Middle Ages). The good teacher doesn't waste his time on marginal nonsense; he sticks to the central truths of the faith—such as the incarnation and the resurrection promise of the life to come. He doesn't teach from the morning's headlines in the local newspaper, but *from the Scriptures.*

Timothy is cautioned to train himself in godliness. When we think of "training" we usually think of training the body; Paul says that training the body is all right provided you don't overdo it. Some people concentrate so much on the health of the body that they neglect the health of mind and soul—which is a lot more important! Someone says, "The Christian is not the athlete of the gymnasium but the athlete of God." Training in godliness—goodliness—develops the *whole* body.

How do we go about training for godliness and goodliness? Dr. Holmes Rolston says: "We can be sure that such training includes the reading of the Word of God, the reading of good books, the practice of prayer, attendance at public worship, the effort to be obedient to the Word of God, stewardship of time, money and abilities. . . ." *That* is what the Christian teacher teaches, and that is what the Christian student must *learn.* Why? Why, because in such teaching and learning *lies all our hope for both the present and the future life.*

Paul puts great stress on the thought that in this life we are getting ready for the next. This life on earth is nothing more than a schoolroom in which we are prepared for our adulthood beyond this earth. The beginning and the end and the meaning of life is to understand that its goal is God and union with Him. For that, the Christian will suffer *anything.* The goal makes the suffering worth while.

II. Let no man despise thy youth, I Timothy 4:12. Timothy was comparatively young—probably between 35 and 40—when he received this letter from Paul. He was young in comparison with Paul, and young in comparison with a lot of the older men at Ephesus, who would surely read this letter, too. Was Paul sending a sly warning to them? Was he telling them that "they didn't know it all," and that this young protégé of his might have something worth listening to when he preached to them and taught them? Maybe so. Too many of us too often look down our noses at those who have the misfortune to be younger than we are!

But mainly, we think, it was directed at young Timothy. Youth needs to be cautioned against improper behavior and pride and disrespect. What Paul was telling Timothy was something like this: "You are young, and you have no need to be ashamed of that. But you can stop all unreasonable criticism of yourself by being an example in speech and conduct in love, in faith, and in purity. Live in such Christian fashion that they will have nothing to criticize!" Be a model youth—not a meddler!

Good advice for *all* teachers!

III. . . . and what you have heard from me before many witnesses entrust to faithful men who will be able to teach others also, II Timothy 2:2 (RSV). Here, Paul goes back to his previous emphasis on the transmission of the faith in all its *purity.* He also makes it plain that the hope of the church rests on those who are teachers—"transmitters"—of the truth. Paul demands that it *be* the truth, not a modified or modernized version of the truth.

As teacher, Timothy is to transmit this truth to faithful men, able, believing, reliable men who can be trusted with so great a treasure, who have the capacity to teach others. It is to be a living chain. . . . How vital the teacher is to Christianity!

SUGGESTIONS TO TEACHERS

Suggested Lesson Emphases:

1. We *must* teach: Christ commanded it.
2. Whatever we teach, we *must* relate it to both (a) life as it is and (b) life as it should be.
3. The teacher's life and faith are more important than his words.
4. The Scriptures should be taught first, all else second.

5. The purpose of teaching is, not to make the student memorize Scripture, but to apply it intelligently.
6. He who does not grow in knowledge of the Christian faith is a sheep lost among wolves.

TOPIC FOR ADULTS
THE CHURCH'S TEACHING MINISTRY

Questioning, Thinking, Believing. Dr. Ben Browne says of the teaching of Jesus: "He did not come to answer all our questions *now*. He came also to provoke our questions. He wanted us to do some thinking of our own. Once, when He was asked for information, He replied, 'Why not judge for yourselves what is right?' After He told His parables His hearers were stirred to questioning. He wanted to quicken the intellects of men. He gave us clues and principles, but He often wanted us to do our own thinking and to work out our own solutions. For did He not require that we not only love God with all our hearts, but also with all our *minds* and with all our *strength?*

"How dull it would have been had He left us His teachings organized like an encyclopedia, a huge dictionary, a textbook, in which we could go searching for rules and regulations! Rather, how wonderful that He left us the stimulus of challenging truth that we might have all the adventure and joy of questioning, thinking and believing." From *The Baptist Leader*, April, 1955.

The church school should never be a brain-washing institution, never a place to encourage children *only* to memorize and repeat Scripture like a human parrot! It is a place to ask vital questions and seek honest answers.

If youth doesn't find those answers in the church, youth goes elsewhere to find them. . . .

The Scriptures. In the course of his life, the average Christian comes in contact with many "Bible" teachers. Some become so bewildered that they just give up. Others use the brains God gave them to pick and choose the best. . . .

We remember one college teacher who wrote an "Outline-of-the-Bible" book when he was very young—and inflicted it on successive generations of students; they merely memorized certain portions of his outlines, got a passing grade, and forgot it. Recently, we heard that the students have asked that his course be dropped from the curriculum. Are you surprised?

We remember another who came into class one day and said, "Gentlemen, I believe that the communist form of government is the finest form ever conceived in the mind of man. Furthermore, I believe the Bible sanctions it. . . ." That started an argument that lasted for days—and a great searching of the Scriptures! Actually, when he had finished we knew that the teacher believed no such thing: he was only asking his students to work out *their own (intelligent) approach to the Bible.* It worked.

Which would you say was the better teacher?

Teachers. A prominent leader in religious education has said: "It stands to reason that a child will learn much more about church history from a trained professional teacher—no matter what his faith, if any,—

than he will from an untrained volunteer." That may be true in the field of church history—but is that the only field with which the church-school teacher is concerned? How about all the rest of life? Is the mind of the teacher more important than his heart in the business of building Christian *character?*

Some other concerned teacher said this: "Consider the modern class-room in a first-rate school: they boast the latest teaching machine, apple-green chalk boards and a language laboratory with individual headsets. And then remember that the Christian faith raced around Asia Minor, invading Greek universities and Roman armies, kings' house-holds and merchants' shops, with none of these teaching aids but simply following the greatest Teacher. Then as now, the best teaching is in the hands of the trained, intelligent, understanding teacher. As Christian educators we must put first emphasis on the teacher and then on the best equipment."

We are not criticizing the use of modern equipment in the public school; we are asking only whether something more than teaching equipment is necessary in the *church* school. Is it? Do both schools have the same *purpose?* Do we dare play down the value of Christian personality in the Christian teacher?

My Teacher. Dr. Henry Van Dyke paraphrased the 23rd Psalm es-pecially for teachers. He made it read:

> The Lord is my teacher, I shall not lose the way.
> He leadeth me in the lowly path of learning;
> He prepareth a lesson for me every day;
> He bringeth me to the fountains of instruction;
> Little by little He showeth me the beauty of truth;
> The world is a great book that He hath written;
> He turneth the leaves for me slowly;
> They are all inscribed with images and letters;
> He poureth light on the pictures and the words.
> He taketh me by the hand to the hilltop of vision;
> And my soul is glad when I perceive His meaning;
> In the valley He also walketh beside me;
> In the dark places He whispereth to my heart,
> Even though my lesson is hard it is not hopeless;
> For the Lord is patient with His new scholar;
> He will wait awhile for my weakness;
> And help me to read the truth through tears.

Questions for Pupils on the Next Lesson: 1. What do we mean by "church renewal?" 2. Why does your church need renewal? 3. What did Paul say we must rid our hearts and church of in order to renew our faith? 4. How does Paul describe the ideal church in Colossians 3? 5. What did he mean by "let the word of Christ dwell in you richly?" 6. How would you start to take a spiritual inventory of your church? 7. Is halfheartedness in the church worse than deliberate sin?

TOPIC FOR YOUTH
WHY A CHURCH TEACHES

Ears. "A ship was in a fog on one of the Canadian lakes. The cap-tain's face suddenly became tense, then perplexed. He rang for slowed engines. The whistle shrieked, but no answer came.

" 'There's something dead ahead,' he declared. 'I get an echo from something.' Just then the fog lifted a little, and not ten feet from the bow was a huge steel scow that had broken loose from harbor and drifted.

"A landsman said he had heard no echo. The captain chuckled. He said, 'It's a matter of an educated hearing. God gave us ears, but we don't always train them.' "—From *The Sunday School Times.*

Religious education isn't sufficiently broad to give you all the answers to everything in this world (only God has all the answers!) but it is broad enough to train your ears and your eyes and your minds to hear and see the danger signals of life and to act accordingly. . . .

Youth. Paul wrote Timothy: "Let no man despise thy youth; but be thou an example . . . (I Timothy 4:12). Let's look at some of the great young men who refused to be despised:

"Alexander the Great conquered the world when he was twenty-three. Hannibal crossed the Alps and commanded the Carthaginian forces at twenty-six. Columbus laid his plans to find India when he was twenty-eight. John Smith staked out a colonial empire in Virginia when he was twenty-seven. Martin Luther started the Reformation when he was thirty. Calvin followed at twenty-one. Joan of Arc did all her work and was burned at the stake at nineteen. Patrick Henry cried, 'Liberty or Death,' at twenty-seven. Hamilton was thirty-two when he was Secretary of the Treasury. A youngster of twenty-six discovered the law of gravitation. Roger Williams was a banished heretic at twenty-nine. Jesus was crucified at thirty."—H. H. Barstow.

One Teacher. "What would a school be without teachers? Not much. And although the Sunday school of necessity has to depend on a staff of volunteer, unpaid teachers, they have given a good account of themselves. Only eternity will reveal the worth of faithful Sunday-school teachers.

"Let me tell you about one of mine. She was my Junior teacher. We had a class of ten or twelve typical Junior boys. We shot spitballs, sailed airplanes made from church bulletins out of the second-story window, and we scuffled. Our teacher an elderly woman with a great capacity to understand and love boys. On my last Sunday in her class (we were moving out of the state), this teacher thought it appropriate to give me a gift. It was a book by the title, *The Silver Trumpet,* and inside she had penned a brief message—'To Billy, one of the finest boys I know.' I look back now and feel that she must have had tongue in cheek when she wrote that, especially after the way I had misbehaved in her class. But as I read that message, God put this thought in my heart: 'If she can love me like this after all the bad things I have done in her class, then when I get big I want to be like [her].' I don't remember her lessons, any particular teaching or instruction during those months in her class, but I do remember *her.* May God give us more like her who will proudly wear the title of teacher and help shape young lives." From *Contact.*

That could be repeated a thousand times in a thousand other lives:

the most effective teacher is the patient, understanding teacher—and often the most obscure. . . .

Humility. "Harry Emerson Fosdick tells of a poor German schoolmaster who lived in a humble house in a small village. Carved over his doorway was this proud inscription: 'Dante, Molière and Goethe live here.' "—Charles L. Wallis.

It might help some of us if over the doorway of the church school we put up the sign, "God lives here. Enter reverently, and listen for His voice."

The teacher is there to help us hear *His* voice. . . .

Percentages. Some years back we read a startling article in some magazine entitled, "Sunday School: the Most Wasted Hour of the Week," or something like that. The author found a lot wrong with the Sunday school. He was right about most of it, but we still think he missed a few good points. For instance:

"Out of the Sunday schools come 95 per cent of the preachers, 85 per cent of the church converts, 95 per cent of the church workers and 75 per cent of the new churches; parents and pastors receive 90 per cent returns from less than a 10 per cent investment in time and energy."—*The Sunday School Journal.*

Anybody know of a better investment?

Sentence Sermon to Remember: The only way we can teach the Word of God is to live the Word of God.—Henrietta Mears.

Questions for Pupils on the Next Lesson: 1. What did Paul mean by, "For ye are dead . . ." (Colossians 3:3)? 2. How can we "mortify our members" for the sake of a better church? 3. What did Paul say we should *stop* doing in the church? 4. What did he say we *should* do? 5. Do you know of any *perfect* church? 6. How seriously do you take Colossians 3:17? 7. Will our modern church be "renewed' 'by (a) new spiritual emphasis or by (b) new social emphasis? 8. Why must the church *always* seek renewal?

LESSON XIII—MAY 28

THE CHURCH'S NEED FOR RENEWAL

Background Scripture: Colossians 3:1-17; I Peter 4:12-19; Revelation
2:1-7; 3:14-22
Devotional Reading: I Peter 2:1-6

KING JAMES VERSION

COLOSSIANS 3 1 If ye then be
risen with Christ, seek those things
which are above, where Christ sitteth
on the right hand of God.

2 Set your affection on things above,
not on things on the earth.

3 For ye are dead, and your life is
hid with Christ in God.

4 When Christ, who is our life, shall
appear, then shall ye also appear with
him in glory.

5 Mortify therefore your members
which are upon the earth; fornica-
tion, uncleanness, inordinate affection,
evil concupiscence, and covetousness,
which is idolatry:

6 For which things' sake the wrath
of God cometh on the children of disobedience:

7 In the which ye also walked sometime, when ye lived in them.

8 But now ye also put off all these;
anger, wrath, malice, blasphemy, filthy
communication out of your mouth.

9 Lie not one to another, seeing
that ye have put off the old man with
his deeds;

10 And have put on the new man,
which is renewed in knowledge after
the image of him that created him:

11 Where there is neither Greek nor
Jew, circumcision nor uncircumcision,
Barbarian, Scythian, bond nor free:
but Christ is all, and in all.

12 Put on therefore, as the elect of
God, holy and beloved, bowels of mercies, kindness, humbleness of mind,
meekness, long-suffering;

13 Forbearing one another, and forgiving one another, if any man have a
quarrel against any: even as Christ
forgave you, so also do ye.

14 And above all these things put
on charity, which is the bond of per-
fectness.

15 And let the peace of God rule in
your hearts, to the which also ye are
called in one body; and be ye thankful.

REVISED STANDARD VERSION

COLOSSIANS 3 1 If then you
have been raised with Christ, seek the
things that are above, where Christ
is, seated at the right hand of God. 2
Set your minds on things that are
above, not on things that are on
earth. 3 For you have died, and your
life is hid with Christ in God. 4 When
Christ who is our life appears, then
you also will appear with him in glory.

5 Put to death therefore what is
earthly in you: immorality, impurity,
passion, evil desire, and covetousness,
which is idolatry. 6 On account of
these the wrath of God is coming.

7 In these you once walked, when
you lived in them. 8 But now put
them all away: anger, wrath, malice,
slander, and foul talk from your
mouth. 9 Do not lie to one another,
seeing that you have put off the old
nature with its practices 10 and have
put on the new nature, which is being
renewed in knowledge after the image of its creator. 11 Here there cannot be Greek and Jew, circumcised
and uncircumcised, barbarian, Scythian, slave, free man, but Christ is all,
and in all.

12 Put on then, as God's chosen
ones, holy and beloved, compassion,
kindness, lowliness, meekness, and patience, 13 forbearing one another and,
if one has a complaint against another, forgiving each other; as the
Lord has forgiven you, so you also
must forgive. 14 And above all these
put on love, which binds everything
together in perfect harmony. 15 And
let the peace of Christ rule in your
hearts, to which indeed you were
called in the one body. And be thankful. 16 Let the word of Christ dwell
in you richly, as you teach and ad-

16 Let the word of Christ dwell in you richly in all wisdom; teaching and admonishing one another in psalms and hymns and spiritual songs, singing with grace in your hearts to the Lord. 17 And whatsoever ye do in word or deed, do all in the name of the Lord Jesus, giving thanks to God and the Father by him.

monish one another in all wisdom, and as you sing psalms and hymns and spiritual songs with thankfulness in your hearts to God. 17 And whatever you do, in word or deed, do everything in the name of the Lord Jesus, giving thanks to God the Father through him.

MEMORY SELECTION: Let this mind be in you, which was also in Christ Jesus. Philippians 2:5.

HOME DAILY BIBLE READINGS

May 22. M. Disorderly Conduct, I Corinthians 11:17-22.
May 23. T. Seeking Higher Standards, Colossians 3:1-6.
May 24. W. "The New Nature," Colossians 3:7-14.
May 25. T. Renewal Through Suffering, I Peter 4:12-19.
May 26. F. Love Grown Cold, Revelation 2:1-7.
May 27. S. Get Hot or Cold! Revelation 3:14-22.
May 28. S. A Spiritual House, I Peter 2:1-6.

BACKGROUND

Colossae was a town in Asia Minor about a hundred miles from Ephesus. Paul had never been there, but he was much interested in a church that had been established there by Epaphras, a citizen of the town. Evidently Epaphras came to Paul and told him that the church at Colossae was rotten with heresy. So Paul wrote this letter to straighten things out.

The heresy was the belief that the universe was filled with a lot of unusual, superhuman beings, of whom Christ was one, and that the Colossian Christians were engaging in angel-worship, living by a lot of man-made rules of conduct, and practicing an extreme asceticism (we met that word last week—remember?). Paul might have been furious about that, but in this letter to the erring Colossians he writes in love, talks of some things that were *good* among them, and pleads for a renewal of profound faith in Christ.

Church renewal! It is much on our tongues today—so much so that we had better understand just what it means.

NOTES ON THE PRINTED TEXT

I. For you have died, and your life is hid with Christ in God, Colossians 3:3 (RSV). In Colossians 2:12, Paul describes baptism as a dying and rising with Christ. The old sins are washed away in baptism; an "old man," a sinful man, dies as in him Christ is born anew. It is a great spiritual experience—or should be!

But there is another great experience which *follows* baptism in Christ: Paul talks about it in terms of the new *moral* life which comes to the Christian as a consequence of baptism. The baptized one—the new Christian—rises into a whole "newness of life." He has been saved from a life of sin and he has begun to live, not according to the rules and morality of men, but according to the rules and morality of Christ, who is now enthroned in heaven—and in the heart of the Christian as well.

His life is "hid with Christ in God" . . . , and because Christ is with God, the Christian's hidden *destiny* is bound up with Christ's, and is with God, too. Some day that destiny will be fully revealed to the Christian: "When Christ, who is our life, shall appear, then shall ye also appear with him in glory" (verse 4). This is surely a reference to the Second Coming.

But while we await that Second Coming, however we interpret it, the Christian needs to put away from himself a lot of the old earthly sins which *can* separate him from Christ and from salvation. Paul names five of them particularly (the number five appears several times in this lesson): immorality, impurity, passion, evil desire and "covetousness, which is idolatry." These are all sins of the flesh and of the world, and every Christian needs to be constantly on guard against them, needs constantly to renew his faith in Christ against them. No Christian, however meaningful or powerful may be his conversion, is immune to temptation; he can be converted a hundred times and still fall . . . !

And there are other sins of the mind and the mouth that should be guarded against: there are five of them—anger (sudden fury), wrath (constant, settled disposition), malice (eagerness to harm your neighbor), blasphemy (or slander) and foul talk. Add lying to this list, and you have the picture of a very poor Christian.

No Christian, no churchman, can be guilty of these "sins of the old man" when he professes faith in Christ. Such morals have no place in the church—and yet the church must struggle constantly against them, must constantly *renew itself* in faith and good Christian behavior. What would happen to our church, we wonder, if we really demanded and enforced Christ's rules against such sinning *within the church?*

Today, we talk a lot about our "image"; that word may be a fad with us, but it wasn't with Paul. Paul reminds us that we were all created *in the image of the creator* (verse 10). Yet, with our sin we have defaced, almost destroyed, that divine image, when we should have been trying to *grow in it.* God hopes, in Christ, to improve our image—but He can do little unless we do much to help Him!

One thing we can do would be to stop thinking of each other as Greeks, Jews, Romans, barbarians, Scythians (savages), slaves, freemen, black, white, yellow, or what have you? Paul says in Galatians 3:28, ". . . for ye are all one in Christ Jesus." Yet what terror and misery on earth have we Christians wrought in deliberately denying *that!*

II. *Put on then, as God's chosen ones, holy and beloved* . . . , Colossians 3:12 (RSV). Having told us what to put off, if we want a renewal of faith and power in the church, Paul tells us what to put *on.* He lists the virtues of the renewed Christian: compassion, kindness, lowliness, meekness, and patience (five of them!). Be forgiving and forbearing. Put on these things—not because Christ tells us to, but *because in love we must.* Forget all the other words and remember this one: love. It is the greatest of all Christian gifts and virtues. It is what brings us together as Christians and what keeps us together. It is what puts the peace of God in our hearts. (Let that peace "rule in your hearts"—as an umpire rules a ball game!)

We want "renewal?" Then we must know the word of God (the gospel); make its home in our hearts. We must sing, and not act like pessimists or look like mournful undertakers! Christianity began as a singing fellowship; the church that stops singing, or sings halfheartedly, is a dying church.

Memorize verse 17: this is the summing up of Paul's formula for church renewal. He puts it concisely: whatever you do, in the church or outside it, do it in the name of Jesus Christ. Archibald M. Hunter says of this verse: "In the ancient world a name had potency; it stood for the personality; it carried the sense of that person's authority. So we still speak of a magistrate as acting in the name of the king or of the law. And therefore, when Paul bids them do all 'in the name of the Lord Jesus,' he means: 'Invoke His help when you act; act with His authority; and let His will be expressed in your action.' 'Giving thanks to God the Father through Him,' issues again the summons to Christian thankfulness with the reminder that Christ is their only true mediator in their approach to God."—Page 139. Volume 22, *The Layman's Bible Commentary*. Quoted by permission of John Knox Press, publishers.

SUGGESTIONS TO TEACHERS

Be warned: this is one of the most difficult lessons of the year to teach. There is much too much for any teacher in one lesson. Concentrate on the following emphases, and let the rest wait for explanation in some other lesson:

1. The need for growth in the Christian graces.
2. The desperate need for renewal in the church.
3. Acceptance of reproof and discipline.
4. The peril of half-heartedness and self-satisfaction.
5. The value of youth's criticism of the church, that it must be awakened to the need of change and growth.

TOPIC FOR ADULTS
NEED FOR RENEWAL

Renewal. The word "renewal" has several meanings; it can mean "making new again," or "to make like new," or "to restore." When it is applied to the church—which meaning is most pertinent? Should we go back to the early church and try to make our churches exactly like that church? Should we "renew" by restoring some teaching, method or theology that once held power, but doesn't now? Get your definitions straight before you begin to "renew!"

We might start with a remark by John Dewey: "It seems to me that the chief danger of religion lies in the fact that it has become so respectable. It has become largely a sanction of what socially exists—a kind of gloss upon institutions and conventions. *Primitive Christianity was devastating in its claims.*"

What claims? What did the primitive church do that we should be doing? Or—should we blaze entirely new paths . . . ? Would that primitive church be as effective in our world as it was in the first two or three centuries?

Reformation. "Emerson said: 'We are reformers in spring and summer;

in autumn and winter we stand by the old—we are reformers in the morning, conservative at night. . . .' Christians should see themselves in this description. The great hope is that the One who makes all things new will keep our spirits young enough to prefer the cost of reform to the ease of the *status quo*.

"Then we might remember the remark of George Bernard Shaw: 'The best reformers the world has ever seen are those who commence on themselves.' What we need is a continuing reformation in the church, and the place to begin, I fear, is with myself. That kind of Reformation . . . would cause considerable discomfort, but it might be a new approach."—Author unknown.

Isn't this the kind of reformation—or renewal—that Paul is talking about in Colossians 3? Can we ever have a church renewed in spirit, faith and effort until we have church *members* so renewed?

What's wrong with us as church members—and how do we correct it?

Not the Church. A poet whose name has been lost put it in these words:

> If you want to have the kind of a church
> Like the kind of church you like,
> You needn't slip your clothes in a grip
> And start on a long, long hike;
> You'll only find what you left behind,
> For there's nothing really new.
> It's a knock at yourself when you knock your church:
> It isn't the church—it's you!
> It's really strange sometimes, you know,
> That things go as well as they do,
> When we think of the little—the very small mite—
> We add to the work of the few.
> We sit, and stand around, and complain of what's done,
> And do very little but fuss!
> Are we bearing our share of the burdens to bear?
> It isn't the church—it's us!

Criticism. "I believe that the citizen who criticizes his country is paying it an implied tribute: at the very least it means that he has not given up on his country, that he still has hopes for it. More often, the critic is motivated by high regard for the society he lives in and for its promise: in this case the vigor of his criticism is the measure of the gap he perceives between promise and performance. I do not think it is 'selling America short' when we ask a great deal of her; on the contrary, it is those who ask nothing, those who see no fault, who are really selling America short. As Thomas Carlyle said, 'The greatest of faults is to be conscious of none.' "—Senator J. W. Fulbright, in *Carolina Israelite*.

Now apply that to the church. Do we help the church by turning deaf ears and blind eyes to the faults of the church mentioned by its critics? Instead of condemning or ignoring them, should we look for truth in what they say, set ourselves to proclaim that truth in renewed devotion—or do *nothing*?

We worry too much about criticism of the church from without and within. The church has been "an anvil on which many hammers have been broken"; it has benefited by listening to its critics, grown stronger and stronger as the storms increased. . . .

Gripes. "A 'Gripe Card' has been suggested by the pastor of an Ohio Methodist church. Properly filled out, it entitles the bearer to gripe about his church.

"The card says:

'1. I attend all the regular and special services of my church.
'2. I pray every day for my church and pastor.
'3. I volunteer for, gladly accept, and enthusiastically carry out all jobs and offices I have in my church's program.
'4. I give at least a tithe of my income to my church.'

"Any member who gives an affirmative answer to all four can gripe."
—From a church bulletin.

Right or wrong? We know another minister who says, "What I need in this church is the presence of an out-and-out disbeliever in a pew every Sunday to check every word I say."

Which is better for the church?

Questions for Pupils on the Next Lesson: 1. What do we mean by "the devotional life," in the Christian sense? 2. Which books in the Bible are known as devotional books? 3. How would you describe a "devout" Christian? 4. Name five world leaders who have a significant devotional life. 5. How did Cornelius go about his "devotions?" 6. Do you think family prayer and/or Bible reading important to Christian living? 7. Why did Cornelius send his men to Peter?

TOPIC FOR YOUTH
NEEDED: BETTER CHURCHES

Church in Need. "A church in a changing neighborhood decides that it will revive itself and launch a ministry to the poor now crowding its doorsteps. So the members rally around and raise some money to launch the new era of ministry. Their first expenditures are to repair the pipe organ and spruce up the stained-glass windows at a cost of eighty thousand dollars. The poor do not batter down the doors to get in, and the church is puzzled. 'Why don't they respond to our efforts to reach them?' . . . Our deeds speak louder than our words, and to invite the poor into our upper middle-class sanctuaries will hardly convince them of our interest. When church members spend millions on themselves and a pittance on others, it is a little difficult to believe that they are 'God's servant people.' "—*The Empty Pulpit,* by Clyde Reid. Quoted by permission of Harper & Row, publishers.

To many a church this is nonsense. Why shouldn't we have fine organs and expensive stained-glass windows? Most good churches have them—*but are most churches good enough?* What would you suggest to "renew" churches in a changing neighborhood to which the poor do *not* come?

Revolution. "Somewhere along the line the church has lost the original spirit of Christianity until it is no longer something revolutionary or the creed of heroes. It is no longer the dynamic force of the early centuries when the world was turned upside down in less than a generation. Today, instead of transforming the social order in which it lives, the church has lost its genius for revolution that characterized its early history; the initiative for revolution in our day has been taken up by the atheistic forces of communism."—John Thompson.

But—we thought there *was* a revolution going on in our churches. Isn't it enough—or is it revolution in the wrong direction, or—what?

We can do only one of three things when we bump into a revolution: we can sit on the fence and watch it, or we can get in and fight, or we can run. Which would you say the church is doing in a time when most of the world is swept up in social, political, and economic revolution? Is it important that we get involved, or should we "stay out of it?"

Which way lies renewal for the church?

This Is My Church. "This is my church. It is composed of people like me. We make it what it is. I want it to be a church that is a light on the paths of pilgrims, leading them to goodness, truth and beauty. It will be, if I am. It will be friendly, if I am. Its pews will be filled, if I help fill them. It will do a great work, if I work. It will bring other people into its work and fellowship, if I bring them. It will be a church of loyalty and love, of fearlessness and faith, if I, who make it what it is, am filled with these.

"Therefore, I dedicate myself to the task of being what I want my church to be."—Brooklyn Central Church Bulletin.

Nuisance. Undoubtedly, Paul was a plain nuisance to many laymen in Colossae and elsewhere, talking as he did. But Paul may have felt it a *duty* to be a nuisance if those churches were to be cleaned up and "renewed."

"The first duty of the layman in his local church is to be a nuisance. This is not easy for him, for all the teaching that he has received in the church from his childhood is that he should be modest, self-effacing, accommodating and obedient—in fact everything but a nuisance. . . . We do not mean that he should be so simply in order to criticize and find fault. . . . He has got to be a nuisance in asking questions: 'Why do we do this or that in the church?' 'What does the minister mean when he says such and such?' He should be a minister in demanding and suggesting action on all kinds of lines, in church and outside. He has got to be a persistent nuisance, for everything will be done to silence him or disregard him."—Mark Gibbs and T. Ralph Morton, in *God's Frozen People.*

Just to make this a bit more constructive, we like to remember the young lady who had just graduated from college; when her father asked her what in her education had made the deepest impression on her, she said, "Once, when I was a junior, one of my professors wrote a comment on a paper I had written."

Was the professor's comment that of a nuisance or a helper—constructive or destructive?

What a nuisance Jesus was to those who feared any criticism of their lives or faith! But. . . !

Sentence Sermon to Remember: A church with a shriveled-up and watered-down gospel has little future in the kind of world we face today; what is needed is not more words but the Word.—W. T. Purkiser.

Questions for Pupils on the Next Lesson: 1. What guiding rules do you have for your devotional life? 2. Is alms-giving devotional (Acts 10:8, 31)? 3. What does Psalm 63:1 tell us about sincerity in devotions? 4. What does the word "Psalm" mean? 5. What elements of faith do you find in the devotions of Cornelius? 6. What have you found to be the best way to communicate with God? 7. What would you add to or drop from the group devotions in your church?

JUNE, JULY, AUGUST, 1972

THE BIBLE AND THE DEVOTIONAL LIFE

LESSON I—JUNE 4

WHAT IS THE DEVOTIONAL LIFE?

Background Scripture: Psalm 63:1–8; Acts 10:1–8,30–33
Devotional Reading: Psalm 63:1–8

KING JAMES VERSION	REVISED STANDARD VERSION
ACTS 10 There was a certain man in Caesarea called Cornelius, a centurion of the band called the Italian band,	ACTS 10 At Caesarea there was a man named Cornelius, a centurion of what was known as the Italian Cohort, 2 a devout man who feared God
2 A devout man, and one that feared God with all his house, which gave much alms to the people, and prayed to God always.	with all his household, gave alms liberally to the people, and prayed constantly to God. 3 About the ninth hour of the day he saw clearly in a vision
3 He saw in a vision evidently, about the ninth hour of the day, an angel of God coming in to him, and saying unto him, Cornelius.	an angel of God coming in and saying to him, "Cornelius." 4 And he stared at him in terror, and said, "What is it, Lord?" And he said to him, "Your
4 And when he looked on him, he was afraid, and said, What is it, Lord? And he said unto him, Thy prayers and thine alms are come up for a memorial before God.	prayers and your alms have ascended as a memorial before God. 5 And now send men to Joppa, and bring one Simon who is called Peter; 6 he is
5 And now send men to Joppa, and call for one Simon, whose surname is Peter:	lodging with Simon, a tanner, whose house is by the seaside." 7 When the angel who spoke to him had departed,
6 He lodgeth with one Simon a tanner, whose house is by the sea side: he shall tell thee what thou oughtest to do.	he called two of his servants and a devout soldier from among those that waited on him, 8 and having related everything to them, he sent them to
7 And when the angel which spake unto Cornelius was departed, he called two of his household servants, and a devout soldier of them that waited on him continually;	Joppa.
8 And when he had declared all these things unto them, he sent them to Joppa.	
30 And Cornelius said, Four days ago I was fasting until this hour; and at the ninth hour I prayed in my house, and, behold, a man stood before me in bright clothing,	30 And Cornelius said, "Four days ago, about this hour, I was keeping the ninth hour of prayer in my house; and behold, a man stood before me in bright apparel, 31 saying, 'Cor-

293

31 And said, Cornelius, thy prayer is heard, and thine alms are had in remembrance in the sight of God.

32 Send therefore to Joppa, and call hither Simon, whose surname is Peter; he is lodged in the house of one Simon a tanner by the sea side: who, when he cometh, shall speak unto thee.

33 Immediately therefore I sent to thee; and thou hast well done that thou art come. Now therefore are we all here present before God, to hear all things that are commanded thee of God.

nelius, your prayer has been heard and your alms have been remembered before God. 32 Send therefore to Joppa and ask for Simon who is called Peter; he is lodging in the house of Simon, a tanner, by the seaside.' 33 So I sent to you at once, and you have been kind enough to come. Now therefore we are all here present in the sight of God, to hear all that you have been commanded by the Lord."

MEMORY SELECTION: O God, thou art my God; early will I seek thee; my soul thirsteth for thee, my flesh longeth for thee in a dry and thirsty land, where no water is. Psalm 63:1.

HOME DAILY BIBLE READINGS

May 29. M. Prayer of the Troubled Heart, Psalm 61:1–8.
May 30. T. Waiting for God, Psalm 62:1–7.
May 31. W. Confidence in God, Psalm 62:8–12.
June 1. T. The Mighty God, Psalm 50:1–6.
June 2. F. Urged to Pray, I Timothy 1:18; 2:7.
June 3. S. Jesus Prayed, Too, Mark 6:45–52.
June 4. S. The Thirsty Soul ,Psalm 63:1–8.

BACKGROUND

The lessons for the next three months are lessons on "The Bible and the Devotional Life." In this series, the lesson for today is important for two reasons: it offers an introduction to the devotional resources of the Bible, and it offers the example of a truly religious man. Strangely enough, this man was not a Christian; Cornelius was a Roman centurion and a Gentile. But, says the *King James Version*, he was a *devout* man, one who feared God and sought communication with Him as God of both Jew and Gentile.

He was the first Gentile to be admitted into the fellowship of the Christian church; his "devoutness" broke the old barriers of prejudice. We are to discover in this man what devoutness really is, what the devotional life is like.

NOTES ON THE PRINTED TEXT

I. A devout man, and one that feared God with all his house, which gave much alms to the people, and prayed to God always, Acts 10:2. The *New English Bible* translates: "He was a religious man, and he and his whole family joined in the worship of God. He gave generously to help the Jewish people, and was regular in his prayers to God." This stamps him as something more than an ordinary man. As a Roman military officer stationed in Caesarea, he was a centurion in what was known as "The Italian Cohort"—a company of freedmen frequently used by the Roman authorities to put down any riots or disorders among the Jews. "Centurions," says an old historian, "are desired not to be overbold and reckless so much as good leaders, *of steady and prudent mind,* not prone

to take the offensive to start fighting wantonly, but able when overwhelmed and hard pressed to stand fast and die at their posts."

Mark those words: "of steady and prudent mind." In such a mind lies
the roots of devotion. Here was a soldier trained in the art of war, accustomed to its brutality, almost instinctive in courage and loyalty to
his superiors and the emperor. But within him burned a greater loyalty
—to God. Above the horror and mercilessness of war, he feared (loved)
God. He was what the New Testament called a "God-fearer"—one who
wanted something better, higher than the worship of the old pagan gods
and the immoralities of their old faiths. Cornelius was like that.

He did his job as a soldier, but "he prayed constantly to God." Despised by the Jews, he still prayed, still worshiped "with all his house"
the one God of the Jewish faith. He did not go all the way with the Jews;
he did not accept circumcision and the law, but he was better than
many a Jew who did accept these things in that he loved both Jew and
Gentile and sought guidance in prayer to be brother to both. That
desire must be present in any man who turns to God for help and
guidance in devotion.

He had his troubles, if not his doubts, about the whisperings of God
in his heart. He did not see this God clearly, completely—*but he wanted
to!* He prayed for that—and God heard him, and through an angel told
him to send for a man who knew God well—Peter, who was then in
Joppa.

We read that Cornelius and his family "gave much alms to the people."
Remember that! While the light within him did not yet reveal fully
the God he longed for, he gave alms—he "gave liberally" (RSV) before
he knew certainly. His devotions included not only prayer but also
service. . . . He practiced what he learned in prayer; that was the pattern of his devotional life.

II. It was kind of you to come, Acts 10:33 *(New English Bible).*
Cornelius stands in the doorway of his house, looking at Peter, who has
just arrived from Joppa: Cornelius the Roman, the Gentile, greeting
Peter the Jew, the Christian: what a confrontation *that* was.

When the messengers of Cornelius reached Joppa they "stood before
the gate"—meaning that they stood at the door. No Gentile aware of
Jewish prejudice ever entered a Jewish house without being invited
in—and rarely if ever did he get such an invitation! The bars of prejudice kept them apart. Now the situation was reversed: a Jew waited at
the door of a Gentile, And the future of the Christian faith hung in the
balance as Peter waited to be welcomed. Would the Gentile invite him
in? Or would the old feeling rise between them to keep them forever
apart?

The words of Cornelius to waiting Peter are enough to make our hearts
weep; he said, almost wistfully, "It was kind of you to come." Kind? It
was courage in capitals. There were not many Gentiles who would have
said it, there were not many Jews who would have come so humbly and
quickly to the Gentile's door. But Peter came—because Peter, like Cornelius, had had a vision. Read the account of it, as it is given in Acts
10. Peter praying on the housetop was prepared there for this confrontation with Cornelius, who had prayed constantly with *his* family. In

prayer both their hearts were washed clean and made ready, the old bigotries and prejudices and racial intolerances were overwhelmed, the old barriers smashed. Driven of God, Cornelius sent for Peter; driven of God, Peter came. Two strong men stood face to face; they knelt together in communication with God.

"Now therefore," says Cornelius, "we are all here present before God. . . ." What a prayer meeting! Teacher and seekers on their knees in devotion, listening for the voice (the commands) of God!

The devotional life? It is a life first of all of *humility*. When a man prays, he knows neither Jew nor Gentile, neither orthodox nor pagan, nor Greek nor Roman nor American nor Japanese nor Russian. He knows only that he needs God desperately, and that he must worship in the spirit of love and brotherhood a God who is Lord of *all*. It is a life of courage; it has no place for fear or compromise, or weak excuse. It is a life of understanding: its heart listens to the longing of every other heart. It is a life born of thirst for God: "O God, . . . my soul thirsts for thee; my flesh faints for thee, as in a dry and weary land where no water is" (Psalm 63:1). It is a life of confident prayer: it expects answers, and gets them.

SUGGESTIONS TO TEACHERS

The following emphases are suggested for this lesson:

1. Define "the devotional life," and "devout."
2. Evaluate the devotional life in today's church.
3. Cornelius as a devout man.
4. The importance of the devotional life for the individual and the church.
5. Name men in church history who had significant devotional lives.
6. Point out some great devotional literature.

TOPIC FOR ADULTS
WHAT IS THE DEVOTIONAL LIFE?

Piety. "There is a revealing paragraph in the autobiography of Miss Petre, the Roman Catholic Modernist. . . . She asks, 'What has kept me to the church of my childhood, and what has kept my religion alive and vital in spite of all the spiritual doubts through which I have passed?' And her answer is: 'The spirit of piety.'

"Piety she defines as 'that spirit of joy and delight above the mere sense of duty in which our religious obligations are fulfilled, the spirit of fellowship with God and her church that exists apart from dogmatic beliefs.' "—J. G. McKenzie.

Did you know that one of the meanings of the word "piety" is "pity"? (Think that over carefully.) Piety isn't a mask you put on in church; it has to do with what you do after you leave the church! (It also means "dutifulness in religion." What *kind* of dutifulness does that refer to?)

Piety Again. "To the question, 'Are we our brother's keeper?' comes the resounding cry, 'More than that; we are our brother's brother, to love as we love ourselves—to love as God loved us.' For there is no such thing as true personal piety without social responsibilities! Imprinted on my memory is a brief moment in a New York elevator a couple of years ago when I, all too casually, greeted a Puerto Rican elevator boy with a cheerful, casual, 'How are you this morning?'

"His answer was straight, 'Terrible!' I asked him why, and he replied, 'I'm tired of being poor.' I was reminded again that cheerful Christians filled with piety will not meet the desperate social needs of our day."— *I Give Up, God,* by Bryan Jay Cannon (Fleming H. Revell Company).

Of what *kind* of piety is the author thinking here? And is it true that religious devoutness has as much to do with practice in the street as it has with prayer in church? What did it mean to Peter and Cornelius?

Devotion's Fruit. "What fairer fruit of devotion could one seek than this: A vision of the true worth of what we do day by day? . . . It is appallingly easy to get all mixed up about the relative worth of what we do. When that happens, chaos moves in. We find ourselves measuring the worth of our lives by the number of organizations we belong to rather than by the quality of what we contribute to them and through them. Mothers bemoan the time their families take, thinking they would rather spend it at the bridge table or on the golf links, or even in church organizations. Husbands and wives count a quiet evening at home as 'lost' and wish for a continuous whirl of activities outside the house. Students feel that they are missing a lot if they concentrate on their studies and give little time to the blinding whirl of campus life.

"If we are not aware of this danger and on guard against it, we will become 'hollow men,' empty of conviction, empty of purpose and empty of any sense of real value at all.

"I cannot say that the habit of daily devotion is a guarantee that this will not happen, but I can say that it is the best guarantee we have. It reminds me of a small boy's description of what salt is: 'salt is what spoils the potatoes when you leave it out.' Devotion is what spoils life when we leave it out. When we put it in and put it in regularly we have our best chance to keep our values in order, our lives in proportion, and our vision of life's meaning bright and beautiful."—*Sermons on the Psalms,* by Harold A. Bosley; pp. 54-55. Quoted by permission of Harper & Row, publishers.

Do your devotions have that effect on you?

Brotherhood. Had it not been for the spirit of Christ working on the sensitive, devotional hearts of Peter and Cornelius, they would have lived and died, the one a Jew and the other a Gentile, with nothing in common. In Christ they discovered that they were brothers.

"How foolish is our racial pride! If you were born today, what choice would you have in the matter? None, of course; only a gambler's odds. The odds would be two out of three that you would be born other than white; only one in twenty that you would be born in America; but they would be one in four that you would be Chinese. And there would be nothing you could do about it, even if you wished. In fact, there is no room for pride when we confront the simple odds of birth. The problem of racial confrontation is one we would like to cloak in forgetfulness, but the true dimensions of this problem must be faced. The world is not too dangerous for anything but truth, and is too small for anything but brotherhood."—*Think Small,* by George T. Tade, Texas University.

Questions for Pupils on the Next Lesson: 1. True or false: "All Scripture is infallibly inspired"? 2. What should parents teach very young children about the Scriptures? 3. For what is Scripture "profitable," according to Paul? 4. What is the meaning of the word "statutes" in Psalm 119:12? 5. What "wondrous things" (Psalm 119:18) have you found in the Bible? 6. Is all Scripture of equal value? 7. How do you use the Bible in your devotional life?

TOPIC FOR YOUTH
DEVELOPING MY DEVOTIONAL LIFE

Devotions. "Charles Kingsley used to lean from his pulpit in the village church in Eversley and say, 'Here we are again, to talk about what is going on in your soul and mind.' Where else but in church does that happen? Every person needs consistently and voluntarily to put himself in an atmosphere where his mind is sensitized to his weaknesses and his sins, and where he catches a glimpse of what he, through Christ, is capable of becoming."—Dr. Kenneth A. Carlson.

Question: Do you know anyone who has developed spiritually and devotionally without the help of the church? Describe him.

The Bloody Jap. Perhaps the greatest lesson in the story of Peter and Cornelius is that when two men meet and follow Christ they can no longer be divided by race, color, creed or . . . !

"During my days in seminary, I met a Japanese divinity student, Toshihito Takami. Other students had told me about him long before I met him. He had been a kamikaze pilot during World II. As you may recall, these pilots would take off in a plane loaded with bombs, without parachute and with only enough fuel for a one-way trip to the target—the American ships. Once over the target, they would proceed to put their planes into a steep dive and crash onto the deck of the ship. (For those of you who are wondering, I might explain that the war ended the day before Toshihito Takami was to make his suicidal flight.)

"I had read books and seen movies depicting these men, so I could not help but see him as my enemy. But I got to know "Tom," as we called him. I worked with him, studied with him, played with him, worshiped with him. I learned how he had been drafted into the air force, and how he had been brainwashed. I came to understand the joys and sorrows of his life. One night, Tom shared with me his plans for returning to Japan to serve Christ in the rural ministry.

"I found that Toshihito Takami was not a 'bloody Jap,' but that, in the deepest sense, he was my brother."—Levon G. King, "The Enemy Within," *Pulpit Digest,* January, 1970. Quoted by permission.

The truly devout Christian is brother to Christ and to all men; his habits of devotion make him like that.

The Holiest Moment. We have all had great, inspiring moments in church as we listened to a stirring sermon, or to a prayer that went deep into our hearts, or as we sat silently praying by ourselves. But Canon Ernest Southcott of England feels that there is another "holiest moment" in our devotions that is as meaningful as these:

"The holiest moment of the church service is the moment when God's people—strengthened by preaching and sacrament—go out of the church door into the world to be the church. We don't go to church; we are the church."

It may be so. It may be that the greatest moments in the devotional lives of Peter and Cornelius were not those moments when they sat with their friends in public worship, but those moments when they knocked on each other's doors. . . .

When? Where? When and where do we develop our devotional lives —and *how?*

We once asked a fine Christian friend of ours when and where and how he prayed and worshiped. As nearly as we can recall, he said something like this:

"Prayer? Worship? I pray constantly. I pray when I fall asleep at night and when I thank God for the morning. I pray when I meet an unfortunate man on the sidewalk. I pray at my desk when I am tempted to "pull off" a shady deal. I pray when I look into the eyes of my children. I pray when I read the headlines of my newspaper. I pray when I hear that a baby has been born or someone has died. Prayer? Worship? I do it constantly, like breathing. . . ."

Sentence Sermon to Remember: Hurried "devotions" become nothing but religious "commotions."—Anonymous.

Questions for Pupils on the Next Lesson: 1. What is the Bible *for?* 2. How early should a child be instructed in the Scriptures? 3. Who taught Timothy when he was a child? 4. Which "Scriptures" did he probably study? 5. Is the Bible inspired against human error? 6. Is Christianity founded on the Bible? 7. What answers to which of your problems have you found in the Bible?

LESSON II—JUNE 11

MEETING GOD THROUGH THE SCRIPTURES

Background Scripture: Psalm 119:9–18, 97–104;
II Timothy 3:14–17
Devotional Reading: Psalm 119:97–104

KING JAMES VERSION

II TIMOTHY 3   14 But continue thou in the things which thou hast learned and hast been assured of, knowing of whom thou hast learned them;

15 And that from a child thou hast known the holy Scriptures, which are able to make thee wise unto salvation through faith which is in Christ Jesus.

16 All Scripture is given by inspiration of God, and is profitable for doctrine, for reproof, for correction, for instruction in righteousness:

17 That the man of God may be perfect, thoroughly furnished unto all good works.

PSALM 119   9 wherewithal shall a young man cleanse his way? by taking heed thereto according to thy word.

10 With my whole heart have I sought thee: O let me not wander from thy commandments.

11 Thy word have I hid in mine heart, that I might not sin against thee.

12 Blessed art thou, O Lord: teach me thy statutes.

13 With my lips have I declared all the judgments of thy mouth.

14 I have rejoiced in the way of thy testimonies, as much as in all riches.

15 I will meditate in thy precepts, and have respect unto thy ways.

16 I will delight myself in thy statutes: I will not forget thy word.

Gimel

17 Deal bountifully with thy servant, that I may live, and keep thy word.

18 Open thou mine eyes, that I may behold wondrous things out of thy law.

REVISED STANDARD VERSION

II TIMOTHY 3   14 But as for you, continue in what you have learned and have firmly believed, knowing from whom you learned it 15 and how from childhood you have been acquainted with the sacred writings which are able to instruct you for salvation through faith in Christ Jesus. 16 All scripture is inspired by God and profitable for teaching, for reproof, for correction, and for training in righteousness, 17 that the man of God may be complete, equipped for every good work.

PSALM 119   9 How can a young man keep his way pure?
By guarding it according to thy word.

10 With my whole heart I seek thee;
let me not wander from thy commandments!

11 I have laid up thy word in my heart,
that I might not sin against thee.

12 Blessed be thou, O Lord;
teach me thy statutes!

13 With my lips I declare
all the ordinances of thy mouth.

14 In the way of thy testimonies I delight
as much as in all riches.

15 I will meditate on thy precepts,
and fix my eyes on thy ways.

16 I will delight in thy statutes;
I will not forget thy word.

17 Deal bountifully with thy servant,
that I may live and observe thy word.

18 Open my eyes, that I may behold
wondrous things out of thy law.

MEMORY SELECTION: With my whole heart I seek thee; let me not wander from thy commandments. Psalm 119:10 (RSV).

HOME DAILY BIBLE READINGS

June 5. M. Keeping God's Laws, Psalm 119:1–8.
June 6. T. Understanding God's Word, Psalm 119:25–32.
June 7. W. Living God's Law, Psalm 119:33–40.
June 8. T. Salvation Through God's Word, Psalm 119:41–48.
June 9. F. Held Steady by God's Word, Psalm 119:129–136.
June 10. S. The Light of God's Word, Psalm 119:105–112.
June 11. S. Love of God's Word, Psalm 119:99–104.

BACKGROUND

This lesson might be titled, "What Is the Bible *For?*" We call it a "library," but it is not a random collection of "sacred writings" gleaned from many centuries. It is a book written with one purpose: to give us a living, working conception of God, and to help us meet Him in the writings of inspired men who had met and loved Him long before we were born.

Two of these writings are offered as Scripture portions for the lesson: one from the Old Testament, one from the New. Timothy, whom Paul loved, is advised to remember what he was taught from childhood up, about the Scriptures; he was undoubtedly taught the meaning of the 119th Psalm, in the most devotional book in all Scripture. That Psalm tells us a great deal about the devotional value of the Bible, but we shall have to find out for ourselves *how* to use it!

The two Scripture portions were written centuries apart, but they have the zest and tang and beauty and power of proven, ancient truth in the heart of a young man. . . .

NOTES ON THE PRINTED TEXT

I. But as for you, continue in what you have learned . . . with sacred writings which are able to instruct you for salvation through faith in Christ Jesus, II Timothy 3:14, 15. Timothy's religious education began the day he was born; he had a religiously devoted mother and grand-mother—Eunice and Lois—and they began very early teaching him the sacred Scriptures of his people. (See Acts 16:1 and II Timothy 1:5). Of his father, a Greek, we know nothing; it was the mother and grand-mother who gave him his religious training. (Isn't it *usually* the mother who "takes care of the religious department" during *our* childhood?) It was so with the Hebrews; someone has said that the Hebrew baby drank the Jewish law in his mother's milk. Bend the twig, and . . . !

What was the Scripture in which they trained him? It was Old Testament Scripture; there was no New Testament when Timothy was born. But the Old is the background of the New, and one cannot understand either until he understands both.

What did these two women teach this boy? They taught him that the Scriptures were *Holy*—sacred; they had a divine purpose: they were "able to make thee wise unto salvation through faith which is in Christ Jesus." They were the *background* of Jesus; they predicted His coming. That was of first importance. Second, he was taught that the Scriptures were "profitable" (or powerful) in telling him what was wrong and what was right in his behavior. It gave him not human but divine standards with which to measure his life. It was food "for correction, for instruction in righteousness" (verse 16). No man ever went wrong following the suggestions and commandments of the Bible! Timothy didn't go wrong; he grew into a consciousness of God in Christ Jesus as he built on the ancient prophets and the law.

He was also taught that "all Scripture is given by inspiration." We can argue over what inspiration is in this sense if we wish—but it will get us nowhere. To most of us the Bible is inspired because it inspires us as no other book, no other writing, can. It is God-inspired because it has confounded and won out over every enemy of God assailing it. It is inspired because it holds truth which cannot be broken. Dr. Barclay, whom we have quoted often in this book, says, "It is perfectly true . . . that Christianity is not founded on a printed book, but on a living person, but the fact remains that the only place in the world where we get a first-hand account of that person and of His teaching is in the New Testament." You can't put it better than that.

So the Bible remains the inevitable and invaluable textbook for Christian teaching. Without it, we teach in darkness.

II. Wherewithal shall a young man cleanse his way? Psalm 119:9. It says a *young* man. A young man, just starting on the road of life—how shall he keep his life clean? Before he dies, he will hear a million voices telling him to go this way, to go that way, to do this but not to do that. The Psalmist instructs the young man to be careful and to choose wisely —and to "take heed" not to the voices of men but "according to *thy* word."

Youth is full of dreams; many doors are open to them, and the dreams all look good until the young man opens them, when he finds—sometimes too late—that he has been deceived into entering what he *thought* was good, only to find it wasn't. Most young men seek the *best;* they want what will be best for them. "With my whole soul have I sought thee: O let me not wander from thy commandments" (verse 10)! There it is —the signpost of God, set at every crossroads of human life. It's clear enough, but either we miss it entirely or ignore it when we see it, and go off down the wrong road.

"Thy word have I hid in mine heart . . ." (verse 11). Most of us got the Word at our mothers' knees, or in the love and teaching of our fathers; one way or another, it was planted in our hearts. But some seed falls on good ground and some falls on barren ground. The world crowds in upon us; sooner or later, said Wordsworth, ". . . getting and spending, we waste our powers. . . ." And "the contagion of the world's slow stain" spreads in heart and character, and the dream is lost, and the man is not what God hoped for in the youth. But the hope never fully dies; it remains in the worst of us, a wistful longing in the heart to be better than we are.

"I will meditate in thy precepts . . ." (verse 15). "I will fix my eyes on thy ways" (RSV). *When?* Near life's end or at its beginning? The Psalmist is pleading with us here to fix our eyes on God at the start, and follow as He directs, not as we *wish* to go. "Thy will, not mine, be done" is a far better guide for the young than "I will work it out for myself, and do as I please." If we "delight" in His law and do not forget His

Word, our lives will be as clean and as profitable as we wish. If not, we walk toward death in a fog.

"Deal bountifully with thy servant. . . . Open thou mine eyes . . ." (verses 17, 18). He will deal bountifully; His patience with us is unbelievable, His mercy wide as the sea—but even the sea has its shores, its limits.

This, then, is the God we meet in the Scriptures: a God who in love lays down the laws and the law, who points the way we should go. This is the God to whom we must listen, in Scripture. This we must know: no man who walks His way ever walks the wrong road.

SUGGESTIONS TO TEACHERS

Think on these things by way of discussion:

1. Define "inspiration" as it relates to Scripture.
2. Is all Scripture of equal value?
3. How to listen to God in Scripture.
4. How to use the Bible in devotional life.
5. The centrality of the Bible for devotional life.

TOPIC FOR ADULTS
MEETING GOD THROUGH THE SCRIPTURES

A Friend. "If a child is brought up with a fair acquaintance with the Bible itself, his intellectual difficulties are resolved as they come along, because he has the materials to work with. But if he first hears the story of Balaam's ass from a drugstore atheist, the story gets what the newspapers call a wrong angle in the mind from the start. If he has been brought up on the Bible, he respects it, and suspends judgment on each apparently conflicting truth as his education proceeds. The book is a friend whose friendship no new acquaintance can easily upset."—Lt. Commander C. Leslie Glenn.

Love Letter. "A young lady, asked to explain what is meant by devotional reading of the Bible, answered: 'Yesterday morning I received a letter from one to whom I had given my heart and devoted my life. I have read that letter five times, not because I did not understand it at the first reading, nor because I expected to commend myself to the author by frequent reading of his epistle. It was not with me a question of duty, but simply one of pleasure. I read it because I am devoted to the one who wrote.'

"To read the Bible with the same motive is to read it devotionally, and to the one who reads it in that spirit it is indeed a love letter."—*The Presbyterian.*

The Bible. "We don't have to defend the Bible. It was not written by angels, as Joseph Smith said the Mormon Bible was, [and] signed, sealed and delivered out of heaven. The Bible is a very earthy, human book. It came up out of the rich mine of human experience with a lot of earth stuff clinging to it. It was not written wholly about good men, or even wholly by bad men. It was written chiefly about sinful men—men and women with streaky natures like our own who, on their own confession, were so dull of mind and spirit that they could not understand the speech of God.

"Some people are disappointed to discover that the Bible is not a textbook with chapters—one, two, three, explaining God—that it does not put down in plain easy words who God is and what He is like. It is not a textbook of answers to our questions. In fact, it is not a book. It's a collection of pamphlets written over a period of at least twelve hundred years in at least three languages by at least thirty persons, many of whom had no idea they were writing anything for the ages. The Bible is the story of the progressive revelation of God to the minds of men through their experiences, and therefore it is the story of a long and patient process in which the Almighty Father teaches His children as you must teach yours—gradually, line upon line, trying to break through the barrier of dullness—with repeated failures and with many words left unspoken because they could not take it in."—*Who Goes There?*, by J. Wallace Hamilton (Fleming H. Revell Company).

Using the Bible. "How have you used the Bible this week? Did you use it to win an argument? Did you defeat your wife, your husband, your mother, your son, your daughter, your neighbor? Did you prove that you were right? Is that the purpose of the Bible? Or did you use it as a pill—to make you forget about your responsibilities in this world?

"Some people have died by only *reading* the Bible. Some people have died spiritually as they have memorized it, but nothing more. Some people have died as they have used the Bible to prove that they were right. But, thank God, many are *alive* today because they have discovered that the Bible is the Word of God. It is the voice of God. It is the voice of God coming to us and saying, 'Believe! Trust! Risk! Go! Do!'

"I think there is a great sign of life in the Christian church. For I believe that Bible *worship* is dying and that once again people are hearing God speak through an instrument called the Bible . . . that once again people are worshiping *God* . . . that once again people love God . . . that once again the Bible is the servant of the living God to bring people to God."—Marcus Gravdal, in *The Lutheran Standard*, September 20, 1966.

Not Enough. "It is not enough to own a Bible; we must read it. It is not enough to read it; we must let it speak to us. It is not enough to let it speak to us; we must believe it. It is not enough to believe it; we must live it."—*Thoughts of a Christian Optimist*, by William Arthur Ward (Froke House).

Priority. "Ask anyone who said the words, 'Of the people, by the people and for the people,' and he will likely respond, 'Lincoln, in his Gettysburg Address.' Yet in John Wycliffe's introduction to his 1382 translation of the Bible, these words occur: 'The Bible is for the government of the people, by the people, and for the people.'"—*Maritime Baptist*.

The Bible isn't just a book to be read for pleasure, even just for comfort; it is the priority book of all literature, to be read in order that we might understand that the head of all man's government is none other than God. . . .

Questions for Pupils on the Next Lesson: 1. How do you define the

word "prayer"? 2. Explain: "They have their reward" (Matthew 6:5).
3. How can you detect hypocrisy in prayer? 4. What does the Lord's
Prayer *demand?* 5. What does "hallowed" mean? 6. Is Matthew 6:11 a
bit selfish? 7. Name three kinds of prayer.

TOPIC FOR YOUTH
MEETING GOD THROUGH THE BIBLE

Revealing. We say that we meet God in the Bible. But what *kind* of
God do we meet there? Leslie D. Weatherhead explains:

> "1. The Bible reveals a God who cares.
> 2. The Bible reveals the purposefulness of God.
> 3. The Bible reveals a God who cannot be defeated.
> 4. The Bible reveals a God who endlessly seeks to be the friend and guide
> and saviour of men."

And He reveals all this in one Person named . . . ?

Something More. "Bobby Richardson, the Yankee baseball star, says
this about the Bible:

"Put a man in a baseball suit, give him a glove and a bat—but that
doesn't make him a star. Nor will all the practice in the world get some
people into the major leagues. Something more important is needed.

"It's also true that if you put a man in church and give him a hymnbook or a Bible, it doesn't make him a Christian. Not singing all the
hymns in the world will do that—not even reading the Bible from cover
to cover will do that.

"That's why something more is needed when you read the Bible. We
call it the Spirit. Read the Bible and let its message live in you, for 'not
the readers of the law are just before God, but the doers shall be justified.' "—*Sourcebook for Speakers,* by Eleanor Doan (Zondervan Publishing House).

The Face. "I have heard of a picture of the Constitution of the United
States very skillfully engraved in copper plate so that when you looked
at it closely it was not anything more than a piece of writing. But when
you looked at it from a distance it was the face of George Washington.
The face shone out in the shading of the letters at a distance, and one
could see the person, not the words or the ideas.

"And that is the way to look at the Scriptures and to understand the
foundation on which they rest. Let men say what they will about this or
that word or idea in the Bible. If you will but stand and look at it, you
will see shining through it and into your heart the face of Jesus Christ."
—Raymond Calkins.

. . . and that is the *purpose* of Bible study. . . .

Faith for the Future. "Some years ago, I was invited to 10 Downing
Street in London by Sir Winston Churchill. It was a dark hour in Britain's
history, and the Prime Minister was deeply discouraged. He had hardly
greeted me before he asked, 'Young man, do you have any hope for the
world?' I took a New Testament from my pocket, saying, 'Mr. Prime
Minister, this book is full of hope.' Quickly, he replied, 'Would you read
me some passages?'

"For the next 30 minutes I read selections that I thought would fit his mood. As I left, he said warmly, 'I thank you. You have given an old man a renewal of faith for the future.'

"I hadn't. But the Bible had."—Billy Graham, *What the Bible Says to Me,* in *Reader's Digest,* May, 1969.

Faith for tomorrow: the Bible offers that to youth. . . .

Lawsuit. A year or so ago (was it 1968?) two ministers, backed by the American Council of Christian Churches, took the University of Washington to court over its offer of a course of study in the Bible. Washington was a state supported university, and the ministers complained that such a university had no right to teach such a course, since the Bible, in their words, is "the infallible revelation from God to man," and as such is not "the proper object of scholarly study."

The case was carried up to the state Supreme Court, which ruled against the ministers; it held that the course was not "slanted" or aimed at a particular theology or interpretation of the Bible.

Well—*should* the Bible be "protected" from scholars . . . ?

A Chapter a Day. Woodrow Wilson and Henry Ford once decided that they would read a chapter of the Bible every day, come what may! They did; they kept the pledge for thirty years.

Said President Wilson: "I should be afraid to go forward if I did not believe that there was, at the foundation of all our schooling and of all of our thought, this unimpeachable and incomparable Word of God. A soul that has been refreshed and made happy early in the morning by prayer and communion with God and His book meets the service, trials and temptations of the day with a power different from that of one who has had no spiritual preparation."

A chapter a day does it!

Sentence Sermon to Remember: I consider an intimate knowledge of the Bible an indispensable qualification of a well-educated man.—Robert A. Millikan.

Questions for Pupils on the Next Lesson: 1. What problems have you about prayer? 2. How selfish are you in prayer? 3. How does God "lead us into temptation"? 4. How does God "reward" prayer? 5. What trespasses did you commit last week? 6. If God knows what we need before we pray, why do we pray at all? 7. Write a prayer in fifty words or less that you can pray anywhere at any time.

LESSON III—JUNE 18

MEETING GOD THROUGH PRAYER

Background Scripture: Matthew 6:1–15
Devotional Reading: Isaiah 55:1–6

KING JAMES VERSION

MATTHEW 6 5 And when thou prayest, thou shalt not be as the hypocrites are: for they love to pray standing in the synagogues and in the corners of the streets, that they may be seen of men. Verily I say unto you, They have their reward.

6 But thou, when thou prayest, enter into thy closet and when thou hast shut thy door, pray to thy Father which is in secret; and thy Father which seeth in secret shall reward thee openly.

7 But when ye pray, use not vain repetitions, as the heathen do: for they think that they shall be heard for their much speaking.

8 Be not ye therefore like unto them: for your Father knoweth what things ye have need of, before ye ask him.

9 After this manner therefore pray ye: Our Father which art in heaven, Hallowed be thy name.

10 Thy kingdom come. Thy will be done in earth, as it is in heaven.

11 Give us this day our daily bread.

12 And forgive us our debts, as we forgive our debtors.

13 And lead us not into temptation, but deliver us from evil: For thine is the kingdom, and the power, and the glory, for ever. Amen.

14 For if ye forgive men their trespasses, your heavenly Father will also forgive you:

15 But if ye forgive not men their trespasses, neither will your Father forgive your trespasses.

REVISED STANDARD VERSION

MATTHEW 6 5 "And when you pray, you must not be like the hypocrites; for they love to stand and pray in the synagogues and at the street corners, that they may be seen by men. Truly, I say to you, they have their reward. 6 But when you pray, go into your room and shut the door and pray to your Father who is in secret; and your Father who sees in secret will reward you.

7 "And in praying do not heap up empty phrases as the Gentiles do; for they think that they will be heard for their many words. 8 Do not be like them, for your Father knows what you need before you ask him. 9 Pray then like this:

Our Father who art in heaven,
Hallowed be thy name.

10 Thy kingdom come,
Thy will be done,
On earth as it is in heaven.

11 Give us this day our daily bread;

12 And forgive us our debts,
As we also have forgiven our debtors;

13 And lead us not into temptation,
But deliver us from evil.

14 For if you forgive men their trespasses, your heavenly Father also will forgive you; 15 but if you do not forgive men their trespasses, neither will your Father forgive your trespasses."

MEMORY SELECTION: Seek ye the Lord while he may be found, call upon him while he is near. Isaiah 55:6.

HOME DAILY BIBLE READINGS

June 12. M. Teach Us to Pray, Luke 11:1–13.
June 13. T. The Nature of Prayer, Luke 18:9–14.
June 14. W. When You Pray, Matthew 6:5–18.

BACKGROUND

Our Scripture for this lesson is a part of Christ's Sermon on the Mount
—and a very important part. Many of us can quote most of it from
memory: there is no other prayer to equal what we call "The Lord's
prayer," so it is well worth memorizing—*and studying.*

In this passage, Jesus deals with three forms or emphases of Jewish
piety: benevolence, prayer, and repentance. And in every one of them,
He calls for one common requisite: genuineness or sincerity. He starts
with what we might call an eleventh Commandment: "Don't be a hypo-
crite!" Then He proceeds to illustrate hypocrisy in prayer. But He doesn't
stop there; Jesus never stopped anywhere with a "Don't!" He gives us a
model prayer as near perfection as any prayer can be. It is altogether
lovely—and *demanding.*

NOTES ON THE PRINTED TEXT

*I. . . . for they love to stand and pray in the synagogues and at the
street corners,* Matthew 6:5 (rsv). This could be retranslated, "When
you pray, don't be a show-off." A well phrased and well thought out
prayer is a joy to the heart, but a prayer that is nothing more than words,
words, words *addressed to people* is hypocrisy. Jesus saw a lot of hypocrisy in prayer among His people. Often in the synagogue people who
wanted to build reputations for piety would stop saying the stated prayers with all the congregation, and, to attract attention, sing out their
own private, self-righteous little personal prayers. On street corners, they
would stand for as much as three hours in the posture of prayer; when
the "hour of prayer" would sound, they were careful to be caught in
some public place, where everybody could see them. To Jesus, this was
a caricature of prayer. Let our prayers be genuinely honest—and not
demonstrative.

Jesus was also suspicious of another tendency in prayer: the tendency
to use "vain repetitions" and "heap up empty phrases." *The New English Bible* translates, "In your prayers do not go babbling like the heathen,
who imagine that the more they say the more likely they are to be heard."
(Forgive us for quoting so much from the NEB; it is a beautiful translation.) It isn't the words in prayer that count; it is the sincerity behind
them, the sincerity most often found in the prayers we offer up *in secret*
—when we stand alone before God. It isn't that Jesus is disparaging
public prayer. He is saying only that corporate prayer can often lack
sincerity and be nothing but a compliance with church ritual. We need
private prayer to add depth to public prayer.

"Do not be like them, for your Father knows what you need before
you ask him" (6:8, rsv). Says J. R. Dummelow here: "Prayer is not to
inform God of our needs, as the heathen think, but that we may have
conscious communion with Him as His children." When Jesus said this,
there was probably someone who asked, "Well, if God knows our needs
before we pray—why pray at all?" It was to answer this question that

Jesus gave His disciples the prayer which bears His name. That prayer ". . . is . . . a giving of our whole selves to God in order that His will may be done in us and by us" (Suzanne de Dietrich).

II. *After this manner therefore pray ye*, Matthew 6:9. The model for prayer which He gave us is divided into two sections: the first section contains petitions related to God; the second, the presenting of the fundamental needs of men.

"Our Father who art in heaven." We have a God who is not a ghost nor an intellectual conception, but a *Father*. Someone has said that "the whole miracle of divine grace is in that single word." Human fathers love as all humans love, but there is a majesty, a holiness about the love of God that passes all understanding. It is not so much a love as a power.

"Hallowed be thy name." Hallowed means "held sacred," or "revered." Old Israel sanctified the name of God in her obedience to Him; she also profaned it in her *disobedience*. So do we; every day of our lives we revere God or desecrate Him *in our conduct*. And we honor Him or insult Him in our ways and attitudes in prayer. Flippant, "smarty" prayers must break His holy heart.

"Thy kingdom come." Some of us pray that line as though the Kingdom were only a wishful hope. But the Kingdom is already here in the lives of those who obey the will of God. The Kingdom is "a society upon earth where God's will is perfectly done, as it is in heaven." We haven't reached such perfection yet, but that doesn't excuse us from trying! The Kingdom will come out of the *individual* will, heart and life. We might well pray, "Bring in thy Kingdom beginning with me." When we pray for the Kingdom we should be praying that *we* may have the courage and the faith to submit ourselves completely to His will. It will never come unless and until we do just that.

"Thy will be done in earth, as it is in heaven." What is in your mind and heart when you say this? Do you say it with a cynical shrug of the shoulders in resentment at some pain or trouble? Or in faith that His will *shall* be done, somehow? Or in resignation, feeling that you can't do or say anything else? Or in love and in determination that at least in *you* His will shall be done? This line in the prayer is no dim hope; it is a call to battle. It is simply a question of struggling until we know the will of God, and then *doing* it.

Now come the sections dealing with the needs of men.

"Give us this day our daily bread." Some scholars say this could be more correctly translated, "Give us our *necessary* bread"—just enough for today, just that which is indispensable to life. He who prays this with understanding of the providence of God has faith that God will care for him tomorrow as well as today; he has no fear of the morrow. . . .

"And forgive us our debts." Sin puts us in debt to God; we can't live long enough to repay *those* debts, so—God, forgive us!—He alone can do that! He will forgive us on one condition: that we have been decent enough to forgive those who have sinned against us. God is the sovereign creditor; to Him we owe *everything*. (Think about that!) We may boast that we "are in debt to no man," but none of us can make that boast to God.

"And lead us not into temptation." This has bothered many of us. Does

God actually tempt us? James says no: "Let no man say when he is tempted, 'I am tempted of God'; for God cannot be tempted with evil, neither tempteth he any man" (1:13, 14). The source of our temptations lies not in God but in our own desires—or it comes from the devil himself (see I Thessalonians 3:5). James is not contradicting Jesus; he knows that God leads us occasionally into circumstances in which our faith is put to the test, as Jesus' faith was put to the test in Gethsemane. Here we might pray, "Lord, lead us not to the test. If it be thy will, spare us this cup, but if we *must* face it, for our own good or for some purpose of thine which we cannot understand, then let us face it like men whose faith cannot be shaken by *any* temptation." We should fear and watch for temptation, and build a faith strong enough to fend it off before it gets its grip on us. Again, the *New English Bible* translates, "And do not bring us to the test, but save us from the evil one."

So ends the Lord's Prayer, except for the closing doxology that sings of the kingdom, the power and the glory. Our Roman Catholic friends are faithful to the original manuscripts in omitting this doxology.

Verse 15 is repetitious; its theme is already stated in verse 12.

SUGGESTIONS TO TEACHERS

It would be easy—too easy!—in this lesson just to talk informally about the Lord's prayer, to take up its teachings, one by one. But that is not the purpose of the lesson: the purpose is to "meet God through prayer." That means that we must know *how* to pray, *what* to pray, where and when to pray, using the Lord's prayer *as a model only*.

Think about it under these headings:

1. The *meaning* of prayer.
2. The centrality of prayer in the devotional life.
3. The problems involved in praying.
4. The *kinds* of prayer.

TOPIC FOR ADULTS
MEETING GOD IN PRAYER

His Prayer. "The first word ('Our') fractured the hermit's life. This plural prayer is not for an only child, but a brotherhood. It smashes barriers, splits the walls of exclusiveness, bursts the little whispering circles and shouts welcome, ringing far and wide. The second word hits harder. 'Are we not all children of one Father?' Others hinted: only Christ dared go so far as to claim Him as Sire. What good is an impersonal God? This prayer is a son's confession, and the rest of it is waste until a man falls to his face, making the prodigal's decision his own: 'I will arise and go to my Father.'"—David A. Redding, "The Lord's Prayer," in *Reader's Digest*, April, 1961.

The Lord's prayer tells us what Jesus thought about the nature of God and what such a God expects us to do. . . .

Prayer Is Reaching. "All prayer is good—the formal, the informal, the talking aloud, the silent, the prayer at desk or table, watching a sunset or a storm; the prayers in church together with one's fellowmen, the prayers in the dark night and the lonely dawn. . . . Prayer is reaching for a hand; prayer is sometimes a spontaneous and selfish petition; prayer is, in secret, a secret. And it always reaches its destination."—Faith Baldwin, in *Science of Mind*.

> Up in Heaven the dear Lord heard and smiled.
> Today she soothed a little, crying child.
> She stopped her work to make old Ella Kloop
> A fragrant, warming bowl of her good soup.
> Her house was orderly, her gardens tended,
> Her children fed, their clothes clean and mended.
> Her husband, home from work, found happiness
> And quiet peace in her deep gentleness.
> The dear Lord smiled again. "Too tired to pray?
> Her hands have offered prayers of love all day."
>
> —Jane Coffin.

Have you noticed that the Lord's Prayer is the shortest in words and longest on action of any prayer ever prayed?

Common Sense Praying. One thing is clear about the Lord's prayer— it is a common sense prayer. It isn't ecstatic, but practical; it goes to the heart of our human problems. It is reverent and relevant, holy and human. We should plan our prayers to resemble His model.

"At our synod, one of the luncheon orators . . . spoke of a lady who had recently arrived among them who was inclined to boast of what she had done in her last church. After a meeting in which she made mention of some of these things, the superintendent closed with prayer, and said, 'Lord, bless Thy servant who has recently come among us. She has worked well for Thy church in other places, so she says. Help her to use common sense, and to work as hard in this corner of Thy vineyard now that she's here.' . . . President Finney of Oberlin had the same habit of directing his prayers both upwards and sideways. At family prayers one morning William, the hired man, heard this petition offered: 'Dear Lord, bless William, and help him to remember to shut the barn doors, for Thou knowest that, if I am encumbered with such cares as these, I cannot give my mind to the care of souls!' "—*Methodist Recorder*.

Irreverent? No! Honest prayer should not only comfort, but inspire; there are times when prayer should *hurt* us into action!

Questions for Pupils on the Next Lesson: 1. What security have you? 2. Why should God be merciful to you? 3. Does this phrase, "My soul is among lions" (Psalm 57:4), apply to you? Describe your lions. 4. What pits (Psalm 57:6) do you fall into *regularly*, and why? 5. Explain the words, "I will awake the dawn" (Psalm 57:8, RSV). 6. What security does the believer in God have that nonbelievers do not have? 7. Do you have any enemies *because you are a Christian?*

TOPIC FOR YOUTH
MEETING GOD THROUGH PRAYER

Finding God. "A friend of mine was talking one day with a friend who was the daughter of Karl Marx. The talk turned, as serious talk naturally turns, to religion.

"The daughter of Marx said, 'I was brought up without any religion. I do not believe in God.' Then she added a little wistfully: 'But the other day in an old German book I came across a German prayer, and if the God of that prayer exists, I think I could believe in Him.'

" 'What was the prayer?' asked my friend.

"She repeated slowly, in German:

> 'Our Father, who art in heaven,
> Hallowed be thy name. Thy kingdom come.
> Thy will be done, on earth as it is in heaven.' "
>
> —Rev. Vincent McNab.

Which Channel? "Football games in some sections of the country are preceded by an invocation, and the invocation often includes phrases like 'that great Quarterback in the Sky.' At last year's Oklahoma-Nebraska game in Norman, Oklahoma, the clergyman concluded by saying, 'and dear Lord, we invite you to take time out from your busy schedule to watch our game this afternoon.' Seconds later a telephone rang in the press box, and a fellow sitting there said, 'He wants to know which channel it's on.' "—*Sports Illustrated,* May 19, 1969.

The "fellow" may seem irreverent to some of us, but he inspires disturbing questions. Is such a prayer in such a place *reverent?* Does prayer belong in a football stadium, or in a prize-fight ring? Do we shame God by thoughtless prayer? And what would He think of the "invitation" mentioned above?

Body, Mind. If the last story tells us how *not* to pray, this one may tell us *how.* . . .

"Lord, deliver me from blinking out my earthly days like a contented toad. Let me find your works forever new, wonderful, challenging. Let me pass on, please, while I'm hepped to the heels in a new project. While I'm here, let me learn to ignore my creaky body. I'll be so grateful, Father, if you help me keep my mental motor running."—Verle Andres, in *We Turn New Leaves.*

God *must* hear a prayer like that!

By All Means! "When the Duke of Wellington was an old man he acquired the habit of making his presence known vocally. Whenever the clergyman who was leading the worship would say, 'Let us pray,' the Duke would bark out in a loud voice, 'By all means!' That gives us an amusing picture of a great man, but it also has a sharp point for remembrance,

"Whenever the invitation to pray is given, the answer should be a hearty, 'By all means,' not vocally, but nevertheless sincerely. Our world needs the power of God, and prayer is a means by which that power comes into life. We cannot chart the way by which God's power finds a channel into the world. But we do know that power for good *has* come into the world through lives that were open to God in praying."—*Christian Herald.*

We and God. "Too many people think of prayer as a kind of magic, a kind of divine Aladdin's lamp in which, in some mysterious way, we command the power of God to work for us. Prayer is not the easy way out. God will never do for us what we can do for ourselves.

"Any wise parent knows that real parenthood does not mean doing things for the child; it means enabling the child to do things for himself. In the same way, prayer is not so much God doing things for us as it is we and God doing things together."—A *Guide to Daily Prayer*, by William Barclay. Copyright 1962 by Harper & Row.

Island Prayer. A Christian minister in Hawaii, Mr. Wong, listened to the prayers read out over the radio by a disc jockey, and he objected that the prayers were for another century. Invited by the jockey to write a prayer for *this* century that he might use on the air, Mr. Wong wrote this one for the people of Hawaii—a people in whose blood flows strains of every racial and national blood known to man:

> Lord, thou hast many hands of mercy
>   in the tenderness of Roman Catholic nuns,
>   in the warm pity of Salvation Army soldiers,
>   and in the caring of Jewish doctors.
> Use us also, if we can no more than say a
>   healing word of love.

That is praying the Lord's prayer in today's language for today's people as Jesus might pray it for us were He here . . . !

Sentence Sermon to Remember: I used to pray that God would do this or that; now I pray that God will make His will known to me.— Mme. Chiang Kai-shek.

Questions for Pupils on the Next Lesson: 1. What is the worst threat to your religious faith? 2. What do we need to be really "secure"? 3. With how much of your life do you trust God? 4. How did Christ escape the plots and pitfalls of His enemies? 5. Do you agree with the words of Job: "Though he slay me, yet will I trust him"? 6. Does God intervene in the affairs of men to protect them? Give evidence. 7. What do you mean when you say that "God is a God who *cares*"?

LESSON IV—JUNE 25

HUNGER FOR SECURITY

Background Scripture: Psalms 57; 90:13–17;
Isaiah 6:1–6; Romans 8:28–39
Devotional Reading: Psalm 90:13–17

KING JAMES VERSION

PSALM 57 Be merciful unto me, O God, be merciful unto me: for my soul trusteth in thee: yea, in the shadow of thy wings will I make my refuge, until these calamities be overpast.

2 I will cry unto God most high; unto God that performeth all things for me.
3 He shall send from heaven, and save me from the reproach of him that would swallow me up. Selah. God shall send forth his mercy and his truth.

4 My soul is among lions: and I lie even among them that are set on fire, even the sons of men, whose teeth are spears and arrows, and their tongue a sharp sword.
5 Be thou exalted, O God, above the heavens; let thy glory be above all the earth.

6 They have prepared a net for my steps; my soul is bowed down: they have digged a pit before me, into the midst whereof they are fallen themselves. Selah.
7 My heart is fixed, O God, my heart is fixed: I will sing and give praise.
8 Awake up, my glory; awake, psaltery and harp: I myself will awake early.
9 I will praise thee, O Lord among the people: I will sing unto thee among the nations.

10 For thy mercy is great unto the heavens, and thy truth unto the clouds.

11 Be thou exalted, O God, above the heavens: let thy glory be above all the earth.

REVISED STANDARD VERSION

PSALM 57 Be merciful to me, O God, be merciful to me,
for in thee my soul takes refuge;
in the shadow of thy wings I will take refuge,
till the storms of destruction pass by.
2 I cry to God Most High,
to God who fulfils his purpose for me.
3 He will send from heaven and save me,
he will put to shame those who trample upon me. *Selah*
God will send forth his steadfast love and his faithfulness!
4 I lie in the midst of lions
that greedily devour the sons of men;
their teeth are spears and arrows,
their tongues sharp swords.
5 Be exalted, O God, above the heavens!
Let thy glory be over all the earth!
6 They set a net for my steps;
my soul was bowed down.
They dug a pit in my way,
but they have fallen into it themselves. *Selah*
7 My heart is steadfast, O God,
my heart is steadfast!
I will sing and make melody!
8 Awake, my soul!
Awake, O harp and lyre!
I will awake the dawn!
9 I will give thanks to thee, O Lord, among the peoples;
I will sing praises to thee among the nations.
10 For thy steadfast love is great to the heavens,
thy faithfulness to the clouds.
11 Be exalted, O God, above the heavens!
Let thy glory be over all the earth!

314

MEMORY SELECTION: For I am persuaded, that neither death, nor life, nor angels, nor principalities, nor powers, nor things present, nor things to come, nor height, nor depth, nor any other creature, shall be able to separate us from the love of God, which is in Christ Jesus our Lord. Romans 8:38, 39.

HOME DAILY BIBLE READINGS

June 19. M. *Longing for Sanctuary*, Psalm 84:1–7, 10–12.
June 20. T. *Deliverance From Death*, Psalm 88:1–9.
June 21. W. *Steadfast in Trouble*, Psalm 57:1–7.
June 22. T. *The Door to Abundant Life*, John 10:1–18.
June 23. F. *Praying for Deliverance*, Psalm 54:1–7.
June 24. S. *God, Source of Security*, Psalm 91:1–12.
June 25. S. *Glad, Even in Affliction*, Psalm 90:13–17.

BACKGROUND

A Psalm is a sacred song or poem; the *Book* of Psalms is a collection of the sacred songs and poems of Israel gathered over a period of centuries, of which at least seventy-three are connected with David in their titles. Whether he wrote them all or inspired them directly, scholars seem not to be certain, but we do know that David had a stimulating influence on the sacred songs and poems used in worship by his people.

We also know that two themes run side by side through all the Psalms: one is the theme of man's constant, never ending search for security; the other describes how he *finds* it.

The 57th Psalm sounds like something that might have been sung or spoken by Daniel in the lions' den . . . or by David in a cave threatened by Saul, or by the wild beasts of the wilderness.

NOTES ON THE PRINTED TEXT

I. . . . in the shadow of thy wings will I make my refuge, Psalm 57:1. It may be poetry, or it may be an experience of David expressed in poetry; it is surely a man pressed desperately by enemies seeking "any port in a storm." The very word "refuge" would suggest a cave, to the soul and mind of a poet or a song writer. To David, a cave often meant the difference between life and death. David brought his father and mother to the cave at Addulam when they were sought by Saul as hostages, and here, too, David brought together his first band of rebel warriors. In another cave he stood over sleeping Saul, wondering whether to kill him or let him go. Caves!

There were other moments of crisis and threatening disaster when David sought just such a refuge. He was a great king who was often tempted. In his youth, a price was put on his head; he ran for his life from one hiding place to another. In his moments of temptation his soul was in danger, and then he fled for refuge to his God.

Not many of us have prices set on our heads—but temptation and the threat of evil against us is as terrifying for us as it was for the Israelites. We are born to trouble, not to peace. The storms begin to beat upon us in childhood, and they never let up. In the midst of it all we turned to God as David did, begging protection (verse 1). As a chick, we run to a mother hen, to security "in the shadow of thy wings." (The Psalmist may have been thinking of the wings of the cherubim, in the

Temple.) When the storm becomes too much for us we turn to God. Inasmuch as He holds the winds and the lightning bolts in His hands, it is natural and not wrong or cowardly for us to turn there. We disagree with Karl Shapiro, that modern poet who said, "I don't have much hope in [the church]. People attend churches as caves to creep into." We agree with Eddie Cantor, who said, "The church must be a very strong and righteous thing, for it has survived every enemy it ever had."

Enemies? The Psalmist is much concerned with them. He speaks of the enemies of good men who would "swallow them up" (verse 3). There are enemies who would trample on whatever and whoever is good; against such, we need God's "steadfast love and his faithfulness." He speaks of lions; there were probably lions in the wilderness where David hid, but, literally speaking, there are no lions on modern Main Street. But there are still beasts in human form, with "teeth [like] spears and arrows" and "tongues [like] sharp swords." There are gossipers, defamers of character, men ruthless enough in business to drive other men to the wall, men ruthless enough to slaughter their brothers in war. Lions all around us, human lions who spread their nets to catch and destroy the innocent and the weak and the unwary, who dig pits in which to trap us.

Do you doubt it? Take a closer look at what we call "modern civilization." Its guiding law seems more and more to be the law of violence. (You can get dozens of illustrations in your morning newspaper of our trend to violence.)

Now, against all this, man needs some power stronger than his own. There come those moments in human life when nothing *human* can help us, when all human "security" proves worthless. It is then that we *must* turn to God. Even Jesus knew those moments. But Jesus had the secret sought by the Psalmist; even when He hung so near death on His cross, when the "lions" in human flesh had done their worst, He cried, "Into thy hands I commend my spirit" (Luke 23:46). In that faith, He had escaped the nets and pitfalls set by His enemies. So, too, can we escape.

II. My heart is steadfast, O God, my heart is steadfast! I will sing . . . , Psalm 57:7 (RSV). Here is the man after the storm has passed, coming out of his "cave" of despondency and thanking God for his deliverance. We have seen him cringing, with his soul almost crushed and defeated; we have seen him trembling in fear of his enemies with their nets and pitfalls—but suddenly the storm breaks, and the sun comes out, the lions are gone, the long night is over and the dawn has come. Usually the man is awakened by the sunrise; now he gets up *before* the sunrise, breaks into song and calls upon the sun to rise! "I will awake the dawn" (verse 8, RSV). He looks up to God; he is so happy at his deliverance that he promises God not to sing alone in the solitude of his cave, not to sing to God only in the Jewish Temple, but to sing it out "among the nations" (verse 9).

This is the singing of a truly devout man—one whose heart has remained "steadfast"—steady in the Lord—in the midst of storm and peril. And it is the song given to Christians to sing to the nations: the song of steadfast faith in God, the unconquerable conviction that there is a God who cares, who will not leave us desolate or beaten, even in death! Cried poor, suffering Job, "Though he slay me, yet will I trust in him!"

SUGGESTIONS TO TEACHERS

Security? We seem to be fresh out of it in the United States. At the moment, we are the best armed nation in the world and the richest in resources. We are also one of the most frightened nations in the world. *Why?*

The teacher could start with asking that question, and go on to discuss security under the following emphases:

1. What are the elements of insecurity?
2. What are the *universal* elements of insecurity?
3. The importance of *change* in material and spiritual security.
4. The Christian's *unique* security.

The temptation will be to spend too much time in talking about material insecurity. Resist it! What we are concerned with here is *trust in God*. . . .

TOPIC FOR ADULTS
HUNGER FOR SECURITY

Nitro. "There was a story some time ago in a Detroit newspaper about a woman who had a hunch that the dark, oily stuff in two old beer bottles, which she found in her basement, was not machine oil. Anyway, before throwing it out, she called the police. She remembered that some thirty-five years before this, a fellow named Joe had brought the bottles and put them in the basement. The police discovered that they were filled with nitroglycerin and that there was enough of the explosive to destroy a city block. The police roped off the streets and kept traffic away. Then, with six squad cars, they took the stuff to a large, open space and destroyed it by burning.

"I kept thinking that, for thirty-five years, that lady and her neighbors stood on the edge of destruction and knew it not. Most of us have something like that deep down in our souls, and there is no security until it is brought out and burned. The tragedy of the President's (John F. Kennedy's) assassination and the killing of the man suspected of the slaying indicated how a nation dwells on top of violence and the jungle. There is no safety for us in our own power, but only when God brings these terrible tendencies under control."—Bishop Gerald Kennedy, in *Pulpit Digest,* February, 1964.

One Desire. Ed McCully, one of the now famous American missionaries killed by the Auca Indians in an Ecuador jungle, wrote these words in a letter to a friend while he was a young law student:

"Since taking this job things have happened. I've been spending my free time studying the Word. Each night the Lord seemed to get hold of me a little more. Night before last I was reading in Nehemiah. I finished the book and read it through again. Here was a man who left everything as far as position was concerned to go do a job that nobody else could handle. And because he went the whole remnant back in Jerusalem got right with the Lord. Obstacles and hindrances fell away and a great work was done. Jim, you couldn't get away from it. The Lord was dealing with me.

"On the way home yesterday morning I took a long walk and came to a decision which I knew was of the Lord. In all honesty before the Lord, I say that no one and nothing beyond Himself and the Word has any bearing upon what I've decided to do. I have one desire now—to live a life of reckless abandon for the Lord, putting all my energy and strength into it. Maybe He'll send me to some place where the name of Jesus Christ is unknown. Jim, I'm taking the Lord at His word, and I'm trusting Him to prove His Word. It's kind of like putting all your eggs in one basket, but we've already put our trust in him for salvation, so why not do it as far as our life is concerned? If there's nothing to this business of eternal life, we might as well load everything in one crack and throw our present life away with our life hereafter. But if there is something to it, then everything else the Lord says may hold true likewise. Pray for me, Jim."—*Through Gates of Splendor,* by Elisabeth Elliot. Quoted by permission of Harper & Row, publishers.

There it is: absolute security born out of absolute trust!

Neurotics. The word "neurotic" is much in our speech today; according to Mr. Webster, one meaning of the word is "nervous." All of us are too nervous about *something* . . . and there is a cure for it:

"You ask, 'What does the man with steady nerves have that the neurotic has not?' He has an amazing inner self-control which nothing outward can decontrol. If you study the neurotic carefully, you will discover that he has hidden away a grudge or resentment, or he is carrying a chip on his shoulder. He feels the world is against him, or jealousy keeps his nerves on edge. He is upset the moment he sees someone having something he wants and does not have himself, or someone doing something and assuming responsibilities which he is too lazy to assume. Dr. Edward Weiss, of Temple University Medical School, told his associates, 'So often we find these patients wearing sacroiliac or abdominal supports, when what they need is inner support. Instead of trying to bolster them up with a crutch, what we ought to do is to try to develop their inner emotional security. We should help them to free their minds of their grudge or resentment, their envy, their jealousy, their feeling that the world is against them" (Source unknown).

No man who understands that this is his Father's world lacks that enviable security *in* the world. He knows and knows well that he can look up and say, "Thou wilt keep him in perfect peace, whose mind is stayed on thee" (Isaiah 26:3).

Questions for Pupils on the Next Lesson: 1. Did Job have a *meaningful* faith? 2. Did Job write the book that bears his name? 3. List two things Job believed, and two things he doubted. 4. Does argument (such as that between Job and his three friends) produce faith? 5. Does Job 23:3 suggest that Job had lost God, or . . . what? 6. How did Job finally "find" God? 7. Have you as much faith as Job had? Prove it!

TOPIC FOR YOUTH
WHOM CAN I TRUST?

Trusting. "A college girl once said to me, 'I have never trusted anyone in my life. How can I trust the Lord Jesus with all the problems of my daily life?'

"Since it was Easter vacation, I asked her how she was going back to college. She said, 'I am going to fly.'

" 'Do you have your ticket?' I asked.

" 'No,' she said, 'I have to find out what time I can get a plane.'

" 'How are you going to do that?'

" 'Well,' she replied, 'I am going to telephone the air line and find out what time the plane leaves and then reserve a seat on that plane. Then I shall take a taxi out to the airport and board the plane.'

"I said, 'Do you know the reservation clerk at the airline?'

"She replied, 'No, I don't.'

"I asked, 'Are you going to taxi to the airport, trusting the information of this unknown clerk?'

" 'Yes, I am.'

" 'Do you know the pilot of this plane?'

" 'No, I don't.'

"Then I said to her, 'You trust the word of an unknown clerk at the airline office, and put your life into the hands of a pilot whom you do not know and probably will not even see. But you will know what real trust is when you take the word of Jesus Christ, who died for you and rose again, and allow Him to pilot your life by His resurrection power.' "
—D. G. Barnhouse.

God Is With Us. "As powerful as the human person is, there is a still greater power. . . . Whenever he became a little shaky, Martin Luther used to go out into his garden and sing, 'A mighty fortress is our God, a bulwark never failing; Our Helper He, amidst the flood of mortal ills prevailing.' This always prepared him to face with confidence whatever might come. He knew that as long as there was a God, he could feel secure.

"One morning I got out of bed, worried about the things I had to do. I had seven sermons to preach in three days and a lot of other things to do. I felt myself getting tired, and it was the worst kind of tiredness. It doesn't hurt you to get tired as a result of something you have done. That is natural. But when you feel tired over something you are planning to do, that is bad!

"But I left home that morning saying to myself, 'The Lord is my shepherd: I shall not want—green pastures—I will fear no evil; for thou art with me; thy rod and thy staff—the house of the Lord forever.' As I saturated my mind with the blessed Twenty-third Psalm, I felt a wonderful calmness, and I thoroughly enjoyed those three days that I had worried about.

"When we think of and use our own abilities with the assurance that God is also with us to supply whatever we may lack, we find that wonderful feeling of security."—*Roads to Radiant Living*, by C. L. Allen (Fleming H. Revell Company).

Alone. Some men say that it is *not* good to have security, for when we have it, we tend to lose our energies and our spirit, to become lazy and "contented," and to do nothing that insecurity forces us to do. That may or may not be true, depending upon the individual; but there is another aspect in which insecurity may be better than security.

For instance—two Englishmen, Ridgway and Blyth, rowed a boat across the Atlantic in 92 days, and in that 92 days they had some hair-raising experiences. Ridgway said, when it was all over and their feet were on *terra firma* again, "We realized in moments of near horror that we were completely and utterly alone . . . now we know there is a God."

Very often, we find that some men have found God when the last shred of confidence and security has been torn from them. It seems a high price to pay, but we still seem to *want* to learn the *hard* way. . . .

Safety. In his autobiography, John Buchan has a little story about storms and safety that is worth repeating. He says that he was caught one day in a snowstorm in the highlands of Scotland; on a distant hillside, he saw a number of sheep walking up out of the deeper places on the hillside to face the storm in the open, without any protection at all. It seemed stupid—until he met the shepherd of the sheep, who explained matters to him. The shepherd said that it wasn't stupid; it was smart! The drifts in snowstorms in that area swept into the low places, and filled them; if the sheep stayed there, they would die! But they had security on the open slopes, where the drifts swept past them, and the snow was not deep.

Now read the Twenty-third Psalm, and see the shepherd caring for His sheep. . . .

Sentence Sermon to Remember: When you cannot trust God you cannot trust anything; and when you cannot trust anything you get the condition of the world as it is today.—Basil King.

Questions for Pupils on the Next Lesson: 1. Do you admire Job; if so, why? 2. What did Job complain about? 3. Why did God make Job suffer? 4. Has any of your suffering strengthened your faith—or weakened it? 5. Does the darkness described in Job 23:17 ever surround you? 6. Explain the meaning of the words, "I have uttered what I did not understand" (Job 42:3) and apply them to yourself. 7. What did it mean to "repent in dust and ashes" (Job 42:6)? Have you ever done anything like that?

This book contains lessons through August 1972. TARBELL'S 1972–73, containing lessons from September 1972 through August 1973, is on sale now at your book store.

LESSON V—JULY 2

DISCOVERING A MEANINGFUL FAITH

Background Scripture: Job 23; 42:1–6; Hebrews 12:5–11;
I Peter 5:6–7
Devotional Reading: Job 40:3–14

KING JAMES VERSION

JOB 23 Then Job answered and said,

2 Even to-day is my complaint bitter: my stroke is heavier than my groaning.

3 Oh that I knew where I might find him! that I might come even to his seat!

4 I would order my cause before him, and fill my mouth with arguments.

16 For God maketh my heart soft, and the Almighty troubleth me:

17 Because I was not cut off before the darkness, neither hath he covered the darkness from my face.

JOB 42 Then Job answered the Lord, and said,

2 I know that thou canst do every thing, and that no thought can be withholden from thee.

3 Who is he that hideth counsel without knowledge? therefore have I uttered that I understood not; things too wonderful for me, which I knew not.

4 Hear, I beseech thee, and I will speak: I will demand of thee, and declare thou unto me.

5 I have heard of thee by the hearing of the ear; but now mine eye seeth thee:

6 Wherefore I abhor myself, and repent in dust and ashes.

REVISED STANDARD VERSION

JOB 23 Then Job answered:

2 "Today also my complaint is bitter,
his hand is heavy in spite of my groaning.

3 Oh, that I knew where I might find him,
that I might come even to his seat!

4 I would lay my case before him
and fill my mouth with arguments.

16 God has made my heart faint;
the Almighty has terrified me;

17 for I am hemmed in by darkness,
and thick darkness covers my face."

JOB 42 Then Job answered the Lord:

2 "I know that thou canst do all things,
and that no purpose of thine can be thwarted.

3 'Who is this that hides counsel without knowledge?'
Therefore I have uttered what I did not understand,
things too wonderful for me, which I did not know.

4 'Hear, and I will speak;
I will question you, and you declare to me.'

5 I had heard of thee by the hearing of the ear,
but now my eye sees thee;

6 therefore I despise myself,
and repent in dust and ashes."

MEMORY SELECTION: *I have heard of thee by the hearing of the ear; but now mine eye seeth thee.* Job 42:5.

HOME DAILY BIBLE READINGS

June 26. M. What Is Faith? Hebrews 11:17–27.
June 27. T. A Growing Faith, Philippians 1:19–26.
June 28. W. Sincere Faith, I Timothy 3:3–11.
June 29. T. A Source of Faith, Romans 10:14–18.
June 30. F. Contend for the Faith, Jude 1–4, 20–21.

July 1. S. A Well-Grounded Faith, II Timothy 1:8–14.
July 2. S. Beyond Man Is God, Job 40:3–14.

BACKGROUND

The Book of Job is a literary masterpiece written (we think!) somewhere between 600–400 B.C. by an author of whom we know nothing.
Whoever he was, he was a poet and philosopher who took a story familiar
in the folklore of Israel and built it into a poetic dialogue that has become immortal. It challenges the old idea that the righteous are rewarded
by God on earth, and that the wicked are punished by Him. It also
throws doubt on the old idea that sin was the cause of suffering. It is a
frank and almost bitter revolt against what we call the justice of God.

It all comes out well in the end, but you will have to read the whole
book to find out about that. Read it! It is not only great poetry and
drama; it is religious experience at its best.

The opening verses of our text show Job complaining about God. . . .

NOTES ON THE PRINTED TEXT

I. Oh that I knew where I might find him! Job 23:3. We have said
that the Book of Job is a dialogue; perhaps we should have said that it
is a four-sided argument between Job and his three friends (Bildad,
Zophar and Eliphaz). It is almost as though they were attorneys in a
courtroom, presenting evidence (or bemoaning the lack of it), stating
different positions, offering different attitudes as they discuss the relationship of God to man. The trouble is that all seem to be attorneys arguing
their cases. But who is on trial here, and who is in the *witness* chair?

Aye, that's the trouble! They are trying Someone who is invisible to the
naked eye. When Job cries, "Oh that I might find him," he is really
crying, "Oh, if only I could put God right up there in that witness chair,
where I could get at Him!" He has a "complaint" to make against God
for the way God has been treating him; that word is a *legal,* courtroom
word. But you must have visible evidence in the courtroom of the accused
and that Someone isn't there!

Job is bitter about it. He admits that he is resentful against God, for
God's hand has been heavy on him in the troubles he has been suffering
(see previous chapters). For the moment, Job is a rebel against God, a
rebel at a loss because God does not condescend to appear before him
in person. He pours out a torrent of wild, rebellious words—and God
doesn't even answer him! It is the old order reversed: God usually complains about man, and here man is trying to make out a case against God.

Job's mouth is filled with arguments, but . . . it's difficult to argue
with an absent witness. Wherever Job looks, behind him or in front, to
the left or to the right—God isn't there. He just can't get the Almighty
into the courtroom, where he might have him judged *on human terms.*
Job is sincere in all this, although to us he sounds like a frustrated little
boy. He is quite "righteous" in demanding that God appear; he feels
that God has wronged him terribly and should be called to account for
it. That would be only fair, wouldn't it?

Yes, by merely human standards that might be all right, but God
doesn't function at human command or by human standards. He does
not stand around waiting to be subpoenaed. God, like the United States,

cannot be sued. In such a sense God is unapproachable, hidden, beyond the beck and call of men. But Job is too angry, too frustrated, to understand that—yet.

Once we heard a fine old lady say to her pastor, "If God doesn't heal me of my sickness, I'll have no more to do with Him." To which the pastor replied, "My dear friend, you can't threaten God into doing anything." Exactly! Job didn't understand that, so his heart was "faint," and the Almighty "terrified" him, and he was hemmed in by this self-created darkness and lack of faith (verses 16, 17). He is overwhelmed by it; he cannot "see" in this darkness, and he cannot understand why God is so indifferent to his beck and call. No man ever found God in such darkness.

II. I have uttered what I did not understand, things too wonderful for me, which I did not know, Job 42:3 (RSV). This comes at the end of the Book of Job; it sums up the great transforming experience of the suffering Job who has come through his sufferings and doubts and bitterness to a new faith in God. It is a confession—two confessions, in fact—from a man who has turned from resentment and blind doubt to wisdom and understanding.

Up to this point, Job had been concerned only with *himself*. Why should God treat *me* this way? *I* have been a righteous man, not a wicked sinner! In most of the book he goes all out to justify *himself*. But now there is a change: now he is thinking only of *God*. Now he knows that, wise as he thinks he is, he is not quite as wise as his God. He confesses: "I know that thou canst do every thing . . ." (verse 2). Now he knows that God may have purposes for him and for all mankind that neither he nor all mankind can fully understand, and that those purposes will not be "thwarted" (RSV).

He understood his own troubles quite well; he did *not* understand God. Do any of us? Do any of us know fully the mind and purposes of God? Never! A border line is drawn between man and God across which no man can ever pass. God is above, beyond us. He governs man's life and actions, not we His. And we must remember that all the argument in the world will not put us one inch across that line, nor bring God one inch closer to us. God, not man, determines in the end who is righteous and who is wicked; God and not man determines the rewards and the retributions and punishments. Job sees this at last.

The second confession comes in the words, "I have heard of thee by the hearing of the ear; but now mine eye seeth thee" (verse 5). He has heard of God in human, intellectual argument; now he sees God through the eyes of faith. *He sees God as a Person*, not as an object of debate, but as a truth to comprehend and to live by. It was like the opening of the eyes of a man who had long been blind. It almost overwhelms him, as most of us are overwhelmed at the moment of conversion. The *King James Version* says that Job abhorred himself and repented in dust and ashes; the *Revised Standard Version* says that he despised himself and repented . . . the *New English Bible* says, "Therefore I melt away!" We like that—melting away. The old creature died and a new creature was born. A doubter became a believer, a sinner a saint. Job had been reconciled. This was justification by faith. Now, the "courtroom" drama seemed a farce; the verdict had been rendered by a God of grace in favor of a man who had become repentant.

Job's book is one of the "Wisdom Books" of our Bible. There is no greater wisdom in any other book ever written by human hands.

SUGGESTIONS TO TEACHERS

William Rainey Harper once asked, "Why didn't someone tell me that I can become a Christian and settle the doubts afterward?" Good! We should *welcome* questions of *honest* doubt in any Christian; it is a sign that he is thinking. And we should be prepared to help him answer those doubts.

Look closely at Job's complaints as we report them in today's lesson. Look closer at God's replies to Job's questions, and closest of all at Job's final affirmation of meaningful faith. Put yourself in Job's sandals—and *listen for the voice of the God, assuaging his doubts.* . . .

And don't expect to answer *all* the questions in one hour.

TOPIC FOR ADULTS
DISCOVERING A MEANINGFUL FAITH

Knowing God. Most of us on this earth live lives of quiet frustration—often noisy frustration! Things just don't work out according to our dreams—and so we turn a cold shoulder to God. The Book of Job was written to show us that there is a better way.

"Frustration, if you let it have its proper effect, says, 'God is your greatest need.' Thomas Carlyle was sitting by his fire on a cozy Sunday afternoon when someone knocked at his door. It was the young minister who had just arrived in the community. The new minister was seeking the wise advice of the great Carlyle. 'Mr. Carlyle,' he said, 'I want to do some real and lasting good in this community. What do you think is the most important thing I can do?'

"Carlyle was silent for a moment. He leaned over to poke the fire. Then he said, 'What this country needs is a man who knows God other than by hearsay.'

"Get to know God and help other people to know Him!"—*Where Are You, God?*, by David A. Ray (Revell).

When Job started his book, he did not know God; at the end he did. Out of that knowing came *meaningful* faith!

You have to know God *first* . . . !

Meaningful. ". . . a young, unmarried, pregnant girl—who says she is afraid to confide in either her parents or her minister—comes to see me to find out how her unborn child can be adopted.

". . . a convict writes to ask if a job might be found for him so that he can be paroled from prison.

". . . a college student, unable to find summer work, borrows twenty dollars.

". . . a woman, who has found another man, wants a divorce from her alcoholic husband.

". . . a Negro is arrested because he protested discrimination in the city.

". . . a seminarian is discouraged and disillusioned about the churches and thinks he cannot and should not be ordained.

". . . an addict wants to get out of the city to try again to kick his habit.

". . . a family is about to be disposessed from its tenement.

"These represent, in my life, the real issues of faith, just as the daily happenings of your life . . . are the real issues of faith for you. . . ." —*Free in Obedience*, by William Stringfellow.

If your faith is meaningful, it is a faith that goes to work on such problems as these. If it isn't strong enough to go to work on such problems it is meaning*less.* . . .

Faith. "Religion without prayer is barren, empty. But prayer without praise is drudgery and unfruitful. The real test of our faith is our ability to sing in the night, when darkness and pain overwhelm us."—Samuel Young, in *Herald of Holiness.*

Beyond Doubt. "Go beyond doubt to commitment. Dr. W. P. Faunce, one-time president of Brown University, used to tell his students that one must learn to question things, 'as the railroad employe tests the car wheels before the train starts out of the station. It is that man's doubt that ensures our safety in travel. But if we do nothing but test car wheels and never really dare to travel, our doubt becomes irrational, paralyzing and preposterous.' In short, doubt is all right as far as it goes, but it doesn't go far enough. As a famous clergyman once said, 'Faith begins with an experiment, and ends with an experience.' Don't let your doubts keep you from the joyous experience that awaits every man who earnestly searches for God. In *Pilgrim's Progress,* John Bunyan's famous allegory, Christian was imprisoned for a while in Doubting Castle, but remember that his journey wasn't over until he reached the Celestial City!"—Donald N. Paulson, in *Watchman-Examiner,* August 24, 1968.

Questions for Pupils on the Next Lesson: 1. From what was Elijah hiding, in I Kings 19? 2. Why did a man as strong as Elijah need the guidance of God? 3. Has God ever helped you to stop running? 4. Did Elijah seek God's guidance out of love or out of fright? 5. Do you seek God's guidance only when trouble comes? 6. Does God speak to you today as He spoke to Elijah? 7. Why didn't God disperse the enemies of Elijah?

TOPIC FOR YOUTH
WHEN I CAN'T UNDERSTAND

A Stranger Coming. "Once, an Indian guide and the poet John Greenleaf Whittier stood watching a milky cataract roar into the canyon below. The poet stood silent before the thunder of the waters. He could hear nothing else.

"Suddenly the Indian pulled at his sleeve and shouted, 'A stranger is coming.'

"Whittier turned in surprise and asked, 'How do you know?'

" 'Because,' replied the Indian, 'I heard a twig break.'

"The question comes: how amidst the thunderous hubbub of voices today can we hear the voice of God? The answer: by having our ears

attuned to His frequency. Jesus sometimes prefaced a parable with
the invitation, 'He that hath ears to hear, let him hear' (Matthew
11:15). He meant, 'He whose ears are eager to hear my message, let
him hear.'

"He also said, 'Every one that is of the truth heareth my voice' (John
18:37), and 'My sheep hear my voice . . . and they follow me' (John
10:27).

"But we can't hear His voice unless we have a tuned-in attitude and
relationship with God."—*Thinkables*, by James C. Hefley (Revell).

Job—and particularly Job's friends—talked too much at first; they
talked so loudly that God's still small voice couldn't get through. We all
talk too much *about* God, too little *with* Him.

Her Troubles. Every Sunday morning a kindly faced but disturbed
woman sat alone in the pew of a big city church; the sexton discovered
that she always left several little wads of crumpled paper behind when
she left the church, bearing such words as "Clara—sick; Lester—no job.
The rent. . . ." He took the wads to the pastor, who after one morning
service, asked the woman about it. She said to him:

"They have meaning for me. You'll think it's silly, I guess—but some
time ago I saw a sign among the advertising posters in a street car. It
said, 'Take your troubles to church with you.' My troubles are written on
those pieces of paper. I wrote them down during the week and brought
them here on Sunday mornings—and left them. I felt that God was
taking care of them.'

" 'God is taking care of them,' the rector replied softly, 'and I shall
ask Him to keep on doing so. Please continue to bring your troubles
here.'

"On his way out of the church he found another note. It contained
three words: 'John—in Korea.'—Adapted from an article in *Guideposts*
by George A. Straley.

Don't stop with taking your troubles to your friends—take them to
God.

Three Kinds. Dwight L. Moody once said that there was not just one
kind of faith; there were three kinds: "Struggling Faith, which is like
a man in deep water; Clinging Faith, which is like a man hanging on to
the side of a boat; and Resting Faith, which finds a man safely within
the boat, and able, moreover, to reach out a hand to help someone else."

Thorn in the Flesh. Dorothea Dix had a thorn in the flesh.

Now not many of the present generation know anything about
Dorothea Dix—and that's *their* misfortune! She was an obscure schoolteacher in Boston when her doctor gave her the bad news that her life
was in danger from a hemorrhaging of the lungs. She closed up her
school and went off to England, where she met a famous mental health
reformer named Dr. Samuel Tuke. Tuke cured her—and gave her life
new meaning besides.

He took her to an insane asylum. Insane asylums in her day (1887)
resembled the lower depths of hell. The patients were kept in chains,
beaten, starved, abused by their keepers and neglected by everyone else.
He told her that the asylums in her own America were as bad or worse

than the asylums of England, and when she came home again she started a crusade to reform those brutal institutions. She moved like a living fire across the land, preaching reform—and Christian concern for the unfortunate insane. She made life miserable for state legislators and even national officials; she was such a nuisance that they instituted reforms to get rid of her! When she died, at 85, she was famous and universally loved. She had transferred her thorn in the flesh to the heart of a great evil—and the evil was lessened, if not wholly overcome. (Were she to come back she would find work to do in *our* insane asylums.)

Thorn in the flesh? Poor Job had a hundred thorns in *his* flesh, but he lost them when he repented in "dust and ashes." You have a thorn in the flesh—perhaps one labeled "Doubt." *Put it to work for God, and watch it disappear!*

Sentence Sermon to Remember: Faith is not belief without proof but trust without reservations.—Elton Trueblood.

Questions for Pupils on the Next Lesson: 1. Elijah's life lacked direction; does yours? 2. Have Elijah's problems ever bothered you? 3. How did Elijah *discover* the will of God? 4. What is the will of God toward present-day communism, and how do you know it is His will? 5. Was Elijah boasting when he said, ". . . only I am left"? 6. Who was Jehu, and what did he do? 7. Did Elijah anoint Elisha?

LESSON VI—JULY 9

FINDING GOD'S GUIDANCE

Background Scripture: I Kings 19:9–18; John 16:7–15
Devotional Reading: John 16: 7–15

KING JAMES VERSION

I KINGS 19 9 And he came thither unto a cave, and lodged there; and, behold, the word of the Lord came to him, and he said unto him, What doest thou here, Elijah?

10 And he said, I have been very jealous for the Lord God of hosts: for the children of Israel have forsaken thy covenant, thrown down thine altars, and slain thy prophets with the sword; and I, even I only, am left; and they seek my life, to take it away.

11 And he said, Go forth, and stand upon the mount before the Lord. And, behold, the Lord passed by, and a great and strong wind rent the mountains, and brake in pieces the rocks before the Lord; but the Lord was not in the wind: and after the wind an earthquake; but the Lord was not in the earthquake:

12 And after the earthquake a fire; but the Lord was not in the fire: and after the fire a still small voice.

13 And it was so, when Elijah heard it, that he wrapped his face in his mantle, and went out, and stood in the entering in of the cave. And, behold, there came a voice unto him, and said, What doest thou here, Elijah?

14 And he said, I have been very jealous for the Lord God of hosts: because the children of Israel have forsaken thy covenant, thrown down thine altars, and slain thy prophets with the sword; and I, even I only, am left; and they seek my life, to take it away.

15 And the Lord said unto him, Go, return on thy way to the wilderness of Damascus: and when thou comest, anoint Hazael to be king over Syria:

16 And Jehu the son of Nimshi shalt thou anoint to be king over Israel: and Elisha the son of Shaphat of Abelmeholah shalt thou anoint to be prophet in thy room.

17 And it shall come to pass, that him that escapeth the sword of Hazael

REVISED STANDARD VERSION

I KINGS 19 9 And there he came to a cave, and lodged there; and behold, the word of the Lord came to him, and he said to him, "What are you doing here, Elijah?" 10 He said, "I have been very jealous for the Lord, the God of hosts; for the people of Israel have forsaken thy covenant, thrown down thy altars, and slain thy prophets with the sword; and I, even I only, am left; and they seek my life, to take it away." 11 And he said, "Go forth, and stand upon the mount before the Lord." And behold, the Lord passed by, and a great and strong wind rent the mountains, and broke in pieces the rocks before the Lord, but the Lord was not in the wind; and after the wind an earthquake, but the Lord was not in the earthquake; 12 and after the earthquake a fire, but the Lord was not in the fire; and after the fire a still small voice. 13 And when Elijah heard it, he wrapped his face in his mantle and went out and stood at the entrance of the cave. And behold, there came a voice to him, and said, "What are you doing here, Elijah?" 14 He said, "I have been very jealous for the Lord, the God of hosts; for the people of Israel have forsaken thy covenant, thrown down thy altars, and slain thy prophets with the sword; and I, even I only, am left; and they seek my life, to take it away." 15 And the Lord said to him, "Go, return on your way to the wilderness of Damascus; and when you arrive, you shall anoint Hazael to be king over Syria; 16 and Jehu the son of Nimshi you shall anoint to be king over Israel; and Elisha the son of Shaphat of Abelmeholah you shall anoint to be prophet in your place. 17 And him who escapes from the sword of Hazael shall Jehu slay; and him who escapes from the sword of Jehu shall Elisha slay. 18 Yet I will leave seven thousand in Israel, all the knees that have not shall Jehu slay: and him that escapeth from the sword of Jehu shall Elisha slay.

18 Yet I have left me seven thousand in Israel, all the knees which have not bowed unto Baal, and every mouth which hath not kissed him.

bowed to Baal, and every mouth that has not kissed him."

MEMORY SELECTION: Shew me thy ways, O Lord; teach me thy paths. Lead me in thy truth, and teach me. . . . Psalm 25:4, 5.

HOME DAILY BIBLE READINGS

July 3. M. Guidance Is Essential, Proverbs 11:14–23.
July 4. T. Lead Me, Psalm 139:1–6, 23–24.
July 5. W. Prayer for Guidance, Psalm 31:1–8.
July 6. T. Guidance in Truth, Psalm 25:4–10.
July 7. F. The Upward Call, Philippians 3:12–21.
July 8. S. The Holy Spirit Guides, John 14:15–24.
July 9. S. The Advantage of Absence, John 16:7–15.

BACKGROUND

Anyone seeking the guidance of God will find help in the story of Elijah hiding in his cave on Horeb. Elijah, as we find him here, is a prophet on the run; he has won a dramatic contest over the priests of Baal (see I Kings 18) and, which was worse, he has defied Queen Jezebel. Her pursuit of him is so determined and so terrifying that he runs into the wilderness and crouches alone in a cave. Literally, he had his back to the wall; he must have thought, "It's all over!"

A man in such a desperate position is a man in great need of God's guidance. Elijah found that guidance: let us see *how* he found it. . . .

NOTES ON THE PRINTED TEXT

I. What doest thou here, Elijah? I Kings 19:9. Elijah was a man of great courage; he had defied a tyrannical, murderous queen, and he had made the priests of Baal look silly and stupid before all the people of Israel, and *that* would never have been accomplished by a weak or hesitant man. But here he is, hiding in a cave, afraid to come out. No wonder "the word of the Lord" whispered in his heart, "What are you doing *here*, brave man?"

For once, he was frightened. But could it be that he was also seeking solitude in which to think over what had happened to him and what he was to do now? We should not be surprised to find him there; the odds against him—the whole army of Jezebel!—were a little too much; to have stayed in the town or the city would have made it easy for Jezebel to catch him. So he went out to be alone, safe in his hiding place, to think and plan. . . . Perhaps we should all do that occasionally; maybe we should periodically "get away from it all," take refuge in quietness and meditation.

But Elijah doesn't explain his hiding in the cave by saying, "I wanted to think it out. . . ." Instead, he replies that he had been very jealous (really *zealous*) in serving God, but he had found the opposition too much for him. The Israelites were backsliding into paganism; they had killed the prophets of God and torn down His altars. Only he, Elijah, was left, and they were after *him* now, to kill him, too. In such a situation, who *wouldn't* run? This mount to which he had fled was the most sacred spot in the world to the Hebrew; it was called Sinai in Judah, Horeb in Israel—the place where Moses had met God, and where the sacred law was given him. What better place was there for Elijah? This was certainly one place where God might be found if he were anywhere in the land.

The voice came again: "Go forth, and stand upon the mount before the Lord." But Elijah doesn't go forth quite yet. From within the shelter of the cave he hears a wind of frightening power rage against the mountain; the floor of his cave shakes in an earthquake and after the earthquake, a fire. In Israel these were the old, traditional signs of the presence of God. But now they are different: they are not only an indication that God was "passing by," but also that something more was to come. All this was only the heralding of God's approach to the torn soul of Elijah in another and quieter way.

God does not always come in the midst of storm, tumult and confusion, not always in wind, earthquake and fire. These may be evidences of His power, but His *presence* may be realized otherwise. It was so here. ". . . *after* the fire, a still small voice" (verse 12). Or, "in a soft whisper," or, even better, in "the sound of a gentle silence."

God guides us not by frightening us, not by threatening doom or punishment, but as gently, as kindly, as an earthy father would guide his children.

II. *And the Lord said unto him, Go* . . . , I Kings 19:15. With the passing of the storm and the earthquake and the fire, courage came back to Elijah; he got up, wrapped his face in his mantle (as once Moses had hidden his face at the burning bush because he was afraid to look into the face of God) and went out of his cave to meet the Lord. The Lord's voice greeted him again with the words, "What doest thou here, Elijah?" Why have you given way to fear, Elijah? Why are you despondent? God is probing; He wants to find out whether Elijah now understands what God would have him do. Elijah doesn't! He mumbles again the words about having worked so hard in the vineyard, and of having been defeated and hounded like an animal before the troops of Jezebel. Then God breaks in and tells him—guides him—in what he is to do.

Certainly, says the Lord, it has been difficult for you. You haven't had the success you hoped for. The way of the righteous is *never* easy; God has never promised any of us that it shall be anything else. But the true soldier, prophet or servant of God doesn't quit with the first blow, or with the hundred and first; he gets up and tries again. God's work still remains to be done, whatever happens to *us!* Get on with it! Go back to your work as a reforming prophet. There is a revolution stirring in Syria; go to Syria and "anoint" Hazael—transmit your spirit to him. Go and speak to Jehu, in Israel. And go and anoint Elisha to be your successor.

We cannot take that word "anoint" literally, for Elijah never anointed Hazael, Jehu or Elisha; but he did make them feel his influence; he understood that God was to use these three in working out His will for Israel. Come victory or defeat to Elijah, he understood at last that he was to act as God's agent.

Verse 18 is a gentle rebuke to Elijah's pride. He had claimed to be the only one left in Israel who could and would stand against the heathen queen and Baal. Not so, Elijah! You are mistaken in thinking that you are the *only* loyal servant left. I have seven thousand in Israel. . . . I have a small band left, made up of courageous men who have not yet bowed to Baal. This is the first mention, in the Bible of the "remnant" —the promise that no matter how low the nation—any nation—might sink in faithlessness and apostasy, there would always be a faithful "remnant" on which God would build his Kingdom.

SUGGESTIONS TO TEACHERS

Many of us will recall Bing Crosby's famous motion picture, "Going My Way." The title was provocative: it made many of us wonder which way or whose way we were going. Every man decides for himself which way he would go—his or God's!

Nine men out of ten lack *direction* in their lives. They just drift. Elijah was drifting in fear when he ran for his cave; others drift in frustration or in inability to face up to their problems, or because they do not know how close and how valuable the guidance of God can be. And the greatest guidance in the world is an awareness of the will of God in our lives and a desire to shape our lives in accordance with that will.

As a starter, it might be good to find out just what we *mean* by "God's will. . . ." Then we might find out whether we *want* to obey His will for us. . . .

TOPIC FOR ADULTS
FINDING GOD'S GUIDANCE

Guidance. "There are four important steps in finding the guidance of God. First, gather information about the issues involved. God does not give guidance in a vacuum. Once you're informed, talk the question over with friends, preferably Christians, for they are likely to be concerned about discovering the mind of God. The Bible can be helpful, too. Reading passages that seem to relate to your problem may result in guidance being given through the words of Scripture.

"Then it comes time to lay the matter before God. In quiet meditation and prayer, there should be a bringing of the issues to Him. There must be a readiness to wait. At last should come a clear conviction as to the way to be taken. We should expect a quiet sense of the pressure of God's spirit on our minds and should then become conscious, through an inner mood of assurance, which is the proper way to take."—Source unknown.

A sense of God's will for us seldom comes *instantaneously;* it comes following mental and spiritual struggle and sweat. . . .

How, Where? How and where do we discover God's will? Dr. Andrew Christian Braun makes the following suggestions about that:

"We find His will through nature's framework. . . . Consider the sense of direction of migratory birds, the constancy in the habits of a setting hen, the fidelity of a dog, the ingenuity of a monkey, the intelligence of a horse. Certainly the handiwork in creation reveals God.

Let us take time to behold His wonders in the heavens and on the earth.

We find His will in the authority of His Word. . . . Man has made millions of laws, but he has not improved on the Ten Commandments . . . he has never bettered the Sermon on the Mount or surpassed the truth in the words of Jesus.

"We find His will by following Him. . . . Willingness to obey Christ, to follow in His light, is the condition of further illumination.

"We find His way in converting our feelings. . . . Make a list of your most ardent wishes and then grade them according to intensity. Is your most prevailing desire to do the will of God? . . . 'Anyone who chooses to do His will shall understand. . . .' To know the will of God we must consecrate our feelings, our dominant desires, to God."—From a sermon by Dr. Braun.

Thy Will, My Will. " 'Everything goes against me,' said a man to Martin Luther. 'None of my wishes comes true. My hopes go wrong. My plans never work out.'

" 'My dear friend, that is your own fault,' said Luther.

" 'My own fault?'

" 'Yes,' said Luther. 'Why do you pray every day, "*Thy* will be done?" You ought to pray, "*My* will be done." But if you pray that God's will be done and not yours, you should be satisfied if God does as you pray.' "
—*Lutheran Witness.*

At times, Martin Luther was a most aggravating man—but he was usually right when it came to religion or theology . . . ! He was certainly right here.

Best Guides. We do not know who it was who said: "A sound head, an honest heart, and a humble spirit are the three best guides through time and eternity," but we wish we had said it.

Good Judgment. When a man is arrested and brought into court to be tried for murder, he sometimes excuses himself by saying, "God told me to do it!" We call that blasphemy, and we call him crazy, and he probably is. But, at times, all the rest of us use quite as bad judgment in blaming God for this or that. For instance:

The year the Minnesota Twins lost the baseball championship of their league to the Boston Red Sox, a woman in Annandale, Minnesota, wrote to a newspaper: "The Twins were virtually the best team in the league. With a little help from God, the pennant would have been theirs. I don't believe it was a coincidence that they lost it in the same year that the State of Minnesota voted to sell liquor on Sunday."

Sports Illustrated remarked on this: "Boston, whose Red Sox beat the Twins in the pennant race, has permitted Sunday liquor selling for a long time."

God gave us brains and common sense to *use;* He expects us to use both in determining His will, and in asking His guidance. . . .

The Cop. "A small child wandered away from home and, after much searching, was located downtown. She had a very logical childish reason for her trip. She was asked, 'Weren't you afraid, in all that traffic?'

"Her reply was, 'No. Every time I got to a corner, a big policeman held up his hand and all the cars stopped and he told me to cross over.'

"A call from God should create such faith; it should make us realize that God will hold traffic, change plans, and take us where we ought to go."—Arthur H. Stainback.

Do we think more of the policeman's guidance than we think of God's?

Questions for Pupils on the Next Lesson: 1. What do you mean when you shout, "Praise the Lord"? 2. What is the "Psalter"? 3. For *what* should we praise God in song? 4. Do *all* of our blessings "flow from God"? 5. Do you approve of the "new" music that is being sung in our churches by our young people? 6. For what do you think God wants us to thank Him? 7. What is there in religion that makes you *want* to sing?

TOPIC FOR YOUTH
HOW CAN I FIND MY WAY?

If I Lose That. "A fine picture was painted by a great artist who set the scene against a night background. Across the dark waters of a lonely lake a solitary man could be seen rowing a small boat. A high wind churned the waters of the lake into white-crested billows which raged around his little skiff. Above was a dark and angry sky. But through the darkness shone one lone star. On this star the rower fixed his gaze, and rowed on through the storm. He was undismayed by the midnight darkness. Beneath the picture the artist had written the words: 'If I lose that, I am lost.' "—W. Harry Freda.

You follow the right path when you fix your eyes on God. . . .

Smithfield. Once, according to Margaret Appelgarth, there was a man who decided to walk to a town called Smithfield. He walked quite a way down the road, until he came to a dividing of the road, where stood a signpost with two arrows telling him that if he took one road he would get to Smithfield, and if he took the other, he wouldn't. Simple enough!

One road was a well paved, smooth, delightful sort of road; the other one, marked, "Smithfield," was rough and stony and steep and un-attractive. The man stood and looked at the signs for quite a while, and then he climbed up and just changed the signs around. Then he went off, singing, down the more delightful road.

He walked and he walked and he walked, but he never reached Smithfield!

God has signposts at every crossroads of our lives, and some of them point the hard way. So many of us are afraid to take the hard, rough, uncomfortable way that, no matter how long we live and walk, we never quite get where we really *want* to go.

His Will? A Canadian minister asks a few questions about our ideas of "the will of God" that are worth consideration:

"The will of God that a car should careen down the street and strike some child? The will of God that men should fill the skies and waterways with poison, make bold to alter the atmosphere itself, and set in motion no man knows what chain reaction? The will of God that babies should be born deformed? The will of God that scientists should find their highest, not to say the most lucrative, pursuit in the manufacture of munitions while cries of hunger fill the air and half the farmers in the world have never seen a tractor?"—From a sermon by N. Bruce McLeod.

Think on these things! Are they all "God's" will—or *ours?* "No," said

Jesus, "it is not the will of my father in heaven that one of these little ones should perish."

Does God steer the careening automobile? Does God guide men into killing each other in war? Does God tell the greedy manufacturer to dump his poisonous wastes into our rivers? Think hard on these things before you speak of God's will!

Dogs. There is an old, old story about a little boy standing out in the street with a huge dog on a leash. They were not moving, but motionless. When a friend asked the youngster where he was taking the dog, he replied, "I don't know. I'm waiting first to see where he's going."

There are a lot of such people—and a lot of such dogs! The dog's names are Custom, Habit, Heedless, Popularity, Fear, Indecision, Selfish, Foolish, Trembler. . . .

Then there are those "Seeing Eye" dogs who lead us if and when we are too blind to find our own way; we trust our very lives to them! Says Charles Crowell: "When we depend on our own wills we are swayed by the varying attractions of the moment, but when our will is to do the will of God He gives us strength to do it."

We like the little verse, whose author we do not know:

> As near as green grass to a hill,
> As petals of gold to a daffodil,
> As near as sunlight is to the sod,
> So near to the human heart is God.

Direction. "The automobile gets its power from external fuel and so do we. Our bodies get theirs from food and our spirits get theirs from God. Without either we can't go far. . . . The car is of no account for transportation without a steering system. It must be guided. You would have little use for a car with a 300 h.p. engine and a fine body and frame, but no steering wheel. Yet many people are like this. They go fast and hard at everything they do, but with so little sense of direction and such little guidance!"—Joseph E. Taylor, in *Arkansas Methodist.*

Sentence Sermon to Remember: I find that doing the will of God leaves me no time for disputing about His plans.—George MacDonald.

Questions for Pupils on the Next Lesson: 1. Give two reasons why the Psalmist *had* to praise God. 2. Do you think the Creator wants the praises of His creations? 3. What is there in nature that makes your heart sing? 4. What praise *patterns* do you find in Psalm 150? 5. Which song of praise in your hymnbook do you like best? 6. What are the "benefits" mentioned in Psalm 103:2? 7. How does praising God renew "your youth . . . like the eagle's" (Psalm 103:5)?

LESSON VII—JULY 16

PRAISING THE LORD

Background Scripture: Psalm 103:1–5; 104; 150
Devotional Reading: Psalm 103:6–18

KING JAMES VERSION

KING JAMES VERSION

PSALM 104 Bless the Lord, O my soul. O Lord my God, thou art very great; thou art clothed with honor and majesty:

5 Who laid the foundations of the earth, that it should not be removed for ever.

6 Thou coveredst it with the deep as with a garment: the waters stood above the mountains.

7 At thy rebuke they fled; at the voice of thy thunder they hasted away.

8 They go up by the mountains; they go down by the valleys unto the place which thou hast founded for them.

14 He causeth the grass to grow for the cattle, and herb for the service of man: that he may bring forth food out of the earth;

15 And wine that maketh glad the heart of man, and oil to make his face to shine, and bread which strengtheneth man's heart.

16 The trees of the Lord are full of sap; the cedars of Lebanon, which he hath planted;

17 Where the birds make their nests: as for the stork, the fir trees are her house.

PSALM 103 Bless the Lord, O my soul: and all that is within me, bless his holy name.

2 Bless the Lord, O my soul, and forget not all his benefits:
3 Who forgiveth all thine iniquities; who healeth all thy diseases;
4 Who redeemeth thy life from destruction; who crowneth thee with

REVISED STANDARD VERSION

PSALM 104 Bless the Lord, O my soul!
O Lord my God, thou art very great!
Thou art clothed with honor and majesty . . .
5 Thou didst set the earth on its foundations,
so that it should never be shaken.
6 Thou didst cover it with the deep as with a garment;
the waters stood above the mountains.
7 At thy rebuke they fled;
at the sound of thy thunder they took to flight.
8 The mountains rose, the valleys sank down
to the place which thou didst appoint for them.
14 Thou dost cause the grass to grow for the cattle,
and plants for man to cultivate,
that he may bring forth food from the earth,
15 and wine to gladden the heart of man,
oil to make his face shine,
and bread to strengthen man's heart.
16 The trees of the Lord are watered abundantly,
the cedars of Lebanon which he planted.
17 In them the birds build their nests;
the stork has her home in the fir trees.
PSALM 103 Bless the Lord, O my soul;
and all that is within me, bless his holy name!
2 Bless the Lord, O my soul,
and forget not all his benefits,
3 who forgives all your iniquity,
who heals all your diseases,
4 who redeems your life from the Pit,

loving-kindness and tender mercies;

5 Who satisfieth thy mouth with good things; so that thy youth is renewed like the eagle's.

who crowns you with steadfast love and mercy,

5 who satisfies you with good as long as you live

so that your youth is renewed like the eagle's.

MEMORY SELECTION: *I will sing unto the Lord as long as I live: I will sing praise to my God while I have my being.* Psalm 104:33.

HOME DAILY BIBLE READINGS

July 10. M. From Despair to Praise, Psalm 13:1–6.
July 11. T. Praise Is Trust, Psalm 37:1–11.
July 12. W. Praise in the Sanctuary, Psalm 150:1–6.
July 13. T. Thanksgiving Through Praise, Isaiah 12:1–6.
July 14. F. Praising in Silence, Habakkuk 2:1–4, 18–20.
July 15. S. Praise and Reverence, Psalm 115:11–18.
July 16. S. Praise for Justice and Mercy, Psalm 103:6–18.

BACKGROUND

The words "Psalm" and "Psalter" are closely related: the Psalter is a book containing Psalms used in the old Jewish liturgies. (Many of our modern churches have rituals in which the congregation and the pastor read alternate verses of the Psalms in what we still call "The Psalter.") Without exception, the Psalms might be called "an invitation to praise God," for we cannot read them without wanting to sing them in the rituals of the church or alone in our devotions at home. And praising God in worship is one of the happiest expressions of the devotional life. The Psalter as we now have it was the hymnbook of the Second Temple.

Some of these Psalms we call "Thanksgiving Psalms." They are songs which the devout just *had* to sing, as they thought of all for which they had to be thankful. Two of these were Psalms 103 and 104, and we are to find out today about some of the beautiful gifts of God for which the devout burst into song to express their gratitude.

NOTES ON THE PRINTED TEXT

I. Bless the Lord, O my soul . . . thou art clothed with honor and majesty, Psalm 104:1. Psalm 104 is one of four songs in the Psalter (8, 19, 29, 104) in which the thought is centered in God as Lord of creation. It begins with a shout. It is as though the people attending divine worship that day leaped to their feet at the beginning of the service and shouted, "Praise God from whom all blessings flow!"

Dr. Kyle M. Yates sees it as a hymn sung by the Psalmist to "call his own soul on the carpet," and that is a good description. For most of the week preceding Sunday our souls are gathering dust in the struggle (some call it the rat race) in the marketplace for survival. We develop many traits and thoughts that are just plain ugly, and all gratitude for the bountiful gifts of God is forgotten. But when we enter the sanctuary something sweeps away the dust and the ugliness and something finer comes into our hearts and souls. Thank God! *Praise* Him for that! The Psalmist calls upon his soul to stand humbly and thankfully before God and to render his thanks in worship.

Why should there be only one Thanksgiving Day in our calendar?
Why not have one every Sunday?

II. *Who laid the foundations of the earth* . . . , Psalm 104:5. The
Psalmist looks on the earth as the basic foundation of man's life, and
he finds it good. He stands in awe at the very sight of the earth: it
could not just have *happened;* it was *created.* He sings a song in praise of
earth which closely parallels the song in Genesis 1, and it is apparent
that the singer was acquainted with the old Babylonian and Canaanite
stories of creation. There are similarities here—and differences. In the
old pagan stories there was a desperate struggle at the moment of
creation; the Psalms speak of no struggle at all. God spoke, and it was
done! He spoke, and the waters separated (see Genesis 7:19–20;
9:11–15).

It is an ancient concept, yes. But who can watch a sunset at sea and
not sing praises to God? Who is so dead in his soul that he can look at
a mountain peak soaring toward heaven and not see God there? Who can
stand on a hill above a valley and not be overwhelmed with a sense of
the peace of the Creator?

The Psalmist is not giving a description of how the earth and the seas
were formed; he is describing the beauty of nature that surrounds him.
He is like Walt Whitman, who listened to a dull lecture on astronomy
and then went out alone into the night and just looked up at the stars in
awe and wonder—and praise!

We have a Psalmlike hymn which *we* sing:

> For the beauty of the earth,
> For the beauty of the skies,
> For the love which from our birth,
> Over and around us lies,—
> Christ our God, to thee we raise
> This our hymn of grateful praise.

From the earth God brought forth grass so that the cattle and even the
wild beasts might eat. He brought forth plants for man to cultivate—
herbs, fruit, grapes for wine, and oil and wheat for bread. And trees to
bear fruit, and the cedars of Lebanon to make the heart of man glad
when he looked upon them, and other trees that the birds of the air
might have safe places in which to build their nests. Even the ugly
stork was provided for!

If you have not thanked God for anything recently thank Him now
for all *that!* He has set us down to live and move and have our being
in a world of beauty . . . and He has given us every mouthful we eat!
Would we be here alive if, somehow, He had forgotten to provide for us?

III. *Who forgiveth all thine iniquities; who healeth all thy diseases;
who redeemeth thy life* . . . , Psalm 103:3, 4. The Psalmist could have
stopped there, but he didn't. He bids his soul lift its eyes above nature
and consider the supernatural. God does more, much more, than merely
to provide a world of beauty and food for the body: He offers us other
"benefits" of forgiveness, healing, redemption from premature death, love,
mercy and the renewal of life. He puts the first crude man down in a
lovely garden east of Eden, in the midst of wild beasts—but He does
not leave man there! He creates a human body prone to disease, but

gives man the intelligence to develop the arts of healing. He stood ready to forgive men who had inherited the crudities and sins of the old Adam; he "crowneth" us with love and kindness and understanding and mercy —and forgiveness! He is still a God "who satisfies you with good as long as you live, so that your youth is renewed like the eagle's" (verse 5). He lifts us from the pits into which we blunder, and sends our spirits soaring like eagles above the mountains. "The eagle is a symbol of renewal both because it is long-lived and because it molts annually" (Arnold B. Rhodes).

This Psalm is an individual expression of grateful praise to God; in early worship, it could well have been sung as a solo in the churches. It is a song we all should sing individually every day of our lives, *everywhere.* . . .

SUGGESTIONS TO TEACHERS

For many people, worship is a matter of asking and thanking—with strong emphasis on the asking. It should be on the thanking! Worship at its highest is an expression of gratitude, appreciation, pure joy in, and adoration of, the Creator.

It might be good to start this lesson by asking your class what they have thanked God for lately. Then examine the thankfulness or praise of the Psalmist. For what did *He* praise God?

If you ever used a blackboard in class, use it now. List the things for which your pupils *should* praise God in thankfulness; then find out what they leave unsaid in their praise. There are hidden blessings from God in the lives of all of us. Today, may our eyes be opened to them—and to the God who gave them!

TOPIC FOR ADULTS
PRAISING THE LORD

Praise Him! We praise our heroes—especially those who have given their lives that others might live and those who, in poverty and hardship, have conquered plagues and opened new paths to health. We offer praise to "successful" men who out of their bounty help us build churches, hospitals, recreation centers and libraries. These things we can *see*. We also see a lot of other things that God gives us out of His bounty, but we don't stop long enough to praise Him for His love and care.

The next time you see a star, praise God. He put it there. You couldn't put it there. It is a touch of beauty which only He can give but all of us can enjoy.

When you see the sun high in the sky, warming the fields for the summer harvest, remember that He hung it there for the purpose. Only He can create a sun and set it in the sky.

When snow covers the earth, praise Him. Only God can cover all the ugly spots on His earth in a single hour, and make it all white and clean. Men can never do that.

When it rains, praise Him. No rain would mean no wheat, no flour, no bread—starvation.

When you sit down to a Thanksgiving dinner, praise Him, thank Him for it—and remember that millions of His children on this earth go to bed hungry every night. Praise Him by feeding them.

"Christians," says someone, "are not called upon to worship God through nature or through any other aspect of creation. Nevertheless, they are to hold Him in reverence as Creator."

Praise is reverent gratitude.

Rich. We are all rich in God, but few of us seem to know it. The lady in the following story knew it, and in a unique way offered her praise to God for it:

"They huddled inside the storm door—two children in ragged outgrown coats.

" 'Any old papers, lady?'

"I was busy. I wanted to say no—until I looked down at their feet. Thin little sandals sopping with snow and slush.

" 'Come in and I'll make you a cup of hot cocoa,' I said. There was no conversation. Their soggy sandals left marks upon the hearthstone.

"Cocoa and toast with jam to fortify against the chill outside. I went back to the kitchen and started again on my household chores.

"The silence in the front room struck through me. I looked in. The girl held the empty cup in her hands, looking at it. The boy asked in a flat voice, 'Lady, are you rich?'

" 'Am I rich? Mercy no! I looked at my shabby slipcovers.

"The girl put her cup back in its saucer—carefully.

" 'Your cups match your saucers,' she said. Her voice was old, with a hunger that was not of the stomach.

"They left then, holding their bundles of papers against the wind. They hadn't said thank you. They didn't need to. They had said more than that. Plain blue pottery cups and saucers. But they matched.

"I checked the potatoes and stirred the gravy. Potatoes and brown gravy . . . a roof over our heads, my husband with a steady job . . . these things matched, too. I moved the chairs back from the fire and tidied the living room. The muddy prints of small sandals were still wet on my hearth. I let them be. I want them in case I ever forget how rich I am."—From *The Gold Star Family Album,* edited by Arthur and Nancy De Moss (Revell).

How was this woman rich? What did she have that you can't have? How did she praise Him who made her rich?

Strawberries. "It was a wise Frenchman many years ago who said that he always put on his spectacles when he ate strawberries, so that they might look larger. A good idea! Perhaps he did not have strawberries very often, so it was a red-letter day when they were on the table. They deserved to be honored with spectacles to make them look larger.

"That is a wise way of dealing with all the blessings of life. Instead of complaining that our gifts are not larger and more plentiful, put on the magnifying glasses of gratitude to God for His mercies. The gifts which are received with thanksgiving to God will be larger and richer because we exercised the grace of gratitude. A good theme song for every day is, 'Bless the Lord, O my soul.' "—*Christian Herald.*

Questions for Pupils on the Next Lesson: 1. How often do you confess?

2. For *exactly* what do you need forgiveness? 3. What difference would it make if God did *not* forgive us for our trespasses against Him? 4. Right or wrong: "We can sin only against God, never against man"? 5. What was hyssop (Psalm 51:7)? 6. How does God hide His face from our sins (Psalm 51:9)? 7. Is a sense of guilt good or bad for man?

TOPIC FOR YOUTH
WHY PRAISE THE LORD?

Singing. When we think of Joan Baez it is to think of her as singing songs of protest; that seems to be her "bag." But she also sang this little song of praise:

"To sing is to love and affirm, to fly and soar, to coast into the hearts of the people who listen, to tell them that life is to live, that love is there, that nothing is a promise, but that beauty exists and must be hunted for and found. That death is a luxury better to be romanticized and sung about than dwelt upon in the face of life. To sing is to praise God and the daffodils, and to praise God is to thank Him, in every note within my small range, and every color in the tones of my voice, with every look into the eyes of my audience, to thank Him. Thank you, God, for letting me be born, for giving me eyes to see the daffodils lean in the wind, all my brothers, all my sisters for giving me ears to hear crying, legs to come running, hands to smooth damp hair, a voice to laugh with, and to sing with . . . to sing to you and the daffodils . . . which are You."—*Daybreak*, by Joan Baez; p. 77. Copyright by Joan Baez, published by Dial Press. Quoted by permission.

What I Am Not. Some of us (the older ones!) will remember Elsie Janis. She sang to us when we were soldiers in World War I; she spread joy and faith in a dark hour. She set these words to music:

When my luck seems all out, and I'm down in the mouth,
When I'm stuck in the North and I want to go South;
When the world seems a blank and there's no one I love,
And it seems even God's not in Heaven above,
I've a cure for my grouch and it works like a shot—
I just think of the things I am glad I am not:

A bird in a cage.
A fish in a bowl.
A pig in a pen.
A fox in a hole.
A bear in a pit.
A wolf in a trap.
A fowl on a spit.
A rug on a lap.
A horse in a stable.
A cow in a shed.
A plate on the table.
The sheet on a bed.
The case on a pillow.
A bell on a door.
A branch on a willow.
A mat on the floor.

When I think of the hundreds of things I might be,
I get down on my knees and thank God that I'm me.
Then my blues disappear, when I think what I've got,
And quite soon I've forgotten the things I have not.

Their Blessings. "One of the finest pictures I can recall showed people in strange dark clothes walking to church. Snow covered the ground, the trees stood gaunt and bare against a grey sky. The men carried muskets, doggedly watching on every side.

"The teacher said that yonder was the wind-swept graveyard on the hill where nearly half their number had been buried during their first winter in this land. Beyond the hill was the dark and forboding wilderness, the continent known as America. Then the teacher added, 'They are walking through the snow and bitter cold and risking attack from the Indians because they want to worship God. They want to thank God for their blessings. They are all alone in a strange land. They don't have much food. Many have become sick and died. They have had much trouble and they know they will have more trouble. But they are thankful for what blessings they have. So they want to worship and serve their God.'

"That is the great reward for those who practice the art of gratitude."
—Bishop Everett W. Palmer, in *Pulpit Preaching*.

Just *why* did they want to worship? Just *what* did they have to be thankful for?

Self-Made Man. " 'Everything I have I have earned for myself,' said a man to me today. I could only look at him with blank disbelief, and answer that I had been more fortunate. I started out as a baby with advantages I had done nothing to earn; I was born into a home I had done nothing to create; I was given the benefits of education I had done nothing to devise; I was greeted with pictures I had not painted, songs I had not composed, domestic conveniences I had not invented. In fact, I am in debt all round. I was reminded of the man who said to Dr. Parker in the City Temple (London), 'Sir, I am a self-made man.' To which Parker replied, 'That lifts a load of responsibility from the shoulders of the Almighty!' "—W. B. J. Martin, in *Presbyterian Outlook*.

Let us sing praises to the Almighty *Creator* . . . !

Sentence Sermon to Remember: God has two dwellings: one in heaven, and the other in a meek and thankful heart.—Izaak Walton.

Questions for Pupils on the Next Lesson: 1. On what conditions does God grant us forgiveness? 2. Is II Samuel 12:1–15 the inspiration David had for Psalm 51? Explain. 3. Of what do you need to be forgiven? 4. What is "trespassing" in the Bible sense? 5. Has there ever been a man who was not a sinner? 6. *How* does God forgive sin? 7. Do you think it would be good for Protestants to have a system of confession like that of the Roman Catholics?

LESSON VIII—JULY 23

CONFESSION AND FORGIVENESS

Background Scripture: II Samuel 12:1–15; Psalm 51;
I John 1:8–9
Devotional Reading: Psalm 32:1–11

KING JAMES VERSION	REVISED STANDARD VERSION
PSALM 51 Have mercy upon me, O God, according to thy loving-kindness: according unto the multitude of thy tender mercies blot out my transgressions.	PSALM 51 Have mercy on me, O God, according to thy steadfast love; according to thy abundant mercy blot out my transgressions.
2 Wash me thoroughly from mine iniquity, and cleanse me from my sin.	2 Wash me thoroughly from my iniquity, and cleanse me from my sin!
3 For I acknowledge my transgressions: and my sin is ever before me.	3 For I know my transgressions, and my sin is ever before me.
4 Against thee, thee only, have I sinned, and done this evil in thy sight: that thou mightest be justified when thou speakest, and be clear when thou judgest.	4 Against thee, thee only, have I sinned, and done that which is evil in thy sight, so that thou art justified in thy sentence and blameless in thy judgment.
5 Behold, I was shapen in iniquity; and in sin did my mother conceive me.	5 Behold, I was brought forth in iniquity, and in sin did my mother conceive me.
6 Behold, thou desirest truth in the inward parts: and in the hidden part thou shalt make me to know wisdom.	6 Behold, thou desirest truth in the inward being; therefore teach me wisdom in my secret heart.
7 Purge me with hyssop, and I shall be clean: wash me, and I shall be whiter than snow.	7 Purge me with hyssop, and I shall be clean; wash me, and I shall be whiter than snow.
8 Make me to hear joy and gladness; that the bones which thou hast broken may rejoice.	8 Fill me with joy and gladness; let the bones which thou hast broken rejoice.
9 Hide thy face from my sins, and blot out all mine iniquities.	9 Hide thy face from my sins, and blot out all my iniquities.
10 Create in me a clean heart, O God; and renew a right spirit within me.	10 Create in me a clean heart, O God, and put a new and right spirit within me.
11 Cast me not away from thy presence; and take not thy Holy Spirit from me.	11 Cast me not away from thy presence, and take not thy holy Spirit from me.
12 Restore unto me the joy of thy salvation; and uphold me *with thy* free Spirit.	12 Restore to me the joy of thy salvation, and uphold me with a willing spirit.

342

MEMORY SELECTION: If we confess our sins, he is faithful and just to forgive us our sins, and to cleanse us from all unrighteousness. I John 1:9.

HOME DAILY BIBLE READINGS

July 17. M. Power of Confession, Hebrews 4:11–16.
July 18. T. Prayer and Confession, James 5:13–20.
July 19. W. Confession Brings Forgiveness, I John 1:1–10.
July 20. T. God Forgives Sin, Luke 5:17–26.
July 21. F. We Have Forgiveness, Colossians 1:9–14.
July 22. S. The Heart of Confession, Luke 24:44–49.
July 23. S. The Blessing of Forgiveness, Psalm 32:1–11.

BACKGROUND

The 51st Psalm is ascribed to David, "when Nathan the prophet came unto him, after he had gone in to Bath-sheba." David had just committed his worst sin, made the most disgusting mistake of his career: he had stolen another man's wife and sent that man out to die. Nathan the prophet comes to him, and condemns him to his face. David admits his crime, and the prophet says, "The Lord also hath put away thy sin . . ." (II Samuel 12).

Now, David may or may not have written this Psalm, but it describes perfectly what happened in the mind and heart of that great man and king when his sin was disclosed. His admission to Nathan, "I have sinned against the Lord . . . ," (II Samuel 12:13), was the beginning of his sincere repentance and forgiveness. Psalm 51 is called the greatest of all penitential Psalms and prayers in all literature. It illustrates perfectly the agony of sin and the beauty of its forgiving.

It was written for us—for every one of us, for every one of us has sinned and stands in need of forgiveness. We should pray daily the prayer of the guilty king. . . .

NOTES ON THE PRINTED TEXT

I. Have mercy upon me, O God . . . , Psalm 51:1. Once we become conscious of the fact that we have insulted God and harmed man in one way or another, we instinctively turn to God for forgiveness for the simple reason that He is the only one who can finally and completely forgive and absolve us. The sinner who repents is the near saint, but that man is *wicked* who refuses to throw himself on the mercy of God; his guilt will haunt him to the end of his life.

We knew a ten-year-old boy who was asked, "Do you believe you have been forgiven for your sins?" He replied, "*What* sins?" It was a good question. The boy asked it not as an adult sinner might ask it, but in sincere search for the truth. *What* sins?

The Psalmist divided sin into three categories.

There is "transgression," which is deliberate violation of a law or command. In the moral and spiritual sense, it is defying the sign that reads, "No Trespassing." It is the sin of a son in rebellion against his father. It is, says someone, like "a private slapping a general in the face."

There is "iniquity"—injustice, corruption, crookedness, or punishment carried too far. Racial bigotry is iniquity; the taking of bribes or graft is iniquity; exaction of vengeance is iniquity.

There is just plain "sin"—which means violation of the divine law, either deliberately or through neglect. The man who knows the right thing to do but doesn't do it is a sinner. The man who silently refuses to accept all other men as brothers is a sinner. The man who cheats God when he thinks he is only cheating his fellow-man is a sinner. Sin is "missing the mark," taking the low road when we know we should be on the high road!

All who are innocent of any of this—stand up! No honest man can stand up. *All* of us are guilty of some sin. All of us need forgiveness. God has three ways of offering forgiveness. He can *blot out* its stain, as we pick up an inkspot with a blotter; He can *wash* out hearts clean of evil and put good in its place; or He can *cleanse* us as a refiner cleanses metal from its dross. (See Malachi 3:3.) All of us are guilty, all dirty. There was only One who was not. . . .

II. *Against thee, thee only, have I sinned. . . . I was shapen in iniquity,* Psalm 51:4, 5. When we wrong a fellow-man we sin not so much against him as against God. Inasmuch as we do it to a brother, we do it to God: A lie to a fellow-man is a denial of God and His law; an indignity or insult offered to anyone is an insult thrown into God's face. To deny any of His commandments is to deny *Him.* Sin is willful turning from God.

The Psalmist hints that often we cannot help sinning: we were born in sin! We all inherit a little of the first sinning Adam in our cradles. "I was brought forth in iniquity, and in sin did my mother conceive me" (verse 5 RSV).

"In connecting sin with his birth he [the Psalmist] was not speaking of the sex act or of ceremonial uncleanliness associated with conception and birth (Leviticus 12:2). Rather he is confessing that he is a sinner born of sinners. This is not an attempt to avoid personal responsibility for his transgressions, but to acknowledge his solidarity with others in the human predicament (compare Isaiah 6:5). All men stand in the need of a salvation which they themselves cannot provide."—Arnold B. Rhodes, in *The Book of Psalms,* p. 86, *The Layman's Bible Commentary.* Quoted by permission of John Knox Press, publishers.

III. *Behold, thou desireth truth in the inward being; therefore teach me wisdom in my secret heart,* Psalm 51:6 (RSV). Verses 6–12 are the most penitential of this whole penitential Psalm; they are really a prayer from the lips of a concerned sinner who wants to stop being a sinner, and to be able to approach God in utter sincerity. He asks God to "purge [him] with hyssop"—an aromatic plant used in the ceremony of purification by persons healed of leprosy (see Leviticus 14:9). He longs to be washed clean of his sin—until "I shall be whiter than snow" (see Isaiah 1:18). But, above all, he asks God, "Create in me a clean heart . . . and put a new and right spirit within me" (verse 10, RSV).

This is important: the Psalmist knew that renewal comes from the inside out, never from the outside in! You can dress up a drunk in a two-hundred-dollar suit, but under those clothes he is still a drunk *until his heart is changed.* This is a prayer that the "right spirit" might get into the heart and make it new; it is also a prayer for emotional and spiritual stability. It is a prayer which understands that only God can give the spirit and renew the heart; the God who created the heavens and the universe uses the same power in rebuilding human life from within.

Now read in II Corinthians 5:16–21 the description of how we can become "new creatures," and in John 3:1–16 the doctrine of the "new birth." Do you see the influence of Psalm 51 on these passages?

"Take not thy holy Spirit from me" (verse 11)! In worship, we are engaged in the business of *constant* soul renewal, and life changing. Ignore worship, and we wither. . . .

SUGGESTIONS TO TEACHERS

Begin teaching today by having one of your class read II Samuel 12:1–13 and stopping him quickly when he comes to verse 13: "I have sinned against the Lord." In these words lies the thrust of the lesson; they are a mirror held to the heart of David's devotional life, and—probably—the inspiration of Psalm 51, which he is reported to have written.

In the truly devotional life shine three great lights: they are called *confession, repentance*, and *forgiveness*. Take them one by one. . . .

TOPIC FOR ADULTS
RECEIVING GOD'S FORGIVENESS

Prescription. "A woman consulted her physician and told him he must do something immediately or she was going to have a nervous breakdown. He told her to spend the first thirty minutes of her day reading the Bible and praying.

"She was incensed; she said, 'I came here for medical treatment, expecting to pay for it, and I don't want to be preached to.' He replied, 'I'm giving you medical treatment. It will cost you fifty dollars, and if you do it you will avert a breakdown.'

"Six months later she came to his office and said, 'Doctor, it worked. I was mad at my husband. I literally hated the woman next door. I couldn't sleep and I was all tied up in knots on the inside. After spending that thirty minutes a day in Bible study and prayer, I've found forgiveness, peace of mind, and happiness.' "—Gaston Foote.

There it is: confession that she was wrong in her anger and hatred, and repentant enough to go to the Bible and prayer as a source of help—where she did find God's forgiveness through study and prayer.

Is there any other way to find His forgiveness?

Forgiveness. The German air force all but wiped out the city of Coventry in World War II; the cathedral in this city was left a heap of charred ruins. It was one of those things that cities and even nations refuse to forget or forgive. Remember the Maine! Remember Pearl Harbor! Remember the Black Hole of Calcutta! Keep your hatred alive and burning—and some fine day get your revenge!

But strange things have happened in postwar Coventry. A working force of young men came from Germany to help build a new cathedral on the ruins of the old. And over the door of the new cathedral is a large cross made of burned wood and melted metal, salvaged from the ruins. On it is the word, "Forgiven!"

If we all felt and acted like that, there would never be another Coventry—or another war. . . .

Restitution. Some of us have the idea that all we have to do to obtain God's forgiveness is to confess our sins and say "I'm sorry," and forget the whole thing. Maybe so. We do not know the mind of God or what He may demand by way of repentance, but this solution seems too easy. We don't let a criminal go scot-free when he says "I'm sorry. . . ."

We like better the repentance of Jim Vaus, who once was a thief, working with a crime syndicate. When he was converted in a Billy Graham crusade, he paid back more than $15,000 of his stolen money. It took his car, his house, his bank accounts and almost everything else that he and his wife owned. We'd call that repentance.

Guilt. Modern psychologists and psychiatrists are telling us that we are silly to keep alive a burden of guilt for our sins; some of them even doubt that there is such a thing as sin. But we have seen too many cases in which this guilt "complex" paid off in positive action—and repentance.

For a century and a half guilt stricken Americans have been sending "conscience money" to the U.S. Treasury in Washington. When a delinquent of 1811 sent in his first tax payment, he said that he was suffering "the most painful pangs of conscience." Another sent a note with his money, saying, "About 25 years ago I cheated on my taxes." An old soldier sent $200 to pay for a mule he had stolen from the army. . . .

Conscience and guilt are stern masters; they demand all-out repentance.

We read somewhere that the government conscience fund now totals something like four million dollars. We wonder what the government has done, or is doing, with the money!

Vengeance or Forgiveness? It is often difficult for men and nations to forgive a crime like mass murder. We remember the case of Adolf Eichmann, the Nazi criminal who was responsible for the death and cremation of thousands of Jews in Nazi Germany. The whole world was repulsed by the slaughter; many demanded that he be hanged with or without a trial. And hanged he was. We called it justice. Was it justice—or only vengeance? Would confinement for life, during which he would have lived with his own guilt, have been a better sentence— a more Christian sentence? None of us wanted to see him go free, but . . . !

On the other hand, there were Mrs. Martin Luther King and Ralph Abernathy, King's successor, who asked that the life of Dr. King's murderer be spared.

Which was the better way? Which do you think was God's way? Lest we forget—Christ prayed for His executioners as He was dying on His cross!

Questions for Pupils on the Next Lesson: 1. Describe your relationship with God. 2. Is your concept of God the same as the concept you held as a child? 3. Give five reasons why you think God is the greatest power in the universe. 4. How do you know that God was in Christ? 5. *Why* should we love God? 6. What other names do we use for "God"? 7. Explain the words of I John 4:12 beginning, "No man hath seen God at any time, . . ."

TOPIC FOR YOUTH
WHEN I FEEL GUILTY

Father, Forgive. "G. A. Johnston Ross told of an incident that occurred years ago during the celebration of the Lord's Supper in a little missionary church in New Zealand. A line of worshipers had just knelt at the altar rail when suddenly from among them a young native arose and returned to his pew. Some minutes later, however, he returned to his place at the rail. Afterward, a friend inquired why he had done this. He replied:

" 'When I went forward and knelt, I found myself side by side with a man who some years ago had slain my father, and whom I had vowed to kill. I found I could not partake with him, and so I returned to my pew. But as I sat there, my mind went back to a picture of the Upper Room, with its table set, and I heard a voice saying, "By this shall all men know that ye are my disciples, if ye have love for one another." And then I saw a cross with a man nailed upon it, and the same voice saying, "Father, forgive them; for they know not what they do." It was then that I arose and returned to the altar rail.' "—Donald Macleod.

That needs no comment or explanation. . . .

Them, Us. Christian Herald recently had a startling cover. There were nineteen words on the cover—and nothing else. The words were: "Father, forgive them; for they know not what they do." And then the words, "Father, forgive us, for we know what we do."

They are terrible words.

Scars. In his day, Eddie Shore was a terror on ice; as a professional hockey player, he was probably more feared and hated than any other defense man in the country. Hockey is a rough and sometimes brutal game; no quarter is asked or expected, and many injuries are inflicted. When Eddie finally retired, he had set a record: he had had more than six hundred stitches taken in his face!

He's an old man now, but still lively—and still, in spite of those stitches, a fine-looking man. He refused to let his scars disfigure him. He massaged his wounds, mercilessly. It took about three years to massage one scar out of existence, he says; some others took a little longer. With steady rubbing and with the help of face creams, the scars were wiped off and out.

Some people love scars and wounds, and do their best to keep them showing. They never forgive or forget. Jesus told them to stop that practice: "How often shall my brother sin against me, and I forgive him? As many as seven times? . . . I do not say to you seven times, but seventy times seven" (Matthew 18:21–22, rsv). Or—indefinitely!

If you expect God to forgive your sins, you forgive your brother—indefinitely.

Confession. While he was pastor of Fifth Avenue Presbyterian Church, in New York City, Dr. John Sutherland Bonnell made a plea for a confessional in Protestant churches. Confession, he said, "should not be regarded as necessarily habitual or compulsory, but thousands of our people who need and desire it should be given a chance to confess their sins." He was pleading for private, not public Protestant confessions, and he reminded us that the great Protestant reformers—Luther, Calvin and Knox—believed that confessions, either public or private, had value under certain circumstances. When we fail to "hear confessions" from our people, Dr. Bonnell said, we turn over to the psychiatrists and psychologists a work that the church should be doing.

We may or may not agree. Confession as we have it in the Roman Catholic Church is too often a ritual, a formality, a "patter" that allows the sinner to confess and be forgiven quickly and easily—and go out and do it all over again! But we must not forget that to the Catholics the church is a *mother,* and mothers, knowing that their children will sin again and again, go on forgiving and forgiving. . . .

If confession is as deep as the heart is deep, and completely honest, it is good. But Francis Xavier once said that he had heard thousands of confessions but never one of covetousness. That, he said, is "a sin we never mention."

Would you like a Protestant confessional ritual?

Three Words. "Many three-word phrases in our language are powerful or significant or informative, but the one that probably gives the greatest over-all peace of mind is 'I was wrong.' "—The Advocate, Allen, Oklahoma.

So few of us have the courage to admit that!

Sentence Sermon to Remember: It is the confession not the priest that gives absolution.—Oscar Wilde.

Questions for Pupils on the Next Lesson: 1. How do we know that God "abides in us"? 2. What does the work and personality of Jesus tell us about God? 3. How may we "have confidence for the day of judgment" (I John 4:17)? 4. How is "every family in heaven and on earth" named, according to John 1:4? 5. Is your God closer to you now than He was ten years ago? 6. What power is working within us (Ephesians 3:20)? 7. How did Jesus Christ become a *living* presence in your heart?

LESSON IX—JULY 30

DEEPENING OUR RELATIONSHIP WITH GOD

Background Scripture: I John 4:13–19; Ephesians 3:14–21
Devotional Reading: Philippians 3:7–16

KING JAMES VERSION

I JOHN 4 13 Hereby know we that we dwell in him, and he in us, because he hath given us of his Spirit.

14 And we have seen and do testify that the Father sent the Son to be the Saviour of the world.

15 Whosoever shall confess that Jesus is the Son of God, God dwelleth in him, and he in God.

16 And we have known and believed the love that God hath to us. God is love; and he that dwelleth in love dwelleth in God, and God in him.

17 Herein is our love made perfect, that we may have boldness in the day of judgment: because as he is, so are we in this world.

18 There is no fear in love; but perfect love casteth out fear: because fear hath torment. He that feareth is not made perfect in love.

19 We love him, because he first loved us.

EPHESIANS 3 14 For this cause I bow my knees unto the Father of our Lord Jesus Christ,

15 Of whom the whole family in heaven and earth is named,

16 That he would grant you, according to the riches of his glory, to be strengthened with might by his Spirit in the inner man;

17 That Christ may dwell in your hearts by faith; that ye, being rooted and grounded in love,

18 May be able to comprehend with all saints what is the breadth, and length, and depth, and height;

19 And to know the love of Christ, which passeth knowledge, that ye might be filled with all the fulness of God.

20 Now unto him that is able to do exceeding abundantly above all that we ask or think, according to the power that worketh in us,

21 Unto him be glory in the church by Christ Jesus throughout all ages, world without end. Amen.

REVISED STANDARD VERSION

I JOHN 4 13 By this we know that we abide in him and he in us, because he has given us of his own Spirit. 14 And we have seen and testify that the Father has sent his Son as the Savior of the world. 15 Whoever confesses that Jesus is the Son of God, God abides in him, and he in God. 16 So we know and believe the love God has for us. God is love, and he who abides in love abides in God, and God abides in him. 17 In this is love perfected with us, that we may have confidence for the day of judgment, because as he is so are we in this world. 18 There is no fear in love, but perfect love casts out fear. For fear has to do with punishment, and he who fears is not perfected in love. 19 We love, because he first loved us.

EPHESIANS 3 14 For this reason I bow my knees before the Father, 15 from whom every family in heaven and on earth is named, 16 that according to the riches of his glory he may grant you to be strengthened with might through his Spirit in the inner man, 17 and that Christ may dwell in your hearts through faith; that you, being rooted and grounded in love, 18 may have power to comprehend with all the saints what is the breadth and length and height and depth, 19 and to know the love of Christ which surpasses knowledge, that you may be filled with all the fullness of God.

20 Now to him who by the power at work within us is able to do far more abundantly than all that we ask or think, 21 to him be glory in the church and in Christ Jesus to all generations, for ever and ever. Amen.

MEMORY SELECTION: . . . it is no longer I who live, but Christ who lives in me; and the life I now live in the flesh I live by faith in the Son of God, who loved me and gave himself for me. Galatians 2:20 (RSV).

HOME DAILY BIBLE READINGS

July 24. M. *The Relationship Begins,* Romans 5:1–11.
July 25. T. *Christ the Basis,* Romans 5:12–21.
July 26. W. *Dead to Sin,* Romans 6:1–14.
July 27. T. *Life in the Spirit,* Romans 8:1–17.
July 28. F. *Relating to God,* Romans 12:9–21.
July 29. S. *Workmen for God,* I Corinthians 3:1–9.
July 30. S. *Righteousness from God,* Philippians 3:7–11.

BACKGROUND

Millions of us worship God every Sunday and throughout all the week, but not many ever stop to work out a really intelligent concept of God, or to try to understand their relationship to Him. Here is the greatest power in the universe, the Creator of it all, who ordains and directs the stars and planets in the heavens, the tides of the seas, the spinning of our earth in space—and here *we* are, crawling about on just one little planet, living fitfully for three-score and ten years, more or less. How are we related to this awesome God, how can we improve and deepen that relationship? It is a question often too big for our little, finite minds—until we approach God through Christ.

Along about the year 90, the Apostle John wrote three short letters in which he discussed all this. Even earlier, about 62, Paul wrote on the same theme in a letter to the Ephesians. Both of them say that a proper relationship between God and man is based on just one attribute, just one *word.* Can you find that word in reading these passages in I John and Ephesians?

NOTES ON THE PRINTED TEXT

I. God is love, I John 4:16. If John I is a sample of apostolic preaching, then that preaching was preaching on fire and abundant with light. John did not preach in any uncertain tones about God; he *knew* God, and no doubt ever shook him, no sneering cynic ever made him "change his tune." To him, God was not just an idea, not a ghostly presence away "out there" in the universe, hopelessly removed from men, hopelessly incomprehensible. He was no God withdrawn from most and known only to a privileged few; He was a God whose other name was Love, whose very inner nature was love. We should see that beyond the shadow of "reasonable doubt," because we have seen Jesus Christ, who was the living, walking, working personification of that love. ". . . his love was disclosed to us in this, that he sent his only Son into the world to bring us life" (verse 9, NEB).

Now, John denies that we are able to love God. Does that disturb you? It need not, when you understand it. What he means is that the love he is talking about is not our love for God, but "the love He showed to us in sending his Son as the remedy for the defilement of our sins" (verse 10, NEB). It is God who loves *us;* we love because He first loved us. We love each other because of what God has done for us in love. We live in an atmosphere of love which came from Him to us. And when we do that, we live *in* God, and He lives *in* us. This is what the Apostle John was thinking of when he said, "No man hath seen God at any time; the only begotten Son . . . he hath declared him" (John 1:18), and what Jesus meant when He said, "God is a Spirit: and they that worship him must worship him in spirit and in truth" (John 4:24). God is the Spirit of love.

John goes on to say that, living in this glow of love, we lose all our *fear*. What a gift *that* is! Every one of us lives in fear of something or someone; it is a universal trait of human character. Some even live in fear of a punishing God! They forget that in the Scriptures, where we are taught to live in the fear of God, what is actually meant is that we are to live in the *love* of God. The fears that haunt us and often destroy us are the result of our lack of love—of a wrong concept of God and an erroneous approach to Him. If we lived completely in His love, fear would be "cast out"—there would be no *room* for fear. "Thou wilt keep him in perfect peace, whose mind is stayed on thee: because he trusteth in thee" (Isaiah 26:3). If we cannot trust a God who Himself is love— whom or what *can* we trust?

II. For this cause I bow my knees unto the Father of our Lord Jesus Christ . . . , Ephesians 3:14. Usually, Jewish worshipers stood when they prayed (see Mark 11:25; Luke 18:11, 13). But Paul *kneels* when he offers this prayer in Ephesians; that marks it as a prayer of unusual earnestness. He addresses the prayer to God the Father "from whom every family in heaven and on earth is named." (Here, the word translated "family" is derived from the word translated "Father." We might paraphrase it: "All *fatherhood*, whether earthy or celestial, derives its name from the Fatherhood of God.") There are three petitions in the prayer:

(1) May God grant them (us) strength and power through His Spirit in the "inner man." Paul says in II Corinthians 4:16 that he does not wonder that we "lose heart" so often, but that one who knows Christ and has the Spirit in his heart, though his "outward humanity is in decay," will find his heart renewed *day by day*, renewed in the strength of the Holy Spirit, which is the driving power of his life in Christ. The Spirit within works to improve his nature and character, to stimulate his reason and enliven his conscience and his will. Let that Spirit die, and Christ dies in us.

(2) May Christ dwell in our hearts by faith. This is something of a repetition of (1). But, in the doctrine of the Trinity, Christ and the Holy Spirit are two as well as one. May they both be alive in our hearts! The memory of Jesus is not enough; lip worship to Him once a week in church is not enough. He must be a *living* presence; the resurrection of Jesus tells us that a dead Christ would have been useless to the ages following Calvary. He must live in living hearts *by faith*. If we cannot have faith in His presence there, we can hardly have faith in anything else we are taught about Him.

(3) May we have "deep roots and firm foundations" (verse 17). Foundations and roots, that is, *in love*. As we worship in love "with all the saints"—with the Christian community. Worshiping with them in spirit and in truth and in love, we can discover the breadth and length

and depth and height of the love of Christ, and the discovery will be something more than we can find through the pursuit of knowledge *about* Christ. Paul doesn't say that knowledge is worthless, only that love is more important than knowledge. Love of God is a greater power than knowledge *about* Christ. What is in the heart is more important than what is in the mind. (You may not agree with that; talk it out!)

Verses 20 and 21 are added as a sort of doxology; it is still used as that, following the sermon, in our Protestant Episcopal churches. Could we say that in essence it means, "May we have a God *big* enough"?

SUGGESTIONS TO TEACHERS

In the Christian home, relationships between parents and children, between husband and wife, are clearly understood and accepted; we know that each member of the family has his "place," that there must be respect for authority, and that behind that authority and obedience there is a law of love holding the whole family together.

In the Christian faith, there is a relationship between God the Father and His children that is not always clearly defined or understood. Few of us can explain intelligently just what our concept of God is, just how we "live with Him," just how much authority He has over our lives. And too few of us understand that it is a relationship of love on both sides!

Today we are to try to work out a clearer understanding of this relationship with God. We can do it by

(1) Recognizing the *greatness* of God.
(2) Basing our relationship with Him on faith in Christ, in whom we find Him most perfectly revealed.
(3) Developing our love for and confidence in God through courageous, Christlike living.
(4) Cultivating a *partnership* with God.

TOPIC FOR ADULTS
DEEPENING OUR RELATIONSHIP WITH GOD

Big Enough? Nearly twenty years ago J. B. Phillips wrote a big little book called *Plain Christianity*. In less than one hundred pages, he tells us more about God than most other men have managed to tell us in five hundred. We quote a sample:

". . . even those of us who profess and call ourselves Christians need to be aware of having a view of God that's too small. We have to beware of confining God to the pages of the Bible (though He certainly does speak there) or to the four walls of a church (though He certainly is present there). I sometimes think that the pictures in our prayer books, instead of being reproductions of religious works of art, should be, for instance, a picture of the Milky Way—to remind us of the vastness of God's creation; a picture of a bowl of flowers—to remind us of His love of beauty; even a picture of the structure of the human eye—to remind us of His meticulous accuracy as Designer.

"And so, if we're going to get to know God the first step for a great many of us today is to clean up our ideas about Him. We must bring to the surface of our minds all the false and inadequate ideas—and see how false and inadequate they are. We must use our adult minds or we shall go through life thinking that God is a childish fancy and no more.

"Having done this, I would suggest that we open every door of our minds and spirits to let in the bigness of God. We need to associate with God all that is lovely and wonderful and mysterious and heart warming. . . . We can never have too big an idea of God."—From *Plain Christianity*, by J. B. Phillips, pp. 43–44. Quoted by permission of The Macmillan Company, publishers.

Partnership. Wallace E. Johnson borrowed $250 in 1939 to set himself up in business. Today he is president of Holiday Inns of America, Inc., employing 110,000 persons. He has built homes and hospitals; he developed a major corporation known as Medicenters of America, Inc., a chain of treatment centers for those who do not need the more expensive care of hospitals. He is a great American "success story." He takes little personal credit for all this:

"I quite frankly admit that I am totally dependent on God for help in everything I do. If I kept Him out of my business I honestly believe it would fall apart in a matter of months. . . . Not too many years ago I was a man of 38 working as a $37.50 a week salesman for a building supply company. I wasn't even very successful at this job. Nothing seemed to go right.

"Instead of a routine, perfunctory prayer, I felt guided to pray to God about my work. I think this is where so many of us fall short. We do not take God along as a partner with us all week in our work. I pray, in essence: 'Lord, I've been trying to make a go of it as a salesman, but I'm not doing very well. What am I doing wrong? Show me, Lord, the direction I should go, the people I should see, the way I should use my time.' "
—Condensed from *Praying Hands*, November–December 1967. Quoted by permission.

It was then that the success story started.

No—working with God doesn't always make a man rich and successful —nor should it! But such a partnership produces a happiness and a sense of accomplishment "more precious than rubies."

Son of God. "He was the world's premier preacher, but we can hardly describe Him accurately by calling Him a pulpiteer. It would seem irreverent to call Him Reverend Jesus. He was the world's greatest teacher, but it would be profane to call Him Professor Jesus. There is only one word big enough to summarize His work: the Man of Nazareth, and because He so completely fulfilled the wholeness of manhood we Christians call him the Son of God."—Kenneth B. Wentzel.

In this Son *was* the Father; our fulfillment is found only in faith in Him, in following His commitment *to* the Father. . . .

God and Man. "A real knowledge of God cannot be taught us by rote, but must be converted into personal experience. Blessed is the man who has more than an intellectual theory of the Lord, and has achieved a sense of living with Him. These religious experiences turn the muck of earth into the firmament of heaven."—George Christian Anderson.

Questions for Pupils on the Next Lesson: 1. Describe the place and importance of the Temple in Jerusalem to the Jews. 2. What is the origin of the word "worship"? 3. Name the "Zion Hymns" and the "Hymns of Pilgrimage" in the Book of Psalms. 4. What values do you find in *congregational* worship? 5. Name three vital elements in congregational worship. 6. Can we worship at a Sunday picnic in the mountains as well as we worship in church? 7. What new patterns would you add to your church's worship?

TOPIC FOR YOUTH
A SPECIAL RELATIONSHIP

The Fine Parts. Frank K. Ellis crashed his plane and woke up in a hospital with his legs paralyzed. He says that only his close relationship to God saved his mind and his life, and enabled him to fly again:

"No man walks alone . . . and it is my personal conviction that God will cast a helpful eye on any man who calls on Him. Conviction, determination, faith . . . these are the fine parts of man, God within us; and if there is tragedy and hopelessness in the world, it is because some men do not grasp these things and hold on to them with a grip of iron. Taken from you may be your arms, or your legs, or your eyes . . . but you can never be defeated while your conviction, determination and faith remain." —From *No Man Walks Alone*, by Frank K. Ellis (Revell).

These are the secrets of a relationship that gives power available nowhere else on our earth. . . .

The Visitor. To some of us, God is a stern lawmaker, a giver of rules, an exacting taskmaster. To others, He is greatly more. For instance:

"I pulled into town last night on week-end business and, being a new Christian, was eager to drop in on one of the local churches. One of those listed at the motel sounded like what I was looking for. I walked in the front door at 9:45 and found the adult Sunday-school class in full swing. I sat down quietly and listened. An elderly man in the class was speaking:

" 'I just don't think it's right for a Christian to play bridge,' he said. 'It can ruin his testimony, for one thing.'

"Then a lady added: 'That's right. It's the same thing with make-up. It's just as sinful the way some people paint themselves up.'

"The teacher of the class nodded in agreement and said the situation in a lot of churches was deteriorating. He even knew some deacons in another church (which he did not name) who practiced the unchristian habit of chewing tobacco. The class then turned into a lively discussion of what things were lawful and unlawful for the believer. I sat there and listened, intrigued and amazed. Playing golf on Sundays, washing cars on Sundays, movie attendance, smoking, eating in places where liquor is served, missing church when away on week ends, and many other subjects were heatedly discussed.

"When the class was finally over, one of the women came over to me and introduced herself. 'It's so nice to have you here visiting with us. What church are you a member of?'

"I explained that I wasn't a member of any church yet and that I had formerly been a Roman Catholic.

" 'Oh, how interesting,' she said. 'It must be nice to come out from under that legalistic system of man-made rules and doctrines.' I just looked at her. And I didn't bother to stay for the service."—Ralph Filicchia, in *Eternity*, April, 1970.

Good for Ralph Filicchia! He had a God bigger than *that*. God doesn't march around with a club demanding little reforms: He comes quietly, saying, *"Love . . . !"*

Seeing Him. "Always Christians had thought and hoped, and dreamed and wondered about God. If only He were this, if only He were that! But at the cross He breaks silence, the veil is rent from top to bottom, and they find themselves looking up into God's very face, seeing Him as He really is, hearing Him speaking, as it were, with His very own voice to them. And what a wonderful message it is that comes through!"— Robert Gossip, in *The Galilean Accent.*

This is what we mean by God in Christ.

His Hand. "If you ask me how I believe in God, how God creates Himself in me, and reveals Himself to me, my answer may perhaps provoke your smiles or laughter, and even scandalize you. I believe in God as I believe in my friends, because I feel the breath of His affection, feel His invisible and intangible hand drawing me, leading me, grasping me."—Miguel de Unamuno.

Sentence Sermon to Remember: God can work only through an unworthy man; those who feel worthy cannot serve God.—George E. Failing.

Questions for Pupils on the Next Lesson: 1. What worship *practices* are described in the 122nd Psalm? 2. What elements of public worship have Protestant Christians borrowed from Judaism? 3. What is meant by the words "provoke unto love" (Hebrews 10:24)? 4. How was Jerusalem "compact together" (Psalm 122:3)? 5. Do you seek the good of others in your church worship (Psalm 122:9)? 6. Should we have more participation by laymen in our congregational worship? 7. Would you prefer worshiping in someone's home with a small group to worshiping with a big congregation in a church? Why, or why not?

LESSON X—AUGUST 6

WORSHIPING IN THE CONGREGATION

Background Scripture: Psalm 122; I Corinthians 11:23–28;
Hebrews 10:23–25
Devotional Reading: Psalm 34:1–10

KING JAMES VERSION

PSALM 122   I was glad when they said unto me, Let us go into the house of the Lord.

2 Our feet shall stand within thy gates, O Jerusalem.
3 Jerusalem is builded as a city that is compact together:
4 Whither the tribes go up, the tribes of the Lord, unto the testimony of Israel, to give thanks unto the name of the Lord.

5 For there are set thrones of judgment, the thrones of the house of David.

6 Pray for the peace of Jerusalem: they shall prosper that love thee.
7 Peace be within thy walls, and prosperity within thy palaces.
8 For my brethren and companions' sakes, I will now say, Peace *be* within thee.
9 Because of the house of the Lord our God I will seek thy good.

HEBREWS 10   23 Let us hold fast the profession of our faith without wavering; for he is faithful that promised;
24 And let us consider one another to provoke unto love and to good works:
25 Not forsaking the assembling of ourselves together, as the manner of some is; but exhorting one another: and so much the more, as ye see the day approaching.

REVISED STANDARD VERSION

PSALM 122   I was glad when they said to me,
"Let us go to the house of the Lord!"
2 Our feet have been standing
within your gates, O Jerusalem!
3 Jerusalem, built as a city
which is bound firmly together,
4 to which the tribes go up,
the tribes of the Lord,
as was decreed for Israel,
to give thanks to the name of the Lord.
5 There thrones for judgment were set,
the thrones of the house of David.
6 Pray for the peace of Jerusalem!
"May they prosper who love you!
7 Peace be within your walls,
and security within your towers!"
8 For my brethren and companions' sake
I will say, "Peace be within you!"
9 For the sake of the house of the Lord our God,
I will seek your good.
HEBREWS 10   23 Let us hold fast the confession of our hope without wavering, for he who promised is faithful; 24 and let us consider how to stir up one another to love and good works, 25 not neglecting to meet together, as is the habit of some, but encouraging one another, and all the more as you see the Day drawing near.

MEMORY SELECTION: *O magnify the Lord with me, and let us exalt his name together.* Psalm 34:3.

HOME DAILY BIBLE READINGS

July 31. M. Jesus "Goes to Church," Luke 4:16–24.
Aug. 1. T. Thoughts for Worship, Psalm 4.
Aug. 2. W. God in His Sanctuary, Psalm 68:24–35.
Aug. 3. T. Affirmations That Aid, Psalm 19.

Aug. 4. F. The Time Is Now! Hebrews 3:7–19.
Aug. 5. S. Attitudes in Worship, Isaiah 6:1–13.
Aug. 6. S. Magnifying the Lord, Psalm 34:1–10.

BACKGROUND

In 621 B.C., while Josiah was king of Judah, the reform code of Deuteronomy became the law of the land—and under that code the Temple at Jerusalem became the legitimate sanctuary for the public worship of God. Under this law, the male population of Judah came three times a year—at the feasts of Passover, Weeks, and Tabernacles—to worship at the Temple. In this worship, they sang two groups of Psalms: the "Zion Hymns" (Psalms 48, 87, 46 and 76) and the "Hymns of Pilgrimage" (Psalms 82 and 122).

As you read the Scripture, think more of the Temple than of the city of Jerusalem. And when you think of the Temple think also of the church as a station along the way of our pilgrimage to "Zion" and of our worship there.

NOTES ON THE PRINTED TEXT

I. Our feet have been standing within thy gates, O Jerusalem, Psalm 122:2. Get the image of the pilgrim in your mind; *after* he has worshiped in the Temple, see him standing there, looking back at it, deeply stirred by what has happened in his heart during the seven days he has spent at the feast. He remembers how glad he was when he was invited to join a party of pilgrims: "I was glad when they said unto me, 'Let us go into the house of the Lord.' Now the worship and the feast are over, and he is about to start home again. His feet have been standing within the gates of the great city of his faith and fathers—Jerusalem! And in Jerusalem he has stood in the Temple. To this pilgrim there was no more sacred spot on earth.

Think of what standing there meant to him. This Temple was the hub of his life's wheel. Religiously, it was the hub of both his faith and his nation, just as the capitol dome is the political hub of the American nation. It was the symbol of the unity of his people. He may have come from some little town like Nazareth or Cana or even Bethlehem, but here he joined with all the Judeans in all Judea in the common worship of a common God. Here he was representative of one of the tribes of Judah and Israel, which "went up" there to give thanks together in the name of God. Here he basked in the memory of great kings—David and Solomon, Asa, Hezekiah, Josiah—standing with all the others on a floor that was level to show that they stood in equality and in unity.

The call to worship is the loveliest call to fall upon the ears of men. Bishop Gerald Kennedy has said, "Whenever I hear any man sounding off against the church, I want to remind him that it is a wonderful thing to have a company of men gathered together once a week to let the sharp light of God penetrate the dark places of our hearts."

Worship in the sanctuary precedes the coming of the light. . . .

II. Pray for the peace of Jerusalem . . . , Psalm 122:6. Now the pilgrim gathers some of his companions around him in the Temple court, and leads them in a prayer of intercession. Together they look on Jerusalem, and pray for peace within its gates, within its Temple. They look out on the humble homes of the little people of the city—on the "tents" of the lowly—and they pray for them as we pray in church today that we may never forget those who have less than we have. They look up at the historic walls and battlements around and above them, where great armies have confronted each other, where the fate of their nation has hung in the balance time and again—and they pray that they may be spared wars tomorrow, that there may be a respite from slaughter— peace—in Jerusalem, and that their Temple may not be destroyed again. They see the palaces of princes and kings, where great things for the people have been planned and executed, where plot and intrigue have threatened disaster, and they pray for an end to all that—for peace in high places as well as in the humble cottage.

The pilgrim leads in prayer that, *beginning with himself,* all in this beloved city and in the Temple may be well. "I will say now, Peace be within thee." In his heart, he will strengthen Jerusalem, and honor the Temple. For the sake of the Lord his God he will seek what is best for all.

This is public prayer, collective worship, as it should be. It is praise, thanksgiving, intercession, hope, faith and love, all in one prayer. This is the attitude in which we should gather when we answer the call to prayer: to seek for His sake, not something *we* want, but what is best for all. These are the values of corporate worship, these are its elements. . . .

III . . . not neglecting to meet together . . . , Hebrews 10:25 (rsv). Some centuries lie between the Psalms and Hebrews, but the same demand is made upon both the Hebrews of the days of the Psalms and the Christians of the day when the Letter to the Hebrews was written. In order to "hold fast" in the faith it was *vital* that they pray and worship together. In fact, the author of Hebrews specifies three things that are necessary: we must come to God in "full assurance of faith" (verse 22), we must "hold fast the profession of our faith without wavering" (verse 23), and we must "stir up one another to love and good works" (verse 24, rsv). The *King James Version* uses the words "*provoke* unto love and good works," and that strikes a responsive chord! Christians *ought* to be provoking people; the common worship of Christians ought to be a provoking process if we are to get things done for the Kingdom of God. For many years, American Christians who had erred or strayed from the path were openly criticized "in meeting." We don't do that any more; it is easy now to become a member of a church, and few questions are ever asked after we get in! Right or wrong?

The *New English Bible* translates verse 25 ". . . . not staying away from our meetings, as some do. . . ." That's good! If we want an education we attend school; if we want *religious* education we go where such education is offered—in "our meetings."

The passage ends with a word of warning: we should not neglect the services of prayer and worship for the simple reason that "the Day" is coming, meaning the Day of Judgment, which was of primary concern in the minds of the early Christians. Today, it is not so stressed. Should it be?

SUGGESTIONS TO TEACHERS

President Coolidge was known as "Silent Cal"; he was a quiet one, but when he did speak, he usually said something. Once he said, "It is only when a man begins to worship that he begins to grow."

Analyze this worship. The church exists to help men worship in groups called congregations. How does that congregation behave in *your* church? How does it worship? Is its worship stale or lively? Rooted and perhaps dying in the past, or relevant to the problems every member of the congregation must face *today?* What *values* are found in congregational worship?

What do we get in congregational worship that we cannot get elsewhere? Why do we go to worship, anyway? Can't we say a prayer at home?

Is your church's program of worship good and fruitful, or could the church get along just as well without it? And why don't more people come to worship with you?

TOPIC FOR ADULTS
WORSHIPING IN THE CONGREGATION

Candles. A young soldier in Vietnam was asked by his chaplain why he had stopped coming to the worship services provided for his company. He replied:

"I seem not to be able to get much out of them any more. They bore me. I've seen some of my buddies pray in those services that their lives might be spared—and then they went out and got blown to pieces. When I get home, I'm not going to waste any time lighting candles in a church; I'm going into politics, where the real decisions are made—and where I may help stop wars *before they begin.*"

But isn't that just what worship is supposed to do? *Have not the greatest peacemakers been worshipful men?* Are not the greatest decisions made when we sit down together with God in worship and in worship develop a community strength to solve the bitter problems that face us?

There has never been a President of the United States who was not a regular—*congregational*—worshiper. Their great decisions are worship based.

Worship. "To give God the service of the body and not of the soul is hypocrisy.

"To give God the service of the soul and not of the body is sacrilege.

"To give God neither is atheism.

"To give God both is worship."—Author unknown.

Now read Psalm 29:2: "Give unto the Lord the glory due unto his name; worship the Lord in the beauty of holiness."

And *now* analyze your church worship services: do they build in you the beauty of holiness—and if not, why not? Would you like to make changes in those services? *What changes?*

Teaching. One Sunday morning we attended a congregational worship service at the famous Drive-In Church (Pasadena Community Church) in St. Petersburg, Florida. It was a church with an average congregation of 2500 and frequently with as many as 10,000 people worshiping together. On this Sunday we heard Wallace Hamilton, the pastor, say this:

"I once heard a man say that if a movement were to take place in the church to help people to pray, to train them in the art of meditation and the habit of prayer, it would meet with a response that would surpass all expectation. I guess that's true. I believe the church is full of people for whom the shine has gone out of religion and the freshness out of life because they don't pray, have never learned how—good people like the disciples, or people . . . wanting to find a deeper meaning for their existence, in whose hearts (if they could understand themselves) is the echo to the disciples' plea, 'Teach us to pray.'"

That is the first value of congregational value: it teaches us to pray—*together*. It teaches us to thank God in song—*together*. Here we are honest in confessing that we are not what we should be—and confessing it *together*. And here we plan our lives together—*as a community*.

Could anything be more valuable?

This preacher added one more value; he said that congregational worship should be "the starting point for a more intimate experience of God." What other value tops that one?

Worshipful Man. "He who neglects worship neglects that which separates man from birds, animals, insects and fishes. Unworshipful man is an anthropoid with a highly developed brain . . . a paragon of morality, but so are bees and ants . . . keenly intelligent, but so are wolves and foxes . . . provides for his family, but so do hyenas and orangutans . . . successful in his affairs, but so are beavers and muskrats . . . artistic— but so are spiders and butterflies. *Worship is the chief concern of highly developed human beings.*"—Dwight Bradley.

Flat Tire. When Bishop Irving Peake Johnson heard a man say that one can worship God just as effectively on Sunday morning by driving through the mountains, he observed, "The only time such people mention the name of God is when they have a flat tire."

Good for the bishop! In the common worship of a congregation we not only mention God—we talk and think with Him, man-to-God.

Questions for Pupils on the Next Lesson: 1. How, when and where does your family worship? 2. What is the "Shema"? 3. Describe the family worship of the Jews. 4. How many families in your church have family prayers at home? 5. What are some obstacles to family worship today? 6. What is a phylactery? 7. Is Roman Catholic family worship and instruction better than it is among Protestants?

TOPIC FOR YOUTH
WORSHIPING WITH OTHERS

Catching Up. "A distinguished explorer spent a couple of years among savages in the upper Amazon. He attempted a forced march through the jungle at high speed. All went well for two days. On the third morning all the natives were sitting on their haunches, looking very solemn. The chief explained: 'They're waiting for their souls to catch up with their bodies.'"—James Truslow Adams.

We worship on Sundays with the congregations to give our souls a chance, to learn how to live as well as how to make a living. . . .

Purpose. "Many years ago a distinguished Methodist pastor—Dr. Pierce Harris, of Atlanta—told of a worship service held during one of his early pastorates in the mountains. Into an afternoon service walked three roughly dressed men who sat down in the rear and did not take off their hats. They chatted, rolled cigarettes, and began to smoke them.

"Dr. Pierce stopped in the middle of his sermon and told them that they were attending a religious service, and they would either comply with the worship etiquette or get out. He went on to point out the fallacy of the sign outside reading 'Everyone Welcome.' If a person goes to church with some other purpose than to worship God, he should not be welcome.

"The purpose of coming to church is to glorify God in worship. No effort to turn all church services into worship experiences is wasted. The only display of anger we have from our Lord came after He entered a place of worship and found that it had become a place of commerce."— A. H. Stainback.

How about disturbing the service by chatting with each other during prayer or sermon? How about all that confusion when the service is over? How about the very small (and innocent!) children whose restlessness destroys the service for the adults? How about . . . well, how about it?

Necessary? "Is going to church necessary? This is not a realistic question, once one understands the meaning of the church in his own life and has, by Christ's presence, become part of Him and His any more than it is a sensible question for a man in love with his wife and committed to his family under normal conditions to ask, 'Is it necessary to go home to one's wife and children?' You wouldn't expect that man to stay at the YMCA when he felt like it and not go home, if it were at all possible. Even if there had been a spat or they were out of sorts with one aonther, naturally you would expect him to return to his family after the working day, expressing the corporateness of being an individual part of the family. It is the same natural expectation of the individual member of the family of God. In twenty centuries, they have felt it necessary to draw together weekly to worship and to work."—*I Give Up, God,* by Bryan Jay Cannon (Revell).

What do we miss if we don't go to worship . . . ?

How? Do we know *how* to worship?

"One Christian leader thinks there is evidence that we do not. 'Time and again,' says Dr. Rovert W. Spike in *To Be a Man,* 'when one gets into a really frank discussion with good active laymen, they confess that they appreciate the purposes of the church, but, to be honest, all that liturgy—hymns, Scripture, communion, etc.—leaves them cold. They like a good talk by the minister, they say, but the rest they suppose they will have to put up with for the sake of the women and "you ministers" who like that sort of thing.'

"One man, who has thought deeply on the inability or reluctance of many of us seriously . . . to engage in vital worship, came up with an interesting explanation. He thinks the major object of worship is 'the pursuit of the spiritual.'

"The word 'spiritual' is a good, important word that often goes wrong.

Too often it means . . . 'out of this world,' nonphysical, 'ideal, pure.' The Biblical understanding is not this kind of mystical, stratospheric concept. In the Scriptures 'spiritual' means 'where the Spirit of God operates.'

"He operates among machines in your offices, at Cape Canaveral, in your kitchens and living rooms, in our banks and in Congress. The Spirit of God operates on the spirits of human beings, and our spirits are not disembodied. They do not hover like a spaceman at certain altitudes in the air, barreling away from the earth and things earthy. Worship is concerned with something more than our feelings. If you do not feel lifted up on the wings of ecstacy in a service, you may still be worshiping in reality and in the Spirit.

"Worship is more than a program, a kind of sacred concert. There is a place in it for smiles and laughter, too; and also for tears, and for expression of our deep hungers."—David A. MacLennan, in *Revell's Minister's Annual* (Revell).

Sentence Sermon to Remember: The whole habit and practice of worship fulfills its purpose in deepening the spirit of fellowship, and in lifting us out of ourselves into a community of love and service for Christ and for one another.—Henry S. Date.

Questions for Pupils on the Next Lesson: 1. Why did the Jews lay such stress on family worship and instruction? 2. Where is Deuteronomy 6:5 repeated in the New Testament? 3. Who taught Timothy when he was a child? 4. How can we glorify God "at home"? 5. True or false: "The family that prays together stays together"? 6. Do you have "grace at meals" in your home? If not, why not? 7. Write a short prayer that would take in every member of your family.

LESSON XI—AUGUST 13

WORSHIPING IN THE FAMILY

Background Scripture: Deuteronomy 6:1–9; Psalm 78:1–8;
II Timothy 1:3–7
Devotional Reading: Psalm 78:1–8

DEUTERONOMY 6 Now these are the commandments, the statutes, and the judgments, which the Lord your God commanded to teach you, that ye might do them in the land whither ye go to possess it:

2 That thou mightest fear the Lord thy God, to keep all his statutes and his commandments, which I command thee, thou, and thy son, and thy son's son, all the days of thy life; and that thy days may be prolonged.

3 Hear therefore, O Israel, and observe to do it; that it may be well with thee, and that ye may increase mightily, as the Lord God of thy fathers hath promised thee, in the land that floweth with milk and honey.

4 Hear, O Israel: The Lord our God is one Lord:

5 And thou shalt love the Lord thy God with all thine heart, and with all thy soul, and with all thy might.

6 And these words, which I command thee this day, shall be in thine heart:

7 And thou shalt teach them diligently unto thy children, and shalt talk of them when thou sittest in thine house, and when thou walkest by the way, and when thou liest down, and when thou risest up.

8 And thou shalt bind them for a sign upon thine hand, and they shall be as frontlets between thine eyes.

9 And thou shalt write them upon the posts of thy house, and on thy gates.

II TIMOTHY 1 3 I thank God, whom I serve from my forefathers with pure conscience, that without ceasing I have remembrance of thee in my prayers night and day;

4 Greatly desiring to see thee, being mindful of thy tears, that I may be filled with joy;

5 When I call to remembrance the unfeigned faith that is in thee, which dwelt first in thy grandmother Lois,

DEUTERONOMY 6 "Now this is the commandment, the statutes and the ordinances which the Lord your God commanded me to teach you, that you may do them in the land to which you are going over, to possess it; 2 that you may fear the Lord your God, you and your son and your son's son, by keeping all his statutes and his commandments, which I command you, all the days of your life; and that your days may be prolonged. 3 Hear therefore, O Israel, and be careful to do them; that it may go well with you, and that you may multiply greatly, as the Lord, the God of your fathers, has promised you, in a land flowing with milk and honey.

4 "Hear, O Israel: The Lord our God is one Lord; 5 and you shall love the Lord your God with all your heart, and with all your soul, and with all your might. 6 And these words which I command you this day shall be upon your heart; 7 and you shall teach them diligently to your children, and shall talk of them when you sit in your house, and when you walk by the way, and when you lie down, and when you rise. 8 And you shall bind them as a sign upon your hand, and they shall be as frontlets between your eyes. 9 And you shall write them on the doorposts of your house and on your gates."

II TIMOTHY 1 3 I thank God whom I serve with a clear conscience, as did my fathers, when I remember you constantly in my prayers. 4 As I remember your tears, I long night and day to see you, that I may be filled with joy. 5 I am reminded of your sincere faith, a faith that dwelt first in your grandmother Lois and your mother Eunice and now, I am sure, dwells in you. 6 Hence I remind and thy mother Eunice; and I am persuaded that in thee also.

6 Wherefore I put thee in remembrance, that thou stir up the gift of God, which is in thee by the putting on of my hands.

7 For God hath not given us the spirit of fear; but of power, and of love, and of a sound mind.

you to rekindle the gift of God that is within you through the laying on of my hands; 7 for God did not give us a spirit of timidity but a spirit of power and love and self-control.

MEMORY SELECTION: . . . as for me and my house, we will serve the Lord. Joshua 24:15.

HOME DAILY BIBLE READINGS

Aug. 7. M. *The Everlasting God,* Isaiah 40:25–31.
Aug. 8. T. *Sing Praise to God,* Isaiah 95:1–7.
Aug. 9. W. *God Glorified at Home,* Deuteronomy 6:1–9.
Aug. 10. T. *Guidance for Wise Living,* Proverbs 1:1–9.
Aug. 11. F. *The Church in the Home,* I Corinthians 16:13–19.
Aug. 12. S. *Solid Foundations,* Luke 6:46–49.
Aug. 13. S. *From Generation to Generation,* Psalm 78:1–8.

BACKGROUND

Jewish history and the Jewish society is based on the Jewish *family.* Scattered all over the world, often deprived of the privilege and freedom of worshiping publicly, the Jew carried his synagogue in his heart and built temples in the hearts of his children through worship and teaching in the home. It is one of the most inspiring demonstrations of faith in any religion.

But—*what did they teach?* And who did the teaching—mothers, fathers, grandparents, who? And to what *purpose* did they teach? To get at all this, Scripture takes us back to Moses and the children of Israel in the wilderness. Moses has just given his people "the commandments, the statutes, and the judgments" of Sinai (Deuteronomy 5), which "the Lord your God commanded (me) to teach you . . ." (Deuteronomy 6:1). These they were to teach to their sons and their descendants "all the days of thy life" (verse 2).

Did they do it? And how did the teaching work out in their history?

NOTES ON THE PRINTED TEXT

I. *Hear, O Israel: the Lord our God is one Lord: and thou shalt love the Lord thy God . . .* , Deuteronomy 6:4, 5. Deuteronomy 6:4–9 is one of the most influential passages of the whole Bible: Judaism, Jesus and the Christian church especially have felt the impact of its spirit and teaching. It is known as "the Shema," which means "Hear!" It is a great confession of faith repeated twice daily by loyal Jews for two millennia. Jesus put Deuteronomy 6:4–5 with Leviticus 19:18 in His summary of the heart of the law in Mark 12:28–34, and so made it of primary interest to all Christians.

Now, there are two requirements in these verses: The first is that we appreciate the unity and the uniqueness of God. Verse 4 makes it clear in the fewest possible words that this is not just another god among a countless number of gods. There is something different about Him, something that demands an unusual devotion from those who believe in Him. There is one God, the Lord above all lesser gods, in place of the many gods of paganism; there is but one supreme God, and He is the God of Israel!

It was important for the people to understand this; their survival depended on it. In those days, they were surrounded with the idols and images and superstitions of other people who worshiped more in fear than in love. Anyone who has seen the horrible expressions on the faces of so many of the "gods" sculptured and painted in the temples of India and China will understand this; they are enough to frighten an unenlightened adult out of his wits, to say nothing of what they might do to children. In this day, there was a bestial god named Moloch; children and even babies were thrown into the fierce fires that raged on the altars of Moloch in a "sacrifice" that was plain murder.

In place of that barbarism, Judaism gave us a god of *love*. Said Moses, in effect, "Don't worship God in fear; worship Him in love." Don't be afraid of Him; love Him "with all your heart, and with all your soul, and with all your might" (verse 5, RSV). This was to be man's response; man was to love and serve a God of love because He first loved *man*.

These words, these laws, of this God *they were to teach their children* from one generation to another, so that the truth about Him should never die. They were to talk about all this "when you sit in your house . . ." (verse 7, RSV). How else? Can we leave all such teaching to the church and the Sunday school and do nothing to emphasize it at home? The Jews thought not; the faith of their fathers was emphasized every day of their lives—at home, as they walked in the streets, as they lay down to sleep and as they got up in the morning. They wore tiny scrolls of parchment on which were written the laws of Exodus 13, Deuteronomy 6 and 11, all wrapped in cases of skin or metal and bound on the left arm and on the forehead when they recited the Shema. They also fastened on their doorposts a *mezuzah*, a small cylinder containing the same verses from the law. They took their religion seriously *at home*. Had they taken it less seriously they would have vanished from the face of the earth.

Teach your children from generation to generation.

II. . . . a faith that dwelt first in your grandmother Lois and your mother Eunice, and now, I am sure, dwells in you, II Timothy 1:5. This is a "quote" from Paul's letter to Timothy—his last word to the young man who was his beloved spiritual son and his last letter to the church. Paul is about to die, and knows it, and this letter is the act of an old man throwing the torch into the hands of a young apostle. He writes, in effect, "I am counting on you who received the faith at the knees of your mother and grandmother to keep this torch burning, this faith alive." Much as he has done for Timothy, there might have been no Christian Timothy at all had it not been for the teachers within his own family.

These verses are supplemented by II Timothy 3:14–15, in which still greater emphasis is laid on the childhood training of the young man about ready to "take over" from Paul. What he learned as a child—his knowledge of the Scriptures, for instance—he should transmit to the churches under his charge. For Christianity, you see, is an assembly line affair; each of us stands at a particular place in the long creative process, with something to contribute to the whole. If we do not contribute, the "line" stops and the whole process suffers. The father contributes what he has to the son, the son to the grandson, or else . . . !

Jesus counted on this, and counted on us, when He said that each generation would do greater things *in His name* than had been done by the previous generation.

SUGGESTIONS TO TEACHERS

Some of us can remember when our families said grace at every meal, often had someone read a passage of Scripture at meal time or just after meals, and at least once a week had prayers together as a family. But the pace of life has changed now, and such family worship seems to be a lost art—or as an incident peculiar to the time. . . .

We can understand how this has happened—but do we realize what we have lost? Or don't we care? Do we get along just as well without it? Why have our Jewish friends insisted upon family worship, while we have been dropping it?

List some historic examples of Christian worship in the home. List its benefits and values. Put over against them all the obstacles to family worship that you can think of. Then take a vote in the class: should they try to keep family worship alive and important, or just let it go?

TOPIC FOR ADULTS
WORSHIPING IN THE FAMILY

The Dew of Religion. "The Quaker, Rufus Jones, said, 'I was born in a home in which religion was a vital part of the air we breathed. I was sprinkled from morning till night with the dew of religion. We never ate a meal which did not begin with the hush of thanksgiving; we never began a day without a family gathering, the reading of a chapter in the Bible, followed by a period of silent worship when we talked to God, who was not far away but very near.'

"Now I imagine that the home from which Rufus Jones came would be especially rich in its atmosphere of faith, and that not very many would equal it. But it is too bad if we are not making an effort to achieve it, because there are not many places where one is going to get it if he does not get it in the home. In the school it has been boiled down to a matter of legality, although Congress seems not to think it is breaking the law when it has a prayer at the opening of a session. It may be highly likely that Congress needs prayer more than the children. But thinking children must find it very puzzling. The church has them for such a short time, and if there is no conscious effort to bring God into the life of the child during the week, he is not likely to put much stock in the brief word he received on Sunday."—Rev. Howard Scharfe, in *Pulpit Preaching*, April, 1969.

Question: How do we expect our children to be impressed by worship in the Sunday school—which we make them attend—when they are denied any emphasis on worship when they get home?

Lost. We don't know who said it, or where we read it, but it is a single line that haunts us, and that will not go away. It is this:

In the lost boyhood of Judas Christ was betrayed.

Lost boyhoods are a dime a dozen in homes where there is no worship of God—or even recognition of Him!

Christ in the Home. "In thousands of homes a number of years ago a certain motto was common: 'Christ Is the Unseen Head of This House.' Or, 'Christ Is the Unseen Guest at Every Meal in This House.' That motto on the walls of homes was a matter of consequence, but the same motto enshrined in the hearts of men and women is of greater significance.

"The test of time demonstrates that when Christ is revered in home life, men and women, boys and girls, are able to fulfill their high purpose in God's Kingdom. Wherever Christ appears on the domestic scene, home life is transformed from a matter of convenience to a matter of conscience, and selfishness gives way to self-giving."—A. T. Howard.

Now read that last sentence, carefully *and thoughtfully.* Does the worship of God in the home transform that home? Or is this author exaggerating? Think of the families you know in which transformation has taken place. Does it always work out this way?

Home, Church. "I wish we could erase the heresy that Christian education is the job of the church only. Actually, the prior task belongs to the family. In the early church this was especially true, for the church was poor and held little property. Christians gathered in homes to worship and in a sense *every home was a little church* within the big church. . . . Do you dare think of your home as a little church?

"Have you ever made this observation about our conversation? With what ease most of us talk about the intimate details of our body—heart, lungs, liver, blood pressure! But with what shyness do we speak of our spiritual lives—prayer, God, Jesus, our spiritual problems! I recently had occasion to dine with a group of ministerial friends. At our table with us was one of our local doctors. As is the trend whenever a doctor is present, conversation eventually turned to the subject of health. One man began to discuss his diet, another described at length his recent bout with the flu, another spoke of vague aches and pains he had noticed recently. I asked our doctor friend, 'Have you ever noticed how conversation turns to health whenever a doctor is present?' 'Yes,' he replied, 'that's the cross we doctors have to bear. You ministers are spared. People just do not talk about God.'

"Make your home a church! Make God, Jesus and the Bible a natural part of your conversation. Don't let your children grow up with the notion that these topics are reserved for the church. Bring dedication into your family circle."—From a sermon by Arthur H. Kolsti.

Questions for Pupils on the Next Lesson: 1. What did Jesus mean when He said, "I am the vine"? 2. What did He mean by "Ye are the branches"? 3. Why did the Jews make the vine the symbol of their nation? 4. What wild grapes have you produced so far in your life? 5. What actions in your life have been *actually* guided by Christ? 6. How is working together with Christ "a devotion and a fellowship"? 7. Explain just how we "abide in Christ."

TOPIC FOR YOUTH
WORSHIPING WITH MY FAMILY

How. Here is how to hold a family worship:

"1. Choose a regular time to hold family worship each day—either in the morning or evening.
"2. The father will be the leader.
"3. Family worship should be a happy gathering, but remember that it should be reverent, too.
"4. Let the Bible be the center of family worship. The Bible reading should be clear, careful and brief.
"5. Follow a definite course of Bible reading, either going through one book at a time—e.g. one of the Gospels—or choosing passages which contain great verses or prayers, or tell of important events or prophecies. Where there are children it is good to use the Psalms.
"6. With young children it is sometimes better to tell a Bible story instead of reading it, or to read from a Bible picture book which will help to hold their interest.
"7. Children should be allowed to ask questions if they wish. They can also recite memory verses.
"8. Prayers should be short, and the children should be encouraged to take part.
"9. Invite friends to share in your family worship when they are visiting in your home.
"10. Remember that saying grace before meals is part of family worship, too!"—Source unknown, quoted by Eleanor Doan in *Sourcebook for Speakers,* pp. 154–5 (Zondervan Publishing House).

It can be longer or shorter than this, as you choose. We know some families in which a short verse of Scripture is read before every meal, then grace is said. That's all, but it is effective!

Practicing the Presence. Here is how family worship was conducted in one home:

"First, there was the constant sense of God's presence. Prayer came almost as naturally as conversation. Whether (mother) was stirring a cooking pot, paring potatoes or scrubbing the floor, God was there.

"Later, I learned about Brother Lawrence, the humble lay brother who worked in the kitchen of a monastery. His conversations, recorded for us in his *The Practice of the Presence of God,* reminded me of my mother. When he broke a dish, he said quite simply, 'Dear Father, I'm clumsy. This is what will happen if you don't help me.'

"Because of the mixture of faiths among our table boarders we never prayed at meal time. On the wall of the dining room, however, was a motto:

God is the unseen guest at every meal,
The silent listener to every conversation.

"This reminded us all throughout the meal that the dinner table was what Rabbi Silver calls 'the altar in the little sanctuary of the home.' Every meal time can be made a time of holy communion if we would make it so."—William H. Genne, in *The Link,* May, 1963.

Home Life. "What is the greatest national emergency facing the United States? Communism? Poverty? Crime? According to a specially chosen federal committee it is none of these. It is the breakdown of the American home. . . . Many homes are not planned. They are moving along without goals or direction. And often the lack of discipline is the beginning of the breakdown of the home. A successful home needs goals —goals that are centered around the Word of God."—Dan Smith, in *Moody Monthly,* June, 1964.

Family Prayer. When the whole family prays, what happens? Bishop Hazen G. Werner, of the United Methodist Church, suggests that these things happen—or could:

> "1. Ill feelings that have resulted from tiffs and quarrels are dissolved.
> 2. One or another member of the family is empowered to ask for forgiveness.
> 3. The home is considered as sacred and family activity as a spiritual vocation."

Well—this is what *should* happen, isn't it? Check these claims of Bishop Werner in your own experience.

The Crown. A poet whose name we shall never know says this:

> The beauty of the house is order;
> The blessing of the house is contentment;
> The glory of the house is hospitality;
> The crown of the house is godliness.

Godliness—does it come with or without worship?

Sentence Sermon to Remember: The family is the church in *your* house.—Nels F. S. Ferre.

Questions for Pupils on the Next Lesson: 1. Explain how you share the work of Christ. 2. When does God "cast forth" a man (John 15:6)? 3. How does a Christian "glorify" God? 4. If we keep God's commandments what can we expect to happen? 5. Does God demand something of us more than, "Only Believe"? 6. Can there be worship without service in real Christianity? 7. In what ways should we dare to "minister" that we have not dared in the past?

LESSON XII—AUGUST 20

SHARING IN CHRIST'S WORK

Background Scripture: Matthew 17:1–20; John 15:1–11
Devotional Reading: John 14:12–21

KING JAMES VERSION

JOHN 15 I am the true vine, and my Father is the husbandman.

2 Every branch in me that beareth not fruit he taketh away: and every branch that beareth fruit, he purgeth it, that it may bring forth more fruit.

3 Now ye are clean through the word which I have spoken unto you.

4 Abide in me, and I in you. As the branch cannot bear fruit of itself, except it abide in the vine; no more can ye, except ye abide in me.

5 I am the vine, ye are the branches. He that abideth in me, and I in him, the same bringeth forth much fruit; for without me ye can do nothing.

6 If a man abide not in me, he is cast forth as a branch, and is withered; and men gather them, and cast them into the fire, and they are burned.

7 If ye abide in me, and my words abide in you, ye shall ask what ye will, and it shall be done unto you.

8 Herein is my Father glorified, that ye bear much fruit; so shall ye be my disciples.

9 As the Father hath loved me, so have I loved you: continue ye in my love.

10 If ye keep my commandments, ye shall abide in my love; even as I have kept my Father's commandments, and abide in his love.

11 These things have I spoken unto you, that my joy might remain in you, and that your joy might be full.

REVISED STANDARD VERSION

JOHN 15 "I am the true vine, and my Father is the vinedresser. 2 Every branch of mine that bears no fruit, he takes away, and every branch that does bear fruit he prunes, that it may bear more fruit. 3 You are already made clean by the word which I have spoken to you. 4 Abide in me, and I in you. As the branch cannot bear fruit by itself, unless it abides in the vine, neither can you, unless you abide in me. 5 I am the vine, you are the branches. He who abides in me, and I in him, he it is that bears much fruit, for apart from me you can do nothing. 6 If a man does not abide in me, he is cast forth as a branch and withers; and the branches are gathered, thrown into the fire and burned. 7 If you abide in me, and my words abide in you, ask whatever you will, and it shall be done for you. 8 By this my Father is glorified, that you bear much fruit, and so prove to be my disciples. 9 As the Father has loved me, so have I loved you; abide in my love. 10 If you keep my commandments, you will abide in my love, just as I have kept my Father's commandments and abide in his love. 11 These things I have spoken to you, that my joy may be in you, and that your joy may be full."

MEMORY SELECTION: He that hath my commandments, and keepeth them, he it is that loveth me. John 14:21.

HOME DAILY BIBLE READINGS

Aug. 14. M. *Jesus and the Father,* John 5:10–18.
Aug. 15. T. *God at Work in You,* Philippians 2:12–18.
Aug. 16. W. *Doing Honest Work,* II Thessalonians 3:6–13.
Aug. 17. T. *Doing Work of God,* John 6:25–33.
Aug. 18. F. *Ministry of Work,* II Corinthians 6:1–10.

Aug. 19. S. *Faith and Work*, Hebrews 11:32–38.
Aug. 20. S. *The Works of Love*, John 14:12–21.

BACKGROUND

The figure of the vine was a prominent and meaningful one in the Jewish faith and society. In the Old Testament, Israel was often called the vine or the vineyard of God; it was inscribed on their coins; it was carved over the door of the Temple. "The vine was part and parcel of Jewish imagery; it was the very symbol of the nation of Israel." (Dr. William Barclay.)

Spiritually, it was a good symbol, for it had to do with life, growth and fruit. When, in the days of the prophets, the spiritual life of Israel began to decline, Hosea cried out, "Israel is an empty vine" (Hosea 10:1)! Jesus may have been thinking of the words of the old prophet when He said, "I am the vine . . ." and gave the whole thing new meaning. . . .

NOTES ON THE PRINTED TEXT

I. I am the true vine . . . , John 15:1. Dr. Barclay calls attention to the interesting fact that in the Old Testament the image or symbol of the vine is almost always used in connection with the idea of degeneration or decay. Isaiah (5:1–7) pictures Israel as a vineyard in which the vines have been allowed to run wild and produce poor grapes; God meant the vineyard to be something better than that, but the people just hadn't taken care of it. In Jeremiah 2 God complains: "Yet I had planted thee a noble vine . . . how then art thou turned into the degenerate plant of a strange vine unto me" (2:21)? We have already quoted Hosea. . . .

Now comes Jesus saying, "*I* am the vine . . . ," Not Israel, but *I*. When He said that He struck at the false pride of the Israelites, who had come to think that as the favored vineyard of the Lord their nation must be perfect and beyond criticism. Weren't they the chosen ones? Weren't they "saved" because they were Jews? Weren't they the one nation picked out of all the nations of the world by God as *His* nation?

It is as if Jesus were saying, "No, you are *not* saved just because you are Jews, just because God has picked you to do something special for Him. The trouble is, you haven't been doing that 'something special.' You are degenerate as a nation and as a people, as your prophets have told you. . . ." It is *never any nation* that is the "true vine," for nations have a way of going wrong, of ignoring God as they become stronger. *Not nations, but Christ.* Not blood, but brotherhood and faith. Not nationality, but living fellowship with and belief in Jesus Christ is the way to salvation.

We Americans should think long and hard about that—we who have so long thought of ourselves as the moral as well as the political guide of the world. . . . Something has happened to that moral vanity and pride since Vietnam began . . . !

II. I am the vine, ye are the branches, John 15:5. Vineyards need careful tending. Farms need a "tender" who gets up at dawn and works until dark, caring for his soil, pruning his vines and trees, digging out weeds and tares. You don't get good vines or grapes or apples or wheat unless you do that! And it wasn't being done in Israel as Jesus spoke. The vines were running wild and bad, fruitless vines were choking the life out of the vines that were producing good fruit.

Now, every farmer and villager in Palestine knew what Jesus was talking about when He spoke of pruning the vines. There were only two kinds of vines and fruit trees; good ones and bad ones. In order that the good might live and give forth good grapes, the non-producing vines were cut off and burned. And the people got the message, too: Jesus was referring indirectly but powerfully to the Jews, who had not taken good care of the vineyard God had given them. They stoned the prophets and crucified Jesus. (Read the parable of the wicked husbandmen in Matthew 21.)

But could He also have been thinking of the "Christians" who were useless "branches," producing nothing? Was He not referring to those who called Him Lord, Lord, and did not as He said—to those who were all leaves and no fruit and would have to be cast out, to those who professed one thing and did another, who went off on picnics when they should have been tending the vineyards? Wasn't He saying that there was no place for drones in the Kingdom of God?

We are the branches! We are those who are supposed to be doing the work of Him who sent us! We are supposed to reflect in our faces the glory that was on His. We are to share His work, working together and with Him in devotion and rich fellowship. We are colaborers with God —or we are hypocrites, useless as a barren branch that must be cut off and thrown into the fire.

What a glorious thing it is to share His work. And how cheaply do we sell the glory for the baubles of the world!

III. If ye abide in me . . . , John 15:7. What does that word "abide" mean? To many of us, it means a mystical experience in which "the Christian is in Christ and Christ is in the Christian." That is a valid experience, much to be desired. But there is another sense in which it means *keeping in contact with Jesus.* We speak of an "abiding" friendship between two people—meaning a friendship that lasts and is effective and beautiful as long as they both live. Keeping in contact with Him is like the branches of a vine keeping in contact with the trunk of the vine from which flows their life.

We knew a fine lawyer once who had been a Bowery derelict in his younger days; he was about ready to commit suicide when an old retired preacher lifted him out of the Bowery gutter, gave him a meal and a new suit of clothes and got him a job and gave him a small golden cross that had been in the preacher's family for generations. It was the turning point: he walked a new road back to respectability in his profession. He had the little cross encased in plastic, and put it on his desk; whenever he was tempted to do what he knew to be wrong, he reached for the cross—and did what he knew to be right. Every move he made he made in the presence of the cross.

That is abiding in Christ! *That* is glorifying God. *That* is keeping His commandments! *That* is sharing Christ's work. (Note: he still carries in

his wallet a broken, crumpled, almost unrecognizable snapshot of his
preacher friend, long dead but still abiding in his heart.)

SUGGESTIONS TO TEACHERS

Henry Ford walked into one of his sales agencies and said to the
manager, "You should change that sign in the window. It reads 'Sales
and Service.' It should read, 'Service and Sales,' because if you give the
service you'll get the sales."

That was good thinking; it could be applied properly to our living as
Christians. To put it rather crudely, we "have something to sell"—faith
in a living Christ. We haven't been doing too well lately in selling it;
perhaps the trouble is that we haven't been demonstrating the value of
our product in our service to mankind. Jesus "sold" Himself even in His
death . . . !

Today we are to discuss ways and means of serving men in His name
—of sharing His work. Start the discussion by pointing to at least two
places in the New Testament where He calls on us to *prove our faith in
service*. Then modernize it: point to the situations in which anyone can
help Him by helping his brother, and in which everyone *should*. . . .

TOPIC FOR ADULTS
SHARING IN CHRIST'S WORK

Working. Somewhere we read of a city preacher who was almost
never to be found at home. He was always "out." One day when a
stranger knocked on his door, the preacher's wife answered the knock;
asked if her husband was at home, she laughed. Asked where the
stranger might find him, she said, "I really haven't the least idea. But
if you will go over on the other side of the railroad tracks, you'll probably find him in some poverty-stricken hole where he thinks Christ
needs him."

If Jesus Christ were to come back to our earth in the flesh, we'd
probably have the same difficulty locating Him. He would no more have a
"home" now than He had then. You'd find Him in the slums, in some
sickroom, or out in the street where a riot was raging, or maybe at the
town jail. Jesus is always to be found where the action is. He left orders
for us to be found there, too, helping Him: "The man who has received
my commands and obeys them—he it is who loves me" (John 14:21,
New English Bible). And His great command was "GO . . . !"

Serving. A wise and experienced minister tells us how to "take to
heart Christ's call to be brother to a world in need":

"1. *Learn*. We can be equipped intellectually, to be knowledgeable
about the needs and the up-to-date facts. . . . Learn. Learn not just
by alert reading but by being led into personal contact with others of
different social, economic and racial positions. . . . Learn!

"2. *Pray*. You can pray knowledgeably. Pray specifically. We should
have on our prayer list not only individuals for whom we bear concern
but also issues of our time, so that we are faithful daily in being God's
instrument of intercession for the world around us.

"3. *Share*. Pour some of your financial resources directly into the stream of healing, lifting and recreating the lives of those struggling with existence. We will never give enough, we know. . . . We can become part of the world's cure, helping to touch them, lift them up, drive out the demons of sickness, hate, despair, hunger and unbelief. . . .

"4. *Give.* Give of yourself. There are untold opportunities to put your life into situations in relationships, personal and corporate, which count and where, person to person, you can be a means by which people in the daily walks of life and the struggle for living can be met, encouraged and helped. . . ."

"Do you see the picture taking form? Masses of black faces that are resentful, fearful, poverty-stricken; white faces that are trapped in sophisticated ignorance or cultural stagnation; the unemployed (by automation) or those elderly people not needed by the bustling nation on the move, who are twisted in distorted fear and apprehension of a changing society; the yellow faces, row on row, in regimented resistance to Western ways and wiles but hungry and lost—a welter of people, many outside the church and the nice polite words we use in theological language, but not outside Christ's open heart. . . . Let your life count. . . . Give yourself up to God, and live!"—*I Give Up, God,* by Bryan Jay Cannon (Revell).

The Brook. God created something altogether lovely when He created brooks. We can sit beside them for hours, watch them, and find peace and inspiration for our souls—which may be what He intended them to do:

"A brook is going somewhere. It is water-on-a-mission. About to present itself to other waters at its destination, it never neglects little wayside opportunities. On its way to make its final offering, it gaily gives itself all along the way. Deer drink of its refreshing coolness with a deep content. Boys of seven and of seventy prod its pools and eddies with their lures and return home at day's end with the brook's gift of speckled trout. Fish, crustaceans, mollusks and water insects find a home in its swirling currents and tranquil pools. From its birth in bubbling springs to its arrival at its final goal the brook is selfless and a happy appearing thing."—Harold E. Kohn.

In God's plan we are all brooks, flowing through life with great potentiality for conquering the thirsts of the soul—provided we can be unselfish enough to work as He worked among men. . . .

Questions for Pupils on the Next Lesson: 1. What is a witness? 2. What do you witness *to* in your religion? 3. Analyze the "witness" of Peter and John in Acts 4:13–21. 4. True or false: "Witnessing is the cornerstone of the devout life"? 5. What do we "share" when we witness? 6. Have we any right to witness unless we "live in Christ"? And how can we do that? 7. Where did you last speak a good word for Christ?

TOPIC FOR YOUTH
MY PART IN CHRIST'S WORK

Grenfell. Dr. Wilfred T. Grenfell might have been a rich doctor anywhere in the world. But he went out to the bitter, freezing coast and seas of Labrador to work as a missionary doctor among a destitute, dying people. Why?

On one occasion he said, "The service we render to others is really the rent we pay for our room on this earth. It is obvious that man is himself a traveler, that the purpose of this world is not 'to have and to hold' but 'to give and to serve.' There can be no other meaning."

That's why.

> There are strange ways of serving God;
> You sweep a room or turn a sod,
> And suddenly, to your surprise,
> You hear the whirl of seraphim,
> And find you're under God's own eyes
> And building palaces for Him.
> —Hermann Hagedorn.

Substitutes. Substitutes are invaluable on a football team—or in the Kingdom of God.

"The substitute is a person who waits on the bench with a hand on his knee, watches every play, listens to all the cheers, always hoping to get in.

"He watches his teammates execute plays which, during practice, he has helped to work to perfection.

"For months he's had the lowly place of submerging himself in loyal desire that teamwork might be made complete, and yet he has not heard his name in the crowd's acclaim.

"The crowd sees him waiting for his chance, the chance perhaps that will never come, but nevertheless he gives his best.

"He is content when thousands laud his teammates, but let us remember that successful teams were never built without the 'sub' who prays, hopes, works and waits."—From *Words of Life*, p. 199. Edited by Charles L. Wallis. Quoted by permission of Harper and Row, publishers.

Substitutes? Timothy substitutes for Paul when the aging apostle was near death. Simon of Cyrene was a "sub"; he carried the cross. Barnabas played "second fiddle" in the apostolic "orchestra," and liked it. Theodore Roosevelt was Vice-President under President McKinley—and proved to be a greater President than McKinley! And Jesus was a "substitute" on Calvary for a criminal named Barabbas.

Obituary. "One morning in 1888, Alfred Nobel, the inventor of dynamite, the man who had spent his life amassing a fortune from the manufacture and sale of weapons of destruction, awoke to read his own obituary. The obituary was printed as a result of a simple journalistic error—Alfred's brother had died, and a French reporter carelessly reported the death of the wrong brother.

"Any man would have been disturbed under the circumstance, but to Alfred Nobel the shock was overwhelming. He saw himself as the world saw him: 'the dynamite King,'—the great industrialist who had made an immense fortune from explosives. This—as far as the general public was concerned—was the entire purpose of his life. None of his true intentions—to break down the barriers that separated men and ideas—were recognized or given serious consideration. He was simply a merchant of death, and for that he would be remembered. . . .

"As he read his obituary with horror, Nobel resolved to make clear to the world the true meaning and purpose of his life. This could be done through the final disposition of his fortune. His last will and testament would be the expression of his life's ideals. . . . The result was the most valued of prizes given to those who have done most for the cause of world peace."—Nicholas Halasz.

There is more than one sermon, more than one teaching, in that. We are all created with built-in dynamite and built-in love; we all use one or the other as weapons in the warfare called life. And it is never too late to change from dynamite to love and peace-making, never too late to stop getting and begin sharing His work and service. . . .

Bernard. "Far upon the Alpine passes the Romans built their roads that travelers might pass from Italy to northern Europe. But in winter snow would cover the roads and travelers would be lost. A man by the name of Bernard devoted himself to dwelling at the highest pass to rescue those who were lost in the storm. They called him St. Bernard. People never forgot his service, and long years afterward when those huge friendly dogs were trained to rescue Alpine travelers, the only name that fitted them was the name of the man who had dedicated his life years before."—Russell J. Clinchy.

Wherever you are, you can share His saving work. . . .

Sentence Sermon to Remember: Lord, do not only count me. Count on me.—Anonymous.

Questions for Pupils on the Next Lesson: 1. What *responsibility* do we have to witness to the gospel? 2. How can you tell a good witness from a poor one? 3. Were Peter and John "unlearned and ignorant men" (Acts 4:13)? 4. Would you call Martin Luther King a witness or a nuisance? 5. Are Jehovah's Witnesses good witnesses? 6. Were Peter and John guilty of disturbing the peace? 7. Would you witness for Christ if it meant going to jail?

LESSON XIII—AUGUST 27

SHARING THROUGH WITNESS

Background Scripture: Acts 4:13–21; 8: 26–40
Devotional Reading: Acts 8:26–40

KING JAMES VERSION

ACTS 4   13 Now when they saw the boldness of Peter and John, and perceived that they were unlearned and ignorant men, they marveled; and they took knowledge of them, that they had been with Jesus.

14 And beholding the man which was healed standing with them, they could say nothing against it.

15 But when they had commanded them to go aside out of the council, they conferred among themselves,

16 Saying, What shall we do to these men? for that indeed a notable miracle hath been done by them is manifest to all them that dwell in Jerusalem; and we cannot deny it.

17 But that it spread no further among the people, let us straitly threaten them, that they speak henceforth to no man in this name.

18 And they called them, and commanded them not to speak at all nor teach in the name of Jesus.

19 But Peter and John answered and said unto them, Whether it be right in the sight of God to hearken unto you more than unto God, judge ye.

20 For we cannot but speak the things which we have seen and heard.

21 So when they had further threatened them, they let them go, finding nothing how they might punish them, because of the people: for all men glorified God for that which was done.

REVISED STANDARD VERSION

ACTS 4   13 Now when they saw the boldness of Peter and John, and perceived that they were uneducated, common men, they wondered; and they recognized that they had been with Jesus. 14 But seeing the man that had been healed standing beside them, they had nothing to say in opposition. 15 But when they had commanded them to go aside out of the council, they conferred with one another, 16 saying, "What shall we do with these men? For that a notable sign has been performed through them is manifest to all the inhabitants of Jerusalem, and we cannot deny it. 17 But in order that it may spread no further among the people, let us warn them to speak no more to any one in this name." 18 So they called them and charged them not to speak or teach at all in the name of Jesus. 19 But Peter and John answered them, "Whether it is right in the sight of God to listen to you rather than to God, you must judge; 20 for we cannot but speak of what we have seen and heard." 21 And when they had further threatened them, they let them go, finding no way to punish them, because of the people; for all men praised God for what had happened.

MEMORY SELECTION: *For we cannot but speak the things which we have seen and heard.* Acts 4:20.

HOME DAILY BIBLE READINGS

Aug. 21. M. *Witness of Christ,* John 5:35–47.
Aug. 22. T. *We Are Witnesses,* Acts 11:1–18.
Aug. 23. W. *Witnesses to All Men,* Acts 22:12–16.
Aug. 24. T. *Empowered Witnesses,* Acts 14:3–18.
Aug. 25. F. *Disciplined Witness,* Hebrews 12:1–11.
Aug. 26. S. *An Affirmative Witness,* John 3:25–30.
Aug. 27. S. *Roadside Witness,* Acts 8:26–40.

BACKGROUND

A "witness" in court does two things: he gives evidence, and (as a "character" witness) he declares his faith in others, whether they be of the prosecution or of the defense. A Christian witness testifies to a truth —the truth he has seen in Jesus Christ. This Christ told His disciples that they had witnessed His ministry—and that they were, in their turn, to "witness" in "Jerusalem, and in all Judea, and in Samaria, and unto the uttermost part of the earth" (Acts 1:8).

So, in this lesson, we find two of the disciples—Peter and John—busy witnessing. We are told *how* they witnessed, what they said and did, the circumstances under which they stood up and declared their faith in Him, and what happened as a result. For those of us who believe that witnessing is an obligation of the devout, devotional life, this short story in Acts 4 lays down the guidelines for *our* witnessing.

NOTES ON THE PRINTED TEXT

I. Now when they saw the boldness of Peter and John . . . , Acts 4:13. "They" were the judges of the Sanhedrin, before whom Peter and John had been summoned for daring to preach in the streets and heal a sick man. They represented the finest families in the land; they were wealthy, intellectual, socially prominent and powerful—and they were the very court which not long before had condemned Jesus to death! Before them stood two humble, obscure men—two *fishermen* from Galilee. The Sanhedrin looked at them and called them unlearned: they had no education worth mentioning. They were also "ignorant"—that is, they were laymen, with no professional qualifications whatever. They were not only uneducated: they were unordained! They had never seen the inside of a college, let alone a theological seminary—and *they* dared to preach! By whose permission did they preach and heal? Preaching should be left to (professional) preachers, who "know how."

This is one of the favorite tricks of those who hate Christ: they do their best to throw contempt on the Christian witness. "Oh, well, after all—he has no education, you know!" Or, "What can a poor fisherman know about God in comparison with our rabbis?" But after all, is this the most important qualification of a witness for Christ? Is it his professional training and status that make him effective in winning others to Christ? Or are there some other strengths in the witness that should be considered? How well "educated" in the schools was Jesus? How many of the disciples might be classified as "drop-outs"? The truth is, is it not, that the first consideration in a disciple *is that he knows Christ?* Much as we value education, we know that a man can be educated into agnosticism, atheism, apostasy *unless he has known Christ.*

The judges looked at this pair—at Peter and John—and as they looked they knew that "they had been with Jesus." There was an air of quiet certainty about them, a dignity, a courage that left the judges helpless to do anything but to tell them, weakly, to stop preaching in the name of Jesus—something the judges knew they would *never* do!

And the lowly witnesses had something else that made the judges look silly: they had a witness of their own. . . .

II. *And beholding the man which was healed standing with them, they could say nothing against it,* Acts 4:14. Peter and John may have been men of lowly status and station, but they were not fools. They didn't come into court unprepared; they brought a *fact* in the flesh of the man they had healed. It was one thing to preach in the streets that Jesus Christ could heal, or that the disciples could heal in His name; it was something else to produce in court the living evidence of one who had been healed! They had "a witness to their witness" which the court could not deny.

We talk so much about the power of Christ, of "proving" this or that about Christianity. These are words, words, *words*. The only proof we need is the proof of a Christian *man;* the only really convincing evidence we need is the evidence of Christian character. We can debate until doomsday about what Christ can do, about what miracles He can work in man, but when a man stands up before us and says, "I know what He can do: He has done it for *me*. . . ." Well, what do we say *then?*

Don't *tell* us about the power of Christ: *show* us!

III. *Whether it is right in the sight of God to listen to you rather than to God, you must judge; for we cannot but speak of what we have seen and heard,* Acts 4:19, 20 (rsv). Courage! There it is, in the raw. Peter and John, despised and ridiculed, proved in these words that they were better men than their judges. They asked, "Which should we obey— men or God?" Should they listen to the voices of the proud on the Sanhedrin bench, or listen to the voice of God? In their hearts, the judges knew which, but they dared not admit it. To admit it would destroy their "prestige" among the people. They were cowards; the two prisoners before them may have been on trial before men, but more than that, *they* were on trial before God! They had no answer for that question.

Today we are a nation torn and divided over the question of civil rights and civil rights "demonstrations." Many men are deliberately dis- obeying the laws of man because, they hold, there is a higher law of God which should be obeyed in preference. To some of us they are right, to some others they are wrong. Is this situation similar to the one described in this lesson? Are the cases of Peter and Paul similar to the case of the modern protestor, or is there something different about them? It isn't a question with an easy answer—but answer it we must, sooner or later. . . .

The real witness of Peter and John, then, was not so much the presence of the healed one in court, not so much the ancient right to listen to God before listening to man; it was the witness of a personal experience with Christ. With the words of Christ sunk and burning in their hearts, they *had* to speak of what they had seen and heard. No man with a great vision can keep quiet about it; he *must* tell others.

It was no second-hand gospel that impelled these disciples; it was first-hand experience with a living Christ. They knew, with eyes that had seen and ears that had heard the Christ that what He said was true, and they were ready to put their lives on the line and die for that truth if that were necessary. They witnessed not by word of mouth alone; they witnessed by throwing all that they had and were into the scales for God.

We could use a few more such witnesses in our church right now!

SUGGESTIONS TO TEACHERS

1. First of all, find out what the Bible means by "witnessing." Acts 5:32 tells us that "we are his witnesses of these things." *What* things? What do we witness to, and for whom? And *why?*

2. Witnessing involves—what? Is it all by word of mouth? Take a look at the witnesses who "went forth" (Hebrews 11), and then list their qualifications as witnesses.

3. Name five witnesses who have lived since you were born who laid down their lives as witnesses.

4. Using Peter and John as examples, ask what your students have done or plan to do that compares with these witnesses.

Ask this question: Can Christianity possibly succeed without witnessing? And this one: Is Christianity failing today because of a lack of honest and all-out witnesses?

TOPIC FOR ADULTS
SHARING THROUGH WITNESS

Sharing. "An American aviator in China was forced down in World War II in enemy territory. Through some woods he saw a mission. All the buildings of the mission were destroyed except the little chapel, which was only partially destroyed. He ran to it for shelter. When he got inside, he was startled to see a Japanese soldier crouching behind the altar. But the Japanese paid no attention to him. As the American approached the altar, he saw that the Japanese soldier was trying to put a bandage on the back of a wounded Russian. The American saw a ring on the Japanese soldier's hand. It was a ring from an American university. Fastened to a chain about his neck was a little cross.

"It was all like a dream. None of them spoke. The American took off his coat and began to help the Japanese take care of the Russian. Then the American went to the front door of the little chapel to stand guard. On the door was a small plaque with a poem written in Chinese. He put the plaque in his pocket, and later a Chinese friend translated the poem:

> Whoe'er thou art that entereth here,
> Forget the struggling world
> And every trembling fear.
> Take from thy heart each evil thought,
> And all that selfishness
> Within thy life has wrought.
> For once inside this place thou'lt find
> No barter, servant's fear,
> Nor master's voice unkind.
> Here all are kin of God above—
> Thou, too, heart; and here
> The rule of life is love.
> —Virgil A. Kraft.

Doran's *Ministers' Manual* 1970, page 63. By permission of Harper & Row, Publishers.

Communism. "Bishop Richard C. Raines reminds us that forty years ago communism was confined to so small a group that they could be seated in the average choir loft. Today it controls the destiny of one-third of the earth's surface and the lives of eight hundred million people. Mr. Khrushchev has predicted that our grandchildren will be communists. That remains to be seen. But if they are, I am sure that it will be because the people called Christians were shallow in their commitment. It will be because we have been apologetic, afraid, or ashamed to express our love for God and to witness to others concerning it. It will be because we have failed to convince the world that the power that supposedly grips us is significant enough to move us."—From a sermon by Rev. Emil D. McAdams.

That is well said. It might also be said that prisons behind the iron curtain are jammed with Christians who would not leave Christ for Lenin. . . .

Anonymous Witnesses. In her book, *Except the Lord* (chapter 59), Joyce Cary tells us dramatically that we are blessed by an innumerable host of unhonored, obscure and vital witnesses. Against an English background, she says:

"Trace now the record of . . . a modest and unconsidered force, an influence little more noticed by the learned and the propagandists, the word-wielders, than the play of the English weather—the daily, weekly ministrations of fifty thousand servants of the Lord. I do not speak here of the mighty (John) Wesley but of those humble and poor men who gave their lives to oblivion. Yea, and among them not only the so-called dissenting pastors, but many a vicar and curate of the English Church, as poor and as ungratefully forgotten; above all, that great anonymous crowd of witnesses, teachers of children, speakers in the way, lay preachers and readers, men like my father, who went among their neighbors speaking mercy, truth, kindness towards all men."

Name five of the witnesses who helped build the church *after* Jesus and Paul were dead. They were rather obscure, weren't they? But what witnesses they were!

Questions for Pupils on the Next Lesson: 1. Describe the general situation of the Hebrews just after Moses died. 2. What was Joshua commanded to do? 3. How were these days completely different from the days in the wilderness? 4. What help did God offer Joshua? 5. How are the times in which *we* live different from any other times? 6. What deathless religious principle is found in Isaiah 40:8? 7. What help does Christ offer *us* in our rapidly changing world (see John 8)?

TOPIC FOR YOUTH
MY WITNESS: GOD IS REAL!

Living Christ, Living People. We were fascinated when we heard Sister Luc-Gabriel sing. She toured this country, singing her witness to the *living* God. She had come out of the shelter and obscurity of a Belgian convent to do this, and we wondered why; she explained:

"The music is my way of evangelizing, *of revealing something alive.* I sing because I believe in Jesus Christ and want to reveal the living Christ to living people."

She won a great many—not to her church, but to an enlivened conviction that God was alive and working with living people. . . . And that is about as fine witnessing as one can find. . . .

Martyrs. Not all martyrs for the faith die: some of them believe it is as necessary to live for Christ as to die for Him. For instance:

"The mysterious kingdom of Nepal is literally on top of the world. The little Arkansas-sized nation spreads across the Himalayas, including Mount Everest, and is a Mecca for mountain climbers. It also serves as a buffer between populous India and communist-controlled Tibet.

"Nepal has always been closed to foreign missionary evangelists, although Wycliffe Bible translators are now analyzing the languages of six tribal groups. Eighty percent of Nepal's ten million people are classified as Hindu, the official religion. The remainder are mainly Buddhist, Muslim and animists. A recent count showed only one hundred and twelve baptized Christians, all prison graduates.

"Every Christian has served at least one year in prison for submitting to baptism. Nepalese pastor Prem Pradhan, the most successful Christian evangelist, has spent five years in seven jails for baptizing eight persons. Authorities shuttled him among different jails to impede his evangelism.

"Now that he has baptized another Nepali he can be sentenced and imprisoned again. However, this may not happen, as Nepal authorities decide that he is less trouble outside than inside a prison where he can preach to captive audiences. . . . What are we doing while Pastor Pradhan and other Nepalese evangelists are increasing Nepal's prison population?"—*Thinkables*, pp. 57–58, by James C. Hefley (Revell).

Some of us are witnessing for the prosecution, saying, "Oh, missionary work is dead, isn't it?" Or, "Why don't we leave the natives alone?" And what do you say—and do?

What a Christian Is. "Witnessing is not just something a Christian says, but what a Christian is.

"Of course, words are important—but they are no substitute for Christlike demeanor. Pious language cannot camouflage profane practice.

"Indeed, words constitute an indictment against the man whose actions contradict what he professes.

"The world will listen if the life manifests Christian character [but] the world will scoff at the emptiness of the words, however pious, *if the witness of life is wanting*.

"Conditioned to demonstration, modern man awaits the confirmation of the claims by the consistent conduct of the claimant.

"Let every serious minded Christian who would be an effective witness for Christ live as though he had to *earn* the right to be heard."—Richard C. Halverson, in *Perspective*.

Witnessing can border on hypocrisy if we don't watch it. How many of us have really earned the right to be heard . . . ?

In the Kitchen. Francis Asbury, the first Methodist bishop in America, rode horseback all up and down the Eastern coast and went as far inland as Ohio, preaching and witnessing. That was rough country. Sometimes he preached to big camp meetings under the open sky; more often he sat in log cabins along the forest trails, with only two or three for a "congregation"—but his witness was just as strong there as it was in the big camp meetings.

We read in his famous *Journal*: "We must preach the gospel in every kitchen."

That struck us deeply, for the most eloquent Christian witness we ever heard was when, as a college student, we washed dishes in a hotel kitchen in Yellowstone Park beside a man who had the beauty of Jesus written all over his face—and his life. We've forgotten a thousand sermons, but, somehow, we can never forget that little fellow who washed dirty dishes for the glory of God. . . .

Sentence Sermon to Remember: Ye are my witnesses, saith the Lord . . . (Isaiah 43:12).

Questions for Pupils on the Next Lesson: 1. Did God promise to be with us in changing times? Give chapter, verse. 2. Should we "change our religion to fit our changing times"? 3. Why does the Bible seem to have less influence over our lives than it had twenty years ago? 4. Name some Christian truths that will never change. 5. What did God promise Joshua (Joshua 1)? 6. How did Joshua face the tremendous changes of his day? 7. Explain how "the word of our God" has *not* been affected by change.

This book contains lessons through August 1972. TARBELL'S 1972–73, containing lessons from September 1972 through August 1973, is on sale now at your book store.